Enlightenment Portraits

Enlightenment Portraits

Edited by
Michel Vovelle

Translated by
Lydia G. Cochrane

THE UNIVERSITY OF CHICAGO PRESS

CHICAGO & LONDON

Michel Vovelle holds the chair of History of the French Revolution at the University of Paris I (Panthéon-Sorbonne) and directs the Institute of French Revolutionary History. He is the author of several major works in eighteenth-century European intellectual history.

The University of Chicago Press, Chicago 60637
The University of Chicago Press Ltd., London
© 1997 by The University of Chicago
All rights reserved. Published 1997
Printed in the United States of America
05 04 03 02 01 00   1 2 3 4 5
ISBN 0-226-86568-1 (cloth)
       0-226-86570-3 (paper)

Originally published by Editori Laterza as *L'uomo dell'illuminismo,*
© 1992, Gius. Laterza & Figli.

Library of Congress Cataloging-in-Publication Data

Uomo del'illuminismo. English
    Enlightenment portraits / [edited by] Michel Vovelle ; translated by Lydia G. Cochrane.
        p.   cm.
    Includes bibliographical references and index.
    Contents: The noble / Pierre Serna—The soldier / Jean-Paul Bertaud—The businessman / Louis Bergeron—The man of letters / Roger Chartier—The man of science / Vincenzo Ferrone—The artist / Daniel Arasse—The explorer / Marie-Noëlle Bourguet—The functionary / Carlo Capra—The priest / Dominique Julia—The woman / Dominique Godineau.
    ISBN 0-226-86568-1 (cloth : alk. paper). — ISBN 0-226-86570-3 (paper : alk. paper)
    1. Enlightenment—France—Influence. 2. Enlightenment—Europe. 3. France—Intellectual life—18th century. 4. Social change—Histroy—18th century. I. Vovelle, Michel. II. Cochrane, Lydia G. III. Title.
DC33.4.U66   1997
944'.034'0922—dc21   96–48853
                                                                            CIP

Contents

Introduction

Michel Vovelle

Enlightenment portraits? The image of the "man of the Enlightenment," in the most literal sense of the term, is forcefully represented by
William Blake's *Glad Day* (1780). Blake's man stands in tranquil, self-
assured nudity, his arms spread wide, before a shadowy background and
within an aureole that seems to emanate from him. He is at the center of
the universe; one might say he is a man of light more than of enlightenment. Regnault presents him in nearly identical terms in his *La liberté ou
la mort,* painted in the thick of the French Revolution. Here too a nude
man stands floating in the sky with outstretched arms, angel or Icarus,
since the artist has given him wings and a celestial flame burning on his
brow. The symbolism is more complex though more explicit. To the
right of the man Liberty, a comely figure poised on a cloud, brandishes a
phrygian cap in one hand and holds in the other the level of Equality. To
the left, as if to counterbalance Liberty, a skeleton of Death, draped in
black and leaning on a scythe, seems to come straight out of a baroque
cenotaph. Man is free, a conqueror, the true master of the universe, because he has exorcized the forces of darkness and of the past.

The Enlightenment View of Man

As we see him strikingly epitomized in image, Enlightenment man justifies (if this were necessary) the present book and its organization. The
eighteenth century—and we might debate its limits—placed man at the
center of its vision of the world; he was the hub around which its entire
thought revolved. This constituted a break with the baroque age and
with a sensibility that had dominated the post-Tridentine era for over a
century and had persisted, disciplined by the classical sense of order—
for how long? I would be tempted to say until midcentury, if setting a

term of that sort did not seem so futile, since it depends upon whether one refers to the anticipations of discoverers working at the end of the seventeenth century, revealed by the "crisis of European consciousness," or to indications of the propagation of ideas, a process that varied enormously from one social group to another and one country to another in a Europe in which the Enlightenment seemed to move out from France and England, then from Germany and Italy, to spread in weakening concentric circles. The end point seems easier to establish: the twilight of the Enlightenment (a convenient metaphor) doubtless came at the end of the century as part of a sequence of events, of which the French Revolution was simply the paroxysm, in which certitudes were shaken, but in which what was irreversible in the turn that the history of humanity had taken was not challenged.

The ambiguity of this investigation of the Enlightenment arises from that base. We will spare the reader the fundamental but insoluble debate—to which all the contributors to this volume are sensitive—on the necessary distinction between the ideal type of the "man of the Enlightenment" and the anonymous and variegated mass of the men and women of the period. We obviously cannot portray them all, and the picture presented here is inevitably elitist. With the possible exception of the portraits of the woman and the soldier—in some respects marginal figures in this universe—we will see here direct actors in history, people who took an active part in the collective adventure and at times paid a high price for it: nobles, priests, entrepreneurs, men of letters, men of science, artists, and explorers. One might be tempted to start by placing them all in one camp or another as fellow participants in the spirit of the age. Peasants and the urban populace are missing, raising the unavoidable question of the position that the common man occupied in the new and evolving model of the *honnête homme* and in a discourse that embraced all of humankind.

We need to start, precisely, from the new discourse on man in general if we want to understand the full variety of the attitudes and representations of the various groups. One obligatory reference is the entry "Homme" (Man) in the great *Encyclopédie* of Diderot and d'Alembert. It offers a few surprises. Thirty-six of its forty-five columns are devoted to human anatomy, eight to "moral man," and a half-column to "political man." An introduction gives the general tone.

> A feeling, reflecting, thinking being, who freely walks the earth,
> who seems to be at the head of all other animals whom he domi-

nates, who lives in society, who has invented the sciences and the arts, who has his particular goodness and badness, who has given himself masters, who has made laws for himself. . . . He can be considered in many ways. . . . Man is composed of two substances, one known as soul . . . the other known as body. The body or the material part of man has been studied a great deal.

The entry continues (after a brief transition conceding that the various perspectives for considering man could be multiplied to infinity, since "there is nothing that cannot be linked to him") to give a full description of the physical man from the fetus through puberty to old age, treating the bones, muscles, and organs, and providing statistics on mortality.[1]

The description of moral man ("article de M. Le Roi") is shorter but no less explicit in its presentation of an analysis visibly inspired by Condillac's sensualism. Recognizing man's advantage in his setting in nature, the article states: "When one regards the immense works of man; when one examines the detail of his arts and the progress of his sciences; when one sees him sail over the seas, measure the heavens, and rival the thunder in its noise and its effect," one is struck by "the lowliness and atrocity" to which "this king of nature has often sunk."

Once the article has posed the problem in this paradoxical manner, it eliminates—with an allowable pinch of aggressiveness—metaphysical explanations based in sin or in man's depraved nature.

Some moralists have recourse to a mixture of good and evil that itself has great need of explanation. Pride, superstition, and fear have produced systems and have loaded knowledge about man with a thousand prejudices that observation must destroy. Religion has taken on the task of leading us on the road to the happiness that it has prepared for us beyond time. Philosophy must study the natural reasons for the actions of man in order to make him better and happier in this transitory life.

And what does philosophy say? Men's actions are ruled by sensations and spring from desires. Man is always what his needs make him, even if, "rubbing elbows with others," he enters society. The "I" is not odious: friendship, love, passion, and ambition (the fruit of a desire to rise in society) exist in function of the degree of utility expected from them. When they are thwarted, these inclinations can lead to unnatural ideas ("see 'Fanaticism'"). There are remedies, however, for this pessimistic picture in which the individual's gaiety disappears when youth flees and societies move from equilibrium to decline: "But the cultivation of experimental physics and the presentation of the picture of nature by men of a strong and rare temper can give the human spirit a spectacle that will extend its views and bring to birth a new order of things."

Although he concurs that "human society is thus a confederation of the wicked united by interest alone," the author of the article concedes that one cannot "mistake in man a sweet sentiment that interests him in the fate of his similars once he is reassured concerning his own."

Men's sensibility can be the source of all virtues and—why not?—the source of "confident happiness" ("see 'Humanity' "). To bring this about requires an entire pedagogy, beginning in infancy. The "virtuous sentiment of the homeland" must be inculcated in the young (the example of Sparta is invoked); they must be taught to opt for the general good and for what furthers society, and they must be brought up not only with right precepts but with good examples. The human machine, governed by pleasure, facilitates this enterprise, given that egotism is corrected by an inclination to imitate: "Men have secret relations with one another that unite them," which are expressed by the fact of living in society; "men are modified by one another," and the Brownian movement of their particular interests is unified in the general mass of the habits of their time. It is legitimate to speak of "Enlightenment man" in a historical perspective, as a reflection of the age: "One speaks of the century of chivalry; one might speak of the century of the fine arts and philosophy, and—may it please God—there may come a time that could be called the century of beneficence and humanity."

The way to attain that ideal was through willpower: "Since it is example and opinion that determine the love of well-being, it follows that men *make themselves* and that it is almost possible to give them whatever form one wishes" [emphasis added]. The article does not avoid the question of the political conditions for such an enterprise: "This can happen above all in a monarchy; the throne is a pedestal on which imitation seeks its model. In republics equality does not allow one man to rise up enough to be ceaselessly on display." But in all cases, it is a good idea to watch general conditions and "situations." A state in which order and ease reign risks sliding into pleasure-seeking and the triumph of individual interests; a troubled state or one vulnerable to war finds in hatred a harmful unifying cement. The formation of the new man followed a narrow path; it reinforced the importance of a carefully thought-out educational pedagogy focused on childhood. Women played a role here.

The author of the *Encyclopédie* article on moral man speaks as a sensationalist philosopher, but it is a physiocrat who speaks in the very short article on political man, a topic treated here in purely technical terms but one that was soon to be debated in terms of citizenship. "There are only two true sources of wealth: man and the land." "Healthy" and "industrious" men are needed, and they can be so only if they are free. This means that commerce too must be free, that fewer workers in luxury crafts and fewer domestic servants are needed, and that farmers must be encouraged: what good are manufactories as long as arable land lies idle?

If men (and land) make up the wealth of nations, they need to be numerous—which returns us to a pedagogy turned toward parents (and nurses). It also brings us back (but less systematically) to the argument of the *Encyclopédie* article on moral man and its discussion of what motivates people: "One enters into a condition only in the hope of an easy life." Hence, the worker must not be driven to despair and his wages must be decent; net profits must be divided not too unequally.

Although the *Encyclopédie* is a cardinal text in the adventure of the Enlightenment—which justifies the prominence given it here—it is far from exhausting the riches of that age. I might add (but the reader will already be aware of this) that it is far from reflecting a consensus universally accepted in the philosophy of the time. The sensationalist discourse that lies behind the article on moral man needs to be contrasted to the Rousseauistic view of man's original goodness, perverted by society, and to the totally different line of argumentation that was to gain increasing prominence during the last decades of the century. The theme of civic virtue, which cannot be reduced to egotistical interests well understood and carefully directed, gained increasing force, as did reflection on citizenship and the affirmation of natural rights, and it found both theoretical and practical expression in the French Revolution. In recent decades, great thematic frescos set in the framework of a new history of ideas have renewed our knowledge concerning the thought of the Enlightenment and established the terms of the debate—Happiness with Robert Mauzi, Nature with Jean Ehrard, Disquietude with Jean Deprun. We do not intend to return to these topics here.

But even if we shun all misguided ambition to raise the question of the "man of the Enlightenment" in the way Kant formulated the question in his "Was ist Aufklärung?" we can recognize that the *Encyclopédie* text permits us to bring together a certain number of general subjects that provide a minimal consensus—above and beyond the controversies—concerning a new vision of the world expressed through a vision of man.

What is most striking at first glance, even if the spirit of the *Encyclopé-die* forces the issue somewhat, is doubtless the repudiation of the theo-centric vision that had formerly dictated the order of the universe. Here man is no longer seen within the framework of the mind of God; the other world fades; the reader is directed to a different entry for the prob-lem of the soul. Guilt and sin enter the sphere of potentially harmful metaphysical speculations ("see 'Fanaticism'").

Reinstated within the order of nature as an animal endowed with particular properties, man in the *Encyclopédie* has his full physical con-sistency, his anatomy, his physiology—all of which are ways to analyze what constitutes the unity of the human species but also its diversity. One thinks immediately of the "dwarf" from Saturn in Voltaire's *Micromegas* (and we know that Voltaire had Fontenelle in mind) who observes the tiny beings of our terraqueous globe and believes that they are actively working to reproduce their kind and exclaims "I have caught Nature in the act!" Like a new Leeuwenhoek, he is an intrepid and imprudent dis-coverer. We will see examples of that same curiosity in the chapter on the man of science, and perhaps even more strikingly in that on the ex-plorer, but also in the chapters on the bureaucrat and even the priest—all persons who were open to a study of behavior, of mores, and of the many varieties of a humanity to be discovered at one's doorstep as well as beyond the seas. The theologian went into hiding or remained en-trenched in his positions. The man of science took his place.

A natural creature and an individual motivated by his own interest, man as depicted in the *Encyclopédie* seems untouched by the constraining hierarchies formerly imposed by the societies of order. If there is a hier-archy, the article on political man tells us, it is determined by a man's social utility and his place in the creation of wealth. Man lives in society, to be sure, but the social contract, reduced here to "a confederation of the wicked united by interest alone" in a minimal expression of a theme that Rousseau treated at much greater length, rests on the essential postulate of freedom as a natural right pertaining to all men.

Master of his fate once he pays the gages of prejudice, religion, and the conditioning that come from his very nature, man is distinct from the other animals as a creature of reason: he has created the arts, the sciences, and wealth-producing activities—in a word, civilization. He is malleable and perfectible. Human history is the history of progress as it can be read on this earth, within the limits of life here below, and to the extent that the ultimate goal that he seeks is earthly happiness. To borrow a phrase from Diderot on the subject of man: "Is he good? Is he evil?" The debate had been joined (as we see here). It led some to conclude that man was originally good but became perverted and others to view man as a combination of individual egotistic interests tempered at times by natural tendencies connected with the "precious sensibility that is the source of all virtues." Sensibility versus reason is another fundamental debate that I do not intend to reopen here. The fact remains that the perfectibility of man, which led to the constantly reiterated question of how to make men happier and more useful, also and inevitably led to a political voluntarism aimed at harmonizing the flux of interests within the framework of a rational city and extending the limits of civilization through the diffusion of Enlightenment. This explains the key role of pedagogy in this mechanism, since in order to prepare him for his role as a man the human being must be molded from infancy, developing his better tendencies and furthering his intellectual acquisitions by appropriate training—an endeavor that the author of the *Encyclopédie* article, showing proof of a broader mind than was universally the case, extends to women.

The problem of the state ineluctably arises in this construction. It is partially eluded in this article, a discretion that cannot be attributed solely to an imposed prudence. It alludes to the republican system only once; the monarchic system appears as the most natural and efficacious reference. This was another consensus that was widely shared, in the age of enlightened despotism, by the great majority of those in the *parti philosophique*. Similarly, it is no surprise to find that the *Encyclopédie* abandons all challenge to the hierarchical social system of the society of orders, attacking it only indirectly through physiocratic argument. This is more than nothing, however, since it leads, by implication, to substituting a system of utility and the production of wealth in the utopian city of the future for the value system of the old order founded on esteem and honors cascading down from the top.

This is how the example that, for lack of space for fuller treatment, we have chosen to analyze here presents Enlightenment man in his ideal formulation. What remains to be seen—and the task is not a small one—is in what measure that discourse was embraced, transmitted, and received. If we want to compare the ideal man, thus broadly defined, and man in the concrete, the ordinary man, even before introducing the major actors in preamble to our authors' chapters, this presupposes disposing of an unavoidable preliminary question: to what degree did the dream of the Enlightenment correspond to reality? In short, was eighteenth-century man—if that expression makes any sense at all— capable of fulfilling that voluntaristic program?

The Common Man

Voltaire's evaluations changed as time went on; we can trace them in the poem "Le Mondain" ("Ah l'heureux temps que ce siècle de fer") and in short stories, for instance in "Le monde comme il va," which ends with the definitive verdict, "Sauve qui peut." Or, even better, in "Les aventures de la Raison," which relates Reason's journey through the world that people call "enlightened" once she has escaped from the well in which she had been imprisoned with her daughter Truth. The result is not all positive: Reason does indeed find cause to hope where enlightened princes reign but she also finds many wars, much barbarity, on occasion even regression. At the end of the story mother and daughter return to their pit to await better days. And Candide, in counterpoint to the great voyages of exploration that we will soon be considering, offers another style of discovery in his disorderly and feverish wanderings, in Europe and the world, from savage wars to the pyres of the Inquisition. Had nothing changed since the picaresque universe of Simplicius Simplicis-simus save the awareness of a tragic absurdity?

We need to turn to today's historians, not for the impossible task of summing up in a few pages how much and up to what point people in the age of the Enlightenment changed in their material condition and their collective representations, but rather to help us recall a few basic, apparently naive facts. That appearance is deceptive, what is more, since historians by no means agree with one another. Pierre Chaunu, for example, in his provocative synthesis of the civilization of the Enlighten-ment, contrasts the time-honored notion of the "glorious eighteenth century" as a world of intellectual ferment and collective progress with the more reserved reading of a historian for whom the great century of revolutions in thought was the seventeenth century, the age of French classicism, which the eighteenth century simply prolonged and drifted away from here and there.

A number of points are indisputable, however. There were more people in Europe: the population exploded, putting an end to the long stagnation of the preceding centuries. Ernest Labrousse's verdict re-garding the advantages and disadvantages of the age for the common mass of urban and (even more) rural people is still unassailable: "Ils y ont au moins gagné la vie" (At least they won the right to live). Demographic increase was notable in England and in France (where the population rose from 20 million to perhaps 28 million), and it was even stronger in central and eastern Europe. In Hungary, for instance, the population exploded spectacularly. Without going into detail about periodization, we can note that the rate of increase was incontestably higher during the second half of the century, varying from one region to another. The reasons for this rise are now firmly established for eastern European lands. Much more than by the revolution in medical and scientific means for controlling disease and death (vaccination among them), surges of mortality were leveled by the decrease, as the century progressed, of both food shortages and the epidemics that followed in their wake and skimmed off the excess births accumulated during the preceding years. This probably lessens the credit—which is nonetheless genuine—that we can attribute to the political voluntarism of agents of the Enlightenment.

In the more advanced parts of Europe collective attitudes toward life, birth, love, marriage and sexuality, and death began to change. Philippe Ariès was one of the first historians to note the age's new regard for the child as children became more precious but at times fewer. Contraception, which was still among the "baleful secrets" that the confessors denounced, can be detected with certainty in more than one place in France, especially from the 1770s on. Illegitimate births increased in Paris and the other major cities. Men's most intimate attitudes had changed—women's as well, and we will soon see within what limits.

People were more numerous, but were they happier? This is another falsely naive question, but one that is directly written into the preoccupations of the Enlightenment elite. War as massacre had declined. That sweeping statement is contestable and perhaps tinged with gallocentrism: France was, by and large, preserved from the scourge of invasion from 1715 to the Revolution. But widespread fighting continued from Flanders to central and eastern Europe, and it was there that Voltaire's Candide found matter for his creator's bitter commentary.

We need to consider the material condition of the population, as expressed in daily life, from the standpoint of a rural world that still accounted for 85 percent of the population of France in 1789 and for an even higher proportion in the less urbanized regions of central and eastern Europe. Was the peasantry prosperous or miserable? There are so many particular cases, so many contradictory discourses. We need to be careful not to be taken in either by the sort of lament still being echoed by Michelet in the following century ("Look at poor Job, lying on his dung heap") or by the rural idyll made fashionable by pastoral poetry, as in the country scenes that Goya painted for the Escorial or in the image of an idealized village society in Rétif de La Bretonne's *La vie de mon père*. To hazard a generalization that risks caricature, let us simply say that agricultural production increased and that in the old, densely populated Europe new land clearing brought the acreage under cultivation to its maximum. We should add that in certain areas—England, Flanders, some parts of France, and the Po Valley—there were the first signs of what would later be called the agricultural revolution. Eastern European agriculture began to play a role by the commercialization, through the Baltic and the North Sea, of wheat from its vast domains.

Still, the condition of the peasantry did not see any spectacular progress. In France during the latter half of the eighteenth century the wages of an agricultural day worker were stagnant, whereas revenues and profits were rising in a society of widening gaps. Above all, the traditional framework of seignorial levies remained unchanged and may have become even more burdensome during times of what has been called the "seignorial reaction" of the final decades of the century. (The concept has been disputed in controversies that we cannot go into here.) But if western Europe reacted against what was left of a moribund feudal system from which England had already freed itself, eastern Europe was undergoing a "second servitude" that reinforced ties of dependency in the framework of the demesnial system.

The industrial revolution, already in course in the British Isles, and forms of proto-industrialization at work in western Europe brought more novelties (in the context that interests us here) to the countryside than to the city. But this entry into an as yet limited modernity was inscribed in people's lives as much in terms of new dependencies, destabilization, and a crisis in the old corporative solidarities as it was in terms of felt progress. We can admit, with Pierre Chaunu, that for the overwhelming majority of workers in both city and country there had not yet been any revolution.

If the century of the Enlightenment was the high point of the tool, celebrated in the plates accompanying the *Encyclopédie,* and of a perfected tool, the machine, which had made its entry into the industrial worlds of textiles and metallurgy, the century nonetheless still largely belonged to an *"Ancien Style"* civilization, as Ernest Labrousse put it. One might object to this judgment, citing the spectacle of the urban world, capitals like London and Paris, and the great ports for trade and trans-atlantic commerce. It is perhaps in such places that we can discern a new man, even in the popular classes. His image was ambiguous for his contemporaries. A negative view prevailed, and not only in Rousseauistic criticism. From Rétif de La Bretonne to Louis-Sébastien Mercier's *Tableau de Paris,* the image of the city was a place of perdition, of both luxury and misery, of debauchery and of corruption in all its aspects—a place crowned by the mephitic vapors that it secreted and rotten to the core. The fact remains that the city—the residence of the aristocratic and bourgeois elites, of a middle and petty bourgeoisie that, outside western Europe, was struggling for affirmation, and, above all, of the vast and composite world of *l'échoppe et la boutique* (the street stall and the shop) of small independent producers—was the place where the ideas percolated and the exchanges took place that allowed novelty to make headway. As Daniel Roche and Arlette Farge have pointed out in recent studies, new customs and new manners of being and appearing arose in the cities. Modernity emerged within structures perpetuated by the guilds and corporations that had not changed globally.

Were people aware of such changes? The problem of the culture of the Enlightenment, of its diffusion, and of its limits lies precisely here. A traveler's remark that he had seen a coachman reading on his perch while waiting for a fare is not enough to settle the question. One might easily cite the contradictory impressions of people—Frenchmen like the Président de Brosses or Englishmen like Arthur Young—who traveled in the age of the Grand Tour and characterized their adventures in the provinces as a plunge if not into savagery at least into the exotic the minute they left the coded network of preestablished contacts and salons waiting to receive them. The same travelers were not always tender toward the provincial elites who entertained them. We can put aside the elites and come back to them later. We have a few rough tests to help us with the problem of the frontier between people of the Enlightenment and people who escaped its diffusion. The criterion of literacy—or at least the ability to sign one's name—offers one global standard for measurement and a sketchy geography.

This criterion distinguishes a more literate northwest Europe, ranging from northern France southward to an imaginary line drawn from Saint-Malo to Geneva, from a southern Europe of lesser literacy and areas of continental Europe of decreasing literacy as one moved from west to east. This frontier long remained stable, but shifts were taking place: literacy progressed during the course of the century, and rough as this indicator is, it does signify something. If not the diffusion of the Enlightenment (who would risk such an imprudent statement?) at least a minimal precondition for some access to written culture. This does not mean, as many thought at the time, that the less literate world was bereft of culture.

That other world was in movement as well. In the French Midi, where Provence had long had a network for male sociability based in the penitential religious confraternities, structures were changing, as Maurice Agulhon reminds us. Recruitment to these groups was becoming more democratic, partly because the elites began to abandon them, finding in the Masonic lodges a framework for sociability better suited to their sensibilities. Denunciations of the confraternities show that they were evolving: was this due to secularization, making it a lay evolution more than a de-Christianization? In fact, the term matters little; the trend remains.

This touches on the domain of religion, a sensitive point and a battlefield for men of the Enlightenment. Is it fair to say that the century displays early signs of a detachment from established religions, even of a "de-Christianization"? It is difficult to sound people's minds and hearts, and we lack the statistical instruments to gauge a religious sociology in contemporary terms. If we want at least to reach beyond what the elites had to say about the masses, we will have to use trickery. This is what I have attempted to do by examining a huge amount of data gathered from thousands of wills drawn up in Provence in the eighteenth century and by analyzing clauses related to spiritual matters—the choice of a tomb, pious bequests, and requests for masses. Other studies have concentrated on Paris (Pierre Chaunu), the French provinces, Italy, or the Iberian Peninsula. Such studies show significantly convergent results, at least in most of France; they vary somewhat elsewhere. Whereas Provence at the end of the seventeenth century shows a massive investment in a profusion of baroque funerary ceremonials on every level of the social scale, a decisive turning point came, generally between 1750 and 1770, at times sooner (around 1730), and earlier still in Paris, where it is clear as early as the beginning of the century. The proportion of wills containing clauses for pious bequests decreases, often by half; this occurs in men's wills more than in women's, in cities and towns more than in rural areas. At the two extremities of the hierarchy of social status, the decline is less marked among nobles and the lower classes, especially in the country, but it is clear among the bourgeoisie and the liberal professions and—one might say by contact—in the world of small shopkeepers and craftsmen. A broader geographical scope puts the French model into perspective: in Spain, Portugal, and most of Italy, the turning point often came later, only in the middle of the following century, and we can discern only a few indications of coming changes. Can one conclude that a decline in baroque piety was a prelude to de-Christianization? Or did it indicate that individuals were turning inward toward an internalized religion based more in both sensibility and reason, as Philippe Ariès would have it? I have no intention of pronouncing one way or the other. What is clear, beyond quarrels about semantics, is that changing attitudes toward death enable us to perceive an essential turning point in collective sensibility, something that is perhaps even more important.

The few inevitably discontinuous and reductive traits by which we have tried to circumscribe the man of the Enlightenment on the level of the anonymous mass leave us with contradictory results. The underlying structures show stability and the framework of daily life remained relatively fixed, but there was a certain mobility reflected in collective attitudes and representations in a more densely populated world in which modernity was making its way thanks to new ways of producing, being, and appearing. This was a fragmented universe (had it been less so before?), divided along lines of social position, urban-rural relations, and geographical location. In the cultural domain as in the economic and social domains, there developed both focal points for the diffusion of novelty and darker zones. The new agents of the transformation—during the Revolution people even dared speak of the "regeneration"—of man in the spirit of the Enlightenment saw a new city to be created and unified according to new norms and thanks to their voluntaristic initiative.

It is to those "happy few" and to the more restricted definition of the man of the Enlightenment that we need to turn now, following the typology proposed by our authors.

Actors and Protagonists

Our operative field of study shrinks spectacularly when we redefine the man of the Enlightenment as participating in a new vision of the world. A polarization emerged in stark contrast to the tripartite division of social orders bequeathed by the Middle Ages that survived in society's official structures: henceforth elite and mass stood opposed as active and passive agents of the recomposition of the world. The French classical age had fashioned the ideal of the *honnête homme*, an ideal still current. On this point there was genuine continuity. One illustration is the "English philosopher" who serves as a spokesman for Abbé Prévost. In France, the "philosopher" states, he has encountered "only a composite of rough-mannered persons who speak no fixed language and have no more taste than resemblance in their fashions in dress and in all their external appearance . . . which means that the only real Frenchmen are the small number of those who are at the head of the others and who are distinct from what is called 'the people.' " But the image of the *honnête homme* had been modified, even if people at times persisted in defining it in elitist terms as "good company." Make way, then, for the elite! As is known, the concept has elicited debate, even concerning its application to eighteenth-century society.

The elite challenged the historical cleavages of the society of orders and overrode class distinctions in the very society in which a new bourgeoisie was growing in numbers and strength—a society founded on a system of broadly shared values whose principle of cohesion was the spirit of the Enlightenment. Was that elite a reality or an illusion? Did it exist? The portrait of the noble, as we shall soon see, shows the force and pertinence of deep-rooted attitudes of caste and class and of an awareness of difference precisely at a time when there seemed to be agreement on a common vision. Moreover, the diversity of social frames of reference from one end of Europe to the other seems to defy the elaboration of a common model.

Yet if we look only at the small group of people who transmitted the new discourse, the century does indeed appear to be one of cosmopolitanism, of exchanges, and of a more intense circulation of men and ideas. There have been altogether too many descriptions of the profound mixing of men during the century for us to dwell on it here— men of letters and scholars, but also administrators and soldiers who moved easily from the service of one state to another in a Europe of enlightened rulers, not to mention adventurers of all sorts, of whom Casanova is the best known if not the most representative example.

That incessant mixing contributed to the idea of a cultural unification perhaps facilitated by the hegemony of the French language within "French Europe" of the century of the Enlightenment, even though that preeminence had begun to be questioned by a growing Anglomania that proved to be more than a passing fancy and by grumbling about French predominance in the German world. The networks of sociability that were created or reinforced—from the academies, whose great century it was, to the phenomenon of Freemasonry, which was born in the British Isles but swept through France to weave a fabric of universal complicity that reached as far as central Europe—seemed to facilitate the elaboration of a common vision within the framework of the Republic of Letters. Unification of the elites was fostered by the circulation of ideas, which in turn was encouraged by proliferating correspondence, both scholarly and within the fashionable world; by the diffusion of the book, both through the channels for official literature and channels for books sold "under the cloak"; and by the circulation of gazettes and journals, which abounded in erudite circles in Germany.

As the century progressed, this dissemination of ideas changed the contours of the enlarged group that participated in it. Historians traditionally insist on social mobility, perhaps more in appearance than reality, in an age in which the barriers of condition seemed abolished. The hierarchy of esteem seemed to have been shaken by the prestige of talent or merit; doors opened to certain commoners, whether they obtained official recognition from the academies or the courts, or, as freelancers and adventurers, they slipped stealthily (or at times scandalously forced their way, like Mesmer and Cagliostro) to the front of the stage.

One might regret that we have failed to reserve a special place for the marginalized, members of a category to some extent new in the Enlightenment, but they are perhaps too easy game. Behind the facade of the bustle of activity that fed the chronicles of the century and contributed to fixing its image, a new distribution of roles was taking place—a recomposition of the social space that we need to investigate to see to what extent it reflects reality, fiction, or simple illusion. In the century in which painting saw a vogue for portraits that repudiated the grand manner in favor of directness, spontaneity and an attachment to the truth of human beings, a "portrait gallery" becomes more than an academic exercise.

As with all enterprises of this sort, the picture that we present cannot fail to leave even its creators with regrets and dissatisfactions. It is inevitably incomplete. The prince is regrettably absent here, although in the age of enlightened despotism he stood at the heart of the overall social machinery. Will some readers object because the philosopher does not have a chapter of his own? It is true that we will encounter multiple images of him in the portraits of the man of letters, the man of science, the artist, even the explorer. Instead of an abstract profile of the bourgeois, we have preferred to focus on the businessman and entrepreneur who brought a more modern face to a new bourgeoisie. As for all those on the fringes of society, adventurers in the broadest sense of the term, they can be encountered everywhere, in nearly all categories, existing inside a system that they helped to challenge.

This means that in one way or another, our picture has come to be organized, without forcing it too much, around several broad themes. First come the *actors,* the mainstays of the "old style" society like the noble and the soldier, or newcomers on the social scene like the entrepreneur. Next come the *spokespersons,* who found their hour of glory as bearers of the new discourse of the Enlightenment, even when they continued to cling to the older world by many ties of dependency. These are the man of letters, the man of science, the artist, and the explorer pushing back the limits of the known world. Finally, the voluntaristic enterprise of remodeling society required agents of transmission, the *cultural intermediaries* who are attracting so much attention today. Did the priest play this new role? In any event, the functionary, an essential player in the framework of enlightened absolutist monarchies who dreamed of rationalizing the state, makes his striking appearance. The woman holds the same ambiguous position in this general scheme of things that the century attributed to her. She enjoyed a social promotion that made her the queen of philosophical salons; she was the object of more intense but also anxious attention that nonetheless kept her, in her overall condition, in a situation of dependency from which she did not emancipate herself for some time.

Let us not regret the loss of a gallery of portraits of the princes of the age of the Enlightenment. It is one we have often visited. What we should recall is not so much the new status of the prince (did it change fundamentally?) as the new image that the ruler took pains to give of himself. Speaking in connection with Ranuce Ernest in *La Chartreuse de Parme* (a work from an only slightly later time), Jean Pomeau, in his *Europe des Lumières,* borrows Stendhal's "a friend speaking among friends." This was a lasting cliché, confirmed by many examples from Frederick II, who brought together the philosophic elite of the time at Sans Souci—Voltaire, Maupertuis, La Mettrie, and the marquis d'Argens—to Catherine II, the "Semiramis of the North" and the protector of Diderot, and to such princely travelers eager for learning as Joseph II and Gustavus III. This was more than a mere facade: when he became the servant of the public good and the artisan of a profound restructuring of the state, the prince, as incarnate in the contrasting personalities of Frederick II and Joseph II (among others), felt himself invested with a new mission, which he carried out directly or by delegation to enlightened ministers—Tanucci, Pombal—through whom he established a

connection with enlightened opinion. The limitations of this rein-
terpretation of the prince that attempted to make him into an anti-
Machiavelli (to borrow the title of Frederick II's work) are just as evident: Catherine II's famous statement to Diderot contrasting the easy
life of the philosopher, who works on paper, to the constraints on the
sovereign, who operates on human skin, brought things back into perspective. The realpolitik of the enlightened monarchs who split up Poland at the same time they cultivated their philosophical contacts gives
their idealized portrait a false likeness that some may find unjust.

Was not the major constraint on the prince, perhaps, that in a world
in turmoil he remained the linchpin of a social system in which he was
both master and servant—a system typified by the primacy of an aristocracy of nobles who still held first place throughout the hierarchy of
honors and powers? Domesticated nobilities (but domesticated in quite
unequal measure if we look at all of Europe) were kept in line by a life at
court at its highest brilliance. The final word on the question—and in
this instance, literally the last word—was perhaps said by Louis XVI, an
enlightened monarch *manqué,* when he declared, at the first rumblings
of the Revolution, "I shall never be separated from *my* clergy and *my* nobility," thus avowing his fundamental solidarity with the old world.

Does this mean that the nobility was the major force of resistance to
the Enlightenment and the incarnation of the past? This was what the
French Revolution said in the context of a merciless struggle against the
aristocratic order that tolerated no halfhearted measures or shades of
opinion. Denounced for its idleness, its usurped privileges, and its moral
decadence, the nobility became for an entire historical tradition the em-
bodiment of the anti-Enlightenment. Pierre Serna's chapter helpfully
recalls the origins of the debate as it was launched by Abbé Coyer and
others even before the Revolution. This cliché (and not all clichés are
false), was once generally accepted but has been seriously revised in recent decades for reasons that Serna recalls. The debate is not recent,
however, as the paradox of a cultivated nobility open to all the currents
of modern thought was pointed out long ago. In its libraries, its salons,
and even in the courts, the aristocracy was far from being closed to the
spirit of the Enlightenment. Recent studies on French provincial academies and on the *sociétés de pensée* give witness to the still important,
even preponderant, place that the aristocracy occupied in the cultural
structures of the time.

Other scholars have reconsidered the nobility in light of what
founded its social power. Some—George V. Taylor, Guy Chaussinand-

Nogaret—have stressed the dynamism of the nobility as it turned agronomist in the age of the physiocrats, manufacturer in leading sectors of metallurgy, trader in the seaports, and speculator in urban real estate. In a word, it was progressive, enabled by its dynamism and its openness to new ideas to claim a more than honorable place within the new elites in formation. The English gentry, regenerated and integrated into the processes of production of an economy in full expansion, immediately springs to mind. Was England the exception that proves the rule? In France, the order of the nobility gave first priority in the collective demands expressed in the *cahiers de doléances* of 1789 to demanding freedoms; the abolition of the seignorial regime came last on their list. Should this seem odd?

Faced with a contradiction deriving from his very position, the noble of the age of the Enlightenment had several options. One was a rear-guard action to defend ancient values and the right of blood, based on arguments often elaborated at the end of the preceding century (by Boulainvilliers's posterity, among others), which generated the characteristic "seignorial" reaction mentioned above. Another was integration into the new elites, a move fraught with ambiguities and misunderstandings.

Some members of the aristocracy did not stop at compromise with the bourgeoisie, and loss of caste took an explosive form for certain Provençal nobles—Sade, Mirabeau, Boyer d'Argens, Antonelle, and Barras—each of whom, in his own manner, violently repudiated the caste and even the world order into which he had been born. The noble descent into debauchery, which in Spain took the form of *majeza* (a flashy elegance and an imitation of cocky, common manners), was the expression of a group pathology symptomatic of a collective malaise. From Molière's don Juan to Mozart's don Giovanni, without going back as far as Tirso de Molina, the emblematic image of the libertine *grand seigneur* had changed. Is there anything more revelatory than the scene of the masked ball in *Don Giovanni*? Don Giovanni's guests cover their faces for an aristocratic festivity—an opportunity for a privileged man whose condition frees him from common constraints to display his appetite for pleasure. The merriment reaches its height, however, in a quasi-revolutionary "Viva la Libertà." Beneath the mask, which is also the mask of the Venetian carnival, the noble is brought to utter words that bear the seed of his own death.

In this context, it is understandable that the full-figure portrait of the man of war, a tradition that seemingly persisted quite naturally from the Middle Ages to the baroque age, changed when it was contrasted to the ideal of the Enlightenment. This might at first sight seem surprising, since the soldier holds a place in this century through the emblematic figure of Frederick II, who was both a warrior and a philosopher, perhaps even more through that of Maréchal de Saxe, whose tomb in Strasbourg, wholly in the spirit of the age, is one of the noblest expressions of the hero's entry into an immortality earned by his merits and his glory. England, too, bowed respectfully before a depiction of the death of General Wolfe on the heights of Montreal, and France wept for Montcalm. But warrior values were no longer lodged at the heart of things in the Enlightenment. They belonged to a world gone by, the world of an aristocracy that still referred to its code of honor but that, in a large portion of Europe, no longer took arms as its primary vocation—although the aristocracy fought hard, in France at the end of the ancien régime, for instance, to reinforce its privileges in the military profession. It is significant that in Jean-Paul Bertaud's chapter on the soldier in the eighteenth century the center of interest shifts from the magnificent hero to the troops—to the simple soldier, often a mercenary, badly treated everywhere, and socially scorned. The soldier was also increasingly professional, thanks to the harsh training and drill for which the Prussian army set an example followed with unequal success in other European lands. The model was long-lived: we can still see it in the first decades of the following century in the tragic image of Büchner's *Woyzeck*. We also know, however, that when the French Revolution created an army of national volunteers it exploded the model of the professional soldier and replaced it with one of the citizen-soldier fighting for liberty.

Everything began to blur at the summit of an Enlightenment cosmopolitan aristocracy seemingly united by a common manner of thinking and behaving. The Prince de Ligne, whose *Mémoires* has been a constant source of discovery for scholars, is representative of the many high-ranking nobles who passed from one role to another and served several masters, one after the other. Was he a general? A diplomat? A wit? A society figure at home in various courts? He was all of those simultaneously, and he boasted of having "six or seven homelands: Empire, Flanders, France, Austria, Poland, Russia, and, almost, Hungary." He was loyal to the emperor; he was well received by the czarina; he was proud of his membership in the top echelon of *honnêtes gens.* He was indisputably a man of the Enlightenment, but was he an enlightened man, in the *philosophes'* sense of the term? Certainly not. He preferred *catins* to *Catons* (whores to Catos).

One might expect to see the bourgeois among the major protagonists of this history, providing a counterpoint to the representatives of
the old world. He is hard to find. Was "the bourgeois" an invention after
the fact, an imaginary creature forged by the nineteenth century? Was
Jaurès dreaming when he countered Michelet's determinedly miserabil-
ist picture of peasant poverty with one of the glorious eighteenth century as a time of the rise, then the affirmation, of the bourgeoisie? We
might well smile at a bourgeoisie that never stops rising from the medieval communes to the Renaissance and beyond. We smile, but there
were some who contested these commonly accepted ideas. Economic
and social historians (Ernest Labrousse, for one) who followed the
Jaurès tradition to highlight the centuries-long rise of bourgeois profits
that paralleled the rise in land revenues have been criticized for using
Marxian terms to characterize the bourgeois of past times. Some
scholars (Taylor, Chaussinand-Nogaret) included in their attack not
only a reconsideration of the new character who had been contrasted to
the noble but also a reevaluation of the role of the aristocracy. The
group of "self-defined" bourgeois that can be encountered in cities and
towns formed an old-style *bourgeoisie rentière* of people of independent
wealth. Such men took noble idleness for their model, lived on revenues
from their landholdings, and aspired to break into privileged circles by
the purchase of the office of counselor or secretary to the king that comported a noble title. The merchants and businessmen in France who
dreamed of little else but purchasing for their sons an office as *conseiller*
to parlement were denounced as traitors. Were the middle run of lawyers, prosecuting attorneys, and members of the liberal professions a
bourgeoisie in the modern sense of the term? Some historians insist that
the bourgeois did not exist; others respond that there was a "mixed"
bourgeoisie "of transition" (Régine Robin).

The bourgeois existed, but he was not yet visible, which is what is
paradoxical about his situation. Jean Ehrard has used literary sources to
show how the bourgeois, a useful man, furnished the age with a model
for a new and positive hero and for domestic virtues. This is reflected in
the birth of the "bourgeois drama" of Sedaine and others. Monsieur
Vanderk, the protagonist of Sedaine's *Le philosophe sans le savoir,* is admittedly an ex-noble who has become a merchant, but both in his activities
and culture he nonetheless represents the ideal of a socially desirable
reconversion.

The affirmation of a new model is not always presented by its protagonists: Daniel Roche's studies of the French provincial academies

have shown how discreet and, in the final analysis, limited the participation of merchants and entrepreneurs was in such structures. They were present in greater number in the Masonic lodges, where merchants (in Bordeaux or Marseilles, for instance) and a bourgeoisie "of talents" made a place for themselves, often an important one. In the dichotomy that was beginning to separate the old world from the new, to which one did the bourgeoisie belong? The ambiguity is perhaps just as striking as for the nobility. The representatives of commercial capitalism—large-scale merchants, bankers, businessmen—operated within the old methods of production and were an integral part of those old ways. It would perhaps be artificial to contrast the two groups, since dividing lines were so fluid between the nobles and the entrepreneurs and manufacturers who were their potential replacements, men who stood ready to propose an alternative in profit-based industry and manufacturing and whose image would prevail in the following century.

This makes us all the more grateful to Louis Bergeron for focusing on the *négociants*—the large-scale merchants—but also on the entrepreneurs. He traces the successive stages of their social promotion, at times as the heirs of merchant families, at others as men of humble beginnings who were the artisans of their own success. It is a different culture that we find sketched out here, one that does not follow the path of a classical education in the humanities but comes out of apprenticeship in the workplace, travel to perfect skills, and, with some, an autodidactic curiosity. It is a culture that led to the birth of new dynasties, that maintained contacts with waged workers and the world of small independent producers, and that was often tinged with a degree of paternalism. French, German, and Swiss examples found a strong echo in England. Can we dispute the right of these representatives of a new world in gestation to figure as men of the Enlightenment? They bear the same characteristic traits: an openness toward the outside world, curiosity, pragmatism, an insistence on social utility. But they also had a conservative side that made them inconspicuous representatives of a changing world. They left the spokesman's role to others.

Spokesmen

The spokesmen occupied center stage. We are open to the charge of simplification, however, when we include among their number the man of letters, the scientist, and the artist. Roles were becoming better defined in a rapidly expanding field of knowledge and expression, and

Roger Chartier rightly bases his analysis of the principles governing that redistribution of roles on the definitions of the man of letters given in dictionaries and commentaries of the time. All of these actors on the social stage benefited from the promotion of the intellectual during the age of Enlightenment. There is nothing really new about this change, and one might argue that from humanism to the age of French classicism a continual evolution had helped in bringing it about. But the increase in knowledge and a developing intellectual world gave such men mastery over opinion just when religious discourse, which had so long dominated thought, declined in relative importance and turned defensive, and just when a limited but genuine liberalization of censorship helped to free speech in the absolutist monarchies.

The framework within which the spokesmen operated was still well defined and constraining. Royal patronage, which had been essential to defining structures in the previous century, remained the rule in the better part of Europe under enlightened rulers, even though it took on a new, perhaps more supple, character. At the same time, however, the *parti philosophique* seemed to be gaining autonomy as a counterpower of opinion, opening the way to a right to criticism that would be tolerated as long as it did not attack established power directly.

Under the direct or indirect aegis of the prince, the intellectual world remained hierarchical and reflected the structures of society. The academy was its prime point of reference, though there were notable differences between academies—an English model, a French model, soon a German model. A small group of high-placed persons (somewhat like honorary members of the *comité d'honneur* of today's France) was joined by a still limited number of associate members and correspondents. This mode of organization might (and on occasion did) result in sclerosis. Voltaire once rather cruelly called the Académie de Marseille "une bonne fille qui n'a jamais fait de mal à personne" (a good-hearted girl who never harmed a soul).

Even with these constraints, the framework exploded under the pressure of collective demand and the very dynamism of knowledge. The phenomenon of the academy spread throughout Europe: in France and in Italy the academies (but also the learned societies) made up a dense and active network. Through the competitions they held and correspondence, they participated in the elaboration of a common market in knowledge and the exchange of ideas.

The personage of the man of letters changed, as did that of the scholar—in its sociology, first. The proportion of literarily inclined clerics tended to shrink, as did that of nobles, who were still well represented, however. For the greater part of the century, the commoners who were part of this group were far from nobodies. Few of them lived on earnings from a profession, subsisting instead on revenues from their lands or their investments, from an official post, or from pensions received. The personage of the author was still a novelty at the end of the century; nonetheless, the figure of the amateur with broad-ranging interests, the cultivated dilettante who collects curiosities for his "cabinet," although characteristic of the century, concealed a growing professionalism, thanks to increasing demand for knowledge, particularly in scientific fields. An engraving of the period might well show Madame du Châtelet offering Voltaire a pair of glasses so that he could read Newton; he would never become a physicist. The itinerary of the scholar (see the career of Lagrange in Vincenzo Ferrone's chapter on the man of science) became more and more precisely defined. Laboratories, observatories, and proliferating places for experimentation all reflect these new approaches, even if many people in this philosophical century were "curious about everything."

What was true for the restricted number of recognized intellectuals at the summit was all the more true of an enlightened opinion whose growth is perhaps one of the most striking features of the century. Paris had its salons, in appearance female spaces, given that ladies—Madame Geoffrin, Madame du Deffand, Mademoiselle de Lespinasse—presided over them, but they were peopled with men. The salons were places where ideas were exchanged in a climate of freedom that included a respect for a certain amount of ritual, but in all-male gatherings (as with the *coterie holbachique* that met at the house of Baron d'Holbach) constraints were fewer. The salon was just one element—the most elitist one—of an entire network of new contacts too well known to require us to linger over them, and based on the diffusion of the book, the learned press, journals and reviews, and the many more informal connections formed through correspondence and travel.

This general overview cries out to have a number of nuances added to it. Local differences need to be highlighted and we should stress the importance of the scientific societies and intellectual associations in England and Italy, which came from a different heritage, the importance of the universities under the Empire and of Masonic lodges in the Habsburg possessions. This is not our purpose. Still, it is appropriate to recall at least some of the results of that multiform activity: a heightened interest in pedagogy, which is inseparable from an interest in learning; and the utilitarian concerns of an approach that, repudiating all metaphysics, strove for a direct grasp of the realities of the physical world in the interest of transforming it. The new role of the explorer falls into this category. At the beginning of the century, the explorer was still close to the spy sent to scout out the enemy; at the end, he stood at the vanguard as a scout for civilization and the agent of a disinterested curiosity (even if that curiosity contributed to gaining mastery over the world that had revealed its secrets). Fontenelle's hardy discoverers and Voltaire's observer who had "caught nature in the act" are of the same breed.

In his report of 18 Floréal, Year II, Robespierre expressed the harshest judgment of the Enlightenment *philosophes* in the person of the encyclopedists. His was not an isolated opinion; Marat, for one, shared it. Robespierre depicts those champions of Liberty as creatures crawling about the antechambers of princes, valets of the ancien régime, which they both undermined and served. We can better understand this retrospective evaluation if we think of the circumstance in which it was expressed. It brings to mind La Fontaine's fable "Le chien et le loup": "Chemin faisant, il vit le cou du chien pelé" (As they made their way together, [the wolf] saw the dog's neck rubbed bare [by his collar]). But no matter how deeply entrenched in the system they may have been, even to the point of being its recognized agents, the spokesmen for the Enlightenment were not its guard dogs. The wolves' hour was soon to come.

Cultural Intermediaries

We make no claim to have exhausted the rich theme of cultural intermediaries in the two illustrative examples presented here, the functionary and the priest. In recent years there has been renewed interest in problems connected with the communication and diffusion of ideas and with these sometimes modest actors who were nonetheless essential for the role that they played. The voluntaristic policies of the enlightened rulers, but also the spontaneous propagation of new ideas, cannot be imagined without recourse to these relay mechanisms. They pose the entire problem of the popular diffusion of the Enlightenment. A large cast of characters began to crowd the stage. They included the *robin* (the "man of the robe," magistrate or official), the notary, the schoolmaster, and—why not?—the tavern-keeper.

But to limit ourselves to the two examples proposed, was the functionary a new personage? The term appeared in France, Carlo Capra reminds us, at the end of the ancien régime. Hence, it seems to have been tied to the new requirements of a modern state in search of a more rational and better-regulated administration. But the traditional monarchies, especially since the beginning of the early modern age, had delegated their powers in matters of administration, finance, and justice in a variety of ways. In France, the system of venal offices had given rise to a body of royal officeholders who were proprietors of their charges, which were transmissible and which in some cases brought personal ennoblement. This was not the only system in practice, however: the *ferme générale* responsible for the collection of taxes had its own personnel, and the system of the revocable "commission" in the direct service of the king began to spread as early as the end of the seventeenth century. Other countries followed a different approach. In England the civil servant made his first appearance in the East India Company; in Russia Peter the Great set up a rigid and hierarchical Table of Ranks *(chin)* listing levels and dignities, civil and military, in the service of the state. What interests us here is not so much the various origins of these structures as a general evolution that affected all of Europe. In quantitative terms this evolution was manifested by a sizable though not precisely ascertainable increase in personnel everywhere to respond to the state's new needs. In qualitative terms it was visible in a vastly swollen bureaucracy in the central state administration, a proliferation of commissions on all levels, and a greater specialization of tasks. Thus France, for example, gained technical personnel of recognized competence in the corps of engineers of the *ponts et chaussées* and the manufacturing inspectors; in the German states, great and small, a methodically implanted bureaucracy emerged. This new pool of talent provided the Enlightenment with partners—men who were often highly motivated and who displayed a spirit not only of rationalism and control but of innovation in the service of both the monarchy and the public good.

Roland de La Platière, the future Girondin minister, had an exemplary career under the ancien régime as an *inspecteur des manufactures*. The Revolution was for France a decisive turning point for innovation that put in place representatives elected by their fellow citizens and a new bureaucracy that was further developed by the Empire. But perhaps we are anticipating too much if we attribute things to the Enlightenment that it only prepared and that found their full realization in the following century in the bureaucrats depicted by Balzac, Gogol, and many others. The social type of the bureaucrat was barely being constituted; it had not yet taken on its definitive characteristics, and both nepotism, which reached the level of a dynastic spirit in offices high and low, and widespread absenteeism demonstrate an esprit de corps that could be read just as easily in terms of archaism as anticipation. Meritocracy was far from having won the day.

It may be stretching the point to enlist the black-robed battalions of parish priests in the service of the Enlightenment state. The post-Tridentine church was a power in its own right, and not one to be trifled with in its domain. In the seventeenth century, the clerical universe was one of the most homogeneous parts of society but also one of the ones that showed the most striking contrasts. Dominique Julia recalls the enormous diversity in the status of the church in Europe and hence the multiformity in the position of the clergy. In the seventeenth century, post-Tridentine reform seemed to have accomplished a number of the goals that the church had set for itself. In France few irregularities remained in either the mores of the clergy or in divine service, and the clergy had attained at least a modest level of doctrinal (if not spiritual) training. Although seminaries were far from presenting a uniformly dense network, they had multiplied and had fulfilled their aims. It would be too much to say that the training they dispensed prepared priests to enter a century in movement; the core of the seminary's teaching was still the Counter Reformation discourse, hardened in the fires of combat against Jansenism.

Still, the French priest of the eighteenth century evolved with the times: the image of the "good priest" as presented in Rétif de La Bretonne's portrait of his brother in *La vie de mon père*—a man close to his flock, whom he supports in distress, a notable among his peers, and a man who, more often than has been said, enjoys a modest ease—is not all fiction. Not all priests conformed to the ideal of the Savoyard Vicar; very few—perhaps a handful—ruminated in their presbytères the sulphurous ideas that Father Meslier, in the beginning of the century, confided to his famous testament—an atheist profession of faith that Voltaire circulated posthumously. Priests did have books, in general books of devotion, but at times books that opened up vistas of another culture. That does not mean that we should see them as agents for the propagation of the Enlightenment, although the point might be debated for the pastors of Lutheran Germany, who were direct dependents of the state. But by that time many priests were prepared to take on the role of professors of morality and civic duty that the Revolution ambitiously attributed to them. The overall picture was of course more complex; even within France there were differences between city and country and from one region to another. There was a marked contrast between areas in which relations between priests and the faithful were more relaxed and a decline in vocations was already being felt (as in the Paris area), and other regions (in the west of France) where a vital clergy assured a successful symbiosis and a real acculturation. And what would we find if we investigated differences between the north and the south in Italy or the apparently monolithic clergy of the Iberian Peninsula?

We have left women aside in the organization of these soundings of the society of the Enlightenment, and this exclusion, although not premeditated, is nonetheless significant. Where are we to place *la plus belle moitié* of humanity (as the French revolutionaries called it)? Everywhere? Or nowhere? Not everywhere, certainly. Excluded from command over the levers of power, participants in the more modest levels of production, women had by no means quashed the old malediction. Traditional religious discourse saw woman as temptress and sinner; *tota mulier in utero* (a woman is a uterus), the physicians of the Enlightenment opined. A more elegant, even a flattering, way to express this was to praise feminine qualities and the mother, and the century was not sparing in this sort of discourse. Can we discern any real progress? Some historians have thought so and have seen the eighteenth century as the "century of the woman," the woman who was the animating spirit of the salons and, in the upper classes at least, won the right to culture and, at times, even the right to speak. The often brutal misogyny of Jean-Jacques Rousseau melts before the image of the strong woman, the Julie of *La nouvelle Héloïse*. But these were only stages on the long road that lay ahead. The French Revolution, which gave women *civil* rights, refused them access to *civic* rights.

This is where the century of the Enlightenment reached its limits and what we still have the right to call its contradictions or its excesses.

When Things Fall Apart

We have given too smooth a picture of the man of the Enlightenment; as if nothing had changed in either the material conditions of people's lives or their mental outlook and their passions; as if the administrative personnel instituted by the monarchies (be they enlightened) and by a society of orders could emerge intact from the sweeping call to change the world by means of the man whom that discourse represents. As each of the following chapters unfolds, there comes a moment when the author shifts from description to an awareness of tensions and movement.

At the end of the century the entire edifice cracked apart. Behind the masks of the aristocratic *fête* we can see the changed face of the old nobility. Even the best-regulated institutions no longer fulfilled their functions; the academies were contested as the refuge of an order that no one wanted any longer.

A new generation began to appear in the Republic of Letters, the world of the sciences, and the world of artistic creation. It did not have an easy job making its way in the world. The time was ripe for the "gutter Rousseaus," as Robert Darnton has called the rabble of authors who contested a self-satisfied establishment. Thanks to a literature of political contestation and pornography that was sold "under the cloak," such men shook settled compromises. In the scientific world, the direct line of scientific discoveries was challenged by the intrusion of new scientists, true and false—Cagliostro, Mesmer . . . and Marat?—who questioned the ordered universe of Newtonian physics that had just won the scientific battles of the century. Could the world be less rational than had been thought?

An awakened sensibility prevailed, and on all fronts the time had come for challenges. As Jean Starobinski writes: "Reason, conscious of its powers, sure of its prerogatives, welcomed the forces of feeling and passion and looked to them as sources of additional energy."[2] But this turning point, which found expression in the Rousseauism of the end of the century, was not without risks: the powers of darkness and dream lay in wait behind that door.

It is revealing that the chapter devoted to the artist of the Enlightenment opens with Füssli and closes with the universe of Goya, though it is true that it passes through David. In Füssli's *The Nightmare* contemporaries contemplated an evocation of the forces of darkness and night. The Goya of *Los Caprichos* (The Caprichos) and *Los desastres de la guerra* (The Disasters of War) revealed a universe of phantasms and of cruelty. These were nonetheless artists of the Enlightenment, and Goya explains his pedagogical aims and his operation of exorcism. The darkness that the Enlightenment denied or whose appearance it attempted to destroy was everywhere; it was part of man's very nature. Sade's theater of cruelty revealed to the human being of the Enlightenment another man in which he recognized himself. In the age in which poetry rediscovered the cemetery and the *roman noir* that France borrowed from the English Gothic novel found a wide reading public, death—whose identity was never denied but which was thought to have been mastered—reappeared.

The apotheosis that concludes *The Magic Flute* with the sun's rays inundating the universe is the final and incantatory expression of the dream of the Enlightenment. Soon Goethe, speaking through Mephistopheles, was to argue the positive qualities of darkness, without which light would not exist. The French Revolution, which brought both violence and Promethean liberation, confronted man with the demands of a liberty to be conquered. A new humanity was seeking its identity; new, but also more aware and more troubled.

Notes

1. *Encyclopédie,* ed. Denis Diderot and Jean Le Rond d'Alembert, 18 vols. (New York: Pergamon Press/Elsevier, 1979); quoted from *Encyclopedia: Selections,* trans. Nelly S. Hoyt and Thomas Cassirer (Indianapolis: Bobbs-Merrill, 1965), 243, 244.

2. Jean Starobinski, *1789: The Emblems of Reason,* trans. Barbara Bray (Charlottesville, Va.: University of Virginia Press, 1982; Cambridge, Mass.: MIT Press, 1988), 136.

1 / The Noble

Pierre Serna

Mais une chose m'a surpris: l'ordre
dans le désordre.

Abbé Coyer
Voyages d'Italie et de Hollande

Jacques le Fataliste: "Un paradoxe
n'est pas toujours une fausseté."

Denis Diderot
Jacques le Fataliste

Abbé Coyer's reflection can be read two ways: either he saw a disorder
organized in a rational manner, or he felt that an existent order had lost
all logical organization. When this remark is applied to the nobility—
which Abbé Coyer discusses in this work—it acquires a completely different depth. Either it implies, subtly and suggestively, differences of
situation, extreme diversity, and perhaps confusion within the second
order of society, or it connotes a real unity within a genuine social diversity. It depends on one's point of view. This is how the nobility of the time
of the Enlightenment appears at first glance: rich and poor, famous and
unknown, conservative and enlightened, new and old. Still, Jacques le
Fataliste, a great traveler and a keen observer of his contemporaries, in-
forms his master that "a paradox is not always a falsity." We need to clarify
the terms of that paradox and to examine the personage of the noble if
we want a closer look at his harlequin costume.

The mode of the portrait implies representation of someone who
is correctly identified and accurately defined. There is a semantic problem in our investigation, however, since a profusion of words syn-

onymous with "noble" muddies the picture: he is, interchangeably, "gentleman," "well-born," "cavalier" *(chevalier),* and "aristocrat" and can be paraphrased as a "member of the elite." All of these terms refer to noble status; each one bears its own meaning, however, adds different nuances to the portrait of the noble, and must be used with precision. This semantic confusion introduces a related problem: the elaboration of a portrait of the noble since the eighteenth century.

The Noble as a Man of the Enlightenment

The history of the relationship between the nobility and the intellectual movement of the Enlightenment has usually been written as seen through the distorting lens of the revolutionary events that started in 1789. Those events, the culminating point of the century, give a first glimpse of the noble we are seeking: for contemporaries of the late eighteenth century, it was the decadence of the order of nobility that brought on the fall of the ancien régime.

The revolutionaries' conception of the noble fallen from his high estate was shared by the partisans of the Restoration when they envisaged a nobility regenerated and broadened by the trials it had undergone during the Revolution. This view persisted into the early twentieth century. Henri Carré depicted the noble as fallen into moral decline, and Pierre de Vaissières showed him sunken into a poverty assumed with dignity. They concurred in presenting a negative general impression of the nobility. Later, in the 1930s, Lucien Febvre depicted the noble as out of phase with his epoch and struggling to preserve his ancestral rights. For Febvre, the noble, trapped within a class-based logic, refused the acquisitions of the ideological movement of the Enlightenment and demanded out-of-date privileges several hundred years old. Up to this point, portraits of the noble did not present an immediately sympathetic, let alone triumphant, personage and did not represent the nobility as a group that was at ease within the elite of the Enlightenment. New perspectives and a different approach came from across the Atlantic toward the end of the 1950s with Robert Forster's partial rehabilitation of the role of the noble within ancien-régime society. Several historians have followed this route, at times putting the nobility in the enlightened, tolerant, and philanthropic avant-garde of the century of the Enlightenment. The reversal of perspective was total. As Emmanuel Le Roy Ladurie put it: "Everything was thus to be for the best in the best of all possible worlds. But how was one to explain, at one and the same time, the great reversal when the nobility turned against the Revolution in the decade of the 1790s, and, conversely, the vast hatred of the sans-culottes toward the *ci-devants* [aristocrats]?"[1] It seemed, in fact, that a laconic, neutral description of the noble (even less, an objective one) was impossible in the midst of a political debate that historians found inescapable. This is perhaps one way of recognizing that the noble is a key personage (perhaps the key personage) for grasping the spirit of the Enlightenment in both its full charge of theoretical novelty and its conservative aspects, but also in its ambiguities, hopes, impasses, scope, and limitations.

Drawing the portrait of a noble in the time of the Enlightenment thus comes down to taking a position on the dialectical relationship that a group at the summit of the social pyramid managed to maintain with a thought that was modern and seductive in its abstractions but risky and, in the long run, dangerous for that group in its practical expressions.

Juridical Status, Types, Numbers

The noble enjoyed a clear juridical status "shown" by intangible attributes. Rooted in a history that was the basis of his pride *(nobilitas),* he occupied a prestigious social function, military in origin and connected with his moral values *(virtus).* Finally, he held land *(certa habitatio).* His "world was that of *constantia,* of an attachment to lasting elements, of tradition, of a scorn for changes and innovations, with a habitual insistence on heredity."[2] This was a theoretical facade; in practice the "second order" contained clearly distinct hierarchies and degrees of preeminence that varied from one county to another.

In France, for example, the dukes and peers allied to the oldest families occupied the most prestigious posts and shared in the life at court. Next in order came the great families of the nobility of the robe, lineages of ministers and secretaries of state. Beneath them came three parallel and distinct groups: the nobility of the robe, who held positions in the judicial system, the military nobility, and the nobility of finance. Last in line came the country gentlemen, who, "without appearing in the cities, resided permanently on their lands, who loved country life and fled fashionable social gatherings. With limited revenues, they could live grandly in the country, where they enjoyed a consideration they would not have found anywhere else."[3] Within each group in this first classification, "an internal hierarchy was created on the basis of antiquity and illustriousness."[4] During the course of the eighteenth century, a third factor—wealth—came to have a determinant importance in this somewhat abstract classification. This remark applies to the whole of Europe and was as true in Spain as it was in Poland.

On the Iberian Peninsula in 1780, there were 119 grandees of Spain, 553 nobles with Castilian titles, and more than 500,000 gentlemen, divided into cavaliers *(caballeros)* and chartered nobles *(hildagos de carta)* named by the king *(de privilegio),* nobles "of 500 sous" *(de devangar quinientos sueldos)* who had served the old kings of Castile, "house-gutter" nobles *(de goteras)* whose privileges were recognized only in their village, and "britches" nobles *(de bragueta)* who had fathered seven males in a row.[5] In Spain, despite subtle juridical distinctions, it was wealth, in particular land revenues, that determined strict classification. The same can be said of the Polish nobility. Poland had a powerful aristocracy that may have been juridically equal to "popular nobilities" close to the peasant masses but was in reality far above the "popular nobles" in wealth, land ownership, and lifestyle.[6]

The noble evolved within a legitimate group arranged hierarchically according to two principles: first, antiquity, which divided it symbolically into an immemorial nobility, a high nobility, and gentlefolk who could claim four degrees of nobility; second, the ability to keep up one's rank thanks to wealth. This awareness of noble identity was accompanied—and this is an early sign, in the beginning of the century, of the influence of a new spirit fascinated by knowledge and by logical reasoning—by an interest in describing the *origin,* the beginning, of the noble condition, and in reflecting on its underlying values. This desire to clarify noble identity was accompanied by an attempt to justify the nobility's preeminence. It soon became necessary for nobles to recognize one another and count their numbers.

First, however, they needed to agree on how to define who was noble and who was not, who should be listed in the registers of nobility and who should not. This was the purpose of the reform of the nobility in France between 1668 and 1672. Jean Meyer remarks about the Breton nobility that "any rationalization of the social structures could not fail to arouse a discontent all the more intense because, basically, the reform of the nobility marked a shift—admittedly incomplete but no less real— from a state of nobility by public reputation and a tacit recognition of social groups in a determined region to a noble estate guaranteed by proofs."[7] Although the Breton reform was not always fully carried through, it permits comparison of a noble estate that often differed from one region to another. In Brittany, for example, only 17 percent of the nobility had an origin more recent than 1550. In Lille, in Franche-Comté, in Lyons, and in Le Maine, "the nucleus of the nobility . . . was of more recent origin."[8] It should be stressed that heavy expenditures were involved in the required operations (searching out letters or charters to authenticate the antiquity of quarters of nobility). For example, the family of the young comte de Tilly, in order to provide Chérin with proof of its nobility, spent considerable sums to dispatch a certain Abbé Guérin to search for documents at the Tower of London, in Denmark, and in Vaneville in Normandy.[9] This confirms the notion that it took wealth to prove the antiquity, hence the legitimacy, of noble status.

The enterprise of counting the nobility was far from exhaustive, however, and in another work Jean Meyer inventories variations in estimates. Abbé Coyer, writing in 1755, put the number of nobles in France at 360,000; Moheau, an *intendant,* estimated them at 80,000 in his *Considérations sur la population de France;* Abbé Sieyès, in *Qu'est-ce que le tiers état?* put the numbers of the second order at 100,000 to 110,000 persons.[10]

These differences reveal the limits of the statistical techniques of the epoch. They also show that the figures were manipulated—which is just as obvious in Abbé Coyer's denunciation of the multitude of poor nobles as it is in Abbé Sieyès's criticism of the minority of the privileged. Another thing that the figures show is the uncertainty that ran throughout the eighteenth century concerning the status of some nobles—the ennobled and the déclassés. Were the first of these truly noble? Should they be counted? How many of them were there? How could one evaluate the validity of their "usurped" title? The more somber question, which also circulated, was who was no longer noble? Could nobles lose their nobility? If so, how? By what criteria should the new codification be implemented? What legitimacy would be established for noble status by that classification?

At least 50,000 persons were ennobled in France between 1710 and 1790. This is a considerable number. How many thousand were to pass quietly, discreetly, from the second order to the third estate? Such social mutations go far toward explaining the sizable differences among estimates of the number of nobles and the acuity of interrogations concerning the nobility's origins. The search for identity and the counts are first expressions of a disquietude regarding the nature of the second order; renewed historical debate, during the eighteenth century, about the origin of the nobility is a second manifestation.

The Origin and Legitimation of the Nobility

Where did the nobility come from? How did it appear in France? What founded its legitimacy? The comte de Montlosier summarized these questions thus:

> The historians of all stripes who have succeeded one another to write our history in one spirit or another, some in the light of Roman law, others in the sense of Frankish law, and still others according to the clergy's views, added new confusion to a terrain that was already filled with confusion. The comte de Boulainvilliers and Abbé Duclos, the first from the noble point of view, the second from that of the people, set the scene for a scandal that the historian Moreau later aggravated in the direct of absolute power.[11]

The stakes were high, and the issue arises often in memoirs and correspondence. Montlosier states: "Were feudalism and, with it, the first nobility, barbarian institutions? Was seignorial justice a usurpation of royal authority? Were the *censives* [feudal levies] a usurpation perpetrated on the people?" He continues: "It was common opinion that the Germanic peoples, when they entered Gaul, took over all possessions and reduced all the inhabitants into servitude. . . . This is why I had no doubts that the lords of the castle were formerly veritable brigands."[12] Such historical "discoveries" embarrassed some nobles who had thought to base their legitimacy in the authenticity of their origins.

They still had the noble values, however, both sacred and profane, that made up a moral code from which they could draw exemplary references. Thus, honor, "the glorious esteem accorded to virtue and courage," was the best quality that the European gentleman could acquire, above all in the profession of arms. Honor gave a sense of belonging to the nobility. This was manifested in two ways: feeling oneself noble implied a particular attitude, bearing, language, and mode of being; being perceived as noble led to a system of representation, recognized and accepted by all, that permitted instant recognition of the well-born. In this quest for identity, the spectacle of the second order, taken as a whole, was presented as social distinction; the principle of legitimacy was confirmed by daily practice.

Dress, for example, took on a special role, unifying the order of the nobility in a common, broadly shared way of life. As Daniel Roche states:

"In an unequal society, the hierarchy of representations ought to coincide with the social hierarchy; it even structured it. . . . If the noble was primarily what he represented and the bourgeois what he produced, the former ought above all to seem and the second to be."[13] Roche goes on to describe the luxurious dress of the wealthy: "It is a small number of very large fortunes which suggest, even magnify, the role of display and luxury and the increase in the ostentatious expenditure of court circles."[14] In this game of social perceptions, it is thus just as important to feel oneself noble as it is to be perceived as noble. Still, dress is only the paradigm of a broader whole summarized as the noble art of living.

If this was notably true in Paris it was even more evident in the provinces. In her study of the city of Aix-en-Provence in the eighteenth century, Monique Cubells insists on the abundance of nobles' domestic servants, the richness of their house furnishings, the value of their collections, the size of their libraries—all clear indications of the lifestyle and the luxurious houses of these *Messieurs du Parlement.* That art of living, which comes over as an immediately apparent distinction, was a sign of power, but it was also a sign of an abuse of power. Thus, even if the facts at times contradict impressions—and Daniel Roche warns us about falling into "the habitual exaggerations impressed on preachers and moralists, and those historians who have swallowed them whole, by the excesses of the tiny group close to the Sun King and his imitators"[15]—by making a spectacle of itself the nobility offered an opportunity to paint a portrait that may well be a caricature but that nonetheless recorded authentic elements of noble life. This is the impression given by the account of a day in the life of a noble, as Henri Carré describes it. Before noon he did little but get dressed; then came dinner, followed by conversation in the salon, reading, singing, visits to his library, promenades, hunting parties, games (*jeu de paume* and other ball games, badminton, billiards, trictrac, chess, dominoes); in the evening, after supper, *fêtes galantes,* theatricals, and balls ended the day. An impression of lightness, idleness, and, above all, superficiality emanates from this agenda, which has quite rightly been corrected by recent studies. Still, it is undeniable that the parts of the noble's day that Henri Carré stresses are moments that were necessary to the elaboration of an aristocratic lifestyle and a noble sociability. In this sense, both their contemporaries' view of them and later historians' views of the nobles may have erred. This faulty perspective still refers, however, to the internalization, on the part of an overwhelming majority of commoners, of a feeling of social distance and inferiority that was desired and even cultivated by the nobility and was experienced by people who were not noble as exclusion from a privileged group.

It remains to be seen how, by the end of the century, these signs of distinction, originally viewed as positive, came to enclose the nobles within systems of representation that bore increasingly negative connotations. My interest here is not in perceiving the nobility as a sum of individuals in the long run more virtuous than has been thought but rather as a unified group with its own solidarity, a group that practiced a noble sociability and elaborated and lived by a certain code and that, when faced with a new conception of being and becoming in society, found its existence challenged.

Unity and Diversity among the Nobility

Theoretical Unity

Group logic clearly implies a unity among the nobility. This was something that posed a problem in the eighteenth century. As a representative of a lineage of which he was the living expression and the receptacle of group values, the noble was, theoretically, on a equal footing with all of his peers; an emergent sentiment of unity was supposed to bind together all the members of the second order. It seems, however, that a portrait of the noble can only be arrived at through a kaleidoscopic sketch revealing not only nuances but cleavages, and at times insurmountable chasms, among nobles everywhere. This makes "the" noble impossible to find; rather, his face varies radically from one place to another. These contrasts are as much geographical as they are historical. It is hard to detect much common ground between "the *hidalgos* who will always consider leisure in the country as inseparable from nobility, and who will judge any activity as incompatible with the splendor of their titles"[16] and the English gentry, whose "essential characteristic is its social permeability," a quality that enabled it to adapt to economic reality and take in new members. The English nobility, "composed of businessmen and of merchants, thus did not bear the burden of an impoverished petty nobility; it is true that the success and the de facto privileges of that gentry can be explained by the reduction of derogation to almost nothing."[17] There were vast differences in nobles' situations for which geographic distance was not the only reason.

To return to France, what unity, hence what cohesiveness, was there among the nobility? Opposing views appear in contemporary discussions, and their polemics communicate an impression of confusion more than a breakdown of the second order. Within a strict hierarchical order there were also differences between the court nobility and the Parisian nobility, and between nobles who owned a residence in Paris and the provincial nobility. The noble's lifestyle was incontestably more luxurious in Paris, where participation in *la vie mondaine* required a certain level of wealth that contrasted with the modesty, even the austerity, of the conditions in which a great many nobles lived. At Versailles the young comte de Tilly observes how difficult it is to be presented at court, to obtain a first honorific charge, to display one's merits when driving out in a carriage. When he visited his uncle in Le Maine, his preoccupations were of a completely different sort. The women there were chaste and everyone went to bed early. His uncle, engrossed by the cultivation of his lands, "would die of fear [at the idea] that château life and the monotony of country living might make a marvelous being like myself, Tilly, die of boredom."[18]

Cultural Differences

The cultural rifts among nobles were even more pronounced. In a century of great intellectual change, a real division seemed to emerge. Some nobles were capable of adapting to new ways of thinking, while others lived in ignorance of philosophical and political novelties or were downright hostile to them. Culture was an important dividing force within the noble order in that access to culture and the acquisition and adoption of new concepts—of social hierarchies in particular—became indicative (though there were exceptions) of different levels of wealth and led, sooner or later, to an ideological divorce within the nobility.

As a child, the young comte de Montlosier read Pluche and Fontenelle's *Les entretiens sur la pluralité des mondes*, then *Gil Blas, Don Quixote, Gulliver's Travels,* and *Robinson Crusoe.* As a young man, a sword at his side (he had a post in the militia) and a scalpel in hand, he studied anatomy, then chemistry. "But this was not enough," he states. "A worthy Irish Capuchin, confessor to my family, proposed that I study public law with him. I went to him, on the one hand, with my Burlamaqui, my Grotius, and my Puffendorf; on the other, with my chemistry texts by Macquer and Beaumé, my anatomical dissections, and my La Faye's *Principles of Surgery* and my Winslow's *Anatomy*."[19] He began to raise questions about religious matters and to read Voltaire, Jean-Jacques Rousseau, Denis Diderot: "In that way, I became what was then called a philosopher. I considered independence to be the first law of nature and equality to be the natural law of societies."[20] He admits, with a touch of irony: "If the revolution had taken me by surprise at that moment of my life, I think I would have said or done fine things."[21] These are telling words about both the broad culture of this young count from the Auvergne and the influence of that culture on the political opinions of his youth.

Vaublanc tells a quite different story about his education at the Collège de La Flèche:

> How far had I gotten after seven years of a cloistered education, counting the two years as a boarding student in Paris? Two cantos of the *Aeneid*, the *Oration Against Catiline*, the first *Oration Against Verres*, and a few passages from Caesar's *Commentaries* were all my meager store. What is more, I could understand without difficulty only the finest bits and the most impassioned lines, for these were so simple that one could understand them as easily as one's own language.[22]

The time that Vaublanc spent at the École Militaire in Paris was no more fruitful. Nonetheless (as his *Mémoires* shows) he opened his mind to the world of the written word and to culture in general. But how many of his fellow students went off to people the garrison towns only half-educated, barely knowing how to write and never reading, proud of their prejudices, unbudging in their political certitudes, and hermetically sealed off from any notion of the reforms that the spirit of the times was bringing about?

Differences in levels of knowledge led to differences in political conception. The nobles' uneven participation in the philosophy of the Enlightenment seems to have operated as a source of disorder among them, undoubtedly because it was superimposed on another source of division that preexisted the eighteenth century: the function of the nobility. Knowledge and culture exacerbated the problem because in the eighteenth century they offered multiple possibilities for exercise and prestige.

Social Differences

George Huppert has shown that, toward the end of the sixteenth century, a "gentry" had been constructed in France of men who were proud of their knowledge and their ability to write well. Nonetheless, this gentry was "bereft of the support of the nation, deeply separated from its origins, and forced to capitulate to the *traisneurs d'espée.*" Huppert concludes:

> The virtues of that ephemeral Fourth Estate, as enumerated by
> Montaigne—peace, profit, learning, justice, and reason—were
> not, after all, to take precedence in public opinion over the virtues of the nobility: war, honor, action, valiance, force. In order
> to achieve the highest honors, it became necessary, once again,
> to embrace the values of the enemy. There was no choice but to
> pretend to be what one was not and to become "an amphibious
> man," to wear the lawyer's gown in the morning and to dress as a
> *gentilhomme* at night.[23]

A century and a half later, this conflict seems to have disappeared.
François Bluche, Jean Meyer, and Monique Cubells have shown in their
studies of various parlements (Paris, Rennes, Aix), that there was no
longer any inequality among nobilities, nor was there any prejudice
against ennoblement "of the robe," by that time borne proudly. "For
now," Cubells suggests, "we need to note that among the families of the
members of the parlements in Provence during the eighteenth century
few were willingly unfaithful to the robe, and even fewer abandoned it
directly for the sword. . . . The [nobility of the] sword does not seem to
have classed itself in a compact block in relation to the robe: neither below, of course, nor above, but rather parallel to it."[24] This impression of
cohesion is corroborated by the matrimonial alliances contracted between families of nobility of the sword and of the robe and by a sociability
in which signs of precedence were not marked from one type of nobility
to the other. The Freemasons' lodges are an example of this:

> The presence within these privileged associations of the most
> illustrious noble houses of the court, of the elite of the magistracy and of a portion of high finance must be interpreted as a
> social dominance. If equality appeared, it was by no means here,
> between a peer of the realm and a hat merchant, between a *receveur des finances* and a vinegar-maker, or between a first president and a musician of the guards, but rather among the three
> categories of nobles whose very joint presence conferred prestige on certain lodges.[25]

Still, whether it was an archaic reflex or a sign of the emergence of a
new division yet to be defined, correspondence and memoirs show
marked scorn toward *la robinocratie*. The young marquis d'Argens ex-

pressed his extreme displeasure at the prospect of becoming a member of Parlement: "The estate that they wanted me to take on seemed horrifying to me; I saw it as the tomb of all pleasures. The sensual life of an officer had much greater charms for me than the painful task of pleading and judging people's suits."[26] Several years later, two other Provençal nobles offered even sharper criticisms. Mirabeau lashed out at the "hundred thousand families risen out of the nation who share our rights," and he described "the delirium and the insolence of the commonality, who attempt to rise out of the crowd and who believe they can become noble by princely letters with a price attached."[27]

From the Bastille, where he was imprisoned, the marquis de Sade imagined what his accuser might have said: "This little runt who is neither a president nor a *maître au compte* thought he could enjoy the privileges of a member of the High Chamber! . . . This little country squire has dared to try to join our ranks, to believe himself permitted to resemble us? What, with no ermine and no round cap?"[28] The very subjectivity of these statements from imprisoned men is interesting, as it clearly shows two reasons for disunity among the nobility: the large number of ennoblements among men who pursued administrative and juridical careers and the increasing influence of money within a more and more selective hierarchy. The total and perfect cohesiveness that the nobility proclaimed for itself was turning out to be impossible.

The Noble Elite

It seems incontestable that—as contemporaries had already perceived—there was a measure of unity among the wealthiest of the nobility and an economic dynamism among many well-born and open-minded entrepreneurs who participated in the elaboration of new ways of regarding the state and social relations. Not without cynicism, Sade presented the protagonists of *Les cent vingt journées de Sodome* in these terms:

> One must not suppose that it was exclusively the low-born and vulgar sort which did this swindling; gentlemen of the highest note led the pack. The Duc de Blangis and his brother the Bishop of X***, each of whom had thuswise amassed immense fortunes [during the Regency], are in themselves solid proof that, like the others, the nobility neglected no opportunities to take this road to wealth. These two illustrious figures, through their pleasures and business [were] closely associated with the famous Durcet and the Président de Curval.[29]

It seems absolutely logical that this dynamic portion of the nobility should have accepted a new code of values and recognized "the eminent dignity of merit, its ability to pick out the exceptional man, to place him outside the ordinary run, and to justify ennoblement as a pure formality and ratification of an existing fact."[30] It was equally logical that this group and the wealthiest members of the third estate should form an elite. This fusion can best be seen in England. For example, "a merchant buys a large estate, settles on his lands, takes on the appearance of a gentleman, stands out for the quality of his conversation and his hospitality. He receives his neighbors with accomplished art, and he lets it be known that he has ancestors of a highly honorable sort. . . . The well-born and the bourgeois can, by and large, merge" to define a new aristocracy.[31]

Consciously or unconsciously, the high aristocracy of Europe—for once in agreement with the monarchical administrations—took sides with the money powers and tended more and more to equate nobility with wealth. Quesnay put it this way: "A nobility of obscure origin and estate attributes less importance to consideration, whereas wealth and illustriousness form the high nobility, our great landowners, our magnates."[32] The political consequences of this state of affairs was an attempt to exclude all the nobles who were economically incapable of keeping up their rank.

Poor Nobles

This was to discount the capacity of resistance of the "poor" nobles who had been excluded from posts that brought prestige and command and had been marginalized, often humiliated. Even if its members had no money, "a petty nobility did exist and they were aware of their individuality and apartness"; moreover, "it would be ludicrous to confuse them with the high nobility which never mingled its blood with theirs."[33] Guy Chaussinand-Nogaret estimates that at least a thousand families had revenues of less than 1,000 livres. "The best-off were peasants, and those most in need were beggars."[34]

Jean Meyer distinguishes between degrees of poverty: "Aside from a nobility who truly lived in misery, in the most literal sense of the term, there was a nobility that felt itself to be poor in relation to its own special needs, without having the third estate and (above all) the people of country areas consider that level of 'wealth' typical of poverty. There was true *misère* and there was relative *misère*."[35] It is nonetheless true that those nobles—who were not as poor as they thought—perceived the threat to their status and developed a discourse against those who had greater wealth but whose noble origins were more dubious or more recent. It is not impossible that this perception gradually came to be shared by those who lived in the small cities, towns, and villages who came in daily contact with these nobles.

Two systems of thought must have cohabited within the order of the nobility: the first enlightened and aristocratic, the second formulated within this less wealthy nobility for whom social identity was based on the past, on dignity, and on reputation. To what extent did the population at large share this way of thinking? Montlosier's villagers "admitted among themselves a sort of nobility, which depended, as it did everywhere, on antiquity, probity, and talent. When these had long been transmitted from father to son, they seemed hereditary within the family. Wealth came only second. I am speaking of new wealth; things were worse when [wealth] was thought ill-gained."[36]

In the final analysis, the struggle among the various groups of nobles led to the implosion of the second order, which came unhinged as a result of its own quarrels. To what extent did the 6,500 families admitted to the nobility during the course of the eighteenth century (by acquiring posts that comported a noble title, through patents of nobility, or, to a lesser degree, by usurpation of a title)[37] share the illusions, ideals, and hopes of the poor nobles who had left only the memory of what they imagined their families had been in their former glory?

That impoverished nobility (a topic too long neglected, too long described through one or two scandalous or exaggeratedly bleak examples) made up a sizable group in some regions that must have influenced the global perception of the second order. "The profusion of Breton nobles can in part be explained by the abundance of the poor nobility, who form a veritable noble plebs. A third of the nobility of Saint-Brieuc is reduced to beggary." At Plouha, only two families paid a head tax *(la capitation)* of 30 livres; one family paid 22 livres; another paid 15 livres; eleven families paid 9 livres; four paid 4 livres, 10 sols; and twenty-four families out of a total of forty-six noble families paid nothing at all. Added to the first third of nobles at the limits of poverty were those who paid less than 10 livres—40 percent of the total in this diocese. And if we include the 7 percent who paid between 10 and 20 livres, this impoverished nobility, often indistinguishable from the rest of the peasant population (as seen in a local proverb: *Noblaz plouha, noblaz netia*), reached the stupefying total of 77 percent.[38] This is an extreme case, and it is attenuated by the option available to the Breton nobility, when economic difficulties became insurmountable, of putting a noble title "in dormition," thus permitting them to engage in activities that would normally imply derogation.

In other regions the spectacle of noble impoverishment had greater political consequences. In Provence the economic distress of some lords in Lubéron freed the village communities from any notion of deference or exaggerated respect toward a "master" who was facing economic disaster. The case of the marquis de Sade, which Michel Vovelle has studied, is illuminating. "If Lacoste did not denounce the marquis, it was perhaps quite simply because without fuss and profiting from the absence of the lord the village had already achieved its prerevolution."[39] The increasing number of suits between villagers and lords and the many complaints against the offices of seignorial justice attest to this rupture of traditional structures, born of the failure of the nobility. Of course, counterexamples exist of economic prosperity and successful symbioses between the seignorial order and villagers.

What is important is not to estimate or count the number of poor nobles, compare them with the rich nobles, and draw systematic conclusions. Nor is it any longer to seek out individual cases of perdition and conclude from them the decadence of the second order as a whole. It seems equally useless to sketch either a "decline of the nobility" or a "rise" of the order during the century of the Enlightenment. Verification by example of one or the other of these theses is not necessarily proof positive. What it does reveal is that the nobility no longer functioned as a totally homogenous social group, and that as the century brought its novelties they shattered the second order, producing sometimes diametrically opposed individual destinies.

The Noble in a Changing World

Was the nobility able to adapt to the new conception that made the individual and his economic function, his monetary value, and his knowledge the foundations of a new social classification? Could it recognize itself in the sum total of such extreme differences? Was there any real awareness of belonging to the same group among those whose "zigzagging careers expressed the instability of the material, social, and political situation of the European aristocracies" and those who were the promoters of new forms of power and were ruled by a more philanthropic philosophy?[40]

One might set up a day-and-night dichotomy between the enlightened portion of the aristocracy and a more obscure fringe group whose malaise reflected a genuine loss of caste—two groups that reflected a social gap within one social order. Among the more dynamic noble, three typical portraits stand out: the industrialist, the landed proprietor, and the army officer.

The Noble Industrialist

We know from the works of Guy Richard, who has studied nearly a thousand noble families, that some nobles took an active part in the economic changes of the eighteenth century by controlling colonial commerce and furthering innovations in the totally renewed industrial sectors of metallurgy, textiles, the chemical industry, and mines.

Thanks to a legal apparatus that eliminated obstacles to derogation and had been set in place over nearly a century, nobles were able to engage in maritime commerce (1669), arms manufacturing and naval construction (1681), maritime insurance (1686), wholesale commerce (1701), and manufacturing and banking (1767).[41] The eighteenth century saw the formation of a veritable business nobility, bourgeois in its preoccupations and feudal in its motivations. "By converting to industrial capitalism, the landed aristocracy was guaranteed continued existence and retained, in the society in gestation, the prime position that it had occupied during the ancien régime."[42]

The Dietrich family in Alsace provides a supreme example of this commercial nobility. Jean III Dietrich (1715–95) inherited ironworks and mines in the Jaegerthal. With the help of a banker named Herman, he managed to amass the 1.1 million livres needed to buy land, finance innovations, and launch construction projects. Social consecration came in 1761, when he obtained letters of nobility. At that point Jean III broke with everything that recalled his bourgeois origins and devoted himself exclusively to his landholdings and his investments in industry. Soon the "king of iron" owned five of the eight blast furnaces in the entire *généralité* and commanded a workforce of 1,500 workers and 300 miners. His son Philippe Frédéric, who held the post of inspector of mines, ironworks, and factories of France and was a member of the Académie des Sciences, took over where he left off.[43]

The Noble Landholder

Nobles in the far south of France provide an equally shining example of the management of their landholdings. Southeast of Toulouse, in

Vieillevigne, a village of a few hundred inhabitants, the marquis d'Es-
couloubres enjoyed a considerable fortune. Besides his own domain, he
owned three *métairies* (share-cropped farms) and four other farms that
brought in a yearly income of 6,000 livres. We would have to add to this
income a number of seignorial fees and dues—the *cens, banalités,* the
retrait féodal (feudal levies), rights to *lods et ventes* (fees on the resale of
property), the *champart,* the *corvée,* and hunting rights.[44] This was by no
means a unique case in the region. Robert Forster has found traces of
the same vitality in Rennes and around Bordeaux. Forster states:

> The seigneurial reaction represented a comprehensive adapta-
> tion of the noble estate to an expanding market for farm pro-
> duce. This adaptation included a number of managerial
> methods applied primarily to the estate proper *(domaine proche).*
> These methods or techniques included more precise estate ac-
> counting joined with the enforcement of seigneurial titles, fore-
> closure of mortgages of indebted peasants and purchases from
> neighboring proprietors, reduction of labor and middleman
> costs through progressive changes in leaseholds, land clearing
> to increase farm production, and stocking and speculation.
> The noble estate owner, moreover, exercised his influence at
> local parlement, estates, or chamber of commerce to champion
> the physiocratic "bon prix" in grain, improvements in commu-
> nication, and suppression of communal rights. This pattern of
> noble activity does not suggest a class of urbanized absentees or
> fossilized relics.[45]

Still, and Forster himself notes the ambiguity, this dynamism might also
have been born of a form of imitation of the bourgeois lifestyle, which
the nobility adopted, as the century progressed, along with bourgeois
values of discipline, rigorous management, and temperance. In this
view, the nobility in fact adapted its instruments of power (land, feudal
law) to a new ethic. Even more, it sacrificed a symbolic prestige based in
great part on a stability and equilibrium in relations with the village communities, which enabled it to accumulate an economic capital that
brought it closer to its rival in business, the bourgeoisie.

   This had predictable political consequences. The problem deserves
to be posed because it suggests that the dynamism and vigor of the nobility may have been a tacit recognition of the economic and social superiority of another model. How could the nobility have negotiated this de
facto *embourgeoisement*? Did the nobles incur no long-term threat to the

legitimacy of their power by appealing to a way of thinking elaborated outside the realm of feudal prejudice and noble preeminence? Was this not also the nub of the ambiguity of the military reform of 1781?

The Noble Career in the Military

If the noble at times successfully engaged in an economic or agronomic adventure, a military career was, in principle, his best career choice and the one in which he justified all his privileges and displayed his true valor. "Genuine nobility derives from arms, and it is through arms that it must be maintained. Making war is an essential condition of both its existence and its survival."[46]

In spite of this statement of principle, the reality of the military profession was not always brilliant. Memoirs frequently note disappointment and quickly abandoned careers. Comte de Tilly had this to say about garrison life:

> I arrived at Falaise, brimming with pride about my marvelous adventure, highly pleased with myself, and persuaded that I would reach the heights. . . . The life we led there was much different from what I had seen thus far. . . . Dragoons continually tormenting [me], officers who showed no great friendliness toward newcomers, ex-legionnaires grown old in subordinate posts . . . military details to be learned in their most minute particulars . . . a fairly ugly town, a few good-looking (and well-supervised) women, others who had no need of supervision, men the Parisians made fun of as if they came from another world.[47]

At times men in uniform came in for severe criticism, and it is true that an army of country squires was not always exemplary. "In Eu in 1756, the lieutenants and captains found it amusing, on some evenings, to toss rockets through the open windows of the burghers' houses." Elsewhere, we are told that in 1671, the young noble in uniform "boasted of caring little for the orders of Monsieur l'Intendant: he did not consider himself to be held to the same obedience as a commoner."[48]

Noble officers often had mediocre careers, punctuated by few acts of bravery, and on many occasions their shaky pecuniary situation was not greatly improved by a return to civilian life: "The provinces are carpeted with crosses of St. Louis, men with pensions who are no older than forty, who are in the full flower of their age, and who could still serve well and long. These are persons useless to the state, who bring it to ruin and dishonor it, and who are neither citizens nor in a position to profit from the advantages that they have extracted."[49]

If there was a degree of malaise, it could also be attributed to indigent nobles whose poverty increasingly distanced them from the military profession and whose places were taken by wealthy commoners. "A way must be found to help the poor nobles, who ask for nothing better than to serve"; if no career possibilities were offered to poor nobles "by giving them training and aiding them so they can fight in the service, they are as many men lost for the king. Their numbers are simply too great."[50]

The nobility had a right to the exercise of arms, and no introduction of a new parameter, be it the power of money, could be accepted without weakening the entire second order. What was comprehensible and acceptable in the conduct of business and the management of landholdings was unthinkable in the military.

> The nobility is humiliated to see itself deprived of the places that its ancestors occupied and cemented with their blood. Wealth, which corrupts everything and breaks all the barriers that honor and glory have erected among citizens, has today become sufficient title for claiming all posts. It is not without reason that I predict the disastrous consequence of this confusion of ranks; it is what is already producing the nobility's efforts to maintain the distinction that was to separate it eternally from the commonality. Demands, intrigues, and petty means are used to rise out of a place once considered honorable but scorned now that people other than one's peers have the right to occupy it.[51]

Reaction against this confusion came to a head in 1781. New military regulations drawn up that year stipulated that an officer's commission could only be granted to gentlemen capable of showing proof of four quarters of nobility on the father's side. David Bien has demonstrated that this reform was not aimed at commoners. "The army commission that discussed and adopted the Ségur regulation knew perfectly well that for some years the officers' corps had been recruited almost exclusively from the nobility."[52] In reality, the desire to better the condition of officers by giving them an indisputable status could be accomplished only by constituting a homogeneous group that was highly motivated, professionally qualified, and recruited by requiring four quarters of nobility. At whom was this regulation aimed, then? The new nobles, the ennobled:

> What the army saw was a group of civilians who appeared to be united as civilians and who were all wealthy: all members [of this group] had been able to purchase a costly post and all (or nearly all) had sons who could afford the expenses involved in military service as an officer. Certain families had left the shop behind them; others were anchored in it by the legal profession or judiciary responsibilities. . . . If the army's intention was to weed out of the officers' corps not commoners but wealthy nobles whose formation was not military, the Ségur regulation was efficacious.[53]

Thus, the aim of the reform drawn up in 1781 and imposed on the nobility was in itself positive because it took into account one of the aspects of the philosophy of the Enlightenment—the benefit of education, upbringing, and environment—for the improvement of the military, which was increasingly considered a profession. Still, as with the noble lords of Toulouse, the military nobility espoused the spirit of the century in the affirmation of a model—the requirement that a candidate for an officer's commission show four quarters of nobility—that was inevitably and logically perceived as retrograde.

These three possible roles for the noble and these three exemplary aristocrats—the industrialist, the country gentleman, and the new officer—reflect an enlightened elite. They are by no means the entire extent of the gallery of noble portraits.

Loss of Caste

The lower end of the second order contains examples of threatened marginality, disorder, contestation, and muffled rebellion that are just as authentic as the success stories we have just seen. If terms such as "downfall" or "decadence" are best avoided because they refer to moral concepts, "loss of caste" perhaps provides a more accurate description of the new social reality that emerged in the latter half of the eighteenth century. The poorest nobles saw loss of caste as inevitable: "The nobility is continually being extinguished in the general mass of common people." There were many nobles, however, who clung to their titles, their last claim to dignity and their last recourse before they plunged into miserable poverty.

In 1765, only one of the four Parigny brothers who had fought the wars in Germany lived to return to his estate of Sainte-Maure in Touraine. Trouble awaited him there. His land had lain fallow for twenty-five years and, as this veteran reported to the first commissioner of the *contrôle générale* in 1766, his woes included "the house absolutely falling apart and open to everyone, its framework removed in several places, as are the doors, the casement windows, the shutters, the locks, even the roofing; the barn and the stables completely ruined, and all the fruit trees cut down." Repairs, land reclamation, and replanting forced Parigny into debt.

By 1771, the situation had grown even worse. Parigny's moneylender had won a suit against him and was hounding him. The stable and half the barn had collapsed. What could the farm laborers, the villagers, and the local farmers possibly have thought of a spectacle of poverty that, although borne with dignity, nonetheless revealed an incontestable loss of caste? What legitimate basis could there be for a nobility of this sort? Between the farmhands' pity and the moneylender's ruthless pursuit, what room was there for respect or even simple social recognition of his noble estate? Parigny preserved his honor and his honesty was never questioned. What are we to think, though, of the many nobles who behaved like outlaws and contributed to an image of noble delinquency?

Representations of the outlaw-noble are many. Although they have at times been exaggerated, they exist, and together they make up a body of instances reflecting what Jean Meyer has called "*le mal d'être* of the eighteenth-century nobility." Obviously, criminal acts were committed by a small minority of nobles; equally clearly, the perpetrators of those acts had severed their connections with the second order or had proven their inability to retain their rank. Since it was the noble's function to offer a virtuous reproduction of a social model and since these men had rejected that function, one obvious reaction was to amplify, even distort, their scandalous doings. Their attitude gave a concrete illustration of the possible fall of the nobility as a whole.

Dueling is an interesting special case. In theory, dueling had been abandoned in the late seventeenth century, but there are few memoirs that fail to mention duels. "People fight for good reason and for no reason; even *robins* draw their swords—on occasion, successfully—against military men."[54] Comte de Montlosier, who was far from a swashbuckling sort, was forced to fight two duels. When his brother killed a young man of good family in a fit of temper, it created serious problems for the family. Tilly confirms this impression:

> France is the homeland of duels. . . . I have not met with this baleful susceptibility anywhere else, this unfortunate disposition to hold oneself insulted and to want to repel an offense. . . . I do not say that this class [duelists] was numerous, but it did exist, which was one more proof of the mania of duels in the nation and of the prejudice that had as if tacitly established that nothing was so noble and so grand as this sort of bravery.

Other observers described the symbolic charge of self-destruction in dueling, pointing out its dangers for a group that was already a small minority.

There were even more dangerous activities, however, more damaging to the reputation of the order of the nobility. There was, for instance, the Beaulieu de Montigny affair in 1737. This young officer killed a husband who had refused to close his eyes to the officer's attentions to his wife. In spite of all that the family could do, the court sentenced the officer to having his head cut off. In 1768, the young duc de Fronsac, the son of Maréchal de Richelieu, arranged to have a young girl kidnaped right in the middle of rue Saint-Honoré. The police found her in the apartment of a procurer. A great effort was made to hush up the affair, because, as the bookseller Hardy reported, "people continue to complain privately to see that when a great personage is involved in a horrible crime he goes unpunished, when the most rigorous punishments would have been applied for any other person." Victor Ysoré, marquis de Pleumartin, provides a significant example of escalating violence.

> He liked somewhat cruel practical jokes. . . . One of his favorite amusements is hanging peasants from the top of a tower and threatening to let them fall into the void below. A break with all morality and public order came on 9 March 1753, however, when the marquis tortured four process-servers. On the following 10 June, the commissioner of police of Chattelerault came to fetch the criminal, who killed two men and seriously wounded another. Finally arrested in January 1755, he died in his prison cell before he could be brought to justice.[55]

Two spectacular cases of noble loss of caste summarize the malaise of a portion of the nobility. The extremist attitudes of the marquis de

Sade and the comte de Mirabeau provide two instructive examples. These two nobles adopted a reactionary stance, clinging to their privileges and, by that token, denying their marginalization, or else they embraced their social fall, predicting, even calling for an end to a regime that no longer guaranteed them a privileged status.

When the marquis de Sade wrote to his wife, "Believe me, we have given sufficient spectacles in the Dauphiné and in Provence. Valence has me registered in its archives next to Mandrin," the dishonor brought to an entire family is clearly perceptible.[56] Here loss of caste is publicly displayed as social scandal; in any event, it is experienced as brigandage.

Michel Vovelle has described the parallels in the social descent of these two noblemen. For both men, their status became more fragile with "economic catastrophe." Sade proved incapable of proper management of his lands: in 1769 his income was 13,329 livres; twenty years later it had risen to only 14,425 livres. Vovelle notes: "This stagnation, at a time in which land revenues were rising everywhere, is already an indication of a decline."[57] Mirabeau's financial failure is even clearer. Between 1772 and 1774, when his annual income was as high as 27,000 livres, he accumulated debts amounting to 161,116 livres.[58] Landholding shows notable disorder, with an increase in forest crimes and in suits between village communities and their lord. "A spendthrift, exploitative, and frivolous nobility offered an utterly debased image of its own class, sacrificing its wealth to worldly pleasures. *La dolce vita* required it."[59]

Imprisonment was another mark of loss of caste. Our two rebels suffered the humiliation of being locked up in the Bastille and in the prisons of Vincennes, Pontarlier, and the Château d'If, and they were ostracized by their peers. This description of group members who had caused trouble being thrust aside might end here were it not that loss of caste was exacerbated by our two libertines, who elaborated a system of thought that turned their exclusion into a mechanism for social criticism. "The libertine is not only someone who gets himself excluded but also someone capable of self-exclusion."[60] Hence, the stand that Sade took regarding religion or Mirabeau's position on the arbitrary nature of the monarchy can be understood as moves aimed at transforming their loss of caste into a destabilization of the reigning order.

In practice, then, sexual disorder became political behavior. For these two nobles, the boudoir was a field for experimentation in which sexual impulses mimicked situations deriving from a conflict with power. Roles in lovemaking were distributed in terms of a clearly expressed social inequality (master/slave; oppressor/oppressed; torturer/victim). The sadist finds pleasure in the fall, the humiliation, and the loss of dignity of his victim; the masochist takes pleasure in his own pain and submission and in an acceptance of his fall. Mirabeau and Sade felt this logic of power physically, but they also expressed it in literature. The perversions imagined and described by these two nobles are paradigms for tormented, exuberant, and (as Michel Foucault called them) "peripheral" sexualities; they reflect a humiliating loss of caste that betrays the truth of their relation to the world. Difficulties inherent in family relations (Mirabeau was pursued by the fury of a father armed with several *lettres de cachet,* who refused to bail him out of his financial troubles; Sade was ceaselessly persecuted by his wife's *robin* family) are an expression of the extreme harshness of relations within these small groups. "It is clear, for example, that the obsessive insistence on incest in Sade's *Les prospérités du vice* and in Mirabeau's *Le rideau levé* has the one meaning and the one function of representing the impossibility of a successful integration."[61]

When he describes the libertine's cruelty and severity, Sade suggests the cruelty and severity of all those who hold power, and all the more so when that power is political. Isolated, suffering sexual loss of caste, the libertine had plenty of leisure to describe what motivated the torturer (on several occasions—in 1768, 1774, and 1775—Sade was imprisoned for violence committed on women or girls).[62] Sade perhaps reached the height of this "social illness" on the morning of 27 June 1772, when, after whipping and being whipped by prostitutes and being sodomized by his valet, he derisively underscored his social "cross-dressing" by addressing Latour, the valet, as "Monsieur le marquis."[63]

In this sense, "sadistic" literature is a negative image: by describing the workings of power, it opened up the possibility of overturning it. For Mirabeau, loss of caste and the divorce from the nobility that he assumed in his rebellion against order took on a more political but no less violent aspect. As early as 1776 he attacked the regime of the absolute monarchy and compared it to "despotism, which is not a form of government. . . . If it were, it would be a criminal brigandage against which all men should join forces."[64]

Power: Theory and Reality

These portraits give an impression of a disintegration that the nobility experienced actively and suffered passively. Still, these men were all nobles; they insisted on their nobility and that very fact prevents a good likeness. The portrait of the noble becomes unfeasible. Within this elusive reality, all nobles thought themselves well-born because they were also the product of an ideological discourse that united them, gave them an identity, guaranteed their social superiority, and justified them in the past, present, and the foreseeable future.

But as soon as the producers of this discourse changed and verities held to be secure and incontestable were challenged, the mask dropped, revealing the fragmentation, even the profound cleavages, within the second order, and throwing new light on the broken destinies of the nobility.

It has been argued that this "crumbling is not necessarily connected to the eighteenth century." Fragmentation withing the noble condition had already been attested in the sixteenth century, and again in the seventeenth century. The nobility's crisis of identity and legitimacy was nothing new. Between 1560 and 1650

> the nobility had doubts about itself, sought itself, defined itself in order to reassure itself; it closed itself within an illusory purity, it clung to superannuated symbols . . . exactly when it was incapable of giving itself a doctrine and a political organization. When administrative tasks were slipping from its grasp. And when its prestige remained immense in the eyes of the rest of society. When it still held large portions of power everywhere. When its material strength was still solid and at times reinforced.[65]

As France emerged from the civil wars and the Fronde, this can in large part be explained by the monarchy's policy of bringing the nobility to court. When it was removed from its power base, the nobility, protected by its statutes, became the most coddled social group. It was distanced from business but drawn closer to the person of the king; it was kept away from decision making but its lifestyle radiated out through the entire kingdom. The multiple destinies of nobles were sublimated by their common reference to the court, the source of fashions to be followed and behavior patterns to be adopted, copied, and imitated. Still, nobles suffered from their lack of political representation. The court was no place for formulating an ideological discourse that might unite the nobility behind a system of coherent demands. In fact, no royal institution gave official expression to the political program of the second order. Even if the various parlements were largely composed of nobles, they did not speak for nobles as a group. France had no Chamber of

Lords as in England, no organized aristocracy as in Venice, no body capable of representing the interests of the group as a whole. As court life lost some of its formal brilliance during the eighteenth century, relations between the state and the nobility inevitably became more tense. Increasingly criticized and challenged, the well-born had no official means for speaking out in their own defense or for expressing their cohesion, their solidarity, and their power as a unified group. They were obliged to place themselves under a benign royal protection that did little to conceal differences within the nobility. Tocqueville observed the "steadily widening" gap between recently ennobled commoners and nobles of ancient date and between the wealthy aristocrats and the increasing numbers of a well-born nobility that, "the more its power declined, the poorer it became."[66] No one institution could claim to structure the nobility or offer it a coherent political position in a climate in which criticism of it grew increasingly violent after 1720.

A New Definition of the Noble: Perceptions

Can we read any unity into a second order that included persons of such different temperaments and with such different destinies, living in such very different social (and above all economic) situations? In reality, the noble becomes perceptible and comprehensible only when he is brought back into a network of interactive relations that shifted between the real and the imaginary and between discourse and practice.

For example, although nobles shared a recognizable lifestyle, their biographies were widely heterogeneous. Similarly, although there was a line of thought that aimed at bringing homogeneity to the second order, nobles were far from agreeing on the values that were to unite them. In short, there is no objective description of practices that can be contrasted to the subjective reality of an ideological discourse. Quite to the contrary, the noble is comprehensible only in a constant interaction between his modes of sociability, as codified and integrated in a system of values, and ideas that he applied, adopted, or made use of. The period of far-reaching reflection that began around 1720 was for the well-born a time of profound intellectual change. Even more certainly, it was a time of important shifts in cultural perceptions of social phenomena that led to a radical transformation in the values of recognition and distinction at the apex of society and resulted in a new conception of the nobility.

This means that it is important for us to reflect on the form and the substance of the discourse whose purpose was to describe, name, define, and recognize the noble. It is also important to know who was writing about the noble—a fellow noble or a commoner—who had an interest in homogenizing the second order through a discourse erecting a common system of values, and who had a stake in constructing a series of critiques presenting the noble as a personage whose psychological, physical, moral, and cultural characteristics had negative connotations. Put simply, we need to inquire into the goals pursued by those who held the power to produce the criteria by which people were ranked in society and who expressed themselves indirectly, between 1720 and 1770, through literature, the theater, the press, and the salons, and in political and philosophical writings.

The "Enlightened" Noble

During that fifty-year period, the noble can be found at the heart of widespread reflection that did much to renew political thought and to recast the foundations of society throughout Europe. The wind of intellectual reform that blew over the Continent challenged the role and the traditional function of the aristocracy in the name of new values. Men of the Enlightenment no longer recognized the noble as a biologically superior being, socially privileged by the fact of his birth and publicly protected solely by his membership in a more or less prestigious lineage. From Lisbon to Moscow a new political discourse was being forged that attempted to redefine social hierarchy and reorganize it on the basis of other values than those of the system of nobility.

Merit was preferred to birth as a quality acquired in humility by a long apprenticeship, symbolized by a rise within a profession, and rewarded by a certain degree of wealth. Courage, bravery, and military exploits were admired less than the virtues of the *honnête homme*—which were a mixture of broad knowledge and wisdom tempered by reason, used to good profit in activities of the mind. Respect for tradition and the order that had been established within historical continuity were valued less than a demand for reform and the advent of a natural equality among all men.

By defining themselves in this fashion, men of the Enlightenment provided a countermodel to the typical portrait of the noble. Obviously, that did not prevent individual nobles from participating in this enlightened dynamic or, at times, from forging the intellectual definition of this new man.

Daniel Roche outlines several levels of participation in the elaboration of this new spirit. Some nobles were its consumers. Noble readers, for example, knew the works of the *philosophes* without necessarily sharing their ideals and made an increasingly large place for those works on their library shelves, usually indirectly in works of history and literature. On the one hand, "an entirely new sort of reflection on society and government was purveyed by the insidious reform of the historical thought of the Enlightenment, [a thought] ambiguous in its social goals and in its hopes for reform"; on the other hand, "reading Voltaire's tales or the novels of Rousseau, which, as is known, were in large part faithful to an ideal of aristocratic behavior, reveals the triumph of the new tastes and of transformed social tastes."[67]

Some nobles who wrote (clandestinely or not) and who spoke in more or less provocative tones in the salons were more deeply involved in the general process of questioning society, hence more compromised. D'Holbach's "coterie" was the archetype of such groups. The *gros baron* was himself an example of integration into the nobility. A wealthy man, he made his oldest son a *conseiller* in the Parlement de Paris, married his daughter to an aristocratic captain of the dragoons, and bought a company for his younger son in Schomberg's regiment. Socially, he occupied a position at the heart of the highest society of his time. Intellectually, there was a flagrant contradiction: "The works of the master abound in denunciations of royal authority, tyranny, the supremacy of the aristocracy, the fanaticism of the church. . . . This contrast between practices and ideology permits us to wonder about the social significance of radical ideas and the intellectuals' attitudes toward change."[68]

The same contrast permits us a better understanding of the subtlety of an intellectual construction that consisted, on the one hand, in elaborating the portrait of the enlightened man—a new man and a model personage born of existing models, noble and commoner, who were living examples of a new spirit—and, on the other hand, in sketching a counterportrait of the noble encumbered with debts and charged with all possible faults, a negative reference, a figure decried as a social reality to be replaced, and the perfect opposite of the first.

Within the critical discourse of the Enlightenment, an image of the noble came to be formed as an idler, useless to the economy of the country, libertine in his mores, scornful and haughty when he was wealthy and a parasite when he was poor, ignorant because he refused the philosophers' audacity, cowardly because the Seven Years' War had shown that he was often unprepared for combat. To be sure, this noble—too rich, too poor, ignorant, and immersed in hedonistic pleasures—never existed. Nonetheless, this description functioned as part of the workings of the ideological machinery manipulated by men of the Enlightenment to disqualify an entire social system. These mechanisms were all the more efficacious because everyone recognized that they referred to the excesses, failings, deviance, poverty, or criminal tendencies of a portion of the nobility—traits that were not only real and exemplified by many individuals present in all regions but that still appeared in critical literature, exaggerated (at times imagined), and that public opinion took for fact.

As for the nobles who possessed the qualities praised by the new philosophical current, their personal destiny was a confirmation that the new values attracted the more capable of all classes, including the well-born. In no case was their good fortune used as an illustration that nobility and its system of values might have contributed to their success, a success that had all the aspects of the honest prudence and the virtuous respectability of the bourgeoisie in place.

The noble found himself faced with an ideological challenge in which the stakes seemed clear: either he could respond to this anti-portrait by creating another image of himself, seeking to give new luster to traditional noble qualities, cleverly contrasting them to a passion for novelty and raising the specter of the risks involved in change, or he could elaborate a radically new system of values. In each case, whether he took his stance with or against the discourse of the Enlightenment, he accepted and submitted to an original political discourse that defined the legitimacy of a new social group founded on the values of virtue, reason, merit, and natural rights—values that stood opposed to a legitimacy of the nobility founded on blood, race, absolutist order, lineage, and appearance.

This cultural challenge was one of the tensions that reveal a struggle for possession of the means of social legitimation and for mastery of the symbolic production goods—both commodities that eventually became common and incontestable signs of distinction in eighteenth-century Europe. In the final analysis, this struggle between two elites was no less intense than the parallel economic struggle to obtain control over the means of production and over materials.

By making its own the new values that had been erected into a positive system and into symbolic signs of social domination, the movement of the Enlightenment forced the nobility to redefine itself and to justify itself anew. Eventually it prompted a struggle for classification in which the noble was virtually dominated and in part demoted. Because the nobility lacked the ability or the power to check the emergence of a typical and admittedly subjective portrait of its faults (which was at times all the more cruel for being painted by a noble), and because it was unable to impose the image of a new noble, self-assured and strong in his confirmed or reconstructed legitimacy, the nobility vacillated.

Abbé Coyer and the Chevalier d'Arcq

We still need to explain why and how the nobility came to be dominated culturally and, as a consequence, discredited ideologically. We still need to retrace the discourse of legitimation that the nobility invented (and it was never passive under critical fire), both within and counter to the spirit of the Enlightenment and quite often under the illusion that adaptation to the form of a new discourse could mask the conservation of ancestral values. The polemic that burst out at the very midst of the period of the Enlightenment between Abbé Coyer and the chevalier d'Arcq is an excellent illustration of this struggle over classification.

Because *La noblesse commerçante* and *La noblesse militaire,* the two works that led to one of the most famous controversies of the century, were so much cited, historians have lost sight of what happened to their authors, Abbé Coyer and the chevalier d'Arcq, and their other works. These works throw new light, however, on the debate concerning the role of the noble in the thought of the Enlightenment.

Behind this intellectual jousting match lie two biographies that go far to explain the gaps, contradictions, and surprises of the epoch. One author, Abbé Coyer, was a commoner, tutor to the prince de Turenne, to whom he was indebted for the ease he enjoyed throughout his life. He was chaplain *(aumonier général)* to the cavalry from 1743 on, and he was a member of the Royal Academy of London (elected in 1768), of the Accademia dell'Arcadia of Rome, and of the Académie de Nancy. Favored and protected by high-ranking aristocrats, his works, long underestimated, reveal a lively and unusually strong critique of the second order. The other author, the chevalier d'Arcq, was noble, the natural son of the comte de Toulouse and a protégé of the duchesse d'Orléans. He obtained a cavalry company and fought brilliantly, earning the Cross of Saint Louis. He had to abandon the military career in 1748, however, at which time he began his literary career. He married a woman of dubious reputation, spent money too liberally, and when he became mixed up in shady financial schemes was exiled to Tulle by a *lettre de cachet.* A decree dated 6 May 1785 even forbade him to use the name "d'Arcq." A second *lettre de cachet* sent him to live in Montauban, where for a short time his behavior raised no comment. This champion of the noble cause, an advocate of aristocratic honor and virtue, was penniless throughout most of his life, had made a bad marriage, did not even have the right to bear his titles, had been exiled, and had suffered loss of caste.

We can learn much from the works of these two men. A superficial reading of *La noblesse commerçante* might lead one to think that Abbé Coyer was content to express some reservations about the idle and impoverished nobility. In fact, however, the words and expressions that he chose are a harsh depiction of a "miserable class" that "spreads indigence and sterility over everything around it."[69] Coyer discredits "all persons incommoded by the cost of foodstuffs in the cities; obtuse men of independent wealth who work neither for themselves nor for the state, gentlemen who amuse themselves counting their ancestors, idlers who intend to subsist doing nothing."[70] He concludes: "You fear scorn and you remain in indigence! You like consideration and you are nullities! Eternal victims of the prejudice that is killing you!"[71] His critical approach was subtle: he used the indigence of a certain portion of the nobility to denounce the whole of the moral and political code of the second order, which he saw as solely responsible for the pauperization of the nobility. The frontispiece to this work shows a gentleman with a parchment that displays the titles from which he had drawn no profit.

Abbé Coyer bitterly criticized Italy. There, he states, "everything is crawling with barons, counts, marquises, and princes. . . . There are so many of them that it is almost a distinction not to be anything."[72] Coyer methodically denounces and dismantles the system of the nobility and its signs, prejudices, blockages, and archaisms, all of which, in the long run, paralyze the dynamism of society. He speaks sarcastically of "the privileges, the heritage of ancestors, the first syllable as an *hors d'oeuvre* that prolongs the name, the stupefying exemption from payment of tallage . . . the vexations and humiliations visited on the bourgeois and on worthy folk, the facilitation for acquiring more knowledge in less time in the universities."[73]

Abbé Coyer invents the story of Chinki, a wise peasant, who observes the king's creation of nobles who "go about thinking that their blood is purer, closer to the great virtues than that of other men . . . and who transmit their privilege to each generation." When he goes to the city to seek work for two of his children, Chinki discovers that simply because he tills the soil his son cannot be a baker, a tailor, a shoemaker, a vinegarmaker, or a locksmith, and that a worker is not judged by the work he does but by his birth. "Does the son of the master inherit his father's skills?" Chinki asks. Coyer notes that the typical noble trait of prejudice regarding birth gets mixed into the way the trade corporations function, blocking professional dynamism and slowing fruitful renewal among artisans. Denouncing the system of recruitment within the crafts and trades enables Abbé Coyer to denounce the contagion of an aristocratic model in the world of labor and the social imitation of sterile practices dangerously propagated to other classes than the nobility.

It was not enough to criticize the nobility; everything in society that had been contaminated by its prejudices and customs stood in need of correction. The corporations, corrupted by the prejudice of birth and blocked by the rule of privileges, required reform in the name of a new philosophy and new values. In his *Bagatelles morales,* Abbé Coyer pursued his campaign against the noble system in the name of virtue, talent, and nature: "This adolescent has vegetated for twenty years; gaming, theatricals, clothing, dogs, and a mistress have taken up all his hours. His father dies, all others withdraw: the child becomes a judge."[74] It is hardly coincidental that as Chinki's adventures draw to a close the country nobility is suppressed and its lands redistributed to the men who work them, while guild masterships and trade corporations vanish.

Coyer's barbs stung all the more because he proposed a coherent solution: replacing the nobility with the new merchant group. If there was a nobility, it was undeniably in trade: "There is one point that I will admit. As long as gaming, pleasures, wild expenditures, luxurious display, and uselessness conserve an air of nobility, commerce will not take it on. If [the man in commerce] gambles, it is only after he has applied himself; if he abandons himself to pleasure, it is after hard work; if he spends, it is with wisdom; if he gives, he has paid his debts."[75] Reading Coyer's works one has the impression that a vocation for commerce is the only title of nobility that should be recognized, and that the old nobility is in a perilous situation and needs to adopt a new deontology as rapidly as possible if it does not want to be replaced. In short: "Commerce can do without nobility, but nobility has great need of [commerce]."

It is hardly surprising that in his search for a social model Abbé Coyer went to England. In London he discovered the worth of "the honest bourgeoisie, that precious portion of the nations that must be consulted."[76] He also found the English nobility praiseworthy for its financial self-sufficiency: its wealth and its function as an integral part of the economy determined its value.

> If the English nobility possesses many means for multiplying and perpetuating itself, it also has many for not falling into poverty or for pulling itself out of poverty. Commerce is open to it at all times, in all of its branches, not one of which can ruffle its sensibilities. While a lord manages the public affairs of the House of Lords, his brother runs a commercial operation without taking fright at the word "derogation" because the thing does not exist.

Coyer saw the English aristocracy as the point of arrival of a social promotion that he thought possible for all "men of merit whatever they may be"—physicians, jurists, university professors—all of whom might be elevated to honors and wealth thanks to their talents, which the king was sure to recognize.

What Abbé Coyer imagined was in fact a pure and simple substitution of a new aristocracy of talent and merit for the old nobility. "The reign of Louis the Great was the century of genius and conquests. May the reign of Louis the Well-Beloved be that of philosophy, commerce, and happiness."[77] Either the old nobility would abandon its false ideas and adopt the commoners' values of the merchants or, marginalized, on its way to impoverishment, and a danger to mores, it would no longer have any excuse for being.

What possible response could the chevalier d'Arcq make to this ultimatum? His argument in defense of the noble was organized around a revelation of the noble's disquietude concerning his status and around his desire to justify that status and give a coherent and positive representation of it. The chevalier d'Arcq was neither closed-minded nor attached to any ridiculous extent to a more or less glorious past, and he fully understood the accuracy of some of Abbé Coyer's criticisms, which he turned into positive qualities of the nobility. Yet he fell into a trap: by arguing the worth of a poor nobility, the danger inherent in confusing social orders, and the abuse of the philosophical spirit, he assented to and even corroborated Abbé Coyer's entire discourse. He did not question the veracity of Coyer's observations, merely criticizing the solutions Coyer had suggested for curing the ills of the nobility.

Indeed, far from contradicting Abbé Coyer on the poverty of the second order, the chevalier d'Arcq saw it as a cause for pride. "I find it all the more honorable," the hero of the *Roman du jour* states, "because in such a situation the person who is abandoned is not the one who should blush." He continues:

The prosperity procured by commerce does not seem to draw out of obscurity those on whom fortune smiles only to plunge them again into a veritable nothingness. Between the two choices, is it not better to choose the road that leads to glory, to truth without opulence but also without risks for probity, and the road to an honest and natural liberty, rather than prefer the choice that takes away a liberty, innocent in itself, that rarely leads to wealth without dulling delicacy, and in which one cannot always enjoy riches without trouble and without bitterness? Between serving one's country and deceiving it, the choice of a thinking man is soon made.[78]

In this reasoning "noble" and "military" had to be synonymous. The chevalier d'Arcq defends the poverty of the nobility because, according to him, it guaranteed a disinterested loyalty to the military, the one authentic career for any nobleman. "One must constantly show scorn for wealth and for life and make glory one's only desire. Modesty, gentleness, humanity, candor, and moderation must be inseparable from the many warlike virtues."[79]

The chevalier d'Arcq fully grasped the cleverness of Abbé Coyer's attack: what introduced the philosophy of the Enlightenment into the political debate was the importance of trade and not the place of the second order within social classifications. And professional activity, taken as a criterion of distinction, emptied the nobility of all prestige. "Then we will find ourselves with a military nobility, a commercial nobility, an agricultural nobility. All that will be lacking is the formation of a manufacturing nobility, and everything will be noble—which is to say that the nobility will no longer exist." The chevalier d'Arcq also understood both what was at stake in Abbé Coyer's criticisms and the force for destabilization that they represented. If "noble" and "military" were one and the same, what was needed was to combat everyone who attempted to practice social confusion. The conservation of honorific status, symbolic functions, and signs of privilege was a means of defense against the new spirit affecting the century. It was a matter of principle that the noble estate was superior to the other estates; the noble's inequality protected him and lent him value: "The state only begins to totter when ranks cease to be distinct from one another, when they mix, when they are confused, when they are absorbed into one another."

Social mobility, attained either through the exercise of a trade and amassing wealth or by ineluctable impoverishment, was the other danger that the chevalier d'Arcq denounced. It was not enough simply to maintain inequality of birth: "It is just as dangerous . . . whether inferior citizens elevate themselves to the upper class . . . or whether the upper class demeans itself to descend to the lower." Should this happen, "ranks will be all the more confused and the state will find itself all the more sliding toward the precipice."[80] Even while he condemned them, the chevalier d'Arcq had a fine appreciation of the social transformations that were effecting a total reclassification of all elites by the introduction of a new code of respectability founded on professional success rather than on birth.

In the final analysis, d'Arcq, seemingly defeated by the abbé's arguments, avoids attacking them either in their content or their form, turning instead to people who made anti-noble statements. He presents the *philosophes* as men suffering social frustration, as if any challenge to an established order inevitably came from people who failed to win their share of privileges: "Such a man, born of obscure rank, with a secret ambition and a somber character . . . suddenly raises his voice arrogantly and exclaims, 'I am a philosopher.' He then gives himself the right to scorn greatness, to insult the great. . . . He thinks he can conceal his own genuine uselessness under the preoccupied air of a reformer."[81] In reality, d'Arcq continues, "The true philosophic spirit does not claim either to reduce all conditions to a sort of slavery under the despotism of one person alone nor to reduce them to the level of equality that some imprudent persons hope for and that would be a common disaster. It only attempts to consolidate order through a wise subordination."

The chevalier d'Arcq offers three arguments in support of his attempt to give the noble a new cultural and political identity: he defends the honor of the poor noble; he denounces the confusion between the order of the nobility and trade, and between social function and wealth; he attacks all the philosophers of the century who were skeptical about the role of the nobility. He also painted an ideal portrait of the noble. As he says in the final passage of *La noblesse militaire,* nobles "in no way want wealth if it costs them their honor; they want no material goods that are not connected with glory."[82] D'Arcq's entire attitude, however, indicates that he was more interested in defending the nobility than in attempting a constructive refutation of Abbé Coyer's vision of the nobility. His sole defense of an economic disorder that was ultimately pitiful was in the name of a principle inherited from an immutable past that he saw as open to criticism only by the embittered and by people excluded from privileges. This was a perfectly possible line or argumentation but it was no match for the abbé's rigorous thought.

Other Perspectives on the Noble

It is possible, however, that satire and literary caricature of the noble did far more to discredit the second order, which for some time was unable to take ideological satire and truculence and turn them back against detractors who moved the combat to the public scene of literature, the theater, and the press. Here too, the various portraits produced of the noble in any one family or in any work or play did not refer to any palpable reality, but they nonetheless ended up reinforcing the image of the parasitic noble.

But even if the character of the noble that was held up to ridicule was not totally "true," the question remains, why did the nobility fail to denounce attacks that could at times be crass? After all, the nobility possessed the financial means to produce and circulate a counter-image in its own literature and its own theater. Why did it not wish to do so, or why was it unable to do so? It was by no means so hypnotized by the new spirit moving over Europe as to deny everything that had made it a privileged class. Did nobles never perceive the danger? Or did they not perceive what was happening as a danger?

Spain is a good laboratory for observation of phenomena that have not been sufficiently studied but offer a wealth of information. In the movement of the Enlightenment on the Iberian Peninsula, as in the rest of Europe, a need for reform and renewal of the nobility was both felt and expressed. Philosophical debate soon turned to the conditions of such changes. A satirical discourse paralleled reflections on a higher plane, and satire, circulated in works of fiction and by the press, attempted to discredit the well-born of Spain through ridicule and sarcastic criticism.

Some thinkers saw the nobility as sick. Extreme libertinism, irreligion and atheism, exaggerated expenditures, and a decline into vulgarity were among the many symptoms that showed the disease to be incurable. Worse, the virus was contagious, and as the century progressed it spread like a gangrene from the top to the bottom of the social scale, paralyzing Spanish society. The only people who were immune to the national disease were the representatives of an enlightened Spain who ceaselessly warned their contemporaries of this contagion.

Jovellanos, who was a judge in Seville, a close friend of Olavide's, the founder of the Asturian Institute at Gijón, and eventually minister of justice under Charles IV, satirized the nobility in these terms:

> What a fine life!
> Worthy of a noble! Would you like a summary?
> He ran after bad women, gambled, lost health and wealth
> And before he reached his fortieth spring
> The hand of pleasure thrust him into the tomb.[83]

Satire attacked a social group primarily interested in appearances, especially in clothing and the bodily attitudes. Thus, writers, essayists, philosophers, chroniclers, and painters worked to unmask the social instability of certain nobles by showing the ridiculous spectacle that they offered with their outlandish fashions and their deformed bodies. Soon satire gave way to a reasoned criticism of the faults, exaggerations, excesses, and fabulations of the nobility. Such works began by contrasting the nobles of the day to their elders, a theme we find repeated until the end of the century:

> The ancient Spaniards of venerable tradition, and even those who until our own glorious times have let themselves be seen walking about the town, attending evening parties, and in campaigns, battles, and other arduous enterprises, were ordinary men in their full virility. . . . But today, our young lords with their fine moustaches, our *curratacos*—little dancers—are delicate, tender cajolers, enemies to any sort of serious occupation.[84]

This comparison, which is hardly flattering to the nobility of the eighteenth century, highlights another trait in this satire, the emasculating refinement, narcissism, and delicacy of these foppish "little lords." Degeneracy began with a loss of sexual identity: "The men are no longer recognizable because they are like women, making an idol of clothing, a serious occupation of hairstyles, a counselor of their mirror, imitation their study, taste their rule, invention a merit, bizarre ornamentation and the escutcheon of the *Petimetre [petit maître]* their quarter of nobility."[85]

One step more—a step that some authors took—and nobility became a disguise and its legitimacy a masquerade. Clavijo y Fajardo clearly perceived the danger, and he lashed out at this segment of the nobility, which public opinion soon identified with the nobility as a whole. In a society of appearances, all "must suit their attire to the qualities of their persons or the nature of their functions, so that there will be distinction among subjects and the confusion introduced can be avoided."[86]

Distinction or confusion—in 1762, Clavijo, a tireless journalist and the editor of *El Pensador,* the great Spanish satirical journal, clearly defined these two poles of the cultural and social challenge that the Enlightenment made to the nobility as nobles struggled with other social groups.

But if loss of caste started with dress, nudity furthered the process and even accentuated the idea of the degeneracy of the nobility. Rather than hiding the body by disguising it, clothing exhibited an emasculated body. Discrediting the noble's body, de-sexing it, was another way to refuse the noble the basic value of the second order, the hereditary transmission of valor and rank. In a satirical novel, Ramírez y Góngora describes only the periphery of the noble's body (his foot, his ear, his waist, his hand, his heart), bodily attributes that would be appropriate, in other circumstances, to the depiction of female charms. Ridiculed, reduced to its "extremities," the body of the noble no longer bore comparison with the body of the ordinary healthy, robust, strong Spaniard who was untouched by this fall from grace. An inversion of political values underlay this satire: nature regenerates bodies by giving them vigor and virility, the only true letters of nobility; noble blood withered the unsubstantial, vice-ridden bodies of the degenerate nobles and emptied them of all vital substance.

Critical verve quite logically turned next to disease and its transmission and contagion, a recurrent, omnipresent theme for the reformers of the eighteenth century. For the Spanish satirists, the noble was not only effeminate and counterfeit, he was also a source of a corruption that undermined the body social. His vices were contagious, and they spread, threatening the rest of the Spanish. Women, too, played a role in this contagion, and Fernández de Moratín describes in his *Arte de las Putas* fine ladies with "poorly dissimulated weaknesses" who bore an illustrious name and indulged in venal love. Anyone who came into contact with this nobility was stricken with its symptoms and was plunged into debauchery, inaction, indecency, and ruin. In Moratín's feverish imagination it was almost natural that this moral contagion should resemble syphilis, the "shameful disease." Syphilis chancres played a symbolic role as the nucleus of a contagion that irradiated everywhere, destroying everything that it touched.

Libertinism and the taste for frivolous expenditure to which the Spanish nobility introduced their compatriots were encouraged by a frequentation of the riffraff of Madrid on the part some of the well-born who became fascinated by the language, physical aspect, customs, and dress of the lower classes. Men of the Enlightenment vilified this *majo* noble for the shame he brought to his illustrious birth by the vulgarity of a life of depredation and sordid duels lived at the limits of crime. The bullfighting ring was the site of an ultimate descent and a promiscuity that both the satirists and the enlightened writers of Spain found odious. One pamphlet that appeared in 1791 contained a violent and sarcastic denunciation of the *plaza de toros:* "Who could fail to conceive sublime ideas about our nobles intent on furnishing barbarous spectacles, rendering honor to the bullfighters, rewarding desperation and folly, and vying with one another to protect the vilest men in the Republic?"[87]

Spain was not unique. In France and Italy as well there were satirical literary works, journals, and plays that skewered the noble, cataloged noble types, and thrashed and made fun of the nobility. In the long run these portrayals imposed the image of a creature who was useless to society, harmful to the spirit of the Enlightenment, and an obstacle to needed reforms.

Nobles Rise to their Own Defense

Were nobles going to stand by and let this happen? Had they no idea of how to fight this battle of symbols by turning their own hands to fashioning an archetype of an aristocrat who embodied the better qualities of the second order? Were no networks of cultural diffusion available to them that could reestablish the balance in their favor and give the eighteenth-century public a more flattering image of their essence? Did they lack the inventiveness and creativity to elaborate a noble type who would occupy the summit of a reconstituted future social hierarchy? Had they even realized that they were slowly being pushed to the periphery of the ideological space in which social models are created, a space where, by the late eighteenth century, the criteria of legitimacy, subjective or objective, were political weapons pointed against the nobles?

Nobles reacted to criticism in three ways. Some joined the system of attacks on the nobility. Although they were in the minority, there were even some nobles who not only had a part in discrediting their own order but at times worked actively toward that end, theorized about it, and made declarations to that effect.[88] Such actions and the divorce from their own group that those actions implied merit reflection. These men were not necessarily people facing social exclusion or marginalization like Sade and Mirabeau. Some abandoned old ways of thinking in full awareness, all the while enjoying consideration and revenues, both of which assured them an enviable position. They did not necessarily play the double game of cultural audacity and respect of social conventions. There were not many such men, but at crucial moments they were nonetheless highly influential.

Among them was the marquis d'Antonelle. A wealthy landowner in Arles and a retired army officer, Antonelle drew up an unending series of reform projects blasting the nobility, whom he considered guilty of a medieval brigandage. He reflected, he read, he wrote. After 1789, he wholeheartedly embraced the consequences of political and social change by becoming one of the instigators of the Revolution in Provence.

A larger group of nobles recognized the accuracy of the theoretical discourses of the Enlightenment, laughed at the foibles of their order along with the *philosophes* and the men of letters, and would have been favorable to a social compromise to permit the constitution of a group in which the wealthiest and best-educated commoners would be on an equal footing with the brightest nobles and those most deeply involved in the economic modernization of the country. This desire was manifested and, at times, realized at the local level. The salons and the academies brought together an elite in the name of such values as virtue, talent, and merit. Gatherings of the sort provided an image of a "possible France" of elites influenced and inspired by the English model: shared social practices and a common enlightened discourse were supposed to lead to understanding. There are signs, however, that elements of divergence, even of division, clouded this rosy picture: religious practices, for example, which varied from one group of participants to another and seem to indicate very different, at times opposite, conceptions of the world.[89] Events soon demonstrated the fragility of the compromise; rather, they soon clarified a misunderstanding. The nobles accepted a new way of thinking, but that did not mean that they were disposed to abandon a hierarchical system that guaranteed their privilege. Welcoming the more outstanding commoners into their group, transforming the nobility into an aristocracy (at the cost of sacrificing the noble who had slipped into poverty) was one thing. Accepting a new society in which the privileges of birth would no longer be recognized was quite another. The anti-revolutionary violence of some enlightened nobles, even before the end of the year 1789, is ample evidence that in France the mixing of the elites did not necessarily imply a shared political ideal.

The Argument of Race

A larger number of nobles attempted to rethink and redefine their own legitimacy, undoubtedly because most in this group were far from recognizing themselves in a criticism that they judged to be a vulgar exaggeration, but also because they had little inclination to enlarge the order of nobility in the name of an economic and philosophical new deal.

What these nobles deemed important was to use the arguments of the age to enhance the nobility as a homogeneous order and to draw up a portrait of the noble that would dissipate sarcasm and stand as irrefutable proof of a need for the nobility's privileges and undisputed position at the apex of society. In a century of widespread reflection on its status, a nobility that was neither passive, immobile, or outdated had to produce a discourse that could refurbish its escutcheon.

Throughout the eighteenth century, nobles worked to conserve what they thought to be the essence of an ancestral heritage by adapting it to a more modern rhetoric. The elaboration of a conceptual system that was certainly more efficacious than it was thought to be during the nineteenth century and part of the twentieth permitted nearly all nobles to imagine a regeneration of their order and provided them with solid and time-honored arguments brought up to date by innovative language.

André Devyver has shown that between 1560 and 1720, the nobility imagined and "ended up believing that it constituted a group apart, historically privileged, [and] biologically superior."[90] By according an excessive importance to heredity and to the genetic transmission of characteristics that made for physical and psychological differences and proved the superiority of a "noble race" of pure blood, the second order maintained and cultivated a sort of racism.

This claim to superiority was all the more deeply anchored because it suited the convenience of highly esteemed nobles and because it was taken up, in the majority of cases, by people who felt that their social status was threatened. "The belief in the excellence of the blood of the ancient lineages in fact permitted a mass of impoverished persons out of phase with the economic evolution of their times to retain an unhoped-for prestige."[91]

Boulainvilliers was certainly the most accomplished theorist of this form of racism. The poverty and the misalliances of a good many gentlemen may have been what motivated him to give the second order "a combat ideology," aimed at explaining the decline of certain lineages through inappropriate marriages and suggesting political means for aiding these ancient families in difficulty. Boulainvilliers's conviction that noble blood was superior was based in his certitude that the French nobility, a virile and warlike race, was made up of the direct descendants of the Franks who had subjugated the indigenous Gallo-Roman population during the Germanic conquest of France. But by the time his volume, *Essai sur la noblesse de France, contenant une dissertation sur son origine et son abaissement* came out in 1732 it was already too late. According to Devyver, the high point of the racist theory came at the end of the seventeenth century and the beginning of the eighteenth, a time when de La Rocque's *Traité de noblesse* went through a number of reprintings. The eighteenth century swept away such fragile "genetic" arguments. "Noble racism . . . soon fell, if not into oblivion, at least into the realm of derision: efficaciously combated by the ideology of merit, it had seemed out-of-date, even to many nobles."[92] Worse, that same ideology was turned against the individuals it was intended to protect. The pamphleteers and patriotic journalists of the end of the century "understood the cutting force of the attacks that could be developed against the 'red-heels'— that is, the last champions of the racist noble discourse—and they were quick to have nobles of their own invention spout the overworked clichés of Père Menestrier, La Rocque, and Boulainvilliers."[93]

By that time, the nobles had adopted the merit argument, accepted it, and adapted to it, but the defense of blood did not totally disappear. It simply took other, more subtle, and in particular more euphemistic, forms. Nobles thought themselves ultimately more meritorious because their blood, which was their natural merit, justified their superiority.

A return to the observation of natural phenomena, an acceptance of scientific rules, and a debate on human and animal species were very much the order of the day when Buffon's *Histoire naturelle* appeared in 1749. The controversy persisted, touching on the existence of species, genus, family, and race. Although Buffon clearly announced the existence of one united human race revitalized and regenerated by a mixing among men, the nobles were probably more interested in his theory of animal "species." Buffon claimed that in accordance with the theory of reproduction, the principal traits and qualities of each group are transmitted from one generation to another by means of a series of individuals situated within fixed families, some of which, "the principal stems," or "the dominant species," were close to an original model, while others were "subordinate species" or "accessory branches that had undergone a real degeneration." We can easily imagine the use nobles could make of this hypothesis. Theirs was a subjective reading that underestimated the innovative depth of Buffon's text and the evolution of his thought, as Jacques Roger has demonstrated. At best, this was a clever reading that aimed at recuperating an enlightened line of thought for the nobles' own purposes. Scientific discourse in Linnaeus, Buffon, and Maupertuis centered on an attempt to classify all living species; this included humankind, organized in a hierarchy from the savage to the most highly civilized man, who, in the opinion of the well-born, was obviously the noble. For nobles, science, and natural science in particular, could be used to justify their privilege. When such men read the article on the horse in Buffon's *Histoire naturelle*, for example, they concentrated on the brilliant image of an aristocratic animal rather than on the utilitarian description of the workhorse in rural society.

And were not Anglomania and a passion for horse racing further signs of just such a faith in blood lines, a faith that seemed to accord with the modern principles of the century? Nicole de Blomac portrays the young French *anglomanes* as noble, wealthy, and well endowed with possessions. They all loved horses, which they rode to war, to the hunt, or in the service of the king: "One can even state that [the nobles] found in this passion a concrete form, even a glorification, of some of the guiding ideas of their century—a fecund liberty, individual merit—but also a striking justification of noble blood and of the primacy of what was called pure blood."[94] In short: "Pedigree was a support for individual merit." This enthusiasm for (and, for the most impassioned among them, identification with) the nobility of the animal implied an aristocratic mode of existence. Moreover, a love of horse racing led quite naturally to the acceptance of a hierarchy of nobility among animals in function of their inherent worth and their performance. Especially after 1770, nobles took to this new fashion as if they had needed a certain amount of time to imagine a style of living that corresponded to a new system for the legitimation of their biological superiority. This defense was clever, as it played on an ambiguity in the word "race," as the comte de Lauraguais noted in 1778 in his *Mémoire inutile sur un sujet important.* The word had different meanings in English and in French, but in horse racing the two merged. "It offers the key to a comportment whose persistence gives one food for thought: a 'race horse' is both a horse who races and a pure-blood, a *cheval de race.*"[95] This new noble ethic was paradoxical, however; it presupposed the acceptance of Enlightenment criticism of the "ideology of blood," a notion in circulation until the early eighteenth century, but it also contradicted rational, naturalistic, and philosophical discourse by arguing the selection of a pure-blooded elite whose strength came from its nobility.

A Summary and a New Argument for Noble Superiority

To repeat my hypothesis: the nobility was not dominated; nor was it reactionary, in love with the past, or degenerate. Quite to the contrary, it maintained a dialogue with the Enlightenment, and it understood the new discourse and its severe criticisms. More than that, it transformed the arguments of the Enlightenment into a system based not on ancient blood but on a noble pedigree, which amounted to a defense of new blood of high quality, "ahead" of others because it was guaranteed by the value of the elements that make up the genealogical record.

It is just as mistaken to believe that an attachment to proofs of nobility, the keeping of family trees, or concern about the value of blood were attitudes linked to the past. Ellery Schalk points out that these concerns were all the more current during the eighteenth century because blood had become the only means to ennoblement. In the sixteenth century, nobility was thought of as a profession or a military function rather than a value transmitted by heredity. Nobility was the military profession. Two centuries later, in the mid-eighteenth century, the nobility was perceived in a totally different way. It was no longer attached to one fixed profession. A noble could, without real derogation, choose his profession or take on a variety of activities. From that moment on, birth alone defined a difference that "no one involved in these debates questioned." Moreover, "People throughout the eighteenth century . . . appeared willing to let birth define nobility, as long as nobility did not make any serious difference in allowing nobles to act like anyone else in society, and in allowing non-nobles not to be especially restricted just because they were not nobles."[96] Everyone agreed that blood made nobility; the nobility had lost its strictly military function. Was this not perhaps a successful ideological response to attacks on the nobility throughout the century? Admittedly, the liveliness of the nobility's reaction cannot conceal the fact that it functioned in *trompe-l'oeil,* fooling the nobles themselves. What they thought was a new discourse was only a skillful makeup job on old beliefs. Only a solid social peace could authenticate the paradox that enabled the nobles to accept an audacious philosophy because it seemed a striking confirmation of their old and illustrious lineages.

Furthermore, if for some individuals of obscure condition the end of the Enlightenment coincided with a possible discovery of the force and power of the irrational, and if future revolutionaries can be found among the followers of mesmerism, for others (that is, for the nobles) the last flames of the epoch were accompanied by an enthusiasm for physiognomy (the political history of which is still to be written) and an insistence on deeply rooted conservative precepts. Lavater's arguments arrived just in time to reassure a group in quest of a confirmation of its pedigree rather than its identity.

At the century's end, Lavater reconciled the society of seeming with its being:

> Physiognomy would accordingly be, the Science of discovering the relation between the exterior and the interior—between the visible surface and the invisible spirit which it covers— between the animated, perceptible matter, and the impercep- tible principle which impresses this character of life upon it— between the apparent effect, and the concealed cause which produces it.[97]

A person's essence could be read in his or her face, bearing, and general allure. Lavater goes even farther: all traits, which invariably reflect moral qualities or faults, are inherited directly from one's parents. A human being cannot be anything but the reflection of two heredities, his or her true personality leaning toward that of the same-sex parent: "We can trace feature by feature, in the son, the character, the temper, and most of the moral qualities of the father."[98]

Wasn't this just the response that the nobles were waiting for, on which they could base their arguments, and that justified new hope? Not only did Lavater permit them to claim superiority, even in degeneration: "You have an explanation of the difficulty, how it comes to pass, that so many persons, whom Nature has endowed with an agreeable figure, and who have become immoral characters, are nevertheless not so ugly as some others."[99] He also confirmed their notion that they were intrin- sically better by bitterly criticizing the idea that intelligence could be the result of a natural coincidence or blind chance. Similarly, he mocked Helvétius and his "amiable enthusiasm" because Helvétius supposed that humankind could be reformed by transforming education and culture.

Lavater's criticism challenged two of the Enlightenment's fundamental acquisitions. The first was a defense of an intelligence distributed to all humankind in ways that one could to some extent perceive but could not explain and could by no means be understood in terms of membership in one kinship group or another. The second was a faith in the virtue of education, which alone could enable intelligence to come forth and develop in the direction of merit, and in the affirmation of individual talents, which were not necessarily inherited.

This negation of the enlightened discourse was also based on an "either-or" system that grouped physical and psychological characteristics according to their "nobility" or their "ignominy." Moral inclinations—a "propensity to goodness"—were noble when they had a "charm irresistibly sweet, varied, yet constant" that would "incessantly attract us toward every thing which tends to the perfection of our nature." Conversely, inclinations were common if they expressed desire, sensuality, or disquietude. Physiognomy was the scientific detection of such traits of character. This "new source of knowledge" would necessarily "awaken in the heart of Man a love of what is noble and beautiful [and] excite an invincible disgust against every thing base and ignoble."[100] Lavater put into his language and his positive extension of the sense of the word "noble" the same determinism that he put into blood heritage: the beautiful and the good were so because they were noble, and vice versa. The well-born could rest assured; the Swiss pastor offered them "scientific reasons" for their difference.

Lavater's discussion of blood, pedigree, and physiognomy contains the structure, even the nub, of a misunderstanding between the greater part of the nobility and the Enlightenment. It was a serious misunderstanding because the overwhelming majority of nobles used "pedigree" to reinvent their dignity, with hardly a second thought, as a unified, coherent group joining in a common cause in the face of criticism. All nobles, rich or poor, famous or unknown, were united by blood, transmitted from generation to generation. Some were persuaded that their success was proof of the purity of their blood; others understood that only their blood permitted them to face trials with honor.

The nobility found in and by means of the Enlightenment an ideological unity and a coherence of thought that reconciled it with itself and with its epoch and the philosophy of that epoch. At least, this is what nobles tried to persuade themselves and what they ended up believing. It was not criticism that weakened the nobility but the integration of the language of the Enlightenment into a typically noble logic, that is, it was the transformation of dangerous and audacious concepts into seeming truths and seemingly reassuring truths. When the nobility refused to join the debate on the hierarchical criterion of blood, and when it persuaded itself that the discourse of the Enlightenment could be read as a new demand for natural selection, it both refused and distorted the current of thought that led, logically, to the abolition of privileges, and it blocked out the intellectual movement that called for the recognition of the equality of all humankind in blood.

The "misunderstanding" and the gap between what the nobility imagined about the discourse of the Enlightenment and what that discourse really implied for nobles does not necessarily reveal any collective blindness, any group unconsciousness, or any attempt to keep up with a situation out of control. This would be too easy. We are perhaps closer to the mark if we see in it a strategy for disarming enlightened criticism by recognizing merit and valor as the distinguishing signs of superior men. Socially, the nobles could find comfort in the thought that the best of the bourgeoisie were attempting to accede to nobility. Was not nobility the sign of successful social promotion for many wealthy commoners? Still, that strategy, which, in the long run, comported high risks, relied on a subtle equilibrium. On the one hand, there was a stable institutional framework embodied in a royalty universally recognized and protective of the privileges of all; on the other, there was a clearly defined ideological arena that had its own rules, code of honor, men of letters, organized polemics, and its ordered jousts and clearly identified combatants— nobles or enlightened commoners. If one of these two elements disappeared or was threatened, the nobility vacillated. "Pedigree," the value and the merit of the nobility, was to take the fight outside the traditional arena, beyond the limits recognized and accepted between 1740 and 1770.

The nobility, in fact, prompted a reaction on two levels. The first was a radicalization of a discourse (pushed to caricature but influential) on the supposed value of blood.[101] The second was a deeper investigation, then an affirmation, of the concept of the equality of all men and the necessary destruction of birth privileges.

After 1762, with Rousseau's *Social Contract,* the Enlightenment debate shifted. Political expression of that discourse was no longer aimed at finding a compromise that would group together nobles and commoners but at imagining a group capable of governing within which prejudices connected with birth would no longer pertain. The nobles either paid no heed to such arguments, condemned them, or scorned them. Perhaps they did not fear them; perhaps they simply could not imagine that they would have any immediate political consequences. More certainly, it was because, sure of themselves, they were engaged in another combat.

If the nobles were superior, they could and must make their voice known to the monarchy, which had bullied them too long. The parlements, whose noble members were proud of their privileges and enlightened by their century, became channels for noble reconquest of effective power. The nearly permanent conflict, after 1775, between the king and the parlements was an acceptance of political challenge on the part of a truly conquering nobility, strong in its "quality," coherent in its struggle against a power that had effectively removed it from real decision making. The nobles in the parlements acted in the name of the Enlightenment—*les Lumières,* but their own *lumières.* The risk was real: when enlightened aristocrats violently attacked the monarchy and denied the radicalization of the political propositions of the third estate, they destroyed the fragile equilibrium that had permitted them to think of themselves as superior.

If the nobility reacted with violence, as it did in 1789, it is perhaps not because it was weak or reactionary but because it believed itself powerful enough, before the Revolution, to assert itself in the face of absolutism, as the most vital force in society, a force regenerated by the thought of the Enlightenment. As it happened, the economic crisis, the convocation of the Estates General in the old form, and the attitude of the second order in the debates of the early days of the Revolution revealed that the nobility's political aim of replacing arbitrary royal power by a government of aristocrats was impossible. In the meantime, the third estate had become a political force, about to prevail, that represented the nation of the French, a nation of equal persons. Between these two political ideologies, inspired by the Enlightenment and born in agreement or disagreement with Enlightenment discourse, the divorce was final.

Conclusion

What, then, was the noble in 1789? How are we to define the nobility? Was it a very heterogeneous, very diverse group shot through with internal contrasts that nonetheless found in the debate of the Enlightenment arguments for a new self-definition when it rallied to support a discourse based in an "ideology of pedigree" that allowed each individual noble to vaunt his "quality," hence the worthiness of his ancestors? Was it a group that thought itself strong enough to invade the political field after 1775 in the hope of reconquering primacy? Was it a group that, in the final analysis, concealed its internal contradictions in order to bolster a cleverly maintained misunderstanding that took the place of a political discourse? Was it a group that failed to grasp the radical transformation of political debate after 1780 and that would be swept away by the events of the final decade of the century?

It was all of that. All nobles felt their "difference" from commoners and were aware of the very great differences among themselves. They all understood that the century was evolving. None abandoned a past that defined the nobility as a group.

Paradoxically, the Revolution brought the second order of society some positive acquisitions. In adversity, in exile, and in hostility, nobles rediscovered a cohesion that the monarchy had never been able to offer them. The nobility—regenerated by its trials, emerging from suffering with its grandeur increased, and clinging to a certain dignity despite a wealth of difficulties—regained a social rank in the early nineteenth century for which it had been incessantly reproached during the eighteenth. In the nineteenth century, it returned en masse to occupy posts that had seemed its due (and that in some cases it had never abandoned, during either the Revolution or the Empire) in finance, the army, and the diplomatic corps. It recovered its landed estates. Does this mean that the nobility "won out" over the Enlightenment, over men of the Enlightenment, and over the Enlightenment's ultimate expression, the Revolution?

That remains to be seen. Although the noble was reinstated in his domains, he had to play a new political game, a game that gained strength as the new century advanced and turned him first into a notable, then an elected representative. He may have remained noble in his inner being, and he may still have been the most important figure in his rural community, but as a bourgeois gentleman, a patron, a mayor in his life as a public man, he gradually become socialized, integrated into a new political framework that recognized his worth, or perhaps just reflected the persistence of tradition in a largely rural France. In any event, by the end of the nineteenth century, the noble was on his way to becoming republicanized.

But Enlightenment thought had done more than that. By according an essential importance to the struggle for classification and the acquisition of the means of cultural and intellectual production; by systematically developing critical reflection; by defining, on the basis of a unified and homogeneous discourse, the imaginary perception that a group might have of itself or that might be given of it; by demonstrating the political importance and the very real social consequences of the production of that discourse; by resolutely carrying the combat into an arena in which psychological manifestations had as much importance as the material reality of facts and events, the movement of the Enlightenment had acquired the means to discredit noble thought durably.

The contrasting intellectual themes that typified the Enlightenment—old/new, liberty/oppression, nature/history, reason/despotism, virtue/libertinism, merit/idleness—inevitably thrust the noble to the negative side, giving him a "typical portrait" that made him repulsive, attributed all possible faults to him, and illustrated "in reverse" the qualities celebrated by the *philosophes*. Men of the Enlightenment ended up taking their depiction of the noble for reality, but more paradoxically—and this shows the force of a combat of "symbols"—in the long run the nobility, too, accepted that unflattering image of itself. The nobility was lastingly "marginalized" and prevented from finding and instituting a stable political regime, at a time when it had effective control of the rural areas, occupied the principal posts in state administration and state institutions, and, after 1815, took leading roles in finance.

How else are we to explain the recurrent image of the noble as degenerate, weak, bastardized, impotent, sterile, and déclassé that haunts French literature of the nineteenth century from Balzac to Huysmans (without forgetting Maupassant)—an image circulated both by advocates for the nobility and its detractors. There is no doubt that Monsieur de Morsauf, devoured by the disease that gradually leads him to insanity, des Esseintes, a *fin-de-siècle, fin-de-race* dandy, or the d'Hubières, a sterile couple forced to buy a child from poor but fecund peasants, are in their own way offspring of the Enlightenment. They are its concrete form in literature, but contemporaries experienced these fictional characters as reality and as true portrayals of the disqualification of the nobility as a force capable of regeneration or of making their own the modernity of the New France imagined by the *philosophes*, glimpsed during the Revolution, and constructed throughout the nineteenth century.

Notes

1. Emmanuel Le Roy Ladurie, foreword to *La Noblesse au XVIIIᵉ siècle: De la féodalité aux Lumières,* by Guy Chaussinand-Nogaret (1976; Brussels: Complexe, 1984), v.

2. Jean Pierre Labatut, *Les noblesses européennes de la fin du XVᵉ siècle à la fin du XVIIIᵉ siècle* (Paris: Presses Universitaires de France, 1978), 7.

3. Henri Carré, *La noblesse de France et l'opinion publique au XVIIIᵉ siècle* (1920; Geneva: Slatkine Reprints, 1977), 107.

4. Labatut, *Les noblesses européennes,* 66.

5. See Georges Desdevises du Dézert, "La société espagnole au XVIIIe siècle," *Revue Historique* 64 (1925): 192–95.

6. Jean Meyer, *Noblesses et pouvoirs dans l'Europe d'Ancien Régime,* Hachette Littérature (Paris: Hachette, 1973), 154.

7. Jean Meyer, *La Noblesse bretonne au XVIIIᵉ siècle* (Paris: Sciences Flammarion, 1972), 53.

8. Ibid., 58.

9. Alexandre de Tilly, *Mémoires du comte Alexandre de Tilly, pour servir à l'histoire des moeurs de la fin du dix-huitième siècle,* 2 vols. (Paris: Le Normand fils, 1828), 1: 320.

10. Jean Meyer, "La noblesse française au XVIIIᵉ siècle: Aperçu des problèmes," *Acta Poloniae Historica* 36 (1977): 9–45.

11. François Dominique, comte de Montlosier, *Mémoires,* 2 vols. (Paris: Dufey, 1830), 1: 126.

12. Ibid., 1: 80.

13. Daniel Roche, *La culture des apparences: Une histoire du vêtement (XVIIᵉ–XVIIIᵉ siècle)* (Paris: Fayard, 1989), 92; quoted from *The Culture of Clothing: Dress and Fashion in the "Ancien Régime,"* trans. Jean Birrel (Cambridge, U.K., and New York: Cambridge University Press, 1994), 91.

14. Roche, *Culture of Clothing,* 96.

15. Ibid., 97.

16. Pedro Rodríguez, conde de Campomanes, *Cartas político-económicas* (Madrid: M. Murillo, 1878), quoted in Desdevises du Dézert, "La société espagnole," 194.

17. Meyer, *Noblesses et pouvoirs,* 221–35.

18. Tilly, *Mémoires,* 155, 214–15.

19. Montlosier, *Mémoires,* 35.

20. Ibid., 36.

21. Ibid., 80.

22. Vincent-Marie, comte de Vaublanc, *Mémoires* (Paris: Firmin Didot, 1857), 20.

23. George Huppert, *Les Bourgeois Gentilshommes: An Essay on the Definition of Elites in Renaissance France* (Chicago and London: University of Chicago Press, 1977), 169–70.

24. Monique Cubells, *La Provence des Lumières: Les parlementaires d'Aix au XVIIIe siècle,* with a foreword by Michel Vovelle (Paris: Maloine, 1984), 58–59.

25. François Bluche, *La vie quotidienne de la noblesse française au XVIIIe siècle* (Paris: Hachette, 1984), 73.

26. Jean-Baptiste de Boyer, marquis d'Argens, *Mémoires* (Paris: Frederic Buisson, 1807), 133.

27. Honoré-Gabriel de Riqueti, comte de Mirabeau, *Des lettres de cachet et des prisons d'État* (Paris: Lecomte et Pougin, 1835), 277.

28. Donatien Alphonse François, marquis de Sade, *Correspondance,* vol. 12 of *Oeuvres complètes* (Paris: Cercle du livre précieux, 1964), 268.

29. Donatien Alphonse François, marquis de Sade, *Sade: Les cent vingt journées de Sodome. . . ,* in *Oeuvres complètes du Marquis de Sade,* ed. Annie Le Brun and Jean-Jacques Pauvert, 15 vols. (Paris: Pauvert, 1986–91), 1: 19; quoted from *The 120 Days of Sodom,* in *The Marquis de Sade: The 120 Days of Sodom and Other Writings,* trans. and comp. Austryn Wainhouse and Richard Seaver, (New York: Grove Press, 1966), 183–595 (quotation, 191).

30. Guy Chaussinand-Nogaret, *La noblesse au XVIIIe siècle: De la féodalité aux Lumières* (1976; Brussels: Complexe, 1981), 59; quoted from *The French Nobility in the Eighteenth Century: From Feudalism to Enlightenment,* trans. William Doyle (Cambridge, U.K., and New York: Cambridge University Press, 1985), 39.

31. Labatut, *Les noblesses européennes,* 149.

32. Quoted in Meyer, *Noblesses et pouvoirs,* 162.

33. Chaussinand-Nogaret, *French Nobility,* 43.

34. Ibid., 62.

35. Jean Meyer, "Un problème mal posé: La noblesse pauvre; l'exemple breton au XVIIIe siècle," *Revue d'Histoire Moderne et Contemporaine* 13 (1971): 161–88.

36. Montlosier, *Mémoires,* 68.

37. See Monique Cubells, "A propos des usurpations de noblesse en Provence sous l'Ancien Régime," *Provence Historique* 81 (July–September 1970): 239–300.

38. Meyer, *La noblesse bretonne,* 35–36.

39. Michel Vovelle, "Sade, Seigneur de village," in *Sade,* Colloquium organized by the Faculty of Aix, 1966 (Paris: A. Colin, 1968), 23–40.

40. Meyer, *Noblesses et pouvoirs,* 21.

41. Guy Richard, *Noblesse d'affaires au XVIIIe siècle,* U Prisme, 37 (Paris: A. Colin, 1974), 18.

42. Ibid., 18–19.

43. Guy Richard, "Les Dietrich en Alsace (1684–1789)," in ibid., 154–62.

44. Robert Forster, *The Nobility of Toulouse in the Eighteenth Century: A Social and Economic Study* (Baltimore: Johns Hopkins University Press, 1960), 31–35.

45. Robert Forster, "The Provincial Noble: A Reappraisal," *American Historical Review* 68, 3 (April 1963): 681–91 (quotation, 684).

46. Pierre de Vaissière, *Gentilhommes campagnards de l'Ancienne France* (1906; Terroir de France, Étrépilly: Presses du Village, 1986), 247.

47. Tilly, *Mémoires,* 151.

48. Bluche, *La vie quotidienne,* 45.

49. Letter from comte de Torcy to the minister, 17 March 1758, quoted in Louis Tuetey, *Les officiers sous l'Ancien Régime: Nobles et roturiers* (Paris: Plon-Nourrit, 1908), 132.

50. Project for military schools and pay raises for second lieutenants (unsigned report written around 1742), quoted in ibid., 34.

51. François-Philippe-Loubat, baron de Bohan, *Examen critique du militaire français* (Geneva, 1781).

52. David Bien, "La réaction aristocratique avant 1789: L'exemple de l'armée," *Annales E.S.C.* 1 (1974): 23–49; 2 (1974): 505–34.

53. Ibid., 515.

54. Bluche, *La vie quotidienne,* 27.

55. Judicial cases referred to in Carré, *La noblesse de France,* 170–71, 298–308.

56. Sade, *Correspondance,* 84–85.

57. Vovelle, "Sade, seigneur de village," 36.

58. *Mémoire à consulter et consultation pour Madame la Comtesse de Mirabeau,* ed. J. B. Monnet (Avignon: Imprimerie des Libraires associés, 1783).

59. Vovelle, "Sade, seigneur de village," 36.

60. Michel Delon, "De *Thérèse philosophe* à *La Philosophie dans le boudoir:* La place de la philosophie," *Romanistiche Zeitschrift für Literaturgeschichte; Cahiers d'Histoire des Littératures Romanes* 1, no. 2 (1983): 76–88.

61. Jacques Rustin, *Le vice à la mode: Étude sur le roman français dans la première moitié du XVIIIᵉ siècle* (Paris: Ophrys, 1979), 239–40.

62. See Gilbert Lély, *Vie du Marquis de Sade* (Paris: J. J. Pauvert aux éditions Garnier, 1984), 170–75; available in English as *The Marquis de Sade: A Biography,* trans. Alec Brown (New York: Grove Press, 1961, 1970), 195–99.

63. Ibid.

64. Honoré-Gabriel de Riqueti, comte de Mirabeau, *Essai sur le despotisme* (1775; Paris: Lecomte et Pougin, 1835), 72.

65. François Billacois, "La crise de la noblesse européenne (1560–1650): Une mise au point," *Revue d'Histoire Moderne et Contemporaine* 18 (1976): 258–77.

66. Alexis de Tocqueville, *L'ancien régime et la Révolution* (Paris: Idées Gallimard, 1967), 155; quoted from *The Old Régime and the French Revolution,* trans. Stuart Gilbert (New York: Doubleday/Anchor Press, 1955), 89, 79.

67. Daniel Roche, *Les républicains des lettres: Gens de culture et Lumières au XVIIIᵉ siècle* (Paris: Fayard, 1988), 99.

68. Ibid., 130.

69. Abbé Gabriel François Coyer, *La noblesse commerçante* (London, 1756), 82.

70. Abbé Gabriel François Coyer, *Trois pièces sur cette question, les nobles doivent ils commercer?* (Paris, 1758), 18.

71. Coyer, *La noblesse commerçante*, 214.

72. Abbé Gabriel François Coyer, *Voyage d'Italie et de Hollande* (Paris, 1755), 253.

73. Abbé Gabriel François Coyer, *Chinki, Histoire cochinchinoise* (London, 1768), 19.

74. Abbé Gabriel François Coyer, *Bagatelles morales* (London, 1754), 85.

75. Coyer, *La noblesse commerçante*, 119–20.

76. Abbé Gabriel François Coyer, *Observations sur l'Angleterre par un voyageur* (Paris, 1779), 17.

77. Coyer, *La noblesse commerçante*, 214.

78. Chevalier d'Arcq, *Le roman du jour, pour servir à l'histoire du siècle* (London, 1754), 63–65.

79. Ibid., 98.

80. Chevalier d'Arcq, *La noblesse militaire ou le patriote français* (Paris, 1757), 35–36.

81. Chevalier d'Arcq, *Mes loisirs* (Paris, 1756), 286–87.

82. D'Arcq, *La noblesse militaire*, 210.

83. Gaspar de Jovellanos, *Satira sobre la mala educación de la nobleza* (1787), ed., with notes, A. Morel Fatio (Paris: Bibliothèque des Universités du Midi, 1899).

84. Don Preciso [Juan Fernández de Rojas], *Elementos de la Ciencia contradanzaria, para que los Currutacos, Pirracas, y Madamitas del Nuevo Cuno puedan aprender por principios a bailar las Contradanzas por sí solos ó con las sillas de su casa* (Madrid: La Viuda de Joseph García, 1796).

85. Don José Gabriel Clavijo y Fajardo, *Pragmática del Zelo y desagravio de las Damas* (Madrid: en la imprenta de los herederos de D. Agustin de Jodevela, 1755).

86. Ibid., 26–27.

87. *Pan y toros y otros papeles sediciosos de fines del siglo XVIII*, collected and presented by Antonio Elorza (Madrid: Editorial Ayuso, 1971), 27.

88. Guy Chaussinand-Nogaret, "Un aspect de la pensée nobiliaire au XVIIIe siècle: L'anti-nobilisme," *Revue d'Histoire Moderne et Contemporaine* 29 (1982): 442–52.

89. Michel Vovelle, "L'élite ou le mensonge des mots," *Annales E.S.C.* 29 (1974): 49–72.

90. André Devyver, "Le sang épuré: La naissance du sentiment et de l'idée de race dans la noblesse française, 1560–1720" (thèse, Brussels, 1973), 2.

91. Ibid.

92. Antoine de Baecque, "Le discours anti-noble (1787–1792) aux origines d'un slogan: 'Le peuple contre les gros,'" *Revue d'Histoire Moderne et Contemporaine* 36 (1989): 3–28.

93. Ibid., 19.

94. Nicole de Blomac, "Élites et généalogie au XVIIIe siècle: Le cheval de

course, cheval de sang, la naissance d'un nouveau concept en France," *Revue d'Histoire Moderne et Contemporaine* 36 (1989): 497–507.

95. Ibid., 506.

96. Ellery Schalk, *From Valor to Pedigree: Ideas of Nobility in France in the Sixteenth and Seventeenth Centuries* (Princeton: Princeton University Press, 1986), 219.

97. Johann Caspare Lavater, *Essai sur la Physiognomie, destiné à faire connaître l'homme et à le faire aimer* (The Hague, n.d.), 22; originally published as *Physiognomische Fragmente zur Beförderung der Menschenkentniss und Menschenliebe* (Leipzig and Winterthur, 1775–78); quoted from *Essays on Physiognomy, Designed to Promote the Knowledge and the Love of Mankind*, trans. Henry Hunter (from French), 5 vols. (London, 1792), 1: 20.

98. Lavater, *Essays*, 1: 144.

99. Ibid., 1: 146.

100. Ibid., 1: 77.

101. See de Baecque, "Le discours anti-noble."

2 / The Soldier

Jean-Paul Bertaud

The eighteenth-century philosopher who dreamed of a new polity based on reason professed a profound horror of violence and war. In the world that he imagined a spirit of peace prevailed. Abbé de Saint-Pierre stated that perpetual peace was possible. What need was there of armed men? War and the man of war, it was said, create disorder in things and immorality in men. War, Jaucourt wrote in the *Encyclopédie,* stifles the voice of nature, justice, religions, and humanity; it is a convulsive disease of the body politic that brings brigandage, ravages, terror, and desolation in its wake. It ultimately perverts all men.

Some raised their voice to disagree, denouncing perpetual peace as a dream. Montesquieu, refuting Hobbes's view that the causes of war lie in man's nature, asserted that war is the product of society. War is a disease of societies, and one difficult to cure. But besides, is it always a bad thing? Wars are unjust when their aim is conquest; they are just when their aim is self-defense, coming to the aid of an ally who has been attacked, correcting an iniquitous treaty, or fending off eventual attack.

For Vauvenargues, "the contemplative man who condemns war while lounging comfortably in a tapestried chamber" is a fool. War is one of the laws of the universe. War is not necessarily a school of vice or the man of war the bearer of all sorts of turpitude. Peace "lets all great talents peter out and weakens peoples. Virtue is combattant, and the love of glory, a strong and noble passion, is the fecund source of human virtues that has brought the world out of barbarity."

Rousseau agreed with Montesquieu about the causes of war and with his distinction between just and unjust wars. He invited peoples and the states who represent them to resist and to defend their homelands. Rousseau disagreed with the cosmopolitanism of Voltaire, who stated that there were no more French, Germans, Spanish, or English, since all humankind had the same customs. Rousseau saw this view as an internationalism demeaning for a people. "Love of the homeland makes up the entire existence of man; he lives his homeland and lives only for it; the minute he is alone he is nothing." But of what use was a homeland if it was not a land of liberty and if it did not contain a nation of citizens made equal and sovereign by social contract? Was not the citizen-soldier a better defender of the homeland than the mercenary or the soldier of despots? Should not every citizen be a soldier and every soldier a citizen, as Diderot had written?

France adopted that principle with the Revolution, and Saint-Just stated that victory depended upon the progress of the republican spirit in the army. But could patriotic enthusiasm alone win the day in an age when war had become a complex art that required professionals? A few years later, Napoleon acknowledged that if love of the homeland and national glory might inspire young troops, it was a good general, good officers, good organization, good training, and good discipline that made good troops, independent of the cause for which they fought.

A national army or a professional army? A citizen militia or professional soldiers? Soldiers with a mission fighting to subvert the established political order of the adversary, or traditional soldiers whose only task was to wield a sword or a gun? Leaving aside theoretical ideas about the soldier, what was the reality of his existence, his training, his mores, and his mind-set? Throughout the early modern age, from the eighteenth century to the French Revolution and the Empire, did not all countries see the formation of a military society that had not existed previously but that proved lasting and imbued all civil society with its values?

From the Mercenary to the Soldier

The Soldier as an Object of Commerce

Tomás, in "El licenciado Vidriera" in Cervantes' *Novelas ejemplares* (Exemplary Novels), is Spanish. He is looking for a master to serve. At the gates of Málaga he meets a gentleman, a captain who is recruiting men for his company. The captain interrogates Tomás and paints a glowing picture of the life of his men, who are about to leave for Italy: beautiful landscapes, the splendors of Lombardy, food in abundance, gold coins clinking in the soldiers' purses—nothing is missing as he attempts to enroll Tomás. He says nothing about the cold, the dangers when attacking the enemy, battle terror, or hunger, the constant companion of the soldier on campaign. Tomás resists temptation and does not sign up for an engagement as a mercenary that many others found attractive. But that was how it worked.

In the sixteenth and seventeenth centuries, the soldier was a piece of merchandise that could be bought or rented within a country or between one city or principality of Europe and another. This commerce created a market that fluctuated according to the season and to states of peace or war. In the seventeenth century, when European armies grew from 100,000 to 1 million men, the market was high more often than low. The price that the soldier commanded depended on his physical qualities, his experience, and his mores: French troops were sought after for their bravery in battle, but were thought unstable, difficult to command, and always ready to mutiny. Austrians commanded a lower price than Italians or Spaniards.

In the weaker states, the Holy Roman Empire and Italy, for example, a contract was signed between the recruit and a captain who owned his unit and sold it to a colonel who in turn was connected with a military entrepreneur. The latter was a businessman, and he was surrounded by a crowd of financiers ranging from a modest managing agent to a major banker—the role that Witte played for Wallenstein. The "general contractors" who operated as war entrepreneurs had lands and lordships, and they raised contributions from the countries occupied by their armies. By renting out ready-to-use war machines to cities or princes they soon rivaled the civil authorities. Colleoni carved out a principality for himself; the Sforzas took over power in Milan. Foreign invasions of Italy brought an end to such dealings, and, in the eighteenth century, war entrepreneurs found a better terrain for their activities in Germany, where hired armies brought desolation, pillage, and rape.

In strong states, such as France or England, the war entrepreneur was the sovereign. He acted directly to engage the services of captains or colonels who owned their units. In those countries as well, the soldier was hired for a more or less limited term. As with the mercenary, it was poverty, a taste for adventure, perhaps a desire to escape the angry father of a girl seduced, but more often a need to escape pursuit by the authorities for a theft committed that urged a man to sign up. Like the church, the king's army was a place of refuge. Nobler motivations appeared in the beginning of the eighteenth century, when the recruit was more likely to be a subject of the king whom he served in defense of a threatened homeland. Military service soon became obligatory, by decree if not by common acceptance. Some were more receptive to doing their duty than others. What most distinguished the king's soldier from the mercenary was that he belonged to a regular army that was better disciplined as time went on and from which it was difficult to escape should he have a mind to do so. A mercenary who decided that the war entrepreneur with whom he had signed a contract had not fulfilled his part of the bargain mutinied: in the Spanish army of the Netherlands there were twenty-one mutinies between 1598 and 1607. The soldier of the king, serving within a regular army, mutinied less but deserted more, even though flight was seldom successful in a well-policed state.

The Creation of Regular Armies

During the eighteenth century, the best-organized regular army was the Prussian army. A country of secondary rank by its size and population, Prussia had one of the most powerful armies in Europe. The *Kanton-system* made the kingdom a military state operating under the iron rule of Frederick II. The *Kanton* was the basic unit of the state, to which the population was tied. All male inhabitants were registered in a *Kanton* commanded by a captain. No one could move about within the country without his authorization. Boys were enrolled at the age of ten, and as *Obligats* they wore a distinguishing red necktie. They participated periodically in military musters. As the *Obligats* emerged from adolescence, the captain selected the tallest among them. The new *Kantonist* underwent complete training as a soldier for a year and a half to two years, after which he took part in annual exercises for two to three months. He was obliged to keep some part of his equipment on his person at all times and to attend Sunday church service in military dress, and his dossier was reviewed annually. The *Kantonist* was given thorough training in arms and was subjected to rigorous discipline meted out with harsh corporal punishment; after his training, his private life continued to be supervised by his commanding officer, who attended his marriage and took a part in successions.

Prussia was by and large administered by former military personnel. The military was given preference everywhere, and the *Kantonist* was aware of the importance of a role that at times freed him from subjection to the seignorial regime.

In France the regular army relied on volunteers. The captain who had a company took leave to return to his native province to "make recruits." If he could not go himself he sent a sergeant accompanied by soldiers. Such military figures were a familiar sight in French towns and villages, striding through the streets, gathering idlers around them, tempting them with the idea of an enrollment bonus and bedazzling them with promises of an easy life. At times enrollment was forced, as when a recruiter invited a man to a tavern, plied him with drink until he was drunk and kidnaped him, perhaps even held him prisoner to keep his family from finding him. Increasingly the captain recruited men who worked in his domains or those of his family or an allied family. Yesterday a lord's peasant, today a soldier, the recruit remained, under his military garb, the "client" of the same individual or his family. Even when the French monarchy gradually phased out the sale of captains' and colonels' commissions, soldiers continued to be recruited in this manner. Examples can be found as late as 1791, when one Colonel Tourville, of the Eighteenth Infantry Regiment, sent an officer named Poncet back to his native Franche-Comté in search of men for the king's service. They had to be at least 5 feet tall and, if possible, over 5 feet 9 inches. Poncet had a doctor examine each recruit for physical defects that would interfere with his ability to perform basic tasks, for example teeth so rotten that the man could not rip open a cartridge paper, hands so hooked that he could not handle a gun, or shoulders so hunched that he could not stand straight and would ruin alignment in the ranks.

When the recruit arrived at his unit, he underwent another examination, and his civic identity, physical appearance, and any physical peculiarities were noted in the regimental books. By this means the military administration could gain a better picture of the state of the troops and track down *rouleurs* who moved from one regiment to another, *passe-volant* ("ghost" soldiers whose names the captain borrowed from another unit to fill his ranks for an inspection), and deserters.

At the beginning of the eighteenth century, the French army had an officers' corps of nobles *de race* (members of the old noble families), recently ennobled men (the sons of businessmen who had bought them a company or a regiment), and men risen from the ranks, commoners whose merits and talent had won them a commission. After midcentury, officers from old noble families began to complain about the ennobled, who often proved unsuited for command. The king introduced a degree of reform into the sale of commissions by creating intermediate grades and an order of promotion. The old nobility was still not satisfied, and it demanded and obtained the gradual elimination of the sale of commissions. But it also demanded that birth no longer be the sole criterion for the recruitment of officers. To be well-born may have implied a vocation for command, but an officer still needed to show proof of talent and have good military training. The monarch created military schools for the training of noble officers (Napoleon among them). The officers' corps was not totally out of the reach of commoners, but only a small minority might hope to win their epaulets in the infantry or the cavalry. Careers in the so-called "learned" branches, the artillery or the engineering corps, were more open. Even there, however, a commoner (Carnot, for example) knew that the higher ranks were reserved for nobles.

Aside from the volunteers in the regular army, the king of France drew from the general pool of his subjects whom the militia had habituated to the notion of a duty to serve. The royal militia was created in 1688 by Louis XIV and Louvois. Bachelors and childless married men were selected by lot; those who drew a "bad" number entered the militia. In times of peace they were given military training in their birthplace; in times of war they were incorporated into the regular troops. Unlike the soldier in the *Kantonsystem,* the French militiaman was not a regular soldier under the permanent orders of an officer. The French militia was composed almost exclusively of country people; on the eve of the Revolution, the *cahiers de doléances* demanded its elimination, although by that time the militia played a less active part in supplementing a regular army that had grown to over 150,000 men.

England had a militia as well. It served as an internal police force and as a force for the country's defense. During the English Revolution, Parliament used the militia as its basic troops. After a reorganization in 1757, the English militia was much reduced in size and its members were chosen by lot, as in France. This "New Militia," which became permanent, was to serve in the defense of England until the nineteenth century.

In the seventeenth century, militias were organized in the colonial possessions of European lands. In the French Antilles the militia played a role in politics during the eighteenth century, and in French Canada a militia was organized on the French model. In England's North American colonies the first militia, created after the English model, appeared in 1611 in Virginia. In 1755, some 500,000 men served in the various militias in the American colonies, and these forces soon played an important role in the colonies' war of independence.

Although the regular armies of the European sovereigns tended to become national, a demand for foreign regiments persisted during the eighteenth century. In the time of Louis XV, one-eighth of the French peacetime army was made up of foreigners—Swiss, Hungarians, Germans, Irish, and Scots. In times of war that proportion rose to one-fourth. On the eve of the French Revolution, the French army still had eleven Swiss regiments, eight German regiments, three Irish regiments, and one regiment from Liège, as well as seventy-nine French regiments. It should be noted, however, that some "foreign" regiments recruited French subjects. The German regiments, for instance, contained Alsatians and Lorrainers.

The "foreign" regiments most frequently found in the pay of the various states were Swiss. Beginning in the sixteenth century, the poverty of the population led the Swiss authorities to organize the recruitment and training of soldiers who were then offered to the ruling heads of Europe. A "capitulation" or treaty accompanied this transfer, specifying the amount of money to be paid but also stipulating that a special code of military justice would pertain for these troops. The recruitment of Swiss soldiers, which was legal since it was carried out by the Swiss cantons, continued up to the early nineteenth century in the Italian states, Prussia, Saxony, and England.

Their high level of technical skill and reputation for keeping their word made the Swiss valued soldiers (the one condition, however, was that they not be asked to fight against their compatriots). The Swiss troops were unfailingly loyal to the king of France until 1790: in August of that year, a regiment commanded by Châteauvieux participated in the revolt of the French soldiers garrisoned in Nancy. On 10 August 1792, other Swiss soldiers died safeguarding the French royal family in the taking of the Palais des Tuileries.

Military Training

In the eighteenth century, when both arms and combat had become more sophisticated, the recruit spent several months being "licked into shape." His body had to be transformed, his senses trained. Throughout Europe, many officers, commissioned and noncommissioned, took lessons from the Prussian army in training their men and strove to inculcate reflexes that would make their soldiers react mechanically to commands. In their attempts to manufacture that automaton, the soldier was schooled intensively and continually; the slightest error brought a reprimand or corporal punishment. In France there were officers who found that sort of method contrary to the "nature" of the

French. The drill instructor should appeal to the recruit's understanding and to his reason; he should show a touch of sensitivity so as to gain the soldier's confidence and bring out the best of the "French fury." Not all high officers were of this mind, however. As late as 1790, soldiers convicted of an offense ran the gauntlet of their comrades, who whipped the offender's bare back with ramrods.

The recruit, who was often of peasant origin, stood with his shoulders forward and a bent back. The instructor taught him to stand up straight. The regiment in battle was like a corps de ballet opening up its ranks or closing them, pivoting swiftly to the right or the left, advancing or retreating. Like the dancer, the recruit learned where to place his feet, how to tense his knees without holding them stiff, how to let his forward foot bear all his weight. There were two basic marching steps, the *pas ordinaire* with a stride of 26½ inches and a rate of 76 steps per minute, and the *pas de charge,* at 120 steps per minute.

Next, the recruit had to learn to handle a gun. During the latter half of the seventeenth century the *fusil* replaced the musket, a firearm over 6 feet long that weighed nearly 15½ pounds. The French *fusil* perfected in 1777 was a weapon just under 5 feet long that weighed a bit less than 9 pounds. Teaching soldiers whose average height was less than it would be today to use this gun without wounding their comrades was a delicate matter. Loading the gun was complicated. Holding his gun horizontally, the soldier disengaged the triggering mechanism *(mettre le chien au repos).* He then ripped open the paper cartridge with his teeth and filled the firing pan with some of the gunpowder in the cartridge. Holding the cartridge between thumb and index finger, he closed the battery and shifted his weapon to a vertical position. Then he placed into the barrel (whose caliber was about 0.67 inch) the rest of the powder, a 0.63-inch ball of shot, and the cartridge envelope, tamping these down with the ramrod housed under the gun barrel. When the ramrod was removed and the trigger cocked *(le chien armé),* the soldier shouldered and fired. A well-trained soldier could fire twice a minute, providing the flint produced a spark to light the powder. (One time out of every fifteen the flint did not function.) Shooting horizontally with a full charge, the flintlock gun had a range of about 220 yards; the shot was spent at 440 yards. Salvos were efficacious at under about 100 yards. This sort of gun did not have an adjustable sight, and the soldier, firing at random, corrected his aim by hand. He usually aimed too high, and the noncommissioned officer always had to be ready to lower the gun barrel with his baton or his sword.

The soldier's apprenticeship was long because training the body was not enough: the recruit also had to learn to control his nerves. Officers were well aware that when a recruit received his baptism of fire he would fire off his gun wildly to calm his nerves. With the invention of the socket bayonet, which could be fixed to the gun barrel without interfering with the weapon's performance, increasing use was made of the bayonet charge, which required special training to make the soldier a good duelist.

The gun was the soldier's mistress. It required a good deal of attention: the barrel had to be cleaned, swabbing and scouring it out with the shot extractor screwed into the ramrod until the water ran clear. The barrel then had to be dried and greased—a mixture of powdered sandstone and olive oil provided good rust protection—and the lock had to be covered with a cloth to protect it from the weather.

The artillery soldier had an even more difficult task. France had cannons made by Gribeauval that were of a quality unsurpassed until the Empire. Cannons were made of bronze; the carriages were made of wood reinforced with metal; the wheels had iron axles. A two-wheeled caisson fitted with a limber could be attached to the front end of the gun carriage to make the artillery piece and its ammunition into a well-balanced vehicle. Detaching the cannon from the limber and reassembling them again was no easy job. The invention of an extension some 26 feet long made the cannon easier to handle, but the cannoneers still had to use both force and skill to place pieces weighing more than a ton, charge them with a projectile or with case-shot, aim them (using an adjustable sight), and fire them. Depending on the crew, cannons could be fired at a rate of from two to seven times per minute for directed fire.

The range of 12-pound and 8-pound cannons was 984 yards. They could shoot effectively at 437 yards. A 12-pound ball could go through over 2 yards of earth, 16 inches of brick wall, or 20 inches of wooden wall at a distance of 437 yards. Well aimed at an attacking column, a cannon-ball could kill dozens of men as it ricocheted, spewing stones about.

The noblest branch of the army remained the cavalry, a branch that required qualities acquired only after months, even years, of practice. In a charge the cavalryman at first had to keep his horse at a walk, keeping in perfect alignment with his fellow cavalrymen, then spur his mount to a gallop near the enemy line. He then needed to find a rise in the terrain where he could rein in his horse or turn him around, all the while laying about with a saber, pistol, or gun.

Combat

In 1715, generals ranged their infantry on the field of battle in long lines parallel to the enemy lines, firing in salvos to create a hail of bullets to stop the enemy and permit one's own troops to advance. Men were placed four or five paces apart and six ranks deep. The army fell into battle array slowly and at some distance from the battlefield. It marched slowly to avoid falling out of ranks, and maneuvers in the presence of the enemy—providing the enemy stood still while waiting for it—were neither easy nor rapid. The Prussian army of Frederick William I, the "sergeant king" (1713–40), changed the traditional troop disposition, adopting an order of presentation that was thinner but more close-packed. The soldiers were placed in three rows, shooting in succession, the first row kneeling, the second standing but crouched, and the third standing straight. The front required fewer men, but remained suffi-ciently spread out to avoid being flanked by the opposing army. The in-fantry marched to the field of battle in columns in which each company was already placed in line. When the column stopped, each company converted to battle array, one wing turning while the other stayed in place, to face the enemy. Once the battle line was in place, each colonel marched his troops to a previously established point. As they advanced, the soldiers fired salvos, holding their guns at their hips. At twenty paces from the enemy the troops fired one last round, then charged, attacking their opponents with their bayonets. The salvos from the infantry guns were accompanied by fire from light cannons drawn by hand to the spaces between battalions. Battles were won, as Frederick II later said, "by superior fire power." He initiated the oblique order of presentation, substituting it for the preceding parallel order. His regiments marched *en tiroir* (by drawers), as Roland Mousnier put it.[1] When he wanted to attack the left flank of an enemy arranged in one long line, he had the first regiment march parallel to the enemy's left flank with the first unit placed a bit ahead of the second, the second ahead of the third, and so on. From a distance, the enemy, who expected the Prussian line to be parallel to its own, was unable to discern differences in the depth of the Prussian line. Suddenly the Prussian army would stop and take up a posi-tion on an alignment oblique to the enemy's line. Frederick, who had put all his reserves behind his most advanced wing, would then have it go around behind the enemy's left flank, forcing it to turn and wiping it out.

French tacticians of the age thought it difficult to adopt this thin battle array, these closely spaced ranks, and murderous salvos. The French soldier, they argued, could not be a disciplined machine and would never attain perfect fire. During the course of the War of Austrian Succession (1740–48) and the Seven Years' War (1756–63), such French tacticians as Maréchal de Saxe (the victor at Fontenoy), Maréchal de Broglie, and the comte de Guibert learned from their observations. They applied their theories in infantry troop maneuvers at Vaussieux (1778), at Strasbourg (1764) and Maubeuge (1766) for the artillery, and at Metz (1788) for the cavalry.

In his *Nouvelles découvertes sur l'art de la guerre* (1724) Chevalier Folard recommended a deep order of presentation for battle rather than the thinly spread one. The troops, arranged in columns of tightly spaced men were spread in a line from 30 to 180 columns wide. They charged the enemy, breaking his ranks by force of a shock enhanced by speed. Mesnil-Durand repeated Folard's ideas, first in 1755 then in 1777, without realizing that these advancing columns offered the adversary an excellent opportunity to destroy them with cannon- and gunfire. In his *Essai général de tactique* (1772), one of the young Bonaparte's bedside books, Guibert criticized this column attack.

At that point, the column was changed. Now made up of only three or four men in a row, it offered less of a target for enemy fire. A distance of a few paces was left between companies to prevent crowding and permit maneuvers. The attack column was used especially for objectives with a narrow front. It advanced rapidly, preceded by sharpshooters who felt out the enemy's troop disposition, tested its nerves, and sowed disorder to prepare the shock of the column's advance. As they moved forward, the troops fired at will (which was deadlier than firing in salvos because it allowed each soldier to take better aim). This way, a simple "right face" or "left face" would turn the men to deploy the column in a line facing the enemy. The shift from column to line and back could be made rapidly. This tactic was used during the Seven Years' War by both Broglie and Guibert. The technique was further improved by the creation of the division, which grouped together infantry, artillery, and cavalry units to form a complete army in miniature. The division, first created to facilitate deployment, was to be used under the Revolution and the Empire to test new ways of maneuvering around the enemy's flanks or to its rear. This was how the infantry became "the queen of battles."

Was this a "war in lace" in which the strategist's genius consisted in placing the enemy in such a difficult position that it would have to retreat, taking refuge in its stronghold, or would soon surrender? In reality, war was already a deadly affair. It was deadly because of cannonfire, gunfire, and bayonets. And it was deadly not so much for the number of men killed on the battlefield as for the number of wounded who died in the hospitals, antechambers of death.

Efforts were made to "humanize" warfare, and in particular to avoid the massacre of prisoners of war. It cost a considerable sum to train a soldier, and taking prisoners opened the way to an exchange of combatants. Opposing forces drew up treaties to facilitate such exchanges, or at least to guarantee tolerable living conditions for the prisoners. As for civilian populations, the generals attempted to avoid pillage, rape, and "scorched earth" tactics. War, Maréchal de Belle-Isle wrote, must be waged "honestly"—a pious wish that all too often went unheeded. Areas where fighting had taken place continued to be devastated, perhaps less cruelly than the Palatinate by the hand of French troops in 1698, but still they were left without great resources.

The Soldier and the Civilian

The soldier was a burden for the populations of the kingdom that he served. Since barracks were unknown, French regiments were obliged to move about through the kingdom, which meant that from 150,000 to 200,000 men—even 300,000 at times—might be in circulation and require lodging. The king's subjects furnished the *ustensile* that the law demanded—a pot, a fire, a candle, a bed or pallet—but the soldier required more and more food and drink. His host might lose his provisions, his linens (and the virtue of his daughters) in the bargain. Many subjects enjoyed "privileges" that exempted them from the obligation of lodging soldiers, which meant that the burden fell on humbler people. When a regiment in search of lodgings moved into the area, some villages emptied, their inhabitants preferring to leave the field free to them, removing whatever they could carry and taking shelter in the woods, in caves, or in a nearby convent. Even though the soldier was increasingly recruited from among the inhabitants of the kingdom, he considered himself almost in enemy territory. Language, customs, habits, and practices differed from one province to another, and often the soldier, far from his birthplace, could not understand the way of living or the thought processes of his fellow Frenchmen.

As nomads, men more accustomed to violence than civilians (who could themselves be violent), and "libertines"—that is, men accustomed to living a life that largely excluded them from the common laws—often drunkards, and at times pimps for the prostitutes who teemed about the edges of a camp, soldiers long inspired fear.

Fear diminished when barracks were established, troops were stationed for longer periods in certain zones (near the frontiers, for instance), and better discipline was instituted. Garrison cities lived with and by the army. Daily life was marked off by the church bells but also by the sound of drums, by the changing of the guard, and by military exercises and parades. The soldier purchased things, but he also sold his physical strength, in spite of regulations forbidding "moonlighting." He was a part-time gardener, field hand, harvester, and craftsman. Closer contact led the soldier and the townsman to know one another better, at times to appreciate one another. The city dweller even came to consider taking up arms an honorable profession that might offer a degree of social promotion, and the bourgeois was less hesitant to accept his son's decision to sign up. The civilian also knew that the king had organized a system of pensions that permitted some military personnel to avoid poverty and beggary on leaving the army. The Hôtel des Invalides offered a refuge to some wounded veterans, and as far as one can judge the soldier's return to civilian life improved as the century progressed. Still, it would be a mistake to extend happy relations between civilians and military personnel to the entire kingdom. In regions that saw the military only episodically the old aversion remained and troop movements created panic. During the Grande Peur of July and August 1789, French peasants were persuaded that the regiments marching toward Versailles announced the imminent arrival of brigands, perhaps even foreign armies, coming to lend a hand to an aristocratic plot to bring the people to its knees.

The Formation of a Military Society

In 1755, Jean-Charles Calais was a soldier. Tired of army life, he put on craftsman's clothing and deserted. At the city gate a lieutenant of the *maréchaussée*, the mounted police corps, recognized his soldierly carriage underneath his journeyman's clothes and arrested him. The army had marked Calais and his companions with an indelible seal. He had a bearing, a way of carrying his head, of walking, and of speaking that betrayed the soldier. He was part of military society, and even in flight he continued to share its mind-set and its culture.

Soldiers, whom civilians too long and too often reproached for setting themselves apart from common folk and having rough manners and vice riveted into their hearts, claimed to belong to a different social group from other men. Where the bourgeois of the eighteenth century proclaimed his "social utility," the soldier argued his spirit of sacrifice and willingness to face death. Military men aiming at improving their condition claimed a moral strength that derived from operating under the aegis of the king in the service of the community as a whole—the homeland, the ancestral land, and the refuge of tradition. They called it "honor."

Honor, for those less imbued with chivalric spirit, was belonging to a community that commanded love and offered protection. That community was, first of all, the battalion or the regiment in which one served, which could be distinguished from the others by the unit's uniform and flag. The flag was an instrument of war. It helped the soldiers to keep their lines and columns straight and to regroup when they broke ranks in the melee. The flag was above all a symbol. As one veteran of Napoleon's Old Guard later said, it was the soldier's "village clock tower." Abandoning the flag was treason of the lowest sort; leaving it in the hands of the enemy was tantamount to disbanding and destroying the community. Every regiment had its own war cry to be shouted in the face of the enemy; it was the voice of the dead resounding in the mouths of the living and reminding them of past glories. Honor commanded soldiers to keep control of themselves on the field of battle, urged them on to heroic acts, inspired them to be loyal to one another. It incited them to keep intact the memory of an epic past, the memory of a military family whose joys and sufferings they shared. Each regiment was like a "little nation" that had its own lifestyle, initiation rites, and customs.

Honor encouraged esprit de corps in a regiment and fostered cohesion, both in the face of the enemy and in relation to other regiments. There were brawls and duels between units, but in the final analysis there was a pride in belonging to an army whose greatness was forged by its trials.

Nonetheless, this military society was never entirely self-contained. On the eve of the French Revolution, the regiments recruited new members from cities and villages in crisis. The crisis of civil society also affected military society: officers complained about officers from the court, arrogant men who were seldom present in their units; noncommissioned officers complained when they were refused promotion; soldiers complained about their living conditions.

From Soldier to Citizen-Soldier

The National Army

What could be done when power had no bayonets at its command? This was the dilemma of the monarchy in 1789. When the first day of insurrection took place in Paris on 27 April, the army—more precisely, the Gardes Françaises—fired on the mob. The following day, desertions began. The population had forged too many bonds with the troops for the soldiers to be insensitive to the fate of the third estate. On the eve of 14 July, the court brought regiments into Paris from the garrison cities. Soldiers harassed by fatigue, ill-lodged, and ill-fed, gathered at the gates of the bivouacs, where patriots crowded around them and questioned them: "Aren't you members of the third estate like us? Will you shoot your brothers?" Some soldiers fled their units, but the troops of the Royal-Allemand took their sabers to the rioters on 12 July. During the night, men in uniform joined the Parisians as they searched for arms. The morning of 14 July, only a few steps away from where the troops were camped in the Champs de Mars, a group of patriots advanced to force the doors of the Hôtel des Invalides. There were soldiers among them. The veterans living in the Hôtel gave over cannons and guns without a struggle. At three in the afternoon the Bastille fell. Again, there were soldiers among the victors, and they had been of great help setting up and aiming the cannons. From July to October, officers reported that although half of the infantry regiments and the cavalry were reliable, the rest of the army was seething with excitement and would refuse to fire on the people.

In August 1790, revolt broke out in the garrison in Nancy. Soldiers protested about their living conditions, accused noble officers of pocketing regimental funds, and formed democratic assemblies that heaped scorn on discipline and hierarchy. The revolt was drowned in blood by troops who had remained loyal to their leaders. From 1790 to 1792, violent outbreaks, brawls, and mutinies developed in a good half of the regiments. Soldiers, at times led by junior officers who were commoners or by "patriot" noble officers like Davout, adopted the cause of city revolutionaries, obliging their officers to retire or emigrate.

The national Constituent Assembly feared that such revolts would turn against it and that a Caesar would emerge to seize power. To avoid that outcome, it worked to move the status of the military closer to that of the citizen. The Assembly proclaimed the duty to serve, maintaining

voluntary enrollment but under tight control. It applied to the army the
principles of the "Declaration of the Rights of Man and of the Citizen":
the recruitment of officers was to be done according to the principle of
equal opportunity based on talent and merit. Discipline was softened.
The soldier who passed the means test for being an "active citizen" could
vote; the soldier who had a good service record would receive rights of
citizenship on his separation from the service. To diminish regimental
esprit de corps, the regimental standards henceforth bore a tricolor
streamer. Regimental names were abandoned and replaced by numbers. The companies were no longer designated by the names of their
commanders but by numbers. Finally, after the flight of the king on
20 June 1791, "commissars" from the Assembly were sent to the army to
receive a vow of loyalty from the troops.

A new body, the Garde Nationale, was formed to serve beside the
royal army, a bourgeois militia composed of "active" (that is, tax-paying)
citizens. Dressed on the model of the Gardes Françaises in blue and red
but with white breeches, the Garde Nationale reflected the colors of the
national flag, standing in contrast to the royal soldiers, who dressed predominantly in white. At the moment of the king's flight and after his
return from Varennes, a national corps of Volunteers was drawn from
the Garde Nationale in the various *départements*. More than 100,000 men
swore to support the homeland in case of conflict and were moved to the
frontiers. The *Volontaires nationaux* had a different pay scale and discipline from the royal troops, and they elected their commanding officers, most of whom were notables, the sons of bourgeois and liberal
nobles.

This new army of men who thought of themselves as citizens underneath their military uniforms was reinforced by a new voluntary enlist-
ment in the summer of 1792, when the war declared in April of that year
threatened the homeland. These 1792 volunteers formed ill-matched
battalions. They were often poor men; the officers were modest men
without military experience. Some had signed up out of democratic enthusiasm, others, out of need. Some were incorporated into the regular
regiments, whose makeup they changed, at times in the direction of a
heightened patriotism. It was this mixed group of soldiers who, after the
fall of the monarchy, withstood hours of cannonfire from the Austro-
Prussian army at Valmy. To cries of "Vive la Nation!" they won a victory
on 20 September 1792 that led, the following day, to the foundation of
the Republic, proclaimed by the Convention.

When their job was done these volunteers went home. They had promised to lend a helping hand to the line army, and when their mission was accomplished they left, in spite of orders from the generals and envoys sent by the governing powers. The revolutionary government ordered another levy in February 1793. This levy of 300,000 men was poorly received by the country populations, who complained that it was always the same people—the poor, who could not afford to buy a replacement as the rich did—who continued to pay the blood tax. They demanded equality: conscript everyone or everyone would refuse to serve! In the west of France the levy set off an explosion of accumulated bitterness against the Revolution and produced a revolt, followed by the formation of a Catholic and royal army, at first commanded by commoners, then by nobles. This was the beginning of a civil war, atrocious on both sides, that did not really end until the Consulate.

In June 1793 the Jacobins, brought to power by the insurrection of the sans-culottes, found themselves facing a coalition (the first) of Prussians, English, Spanish, Portuguese, Sardinians, and Neapolitans. It was *vaincre ou mourir.* The sans-culottes brought the Terror into the army: they demanded the eviction of aristocrat officers and their replacement by patriots, a *levée en masse* of all citizens for a mass war, and a patriotic war to replace the "learned" war of the king's creatures. In one day and one night, a combat that involved all Frenchmen was to sweep out the prince's mercenaries. Since the Jacobins were realists, they transformed the total levy of the French people demanded by the sans-culottes into a requisition. The decree of 23 August 1793 stated that all bachelors and childless widowers from the ages of eighteen to twenty-five were requisitioned for army service until the reestablishment of peace. This was a requisition of soldiers and of all citizens: those not enlisted in the army were to work to provision and arm the troops. Women and children were urged to help in the war effort, and the aged were to preach hatred of kings. There was no more front, no more rear, but only a united people standing up against tyrants! This was the Jacobins' order of the day, inscribed on flags that by then bore the national colors.

Unity of the nation required unity of the army. The law of amalgamation voted in February 1793 decreed that all soldiers would wear the same uniform, that of the Volunteers. This measure was designed to eliminate the particularism of the formerly royal regiments and put an end to brawls between *culs blancs*—the regular soldiers in their white britches—and the *porcelaine bleue*—"blue china," a scornful term that the ex-soldiers of the king used to designate the Volunteers. All men were to wear the same uniform, receive equal pay, and experience iden-

tical discipline. A third of the officers were to be promoted by seniority
of service, and the other two-thirds elected by immediate subordinates
or coopted from among the officers qualified to hold the rank in question. The law further specified the formation of *demi-brigades* (regiments) made up of one unit from the old army and two units of
Volunteers. Volunteers were to transmit their patriotism to the old soldiers, who in turn would teach them the art of war. This amalgamation,
realized only gradually, was begun in the summer of 1793 but completed
only in late 1794 and the beginning of 1795.

From that moment on, military personnel from the army of the ancien régime, Volunteers who had signed up in 1791, 1792, or 1793, and
the enlistees from the requisitions of 1793 and 1794 lived together,
shared tents, and filled their mess-kits from the same stew pot. Louis
Glence, a junior officer in the army of Louis XVI, born in Brittany in
1756 into a family of wig-makers, lived side by side with Henri Grimal, a
56-year-old man from Lorraine who had volunteered in 1791; Jean Tar-
dif, a 23-year-old laborer born in Burgundy who had volunteered in
1792; and two enlistees by requisition, Pierre Lassia, a mathematics
teacher from Paris, and one Bessa, a shopkeeper also from Paris. The
new army was a melting-pot not only of army personnel but of the new
nation. It included men from all professions and all levels of wealth from
farmers' sons to the sons of merchants and members of the liberal professions. An Alsatian learned to live with a Provençal, the one speaking
with the rough accent of northeastern France, the other with the singing
inflections of the south; the one accustomed to cooking with butter, the
other with olive oil. As they lived side by side they exchanged the customs and the songs of their birthplaces. Beyond their cultural differences they saw themselves as French. But were they all French? The army
included non-French patriots—Belgians, Batavians (that is, Dutch),
Germans, Italians, and Poles who formed foreign legions working to
bring an end to the reign of princes and aristocrats in their own lands.
Sulkowski, for example, was a Pole who became an aide-de-camp to
Napoleon Bonaparte in Italy.

A Republican Army

The Jacobin of Year II kept watch over the civic education of this new
army. Through the *représentants en mission*, deputies of the Convention
granted full powers, and through a number of government agents that
ranged from the war commissars to military judges, the Montagnard Jac-

obin legislators taught soldiers what they were fighting for: the total destruction of "feudalism," freedom of the land and of man, equality, and the unity of a nation at war with the aristocracy of France and all of Europe. The discourses of the representatives on mission, the civic festivities in which soldiers and citizens mingled, the clubs and popular societies in which they met one another, patriotic songs like the *Marseillaise* or couplets made up on its melody, and theatrical works were all instruments used by the pedagogues of the Republic.

The militants in the army ranged from ultrarevolutionaries indoctrinated by Hébert, who distributed his journal *Le Père Duchesne* to the troops, to Jacobins who read the *Antifédéraliste* or the *Bulletin des Lois* and somewhat less "ultra" revolutionaries close to Danton or Camille Desmoulins. Just as the Montagnards worked to reduce "factions" in the body civic, they worked against factions in the army, which they subjected to a strict discipline. Were soldiers lesser citizens? They voted, but the practice of that civic act was very often tinged with conformity. They retained the admittedly limited right to elect their officers, their *conseils d'administration*—administrative councils within the regiment that functioned like a municipal council in miniature and drew up the rules that governed their lives—and the juries that served in military trials.

The Jacobins' aim was to make these soldiers into model citizens. They boasted about the soldiers' merit, their spirit of sacrifice for the national cause, and their solidarity, both among themselves and with civilians. The *Recueil des actions héroïques* composed by the Convention and distributed to city governments and schoolchildren, related notable acts of the nation's warriors. The dead soldier would not just disappear: the Jacobins worked to combat de-Christianization in both the army and civil society, and some soldiers played a part in the fight against Catholicism. When the Montagnard Convention created the cult of the Supreme Being and recognized the immortality of the soul, it brought that cult to the army. Associated with a cult of the homeland, whose ardent champions soldiers were supposed to be, the cult of the Supreme Being taught that the shades of departed soldiers kept watch over their companions in arms. The Convention made much of adolescent soldiers like Viala and Bara who gave their lives, and it produced the first monuments to the revolutionary dead.

The soldier was encouraged to substitute civic virtue for the older notion of the soldier's honor. Civic virtue was forgetting oneself for the benefit of the whole community. It found application in obedience to the laws and the representatives of the sovereign nation, and in a respect for property, particularly in foreign lands: "War to the châteaux; peace to the thatched cottages" was the word passed on to the republican army.

This Jacobinism had various effects within the army. Along with convinced militants, the army also contained moderates and indifferents. Beside soldiers intent on de-Christianization, there were Catholics who continued to profess their faith (some battalions had clandestine chaplains until Year II). The "virtuous" soldier who shared "the black bread of liberty" with the inhabitants of the lands the army conquered fought side by side with a soldier bent on pillage who mocked a system of justice that promised him a death sentence. The soldier who respected prisoners of war was the companion of another who massacred his adversaries. The Convention itself recommended killing prisoners of war as a response to atrocities committed by some enemy troops. There was often a gulf between law and practice, and the revolutionary government— like governments of the ancien régime—understood the need to safeguard combatants who could be exchanged for one's own soldiers who had been taken prisoner.

All these soldiers cast in the role of missionaries of liberty ended up, in varying degree, participating in the exaltation of an all-conquering Great Nation that would level differences. They were all guilty of chauvinism. As well as the soldier who was conscious of remaining a citizen, there were the old and the new professional soldiers. It was to the latter that Carnot, on the eve of 9 Thermidor, addressed his journal *La Soirée des camps*, a publication that tended, contrary to the Jacobin spirit, to see the citizen in arms first and foremost as a military man and a member of a special society. In the social domain Jacobinism applied an assistance policy that offered benefits to soldier and civilian alike. Carnot felt that the military man had a greater claim to this assistance than the civilian because his role was technical—he was the technician most useful to the whole body social.

From Patriot Soldier to Technician of War

In 1794 the French army became a mass army. It counted nearly 800,000 men (the million combatants announced from the tribune of the Convention was a myth designed to inspire fear in the enemy and give the nation a sense of security). The army of the Revolution was immeasurably bigger than the army of the monarchy. During the Seven Years' War (1756–62), the king of France recruited 270,000 men, 70,000 of them non-French. In the sixty-two years from 1701 to 1763, the monarchy levied 460,000 men and trained 1,545,000 men so as to have, at any given time a war-ready standing army of 160,000 men. In all, this meant a total of 2,030,000 soldiers, 360,000 of them foreigners. In not much more than a year, the Republic organized an army equal in numbers to nearly half of the "nationals" levied in over a half-century by the monarchy.

This was not only a considerable mass of men, but a mass that, by and large, had everything to learn about the profession of arms. At the beginning, the soldier learned warfare by marching. Warfare changed from a war of positions to a war of movement that was, as the Jacobins said, as rapid as "the electric spark." Even more than before, the soldier was a *pied-poudreux,* a "dusty-foot." His kit bag on one shoulder, his gun slung across his back, he was expected to rise above fatigue as he marched under the burning summer sun or on the icy roads of winter. War no longer had seasons. The logbooks of these soldiers tell of short halts, constant alerts, the contents of the mess-kit swallowed fast, the common pot overturned to extinguish the bivouac fire, and incessant marches. In seven years of war a volunteer from Paris named Aymez, who had enlisted in 1792, marched through the Paris region, northern France, Belgium, western Germany, Switzerland, and northern Italy. In six months in 1796 he covered more than 850 miles. Distances varied from day to day: on 7 September he and his companions marched only five miles; on 25 September, twenty-nine miles, fighting the entire time.

Aymez admits that at times he and his comrades in arms slept as they marched. The effect of this sort of physical exertion can be read in the troop records and in the lists of the sick and wounded. There were soldiers deafened by cannonfire, men with organs out of place as a result of such violent exertions that they eventually had voluminous hernias. Poor living conditions, combined with excessive and irregular effort, resulted in large numbers of soldiers with rheumatism or chronic kidney pains. Poor nutrition, living out of doors in cold and unhealthy regions, always in combination with exhausting marches, led to depression or weak lungs. All these ills, which already existed in the armies of the eighteenth century, escalated with the wars of the Revolution and the Empire. Other diseases were added: halts were altogether too often dedicated to Bacchus and Venus. Alcoholism was a typical disease of the army, and the venereal diseases contracted from the thousands of prostitutes who followed the army despite governmental orders became— along with scurvy—a veritable scourge. Living conditions in the army transformed a twenty-year-old into an old man in only a few years. When Jacquin came marching home again, his loved ones—even his mother—could hardly believe he was their kin.

On the road or in camp, the young recruit learned the rudiments of his profession—marching, fighting, and learning to handle weapons—from the old hand. This means that the first revolutionary battles were fought by awkward apprentice soldiers who were terror-stricken and scattered when they came under fire. Despite all the efforts of the revolutionary government, arms were at times lacking or were of poor quality. Guns left from the ancien régime were used; others were manufactured; still more were requisitioned from the population at large. These guns were not always without danger for their user: they tended to blow up in one's face, especially if not kept in good condition.

For some revolutionary soldiers, fire power was less important than steel: the bayonet, the saber, even the pike. These weapons had something mythical about them for the patriot, who saw typical weapons of insurrections as the ones most efficacious for the face-to-face attack appropriate to citizen-soldiers. The simplest way to improve on the traditional arts of war was the use of mass force, that is, assembling the largest possible number of soldiers at the point chosen for the attack, then mounting an assault, bayonets raised, a patriotic song on the soldiers' lips, striking the enemy hard, sowing disorder among the enemy troops, and destroying them. Away with the old tactics, the sans-culottes proclaimed; they were for the king's mercenaries. Revolutionary warfare must have a new style. "Attack! Attack always, without stint, in compact columns, with fixed bayonets!" the representatives on mission commanded. At first, this mass warfare was accompanied by a "psychological warfare" of subversion. Repeating Rousseau's injunction to destroy the public convention of the enemy state, the military authorities distributed tracts to enemy soldiers inviting them to desert the cause of kings and join with the people's cause.

As a result of this new sort of warfare, the initial reversals were followed by victories with a high cost in human lives. The bloodletting was so great in some units that even when they remained masters of the battlefield they were unable to follow the Convention's orders to pursue the adversary and annihilate it. Houchard, the victor at Hondschoote on 8 September 1793, was guillotined for failing to follow up his advantage by pursuing and destroying the enemy army.

The revolutionary government drew a lesson from such hecatombs. It suspended the purge of noble officers, nearly a thousand of whom were retained and assigned to work in the war office under Carnot, where they went right back to plans and projects elaborated under the monarchy. When he was a staff officer, Barthélemy set up divisions of fighting units, as in the old days. By combining two *demi-brigades* of heavy or light infantry with cavalry and artillery, he formed divisions of 5,000 to 10,000 men. The mass became operational and "active," but the officers were better trained as well. The government of Year II launched a widespread search for talent, and units were passed in review in search of men who could read, write, count, and draw and understand campaign maps. Promoted, such men were sent to camps established behind the front. There, in the company of other ex-soldiers and noncommissioned officers, they were given a short course in the rudiments of tactics. On their return to their battalions, they in turn taught others.

The young generals learned from their adversaries, drew lessons from combat, and gradually became more skilled at leading mixed units. They encouraged better training for their men, and they used the attack in columns as well as in lines and defensive squares. The instrument of war that the Republic bequeathed to Bonaparte was a good deal better than some historians would have us think, and Bonaparte knew how to use it to best advantage. Here, for example, is what a combatant in the Egyptian campaign, Vigo-Roussillon, had to say about one episode during the Battle of the Pyramids:

General Bon[aparte] ordered one-half of the first side of his square to advance and attack the enemy's camp. All the even-numbered platoons of that side, backed up by the carabineers of the Fourth Light, marched toward the enemy retrenchments. We were at about 200 paces when we were charged, with the greatest intrepidity, by a multitude of cavalry. Our platoons marched separated, due to General Bon's error in detaching only even-numbered platoons and not having them close ranks to advance. Happily, each platoon was made up of six ranks, and although surrounded and separated from one another, formed small masses like filled squares when the three last ranks turned around and faced backwards. . . . We fired at ten paces and covered the earth with men and horses. At the same time, we continued to advance, still surrounded, toward the retrenchments. Suddenly the battalion commander, Duranteau, gave the order to advance at a run to the village of Embabeth, a support point to the left of the camp. We took it swiftly, and found ourselves masters of the only way out of the enemy camp. The Mamelukes tried to escape, but in an instant the entrance to the village was blocked by the bodies of men, horses, and camels fallen under our fire. They formed a high barricade. The carnage was horrible.

The fury of such battles cost the armies of the Revolution losses of over 480,000 men. Even more died in the hospitals, victims of epidemics. Overworked surgeons cut flesh and sawed through bones while the wounded soldier gripped his pipe between his teeth. If the pipe fell and broke, it meant that the soldier was dead.

Violence touched the civilian population as well. Generals (including Bonaparte) prohibited marauding, but in vain; ill-nourished soldiers spread out over the countryside, robbing and raping. At the end of the Revolution, some officers went back to the old mercenary customs and demanded tribute from cities when a siege was raised, ransomed the cities' inhabitants, and diverted funds to their own war chests. In retreat the routed army gave no quarter. In 1796 Captain Humblot described the army's retreat from Sambre-et-Meuse in these terms:

> I saw the inhabitants reduced to beggary when their animals, their foodstuffs, and provisions of all sorts were carried off, leaving them barely a bit of bread that they moistened with their tears and that a barbaric soldier came to snatch from them. Inhumanity was not yet at its height. [The soldiers] further demanded, by the most cruel treatments, that these victims of their fury produce sums of money, even though they no longer possessed a penny, having already made the last sacrifices twenty times over to buy their lives.

The Return of the Professional Soldier

The army was exhausted. In 1798, threatened by a second coalition, France promulgated the Jourdan Law replacing requisition with conscription. Henceforth all bachelors and childless widowers who reached the age of twenty had their names and physical descriptions registered. Men between the ages of twenty-one and twenty-five formed four other classes. Lots were drawn in the various age classes to form a contingent for the army. This conscription, which established and regulated obligatory military service, lasted until the nineteenth century. The law was soon vitiated, however, by the conscripts' option to purchase a replacement, a commerce in men that permitted the wealthy to avoid service.

Napoleon Bonaparte reinstated conscription, but it continued to be viewed with a jaundiced eye. A number of recalcitrants went into hiding, and the hundreds of thousands of conscripts promised at the end of the Directory produced a contingent that although sizable was powerless to change the composition of the army. This meant that the army was predominantly made up of men who had been fighting for some time, some as long as seven years.

Citizen-soldiers became professionals. Since they lived for years far from their birthplaces, they remained in large part out of the reach of the civil authorities and fell under the sway of their generals. The generals gave them the gold and silver of the conquered countries, organized the recruitment of officers for their armies, and controlled military justice. They transferred the cult of the homeland to a cult of their own persons; they revived an esprit de corps by bringing back regimental flags that bore the names of the battles in which each unit had participated and by distributing honorary sabers, the first form of military decoration under the Republic. Before he was a soldier of the Republic, a man was a soldier of the regiment in which he served; before serving the homeland, he served in "Bonaparte's army" or "Bernadotte's army." Bonaparte's men, who still had a certain Jacobin spirit, called Bernadotte's troops "aristocrats" or *Messieurs* and challenged them to individual or collective duels. Thus, every general had a "clientele" that allowed him to make and unmake the governments of the occupied countries and to bypass civilian authorities to sign treaties of peace. Thanks to this proconsuls' game, the generals acquired a taste for civil power and dreamed of playing a role in France's internal political struggles. The political class, threatened in 1797 by the royalists, invited them to do so. Bonaparte and Hoche both sent officers and soldiers to France to take part in a coup d'état. At the same time, Bonaparte indoctrinated his soldiers, reconstructed a cult of the dead for military society alone, and exalted the heroism of combatants, whose mores he praised as superior to those of the dissolute politicians. He encouraged his soldiers to write threatening messages to the constituted powers: "Maintain the Republic, or the army will intervene!"

The generals were involved in politics on the eve of the coup d'état of 18 Brumaire in 1799, even before Bonaparte's return from Egypt. Some of them sided with the neo-Jacobins; others with revisionists who, like Abbé Sieyès, wanted to change institutions. After his return, Bonaparte succeeded in charming them all and in manipulating the assemblies through his brother Lucien, and he set up a propaganda machine favorable to himself in the press. He was the choice of the revisionists and of notables frightened by the second coalition and the resurgence of the Jacobins. The plan set up to induce the political assemblies to transform the constitution went without a hitch on 18 Brumaire, when the deputies accepted a transfer of venue to Saint-Cloud. On the following day events took a dramatic turn. Some deputies called Bonaparte a dictator and threatened to send him to prison. Bonaparte became confused and was saved only by his brother Lucien's quick thinking. The army that had been called out to protect the deputies turned into the army for the coup d'état. Murat burst into the assembly hall and ordered his followers to "throw all those people out." The Consulate was installed in the shadow of bayonets. Was France heading for a military dictatorship? Some soldiers hoped so, arguing that a nation at war should be militarized. The middle class feared falling "under the rod of a dictatorship" of a soldier rabble that scorned them. Bonaparte had the wit to appear more as head of the civil state than as a general. He reconciled the "parties," arranged a rapprochement between notables of the Republic and émigré nobles returned from abroad, and pacified France internally and externally. In 1802, many French men and women regarded him as a "savior." Still, the First Consul had to take the army into account, and with it the clienteles of generals who plotted against him. He needed time, and only became the absolute master of the army in 1804.

The Napoleonic Soldier

A National Army or a Professional Army?

Under the Empire, army recruitment relied in part on volunteers but above all on conscription. Conscription was applied unequally from one social class or region to another and between urban and rural areas. The army was often made up of poor peasants. France was asked for a relatively light contribution in men under the Consulate and the Empire, but levies rose constantly, growing from 113,000 men in 1805 to 165,000 men in 1806 and over a million for the levies of 1812 and 1813. In all, 2 million men were enlisted, or 37 percent of all men of military age and 7 percent of the population as a whole. Many conscripts refused to serve or deserted. The authorities only managed to stop the hemorrhage in 1810, when the refractory fell in number from 68,000 to 9,000.

This national army still contained a large nucleus of veterans of the revolutionary wars: in 1803, 174,000 men who had been enlisted from 1792 to 1799 were still serving in the army. The conscripts who joined them left the military only through the hospital or death. Thus, under the cover of a national army, France really had a self-perpetuating professional army that taught newcomers the rules and customs of military society.

A National Army or an Army of the Nations?

This national army was just as much of a melting-pot of the nation as it had been during the Revolution. In one way or another, all French men wound their way to the camps to take part in military life. Conscription, Napoleon said at Saint Helena, was an institution that had become an integral part of French mores, and no one but their mothers still tried to dissuade sons from their duty to serve. He was forgetting that before 1815 there were always defectors, and that after the Russian campaign their numbers swelled to form large bands.

Was it a national army? As time went on, the Napoleonic Grand Army became an army of the subjugated or satellite nations. Until 1814, the Cisalpine Republic, which had become the Kingdom of Italy, furnished 218,000 men; the Kingdom of Naples, 60,000; Spain, 15,000; the Confederation of the Rhine, 120,000; Switzerland, 10,000; and Holland, 36,000. Portuguese and Polish troops should be added to these numbers.

In this army of the nations, Bonaparte extended the principle of equal opportunity to conscripts from annexed countries. Anyone might be promoted to an officer. A young conscript named Traversa offers one example: he was an Italian born in Alessandria, the capital city of the *département* of Marengo. Conscripted at the age of twenty, his courage and his talent for the military soon brought him a second lieutenancy in a regiment of light infantry in 1813. Napoleon's military schools also opened their doors to the sons of non-French notables. Men from the Illyrian Provinces, for example, received scholarships to study at Saint-Cyr or the École Polytechnique. In the emperor's mind, the army must be a melting-pot to forge the unity of the various populations of his empire.

The Soldier and the "Pékin"

Napoleon worked to reconnect military and civilian society, but he succeeded in doing so only in part. The middle class retained some of its mistrust of the military, and soldiers still treated the civilian with arrogance and gave him the pejorative nickname of *pékin*.

At first Napoleon sought to attract notables' sons—the sons of bourgeois or of nobles who rallied to his cause—to his officers' schools. He counted on such institutions to furnish him with good technicians, but the schools also opened their doors to civilians and they brought together elites that the Revolution had fought. The needs of war were so great that Napoleon never succeeded in raising the proportion of officers trained in the schools to more than 10 percent of the officers' corps. Besides the officers who graduated from Saint-Cyr or the École Polytechnique there were officers who had risen from the ranks, among them many sons of the petty bourgeoisie attracted by the brilliance and glory of the military profession. Statistics from inspection rolls prove that the officers' corps in Napoleon's army was largely made up of the middle classes. Contrary to the legend, not all soldiers carried a marshal's baton in their cartridge-pouch.

Napoleon also wanted officers to be notables comparable to the ones who provided him with a power base in civil society. Although a junior officer's pay barely allowed him to hold his rank, the emperor added a good many advantages to it: noble titles or decorations with an annual stipend attached, a juridical status that put the officer above the common herd, scholarships to the military schools for officers' sons and places for their daughters in the Maison de la Légion d'Honneur. What counted more than anything else in a France determined to be egalitarian was *l'étiquette*—the "label"—connected with honors and privileges and recognized in public manifestations. The 1804 code favored the military over civilians in this regard.

The marshals and the generals of the Empire were also known for their wealth. Aside from their generous pay (on occasion they held more than one commission), the "top brass" had a further source of income in annual grants approved by the emperor. Berthier had an annual income of over a million francs. Masséna and Davout had revenues close to that sum. Money did not erase one's origins or lack of education, however. For every one man like Davout, a noble of the ancien régime who was accepted in high society, there were many like Lefebvre, the son of a gate-keeper in an Alsatian city, once a sergeant in the royal army and the husband of a former company washerwoman, Catherine Hübscher, known as "Madame Sans-Gêne." That couple was a laughing stock not only among the notables but also among the many generals—in 1814, 166 out of 277—who were ancien-régime nobles.

Finally, Napoleon saw the military as a channel for giving greater moral stamina to the society he sought to create. The soldier should stand out among civilians, who were primarily motivated by individualism and a quest for wealth. He should be a pedagogue of honor. The emperor used the ancien-régime officers' vision of honor and the Republic's vision of virtue, and turned them toward his own person. In one symbolic gesture that made the soldier the heir of the chivalry of times gone by, the first decorations of the Legion of Honor were picked out of the helmet of Bayard, the *chevalier sans peur et sans reproche*. As the heir of republican virtue as well, the soldier was expected to put aside everything—love, family, personal interest—to face the supreme sacrifice for a homeland henceforth embodied in the person of Napoleon. In the discourses that he delivered at the military schools or had written for them, Napoleon ceaselessly taught that the soldier must imbue civil society with the honor of the camps. Not many soldiers took on the mission.

If it was true that military exercises and parades and the *Bulletin de la Grande Armée*, which was circulated everywhere, communicated the values of military society to civil society—as Vigny and Musset experienced and as they wrote—there was still a barrier between the military man and the *pékin*. Military society kept its initiation rites, customs, and culture—which differed from that of civil society. The soldier remained a nomad who founded a family only at an advanced age. A glorious nomad, he could be proud (at times that pride was more like vanity) of defining himself by the sword and by the victories won by the elite of the Great Nation. The military man might meet civilians in society, in the salons that were at times open to him, in balls at court or at the Hôtel de Ville, but he never really associated with them. Soldiers continued to treat civilians with condescension, if not with scorn. "What could men like us have in common with people shut up in their shops or hemmed in by their businesses, living a mediocre life in the pursuit of wealth?" asked military men, who were just as accustomed to spending money without counting or throwing their gold on the gambling tables as they were to throwing themselves into combat. When military men were Freemasons, they joined military lodges. Often atheists and anticlerical, they mocked the hypocritical bigotry of the bourgeois. Although their regiment provided the framework of their lives, theirs was not the limited horizon of the bourgeois but that of the whole of Europe, which they had traveled over and held under their sway. In the final analysis, what attached them to the nation was the person of Napoleon. Although they might grumble about him, Napoleon remained for them (with the exception of the marshals who were to betray him) the "little bald man," the "little corporal," the leader of men whom he alternately fawned on or browbeat but to whom he brought glory. Napoleon, like his soldiers, was a "gambler" capable of betting his destiny in a single battle.

The Fury of War

Napoleon Bonaparte took the instrument of war that the Revolution had delivered over to him, and, with a mastery the world had never before seen, he applied that instrument to the art of war as it had been perfected before 1789. His overall systematic strategy was to engage battle and pursue the total destruction of the enemy.

His technique involved reflection and meditation, as he himself said. "No genie suddenly reveals to me in secret what I have to say or do in circumstances that others do not expect." He worked out a guiding idea for every campaign, but he eliminated no solution, and he remained ready to change his plans at the last minute. His general principle was to economize his strength and manage his forces well—to be strongest at the place where he had decided to strike the decisive blow. He applied this principle in maneuvers either at the enemy's rear or at the center of the front. He used the first technique when he had numerical superiority over his adversary, throwing his army on the enemy's rear to gather it in as if in a net. He concentrated his forces to face the enemy's front when his troops did not have numerical superiority. By dividing the enemy forces in two, his central position between the two enemy groups enabled him to crush each portion in turn.

Speed was an absolute necessity if force was to be concentrated in one place or the opposing army was to be taken by surprise. Napoleon won a great many of his battles thanks to the legs of his soldiers, from whom he demanded long, rapid, and exhausting forced marches.

On the field of battle he disposed his forces in various ways. The infantry might be arranged in two lines, the second independent of the first; or it might be deployed in one long line or arranged in a series of battalions, some deployed, others in columns to provide backup. At the beginning of the Empire, columns were deployed with open spaces between them, but the troops' lack of training made it necessary to have them maneuver in tight columns, which made alignment easier to maintain but made the massed troops less mobile and left them more exposed to enemy fire. Use of a firing line was an exception; sharpshooter fire was more often used, since firing at will left the initiative to the soldiers, was more unsettling to the enemy, and killed more enemy soldiers. The cavalry was disposed in two lines behind the infantry, the second line acting as a reserve for the first and operating independently of it. The cavalry attacked in successive waves, and when it had penetrated the enemy lines it pursued the routed troops, slashing at them with sabers. The artillery was placed throughout the front in small groups of two to eight pieces, at times stationed in the spaces between battalions, at other times, when it could take advantage of a rise in the terrain that offered a dominating position, behind the first line. The artillery pieces could be hauled about, so artillery was more mobile than it had been under the Revolution; hence, it could be concentrated swiftly at selected points and sow havoc in the opposing front with a deluge of fire. This technique was used more and more after 1807. The Imperial Guard, a mix of infantry, cavalry, and artillerymen with a strength of 9,798 men in 1804 and 56,169 in 1812, was a maneuverable mass to be used only at the most critical moments. The other units laughed at the arrogant guardsmen who did not always see action, calling them "the immortals." When it did see action, the Imperial Guard nearly always did so successfully, as at Eylau, at Somosierra Pass, and during the Russian campaign. It sacrificed itself at Waterloo, when the last square formations of *braves* surrounded Cambronne.

The emperor demanded discipline, training, organization, and blind obedience from his soldiers. As long as contact had not been made with the enemy, Napoleon closed his eyes to soldiers who wandered off, marauded, invaded the peasants' chicken coops or rifled their provisions cellars. On the eve of a battle, however, soldiers had to be present or face arrest followed by a death sentence. At first, the emperor took great pains to supervise training maneuvers, which he had his troops repeat tirelessly in camp, for instance at Boulogne. Later, the pace of military operations prohibited thorough training, and toward the end, the "Marie-Louise"—young recruits—learned the art of war, as in years past, at the side of the veteran soldiers. There were some chinks in this army's organizational armor. The support services charged with provisions were often lacking, thus obliging the men to live on the land, which was bad for the men but worse for the malnourished cavalry horses, many of whom died of disease (in Russia, for example). The mobility and rapidity of troop movements were often impeded. In spite of attempts to organize ambulances and special corps of stretcher-bearers, medical services could never keep up with the level of butchery of the battlefield. The losses of Napoleon's army have been estimated at over 900,000 men, and, once again, the hospitals killed more men than battle fire.

The custom of disputing orders, which had been possible under the Revolution, was eradicated. The private followed his captain's orders; the captain, those of the general; the general was not expected to act on his own initiative but received orders that he was to execute without flinching. Napoleon demanded that his young general staff (the average age of his generals was forty-one) execute his orders and be charismatic leaders of men. One sign of the latter was a willingness to expose themselves to enemy fire at the head of their troops. Oudinot, for example, bore twenty-three scars on his body. But here too there was a fault in the Napoleonic system, a fissure that was to be exploited by turncoat French generals like Bernadotte who passed to the opposing side. When the generals had large forces under their command, as during the Russian or the German campaigns, they proved poor strategists. There were exceptions, however, such as Lannes and Davout.

Blind obedience did not mean that the Napoleonic army was made up of robots. Napoleon knew that his men had inherited from the revolutionary epoch (if not from the monarchic age) a desire to know where they were being led. The emperor long continued the habit of haranguing them on the eve of combat. He claimed that he did so to quash the insinuations and rumors that ran through the camp and to keep moral high. But the emperor's orders of the day also responded to the expectations of his men by laying out the general outlines of what the next day's action would bring.

Neither was obedience absolute on the field of battle. In minor encounters the clashing armies might designate champions to fight in single combat, just as under the ancien régime or the Revolution. Moreover, the soldier always had his eye out for an enemy soldier with a fine mount or well-filled saddlebags whom he could attack, capture, and strip of his belongings. At the rear, the soldiers regained the individuality they lost in the attack columns and front lines, and despite Napoleon's prohibitions they fought duels. Among the rites of initiation for the new recruit or young officer was not only "greasing the pot" and paying for a bottle but also taking on the *crânes*—soldiers known as redoubtable duelists who always stood ready to provoke a young soldier to a fight. Fighting a duel was proof that a soldier did not hold his life too dear and would be capable of preserving the honor of the flag and being a companion one could count on in combat.

Continuity and Rupture

Nearly twenty years of uninterrupted war brought few changes to armaments. The soldier continued to fight with the same arms. The Prussian gun had been improved only in its charging mechanism. This now bore a cutting blade with which the soldier could open the cartridge without having to use his teeth, thus accelerating the gun's rate of fire. Napoleon refused to adopt this new technique. He also rejected the use of the balloon, he refused to replace the saltpeter in gunpowder with potassium chlorate, and he continued to use flintlock guns rather than the percussion lock invented by Forsyth, which used a "fulminating powder" as priming to ignite the charge when it was struck by the hammer. The artillery still used Gribeauval cannons. This absence of any "technological revolution" was not only attributable to the state of the steel industry in France; narrowly conservative generals rejected the proposed changes.

In appearance, tactics were also little changed. The generals applied techniques that had been worked out on the eve of the Revolution. Whether French or non-French, they applied these same methods but with more brio, and they were obliged to accept the "lightning war" that Napoleon imposed. This "lightning war" was increasingly difficult to carry out, given that rapid movement and surprise did not work as well with mass forces. Von Clausewitz, the Prussian general who summed up all that he had learned in the Napoleonic wars in his *On War,* understood early on that "any offensive is weakened by the very fact of its advance." "Five hundred thousand men crossed the Nemen," he stated, "120,000 fought at Borodino, and even fewer reached Moscow," which led Clausewitz to conclude that "the defensive form of warfare is intrinsically stronger than the offensive." This was even more true when Napoleon invaded Russia, a land so vast that the adversary could always refuse combat, draw back, and leave poorly supplied, exhausted troops.

Wellington sorely tried Napoleon's tactics as well. Taking a lesson from his experience on the Iberian Peninsula, Wellington made better use of the terrain by digging a series of parallel retrenchments that slowed and eventually stopped the French assaults. There was another thing that Napoleon overlooked. As war became total, it prompted a reaction from the various peoples involved. Nationalism was on the rise, and from the *guerillos* active in the sierras of Spain to the partisans in the Tyrolian Alps who rose up under Andreas Höfer and the swarms of peasants in movement on the plains of Russia who were urged to fanaticism by their priests, the French army met with a style of war to which its only response was a redoubled violence that brought on the horrors of war depicted by Goya.

Another change was a more intensive use of artillery. The infantry remained "the queen of battles," but an army's fire power was much enhanced by the number of cannons it used and their mobility. At Leipzig, in the battle of 16–19 October 1813 that involved ten nations, 500,000 men, and more than 3,000 artillery pieces, the French artillery alone fired off more than 220,000 shots.

War became a "butchery" that peopled the great military cemetery of all the peoples of Europe. This paroxysm of violence influenced the soldier's mind-set and his attitude toward civilians, whether they were his compatriots or foreigners. Just before demobilization in 1815, there was widespread fear that there would soon be hundreds of thousands of men in the streets who knew how to do nothing but kill. The French Revolution had developed a policy of social assistance to the veteran. The Empire kept up this nationalized relief program but eliminated its egalitarian character, and the veterans' hospitals and army camps could not possibly have received tens of thousands of men. Under the Restoration these veterans were put on half-pay and left to parade their poverty and their bitterness from the street to the café, from the tobacco den to the public square, as they shared their memories of epic times with the people. In the early years many of them still inspired fear since the brutal treatment they had given and received left some of them suffering from psychiatric disturbances, even madness.

The century of the Enlightenment had dreamed of a universal peace or the submission of war to the rule of law. War would no longer be the "commerce of kings," as Thomas Paine wrote, but would be humanized and would respect the rights of all peoples. In 1815, Europe woke up in the middle of general slaughter. In all lands, men had looked to France for liberation from despotism, and these "enlightened" men—Goya for one—found themselves torn. The war of liberation had been transformed, as Robespierre had predicted, into a war of enslavement that inspired hatred and murder in both victor and vanquished. Europe needed time before it could find its way back to a democracy that had been "frozen" by the military and to an equality that had been forgotten in the turmoil of war.

The soldier's place in society was affected by this. For more than twenty years, the military man had been presented as a model by the revolutionaries and had been an object of adulation under the Empire. In France, as in Prussia where York's reforms had begun to open the way for commoners to earn an officer's commission and to gain appointments to higher functions, the people had believed in social promotion by the "red," the military uniform. Promotions to the junior officer level permitted a degree of social advancement, from which the middle class profited more than the peasant or the craftsman, and the ancien-régime noble more than the bourgeois. A gulf was often apparent between officers risen from the ranks and those who came from the schools and enjoyed rapid promotion.

An entire "ardent, pale, and nervous" generation was brought up focused exclusively on the glory of arms. Thousands of children who had been conceived between two battles and educated in the secondary schools to the sound of drums stopped short to look at one another. As Musset wrote in *La confession d'un enfant du siècle:* "They flexed their puny muscles. From time to time their blood-stained fathers appeared, picked them up to their gold-bedecked chests, then put them down again and got back on their horses. . . . And if they should die, what of it? Death was so beautiful then, so grand, so magnificent in its purple smoke!"

Peace came and "seated an anxious younger generation on top of a world in ruins." The young had hoped to participate in the exaltation created by an epic. What followed that epic no longer offered them more than a mediocre life as a shopkeeper or merchant. Behind this *mal de siècle* that gripped an entire generation lay the end of the myth of the soldier. Romanticism replaced the romance of idealized war.

Notes

1. Roland Mousnier with Ernest Labrousse, *Le XVIIIe siècle* (1953; Paris: Quadrige, Presses Universitaires de France 1984), 98.

Bibliography

France

Bertaud, Jean-Paul. *La révolution armée: Les soldats citoyens et la Révolution Française.* Les hommes et l'histoire. Paris: Laffont, 1979. Available in English as *The Army of the French Revolution: From Citizen-Soldiers to Instrument of Power.* Translated by R. B. Palmer. Princeton: Princeton University Press, 1988.

Bertaud, Jean-Paul, and Daniel Reichel, eds. *L'armée et la guerre.* Vol. 3 of *Atlas de la Révolution,* edited by Serge Bonin and Claude Langlois. Paris: École des Hautes Études en Sciences Sociales, 1987–93.

Corvisier, André. *L'armée française de la fin du XVIIᵉ siècle au Ministère de Choiseul: Le soldat.* 2 vols. Paris: Presses Universitaires de France, 1964.

Léonard, Émile G. *L'armée et ses problèmes au XVIIIᵉ siècle.* Paris: Plon, 1958.

Rothenberg, Gunther Erich. *The Art of Warfare in the Age of Napoleon.* Bloomington: Indiana University Press, 1978.

Scott, Samuel F. *The Response of the Royal Army to the French Revolution: The Role and Development of the Line Army, 1787–1793.* Oxford: Clarendon Press, 1978.

Italy

Actes du Colloque Napoléon et l'Europe. Special issue, *Rivista di studi napoleonici* 1 (1988).

Brancaccio, Nicola. *L'esercito del vecchio Piemonte.* 2 vols. Rome: L'amministrazione della guerra, 1922–23.

Pieri, Piero. *Guerra e politica negli scrittori italiani.* Milan: Ricciardi, 1955.

Quazza, Guido. *Le riforme in Piemonte nella prima metà del Settecento.* Collezione storico del Risorgimento italiano, 3, nos. 51–52. 2 vols. Modena: Società tipografica editrice Modenese, 1957.

Zaghi, Carlo. *L'Italia di Napoleone dalla Cisalpina al Regno. Storia d'Italia.* Vol. 13, 539–64. Turin: UTET, 1986.

Germany

Barker, Thomas M. "Military Entrepreneurship and Absolutism: Habsburg Models." *Journal of European Studies* 4 (1974): 19–42.

———. "Officers' Recruitment in the Habsburg Army of the Seventeenth and Early Eighteenth Centuries." In *Recrutement, mentalités, sociétés.* Colloque international d'histoire militaire, Montpellier, 1974. Montpellier: Université Paul-Valéry, 1975.

Büsch, Otto. *Militärsystem und Sozialleben im alten Preussen, 1713–1807.* Berlin: W. de Gruyter, 1962.

Duffy, Charles. "Recruitment and Mentality in the Army of Maria Theresa (1740–1780)." In *Recrutement, mentalités, sociétés.* Colloque international d'histoire militaire, Montpellier, 1974. Montpellier: Université Paul-Valéry, 1975.

Redlich, Fritz. *The German Military Enterpriser and his Work Force.* 2 vols. Wiesbaden: F. Steiner, 1964.

Spain

Diccionario bibliográfico de la guerra de Independencia española. 3 vols. Madrid: Servicio geográfico del ejérjito, 1944–52.

Estudios de la guerra de Independencia. II Congreso histórico internacional de la guerra de Independencia y su época, Zaragoza. 1944–52.

Great Britain

Fortescue, Sir John William. *A History of the British Army.* 13 vols. London, 1910–35. New York: AMS Press, 1976.

Sweden

Nordmann, Claude J. *Grandeur et liberté de la Suède, 1660–1792*. Travaux du Centre de recherches sur la civilisation de l'Europe moderne, 9. Paris and Louvain: Béatrice-Nauwelaerts, 1971.

General

Clausewitz, Karl von. *Vom Kriege*. 3 vols. Berlin: F. Dümmler, 1832–34. Available in English as *On War*. Edited and translated by Michael Howard and Peter Paret. Princeton: Princeton University Press, 1976.

Corvisier, André. *Armées et sociétés en Europe de 1494 à 1798*. Paris: Presses Universitaires de France, 1976. Available in English as *Armies and Societies in Europe, 1494–1798*. Translated by Abigail T. Siddall. Bloomington: Indiana University Press, 1979.

Hughes, B. P. *Firepower: Weapons Effectiveness on the Battlefield, 1630–1850*. London: Arms and Armour Press, 1974.

Jomini, Baron Henri. *Histoire critique et militaire des guerres de la Révolution*. 15 vols. 4 atlases. Paris, 1820–24.

———. *Précis de l'art de la guerre*. 1837. Paris, 1977. Available in English as *The Art of War*. Translated by G. H. Mendell and W. P. Craighill. New ed. The West Point Military Library. Westport, Conn.: Greenwood Press, 1971.

3 / The Businessman

Louis Bergeron

In the age of the Enlightenment was there a specific figure who could be called a "businessman"? Admittedly, production, exchange, and the people involved in them lay at the heart of some of the major debates of the eighteenth century—on freedom of commerce and labor; on the *négociant* (a generic term that included the full range of people in trade and commerce), his place in the social hierarchy, and his ennoblement through commerce; or on the need to reassess the values of labor and earned wealth. Moreover, a noted biography of Christophe-Philippe Oberkampf written some fifteen years ago by Serge Chassagne has the apparently positive subtitle, "A Capitalist Entrepreneur in the Age of the Enlightenment."[1] Still, the Enlightenment does not seem, in and of itself, to have had any direct influence on either the structure or the culture of this socioprofessional group. The real causes of its transformation are to be sought elsewhere, in technological and economic change, new ways of organizing work, and the new conditions created by the French Revolution.

The *négociant* or *marchand* who traded in merchandise, commercial instruments, or coinable and coined metals, or who on occasion used resources not tied up in exchange transactions to accumulate credit or make a number of other investments to complement his holdings, thus operating in ways approaching banking, remained substantially just as he had been from the end of the Middle Ages and the time when the voyages of discovery and the first colonial economies expanded world commerce. The eighteenth century might seem to be the golden age of this social type, thanks to a lively increase in intercontinental exchange and the thriving fortunes, described in a number of monographs, of the bourgeoisie of port cities from Marseilles to Bordeaux and Nantes, from Bristol to London, and from Amsterdam to Hamburg. The eighteenth century was certainly the time of the most thoroughgoing codification of merchant culture. Basel, the example we shall examine here, was a city set in a region that had long been at the hub of international exchange on the European continent and that became one of its most dynamic centers of early industrialization.

What did the writers of the age consider necessary for a successful career as a merchant in a major commercial center?[2] The question needs to be asked because the culture of the late-eighteenth-century merchant was the common trunk onto which the traits of the entrepreneurs of the following generations were grafted. This culture was extremely broad and very open; it was both encyclopedic and practical, general and technical—the result of both knowledge and experience acquired over a long span of time.

As one contemporary put it, the merchant had to know his merchandise; bookkeeping and the calculation of exchange rates; negotiation procedures; commercial language and its technical terms; foreign languages; proper spelling; moneys, weights, and measures and their equivalents; commercial marks; the major manufactories; geography; the commercial customs of the places in which he did business; navigation; the postal system; and land, maritime, and commercial law.[3] As if this were not enough, the merchant should make good contacts; frequent the more important fairs regularly; keep up with current happenings through the press, private correspondence, and business trips; and verify the financial solidity of his clients.

For another contemporary, he must speak proper German and have a fine writing hand (long a decisive criterion for engaging a clerk in a commercial house); he should also have a good knowledge of French and Italian and know some Latin for juridical reasons; he should cultivate his epistolary style, have some notions of statistics, history, law, natural sciences, and agriculture; he should draw up periodic balance sheets and inventories.[4] The two differ in one respect: only the second recommends that the merchant take physical exercise and develop an interest in letters and the fine arts.

Thanks to reconstructions of tens of careers, we can gain a concrete notion of how the future merchant was trained. His formation began toward the age of fifteen, when he was put into a commercial apprenticeship regulated by a contract between his parents and a merchant. This apprenticeship period lasted a minimum of three years, more often four or five, and it might be prolonged, without contract, to a total of seven or eight. In the Basel area the best places for finding commercial apprenticeships, aside from Basel itself, were Geneva, Lyons, and, less often, Strasbourg, Frankfurt, or Paris.

At about twenty years of age, the young man moved on to the next step in his formation: a tour of the region, or *Bildungsreise*. This was a cultural voyage that would take him to various commercial centers within the area of Basel's commercial relations: Frankfurt, Ulm, Augsburg, Geneva, and towns in Alsace, Lorraine, Burgundy, and Franche-Comté. His travels might range much farther to touch on the principal countries of Europe. Out of a sample of sixty-two cases, we note forty-nine sojourns in France, twenty-nine in Holland and the Austrian Netherlands, twenty-eight in Germany, seventeen in England, and only ten in Italy. Trips to eastern Europe were rare: the limits of these voyages of exploration were Vienna and Hungary, Leipzig, Berlin, Danzig, and Königsberg. Quite exceptionally a trip included Russia. What did the young man spend his time doing on such trips? He observed commercial life, paid visits to his father's business contacts, made contacts of his own for future use, and visited the most notable local curiosities— palaces, gardens, castles, and churches. Young merchants from Basel who went to Paris hastened to Versailles. There, thanks to contacts in high places and a generous distribution of tips, he might attend a royal meal. On one such occasion in 1701, a young merchant had an opportunity to observe Louis XIV: "A monstrosity," he reported, "evoking Mongolia more than the West." The king had wine dribbling down his cheeks; he gobbled down an extraordinary quantity of food, which he ate with his fingers, ignoring the gold flatware set before him; he was nearly toothless. Another young man from Basel who was visiting the apartments of the dauphin was summarily thrown out of the palace in 1757 for having accidentally damaged a large landscape painting that the dauphin was copying.

After his educational tour, the young man might not return immediately to Basel, choosing to complete his education by taking employment for a few years as a clerk in another commercial center. This custom seems to have been tied to the professional code of the Basel merchants, which prohibited apprentices from passing directly into the service of another house, a measure that worked to guard business secrets but forced the young to seek work in another city for three or four years. The length of these *Wanderjahre* generally meant that the young merchant married relatively late, at closer to thirty than twenty years of age. By that time working on his own, the merchant—according to the same sample—kept informed through private correspondence and by reading journals, which tended to be printed in commercial centers.

The greatest change in the culture of the "entrepreneur," in the broadest sense of the term and as distinguished from the culture of the "generalist" whose formative years we have just seen, seems to me to have come in the latter half of the eighteenth century as a result of developments in the early stages of modern industrial enterprise. The distinctive signs of the appearance of modern industry can be seen, first, in early forms of a labor force concentrated in units of production (by gathering workers in proto-factories or by means of commercial control over a large number of dispersed workers); and second, in an increasing technological specialization of manufacturing procedures and tools that obliged the proprietor-entrepreneur (well before the age of the engineer) to broaden his expertise if he wanted to avoid total dependence on specialists whom he would have to bring in at great expense. A third sign was the need for a new sort of information about the market and consumers, and for new ways to predict future demand, given that the new manufactured articles did not necessarily respond to the same mechanisms that had regulated the sale of traditional commercial products. The merchant who had become a manufacturer had to have a feeling for new ways to organize work and command men; he needed not only a different technical culture, but decisiveness and a "nose" for new products and clienteles backed by a penchant for innovation, calculation, and psychology.

The manufacturer in a changing eighteenth century was no mythical being arrived from beyond; he was often a merchant who diversified his activities, a wealthy peasant who had moved on to trading in agricultural products or processing them on an industrial scale, or an inventive and lucky artisan. Nonetheless, this new sort of businessman might also be the product of the migration of qualified workers, techniques, or capital from England, Wallonia, southern Germany, or northern Switzerland. Often, a textile manufacturer of calicos and other cottons, a chemicals manufacturer, or an industrialist in metallurgy had already had a highly successful career as an entrepreneur somewhere else than his birthplace. Another theoretical model suggests that a spirit of enterprise was sparked or stimulated by the circulation of cultural influences in places that lay at the crossroads of trade. In the east of France this was surely the case in the region of southern Alsace and the Jura Mountains, between Mulhouse and Montbéliard, a region bordering on Switzerland, Germany, and France and a contact zone for the languages, religious confessions, and complementary cultures of the Rhine Valley. It is our good fortune to have texts and studies that permit us to trace the rise of modern industry in that area, but one might equally well trace its genesis in the Caux region, in the environs of Lille, or at Ghent, Verviers, Paris, and elsewhere.

A good place to begin is with the brief but suggestive autobiography of Jean Zuber the elder (born 1772, active from 1791 to 1835), the founder of a famous wallpaper manufactory at Rixheim, near Mulhouse.[5] In this text, written in his old age for the instruction of his children, Zuber states: "Happiness and the consideration of men can have no other bases, aside from God's blessing, than in assiduous and conscientious labor. May my descendants always observe this precious rule." Be that as it may, this text is also valuable as evidence that, as Serge Chassagne says, "one clearly could not improvise one's way to being an entrepreneur." It also provides a "real-life" example of cultural transition from the traditional merchant to the modern industrial entrepreneur, a transition that in this case occurred in the middle of a period of instability, both in France and throughout Europe. The old methods of training and apprenticeship still pertained; the essential qualities of the successful merchant remained a solid character, moral rigor, and quick and accurate judgment of commercial and political situations. Henceforth, however, the budding entrepreneur also needed other and technical capacities, notably, an understanding of manufacturing procedures and a knowledge of mechanical tools. He also needed management skills and a gift for commanding men, just as if the manufacturer had become an army officer with civilian troops under his orders.

Jean Zuber was the son of a master cloth manufacturer. He was allied by marriage to the Schmaltzer family—even before 1750 one of the founding families of the Mulhouse textile industry—a connection that brought him membership in a solid network of kinship and solidarity within the microcosm of the craftsmen and merchants of the little republic. The city school taught him little more than the rudiments of writing and arithmetic, but two uncles took over from a negligent father and, when it proved impossible to hire a tutor or send young Jean to school outside Mulhouse, they sent him to a private school. Zuber states: "A kindly old man . . . the founder of a famous method of writing . . . gave me my first French lessons. I did my best to imitate his fine hand." Zuber was eleven at the time, and to help his mother he spent his after-school hours "making linen ties, which were used by the laundries to tie down the lengths of cotton cloth on the fields"—an occupation that helped him to acquire both a sense of the price of labor and direct experience with manual work. At thirteen, he had the good luck to share in the lessons given to a small number of boys "of good family" by a vicar recently named to the town, an "excellent teacher" and a man who was his friend for life and who exerted an undeniable spiritual influence on him. At the same time, young Zuber saved up to buy a spinet, then a small organ (which he repaired himself), paying for lessons by copying out scores for his music teacher. The length of the passages in his journal devoted to such matters shows how important he considered this artistic self-education to have been for the personal equilibrium of a future industrialist and businessman.

Zuber's formal studies ended at this point. At the age of fifteen, he began a four-year apprenticeship with Heilmann, Blech & Co, one of the oldest manufactories of *indiennes* ("Indian cloth" or calico), founded in 1764. He states: "A young apprentice . . . was expected to be the first to arrive every morning. He swept the office floors, did all the errands in town, carried letters and packages, then copied everything that was written in the office. . . . An elderly clerk . . . befriended me and helped me in everything." A Schlumberger cousin, the son of one of the partners in the firm, initiated Zuber "into the mysteries of double-entry bookkeeping and exchange transactions." Once his apprenticeship had ended, he was offered a chance to stay another year as a clerk, at 600 livres a year, while he waited to find "a good position." The French Revolution did him an enormous service: one of his tasks was to ride on horseback to neighboring towns to exchange the promissory notes that had been received from buyers for cash to pay the workers. As he was riding to Guebwiller "one Sunday . . . on a superb summer morning," he met Nicolas Dollfus. This man had opened a wallpaper factory in Dornach in 1790 and had engaged Laurent Malaine, a painter who specialized in flowers and who had previously worked in the Gobelins tapestry works, paying him the comfortable annual salary of 4,000 livres, plus 10 percent of the profits. Dollfus hired Jean Zuber on a four-year contract, and, turning his back on his father's profession of weaving, Zuber entered an industry with a bright future and a rapidly expanding market.

This new turn of events enabled Zuber to take a training voyage, something that his education as a merchant had lacked. In reality, however, it was his first professional trip (he was eighteen at the time), and, unlike the typical travels of young merchants from Basel, its itinerary was strictly defined by the commercial needs of the firm: his task was to explore possibilities for selling wallpaper all over the Italian Peninsula. We know that Mulhouse had few contacts with Italy because Jean Zuber had great difficulty finding anyone in the city who could teach him the rudiments of Italian. There are two intertwined themes in his report on the trip (November 1791 to June 1792). First, he was obsessed with obtaining orders, but Italy proved only a mediocre market and he found little interest in imported wallpaper. Second, his lively aesthetic and social sensitivity helped him to learn the language quickly, and he proved skillful in making friends among families who could provide him with introductions. He was also highly receptive to new things whose fascination he had not even imagined: the episcopal library at Saint Gall; the passage over the Alps by the Splügen Pass and the descent to Lake Como; the cathedral in Milan; and life in the courts of Parma, Modena, Tuscany, Rome, and Naples (the high points of which were for him the Teatro San Carlo and the crater of Vesuvius). He returned by way of Trieste, Venice, Genoa, and Turin. A second voyage (November 1792 to May 1794) in wartime, took Zuber from Italy to Corsica and to the Iberian Peninsula, where he followed the coast to Bilbao before returning to Barcelona by land and to Italy by sea. His travels gave the young merchant an opportunity to face dangers of all sorts—meteorological, military, and political—which explains why, a few years later (August to October 1796), he did not hesitate to travel in southern Germany when it was a war theater. Going from Frankfurt to Cologne, Kassel, Hannover, Hamburg, Lübeck, and Leipzig, he combined a business trip with a honeymoon, both in order to save money and out of professional obligation.

Between trips and after 1797, when he became a partner in the Dollfus firm, Jean Zuber worked in the workshops and shifted his interests from being a salesman and merchant to being an entrepreneur passionately involved in the manufacturing side of the industry. While still a salesman, his employers made a decision from which Zuber was to profit greatly. They moved the manufactory to Rixheim, a town just outside Mulhouse in French territory, where they bought a superb commandery that had been declared national property. In this way, even before Mulhouse became French again in 1798, the company found a way to circumvent the customs block that had hampered business development in that little republic.

The move to Rixheim in 1797 allowed Zuber to demonstrate his full talents as manager of the workshops. He organized the workspace and the workers' lodgings, installed the equipment (notably, forty-eight long workbenches for printing the paper from plates), and set up a "color

kitchen"—a chemical laboratory that was the domain of a color specialist recruited in Bern. "This colorist," Zuber wrote, "knew how to obtain
greens and blues from copper precipitate better than anyone else.
Thanks to him, we succeeded in producing the beautiful meadow-grass
green that was long one of our principal articles and brought us fine
profits." Zuber, who had by then become a 30-percent partner in the
business with "rights of common property," was motivated both by a
sense of vocation and by personal ambition. "I had identified so completely with that industry that I could no longer separate myself from it,"
he wrote. His only thought, when sales picked up, was to become the sole
proprietor of a firm for which he had high ambitions. When his partners' poor management of a warehouse that the firm had opened in
Paris nearly sent the company into bankruptcy, it gave him the opportunity he was waiting for. Early in 1802, when the company was about to
be dissolved, he wrested control out of their hands, and in 1803 he
brought the liquidation to an honorable conclusion. At this point he
wrote triumphantly in his autobiography: "Now the sole proprietor of
the fine industry to which I had given all my energies for eleven years
and in which I hoped, in all confidence, to find secure profits, I could
finally breathe freely."

In 1804 he began to give free rein to his audacity as an entrepreneur
and innovator. He decided to offer a new product that would give him a
foothold in the French and international markets: scenic wallpapers
that depict a panoramic landscape covering the four walls of a room.
Nearly two centuries later, such papers are still being printed and sold as
a luxury item. Zuber hired a new painter from Paris and commissioned
him to paint Swiss landscapes, which were soon followed by a Hindustani
landscape. The firm won a silver medal at the Exposition of National
Industrial Products organized in Paris in 1806. While in Paris, Zuber recruited a chemist whom he brought to Rixheim to set up a color research laboratory (the scenic papers required as many as 250 different
hues). These papers, which the landscape painter Mongin, a pupil of
Doyen's, had in fact inaugurated some time earlier for a Parisian wallpaper manufacturer, became the stock-in-trade of the young industrialist in Mulhouse.

All the traits of character that we have seen in Zuber combined to
make him an archetype of the early modern entrepreneur: his careful
pretesting of the market (a task for which he had been well prepared by
his years as a salesman); his determination to bring the management of
capital and the direction of manufacturing together in his own hands;

his constant concern to use technological advances to improve the articles he offered; his fine sense for the public's taste and flair for locating new market niches for wallpaper—all catalyzed by a passion for hard work and a deep love of his trade. One might add to this list a keen grasp of economics, something we can see clearly in his decision (in 1805) to complement his workshops for designing, engraving, and printing wallpaper with a paperworks that he bought from a merchant family in Basel. As he stated: "We were finally able to realize our longstanding desire to make ourselves the paper we need. Up until then, the paper that we brought in from various sources was often substandard."

Throughout the nineteenth century, the founder's spirit of innovation continued to bring success to the firm as it constantly sought out new "effects." Technical superiority put Zuber's firm at the top of the profession, obliging Paris and Lyons to share their earlier primacy with Rixheim. From the moral viewpoint as well, Zuber fulfilled the portrait of the head of the firm who exerted a dynamic influence on all members of his family, in good times and bad, and on the "extended family" of technicians and workers (nearly all of whom were specialized) who felt themselves close to the family, with whom they formed what the *patron* called "our colony." Zuber's authority was avowedly paternal, but it was based on his commercial success and his proven professional competence.

The history of a near contemporary of Jean Zuber's, the Paris brewer Antoine-Joseph Santerre,[6] confirms this impression of the emergence, in this borderline moment between the age of the Enlightenment and the changes brought by the Revolution, of a new generation of businessmen who sought economic success through an increased emphasis on technology. Although Santerre belonged, like Jean Zuber, to a lineage of master craftsmen and to the crafts world, his family had risen, professionally and socially, and had moved from near Cambrai and the Thiérache region in northern France to Paris, where members of the family ran a number of sizable establishments. In the 1780s, Santerre himself belonged to an elite of entrepreneurs of the Faubourg Saint-Antoine, where a neighbor named Réveillon was a wallpaper manufacturer.

Santerre's training was less complex than that of Jean Zuber, since he went directly from secondary school to an apprenticeship in his father's brewery. The two men were alike, however, in their curiosity about technical matters and their interest in providing enlightened customers with a new product of high quality. Neither man had reached the stage—for Santerre, in the brewing of beer; for Zuber, in the fabrication of delicate colors for the printing of wallpaper—of a cooperation between scientific research and its industrial applications. Both men belonged to a world of empirical knowledge and business "recipes" dictated by experience and observation in which the brewer's "kitchen" resembled the colorist's laboratory—a world that left room for personal taste, intuition, and a savoir faire at least in part subjective. Both men were also fascinated by novelty. For Santerre, this meant beer *à l'anglaise*—English beer—which he did his utmost to copy. For Zuber it meant from the start borrowing artists from Paris and samples from Lyons. They were not far from the sort of industrial espionage that was practiced for the mechanization of the cotton industry or improvements in steel manufacturing. In Santerre's case, observation meant an aptitude for judging proportions and evaluating grains and flour from their aspect, for knowing what consistency an infusion should have, and, above all, for recognizing perfect fermentation by its "look" and its signs. Experimentation and attempts to surpass previous performance depended, for instance, on the use of a thermometer to control the temperature of the malting process and an aerometer to ascertain the density of well-water. Santerre, like Zuber, personally controlled everything from the supply of raw materials (family connections in northern France assured him good shipments of hops and barley) to the sale of his beer.

In the Faubourg Saint-Antoine, as Zuber had in Rixheim, Santerre employed a few tens of workers. In both cases this was enough to raise the question of authority in work and production. "You have to be the inspector of everyone, and without pause, if you want to succeed completely," Santerre wrote. It is true that the wage-worker milieu was in many ways less disciplined in Paris than it was in southern Alsace: regularity on the job, stability of employment, and respect for the person and the property of the employer. Both men took an interest in their firms' buildings and in using space rationally. Finally, both were interested in transmitting a legacy consisting not only of their wealth and their holdings but also of their technical and managerial experience. To bolster the continuity of a family industrial endeavor and pass it on to the next generation (a move that was for them the normal procedure), each man, toward the end of his life, wrote a text. For Santerre, who died in 1809, this was a book dedicated to his sons, *L'art du brasseur* (1807), a remarkably complete work that deals with every aspect of brewing.

The age of the Enlightenment and the Revolution thus appear as a time of diversification and increasing complexity in the culture of entrepreneurs, both because the merchant, the trader, or the trader-banker at times added to his usual activities those of the industrial entrepreneur, and because the manufacturer tended to emerge as a distinct personality. This is true even if (in France at least) he often attempted to hide his true identity as a manufacturer under the seemingly more prestigious guise of the *négociant* or the *propriétaire.*

This diversification was the product of a requisite acquisition of supplementary skills, but it was also connected with local sociocultural contexts that favored, in varying degree, a transition from one type of capitalism to another or that gave rise to manufacturing cultures. For centuries, the realm of business transactions had displayed a remarkable unity of techniques, practices, and mentalities, in particular at the level of international trade. This unity was accentuated by ethnic mixing (as in the foreign "colonies" that existed in all the major port cities of Europe). Now those old ways seemed to give way to an age of more varied, more regional industrial cultures. This helps to explain all sorts of contrasts: some regions show a continuity between a proto-industrial system for the organization of labor and a modern form of industrialization, while others show a clear break; in some regions or nations industrialization was more dynamic than in others or occurred sooner than in others. At the end of the eighteenth century, when new forms of production already coexisted with the older forms, the region on which we have concentrated here and that bordered France, Germany, and Switzerland provides a striking example of just such a cultural diversity.

A recent study of the industrial dynasty of the Japy family of Montbéliard, a small city not far from Mulhouse, provides an interesting view of the emergence of a quite different milieu with a strong industrial culture.[7]

Frédéric Japy, the founder of the dynasty, was born in the village of Beaucourt. His family, who had long been farmers and stockmen, enjoyed a secure position; Japy's father was a blacksmith. In any event, the family was wealthy enough to send Frédéric to school for several years in Montbéliard, at the time a principality under the dual control of Württemberg and France, where there were good Protestant schools. Originally largely rural, Montbéliard had been infiltrated by industry— textile works and metalworking concerns of all sorts from forges to firms that made small mechanical devices, notably clocks—all of which was controlled by the merchant-manufacturers of Montbéliard. The second stage in Frédéric Japy's formation was a sojourn (around 1770) in Le Locle on the other side of the Jura Mountains, first with one Perrelet, then with Jeanneret-Gris, a man who came from a family of inventors whose specialties were precision mechanisms and improved watchmaking techniques. On his return to Montbéliard, Japy made his entry into the crafts production system, setting up a small shop for making clock and watch parts and selling his unassembled mechanisms at La Chaux-de-Fonds. He joined the *chonffe* (guild) of Saint-Eloi, the "society that strikes the hammer on the anvil," and in 1773 he married the daughter of an Anabaptist farmer, thus providing him contacts with a milieu of strong communitarian traditions.

In 1776–77, when he was not yet thirty years old, Frédéric Japy made a radical move. He bought out Jeanneret-Gris (who, Pierre Lamard tells us, was "defeated by the inertia of the artisanal world"), paying him 600 louis d'or for his machines and inventions, and he commissioned Jeanneret-Gris to make him ten machines for manufacturing the eighty-three parts that his clock and watch mechanisms required. These machine tools enabled Japy to move on to mass production, and their simplicity of operation meant that he could include women and the elderly in his workforce and produce his articles more cheaply. The construction in 1777 of a new workplace is no less symbolic of an entry into a new sphere than the acquisition of machines. Japy purchased a rocky piece of infertile, hence inexpensive, land on a hill near Beaucourt, and he used stone quarried from his plot to construct a building capable of housing some fifty specialized workers. (He also sent out piece-work that was done in workers' homes.) When he added assembly and completion of the finished product—something that had been the province of the clockmakers of Montbéliard—to manufacturing the mechanisms, he placed himself outside the guild system and in competition with it. In fact, he offered it "a devastating competition."

Frédéric Japy got his start as an entrepreneur and innovator during the years of the French Revolution and the Republic. The new order brought him nothing but advantages, from the abolition of limitations on the freedom to work to the acquisition of properties confiscated from Prince Frédéric-Eugène of Württemberg after 1792, which allowed Japy to acquire handsome, solid buildings that he could use for future expansion of his workshops or as collateral for loans. His patriotism led him to name his last daughter, born in 1793, Jacobine-Angélique, and he was later one of the first chevaliers of the Legion of Honor named in the district of Belfort. Japy's library contained not only scientific and technical dictionaries but the *Encyclopédie* and works of Montesquieu, Voltaire, and Rousseau.

The years of the continental blockade brought Japy an opportunity to diversify his production. When competition from English hardware dried up, he began to manufacture wood screws, a product that became a mainstay of his company's activities and that he sold in Germany and throughout France, along with a full range of other products—bolts, hooks, eye-bolts, nails, pins, chains, and buckles. Diversification was for tens of years to remain the keystone of the firm's prosperity. It was in the same early years of the nineteenth century that Japy, feeling that he was getting on in years, set up a system by which his three eldest sons would succeed him at the helm of his business. In doing so, he showed a significant concern for the future of a firm that was becoming detached from his person to become a moral entity in succeeding generations.

Japy's originality in terms of a manufacturer's culture lies elsewhere, however—in his special and precocious attempt to devise a system of relations in the workplace that would guarantee the efficiency and regularity of manufacturing operations, something that is the prime obsession of all entrepreneurs.

Beaucourt differed from Rixheim in that Japy faced the difficult problem of obtaining an industrial rate of production from a peasant workforce. A first difficulty was that the entire labor force he required was not be found in the immediate locality and had to be recruited at a certain distance; a second problem was to lure workers away from home piece-work and crafts methods. Japy understood that in order to prevent this new sort of wage workers from rebelling or quitting, he had to find a new way to organize work and to invent a new sort of life capable of giving the workers a sense of well-being and security. This should not be seen as prefiguring the idea, typical of the nineteenth century, of encouraging workers to settle in one place as a way to increase worker production rates. The inspiration and the practice of the "Japy system," which developed as the enterprise grew, seem to have been patterned on the lifestyle of rural Anabaptist families and on the organization of aid as Japy had observed it in the guilds—*chonffes* or *Zünfte*—of Montbéliard or in the valleys of the Swiss Jura around Le Locle. This system emphasized organization imbued with a very strong sense of solidarity and based in collective customs and rules. In short, Japy was able to adapt old formulas to a new situation and to make them evolve under later developments.

The Japy system was neither a utopian project nor a foretaste of the later *familistère,* a form of workers' production cooperative. In its first form it evoked the traditional structures of a life centered on religion. Japy had a building constructed with a central portion three stories high (plus another story under the mansard roof), where the work spaces were located. Wings to either side of this center building each contained a kitchen and a dining room on the ground floor and bedrooms and dormitories above. The day's schedule covered the entire day, not just the working hours, and it was followed under the watchful eye of the head of the firm, who was also the head of the family. "I want my workers to make one and the same family with me and mine," Frédéric Japy stated. "My workers must be my children and, at the same time, my fellow operators." Work, preceded by breakfast, began at sunrise; at one o'clock in the afternoon it stopped for one hour; and it continued until eight o'clock in the evening. Supper was then served, presided over by Frédéric Japy, *le Père,* who sat at a big table surrounded by all the male workers, while his wife, Suzanne-Catherine Amstoutz, *la Maman,* did the same for the female workers in the other wing of the building. She and their daughters did the household tasks. The provisions came from farms on lands that Japy had acquired, and a shop in the building sold articles for everyday needs. The owner and his wife took charge of both elementary education and religious education: every Sunday, after the evening meal, Frédéric Japy would read a chapter from the Bible, followed by prayer. As a matter of course the workers' conduct and morality came under his supervision. He offered guaranteed benefits to cover sickness, old age, widowhood, and burial. The staff grew from fifty workers in 1777 to five hundred in 1802 (the village of Beaucourt had a total population of only 263 inhabitants in 1791).

Even if we take it into account that these figures include workers who did piece-work at home, this centralized and personalized system was certainly close to its limits of viability. The system began to fall apart in 1806, when Japy's three elder sons took over joint direction of the firm. Moreover, the diversification of the products that they manufactured gradually led to a breakup of production among a number of sites, thus limiting the risks of an excessive concentration of workers in one place. I might note in passing that the history of the Japy firm is a perfect illustration of the institution, as early as the eighteenth century, of a system of capitalistic production (a system violently felt to be capitalistic by the craftsmen of the traditional sort, as shown by riots aimed at Japy in 1801) that was to have widespread success in nineteenth-century France. It was a system in which the firm reached out to rural areas to seek available reserves of manpower, thus setting up industries in the countryside in units that could be called big if compared to the craft unit but that for some time continued to be of quite limited size. It was also a system that dovetailed the rural world and the industrial world, uprooting fewer people and limiting urbanization.

On the human and ethical plane the Japy system in its first thirty years was indeed a paternalism—one might even say, at the risk of tautology, a patriarchal paternalism. Historians have been in the habit of using the term "paternalism" to cover an entire set of policies, practices, and institutions in business initiatives that later, in a wide variety of places and sectors, accompanied the growth of industry and became an integral part of a genuine business strategy, even when the industrial firm strove to retain something of the family spirit of what was already viewed as its "golden age." In Japy's case, however, we see paternalism at its birth, as a product of the late eighteenth century, when paternalistic methods looked much more toward the past than toward the future and were invested with the mission of effecting a "soft" transition to industrialization. As Pierre Lamard has rightly remarked, "The paternalism of Beaucourt . . . constitutes . . . one of the few links between the crafts world of the eighteenth century and the more industrialized society of the nineteenth." He adds, "A continuity in social practices undoubtedly guaranteed a delicate transition"—a transition that worked to renew the lease on life of a system of material and moral protection that operated particularly effectively in the Montbéliard area, where "a Germanic version of *compagnonnage*" (French journeymen's craft association) led to "a strong awareness of a sense of solidarity." Such hypotheses support the notions of continuity rather than rupture and of heterogeneity between the two major stages in industrialization. Nonetheless, it should be noted that in the new socioindustrial culture, relations between employer and employee were closed behind the plant walls, while in the corporative structure they were immersed in a more open and more transparent urban structure.

Until now, historians have insisted on the bifurcation that took place during the second half or the last quarter of the eighteenth century between two professional and cultural categories in the small world of businessmen—between the traditional figure of the *négociant* and the new figure of the manufacturer, who is defined above all by his capacity for innovation. This was a way to focus attention on all that the nineteenth century, as it became more and more industrialized, owed to its predecessor.

Whether *négociants* or manufacturers, all businessmen of the century of the Enlightenment and the Revolution of 1789 reacted in the same way to the great ideological debates of the age and to their impact on working conditions and the social status of the group to which they belonged. Those debates turned around the two central notions of liberty and equality, notions whose definition and, even more, whose transfer to practice in institutions and mores eventually pointed to ambiguities and contradictions within the elites who ran the economy.

In principle, the century of the Enlightenment claimed that liberty was the soul of commerce and industry. The battle to liberalize the laws was fought on many fronts: traders and shippers in French port cities fought for the abolition of the monopoly of the companies that held special privileges; the "American" colonists of the Antilles fought against the system of exclusive trade rights that hampered the establishment of direct exchanges between the islands and their partners in the English or Spanish empires; everyone engaged in domestic commerce fought against the maintenance of tolls; merchants, landowners, and farmers joined forces to fight for the free circulation and exportation of grains and cereals.

But the moment the delicate question of customs duties arose, it was clear that French trade and manufacturing interests looked to the eventual triumph of absolute liberalism with fear and trepidation. The famous treaty of 1786 with England set off howls of complaint. The protests in fact arose out of a crisis in entire sectors of the proto-industrial textile business in northwestern France, a crisis echoed in the *cahiers de doléances* that contributed to the broader economic crisis of the end of the ancien régime. On the other hand, when Pierre-Samuel Dupont de Nemours was charged by Vergennes to inquire into the effects of the commercial treaty, he dared to defend it in his "Lettre à la Chambre de Commerce de Normandie" (1788). Manufacturers in Elbeuf also thought they could turn the treaty to their advantage: since their specialty was fine-quality cloth, they hoped to improve their sales across the Channel, given that the English market had no native-made goods of comparable quality. Normandy, whose situation in the lower Seine Valley turned it toward London, had long benefited from a free circulation of men and techniques, and its early industrial take-off had made use of advances introduced by English technicians, many of whom later made a fortune as industrialists. Still, those who saw that free competition might have a stimulating effect in the midterm remained in the minority in relation to a more fearful majority whose dogma it was that commerce and manufacturing had a right to state protection, even to fiscal advantages. Jean-Pierre Hirsch has clearly shown that commerce oscillated between audacity and conservatism and between a desire for independence and a search for a beneficial surveillance.[8] Hirsch finds such deep-seated but contradictory aspirations among men of the business community in Lille, another milieu of precocious industrial development. Soon the revolutionary assemblies followed the monarchy's policies, contravening their own theoretical principles by maintaining defensive tariffs.

The same ballet took place in people's attitudes toward the dilemma of the freedom or the regulation of labor in such matters as leadership among, and supervision of, the workforce; quality control for products; and limitations to the number of business enterprises. Freedom to engage in business, for example, aroused great hopes. This was evident among merchants who, when they turned to manufacturing, went beyond the zones where labor was regulated (essentially, urban areas) to recruit rural workers for cottage industry, but expectations were equally high among the many journeymen who were denied access to master's status. The aspiration to break away from wage earning and set up shop as a small independent proprietor has contributed, from the eighteenth century to our own day, to revolutionary action, eventually becoming a simple mechanism of social promotion or petering out as a mirage or in failure. But freedom of labor also meant increasingly concentrated competition, uncertainty in the quality of manufactured products, and increased volatility and disrespect for discipline in the labor force (a subject for complaint even under the guild regime). Could economic society withstand fragmentation? As soon as the Revolution moved into its downward phase, the most timorous—and these were not only former master workers dispossessed of their monopoly—demanded a return to a degree of corporatism and control and the reestablishment of specific institutions to represent economic interests. Custom and the provisions of a new law were invoked to authorize the regulation of both bankruptcies and work contracts.

For businessmen of the eighteenth century, authority, discipline, and a respect of rules between partners were no less indispensable to prosperity than peace or freedom of initiative for people with capital. This means that for a trader or manufacturer, equality was just as much of a burning question as liberty. How were they to accept the emancipation of the black workers in the colonial plantations? How could one imagine equality of supply and demand in the labor force, or between the proprietor and the worker in the workplace? All of the nineteenth century (and some of the twentieth) was to pass before employers accepted work relations of a democratic type, established by contract, or recognized (for example) the validity and utility of union organization or collective bargaining. Before that happened, employers alternated between accepting open confrontation and deploying a variety of strategies in the hope of reestablishing a nonegalitarian relationship in the workplace where, in the best of instances, the workers' submission was compensated by management's respect for a certain work ethic.

In reality, the businessman or the entrepreneur of the transition period in which the Enlightenment moved into the Revolution faced a doubly uncomfortable situation. He was under pressure on one side from a mounting popular insubordination that arose much earlier, in a city like Paris, than the explosion of the Revolution, while on the other side—that is, from the higher echelons of the social scale—he found it difficult to obtain recognition of his merits. Saint-Simon's ideas found expression in France a good half-century before his followers took over the levers of command, and even before Saint-Simon, a certain Enlightenment discourse on the honor and social utility of men whose capacities, savoir faire, and capital were related to work was in no way representative of the average state of enlightened opinion, still unconverted to that viewpoint.

The businessman's social status is visible in the way ennoblement by royal letters patent functioned during the last decades of the absolute monarchy. The *négociant* worthy of being assimilated into the aristocracy was always someone who, in one way or another, had served the interests and the views of power. A few examples, restricted to the final decade, 1780–89, will illustrate this point. Louis Tourton, a banker who received his letters of ennoblement in 1783, was the administrator of the Caisse d'Escompte, the central discount bank. He belonged to "one of the oldest and most important bourgeois families of Annonay," a family that could boast of including nine notaries since 1551. Tourton had been a director of the Compagnie des Indes for twenty years, and he supplied the French troops in Germany with arms. Papion, the only member of his family not to be ennobled before he received his letters in 1782, and a man allied to "very distinguished families in the magistracy," was director of the royal damask manufactory that had been established in Tours in 1760, a post in which he "gave a living to eight hundred families and kept down untoward expenditures." Delaunay (ennobled in 1785), a merchant in Laval, headed a textile works that made cloth for the navy. Denis Montessuy and the Leleu brothers (ennobled in 1782), Paris merchants, were provisioners for the navy; they also furnished Paris with wheat and administered flour mills in Corbeil. Gamba (ennobled in 1786), a Dunkerque merchant, came from a Piedmontese family that was ennobled by both Emperor Joseph I and the king of Sardinia and was a man who "nobly exercised his profession." There were exceptions: in 1762, a master of the forges of Ruffec was ennobled for having introduced technological improvements in methods for forging and casting iron; and even Oberkampf owed his ennoblement in 1787 to the excellence of his products. In general, however, social promotions arose out of specific uses of wealth and previously established connections with the privileged classes. Men were not ennobled simply for having run their businesses well and amassing a large fortune. Making money was not a title of nobility, and Emperor Napoleon I was guided by the same principles as Louis XV or Louis XVI when it came to selecting notables to fill high-ranking posts and candidates for ennoblement.

This being the case, merchants quite understandably attempted to get around these obstacles by purifying their money through the purchase of an office, for example, as a king's secretary. Out of 1,475 offices of that type sold by the Grande Chancellerie of Paris between 1702 and 1789, 357, or one-quarter, went to merchants. Another indirect road to social promotion was the development of landholdings, thus establishing a de facto relationship with the landed aristocracy. Some scholars still view the French merchant's acquisition of land as the expression of a desire to leave his profession behind him. It would probably be more accurate to interpret it as a way for the businessman to earn a social recognition that his professional virtues alone did not permit him. Land ownership demonstrates yet another continuity in the social operations of the businessman before and after 1789. Is it so astonishing that merchants should have wanted to cut themselves a large share in the sale of properties that had been nationalized when the Constituent Assembly opened the way to a political regime based both on property and on an elective system that covered a large number of posts? With the broadening of his property base, the merchant could consolidate his social prestige and gain access, at least on the local and departmental level, to a number of offices.

The French Revolution opened a large breach in the defenses that, until that time, had limited and delayed the social promotion of the economic elites. One might be tempted to say that the merchants' immediate political gain was greater than the long-term advantages promised by liberalized conditions for the exercise of economic activities. In any event, the Revolution allowed the *négociant* to savor his triumph when he became a full-fledged, rather than a second-class, notable. It is true, however, that when he demanded to be valued first as a landed proprietor his gain came at the price of a loss of identity and financial losses, at times substantial ones, inflicted by political and military events on fortunes and businesses of all sorts. All in all, the Revolution had not overturned everything in the scale of values.[9]

Notes

1. Serge Chassagne, *Oberkampf: Un entrepreneur capitaliste au Siècle des Lumières* (Paris: Aubier, 1980). See also Serge Chassagne, ed., *Une femme d'affaires au XVIIIe siècle: La correspondance de Madame de Maraise, collaboratrice d'Oberkampf* (Toulouse: Privat, 1981).

2. On this topic, see Niklaus Röthlin, *Die Basler Handelspolitik und deren Träger in der zweiten Hälfte des 17. und im 18. Jahrhundert* (Basel and Frankfurt am Main: Helbing & Lichtenhahn, 1986).

3. Rudolf Meyer, *Theoretische Einleitung in die praktische Wechsel- und Warenhandlung* (Hanau, 1782).

4. Jakob Sarasin (1742–1802) owned a library that was among the best furnished with works on the training of the merchant.

5. Jean Zuber the Elder, *Réminiscences et souvenirs de Jean Zuber père* (Mulhouse: Veuve Bader, 1895).

6. See Raymonde Monnier, "Antoine-Joseph Santerre, brasseur et spéculateur foncier," in *La Révolution française et le développement du capitalisme,* Actes du colloque de Lille, 19–21 November 1987, ed. Gérard Gayot and Jean-Pierre Hirsch, *Revue du Nord,* Hors série, collection histoire, 5 (Villeneuve d'Ascq: Revue du Nord, 1989), 333–46.

7. Here and below in this chapter, see Pierre Lamard, *Histoire d'un capital familial au XIXe siècle: Le capital Japy (1777–1910)* (Belfort: Société Belfortaine d'Émulation, 1988); see also Pierre Lamard, "Japy et ses ouvriers au XIXe siècle," *Société d'Émulation de Montbéliard* 81, fasc. 108 (1985 [1986]): 103–33.

8. Jean-Pierre Hirsch, *Les deux rêves du commerce: Entreprise et institution dans la région lilloise (1780–1860)* (Paris: École des Hautes Études en Sciences Sociales, 1991).

9. Louis Bergeron, *Banquiers, négociants et manufacturiers parisiens du Directoire à l'Empire* (Paris: École des Hautes Études en Sciences Sociales; The Hague and New York: Mouton, 1978).

4 / The Man of Letters

Roger Chartier

The entry "Gens de Lettres" in the *Encyclopédie* states that it is an "article by M. de Voltaire."[1] In it Voltaire defines the man of letters by means of two contrasts. He states first: "This name is not given to a man whose knowledge is limited and who cultivates only one genre of literature," and second: "Universal knowledge is no longer within man's reach; the true literati cover various fields, although they cannot do them all." Hence, the man of letters was a modern version of the grammarian of classical antiquity, "not someone who was merely versed in grammar—the basis of all knowledge—but a man familiar with geometry, philosophy, and general and particular history, a man whose special studies were poetry and eloquence." The definition of the man of letters given in the *Encyclopédie* was thus that of an encyclopedist: he was not a scholar who had acquired profound knowledge in a specialized field but a studious man who had some acquaintance with all fields of knowledge.

For Voltaire, then, "letters" were not "literature." His definition is closer to the one given in Furetière's dictionary in 1690 ("*Lettres:* also said of the sciences. . . . One calls *lettres humaines* and, improperly, *belles lettres,* knowing about the Poets and the Orators, whereas true *belles lettres* are Philosophy, Geometry, and the solid sciences") than it is to the definition in Richelet's dictionary, published ten years earlier than Furetière's ("*Les belles lettres:* this is knowledge of the Orators, the Poets, and the Historians"). I might note that the article "Lettres" of the *Encyclopédie* prefers Richelet to Furetière when it distinguishes between "belles lettres or literature" and the "sciences, properly speaking" and between "men of letters, who cultivate only a varied erudition full of amenities" and "those who dedicate themselves to the abstract sciences and [the sciences] of more conspicuous utility." Even though the article states that the sciences and letters share a "linking, connections, and relations of the narrowest sort" and recognizes that "the man attached to the sciences and the man of letters have intimate connections through their common interests and natural needs," it nonetheless establishes a division whose very principle Voltaire rejects. For Voltaire, faithful to the traditional definitions, the man of letters was also a man of science.

Voltaire's man of letters was not a scholar; nor was he a *bel esprit:* "A man of letters is not what we call a wit. One does not need to know philosophy to be a wit, nor does one need to be so learned and cultivated. To be a wit requires above all a brilliant imagination, a mastery of the art of conversation, and wide reading." If men of letters had become for the most part "as much at ease in good society as in their study," that by no means meant that their competence in particular disciplines was less. Quite the contrary: like fashionable people—*gens du monde*—they had wit and took pleasure in the charms of conversation and in parlor games, but above all they were men of letters—that is, men dedicated to study, to reading, and to their *cabinet.* It was thanks to the maintenance of this difference (tempered, however, by the "spirit of the age") that it was thinkable—and praiseworthy—for men of letters both to participate in aristocratic society and be considered superior to their predecessors: "Up to the time of Balzac and Voiture they were not admitted to society; since that time they have become a necessary part of it."

The Philosophical Spirit and Royal Patronage

Two major developments, Voltaire declared, had profoundly transformed the role and the status of men of letters. The first was a conversion of philological criticism to philosophical spirit.

> Formerly, in the sixteenth century and well into the seventeenth, men of letters devoted much time to grammatical criticism of Greek and Latin authors. To their labors we owe dictionaries, correct editions, and commentaries on the masterpieces of antiquity. Today this criticism is no longer so necessary, and has given way to the philosophic spirit. This spirit seems to characterize men of letters; and when it is combined with good taste, it produces a perfect literary man.

Long hemmed in by its focus on the establishment of ancient texts, critical activity moved on to a consideration of beliefs and doctrines. In doing so it "destroyed all the prejudices with which society was afflicted: astrologers' predictions, the divining of magicians, all types of witchcraft, false prodigies, false marvels, and superstitious customs. This philosophy has relegated to the schools thousands of childish disputations which had formerly been dangerous and have now become objects of scorn. In this way men of letters have in fact served the state." The empire of criticism, which was that of *saine philosophie,* had thus subjected not only popular superstitions but also, as this text states between the lines, the dogmas of religion. Here Voltaire's definition at least in part anticipates Kant's remark in the preface to the first edition of *The Critique of Pure Reason* (1781):

> Our age is the age of criticism, to which everything must be subjected. The sacredness of religion, and the authority of legislation, are by many regarded as grounds of exemption from the examination of this tribunal. But, if they are exempted, they become the subjects of just suspicion, and cannot lay claim to sincere respect, which reason accords only that which has stood the test of a free and public examination.[2]

Men of letters were the first jury to judge this "free and public examination."

The second change that Voltaire points out seems paradoxical to a twentieth-century observer in that it couples the independence necessary to men of letters with the protection that royal patronage brought them: "They are ordinarily more independent of mind than other men. Those who were born poor easily find in the endowments established by Louis XIV the means to strengthen this intellectual independence. We no longer encounter, as formerly, those dedicatory epistles offered to vanity by self-interest and servility." For anyone unable to live on his landholdings, his posts, or his income, the pensions and gratifications granted by the prince were the only way to avoid the humiliating dependency of a clientage relation. Far from destroying the critical freedom that was the mark of the man of letters, the sovereign's generosity made that freedom possible because it rescued the less wealthy among them from the tyranny of private protectors.

This explains why Voltaire should celebrate the great king's munificence (which reached beyond the borders of France) in his *The Century of Louis XIV,* published in 1751:

> What gave him the greatest glory in Europe was his liberality, which was unprecedented. The idea was suggested to him by a

conversation with the Duke de Saint-Aignan, who related to him how Cardinal Richelieu had sent presents to certain foreign scholars, who had written in his praise. The king did not wait to be praised, but sure of his desert he bade his ministers, Lyonne and Colbert, make a choice of a number of Frenchmen and foreigners upon whom he wished to confer marks of his generosity.[3]

It also explains Voltaire's criticism, in the Amsterdam edition of the *Dictionnaire philosophique portatif* of 1765, of the ridiculousness and the constraints of private patronage: "Compose odes in praise of Lord Superbus Fatus, madrigals for his mistress; dedicate a book of geography to his porter, and you will be well received. Enlighten men, and you will be crushed."[4]

The demands of private patronage were not the only threat to men of letters. There was another, which struck all who considered letters as a "profession"—that is, an occupation that should enable them to make a living. To be reduced to living by one's pen, to become an "author," was to expose oneself to a number of disagreeable things: the rapacity of the bookseller-publishers, the jealousy of one's peers, and the judgment of fools. Voltaire praised the liberty and tranquility of full financial independence over any professionalization of the writer's craft that might bring an insufferable dependence on the operations of the literary marketplace. He states in "Men of Letters":

> There are many men of letters who do not publish anything. They are probably the happiest of all. They are spared the humiliations that the profession of author sometimes brings with it, as well as the quarrels occasioned by rivalry, partisan spite, and unfounded opinions. They live in greater concord with each other, they enjoy sociability more, they are the judges while the others suffer judgment.[5]

Unlike Duclos in his *Considérations sur les moeurs de ce siècle* (1750) or d'Alembert in his *Essai sur la société des gens de lettres et des grands, sur la réputation, sur les mécènes et sur les récompenses littéraires* (1752), Voltaire's article in the *Encyclopédie* rejects the assimilation of the activity of men of letters to a "profession." Just as the search for aristocratic patronage obliged men of letters to submit to the ridiculous caprices of their protectors, the status of author delivered them over to the capricious demands of the bookseller-publishers and the public, and enmeshed them in the conflicts common to all trade communities.

In several articles written for the *Dictionnaire philosophique* Voltaire tears to pieces those whom he designates as "the unhappy class who write in order to live." Such men eked out a living producing useless writings: "A hundred authors compile to get their bread, and twenty fools extract, criticize, apologize, and satirize these compilations to get bread also, because they have no profession." They fight tooth and nail to get work: "These poor people are divided into two or three bands, and go begging like mendicant friars; but not having taken vows their society lasts only for a few days, for they betray one another like priests who run after the same benefice, though they have no benefice to hope for. But they still call themselves authors!" Letters could not be a craft, and it would have been better if these unfortunate people could have found a good post:

> The misfortune of these men is that their fathers did not make them learn a trade, which is a great defect in modern policy. Every man of the people who can bring up his son in a useful art, and does not, merits punishment. The son of a Mason becomes a Jesuit at seventeen; he is chased from society at four and twenty, because the levity of his manners is too glaring. Behold him without bread! He turns journalist, he cultivates the lowest kind of literature, and becomes the contempt and horror of even the mob. And such as these, again, call themselves authors![6]

The ideal of the man of letters, the negative image of which was given in Voltaire's scathing description of *la canaille de la littérature,* incontrovertibly associated the sovereign's protection and the philosophical spirit. Because it liberated the writer from the obligations of clientage, protected him from the perversions of the market, and recognized true scholars, monarchical patronage as it was instituted by Louis XIV, was a prime condition for men of letters worthy of the name to exercise the independence of their minds freely and without constraint or censorship. Voltaire noted in the 1765 edition of the *Dictionnaire philosophique:* "The literary man is without aid; he resembles the flying fish; if he rises a little, the birds devour him; if he dives, the fishes eat him up." His only recourse lay in the magnanimity of an enlightened prince.

Men of Letters, Academicians, and Pamphleteers

Did the real social world confirm this ideal figure of an independent, well-protected man of letters? There have been several recent studies that have attempted an evaluation and a sociological definition of the French man of letters. The first is Robert Darnton's inventory of the literary population of France as revealed by the lists of authors given in *La France littéraire,* a literary almanac published starting in 1755, which offered information on "all the men of letters who have lived in France from the beginning of the century to the present."[7] The listings in *La France littéraire,* which were based in a broad definition of the man of letters, since anyone who had published anything (not necessarily a book) was listed in the publication, attest, first, to an increase in the number of authors. The 1757 edition gives 1,187 names; in the 1769 edition there are 2,367; the 1784 edition (the last edition of a work that had become a veritable annual) lists 2,819 authors still living at that date. Darnton writes, taking probable omissions into account, "I think it safe to conclude that by 1789 France had at least 3,000 writers, more than twice the number in 1750."[8]

La France littéraire gives an "estate" or a profession for 53 percent of the men of letters it lists for 1784 (1,493 out of 2,819 writers). Three models emerge. The first shows writing activities backed up by solid revenues from a title, a benefice, a post, or an office. This includes clerics (who account for 20 percent of writers; 21 percent if one includes Protestant pastors); nobles of the sword or of the robe (14 percent); and officials, administrators, or engineers who were commoners (6 percent). The second model ties intellectual activity to professionals who required knowledge and skills such as lawyers (11 percent); physicians and apothecaries (17 percent); and professors (11 percent). The third model includes all the occupations (secretary, librarian, interpreter, tutor, etc.) that depended directly on the protection of an important personage or the king and accounts for 8 percent of authors in 1784.

Two groups emerge from the sociological description of authors provided by *La France littéraire.* In the first, which was traditional and might be called Voltairean, we can see the coexistence, in unequal measure, of some people whose status and wealth sheltered them from need and others who benefited from the positions and remunerations offered by service to the great. In the second, which shows that the century was evolving, we can see the affirmation of a *bourgeoisie à talents* that rooted its writing activities in the exercise of an intellectual profession.

Two comparisons may clarify this dual image. The reports drafted between 1748 and 1751 by a police officer who was inspector of the book trade, Joseph d'Hémery, about the authors living in Paris show a different balance.[9] D'Hémery's criteria were more demanding than those of *La France littéraire:* he included only writers who had written a genuine work, and, as might be imagined, he gave special attention to those whom he held to be "dangerous." If we take the 333 authors whose social identity d'Hémery provides and divide them according to the three sociological groups that we have seen in connection with *La France littéraire,* we see that the first category (clerics, nobles, and commoner officials and administrators) is of equal proportion in the two listings, accounting here for 40 percent of the total. The differences lie in the smaller proportion of clergy (12 percent as opposed to 20 percent in *La France littéraire*) and the greater proportion of commoners in the service of the judicial system or the royal administration (12 percent compared with 6 percent). But in Inspector d'Hémery's files there were many more men who held positions that depended on patronage than men in the liberal professions: 33 percent of the authors he describes served a protector in some capacity (twenty-five were secretaries; thirty-five were tutors), whereas only 13 percent were lawyers, professors, or physicians. At midcentury and for the literary figures most involved in the book trade, we must agree with Robert Darnton that "protection functioned as the basic principle of literary life."[10]

Was the social world of *La France littéraire* closer to the society of the provincial academicians, as reconstructed by Daniel Roche, than to the Parisian Republic of Letters that fell under police surveillance?[11] The sociology of men of letters and that of the academicians both reserved a prominent place for the traditional elites, and although the clergy was present in nearly equal proportion (22 percent of ordinary members of the academies instituted in thirty-two provincial French cities were clerics, as were 20 percent of authors), the proportion of nobles was quite different, with 40 percent of academicians in the second order, as compared to only 14 percent of authors. Within the third estate the two listings are quite similar, showing nearly identical percentages for physicians (28 percent of academicians who were commoners; 28 percent of authors) and for merchants and manufacturers (8 percent of academicians; 7 percent of authors). There is only one gap but it is a significant one: the world of the robe—officials, lawyers, administrators—accounted for 51 percent of the commoners who were ordinary members of the academies and for only 25 percent among men of letters. Inversely, the intellectual professions, in the strong minority among commoner academicians (only 13 percent), account for 32 percent of the commoner authors listed by the editors of *La France littéraire*. The world of authors in its broadest interpretation (as in *La France littéraire*) thus fairly closely resembled the society of provincial literati who made up the academic network.

But what was the situation of Voltaire's "unhappy class who write in order to live"—those who hoped to survive on the "commercial value" of their works, which meant ceding what they produced to the bookseller-publishers? Was there a sizable number of people who hoped to cover the better part of their expenses from revenues from the sale of their manuscripts? Diderot justified their hopes in his *Lettre sur le commerce de la librairie* when he pointed out that the affirmation that the bookseller-publisher's "privilege" was inalienable implied a recognition of the author's full rights of ownership to the work that he ceded in exchange for just remuneration.[12] Rousseau set them an example by entering into negotiations for the same work several times, selling it, after making a few changes or additions, to different publishers inside and outside of France. He sold rights to *La nouvelle Héloïse* three times: Marc-Michel Rey acquired the original manuscript for 2,160 livres; Robin and Grangé paid 1,000 livres for an expurgated version that would be sure of authorization by the French authorities; and Duchesne spent 1,200 livres to buy the text augmented by the "Préface de Julie, ou, Entretien sur les Romans," in which the author explained, "I thought it best to wait for the book to have its effect before discussing its advantages and drawbacks, since I wanted neither to harm the booksellers nor to beg the indulgence of the public."[13]

In Inspector d'Hémery's reports as in the listings of *La France littéraire*, no profession or "estate" is given for a number of authors. The proportion of these men of letters with no employment listed or otherwise ascertainable increases from one source to another. This is the case of 101 out of the 434 writers described by d'Hémery between 1748 and 1753 (23 percent of the total), but it is also true of 1,326 out of the 2,819 authors (47 percent) listed in *La France littéraire* in 1784. In the 1757 edition of that publication, this was true of 27 percent of the authors listed; in the 1769 edition, of 33 percent. It would of course be extremely hazardous to conclude from this that these growing numbers of literati with neither a title nor a craft were all professional writers. Nonetheless, one might reasonably suppose that many among those with no post or sinecure tried to live by their pens. But they weren't all Rousseau. The first

resource for such men lay in the large publishing enterprises—
encyclopedias, dictionaries, collections, abridgements, translations—
that required a number of collaborators. As Louis-Sébastien Mercier
observed, it was these initiatives that gave a living to the writers whom he
scornfully calls *demi-littérateurs* and *écrivailleurs*. He said of the dictionaries: "Panckoucke and Vincent commission them from every compiler armed with scribes; one builds volumes by the alphabet just as a
building is built, in the space of a few months. The work is sure with this
manpower. Everything has been put into dictionaries."[14]

It was from the ranks of such writers that the various factions recruited pamphleteers to carry on the pamphlet wars attacking other factions or the ministers, the court, or the queen. Propaganda campaigns
of this sort always sprang out of divisions among the elites, each *parti*
attempting to put public opinion on its side. As Jeremy Popkin writes:
"The collusion of important members of the Court, the ministerial elite
or wealthy financiers was necessary for the publication and circulation
of almost all the controversial pamphlet literature of the period up to
the crisis of 1788."[15] This was a new type of patronage that enrolled the
most impecunious men of letters in the service of the interests of the
people who commissioned their writings. Obviously, not all libelists were
"gutter Rousseaus." Pidansat de Mairobert was secretary to the king, *secrétaire des commandements* to the duc de Chartres, royal censor, and a
shareholder in the Compagnie des Indes; Théveneau de Morande was
engaged by the French government to publish a periodical financed by
Versailles, *Le Courrier de l'Europe*. Still, a good many pamphleteers came
from the world of writers who had no "estate" or fortune and who fulfilled their needs by entering into a clientage relationship. This was true
of Brissot: after his stay in the Bastille and financial ruin, he wrote a number of pamphlets (not necessarily published in his own name but often
under Mirabeau's) for the Geneva banker Clavière, who was attempting
to manipulate the stock market. This made Brissot the perfect example
of a "typical hack, making compromises and writing for money."[16]

Comparisons

Did the characteristics of the French man of letters hold true everywhere in Europe? Two points of comparison may be of help. In the
German states, authors seem to have increased markedly in number during the last third of the eighteenth century. The annual published by
Johann Georg Meusels entitled *Das gelehrte Teutschland oder Lexicon der*

Letzt lebenden teutschen Schriftsteller lists 3,000 authors in 1766, 4,300 in 1776, 6,200 in 1788, about 8,000 in 1795, and nearly 11,000 in 1806, or a four-fold increase in four decades.[17] During the 1780s, the population of men of letters in German lands was thus twice as large as it was in France.

Comparison between France and Italy is of another order, since in Italy it is based on a sample of 219 authors born between 1720 and 1780. The definition of the man of letters in this sample is narrow because it does not include philosophers, theologians, economists, men of science, or scholars, and lists only authors of works of fiction, critics and historians of literature, and editors of ancient texts.[18] The milieu of men of letters in Italy, circumscribed in this manner, shows, first, a decline in the number of clerics, who made up 51 percent of the authors born between 1720 and 1740, 37 percent of those born between 1741 and 1760, and 35 percent of those born between 1761 and 1780. This is a sizable reduction, but it should be noted that clergy accounted for a much higher proportion of authors than in *La France littéraire* (20 percent in 1784). We have to wait for the generation born between 1781 and 1800 to see a real reduction in clerical authors in Italy, when they account for only 15 percent of all authors.

Second, in the Italian states as in France, writing was nearly always a secondary activity made possible because the writer belonged to a privileged elite or exercised a profession. In the first case, the condition of man of letters fitted into an aristocratic and lordly existence of financial ease and leisure. This happened frequently in Italy, where 27 percent of the authors born between 1720 and 1780 were nobles and members of the laity (compared with 14 percent in *La France littéraire* in 1784). In the second case, literary production depended upon profitable use of the time left over from the writer's principal occupation, which might be a teaching position, an intellectual responsibility (as secretary, librarian, etc.), an administrative office, or the exercise of a liberal profession. These various activities, practiced by clerics, nobles, and laymen, account, respectively, for 25, 17, 17, and 8 percent of the population of the 219 authors examined. This means that, all in all, there were few "professional" men of letters: "The case of 'professional' writers—that is, of writers for whom writing was not a second profession—is objectively rare: a court poet here and there or a dramatic poet (who might also be an actor)."[19] If we add the few journalists of the age, the figure rises to 13 percent of the sample.

Although the notion of literary property had been asserted and various legislative bodies had recognized it in one form or another,[20] the men of letters whose material existence did not depend upon a situation, a profession, or on state or private patronage remained a very small minority. "I did not believe I could live by the trade of man of letters," Abbé Morellet wrote in his *Mémoires,* a state of affairs that led him to remain within the church, to become the tutor of the son of the marquis de La Galaizière, and, lending his pen to the service of Trudaine, Maynon d'Invault, and Turgot, to accumulate pensions, incomes, and sinecures. Robert Darnton, who has followed Morellet's irresistible rise, figures his annual income on the eve of the Revolution at 28,275 livres: 16,000 livres that came to him from land revenues and rights pertaining to his benefice (the priory of Thimert, near Chartres); 11,275 livres from gratifications and pensions paid, for the most part, by the Caisse du Commerce or the Ministry of Finance; and only 1,000 livres of direct revenues from literary labors to prepare a *Dictionnaire de commerce* (which was never published).[21]

Similarly, Marmontel indicates in his *Mémoires* how he subordinated his entry into a literary career to obtaining a stable and sufficient income. When he became a contributor to the *Encyclopédie* (he was at the time *secrétaire des bâtiments du roi*—secretary for the royal building projects—at Versailles in the service of the marquis de Marigny, Madame de Pompadour's brother), Marmontel found the "society of men of letters" attractive: "Such of them as I most loved and respected were kind enough to say that we were formed for living together, and they held out the French Academy as a prospect on which I might fix my views. From time to time, therefore, I felt a renewal of my desire to enter into the career of literature. But, as a previous step, I wished to secure a fixed and independent livelihood." Madame de Pompadour's protection, a pension of 1,200 livres pledged from the revenues of *Le Mercure de France,* and the "privilege" to put out that periodical, which brought, he tells us, 25,000 livres to the review's proprietor, assured him the liberty he sought, but, unfortunately for him, not the security he desired. When, at Madame Geoffrin's house, he recited some fifty lines of verse of a satire directed at the duc d'Aumont, he was accused of having written the piece. Despite his denials, Marmontel was sent for a few days to the Bastille, where he was treated with great courtesy ("There was a library in the Bastille, and the governor sent me the catalogue and desired me to make my choice of the books which it contained"). In a more serious punishment, the patent for the *Mercure* was taken away from him. Supported only tepidly by his protectress, Marmontel failed in his attempt to get back his "privilege," which was "granted to a person of the name of Lagarde, Madame de Pompadour's librarian, and the worthy favorite of Collin, her man of business." He did manage to retain a pension connected with the periodical that gave him 1,000 écus (3,000 livres). He got his revenge later, with his election to the Académie Française in 1763 and, in 1772, with his installation, thanks to the protection of the duc d'Aiguillon, as official historian of France.[22]

The Aristocracy of Men of Letters: Parisian Salons and Dinners

What made the man of letters in the eighteenth century was not so much living by his writing as participating in the "society of men of letters," as Marmontel wrote. At first, that society took the form of select companies of people who took pleasure in meeting and conversing with one another in the salon or at dinners. Nothing better illustrates the necessary connection between intellectual activity and worldly sociability than the correspondence of Abbé Galiani after his forced departure from Paris in 1769 and his recall to Naples (at the demand of the duc de Choiseul, who was irritated by the relations that Galiani had established, counter to French and Spanish interests, with the ambassador of Denmark at Naples, Baron Gleichen). Thus, after ten years in Paris as secretary to the ambassador from the Kingdom of Naples, Galiani was obliged to leave Paris and return to Naples, where he occupied a post in the Supreme Court of Commerce.

Galiani viewed this return as a veritable exile that deprived him of all literary society. He wrote to Baron d'Holbach on 7 April 1770: "As for me, I am mortally bored. I see only two or three Frenchmen. I am Gulliver returned to the land of the Houyhnhnms, whose only remaining society is two horses. I go to pay courtesy visits to the wives of two ministers, of state and of finance. For the rest, I sleep or I dream. What a life! Nothing is amusing here. . . . Life is of a killing monotony. No one discusses anything, not even religion. Ah! my beloved Paris! Oh how I miss it!" In his "desert" Galiani sought to recreate something of the pleasures he had lost. On 22 December 1770, he declared to Madame d'Épinay, his faithful correspondent who had promised to send him a letter every week: "I have arranged a sample of Paris here. Gleichen, General Koch [an army officer and an Austrian agent], a resident of Venice, the secretary of the French embassy, and I dine together. We get together and we play at Paris, just as Nicolet plays Molière at the fair. I thoroughly amused this dinner with Voltaire's letter and with his prose ode, which you were kind enough to send me. I thank you for them from the bottom of my heart, and I beg you, in the name of the *coterie* and in my own name, to send me everything striking and amusing that appears in Paris."

The imitation proved a disappointment. It lacked what made the charm of the Paris salons and dinners—the intellectual governance of women and a company of witty people. "There is no way to make Naples resemble Paris if we cannot find a woman to guide us, to govern us, to 'Geoffrinize' us," Galiani wrote to Madame d'Épinay on 13 April 1771 (a bow to Madame Geoffrin's dinners). On 5 April 1772 he responded to Diderot: "You ask if I have read Abbé Raynal? No. Why? Because I no longer have either the time or the taste for literature. Reading alone, with no one to talk to, to discuss things with or be witty with, to listen to or to listen to me, is impossible. Europe is dead for me. They have put me in the Bastille."[23] It was difficult to adjust the role of a man of letters to retirement, solitude, or distance from the capital of the Republic of Letters. Upholding that role presupposed the sense of connivance that bound together the little societies in which men of letters enjoyed conversing and disputing.

All Europe envied Paris these societies, of which the salon was the primordial form. According to Dena Goodman (and Galiani), what distinguished the salon from all other forms of intellectual encounter was the dominant and guiding place that women occupied in it.[24] Although women had only a modest share of mentions in listings of authors (in *La France littéraire* as in d'Hémery's reports, they count for only 3 percent), their role was decisive in the literate sociability that brought together men of letters and people from the fashionable world. In the memoirs that they wrote after the Revolution some habitués of Paris salons recalled how their female governance operated. Marmontel, for example, describes (with a touch of condescension toward the lady of the house) the two societies that met in Madame Geoffrin's salon:

> She was rich enough to make her house the rendezvous of literature and the arts; and seeing that this would afford her old age an amusing society and a respectable character in the world, Madame Geoffrin had established at her house two weekly dinners, one on Mondays for artists, another on Wednesdays for men of letters. It is very remarkable that, though this woman had no knowledge either of the arts or of literature, and had never learned anything thoroughly in her life, yet, when placed in the midst of these two societies, she did not seem out of place.

She was even quite at ease, for she had good sense enough never to speak of anything she did not know very well; while on every other subject she gave place to persons who were better informed. She was always politely attentive, and never seemed to tire of what she did not understand. But her great art consisted in presiding, in watching, in keeping up her authority over two classes of men who are naturally fond of freedom. She set bounds, however, to this liberty, and by a word or a gesture, as by an invisible thread, could recall any one who attempted to escape. "Well said, indeed," was commonly the signal of caution which she gave her guests.

The comparison changes tone but not meaning when Marmontel recalls the circle assembled at the house of Mademoiselle de Lespinasse:

This circle was composed of persons who had no connection together. She had collected them out of a variety of different societies, but had suited them so well together that when they met they appeared to be in harmony, like the strings of an instrument tuned by a skillful hand. Pursuing the comparison, I may say that she played on this instrument with an art that bordered on genius; she seemed to know the sound that would be yielded by the string she was about to touch; that is to say, our minds and character were so fully known to her, that a word was sufficient to bring them into action. Nowhere was conversation more lively, more brilliant, or under better regulation.[25]

Only a woman's light touch and skill seemed capable of keeping within the limits of civility the "balance of tensions" (to quote Norbert Elias) inherent in literary disputes.

The role of mistress of a salon required initiation and was open to imitation. Hence the continuities (which, on occasion, turned into fierce rivalries), among the various salons. Madame Geoffrin had long frequented the salon of Madame de Tencin, who said about her, "Do you know why Geoffrin comes here? She wishes to see how much she can pick up out of my inventory."[26] Her rival, Madame du Deffand, had been familiar with the "court" that assembled at Sceaux around the duchesse de Maine and that later participated in the salon of the marquise de Lambert. For twelve years before she established her own circle, Mademoiselle de Lespinasse had been the companion of Madame du Deffand. Madame Necker had frequented Madame Geoffrin's salon. Thus, from one society to another the quintessential female art of governing men's minds, which required an invisible and discreet authority, was transmitted from one woman to the other. As Dena Goodman writes, "Enlightenment salons were places where male egos were brought into harmony through the agency of female selflessness."[27]

If we give credence to the memoirs of Marmontel or Morellet, female control over discourse did not stifle the desire for an exclusively masculine sociability, which such memoirs present (perhaps with a dose of retrospective illusion and an interest in self-justification) as freer and more audacious. Marmontel recalled the dinners for men alone given by Pelletier:

> Madame Geoffrin's society wanted one of the pleasures on which I set the greatest value, and that was freedom of thought. With her mild "Well said, indeed," she kept our minds always, as it were, in leading strings; and I partook of dinner elsewhere, where we were more at our ease. The freest, or rather the most licentious of all, was that given by a wealthy farmer-general, of the name of Pelletier, to eight or ten bachelors, who were all fond of gaiety.

Marmontel also recalled dinners given by d'Holbach:

> Nevertheless, however interesting as a source of mental improvement I found the society of these agreeable women, it did not prevent me from strengthening and exalting my soul, from opening and enriching my ideas in a society of men whose minds gave warmth and light to my own. The house of the Baron d'Holbach, and for some time past that of Helvétius, formed a rendezvous for this society, which consisted partly of the flower of Madame Geoffrin's guests, and partly of some heads which had appeared to Madame Geoffrin too bold and too hazardous to be admitted to her dinners.[28]

Morellet made similar comparisons between the dinners given by Madame Geoffrin and a more rebellious, more unfettered, all-male society. There were open-air meetings in the Tuileries as well: "After our dinners at her house, we often went to the Tuileries—d'Alembert, Raynal, Helvétius, Galiani, Marmontel, Thomas, etc.—to meet other friends, to hear the latest news, to criticize the government, and to philosophize as we wished. We sat in a circle at the foot of a tree in the central *allée*, abandoning ourselves to a conversation as animated and free as the air that we breathed." There were also dinners at d'Holbach's:

> The Baron d'Holbach regularly had two dinners a week, on Sundays and Thursdays. Ten, twelve, and even fifteen or twenty men of letters, men of the world, or foreigners, all of whom loved and cultivated the same arts of the mind met there, without the prejudices of some other days. Rough but good fare, excellent wine, excellent coffee, much disputation, never an argument; simplicity of manners, as is proper among reasonable and educated men, but which never degenerated into vulgarity; a true but not wild gaiety: in short, a truly pleasurable company, which could be seen by the one symptom that having come at two in the afternoon, according to the custom of those times, often nearly all of us were still there at seven or eight o'clock in the evening.

There were dinners at Helvétius's house, although these were somewhat dampened by the conduct of the lady of the house, who never learned how to stay out of the conversation or how to direct it skillfully:

> Roughly the same persons met at Helvétius's house as at Baron d'Holbach's, on different days, but the conversation was less good and less consistent. The lady of the house, drawing about her the persons whom she liked best (and not choosing the worst) broke up the society somewhat. She liked philosophy no less than Madame d'Holbach, but the latter, keeping to her corner without saying a word or chatting quietly with one or two of her more intimate friends, was no hindrance, whereas Madame Helvétius, who was handsome and of an original mind and a natural sharpness, disturbed the philosophical discussions considerably.[29]

It is clear from the memoirs that the difference between female governance and masculine sociability was in fact experienced as a succession of meetings whose advantages and pleasures complemented one another, either during one day or throughout the week. Each Wednesday, for example, Marmontel participated first in the dinner "presided over" by Madame Geoffrin at which the company, with the exception of Mademoiselle de Lespinasse, was entirely male (the habitués he names are d'Alembert, Dortous de Mairan, Marivaux, Chastellux, Abbé Morellet, Saint-Lambert, Helvétius, and Thomas and, among the foreigners,

Abbé Galiani, the marchese di Caraccioli, and Count Creutz). He then went to the Tuileries with some of his friends before returning to Madame Geoffrin's to rejoin a more fashionable and more female company. He states: "After dining at Madame Geoffrin's with literary men or with artists, I spent the evening with her in a more intimate society, for she had also done me the favour of admitting me to her private supper parties. . . . The company was small, and consisted at most of five or six particular friends, or three or four men and women of the highest fashion, suited to each other's taste, and all of whom were pleased to be together."[30] For the aristocracy of the men of letters, the weekly schedule also offered complementary occasions for sociability. When Madame Necker decided to launch a salon of her own, the problem was to find a day: "Madame Necker turned to the three of us [Marmontel, Raynal, and Morellet] to lay the foundations of her literary society. We chose a day that would not conflict with the Mondays and the Wednesdays of Madame Geoffrin, the Tuesdays of Helvétius, the Thursdays and Sundays of Baron d'Holbach. Friday was Madame Necker's day."[31]

"What the eighteenth-century salonnières did was to transform a noble and thus leisure form of social gathering into a serious working space," Dena Goodman writes.[32] There were notable differences between the salons of the seventeenth century[33] and the eighteenth-century gatherings, which contemporaries rarely called "salons," preferring such terms as *maison, société, compagnie,* or *dîner.* A sociability with a strong female contingent was succeeded by companies of men governed by one woman, the mistress of the house and mistress of the conversation. Where before literary games had predominated, now information was exchanged, ideas were discussed, critical functions were exercised, and philosophical projects were elaborated. Whereas the earlier groups had been preponderantly noble, in the later societies nobles and commoners mingled, and differences of condition and estate bowed before the equality that intellectual debate required. Whereas the salons of the *précieuses* participated in the society of the court—hence they belonged within the domain of public authority in its absolutist form—the dinners of the Enlightenment were the first private spaces to support the emergence of a public sphere distinct from the monarchy and critical of it.

The Art of Conversation

What the salons of the seventeenth century and the companies of the eighteenth century had in common was the similarity of their literary practices (although, as we have seen, these practices had quite different ends in mind). The most essential of them was conversation. The true man of letters of the eighteenth century, according to the criteria of the literary "establishment" at least, was primarily a master of discourse in society. Garat gives striking witness to this in his *Mémoires historiques sur le XVIIIe siècle et sur M. Suard,* published in 1821. According to Garat, the literary and philosophical merit of Suard (who accumulated protections, pensions, and posts, and who received the supreme consecration of election to the Académie Française) lay wholly in his eloquence:

> Monsieur Suard has spoken much more than he has written. He has dispersed much wit and talent in scattered fragments, and even more in society and conversations. . . . We [who are] so close to Monsieur Suard and [are] so full of his memory cannot possibly refuse to rescue from oblivion and usurpation some of the precious things he lavished [on us], with no thought to his memory, when he was alive. But it was within the circles, the *cabinets,* and encounters that he so to speak threw them about.

A theoretician of his own practice, Suard had planned to write (Garat says, "to touch upon in a very little volume") a "history of conversations in France since the tenth century":

> He thought—something that is not generally admitted but that is highly evident—that the centuries would be better depicted through a history of their conversations than through histories of their literatures because few persons write and many converse, because it is only too common that writers imitate and copy one another, even at many years' distance, and because it is by no means rare that one is happily constrained to speak as one feels and thinks.

Applying this notion to the eighteenth century, Garat imputes to the power of the spoken word the upheavals that ended that century:

> If the influence [of the "philosophic spirit"] had operated only through books and through reading, it would have been far from so rapidly producing such important and widespread results. It was in conversations that it drew that ever-stronger force, which nothing could defeat and which was to change everything. That force was practiced and it increased principally in the societies in which Monsieur Suard lived, where a taste for the arts and for letters brought together the men who had the

greatest hold on opinion by their enlightenment, their rank, and their positions.[34]

The decisive importance that contemporaries attributed to conversation, understood as a veritable genre with its own rules and conventions, is evident in two articles that Morellet wrote for *Le Mercure de France* in 1778, "Essai sur la conversation" (inspired by Jonathan Swift's *Hints Toward an Essay on Conversation*), and "De l'esprit de contradiction."[35] Morellet reworked and modified these two pieces in treatises published under the same titles in 1812 in a collective volume entitled *Éloges de Mme Geoffrin*. In these texts Morellet defines conversation as a major genre of the practice of letters because when the confrontation—even the opposition—of ideas is placed under the constraints of worldly politeness it enables truth to be established without allowing too-lively tensions to destroy the bond of sociability. Like the "dialogue style" in music that became popular in Paris around 1760, a well-conducted conversation— "neither rigorously methodical nor absolutely incoherent"; neither pedantic nor frivolous—brought a variety of voices into harmony. The salon was like a concert in which a skilled *maîtresse de musique* directed the various parts.

Criticism of the Salon

Female governance of the Republic of Letters, in the form it took in the society of the Paris salons, was not to everybody's taste. Rousseau rejected it in his letter to d'Alembert "Sur son article Genève dans le VIIe Volume de l'Encyclopédie, et particulièrement, sur le projet d'établir un théâtre de comédie en cette Ville," published in 1758. He did so in the name of a necessary separation between the sexes: "Let us follow the indications of nature, let us consult the good of society; we should find that the two sexes ought to come together sometimes and to live separated ordinarily" and out of respect for the duties particular to each sex. Parisian salons, a detestable opposite of Sparta and the happy society of the *Montagnons,* made a merit of immodesty: "With us . . . the most esteemed woman is the one who has the greatest renown, about whom the most is said, who is the most often seen in society, at whose home one dines the most, who most imperiously sets the tone, who judges, resolves, pronounces, assigns talents, merit, and virtues their degrees and places, and whose favor is most ignominiously begged for by humble, learned men." Worse, the salons corrupted the women and softened the men, thus destroying the virtues that should be proper to each sex: "Meanly devoted to the wills of the sex that we ought to protect and not serve, we have learned to despise it in obeying it, to insult it by our derisive attentions; and every woman at Paris gathers in her apartment a harem of men more womanish than she, who know how to render all sorts of homage to beauty except that of the heart, which is her due." Imprisoned, rendered spineless and languid by women's "sedentary and homebound life," men of letters dedicated their talents to frivolous and ephemeral writings and lost all genius: "Imagine what can be the temper of the soul of a man who is uniquely occupied with the important business of amusing women, and who spends his entire life doing for them what they ought to do for us when, exhausted by labors of which they are incapable, our minds have need of relaxation."[36]

When he visited Paris between 28 January and 9 May 1763, Edward Gibbon frequented literary dinners thanks to letters of recommendation that he had collected in London. He states: "Four days in the week I had a place without invitation at the hospitable tables of Mesdames Geoffrin and du Bocage, of the celebrated Helvétius, and of the Baron d'Olbach." His impression, as reported in the memoirs he wrote in 1789–90, was mixed. On the one hand, the society he frequented conformed with his idea of the French as "a polished and amiable people": "In these *Symposia* the pleasures of the table were improved by lively and liberal conversation; the company was select, though various and voluntary." On the other hand, Gibbon found the despotism of female governance and the intolerance of the men of letters odious: "Yet I was often disgusted with the capricious tyranny of Madame Geoffrin, nor could I approve the intolerant zeal of the philosophers and the Encyclopedists, the friends of d'Olbach and Helvétius; they laughed at the scepticism of Hume, preached the tenets of atheism with the bigotry of dogmatists, and damned all believers with ridicule and contempt."

Gibbon found this company lighthearted, and he preferred private visits to men of letters in the morning, before dinner. "Alone in a morning visit I commonly found the wits and authors of Paris less vain and more reasonable than in the circles of their equals, with whom they mingle in the houses of the rich." He also enjoyed conversations among scholars ("The evening conversations of M. de Foncemagne were supported by the good sense and learning of the principal members of the Academy of Inscriptions"), the theater, and the company of Madame Bontems, about whom he observed that "in the middle season of life, her beauty was still an object of desire." Gibbon long remembered this happy encounter ("Fourteen weeks insensibly stole away; but had I been

rich and independent, I should have prolonged and perhaps fixed my
residence at Paris"). Twenty years after his weeks in Paris, however, Gibbon felt no need to stop there on his way from London to his retreat in
Lausanne and took the shortest route to Switzerland.[37]

The last witness for the prosecution in criticism of the society of the
salons had quite different reasons for his dissatisfaction. When Jacques-
Pierre Brissot wrote his memoirs during his imprisonment he expressed
an aversion for *femmes littérateurs* and for "the pedantic bureaus sprout-
ing up all over Paris" because "the wife of the academician and the prosecuting attorney, the bourgeois and the great lord, the *contrôleur des
finances* and the simple financier all want to have a bureau to preside
over." Brissot was writing as a frustrated young man whom the world of
letters refused to recognize as one of its peers. Brissot treated to equal
scorn the *bureaux de bel esprit* of the mistresses of the salons and egotistical and indifferent men of letters—d'Alembert first among them. He
states:

> As a young neophyte, a stranger to these individuals and come
> here to admire great men, or at least to listen to philosophers, I
> expected to find them affable and full of good will, as they paint
> themselves in their works; human and tolerant, since they speak
> ceaselessly of tolerance and humanity. When I saw them de-
> scend from their pedestals and could consider them at closer
> range, my illusions were soon dissipated. I loved philosophy
> with no less ardor, but I thought little of certain philosophers.

He thought equally little of academicians imbued with prejudices and
jealous of one another. This was what led Brissot to support Marat
against Laplace because, as he said, "I could not bear his treating a physician with insolence and despotism because, unlike himself, he did not
enjoy a seat [in the Academy]."[38] Even if they too are marked by retrospective illusion and a posteriori reconstruction, Brissot's memoirs
forcefully depict the wall of hatred that separated all less-fortunate authors in search of legitimacy and remunerations and the men of letters
who monopolized protections, pensions, and positions.

The Voyages of Reason: Berlin

To be admitted to the dinners and companies in Paris (and only in Paris)
that consecrated the true man of letters who was also a man of the world
and a philosopher was the ambition of many people who thought and

wrote in the French provinces and outside of France. Still, the Paris salons were only one expression—albeit the most visible and the most envied one—of a number of places for intellectual sociability that qualified those who participated in them as citizens of a Republic of Letters with no one capital and no impenetrable frontiers. There was a dual logic to this network that extended throughout Europe. The first logic was geographical and was based on varying degrees of penetration of the philosophic spirit; the second logic was institutional—in it instances of legitimation strictly dependent upon the sovereign power stood opposed to free and voluntary sociabilities in which the exercise of criticism could be pursued more at ease.

The Monsieur André in Voltaire's *L'homme aux quarante écus* drew an ironic map of a Europe unequally open to the "progress of the human spirit" because it offered an unequal welcome to those who made that progress possible:

> He recently remarked to me that Reason travels by slow journeys from north to south, in company with her two intimate friends, Experience and Toleration. Agriculture and Commerce attend them. When Reason presented herself in Italy the congregation of the Index sternly repulsed her. All she could do was to secretly send some of her agents, who, in spite of her enemies, do some good. Let but some years pass, and it is to be hoped that the country of the Scipios will no longer be that of harlequins in monks' habits. She has sometimes met with cruel foes in France; but she has now so many friends in that kingdom that she stands a good chance of at length becoming first minister there. When she presented herself in Bavaria and Austria, she found two or three great wig-blocks that stared at her with stupid and astonished eyes. Their greeting was: "Madam, we never heard of you; we do not know you." Her answer to which was: "Gentlemen, in time you will come to know me and to love me. I have been well received at Berlin, at Moscow, at Copenhagen, at Stockholm. It is long ago that I have been naturalized by Act of Parliament in England, through the labors of Locke, Gordon, Trenchard, Lord Shaftesbury, and a number of others of the same nation. You will, some day or other, confer on me the like grant. I am the daughter of Time. I expect everything from my father." When she passed over the frontiers of Spain and Portugal, she blessed God on observing that the fires of the

Inquisition were less frequently kindled. She rejoiced on seeing the Jesuits expelled; but was afraid that, while the country had been cleared of foxes, it was still left exposed to the ravages of wolves.[39]

We need to look more closely at the geography that Voltaire outlined in 1768. Reason declares she has been "well received at Berlin." In the capital of Prussia men of letters were members of several groups. The most official of these was the Royal Academy of Sciences, founded in 1700 and reformed by Frederick the Great in 1740. For some time it was dominated by the French *philosophes,* and (until the king's death in 1786) it was not particularly open to the Prussian *Aufklärer.* Enlightened Prussians were more apt to frequent their own societies, where they rubbed elbows with public officials, administrators, and professors. These societies included the *Montagsclub,* founded in 1749, the *Fesslersche Lesegesellschaft,* and the *Mittwochgesellschaft,* a secret society of twenty-four members that had been founded to counterbalance the anti-Enlightenment tendencies of another secret society, the *Bruderschaft der Gold- und Rosenkreuzer.* During the last decade of the eighteenth century, the new literary generation drifted away from the enlightened societies, preferring the romantic salons, fourteen of which existed in Berlin by 1806. Although the deliberations of the *Mittwochgesellschaft* were secret, the society reached the public through a periodical closely tied to it, the *Berlinische Monatsschrift.* This journal published some of the lectures given by members of the society (Johann Friedrich Zöllner, Moses Mendelssohn, Christian Gottlieb Selle, and Carl Gottlieb Svarez), and it organized debates that paralleled those that took place within the society. One of these was on the famous question *Was ist Aufklärung?* (What is Enlightenment?), a question posed by Zöllner in the journal in 1783 and in the society by Karl Wilhelm Möhsen; another touched on legislative reform and the elaboration of the Prussian General Code, the *Allgemeines Landrecht für die Preussischen Staaten.*[40]

The scene in Berlin, which was reproduced on a smaller scale in a number of small capital cities, illustrates two fundamental characteristics of the milieu of German men of letters. The first is the essential role played by periodicals whose circulation provided shared opportunities for publication and discussion in spite of the absence of an intellectual capital comparable to Paris and in spite of Germany's many nation-states. The number of new and more or less durable periodicals increased markedly: 316 new journals and reviews were published between

1701 and 1730; 767 between 1731 and 1760; 2,353 between 1761 and 1790 (1,225 in the last decade alone). Learned journals, which predominated during the first half of the century, were overtaken by periodicals that encouraged and organized public discussion and criticism: out of a sample of 160 periodicals published between 1750 and 1800, articles concerning contemporary problems (social, economic, juridical, political, pedagogical) accounted for 41.5 percent of all articles published.[41] This points to a second characteristic of men of letters in the German states: their close connections with men who held posts and offices in the service of the state or who sometimes participated directly in the bureaucracies constructed by absolute (on occasion, enlightened) German princes. We can thus apply to German men of letters Anthony La Vopa's judgment of Enlightenment society: "It was precisely this multitiered service elite, more or less directly implicated in the workings of 'absolutism,' that formed the center of gravity for the Enlightenment's new sociability. By and large the new social spaces, Masonic lodges prominent among them, were occupied by the groups who constituted the state. If they were private retreats from absolutism, they were also its informal extensions."[42] Hence the ambivalence of men of letters (particularly but not exclusively in Germany) toward the absolutist state, which they criticized but with which they also identified.

Paris and the Provinces: Institutions of Consecration and Places of Sociability

In France, according to Voltaire's Monsieur André, a battle was raging between the enemies and the friends of Reason. Control of the most prestigious institutions was a decisive stake in this combat. After d'Alembert's election to the Académie Française in 1754, the philosophical faction *(le parti philosophique)* launched an assault on that bastion of intellectual legitimacy. The fight was rough and conquest was slow. In 1763, when Marmontel was lobbying for the seat left vacant by Marivaux's death, its gains were still fragile: "The Academy contained four members who went by the name of philosophers, an appellation which was then odious. The academicians thus designated were Duclos, d'Alembert, Saurin, and Watelet." Sure of the support of these members (even though at the time d'Alembert and Duclos had quarreled bitterly), Marmontel made the visits that tradition required, but he ran into fierce opposition from a minister, the duc de Praslin. The only way to get around the hostility of such a powerful personage was to win the favor of the king. To do that, the philosophers' candidate, helped by his protectress, returned to the most traditional of the gestures of submission of the man of letters—the presentation to the sovereign of a richly bound copy of one of his works:

> The printing of my "Art of Poetry" being at last completed, I besought Madame de Pompadour to obtain permission from the King that a work which filled up a blank in our literature should be presented to him. "This," said I, "is a favour which will cost neither the King nor the State anything, and which will prove that the King is well inclined towards me." I owe this testimony to the memory of this beneficent woman, that, on hearing of this easy and simple mode of publicly determining the King in my favour, her fine countenance sparkled with joy. "Willingly," said she, "will I ask this favour from the King, and I shall obtain it." She obtained it without difficulty, and said, when she announced it, "You must give this presentation every possible solemnity; all the royal family and all the ministers must, on the same day, receive the work from your own hand." I disclosed this secret only to my intimate friends; and, having got my copies very magnificently bound (for I spared no cost on them), I went one Saturday evening to Versailles with my packet. Next day I was introduced by the Duke de Duras. The King was at his levee, and never did I see him look so handsome. He received my homage with an enchanting look. My joy would have been at its height had he just spoken three words, but his eyes spoke for him. . . . When I went to call on Madame de Pompadour, to whom I had already presented my work, she said, "Go to M. de Choiseul and offer him his copy; you will meet a friendly reception. Leave me that of M. de Praslin with me; I will present it myself." After my expedition, I went immediately and informed d'Alembert and Duclos of the success I had met with. I distributed copies to such of the academicians as I knew to be my friends.

The distribution of the *Poétique Française* did its job, since, once a final intrigue was disposed of (Praslin's attempt to get Thomas, at the time his private secretary, to present his own candidacy), Marmontel was finally elected to the Académie.[43] The story seems exemplary of the discipline maintained between the new definition of the man of letters (according to Voltaire, a *littérateur accompli* and an adept of the *esprit philosophique*) and the most traditional forms of princely patronage, with the king as supreme dispenser of graces and the final arbiter of literary rivalries.

All those who were unable to gain access to the most prestigious institutions or posts of the monarchical cultural apparatus were obliged to frequent or invent other forms of sociability—forms that also attest to the figure of the man of letters, but in a different way. In France during the final decades of the ancien régime these new forms drew inspiration from a variety of models. The first of them, the café, was modeled on the coffee-houses of London, which already numbered three thousand at the beginning of the eighteenth century.[44] As Robert Darnton put it, "the café functioned as the antithesis of the salon."[45] Rather than gathering together a select society, it was open to all; it was by no means governed by a female presence but was exclusively male. The second model was that of the literary society, which was defined both in contrast to the academy and in imitation of it. Young provincials of literary proclivities who waited eagerly at the doors of academies established on the Parisian model found in these freer associations, which demanded no letters patent or official recognition, a way to assuage their impatience. Finally, the proliferation of museums and lyceums, with their less utilitarian and more pedagogical aims than the academies, offered an outlet for persons of a literary bent who were excluded from the more legitimate forms of recognition.[46]

The new form of intellectual sociability could be a vehicle for subversion. This was the case with Brissot, who recalled his attempt to found the Lyceum of London in 1782–83 with a retrospective and justificatory embellishment typical of memory. The project was an ambitious one:

> I was to create a Lyceum, a Museum in which, on certain days of the week, the scholars and philosophers of the entire universe would meet and in which the products of all the arts would be brought together. I also dreamed of having a journal dedicated to publicizing the results of these scientific encounters, which would serve to transmit the philosophical and political truths with which to inoculate all French minds.

Brissot's plan was to bring together the "intrepid and enlightened friends of liberty" in London; to have their works published in that city, "where individual liberty was at the highest point"; then to have those works reprinted in Switzerland, Germany, and Holland, and eventually introduced into France. The London Lyceum was to fulfill two roles. On the one hand, "externally, it was an institution similar to the *lycées* and *musées* that existed in France"—and in fact the idea was based on a project of Mammès-Claude Pahin de la Blancherie, who also wanted to group together scholars of all countries and combine this group with correspondence and a periodical. On the other hand, Brissot insisted:

> This Lyceum was not supposed to be constricted within the severe limits that the tyranny of the ministry had put on the ones in Paris. It was not spectacle, amusement, instruction, news, music, or paintings that were to attract people to my Lyceum; it was uniquely the utility that the friends of letters could draw from one another's company, a utility redoubled in a land in which nothing hinders liberty; a utility transformed into necessity when one thought of the character of the English scholars and of the absolute lack of communications.

The realization of Brissot's project fell short of his ambitions, and only twelve issues of the *Journal du Licée de Londres, ou Tableau de l'État présent des Sciences et des Arts en Angleterre* were published in 1784 and 1785, a time when Brissot had a number of personal troubles: he was imprisoned for debt in London, his periodical was forbidden by Vergennes, he spent two months imprisoned in the Bastille, and he was unable to return to England.[47]

Visits and Correspondence

Even when it did not have the immediately subversive goals assigned to it by Brissot, the idea of a sole organization and a central government of the Republic of Letters inspired a number of projects throughout the eighteenth century, from the anonymous "Projet pour l'établissement d'un bureau général de la République des Lettres," published in Amsterdam in 1747 in the *Bibliothèque raisonnée des ouvrages des savans de l'Europe,* to the "Plan d'association générale entre les savants, gens de lettres et artistes, pour accélérer les progrès des bonnes moeurs et des lumières" proposed by Abbé Grégoire after the French Revolution, in which he suggested holding a first worldwide convention of *lettrés* or *savants* (he uses the two terms interchangeably) in 1817 in Frankfurt am Main. Voyages and correspondence, which were not hampered by this lack of unity, created a community of men of letters that reached beyond national frontiers.

Jean-François Séguier, a man who, precisely, was not a leading figure in the intellectual world, was a member of the Académie de Nîmes and eventually became its director and perpetual secretary.[48] As the traveling companion of the marchese di Maffei Séguier visited libraries and *cabinets de curiosité* throughout Europe before returning to his native city, where he created a botanical garden and an archaeological collection. From Nîmes he carried on a sizable and regular exchange of letters with 338 correspondents: aristocrats in Languedoc, scholars and erudite personalities throughout southern France, but also (and these accounted for a third of his correspondence) foreign literary correspondents, more of half of them in Italy and in Spain. The Italian and Spanish correspondents show the originality of Séguier's network of contacts, which was much more strongly Mediterranean than those of such great writers of the Enlightenment as Voltaire or Diderot, who concentrated on exchanges in northern and Protestant Europe.[49] If Séguier was a zealous letter writer he was also an excellent host: between 1773 and 1783, 1,383 visitors came to see him, some of them returning several times. Of these visitors 65 percent were French: men of the court and the administration, or men of learning; 35 percent of them came from abroad, in particular, from northern Europe (foreign visitors account for a higher proportion of total visitors than foreigners among Séguier's correspondents).

Séguier's correspondents and his visitors are not wholly typical of the epistolary exchanges and acquaintances of men of letters because most of them were members of the governing aristocracies or scholars. They do demonstrate, however, that a society not limited to people who lived in the immediate area could be constituted on a provincial scale. As Galiani wrote to Suard from his Neapolitan exile, "My letters are like St. Paul's, *Ecclesiae quae Parisiis*. So please read them to my friends."[50] Reading aloud a letter that one had received maintained the author's presence despite geographical separation, and it attested to common membership in the same company.

A Moral Model: Retreat and Disinterest

If the status of the man of letters was defined by his active membership in the various institutions and sociabilities of the society of literary people, it was also defined by the many and contradictory discourses that gave it objective expression. These discourses developed concurrently on several levels. The most traditional one had an undercurrent of moral and pedagogical intent. Its roots lay in the earliest work explicitly dedicated to the man of letters, the *Dell'Huomo di lettere difeso e emendato parti due* by a

Jesuit, Daniello Bartoli, a work published in Rome in 1645 and reprinted eight times in that same year. Bartoli's book was translated into French in 1654 by Father Le Blanc, also a Jesuit, as *La Guide des Beaux-Esprits* (Pont-à-Mousson). The work was highly successful; it went through nineteen Italian editions between 1645 and 1689 and was translated into English (1660), German (1677), Castilian (1678), and Latin (1693). It was translated into French a second time during the eighteenth century by another Jesuit, Father Delivoy, as *L'homme de lettres* (3 vols., Paris, 1769). The work stresses the dignity of the career of letters against all detractors, and it draws a close connection between intellectual activity and absolute disinterest, proposing to the man of letters that he take as a model the sage of classical antiquity, and to the powerful, the model of the patron.[51]

Five years before the publication of Father Delivoy's translation of Bartoli, Jean-Jacques Garnier, royal professor of Hebrew and member of the Académie des Inscriptions et Belles-Lettres, published another work entitled *L'homme de lettres,* which perpetuated the same set of representations. Garnier states, "I define the Man of Letters as one whose principal employment consists in cultivating his mind through study in order to make himself better and more useful to society." On the basis of this definition, which he distinguishes from the definition of the "people," who "confuse the Man of Letters with the author," and the definition of "fashionable people," who "only imagine in the Man of Letters the amusing man and the fine talker," Garnier worked out a model that he contrasts, point by point, with the practices and the aspirations of the habitués of the salons and the contributors to the *Encyclopédie.* For him, the "occupation" of men of letters presupposed withdrawal from the world, far from passions and distractions: "By losing a taste for retirement, one soon abandons the desire to cultivate one's mind, and, as a necessary consequence, one ceases to be truly a man of letters to become a man of society." That occupation posited the superiority of "composition" (that is, writing) to conversation: "One meets every day persons whose conversation is enchanting and who cannot put two ideas together with a pen in their hands." It also implied acceptance of an honest poverty that sought neither "gratifications" nor pensions—things that absolutely had to be banished because in order to obtain them one had to seek protection and patronage and because, once granted, they were an incitement to softness and laziness. The only legitimate "literary rewards" were "distinctions, charges, employments, places, consideration, and all that can stimulate emulation and flatter self-love," which the state would concede, with discernment, to those worthy of them. Garnier thought he could prove the advantage of posts over pensions by demonstrating, against Voltaire, that the reign of Francis I was superior, in literary terms, to that of Louis XIV.

For Garnier, the man of letters was like a lay cleric, vowed to celibacy: "The indispensable cares and burdens of marriage are ill-suited to the calm and the indifference that are so necessary to the exercises of the mind." He must be disinterested in his practice of the sciences and the arts: those who made these "their principal occupation" might merit the title of man of letters "provided they seek in them less sordid gain than useful knowledge, and that they be more jealous of advances in their art than in their fortune." Although he recognized no authority superior to that of reason, Garnier was wary of the critical activity that, in Voltaire's definition, was reason's identity and special mission. To counter the evolution that made a philosopher of the man of letters, Garnier remarks that the latter's "total independence in no way infringes on the established laws, unless they are iniquitous. The Man of Letters, it is true, does not submit to these laws out of a fear of punishment, like a vile slave, but out of a love of order, for he knows better than anyone both their advantages and the need for them in all established societies. Hence he will be their most ardent defender."[52] Unlike the new definitions of the man of letters (those elaborated by Duclos or d'Alembert, for example), and unlike the social practices of the Parisian world, the books of Jean-Jacques Garnier the scholar and Delivoy the Jesuit continued, throughout the century, to perpetuate a traditional model in which many people endowed with a situation or an employment and dedicated to an unquestioning, respectful, and tranquil erudition were happy to see themselves.

The Author as Proprietor of his Work

Bookseller-publishers intent on defining their special privileges created another discourse in publishing and juridical circles that varied from this traditional discourse. The movement arose particularly early in England. As Mark Rose writes, "It might be said that the London booksellers invented the modern proprietary author, constructing him as a weapon in their struggle with the booksellers of the provinces."[53] In 1709, a statute voted by the Parliament, titled An Act for the Encouragement of Learning, by Vesting the Copies of Printed Books in the Authors or Purchasers of such Copies, during the Times therein mentioned, destroyed the old publishing system that had operated to the over-whelming advantage of the booksellers of London. Under the system of self-regulation by the book-publishing community, "entering" a title in the register of the Stationers' Company guaranteed the bookseller who had obtained the work thus registered full and inviolable ownership of it (which meant that such ownership was transmissible, divisible, and ex-changeable). The 1709 statute did two things to dismantle the old sys-tem. First, it limited the duration of the copyright to fourteen years (plus a further fourteen years if the author were still alive) or to twenty-one years for works that had already been published; second, it authorized authors to demand a copyright for themselves. The London booksellers lost both their monopoly on obtaining copyrights and the perpetuity of their rights, which left the field free for their provincial colleagues, Irish or Scottish, to reprint titles when their copyright expired.

The only way that the booksellers of the Stationers' Company could reassert their traditional dominance was to work for recognition of the author's perpetual rights over his own work and hence the equally per-petual rights of anyone who had acquired that work. Thus, in a certain sense, they had to invent the man of letters as an author-proprietor. The London booksellers developed a dual line of argumentation in a series of suits aimed at the booksellers who reprinted titles for which the Lon-doners claimed to hold an imprescriptible privilege. Their first point was founded on a theory of property derived from Locke that sustained that a man, as the proprietor of his own person, is also the owner of all the products of his labor, both literary and nonliterary: "Labour gives a man a natural right of property in that which he produces: literary com-positions are the effect of labour; authors have therefore a natural right of property in their works."[54] Their second argument was based on an aesthetic theory of the originality inherent in literary compositions that made them incompatible with mechanical inventions that were subject to "patents" that granted a monopoly for only fourteen years. As William Blackstone stated:

> Style and sentiment are the essentials of a literary composition. These alone constitute its identity. The paper and print are merely accidents, which serve as vehicles to convey that style and sentiment to a distance. Every duplicate therefore of a work, whether ten or ten thousands, if it conveys the same style and sentiment, is the same identical work, which was produced by the author's invention and labour.

In this way, Blackstone justified equating literary property with an inalienable "common law right" whose perpetuity was transmitted from the author to the bookseller.[55]

The juridical and judiciary debates engaged in England after the passing of the statute of 1709 went on without any direct intervention on the part of the authors themselves. It was the booksellers, the lawyers, and the judges who drew up a new definition of the man of letters as proprietor of his works, hence as deserving of recompense for a sort of labor unlike any other. A new model for literary activity thus came to be opposed, term for term, to the ancient and aristocratic figure of the "gentleman writer" or the "gentleman amateur" disdainful of the bookselling business and its monetary rewards.[56] In 1774 Lord Camden stated, in defense of this traditional concept: "Glory is the Reward of Science, and those who deserve it, scorn all meaner Views. I speak not of the Scribblers for bread, who teize the Press with their wretched Productions. . . . It was not for Gain that *Bacon, Newton, Milton, Locke* instructed and delighted the World; it would be unworthy such Men to traffic with a dirty Bookseller for so much as a Sheet of Letter-press."[57] The new representation of the man of letters constructed by the booksellers and the jurists as a polemic weapon was hard to reconcile with reality. Until the end of the century, very few authors were able to live from their literary endeavors. The practice of the definitive cession of the manuscript to the bookseller, with no share in the profits deriving from the work's eventual success, along with the aristocratic prejudice disdaining anyone who wrote for money, often made the author-proprietor created by this discourse a proprietor with no revenues.[58]

The only exceptions to this rule arose out of the particular nature or the success of certain genres: drama, where revenues from the publication of the text were accompanied by gate receipts from performances; translations (they made Pope a wealthy man); and, at the end of the century, widely read history books whose authors—Hume, Gibbon, Robertson—were among the first to receive royalties on sales. But the only true literary professionalization in eighteenth-century England was tied, paradoxically, to an activity that hardly ever recognized the author as proprietor and rarely recognized him as a man of letters—journalism.[59] If after 1695 and the Licensing Act (which did away with all pre-publication censorship) the multiplication of periodicals of all sorts created new roles and new employments for writers in the collection of short stories, translation projects, column writing for periodicals, and editorial work, and if some writers (Samuel Johnson, for one) realized handsome revenues from periodical literature, it kept most of the "Grub Street" writers who wrote for the booksellers (and who owned the periodicals) in miserable poverty.[60] James Ralph spoke of these unfortunate writers in 1758 in a pamphlet entitled *The Case of Authors by Profession or Trade Stated:*

> Thus there is no Difference between the Writer in his Garret and the Slave in the Mines; but that the former has his Situation in the Air, the latter in the Bowels of the Earth: Both have their Tasks assigned them alike: Both must drudge and starve; and neither can hope for Deliverance. The Compiler must compile; the Composer must compose on; sick or well; in Spirit or out; whether furnish'd with Matter or not; till by the joint Pressure of Labour, Penury and Sorrow, he has worn out his Parts, his Constitution, and all the little Stock of Reputation he had acquir'd among the Trade.

To resist this enslavement in which labor was no guarantee of ownership and the author no longer possessed himself, James Ralph exhorts writers to band together and strike, refusing to write:

> Were only the *Journals, Chronicals, Magazines,* and other periodicals as well as occasional Productions (which at present contribute so much to the Amusement and Chit-Chat of the day) to be discontinued all at once, how doubly loaded with all the Horrors of vacancy would every Hour limp off? . . . Combine! And perhaps you would need neither Patrons nor Establishments! Combine, and you might out-combine the very Booksellers themselves.[61]

There was thus a sizable gap between the construction of the man of letters as a sovereign and perpetual proprietor of his work, as depicted in the arguments in favor of booksellers anxious to defend their own privileges, and the reality of a situation that only authorized the professionalization of the activity of writing under conditions of submission and precariousness.

Elsewhere in Europe the proliferation of periodicals was not necessarily based on the constitution of an intellectual proletariat that resembled the miserable hack writers of Grub Street. In France it was by and large authors who had a situation or a profession who carried on journalistic activities. In a sample of 274 journalists active between 1725 and

1789, clergy account for 15 percent; officeholders and administrative personnel, 12 percent; men with an independent income, 6 percent; physicians and surgeons, 8 percent; and lawyers, 4 percent. Members of the intellectual professions (professors, tutors, librarians, secretaries) make up 23 percent of the total; and bookseller-publishers, 6 percent. Thus, fewer than a fourth of French journalists (22 percent) belonged to the world of the men of letters who lived essentially on their various writing activities.[62]

In the Italian states the rise in the number of journal titles (some 358 periodicals have been identified between the mid-seventeenth century and the end of the eighteenth century) and the diversification of periodical genres available to the reading public led to a first stage in the professionalization of writing.[63] Giuseppe Ricuperati dates this development in the second half of the century. At that time

> lay professionals began to emerge who took up the trade of journalist in its diverse and by now complex forms as their principal activity. This was the case of Gasparo Gozzi . . . of the Caminers, father and daughter, of Giuseppe Compagnoni, of Giovanni Ristori, of Saverio Catani, and many others. Naturally, the journalist could not live on his earnings from contributing to or editing one periodical alone, especially if it was of the literary sort. Almost always, he combined a number of activities in the same field—those of the gazetteer, the contemporary historian, the editor, and the translator.[64]

Even as journalism was emerging as a specialized occupation, however, the publication of a periodical was still strongly linked to the existence of a particular intellectual milieu. The composition of such circles varied, but all their members were united by bonds of literary sociability. *Il Caffé* is a good example. This journal, modeled on the *Spectator,* arose out of the meetings and conversations of a group of friends in Milan: Pietro Verri, his brother Alessandro, Cesare Beccaria, Gian Rinaldo Carli, Giuseppe Visconti, and Luigi Lambertenghi. What is more, although the journal was well received by its readers, it ceased publication when the group disbanded: "The little society of friends who have written these pages has dissolved; some have gone on a trip, others are occupied by business. Necessity dictates the termination of a project that, according to plans, should not have ended so soon, and this happens at a time at which the favorable welcome of the public more than ever invited its continued existence."[65]

The Pathology of the Man of Letters

The third discourse that provides an objective description of the status of the man of letters is less predictable because its description is medical. In 1766, Tissot delivered a lecture on the topic *de valetudine litteratorum* to inaugurate the chair he had just been offered at the College of Medicine at Lausanne. Two years later, in response to a faulty and abridged translation of that dissertation, he published a corrected and enlarged version in French, which he entitled *De la santé des gens de lettres*. In his preface Tissot recalled that the topic had already been treated in several lectures (by Ramazzini and by Platner) and in a book, *Della preservatione della salute de' Letterati,* written by a professor from Padua named Pujati and published in Venice in 1762. Tissot's interest lay elsewhere, however, since his aim was to "provide a grasp of all the particular circumstances relative to health that distinguish the state of Scholars from that of the other orders of society"—or, in practical terms, to show how the mode of existence of men of letters was as far removed as it could be from the ideal of a life that was natural, "aerated," active, and balanced. It was by the gauge of a convinced Rousseauism that Tissot measured the aberrant behavior that ruined the health of men of letters.

Tissot distinguishes nine causes of their ills. The first two, a tense mind and an inactive body, are the most important. Excessive mental work (which Tissot defines as "literary exhaustion") makes the blood and the vital humors flow to the brain, causing illnesses of the brain (tumors, aneurysms, delirium, convulsions, insomnia, etc.), derangement of the nerves, which depend on the brain, and digestive disorders ("the man who thinks the most is the one who digests the most poorly"). Moreover, Tissot continues, the sedentary life destroys the muscles, impedes the circulation of the blood and the fluids, and engorges the stomach and the intestines, all of which make the man of letters vulnerable to dropsy, bladder troubles, and, especially, hypochondria. Because of its dual etiology (it could produce "weakening of a nervous sort" or "engorgement of the viscera of the lower stomach"), hypochondria is identified as the prime illness of the man of letters: "It is rare for them not to be affected by it in varying degree, and it is difficult to cure them of it completely."

As if this clinical picture were not sufficiently disquieting, Tissot adds other characteristics. The specific ills that men of letters suffer from, he states, can be assigned to various causes: their habits (poor posture, which causes hemorrhoids; keeping excessively late hours, which disturbs sleep; reading during meals, which prevents good digestion), their negligence (they fail to renew the air in their bed chambers every day; they neglect bodily cleanliness; they imprudently "retain their urine for a long time and defer evacuation"), and their retirement from the world. Retirement may well be praiseworthy in moral discourse but the physician judged it to be dangerous: "I do not hesitate to regard as the ninth cause of the illnesses of Scholars their renunciation of society. . . . Men were created for men; their mutual commerce has advantages one does not renounce with impunity, and it has rightly been remarked that solitude throws one into languor. . . . It produces a misanthropy, a vexatious spirit, a discontent, and a disgust of everything that can be considered the worst of all ills because they prevent enjoyment of all good things."

In order to reestablish a health so dangerously compromised (and, if possible, preserve it), Tissot proposes a number of "preservatives" to correct the disorders of the studious life. To counter an overloaded brain, the mind must be offered relaxation, and the scholar must realize that study is not always useful:

> Most people waste time and health for nothing; one compiles the commonest sort of things, another repeats what has already been said a hundred times, a third busies himself with totally useless research; this one is killing himself over the most frivolous compositions, that one composes utterly boring works— and none think of the harm they are doing to themselves or the little profit that the public will draw from it.

To counteract bodily inaction, the man of letters must take physical exercise: "The exercises that I hold best and that are most appropriate for men of letters are those that exercise all the parts of the body, such as tennis, badminton, billiards, croquet, hunting, bowling, lawn bowls, even quoits." A house should be positioned so as to counteract the dangers of bad air. If a country residence proves impossible—and the country is "the place in which one thinks best and breathes the purest air"—one should at least find a city lodging "that is high, well lit, exposed to the wind in the summer and to the sun in winter, and that is far from neighborhoods that have unhealthy exhalations."[66] This means that in Tissot's medical discourse men of letters were considered (negatively) to comprise a particular population distinguished from the rest of society by its mode of life, activity, and habits (in general, its bad habits).

He set up a pitiful image of the literary man as an invalid, in contrast to the more heroic picture of him as a philosopher and guide for humanity.

From the Glories of Parnassus to the Citizen of the Republic of Letters

The image that men of letters gave of themselves provides the last group of representations that we need to consider here. These representations are inscribed in a great variety of literary genres—*éloges, anas, extraits, mélanges,* and more—that aimed at perpetuating the memory of one particular author (by gathering together his writings or his witticisms or by giving an account of his actions) and, beyond the individual portrait, at tracing the ideal image of the man of letters.[67]

On exceptional occasions those representations took the form of a monument. This happened in 1718 and again in 1776. In 1718, the sculptor Louis Garnier finished a bronze statue representing the French Parnassus, a work commissioned and paid for by Titon du Tillet. The latter, who came from a family of nobles "of the robe" and who first had been a captain of dragoons and then *maître d'hôtel* to the dauphine, Marie-Adélaïde of Savoy, was a man of letters who sought (and obtained) academic honors: in his life he was a member of twenty-seven academies—eight in Italy, two in Madrid, one in Lisbon, and sixteen in provincial French cities. His intention was "to raise to the Famous Poets and Musicians a Monument that I have called *The French Parnassus,* presided over by Louis the Great, the August Protector of the Sciences and of the Fine Arts." Parnassus was "represented by an isolated Mountain, somewhat steep and of handsome form, on which are scattered Laurels, Palms, Myrtle branches, and trunks of Oak covered with Ivy." On the slopes of the mountain Louis Garnier, the sculptor, placed thirty-six figures. The fourteen principal statues represented Apollo (that is, Louis XIV), the three graces (Mesdames de La Suze and Deshoulières and Mademoiselle de Scudéry), the nymph of the Seine, and, in imitation of the nine muses, eight poets (Pierre Corneille, Molière, Racan, Segrais, La Fontaine, Chapelle, Racine, and Boileau) and one musician, Lully, who carried on one arm a medallion with a portrait of Quinault. Twenty-two smaller figures held either medallions showing the effigies of other poets and musicians or three scrolls on which their names were inscribed—ninety-one persons in all, including eleven women. Titon du Tillet had thought to leave room so that new writers or composers could be admitted to his Parnassus on their death: their pictures or names could figure on a fourth scroll, on new medallions, or, if one of them should prove worthy of the honor, in a tenth authorial figure.[68]

Titon du Tillet's monument was realized in a reduced format that could be placed in a salon or a gallery. It is depicted in an engraving by Jean Audran that was presented to the king and the principal courtiers in 1723, its more grandiose realization awaiting the sovereign's will: "One might regard this *Parnassus* as a trial for a bigger and more superb one that I would be delighted to see erected with all possible magnificence and the most exquisite taste, but the will to execute something grand must in some way be provided for when private means cannot reach that far." The monument, which was conceived to be installed in a public place in Paris or in the courtyard of the Louvre, was to have figures of "at least natural size" and to be placed on a pedestal of white marble. At its base there was to be "a heap of stones and rocks, thrown there as if by chance" and it was to be enlivened by cascading waters falling into a basin of fine marble. The project was never executed, but as Titon du Tillet imagined it, the monument nonetheless bears witness to a representation using an allegorical and analogical language to construct a pantheon of literary figures whose talents had blossomed thanks to the protection of the prince who governed them.

Fifty years later, Pigalle made a statue of a totally different sort. This one was realistic rather than allegorical; it neither exalted the sovereign's munificence nor celebrated past literary glories. Instead, it offered a true likeness, in the nude, of a contemporary—Voltaire. In a letter to Galiani dated 13 April 1770, Madame d'Épinay tells how the project got started:

> The Sunday gatherings of the rue Royale [the salon of Baron d'Holbach], the Thursdays of the rue Sainte-Anne [at the house of Helvétius, who lived on the same street as Madame d'Épinay], and the Fridays of the rue de Cléry [Madame Necker's salon] got the idea of taking up a collection to erect a statue to Voltaire and of placing it in the new hall of the Comédie Française, which is under construction. Pigalle has been asked to do it; he is asking 10,000 livres and [it will take] two years. Panurge [Abbé Morellet] immediately took charge of the project, and he has drawn up a financial prospectus for its execution. The first rule is that one must be a man of letters whose works have appeared in print in order to subscribe, and he set the subscription levels at 2 louis, 10 louis, and 2,000 livres. D'Al-

Jean Baptiste Pigalle's statue of Voltaire, 1776. Musée du Louvre, Paris.
Giraudon/Art Resource, NY.

embert will act as treasurer and hold the requests and the
money, and Panurge insists that the amounts and the name of
each subscriber be kept secret. And to cap his despotism, he has
drawn up a list prescribing, without consulting them, what all
the associates must contribute.

A week later, Madame d'Épinay informed her correspondent that the
subscription conditions had been broadened so that it was no longer
necessary to have published to participate: "A plurality of votes went
against Panurge, and all *gens de lettres* or amateurs can subscribe for the

statue erected to Voltaire. The epigraph says, 'A Voltaire de son vivant par les gens de lettres ses compatriotes.' "

On 5 May, Galiani, who was at the time absorbed by the publication of his *Dialogue sur les blés* and his controversy with Morellet and the "economists" (that is, the physiocrats), responded jokingly to the first letter:

> I will only subscribe for the statue of Voltaire if I get my turn. One must be erected to me in the handsome rotunda of the new market hall at the Hôtel de Soissons. I would be marvelously at home there, among the flours and the prostitutes of Paris. I will have everything I need for nourishment and for population, and the new philosophers could demand no better. I want it colossal in order to hide from posterity how short I am.

Galiani went on to invent the Latin inscriptions and the medallions that should adorn his monument: "An economist, bowed in adoration before the great god of gardens, who shows his behind as he bows"; "A lady economist who makes an offering of fruits and flowers to Pomona and who, as she offers them, picks her skirts up too high in front"; the two abbés, "Panurge and Badot who sacrifice their writings on a rustic altar to Harpocrates, the god of silence, sleep, and oblivion." On 12 May, Galiani answered a second letter from Madame d'Épinay in a somewhat more serious vein:

> The inscription that is to be placed at the base of the statue of Voltaire would be sublime if all the people of letters of Europe were admitted to the subscription. It would be a fine thing to call the Englishman, the German, and the Italian *comprapatriotes* of Voltaire [a play on words blending "compatriots" and the Italian verb, *comprare*, to buy], and even the emperor of China, who has just written a poem. But if there were only Frenchmen the inscription would fall flat, and it would be better as *A Voltaire par un transport d'admiration.* This would be even better in Latin: *Voltario devicta invidia. Saeculi sui miraculo. Aere eruditorum conlato* [To Voltaire, the destroyer of envy. Miracle of his century. With the money of erudite persons gathered by subscription]. Latin is the language of inscriptions, and the French will never accomplish this miracle in their language.[69]

This initiative, which *La Correspondance Littéraire* attributed to "an assembly of seventeen venerable philosophers, at which, after they had duly invoked the Holy Spirit, copiously dined, and talked at random, it was unanimously decided to erect a statue to Monsieur de Voltaire,"[70] created a scandal. No man of letters had as yet received an homage of this sort during his lifetime. That honor was customarily reserved to sovereigns, a principle that had been respected in the *Parnasse Français,* which celebrated only dead poets. By commissioning a statue of Voltaire, the "House of Lords of literature" (as *La Correspondance Littéraire* wrote) that gathered at Madame Necker's house intended not only to exalt the merits of a man but also to present a representation of the new definition of the man of letters. The subscription, which emanated from the narrowest circle among the literary folk who made up the intellectual sociability of Paris, offered a broader milieu not only an opportunity to declare its candidacy as participants in the Republic of Letters but also a chance to be recognized by the sponsors of the enterprise. As Dena Goodman writes, "By subscribing to the statue of Voltaire, one thus made a political statement: one asserted oneself as a citizen of the Republic of Letters."

Notified of the project by private correspondence (see Madame d'Épinay's letters to Galiani) and by *nouvelles à la main* (manuscript newsletters), eighty persons subscribed. They represented the two aspects of the Enlightenment in its most legitimate definition: within the kingdom of France, wealthy men of letters who had "arrived" (the average age of subscribers was high: forty-five), many of whom held offices or charges in the royal administration or were members of academies, and one-fourth of whom were occasional or regular correspondents of Voltaire's; outside France, the princes of enlightened Europe.[71] Morellet recalled in his memoirs the importance of this princely participation— which was political more than financial, since the size of the contributions was limited to preserve at least the fiction of equality among the subscribers: "What put the final touch on determining the execution of the project was the part played by the king of Denmark, the empress of Russia, Frederick the Great, and several German princes."[72]

Pigalle's statue of Voltaire (Pigalle was also the sculptor of the statue of Louis XV commissioned for the Place Royale in Reims in 1755) showed the writer nude but for an unrolled scroll held in one hand and a quill pen in the other. As a representation of the man of letters it was less than fully appreciated by contemporaries. Morellet declared: "Persons of taste generally criticized the execution. In order to demonstrate his knowledge of anatomy, Pigalle has made a nude, fleshless old man, a skeleton—a defect barely remedied by the verity and the life to be admired in the physiognomy and the oldster's attitude."[73]

Nonetheless, when he sculpted Voltaire in his full humanity, without monumentality and without aestheticizing him, Pigalle displayed the fundamental and necessary equality among all citizens of the Republic of Letters, but also the dignity inherent in all citizens. The statue of Voltaire—sponsored by the very aristocratic and very exclusive society of the Paris salons, supported by the literary milieus that were both the wealthiest and the most solidly established within a society of orders and bodies, supported by the enlightened (if despotic) princes of northern Europe—nevertheless offered a representation of the values of a new literary and political order. It was a perfect incarnation of the contradictions that permeated both the definition and the status of the man of letters in the age of the Enlightenment: privilege and equality, protection and independence, prudent reformism and utopian aspiration.[74]

Notes

1. "Gens de lettres," in *Encyclopédie, ou Dictionnaire raisonnée des sciences, des arts et des métiers, par une société de gens de lettres* (Paris: 1751–72); quoted here and below in this chapter from "Men of Letters," in *Encyclopedia: Selections*, trans. Nelly S. Hoyt and Thomas Cassirer (Indianapolis: Bobbs-Merrill, 1965), 247–49 (quotation, 247). See also the articles "Lettres" and "Littérature" in *Encyclopédie*.

2. Immanuel Kant, preface to the First Edition, *The Critique of Pure Reason*, Meiklejohn translation revised and expanded, ed. Vasilis Politis, Everyman (London: J. M. Dent; Rutland, Vt.: E. Tuttle, 1993), 5.

3. Voltaire, *Le siècle de Louis XIV* (1751), 2 vols. (Paris: Garnier-Flammarion, 1966), 1: 327–29; quoted from *The Age of Louis XIV*, trans. Martyn P. Pollack (London and Toronto, J. M. Dent & Sons; New York, E. P. Dutton, 1926), 275.

4. Voltaire, "Lettres, Gens de lettres, ou Lettrés," in *Dictionnaire philosophique, comprenant les 118 articles parus sous ce titre du vivant de Voltaire avec leurs suppléments parus dans les Questions de l'Encyclopédie* (Paris: Garnier Frères, 1961), 271–74; quoted from "Letters (Men of)," *Philosophical Dictionary, The Works of Voltaire*, trans. William F. Fleming, 42 vols. (London: E. R. Dumont, 1901), 11: 118.

5. Quoted from *Encyclopedia: Selections*, 249.

6. Voltaire, "Auteurs," in *Dictionnaire philosophique*, in his *Oeuvres complètes* (Paris: Garnier Frères, 1878–79), 1: 496–501; quoted from "Authors," in *Philosophical Dictionary, The Works of Voltaire*, 6: 173, 175–76.

7. Robert Darnton, "The Facts of Literary Life in Eighteenth-Century France," in *The Political Culture of the Old Régime*, ed. Keith M. Baker, vol. 1 of *The*

French Revolution and the Creation of Modern Political Culture (Oxford and New York: Pergamon Press, 1987–94), 261–91 (quotation, 264).

8. Ibid., 267.

9. Robert Darnton, "A Police Inspector Sorts His Files: The Anatomy of the Republic of Letters," in *The Great Cat Massacre and Other Episodes in French Cultural History* (New York: Basic Books, 1984), 144–89.

10. Ibid., 168.

11. Daniel Roche, *Le siècle des Lumières en province: Académies et académiciens provinciaux, 1680–1789,* Civilisation et sociétés, 62, 2 vols. (Paris and The Hague: Mouton, 1978), 1: 185–255; table 16, 2: 385; table 30, 2: 406–7.

12. Denis Diderot, *Sur la liberté de la presse,* partial text established, presented, and provided with notes by Jacques Proust (Paris: Éditions Sociales, 1964). On this text, see Roger Chartier, *Les origines culturelles de la Révolution française* (Paris: Seuil, 1990), 69–80; available in English as *The Cultural Origins of the French Revolution,* trans. Lydia G. Cochrane (Durham, NC, and London: Duke University Press, 1991), 38–66.

13. Raymond Birn, "Rousseau et ses éditeurs," *Revue d'Histoire Moderne et Contemporaine* 40, 1 (1993): 120–36.

14. Louis-Sébastien Mercier, "Dictionnaires," in *Tableau de Paris: Nouvelle édition revue et augmentée,* 12 vols. (Amsterdam, 1782–83), 6: 294–95; for a modern edition, see *Tableau de Paris,* ed. Jean-Claude Bonnet, 2 vols. (Paris: Mercure de France, 1994).

15. Jeremy Popkin, "Pamphlet Journalism at the End of the Old Regime," *The French Revolution in Culture,* special issue of *Eighteenth-Century Studies* 22, 3 (1989): 351–67 (quotation, 361).

16. Robert Darnton, "Ideology on the Bourse," in *L'image de la Révolution Française,* ed. Michel Vovelle. Papers presented at the Congrès mondial pour le bicentenaire de la Révolution, Sorbonne, Paris, 6–12 June 1989. 4 vols. (Paris and New York: Pergamon, 1990), 1: 124–39; Darnton's paper is available in French translation as "L'idéologie à la Bourse," in his *Gens de lettres, gens du livre,* trans. Marie-Alyx Revellat (Paris: Éditions Odile Jacob, 1992), 85–98. On Brissot, see the exchange between Frederick A. de Luna and Robert Darnton in *French Historical Studies* 17, 1 (Spring 1991): 159–208 (quotation, 199).

17. Reinhard Wittmann, "Der Dichter auf dem Markt—Die Entstehung des freien Schriftstellers," chap. 5 in *Geschichte des deutschen Buchandels* (Munich: Verlag C. H. Beck, 1991), 143–70, esp. 147. See also Albert Ward, *Book Production, Fiction, and the German Reading Public, 1740–1800* (Oxford: Clarendon Press, 1974), 88.

18. Claudio Colaiacomo, "Crisi dell' 'ancien régime': Dall'uomo di lettere al letterato borghese," in *Produzione e consumo,* vol. 2 of *Letteratura Italiana,* ed. Alberto Asor Rosa (Turin: Einaudi, 1982–83), 363–412.

19. Ibid., 363.

20. On the rise of the concept of literary property, see the studies of Martha

Woodmansee, "The Genius and the Copyright: Economic and Legal Conditions of the Emergence of the 'Author,' " *Eighteenth-Century Studies* 17, 4 (1984): 425–85, and *The Author, Art, and the Market: Rereading the History of Aesthetics* (New York: Columbia University Press, 1994) (for Germany); Mark Rose, "The Author as Proprietor: *Donaldson v. Becket* and the Genealogy of Modern Authorship," *Representations* 23 (1988): 51–85, and *Authors and Owners: The Invention of Copyright* (Cambridge, Mass., and London: Harvard University Press, 1993) (for England); Carla Hesse, "Enlightenment Epistemology and the Laws of Authorship in Revolutionary France, 1777–1793," *Representations* 30 (1990): 109–37 (for France); Joaquín Alvarez Barrientos, François Lopez, and Immaculada Urzainqui, *La República de las Letras en la España del Siglo XVIII* (Madrid: Consejo Superior de Investigaciones Científicas, 1995) (for Spain). See also Roger Chartier, "Figures de l'auteur," chap. 2 in *L'ordre des livres: Lecteurs, auteurs, bibliothèques en Europe entre XIVᵉ et XVIIIᵉ siècle* (Aix-en-Provence: Alinéa, 1992), 35–67; available in English as "Figures of the Author," in *The Order of Books: Readers, Authors, and Libraries in Europe between the Fourteenth and Eighteenth Centuries,* trans. Lydia G. Cochrane (Cambridge, U.K.: Polity Press, 1994), 25–60.

21. *Mémoires de l'abbé Morellet de l'Académie française sur le XVIIIᵉ siècle et sur la Révolution,* with introduction and notes by Jean-Pierre Guicciardi (Paris: Le Mercure de France, 1988), 54. For a complete edition of Morellet's correspondence, see *Lettres d'André Morellet,* ed. Dorothy Medlin, Jean-Claude David, and Paul Leclerc, 2 vols. (Oxford, Voltaire Foundation, Taylor Institution, 1991—), esp. vol. 1. On Morellet's career, see Robert Darnton, "Une carrière littéraire exemplaire," in *Gens de lettres, gens du livre,* 47–67. On Morellet's projected commercial dictionary, see Jean-Claude Perrot, "Les dictionnaires de commerce au XVIIIᵉ siècle," *Revue d'Histoire Moderne et Contemporaine* 28 (1981): 36–67, reprinted in Jean-Claude Perrot, *Une Histoire intellectuelle de l'économie politique, XVIIᵉ–XVIIIᵉ siècle* (Paris: École des Hautes Études en Sciences Sociales, 1992), 97–126.

22. Jean François Marmontel, *Mémoires,* critical edition by John Renwick, 2 vols. (Clermont-Ferrand: G. De Bussac, 1972), 1: 143, 179, 188; quoted here and below in this chapter from *Memoirs of Marmontel,* Courtiers and Favourites of Royalty, ed. Léon Vallée, 2 vols. (Paris: Société des Bibliophiles; New York: Merrill D. Baker, 1903), 1: 223, 283, 299.

23. Abbé Ferdinando Galiani, *Correspondance,* ed. Lucien Perey and Gaston Maugras, 2 vols. (Paris: Calmann-Lévy, 1889–90), 1: 93–94, 328, 380; 2: 110. For a complete edition of Galiani's correspondence with Madame d'Épinay, see Ferdinando Galiani and Louise d'Épinay, *Correspondance,* presented by Georges Dulac, ed. Daniel Maggetti, 4 vols. (Paris: Éditions Desjonquères, distribution Presses Universitaires de France, 1992—), 1: 1–20.

24. The study of Paris salons was profoundly revitalized by several studies by Dena Goodman: "Enlightenment Salons: The Convergence of Female and Philosophic Ambitions," *Eighteenth-Century Studies* 22, 3 (1989): 329–50; "Governing the Republic of Letters: The Politics of Culture in the French Enlighten-

ment," *History of European Ideas* 13, 3 (1991): 183–99; "Public Sphere and Private Life: Toward a Synthesis of Current Historiographical Approaches to the Old Regime," *History and Theory* 31, 1 (1992): 1–20. See also Dena Goodman, *The Republic of Letters: A Cultural History of the French Enlightenment* (Ithaca: Cornell University Press, 1994).

25. Marmontel, *Memoirs of Marmontel,* 1: 251–52, 350.

26. Ibid., 250.

27. Goodman, "Governing the Republic of Letters," 187.

28. Marmontel, *Memoirs of Marmontel,* 1: 269, 357. On the dinners given by d'Holbach, see Alan Charles Kors, *D'Holbach's Coterie: An Enlightenment in Paris* (Princeton: Princeton University Press, 1977); Daniel Roche, "Lumières et engagement politique: La coterie d'Holbach dévoilée," in *Les Républicains des Lettres: Gens de culture et Lumières au XVIIIᵉ siècle* (Paris: Fayard, 1988), 242–53.

29. Morellet, *Mémoires,* 96–97, 129–30, 135.

30. Marmontel, *Memoirs of Marmontel,* 1: 266.

31. Morellet, *Mémoires,* 143–44.

32. Goodman, "Enlightenment Salons," 338.

33. Carolyn C. Lougee, *Le Paradis de Femmes: Women, Salons, and Social Stratification in Seventeenth-Century France* (Princeton: Princeton University Press, 1976).

34. Dominique Joseph Garat, *Mémoires historiques sur la vie de M. Suard, sur ses écrits, et sur le XVIIIᵉ siècle,* 2 vols. (Paris: A. Belin, 1820–21), 1: 173, 172, 170. On Suard's career, see Robert Darnton, "The High Enlightenment and the Low-life of Literature in Prerevolutionary France," *Past and Present* 51 (1971): 81–115.

35. André Morellet, *De la conversation, suivi d'un essai de Jonathan Swift,* with a foreword by Chantal Thomas (Paris: Rivage poche/Petite Bibliothèque, 1995). On Morellet's texts, see Daniel Gordon, "'Public Opinion' and the Civilizing Process in France: The Example of Morellet," *Eighteenth-Century Studies* 22, 3 (1989): 302–28; Barbara R. Hanning, "Conversation and Musical Style in the Late Eighteenth-Century Parisian Salon," *Eighteenth-Century Studies* 22, 4 (1989): 512–28 (quotation, 518). On conversation as a genre, see Marc Fumaroli, *Le genre des genres littéraires français: La conversation* (Oxford: Clarendon Press, 1992).

36. Jean-Jacques Rousseau, *Lettre à M. d'Alembert sur son article Genève* (Paris: Flammarion, 1967), 195, 115, 197–99; quoted from *Politics and the Arts: Letter to M. d'Alembert on the Theatre,* trans., with introduction and notes, Allan Bloom (1960; Ithaca: Cornell University Press, 1968), 100, 49, 101–2, 103.

37. Edward Gibbon, *Memoirs of My Life.* ed., with introduction, Betty Radice (London and New York: Penguin, 1984), 136, 137.

38. Jacques-Pierre Brissot de Warville, *Mémoires (1754–1793),* 2 vols. (Paris: Picard, 1912), 1: 126–28, 122–23, 199.

39. Voltaire, *L'homme aux quarante écus* (1768), in *Zadig ou la destinée, Micromegas et autres contes* (Paris: Le Livre de Poche, 1983), 2: 201–78 (quotation, 271);

quoted here from "The Man Worth Forty Crowns," in *The Works of Voltaire*, trans. William F. Fleming, 42 vols. (Paris, E. R. DuMont, 1901), 2: 298–99.

40. Horst Möller, "Enlightened Societies in the Metropolis: The Case of Berlin," in *The Transformation of Political Culture: England and Germany in the Late Eighteenth Century*, ed. Eckhart Hellmuth (London: German Historical Institute; Oxford and New York: Oxford University Press, 1990), 219–33.

41. Hans Erich Bödeker, "Journals and Public Opinion: The Politicization of the German Enlightenment in the Second Half of the Eighteenth Century," in *The Transformation of Political Culture*, ed. Eckhart Hellmuth (London: The German Historical Institute; Oxford and New York: Oxford University Press, 1990), 423–45, esp. tables on 428, 436.

42. Anthony J. La Vopa, "Conceiving a Public: Ideas and Society in Eighteenth-Century Europe," *Journal of Modern History* 64 (1992): 79–116 (quotation, 89). See also Franklin Kopitzsch, "Esquisse d'une histoire sociale de l'*Aufklärung* en Allemagne," in *La Révolution, la France et l'Allemagne: Deux modèles opposés de changement social?* ed. Helmut Berding, Étienne François, and Hans-Peter Ullmann (Paris: Maison des Sciences de l'Homme, 1989), 348–65.

43. Marmontel, *Memoirs of Marmontel*, 1: 337, 338–40.

44. On the English coffee-houses, see Aytoun Ellis, *The Penny Universities: A History of the Coffee-Houses* (London: Secker and Warburg, 1956); E. J. Clery, "Women, Publicity, and the Coffee-House Myth," *Women: A Cultural Review* 2, 2 (1991): 168–77, an article that reevaluates female sociability in the coffee-houses; Steve Pincus, "'Coffee Politicians Does Create': Coffeehouses and Restoration Political Culture," *Journal of Modern History* 67, 4 (1995): 807–34.

45. Darnton, "The High Enlightenment," 100.

46. Roche, *Le siècle des Lumières en province*, 1: 63–68.

47. Brissot, *Mémoires*, 1: 238–43, 338–39 (quotations, 239, 329). On the *Journal du Lycée de Londres*, see Jean Sgard, ed., *Dictionnaire des journaux, 1600–1789*, 2 vols. (Paris: Universitas, 1991), 2: 659–60.

48. Daniel Roche, "Correspondance et voyage au XVIIIᵉ siècle: Le réseau des sociabilités d'un académicien provincial, Séguier de Nîmes," in *Les Républicains des lettres*, 263–80.

49. Roche, *Le siècle des Lumières en province*, 1: 319–22; 2: 509–13.

50. Galiani, Correspondance, 1: 188.

51. On this work, see Claude Cristin, *Aux origines de l'histoire littéraire*, Hypothèse, 3 (Saint-Martin d'Hères: Presses Universitaires de Grenoble, 1973).

52. Jean-Jacques Garnier, *L'homme de lettres* (Paris: Panckoucke, 1764), 7, 45, 118, 121, 192, 8–9, 198.

53. Rose, "The Author as Proprietor," 42.

54. William Enfield, *Observations on Literary Property* (London, 1774); quoted from Rose, "The Author as Proprietor," 59.

55. William Blackstone, *Tonson v. Collins* in *The English Reports, Full Reprints*, 176 vols. (Edinburgh and London, 1900–30), 96: 189; quoted from Rose, "The Author as Proprietor," 63.

56. On the status of the man of letters in England during the eighteenth century, see the two classic studies of Arthur Simons Collins: *Authorship in the Days of Johnson: Being a Study of the Relation Between Author, Patron, Publisher, and Public, 1726–1780* (London: Robert Holden and Co., 1927), and *The Profession of Letters: A Study of the Relation of Author to Patron, Publisher, and Public, 1780–1832* (London: George Routledge & Sons, 1928). See also Alvin B. Kernan, *Printing Technology, Letters, & Samuel Johnson* (Princeton: Princeton University Press, 1987).

57. Lord Camden, in *The Cases of the Appellants and Respondents in the Cause of Literary Property Before the House of Lords* (London, 1774), 54, quoted in Rose, "The Author as Proprietor," 54.

58. Terry Belanger, "Publishers and Writers in Eighteenth-Century England," in *Books and their Readers in Eighteenth-Century England*, ed. Isabel Rivers (New York: St. Martin's Press, 1982), 5–25.

59. Michael Harris, "Journalism as a Profession or Trade in the Eighteenth Century," in *Author/Publisher Relations during the Eighteenth and Nineteenth Centuries*, ed. Robin Myers and Michael Harris (Oxford: Oxford Polytechnic Press, 1983), 37–62.

60. On the literary proletariat of England, see the studies of Pat Rogers: *Grub Street: Studies in a Subculture* (London: Methuen; U.S. distribution, Harper & Row, Barnes & Noble, 1972), and *Hacks and Dunces: Pope, Swift and Grub Street* (London and New York: Methuen, 1980).

61. James Ralph, *The Case of Authors by Profession or Trade Stated* (London, 1758), quoted in Harris, "Journalism as a Profession or Trade," 37–38.

62. Jean Sgard, "Journale und Journalisten im Zeitalter der Aufklärung," in *Sozialgeschichte der Aufklärung in Frankreich: 12 Original-Beiträge*, ed. Hans Ulrich Gumbrecht, Rolf Reichardt, and Thomas Schleich, Ancien régime, Aufklärung und Revolution, 4, 2 vols. (Munich and Vienna: Oldenbourg, 1981), 2: 3–33 (table, 28).

63. Giuseppe Ricuperati, "Giornali e società nell'Italia dell'Ancien Régime (1668–1789)," and Mario Cuaz, "Elenco delle testate," in *La Stampa italiana dal Cinquecento all'Ottocento*, ed. Valerio Castronovo, Giuseppe Ricuperati, and Carlo Capra (Rome and Bari: Laterza, 1976–78), 67–365 and 366–72, respectively.

64. Giuseppe Ricuperati, "Periodici eruditi, riviste e giornali di varia umanità dalle origini a metà Ottocento," in *Il letterato e le istituzioni*, vol. 1 of *Letteratura italiana*, ed. Alberto Asor Rosa, 921–43 (quotation, 928).

65. On *Il Caffè*, see Ricuperati, "Giornali e società," 208–15 (quotation, 215).

66. Samuel Tissot, *De la santé des gens de lettres* (1768; reprint, presentation by

François Azouvi, Geneva and Paris: Slatkine Reprints, 1981), xii–xiii, 23, 25, 69, 93, 95–96, 125, 136, 200.

67. On the genre and the themes of the academic eulogy, see Roche, *Le siècle des Lumières en province,* 1: 166–81.

68. Évrard Titon du Tillet, *Description du Parnasse François, exécuté en bronze, suivie d'une liste alphabétique des poètes, et des musiciens rassemblés sur ce monument* (Paris, 1727), xxiii, 1, xxv–xxvi. On this monument and its commissioner, see Roche, *Le siècle des Lumières en province,* 1: 302–4; 2: 120.

69. Galiani and d'Épinay, *Correspondance,* 1: 140, 144, 158–59, 165.

70. Friedrich Melchior Grimm et al., *La Correspondance Littéraire, Philosophique et Critique . . . ,* ed. Maurice Tourneux, 16 vols. (Paris: Garnier, 1879), 9: 15–16. The seventeen philosophers listed were Madame Necker, Diderot, Suard, the Chevalier de Chastellux, Grimm, the comte de Schomberg, Marmontel, d'Alembert, Thomas, Necker, Saint-Lambert, Saurin, Abbé Raynal, Helvétius, Bernard, Abbé Arnaud, and Abbé Morellet.

71. Dena Goodman, "Pigalle's *Voltaire nu:* The Republic of Letters Represents Itself to the World," *Representations* 16 (1986): 86–109 (quotation, 96).

72. Morellet, *Mémoires,* 175.

73. Ibid.

74. Franco Venturi, *Utopia e riforma nell'illuminismo* (Turin: Einaudi, 1970); available in English as *Utopia and Reform in the Enlightenment,* Trevelyan Lectures, 1969 (Cambridge, U.K.: Cambridge University Press, 1971). See also the critical note on the English translation of this work by Bronislaw Baczko, "L'énigme des Lumières," *Annales E.S.C.* 28 (1973): 1515–20.

5 / The Man of Science

Vincenzo Ferrone

If during the seventeenth century science, though not yet the scientist, began to take form, they both played a major role in the age of the Enlightenment. Obviously, we need to agree on what we mean by the term "scientist," taking into account contexts and historical moments and doing our best to avoid forced comparisons and anachronisms. The guiding thread of the present chapter is the hypothesis that for the man of science the eighteenth century represented not so much a transition phase leading to the contemporary scientist (who appeared in the nineteenth century), but rather a laboratory stage of modernity. It was during the eighteenth century that long-term processes reached maturity—a new knowledge achieved definitive recognition, gained legitimacy, and acquired the institutional consolidation necessary to lay the foundations of a true profession. New and lacerating questions appeared on the horizon, among them the great topic of demarcation, debated officially for the first time—that is, deciding what should be considered science and what should not.

But if we are to comprehend the eighteenth-century view of the man of science we need first to recall that he had behind him at least two centuries of the so-called scientific revolution. University professors, clerics, physicians, philosophers, mathematicians, astrologers, artists, architects, and engineers had worked to bring to life a new sort of knowledge and to invent the new figure of the intellectual determined to investigate natural phenomena with empirical methods and to measure them and verify them experimentally. This new man had a language and objectives that differed from those of the traditional disciplines of philosophy, theology, jurisprudence, and literature. A key moment in the formation of this distinction occurred during the seventeenth century, when an aggressive movement to propagandize science as an autonomous and original form of knowledge—one deserving of dignity and prestige thanks to its social utility—encountered an emergent academic movement often in open disagreement with the university corporation. It was within the academies that the man of science began the long march that was to lead him to take on scientific investigation as a profession.

This long and laborious process was successful, despite its first clamorous failure in Italy, but it took two centuries. In Italy, where both modern science and, before it, the academic movement were born, the omnipotent figure of the theologian still reigned supreme and the scientific academies failed to take root. Galileo's condemnation, the experience of the Accademia dei Lincei and the Accademia del Cimento, and later (in the early eighteenth century) that of the enlightened Catholics under the leadership of Celestino Galiani were all stages in a gradual and melancholy marginalization of the man of science in relation to literati and philosophers more sensitive to the "reason of the church" imposed by the Council of Trent.

The English man of science fared better, and across the Channel scientific propaganda soon overcame all resistance. In London the harmonization of science and religion that was impossible in Rome became the fulcrum of a genuine cultural revolution, to the point that some scholars speak of the "Anglican origins of modern science." The millenarian inspiration in English Protestantism had immediately grasped the utilitarian dimension of the new knowledge. Bacon and many Puritan thinkers after him saw the task of science as producing wealth, improving health, developing trade, and creating an encyclopedia of all knowledge—an *Instauratio Magna*—to effect a return to Eden. The mechanistic universe of Isaac Newton and the famous Boyle Lectures delivered and circulated to combat "freethinkers" and radical republicans contributed to the definition of an ideology of the "establishment" that had emerged victorious from the Glorious Revolution of 1689 and had made the Royal Society (founded in 1662) the leading scientific institution of Europe. From that moment on, science was considered an integral and decisive part of the education of the new elites of England. Nonetheless, the undisputed primacy that the British man of science had enjoyed in Europe during the latter half of the seventeenth century proved more fragile than had been foreseen. Paradoxically, the very qualities that had made him so extraordinarily successful worked against his fortunes in the coming phase of rapidly changing problems and methods of investigation. The Baconian model of the "natural philosopher" as a pious Christian and a dilettante and the private societies that grew out of that model were ill-adapted to a growing specialization and its concomitant need to train people to something approaching a professional level in a reasonable amount of time.

During the eighteenth century, the Royal Society yielded to its sister society in Paris, the Académie des Sciences, which flourished under the pensions and privileges lavished on it by Louis XIV. Throughout the new century, the much-admired fellow of the Royal Society remained true to the Baconian model of the natural philosopher, ceding leadership to the more open-minded, more modern Parisian *savant*.

The Ancien-Régime Man of Science and French Primacy

Lagrange was not altogether to be blamed when he responded, in 1787, to the pressing invitation of the new king of Piedmont, Victor Amadeus III, to return to Turin, saying that he could not refuse the offer made to him by the Académie des Sciences in Paris. "The Académie has a great attraction for me," Lagrange wrote, "as it is the leading tribunal of Europe for the sciences." The French scientific community was unrivaled in all disciplines. All Europe admired and imitated the model of the *savant* in the service of the state, a model created over a century of Bourbon absolutism by the efficacious and forward-looking cultural policy of royal patronage initiated by Richelieu and Colbert. The Académie des Sciences, later the keystone of the entire French academic system, was founded in 1666, many years after the much more famous Académie Française and a few years after the Académie des Inscriptions et Belles-Lettres. The creation of a body to promote the advancement of the sciences was urged by such scholars as Auzout, Petit, Huygens, Thévenot, and Sorbière, all men who had been formed in the schools of Galileo, Descartes, and Bacon. Their conception of the organization of scientific research was strongly influenced by the democratic tendencies of the Baconian model but also by a vision of the academic world financed by princely patronage, as in the Italian Renaissance, that had persisted in the academies of the Lincei and the Cimento. It is hardly surprising that the activities of the first decades of the Académie reflected the underlying notions of Thévenot's 1665 project for a Compagnie des Sciences et des Arts in which scholars were to work and publish collectively and anonymously in order to guarantee absolute equality to the members of that revival of the "House of Solomon." The first official publications of the Académie des Sciences appeared without mention of their authors' names, while the king played the time-honored role of the wealthy patron.

It was only in 1699, with the new rules for the Académie drafted by Abbé Bignon (approved in final form by the Parlement de Paris in 1713), that the French man of science—and, more generally, the European man of science—emerged. This was a totally original figure, different in many ways from both Bacon's "new philosopher" and the earlier "scientists." In homage to France, his native land, this new figure might be defined as the *savant* of the ancien régime—that is, an intellectual who functioned as an organic part of the apparatus of state and who wholly accepted the logic and the values of a society that was hierarchical, prescriptive, and organized into orders, strata, and bodies emphasizing dignities, honors, and a constant presence of privilege and rank. The integration of the man of science into this markedly inegalitarian social order was without doubt the most characteristic feature of the *Règlement* of 1699: "In virtue of its rules," Fontenelle wrote with notable satisfaction, "the Académie des Sciences becomes a body established in proper form by royal authority—something that it was not before." It was not only a *corps* but a *corps savant* determined to find a prominent place for itself, a specific identity, and full legitimation among the various *corps d'état*. To further these aims, the Académie took steps to create a ritual and a rigid etiquette, formulating written norms of comportment and detailed guidelines for judging works and propagandizing the merits and conquests of its learned members to the outside world. The members of the Académie debated the choice of an image, a motto, and symbols that would represent the nascent community in the collective imagination. The symbol chosen, as the academy's first great secretary and its historian, Fontenelle, relates, was "a sun, symbol of the King and of the sciences, between three fleurs-de-lys"; and the academy's device was "a Minerva surrounded by the instruments of the sciences and the arts, with the Latin words *invenit et perficit.*"

To effect the crucial connection between historical memory and the new body, the practice of delivering an *éloge* in commemoration of a deceased *savant* was instituted. Such eulogies, which were published periodically, became, in time, a genuine literary genre and a formidable contribution to the "history of the sciences" to which Condorcet assigned the task, toward the end of the century of the Enlightenment, of providing the nub of a progressive ideology to further the "advance of the human mind" under the banner of scientific knowledge.

The new *corps d'état* of *mathématiciens, physiciens, médecins, chymistes,* and *savants anatomistes,* although "open to merit," as Fontenelle proudly insisted, was organized according to the vertical logic of a stratified French society. The rules of the Académie grouped the *savants* in a hierarchical order. At the summit were the *honoraires,* all men of the high clergy, the nobility, or the government, most of them dilettantes of no scientific merit. This group, which is not mentioned in the original acts of foundation, appears in the new rules drawn up in 1699, thus ratifying the presence of the absolutist state and the academy's adherence to the social principles of the ancien régime. Second in rank came the *pensionnaires,* authoritative men of science who received compensation for their investigations. They were followed by *associés,* foreign and French *correspondants,* and *élèves,* also called *adjoints.* In all more than three hundred people contributed to what might be defined as the first "scientific enterprise" of modern times.

The crown not only held administrative control of the Académie (divided between the ministries of the Bâtiments du Roi and the Maison du Roi) but chose the most prominent *honoraires,* thus sanctioning the academy's definitive change, after 1699, from a semiprivate structure supported by royal patronage and administered by the scholars themselves to a genuine state institution with functions resembling those of a modern technical and scientific consultative body. This radical change brought the Académie new tasks: first, the duty to examine scientific novelties that emerged in France or elsewhere; next, the control and guidance of research through a strategy of competitions that (for the first time in history) offered sizable rewards for the best solutions to problems in a variety of disciplines; finally, the creation of the bases for the balanced and controlled development of a more modern technology. This third and highly important task, which included the formulation of norms and criteria for global evaluations covering all "inventors," was furthered by the famous *privilège* that the Académie granted to artisans and inventors and by the publication of the volumes of its *Description des arts et des métiers.*

The Académie also had the mandate (soon transformed into a monopoly) to supervise everything published in the sciences, not only the articles that appeared in its own *Mémoires* but, in practice, everything produced within the borders of the kingdom. This included supervisory powers over the *Journal des Savants* and production of the astronomical almanac compiled by the Observatoire.

Carrying out these institutional duties brought ample rewards and recognition. The king gave the *pensionnaires* (with the *honoraires,* the real masters of the Académie) 2,000 livres per year, plus one *jeton* (a token representing a cash payment) for each meeting they attended. This was a modest sum but it was accompanied by other and hardly negligible rewards in the form of nominations reserved for academicians to posts in public administration, teaching positions, or positions as consultants for the Bureau de Commerce. Following the custom and the logic of the ancien régime, the state granted precise privileges and honors to each class of *académiciens*. These ranged from partial exemption from taxes on their earnings to exemption from military service; from a highly prized opportunity to be admitted into the presence of the king to formal recognition and a specified place at court ceremonies and public manifestations, along with the other *corps d'état*. Only the *pensionnaires* and the *honoraires* could vote to elect new members, whose nomination was ratified by the king. Even service on committees and commissions, and participation in discussion on particular topics when the Académie met in formal sessions were governed by a protocol based on hierarchy that displayed an ironclad respect for seniority and rank.

In short, a spirit inherited from feudalism that had nothing in common with the democratic tone of the "House of Solomon" of Bacon's dreams unquestionably still reigned in the halls of the Louvre in which the members of the Académie met twice weekly, filing in with silent and respectful reserve according to a precise ceremonial. Through the Académie, the *savant* took his place within the dialectic of status. Nonetheless—and paradoxically—beyond appearances and in spite of the marked contrast between the innovative system of values of the new science and the unbudging reality of a stratified society, precisely because the *Règlement* of the Académie fitted in with the corporative logic of the ancien régime it considerably accelerated the process of creation of the modern *savant*. The man of science became one of the protagonists in the process of formation of the new elites of merit that created a place for themselves beside the nobility and the *grands* of the kingdom. The compromise with absolutism and with its patronage-based system for the organization of intellectual life permitted them (among other advantages) an opportunity for the full development of the potential of the scientific method and for enlarging their ranks, thanks to the financial aid, pensions, and privileges accorded by the king.

The European man of science who visited Paris in the eighteenth century in a sort of lay pilgrimage would be shown with pride the city's many centers of study, unequaled throughout the Continent, its laboratories, and its well-stocked specialized libraries. The Académie des Sciences stood at the pinnacle of the system, but there were other highly prestigious institutions financed by the state such as the Société de Médicine and the Observatoire. Bailly and Lalande worked in the monumental building that the Sun King had constructed in 1667 for the Observatoire, for decades administered by the famous Cassini family. The Observatoire, in collaboration with a network of telescopes at the Collège des Quatre Nations, the École Militaire, and the Collège de Cluny, coordinated the research of a number of scholars—Delambre, Maraldi, Lecaille, La Condamine, and Legendre—and astronomers throughout Europe. Their work enlarged knowledge in the fields of cartography, geodetics, and star mapping, and the institutions mobilized resources and manpower for spectacular voyages to the equator and other far-off parts of the globe.

The troubled existence of the Société de Médecine casts light on the complex relationship between scientific circles and public power during the eighteenth century. Founded by letters patent granted by the king in 1778 and directed with great authority by Vicq d'Azyr, who was a friend of Turgot's, the Société was granted ample jurisdiction over the health policies of the kingdom. This was in open contradiction with the privileges of the powerful Faculté de Médecine, which reacted by appealing to the Parlement de Paris. The administration allocated to the Société responsibility for acting to control epidemics, for the scientific analysis of pharmaceuticals in view of their commercialization, and for coordinating the nascent study of meteorology and the study of diseases, which it carried out by collecting reports on all manner of diseases from corresponding members in the provinces.

There were other institutions organically connected with the bureaucratic apparatus of state that swelled the number of Parisian men of science. One body that immediately springs to mind is the prestigious Collège de France, justly considered the first modern structure for advanced scientific instruction. In its lecture halls next to the Sorbonne opened by royal patronage to private citizens in 1550 in order to communicate knowledge often not offered at the university, eight of the nineteen disciplines taught were scientific, thus confirming the public's growing interest. Among others, Daubenton, Poissonier, and Lalande lectured in astronomy at the Collège, as did Darcet in chemistry, Girault de Kéroudou in mechanics, and Lefèvre de Gineau in experimental physics. Public lectures were also given by the personnel of the Jardin des Plantes, another famous institution, in which Buffon and his students worked to extend knowledge in the fields of natural history, botany, zoology, and geology.

If we are to grasp the full weight and breadth of French science, however, or the underlying reasons for its primacy during the Enlightenment, we need to take into account the organic nature of the entire self-sustaining system to which the various disciplines and institutions contributed. Long-term structural demands entered into this picture, such as the state's need to coordinate and encourage the nation's slow but constant economic and technological development through a system of technical schools. Another factor was the need to support research in military technology. Here the French man of science found a particularly fertile terrain for developing his potential, encouraging the trend toward professionalization. A connection between science and war existed in many other European countries from Prussia to the kingdom of Naples and the Russian Empire of Peter the Great and Catherine II. Piedmont under Charles Emmanuel III provides perhaps the most obvious example of how the military world and the bureaucratic apparatus could facilitate the rise of a great scientific culture out of almost nothing. In Turin, the need to modernize the army meant that the roots of the Reale Accademia delle Scienze, created in 1783, reached deep into the fertile terrain prepared by the Reali Scuole d'Artiglieria, founded in 1739, and the chemical laboratories of the Arsenale.

The so-called "learned branches" of the army—the artillery and the corps of engineers—had always led in research. Sovereigns and governments invested large sums in advanced laboratories, libraries, and schools for the study of ballistics, the chemistry of gunpowder, and metallurgy—in general, the sectors of the "technology of the cannon" that had fascinated Galileo and Newton and that now appealed to Euler, Lavoisier, Monge, and many others. In France, the creation in 1748 of the École Royale du Génie at Mézières, in the Ardennes, brought the powerful and always tragic synergy between war and science to new heights. The École in fact produced an incredible number of high-level men of science: Nollet, Monge, Carnot, Coulomb, Borda, Bossut, Bézout, and others.

This was not enough, however: there were specific economic interests and administrative needs that revolved around the military world and its problems, and that directly involved important questions in the field of scientific and technological innovation. One classic example of the use of men of science in the role of technocrats was the directorship of the Régie des Poudres and the laboratory of the Arsenal by an authoritative academician, Antoine Lavoisier, the father of the chemical revolution. Under Lavoisier's able direction, interests of a scientific and economic nature were merged with notably positive results. Not only did France once again become self-sufficient in gunpowder production, thanks to a greatly increased productivity, but the more than 6 million livres that the Régie poured into the treasury in the thirteen years after 1775 enabled France to begin to modernize machine tools and manufacturing techniques and to finance research on nitric acid. Turgot even offered a competition in the Académie des Sciences on the topic.

It was when Turgot became controller general of finance that the use of the *savant* as a technocrat and a functionary reached its height. The symbiosis between scientific knowledge and administration demonstrated its full potential by creating the technological preconditions for the development of the mining, paper, and textile industries, and it even permeated the agronomic activities of the nascent agricultural societies. The *Voyages métallurgiques* (1774) of Gabriel Jars was a monument to the feverish activity of the pioneer technocrats in the service of both the state and science who were trained in such major schools as the École Royale des Ponts et Chaussées and the École des Mines.

The most concrete aid lent to scientific research by the needs of industry and production came through the laboratories connected with the royal manufactories. It was in the royal tapestry works of the Manufacture des Gobelins that the Savoyard Louis Berthollet, the director of its laboratories and an academician, carried out the experiments that he published in 1791 in his *Eléments de l'art de la teinture*. Scientists as highly qualified as Réamur, Macquer, and Darcet worked at various times in the Sèvres porcelain works. For the study of the properties of steel, a field in which commercial competition with the nations of northern Europe was keen, the French state mobilized notable resources under the guidance of Monge, Vandermonde, and Berthollet. Analogous efforts were made in such sectors of production as paper and the design and construction of new machinery for the textile industry. The Académie des Sciences may have been bogged down in its routine, but behind it there lay a network of public institutions, a moving web of men and powerful interests backed by a conscious and efficacious policy of state aid. Thus, throughout the eighteenth century, the identity, prestige, and fascination of the *savant* were not only backed by an ideology that dated from the earliest phases of the scientific revolution, but also (and above all) they were openly recognized and legitimated—socially and economically—by the supreme political power.

Nonetheless, the reasons for the primacy of Paris were not exclusively internal, and they did not depend solely on propagation of the effects of the model of patronage adopted by French absolutism. There were also external reasons that become clear when we look at the great chain of scientific societies and academies that existed throughout the Continent, all of which were organically tied to France and out of which the first true international scientific community was born.

The "New Atlantis": Between Utopia and Reality

During the 1770s, when he had become secretary to the Académie des Sciences, Condorcet began to think about how scientific research should be reorganized and, more generally, he began to reflect on the extraordinary function of science in the history of humankind. In the tumultuous years before the Revolution brought collapse, the years in which Turgot was gathering together *savants* and *philosophes* for one last grand attempt at reform under the sign of the Enlightenment, Condorcet began to reflect on questions that found mature expression in the prophetic fresco of the *Esquisse d'un tableau historique des progrès de l'esprit humain*. In particular, Condorcet wrote *Réflexions sur l'Atlantide*, a work that clarifies his project for relaunching the Baconian dream of a profound transformation of humanity through a new politics of scientific knowledge and the realization of the *Instauratio Magna* (Encyclopedia of Knowledge). In returning to the myth and the objectives of the "New Atlantis," Condorcet was not suggesting a return to the egalitarian organization of the "House of Solomon" but rather a centralized and hierarchical "New Atlantis" based in merit and talent. In his scheme for the practical realization of this project, the French provincial academies would rely directly on Paris for the organization of their work projects, while the societies of the broader network throughout Europe would reinforce their own hierarchical ties with the leading French academies. This was an obviously utopian project and one that presupposed a high level of cultural homogeneity within the scientific community throughout the Continent and a commonality of ideology and purpose that was far from being the case. Reactions to Condorcet's proposals were universally chilly, if not downright negative.

Condorcet was not merely daydreaming, though. Between myth

and reality there really was something cosmopolitan in western Europe, something endowed with common values and practices and that resembled a "New Atlantis." Recent studies have thrown light on the extent and the importance of the widespread network of academies and societies. The academies, directly influenced by absolutism and by the society of the ancien régime, responded to the fascination of the Académie des Sciences of Paris; the societies, which were more open, potentially more democratic, and certainly less professional, followed the example of the Royal Society and its fellows. Both forms of association were further divided into public and private institutions according to their degree of state recognition, the concession of letters patent by the sovereign, their pensions, and their modes of financing. During the latter half of the eighteenth century, there were some seventy public academies and societies in operation in western Europe and over a hundred private ones, not counting the twenty or so small scientific circles that existed thanks to the support of a private patron.

Although the scholars of the age never failed to appeal to the egalitarian and utopian model of the "Republic of the Sciences," in practice their endeavors were structured by a hierarchical principle based on the importance and authority of the various centers. The result was a pyramid that granted de facto primacy and the most prestige to the great state academies of France, England, Prussia, Russia, and Sweden. The only countries missing among this restricted elite were Spain and Austria—the first because it was objectively backward, and the second because it had chosen a polycentric model for the organization of scientific investigation that located academies on the periphery of its empire. Immediately after these major institutions came the academies and societies of Bordeaux, Edinburgh, Dijon, Montpellier, Göttingen, Turin, Naples, Mannheim, and Philadelphia. Less wealthy institutions with fewer major talents, less well equipped laboratories, and more irregular publications brought up the rear: Brussels, Copenhagen, Barcelona, Marseilles, Munich, Rotterdam, and Toulouse.

From Russia to Brazil, from Ireland to Switzerland, from the Thames to the shores of the Mediterranean, the rapid development of the academic circuit during the eighteenth century clearly prefigured what today we would call the modern international scientific community. This singular world came into being gradually, at different times and in different ways. Although it followed the cosmopolitan and universal myths and values of the propaganda for the scientific movement that had begun in the seventeenth century, it developed according to specific functions, tasks, and characteristics dictated by its various historical contexts that it would be unwise to underestimate.

In Russia, for example, the Academia Scientiarum Imperialis Petropolitana, founded in 1724, functioned as the origin and the focus of the entire process of acculturation "by decree" inaugurated by Peter the Great and continued by Catherine II. By spending 24,000 rubles a year on the academy, the Russian state acquired not only the services of an organism of technical consultation and a center for the promotion of research but also the academicians' services as professors, a vital function in a country that had no real university before the foundation of the University of Moscow in 1755. It was on the banks of the Neva, thanks to the presence of a sizable number of foreign mathematicians, physicists, and chemists (Swiss and German for the most part) that included Euler, Bilfinger, Hermann, and Nikolaus and Daniel Bernoulli, that the cultural "take-off" connecting Russia with European civilization began.

In Sweden, which had a stronger scientific tradition than Russia (we need only think of the work of the Societas Regia Scientiarum Upsalensis, founded in 1728 by Berzelius; of Polhem, the leading engineer and technologist of the age; or of Swedenborg), the state academy of Stockholm had a personality of its own and was an eager participant in the activities of the "New Atlantis." The institutional responsibility of the Konglika Swenska Vetenskaps Akademien (founded in 1755) was to channel all the revenues from a monopoly on almanacs and calendars (which the crown had granted it) into support of immediately useful research in the fields of technology, mining, agriculture, and the navy. In 1744, with the nomination of the astronomer Wargentin, the scientific potential that the presence of Celsius, Linnaeus, Scheele, Bergmann, and others guaranteed the Swedish Academy came to be fully realized, and the launching of an impressive series of well-funded competitions in scientific sectors of research placed Stockholm on the same plane as Paris, Berlin, and St. Petersburg.

In Italy the European academic circuit could count above all on Turin. The Reale Accademia delle Scienze, founded on the Parisian model in 1783, had behind it technical institutions and economic and military interests similar to those of its Parisian counterpart. It was the leader of what might be defined as a true scientific renascence in Italy at the end of the eighteenth century—a renascence affecting only the northern part of the peninsula, however, in city universities like the Pavia of Boscovich, Volta, and Spallanzani and in the active and flourishing scientific societies of the Veneto, Tuscany, and Emilia. The situation was quite different in southern Italy. One should not be deceived by the large sums of money that the Bourbon rulers of Naples spent on the foundation, in 1787, of the Reale Accademia di Scienze e Belle Lettere, structured in imitation of the Berlin Academy. The Neapolitan Accademia took from its prestigious model only its organization and its aims, certainly not its efficacy or productivity. Within only a few years the Neapolitan experiment proved by and large a failure, dominated by a courtier mentality that separated the Neapolitan science of southern Italy from the science of the rest of Europe.

The situation was a good deal more complex in both Germany and England. With the decline of the Royal Society in the eighteenth century, England saw the tumultuous rise of so-called "scientific societies" in the provincial cities. From Manchester to Derby, from Newcastle to Birmingham, small but enterprising groups of devoted amateur "natural philosophers" (who were light years distant from the Parisian *savants*) determinedly pursued the Baconian and Puritan dream of the *Instauratio Magna*, inventing machines, performing chemical and electrical experiments, and reflecting with utilitarian zeal on the industrial applications of the new findings. These were the men who created the preconditions—ideological as well as technical and scientific—for the industrial revolution (a topic recently studied by Margaret C. Jacob in her *The Cultural Meaning of the Scientific Revolution*).

The scientific movement that exploded in the societies and academies of German lands during the latter half of the eighteenth century deserves a chapter of its own. Although at first these societies imitated the Societas Regia Scientiarum of Berlin (founded in 1700 at Leibnitz's suggestion, which became the Académie Royale des Sciences et Belles-Lettres de Prusse with the reform of Frederick II in 1744), they soon developed specific regional characteristics, and they stood out as an important focus for many other associations and as important channels of communication with the university world. The Göttingen Academy (the Königliche Societät der Wissenschaften), presided over by Haller and directly financed by the Hannover dynasty through the channel of the customary monopoly on almanacs, worked in close cooperation with the professors of the prestigious University of Göttingen. In Erfurt the Akademie Gemeinnütziger Wissenschaften became the center of joint ventures between men of science and economic and patriotic societies. Scientific laboratories, observatories, and centers of study specializing in such areas as meteorology and magnetism were founded in Munich (1759), Mannheim (1763), and Lipsia (1768), laying the groundwork for the great advances in science in nineteenth-century Germany. One could draw up a long list of other attempts at scientific association under the sign of absolutism. The Austrian monarchy implanted important provincial state academies in Prague, Brussels, and Mantua; others on the private model were founded in the United States of America and in the United Provinces. Each of these initiatives had a claim to originality; each was conditioned by its historical context and had political and programmatic objectives of its own. Still, they all shared a horizon of reference and the same framework of values, language, and practice. The "New Atlantis" was a cultural community whose characteristics are incomprehensible if they are not related to the growing strength and success of the entire academic movement in the eighteenth century.

We know from Daniel Roche's masterly works how much that success relied upon the diffusion of the so-called "academic ideology." This ideology of compromise and social integration reflected one of the principal forms of political struggle practiced by enlightened absolutism as it attempted to achieve a painless reconciliation of the old and the new, tradition and innovation, the old privileges of blood and rank and the new rights of merit and talent. Although the primary function of the academies was to celebrate the cultural legitimation of authority, within their ranks they moved toward a new ideal of civil service and toward a ritual sublimation of conflict between social levels that tended to balance social heterogeneity with a cultural and intellectual homogeneity. Within this process, which involved men of letters, artists, and scholars, men of science and their world formed an undisputed elite of the academic movement, its most self-conscious and organic community, and a veritable *imperium in imperio*. As Samuel Formey, the secretary of the Berlin Academy, proudly declared:

> What a revolution, gentlemen! . . . Everywhere, to the ice floes of the pole, the academies are capitals of the sciences that the capitals of empires should not, or even cannot, do without. It seems to me that I can already see them crossing those straits, so long sought-after and whose discovery seems within reach, that separate Europe and America, and procuring for our globe an advantage that the Sun himself, although the father of the day, cannot enjoy, which is to light the two hemispheres at once.

Among the institutions of the Republic of Letters, only the chain of Freemasons' lodges (which, hardly by chance, could often be superimposed on the map of the scientific societies) could boast of a similar international dimension and a comparable cultural homogeneity. We can see proof of this in such academic publications as the *Novi Commentarii* of St. Petersburg, the *Historiae* of Mannheim, the *Mémoires* of the Paris Académie, or the *Miscellaneae* of Turin. The official iconography that appears in the frontispieces of these texts is nearly identical, enclosing within a limited number of images the entire ideology and history of the scientific movement. We see instruments of measurement, Minerva, the Sun illuminating men's minds, the mythical Columns of Hercules taken from Bacon's *New Atlantis,* the sovereign's symbol, etc. The pages that follow these images always refer to the myth of Prometheus and present a wholly positive history of science made only of successes, discoveries, and inventions—a history to which each society brought its small but important contribution.

That cultural community was guaranteed a solid base by more than a shared system of beliefs founded on an ideology of progress in turn driven by the social utility of science and scientific values (although these would have sufficed to cement group solidarity). Other factors combined to make that solidarity particularly homogeneous, both internally, within the scientific community, and externally, in its relations with the outside world. The scientific societies shared the academic practices of the literary and artistic societies—mechanisms for election, the ceremonial of public sessions, the ritual of the academic voyage—but they were also dedicated to the scientific method, a formidable vehicle for a common identity. That is, they accepted a common language that permitted a man of science in Turin to operate with the same procedures and the same criteria of rational analysis and experimental verification of results as his counterpart in Philadelphia or Stockholm. This permitted the creation and persistence of other and no less powerful mechanisms for cultural homogeneity. One of these was the practice of institutions in different countries organizing scientific enterprises that brought together people of different nationalities who worked side by side with no problems of understanding. Moreover, one person might belong to more than one academy, thus opening the way to an intellectual mobility determined solely by remuneration and better working conditions.

Finally, international competitions had an impact. Competitions are definitive proof of the existence of a cultural community that now took questions and problems in physics, mathematics, hydraulics, and chemistry to be of common concern. The seventy-five prizes of the Académie des Sciences of Paris (totaling more than 200,000 livres), the forty-five prizes offered by the Berlin Academy, and the 125 competitions of the Copenhagen Academy were ongoing opportunities for joint projects, research, and comparison totally removed from questions of the participants' religious convictions, national cultures, and political frontiers. The papers of the men of science of the age show them to have been fully aware of belonging to a cultural elite of international dimensions endowed with well-defined characteristics and a common scientific language. It is true, however, that the idealistic sentiment of being *confrères* (a word that crops up often in letters between academicians) was insufficient to cover up some of the negative aspects of a strong sense of identity: the esprit de corps of men of science clearly hints that what was to become one of the most powerful and envied corporative bodies of the ancien régime had a strongly normative and prescriptive nature.

The "Noble Career of the Sciences": Between Community and Corporation

The late eighteenth century undeniably signaled the "triumph of science" (Hahn 1971) and its definitive legitimation in the eyes of a nascent public opinion. It was also the moment of its first serious institutional and epistemological crisis, one that shook the prestige of the French-style *savant* to its very foundations. It is difficult today for us to comprehend the full psychological effect and the impact on collective mentality of the astonishment, marvel, and excitement of the masses of people who thronged to the public squares of all Europe to watch the first flights of aerostatic balloons. Useful inventions (the lightning rod, for one) came in quick succession; the gazettes were filled with heated polemics about miraculous cures obtained by healers who used animal magnetism or with debates on the existence of phlogiston. These fed the frenetic curiosity of the salons and the princely courts, where people talked about the marvelous experiments in electricity of which the great Benjamin Franklin was the master.

By the century's end the man of science was truly *à la mode*. Everyone wanted to play the *petit-maître physicien* and help, even as a dilettante, to spread the feeling of omnipotence typical of general commentary and journalism regarding science and technology. Priestley speaks, with good reason, of "universal enthusiasm" in one of the many editions of his *History and Present State of Electricity*. In an issue of the *Journal Historique et Politique* of Geneva published in 1784, Mallet Du Pan evoked the incredible interest that such topics evoked: "The arts, the sciences, everything today teems with inventions, prodigies, and supernatural talents. A crowd of people of all estates, who never thought they were chemists, geometers, mechanicians, etc., come forth every day with marvels of every sort." Louis-Sébastien Mercier was no less astonished by the rapid change in the interests of the cultivated public and by the rampant success of the sciences. He states in his *Tableau de Paris:* "The reign of letters has passed; physicists replace the poets and the novelists; the electric machine supplants the play."

Research on the sort of books present in French libraries during the eighteenth century provides tangible evidence of this shift in interests. If during the 1720s, volumes of a scientific nature account for 18 percent of books in French libraries, at the beginning of the 1780s the proportion rises rapidly to 30 percent. But more than in book production, it is in the gazettes, the undisputed agents of the birth of public opinion in Europe, that we see proof of a genuine triumph of the sciences: they not only publicized the great scientific controversies of the age but also found space for the more mundane polemics and quarrels within a community in full effervescence that long before had achieved the legitimate existence that it had so tenaciously pursued in the seventeenth century. The first daily newspaper in France, the *Journal de Paris,* provides valuable evidence of this. It published a detailed chronicle of scientific debate in the capital and the working agenda of the Académie des Sciences, but it also reported on the petty diatribes among its membership. Italian, German, and English periodicals devoted large amounts of space to the activities of the provincial and national academies and to competitions, debates, and such scientific quarrels as those between supporters and critics of Lavoisier's revolution in chemistry or Franklin's interpretations of electrical phenomena.

Science was also a rapidly spreading fashion that had its excesses as intellectuals, bourgeois, ladies of the aristocracy, queens, and sovereigns throughout the Continent could hardly believe their eyes as they observed the miraculous phenomena of the electrical machines or sighed at the terrible tragedy of Pilâtre de Rozier, an ill-fated Icarus who was burned to death in June 1785 during an attempted balloon crossing of the English Channel. But behind these showy events a profound change was taking place in the traditional frames of reference of Western culture. Scientific culture came to take a rightful place in the intellectual education of the modern urban elites.

In the provincial French academies between 1700 and 1789, according to the data furnished by Daniel Roche (an analogous change took place in the rest of Europe, however), 50 percent of the more than two thousand competitions offered were reserved for scientific and technological topics. Societies in Montpellier, Brest, Bordeaux, Orléans, Metz, Valence, and Toulouse that had arisen as predominantly literary societies became *sociétés savantes* during the latter half of the eighteenth century, dedicating 80 percent of their publications to the sciences. To be sure, the members of those societies were for the most part dilettantes and these forums for the diffusion of science were at times highly superficial. Still, their optimistic ideology of human progress to be obtained through experimentation, observation, and fidelity to the scientific method had an enormous impact on society in general, and in the long run it proved its efficacy and won out over resistance and prejudice. Its suggestive power reached out in all directions. In northern Italy, for example, provincial academies and agrarian societies launched a strategy for the popularization of science through almanacs that combined the more traditional astrological predictions with articles on Newton, the Montgolfier brothers, and the discovery of the new planet, Uranus. This strategy produced a profound change in the collective imagination of the age, and it served to legitimate scientific knowledge as a formidable instrument for transformation and secularization at all levels of society.

The so-called "second scientific revolution" accompanied the "triumph of science" in the salons, the gazettes, and the small provincial societies of the age, almost as if to aliment and justify the flowering of that singular fashion. Its portentous fruits matured silently in the laboratories of the state-sponsored societies, and they became known in the increasingly specialized language of the solemn *Mémoires* and *Acts* of the academies. Lavoisier completed the experiments that gave modern chemistry a quantitative base, abandoning once and for all the ancient symbolism inherited from alchemy; Lagrange's calculus of variations laid the mathematical foundations for mechanics; Laplace refined theorems and formulas for the calculation of probability and applied Newton's law of numbers to all stellar motion. The pioneering and spectacular electrical experiments of the beginning of the century that so astonished and fascinated the ladies of the salons of all Europe eventually developed into physical and mathematical analyses of electrodynamic phenomena in the works of Cavendish, Coulomb, and Aepinus. Other branches of science acquired status and rigor: meteorology; hydraulics, with the kinetic theory of fluids, based on the atomism of Daniel Bernoulli and Mikhail Lomonosov; biology, with the painstaking experimental protocols that Spallanzani had elaborated.

A scientific community that had come of age set itself the problem of how to go beyond the old system of communication among research centers anchored in the seventeenth-century formula of publishing academic *Acts*. The solution to this problem came in the 1770s with the appearance of the first scientific periodicals, an innovation that almost symbolically marks the changed times. The *Journal de Physique* of Abbé Rozier dates from 1771. Still in France, the *Annales de Chimie* appeared in 1783. In Germany, Lorenz Crell, the great opponent of Lavoisier's theories, inspired analogous enterprises, among them the *Chemisches Journal* (1784). In Italy the Milanese and Torinese publications of the *Scelta di Opuscoli*, whose first number appeared in 1775, enjoyed great success, as did the many specialized periodicals promoted from Pavia by Luigi Brugnatelli. The contents of these periodicals were directed at men of science, but they openly competed with the stuffy and slow official communications of the academies and just as openly attacked the popularizing and scandal-mongering chronicles of the various gazettes.

What was new about these periodicals was their specialization by discipline. They were yet another sign of the maturity of a scientific community in which a solid base of aspiring scholars encouraged by the public's growing sympathy for the sciences was beginning to produce its first genuine celebrities. These men, stars of the first magnitude, were celebrated by the periodicals and gazettes, rewarded and received at all the courts of Europe, and contested by state academies that competed with one another in an eighteenth-century version of a scientific employment market. They tended to be aware of living in an age in which scientific research and organization had progressed far beyond their beginnings in the age of Galileo and Newton. Even though these men operated within different contexts and traditions, they opened the way to a new career whose characteristics, obligatory stages, *cursus honorum,* and goals were already clear in the eighteenth century. A few exemplary biographies will illustrate the historical forms of that career.

The most clamorous example of a professional scientist *avant la lettre* is certainly Joseph-Louis Lagrange. Born in Turin in 1736, Lagrange was named a professor of "sublime analysis" in the Reali Scuole d'Artiglieria at the tender age of nineteen. Although his career was hardly typical, it provides an ideal type of the *savant* of the age of the Enlightenment. In 1757, together with other men of science in Piedmont, most of whom were in the military, he founded the Società Privata Torinese, the nucleus of the future state academy, which was founded in 1783. Lagrange's exceptional talents as a physicist and mathematician were known and admired throughout the Continent thanks to the *Mélanges* of that little society. In 1763, like many young men of the scientific world in Europe, he took an academic journey, a veritable rite of initiation. He went to Basel, Berlin, and Paris to meet and pay homage to his future *confrères*. In Paris he frequented the leading salons; he became a firm friend of d'Alembert's, and the two men later managed the entire circuit of the European academies like patriarchs. After his academic journey, Lagrange became associated with the major academies, enjoyed his first (and richly rewarded) victories in competitions in astronomy, physics, and mathematics, and, in 1766, won the post he yearned for—director of the mathematics section of the Berlin Academy. As a man of science and an academician, Lagrange had reached his goal. At only thirty years of age, at the peak of his swift rise, he could finally permit himself the luxury of full-time research (a privilege given to few in the eighteenth century), limiting his institutional responsibilities to evaluating his colleagues' contributions and producing admirable constructions whose thought still fascinates us for its intellectual daring. In the 1780s, Lagrange, by then a great and famous figure, discreetly put his name on the market. The academies of St. Petersburg, Naples, and Turin fought over him, offering generous conditions, but he chose to go to Paris. There he passed unharmed through the Terror, Thermidor, and the Empire. His genius and his prudence won him a place in the Pantheon, the first scientist to figure among the fathers of modern France.

Leonhard Euler (1707–83), a major figure among the many German-speaking Swiss men of science (the Bernoullis are on that list as well) had an equally extraordinary life. Euler's career—and, for that matter, that of most of the scholars of the age who dedicated themselves to studying the sciences—followed many of the same career stages as Lagrange's. Euler's early mathematical works were published in the *Acta eruditorum;* he was called to the Academy of St. Petersburg in 1726; he won twelve prizes between 1738 and 1772; his works were published in the official *Acts* of the major state academies. He spent the years from 1727 to 1744 in Russia, after which he accepted a generous offer from Frederick II and moved to Berlin. For some time he continued to draw pay from both academies as a technical and scientific consultant for the two governments. In both Russia and Prussia Euler's duties included the organization of research and teaching, but he also studied hydraulics, and compiled maps, calendars, and manuals of artillery and navigation. He worked energetically, through journals and reviews, to spread the major scientific and philosophical ideas of the century and discuss their relationship with religion. One of the best-sellers of the age was his famous *Letters to a German Princess,* a work that went through twelve editions in French and was translated into many other languages, among them English (nine editions), German (six), and Russian (four). There was one element in Euler's career that Lagrange lacked: a stubborn passion for teaching. He trained the first generation of Russian physicists and chemists, men capable of competing with their colleagues throughout Europe. Russia owed to his efforts the entry onto the intellectual scene of Kotel'nikov, Roumovskii, Sofronov, and, above all, Mikhail Vasilyevich Lomonosov, the "Siberian Lavoisier," who was born in 1711 in the province of Archangel.

Among the men of science of the age of the Enlightenment, Lomonosov is a particularly interesting case: his scientific career blossomed in a context of cultural underdevelopment, and he was almost an *in vitro* product of the mechanisms of reproduction of the European academic circuit.

After studying with Wolff in Marburg, Lomonosov followed the entire traditional *cursus honorum* to become a member of the Academy of St. Petersburg in 1742. In that monumental city built by Peter the Great's decree as Russia's portal to the West, he created chemistry laboratories, drew up projects for the University of Moscow, and elaborated (with notable success) refined mathematical models of a kinetic theory of gases based on an atomistic theory of matter. Like his colleagues in Paris, Berlin, and Turin, Lomonosov was a technical consultant for the government, and he spent a good deal of time on metallurgy, geodesy, and hydraulics, and compiled school manuals. Above all, his translations laid the foundations for Russian scientific language. Throughout his brilliant career as a man of science and a militant intellectual, Lomonosov remained loyal to a sort of dual identity that permitted him, on the one hand, to embrace and propagandize encyclopedism and the scientistic ideology of progress and to feel himself part of and in tune with the cosmopolitan values of what he was fond of calling "the Republic of the Sciences," and, on the other hand, to hold fast to the French model of the scientist organically tied to the state.

Not all men of science of the eighteenth century had careers that followed the academic pattern of these examples, though. There were many intermediate articulations between the rigid typology of the academic model and the opposite pole, the Baconian "natural philosopher," a model that was particularly popular in England, the United States, and the United Provinces. The career of another great scholar of the late eighteenth century, Joseph Priestley, the discoverer of oxygen and the great opponent and rival of Lavoisier, can serve as an example here.

It is difficult to measure the distance separating a "professional" like Lagrange and a "dilettante" like Priestley. The two men represent two different cultural universes that were institutionally and socially quite unlike one another, at times irreducibly so. Lagrange belonged wholly to a closed and corporative society dominated by the logic of the absolutist state; Priestley reflected a more open and dynamic civil society in the making in which the state played a much more circumscribed role. If the identity of the *savant* had emerged by acquiring a place among the *corps d'état*, the "natural philosopher" had behind him the myth of egalitarian intelligence that had been formulated by Bacon and the Newtonian Boyle Lectures. This was Priestley's preparation. Priestley's career was as a self-taught man hostile to the notion of an increasing specialization and professionalization of scientific knowledge that risked losing sight of the fertile connections between science and politics, religion, and philosophy. Priestley came late to his research in electrical phenomena and "airs"—now the chemistry of gases. His first works were explanations of and commentary on the radical politics and the Socinian religious tradition that were dear to his heart. He taught for a living, was a journalist, and wrote manuals for schoolchildren. When he decided to devote part of his time to scientific research, he followed the model of the natural philosopher to the letter, participating in the projects of the Lunar Society of Birmingham, a provincial private society in which gentlemen and scholars—Samuel Galton, James Watt, Erasmus Darwin, and others—met to discuss scientific topics on a plane of absolute equality and under the sign of utilitarianism and industrialism. Priestley published a number of well-received books, translated into a number of languages, that publicized and propagandized the conquests of science in the service of humanity. He did hundreds of experiments (leading to important discoveries) in his own house, fashioning his own instruments and equipment. Like another famous eighteenth-century natural philosopher, Benjamin Franklin, he had little fondness either for mathematics or the revolutionary quantitative methods of Lavoisier or for the abstract and intellectual theorization of Laplace. Throughout his life, Priestley remained a dilettante engrossed in experimentation and de-

voted to a way of conceiving of and practicing science that was far from
being in the minority or marginal in the age of the Enlightenment. It was
only at the end of the nineteenth century that the Anglo-Saxon world
confirmed, on the linguistic level, the definitive disappearance of the
seventeenth-century "natural philosopher" and preferred the modern
term "scientist" (Ross 1962).

   In many parts of Europe that transformation progressed rapidly and
might be considered complete by the end of the eighteenth century.
One could debate ad infinitum on the *vexata quaestio* of the professionalization of the eighteenth-century man of science. In light of objective
sociological criteria (the definition of a body of knowledge, remune-
rated employment, the autonomous organization of training and activities) the scientist cannot be said to have achieved professional status.
For example, being a scientist was not yet a true "trade" and did not
define an occupational category. In practice, most men of science
worked part-time: a few exceptions aside, they were generally state functionaries. As far as we can tell, European archives never mention "scientist" as a specific profession. Still, from the historical viewpoint there can
be no doubt that by that time a figure and even a career very similar to
those of the modern scientist had appeared. That figure, however, must
still be evaluated with its particularities and in forms conditioned by the
historical context of the ancien régime. One interesting parameter that
needs to be taken into account is how aware contemporaries were of the
special status of the scientist.

   Voltaire included people who study scientific matters in the more
generic category of *hommes instruits* that he discussed in the entry "Gens
de lettres" of the *Encyclopédie*, but d'Alembert spoke in 1753 of the "noble career of the sciences," clearly distinguishing between the *homme de
lettres* and the *savant*. "When I say *savants*," he writes in his *Essai sur la
société des gens de lettres et les grands*, "I do not mean by that those who are
called *érudits*" but rather, he explains, those among the *gens de lettres*
"who occupy themselves with the exact sciences." Both in Condorcet's
Eloges and in the articles printed in the leading gazettes of the Continent, the man of science was a personage who was both recognizable
and recognized, clearly distinguishable from the philosopher, the theologian, and above all the man of letters. In fact, the genuine antagonism
that developed in the 1780s between men of science and of letters provides a clear sign of a firm connection between the terms *savant* or *scienzato* and investigative activities in a specific sector of knowledge.

   In late-eighteenth-century Italy it became common to oppose the *letterato* and the *scienzato*. The Neapolitan *illuministi* Galanti and Filangieri clearly express this contrast. In his *Del principe e delle lettere,* a work written to establish the "difference between belles lettres and the sciences," Vittorio Alfieri writes as clearly as a modern sociologist of science. Alfieri strongly attacks the *scienzato* (his use of the term is consonant with today's usage), denouncing his tacit pact with power and his "servitude," and outlining what Alfieri considered to be the underlying nature of a sort of scientific knowledge for whose existence and advancement the economic support of the great state academies was absolutely indispensable. The *letterato* was in a quite different position: he could pursue his activities without constantly being preoccupied by financing, hence he could easily do without the prince if he so desired. When he freed himself of that moral grip, the *letterato* had won a private dimension for his work (a dimension guaranteed by the growing success of the struggle for recognition of authors' proprietary rights), and this permitted him to denounce despotism, preach virtue, and educate the people.

Of course Alfieri was not the only writer who criticized scientists during the 1780s or denounced the negative aspects of the "New Atlantis," nor was he the only person to compare the man of science and the man of letters in terms of public and private activity or despotism and liberty. More than a decade of virulent polemics aimed at the entire academic world preceded and prepared the ground for the clamorous decree promulgated by the Convention in August 1793 calling for the immediate suppression of every sort of state-supported academy and society. This was a genuine dismantling of the system of state patronage of culture that had come to cost the French government well over 250,000 livres in pensions for the year 1785 alone. The reasons behind such a drastic measure were outlined by Abbé Grégoire in a harsh speech to the members of the Convention. It deserves summarizing for its exemplary clarity.

In Grégoire's opinion, the democratic and egalitarian ideals of the Republic of Letters had been betrayed by the mechanisms of the *corps savants,* special privileges, and pensions. Accepting a change from a principle of cultural community to a corporative structure had inevitably led to "a sort of hierarchy among men" that left no room for talent and merit. The shift from community to the "academic corporation" had brought degeneration, to the point that the members of that corporation had become "inquisitors of the thought" of others whom they excluded from membership. Esprit de corps was expressed as arrogance and especially as the marginalization of all innovators and anticonformists. Academicians now fulfilled the humiliating public function of "panegyrists" and the "slaves" of "despots."

Men of science, the keystone of the entire academic system, had long operated in the eye of the storm. The academic corporation attacked them furiously for the way they organized their research, for their methods, and for their social role; it even cast doubts on the image of science that had emerged triumphant from the first scientific revolution of Galileo and Newton. Exactly how all this occurred and how it prompted a serious identity crisis in the eighteenth-century man of science is a question still being investigated and debated by historians, who have long underestimated the lacerating polemics within the European scientific community at the end of the century.

The Man of Science and the Identity Crisis of the Late Eighteenth Century

In May 1784, the Italian gazette *Notizie del Mondo* satirized the "instability of Parisian brains," giving full particulars on how "the mania for flying balloons" had been replaced by a mania for "animal magnetism." It added, "Everyone competes to run to Delon to see Mr. Mesmer who, with a touch of his hand, cures without the aid of any medicine." Another Italian gazette, Lorenzo Manini's *Notizie Diverse* of Cremona, reported on the cures effected by the Austrian physician Franz Anton Mesmer with less levity, preferring to present them as puzzling, and showing some inclination to take Mesmer's healing powers seriously.

The division between those who held Mesmer to be a charlatan (a word that suddenly became popular in Paris in those years) and those who thought him a great scientist, misunderstood and denigrated by the arrogant *académiciens,* was echoed in gazettes in France, Germany, and the United Provinces. Everywhere in Europe in the early 1780s people argued over whether or not "magnetic animal fluid" existed. These were polemics that touched not only a credulous populace but even (and especially) illustrious scientists, famous men of letters, princely courts, academies, and men of the Enlightenment, all of whom took sides. In Germany during the same years, there was a reemergence of interest, both among individual intellectuals and in prestigious universities, in physiognomy and dowsing—a passion that soon spread to the rest of Europe. In the nascent field of meteorology there was a curious revival of the theoretical bases of natural astrology, which Giuseppe Toaldo, the courageous publisher of Galileo's works and Galileo's successor at the University of Padua, had succeeded in stripping of all magical contamination.

These enthusiasms were an obvious return to ancient forms of rationalization whose matrix was empirical and divinatory that had already been present at the dawn of the scientific revolution and now were relaunched as possible forms of knowledge alternative to the physical and mathematical paradigm of the Newtonian mechanistic universe that predominated in the great state academies. Writers who defended these sorts of science (or pseudo-science, depending on one's point of view) called them "popular" not because they were cultural expressions of a "lower" social level but because they were simple, elementary, and had little to do with the abstract and at times incomprehensible intellectual theorizing about reality of Condorcet and Laplace.

Denis Diderot had been one of the first fathers of the new "sciences" in the age of the Enlightenment. In his *De l'interprétation de la nature* (1754), he clarified the epistemological bases of the opposition between the traditional image of a Galilean and Newtonian science made of eternal mathematical laws to be grasped through *numero, pondere et mensura,* and an image of science defined solely by the usefulness of its results, the simplicity of its qualitative and experimental instruments of knowledge, and its goal of arriving at a morphology of a nature as changeable, dynamic, and in perennial transformation. Diderot rightly predicted that in the future his epistemological reflections would find widespread echoes among the multitude of dilettantes who, at the end of the century, threw themselves into the practice of the sciences, suddenly all the rage. The scope and implications of the success of the "popular sciences" within intellectual circles and with public opinion greatly alarmed scholars like Volta, Condorcet, and Lavoisier, who felt obliged to speak out and take a public stand on the question. The accusation of charlatanism was hurled on both sides, leading to confusion. This was the first time that the definition of scientific knowledge—acquired with great difficulty and agreed upon by all European men of science—had been challenged.

But if historians now concur that such quarrels were the cultural event of greatest political, social, and ideological significance before the French Revolution (Darnton 1968; Venturi 1984 [1991]), they are far from agreeing on how to interpret those polemics. Some have seen that *querelle* uniquely (and simplistically) in terms of a triumphant return of magic, forgetting that there were few occultists in Europe and that the overwhelming majority of Mesmer's followers and the supporters of the "popular sciences" were convinced rationalists, disciples of the encyclopedist tradition, even sworn enemies of any recourse to the supernatural, which they derided and depreciated in their writings. The works of one follower of Mesmer, Brissot de Warville, are a case in point. Another hypothesis—and to date the prevailing one—takes the irrationality of these movements for granted and credits them with the decline, even the demise, of the Enlightenment beginning as early as the 1780s. In reality, the disagreements between Condorcet and Marat and between Mesmer and the academicians over whether or not the methods of investigation typical of the "popular sciences" could be called scientific (and even the arguments against the *corps savants*) can and must be reinterpreted with a more stringent critical look at overly rigid definitions and categories of rationality and scientific knowledge that belong to the past, and which have in fact been questioned repeatedly in recent times by authoritative philosophers and epistemologists.

Historians agree on one point, however: the squall among men of science was, on closer inspection, the first great attack, forcefully unleashed and with a budding prerevolutionary sensibility, on the institutions of the ancien régime and on the "New Atlantis" that was the heart of the corporative cultural system. This is where we need to start if we want to understand a phenomenon that conditioned both the basic characteristics of the Enlightenment and later historiographical interpretations of those characteristics.

Paradoxically, it was precisely the "triumph of science" that created the social and ideological bases of the conflict. That triumph was freighted with collateral phenomena that inevitably determined a crisis of growth that had serious consequences. For example, the increased number of *amateurs,* dilettantes who formed little private societies everywhere and who proudly resisted any form of control by the state academies, helped to create tension. Freemasonry did its part through a propaganda strategy that encouraged popular scientific education by founding academies, museums, and periodicals, thus broadening the base of scientific practitioners at the price of a loss of rigor in scientific investigation. Finally, the growing competition between academicians and university professors for control of their professions was a thorny question of pan-European dimensions.

All of these sources of pressure on the scientific community were external, but the worm of contestation also lodged within the Académie des Sciences. During the latter half of the eighteenth century, contestation made a public and noisy appearance. Even some academicians found the inequality and the privilege sanctioned by the 1699 *Règlement* odious. D'Alembert was among the first to speak (in 1753) of the "spirit of despotism" that had become the insufferable rule in relations among *gens de lettres*, claiming that "the democratic form pertains better than any other to a state such as the Republic of Letters, which lives on its liberty alone." Yet the same d'Alembert who had helped to politicize (so to speak) the debate on the organization of scientific investigation stood in the front lines in the quarrel that raged at the end of the century, side by side with Condorcet, Lavoisier, and Vicq d'Azyr in a rigid defense of the academic corporation against Mesmer, Marat, Brissot, and many others whom that corporation excluded. The fact is that the attack on official science was so radical and so dangerous in its institutional, political, and epistemological implications that defection from a common stance and tolerance of difference were no longer permissible. As long as criticism remained on the level of Deleyre's feeble and Baconian denunciation of the *abus des sciences* on the part of the *savants* in his *Analyse de la philosophie du chancelier François Bacon* (1755), response to it could be acceptance of and even agreement with some of its complaints. The corrosive accusations brought by supporters of the "popular sciences" were quite another matter.

In 1782, Brissot de Warville used vigor and subtlety to summarize the notions that had the greatest impact on public opinion. His pamphlet, *De la vérité,* became a sort of catechism for contestation and a source of arguments and suggestions that fed polemics in occasional works and gazettes throughout Europe. In order to demonstrate that the academies "impede the search for truth," Brissot established a parallel, echoing Rousseau, between the virtuous and free knowledge of the ancients and the bold-faced arrogance and mania for "glory" and "fortune" of the moderns. Athens and Rome had no intellectuals "by patent." No one in those days had ever conceived of "bodies as bizarre as our academies." Only "the moderns have introduced a sort of elective aristocracy into the empire of the sciences." The costs had become heavy, Brissot continues, not only on the moral plane and on the plane of civil cohabitation but also and above all because of the problems that the institution of an elite posed for the advancement of knowledge.

This was in fact one of the truly sore points in the controversy. Like all bureaucratic bodies, the state academies had ended up placing a heavy veil of ideology, impermeable to novelty, over the free cultural community of men of science, thus encouraging a codified, immobile, and normative type of knowledge. The great scientists henceforth felt themselves the "infallible depositories of the verities"; all novelty was branded as "heresy." The categorical affirmation that became the ironic slogan of the charlatans, "No salvation outside of Newton," sanctioned a conservative, systematic knowledge typical of "normal science" (to use Thomas Kuhn's term) through which *le préjugé académique* could speak freely. In order to be admitted to the corporation, one had to accept the dominant scientific paradigm of the grand masters, "repeating and scrupulously believing all their ideas."

That there was some truth to these exacerbated reflections seems evident not only from the furious attacks on anyone who dared criticize Newtonian theories but also from the intransigent works of Samuel Formey, a powerful figure whose opinions were much heeded. As early as 1767, he attacked *demi-savants* whom he accused of diffusing "false knowledge" in Germany, and he demanded that the academies be granted "a half-century of . . . dictatorship." He stated that if "the church keeps watch over the sacred trust of religion, the courts over the maintenance of the laws, it is up to the academies to enforce the reign of a purified, solid knowledge." That this was not an idle threat is clear from the academies' official intervention in the sensational controversies of the end of the century.

In 1784, with the nomination of royal commissions within the Académie des Sciences and the Société de Médecine, procedures for establishing the scientific basis of animal magnetism were set in place in Paris. Several years later in Turin, the Reale Accademia delle Scienze ordered an investigation into the phenomena of dowsing and divining rods. In Germany illustrious scholars from prestigious universities gave battle in commissions named for the purpose of determining the theoretical bases of physiognomy and a possible morphological science of nature behind the disquieting mystical reading of nature of Lavater and some Masonic circles.

For the first time, debate in Europe exploded on the official cultural level on the great epistemological question of "demarcation." What is science? What are the criteria of the scientific? Who decides on those criteria? Is it legitimate to impose them and link them with truth? What surfaced in the minutes of the royal commission on magnetism, which were published and commented on in gazettes throughout Europe (as if these represented a singular and disconcerting prefiguration of the debate in the 1930s on the definition of science between Karl R. Popper, a logical neopositivist, and the supporters of psychoanalysis), were two irre-

ducibly different images of scientific reality. The royal commissioners—
Lavoisier, Franklin, and Bailly—insisted that the key question by which
mesmerism should be judged was whether or not "animal fluid" existed
and if it could be proven experimentally. For their adversaries, the sole
criterion of whether or not mesmerism was scientific lay in verification
by the practical utility of its method of healing, as evidenced by cures.
One side made a last-ditch defense of a science that, in historical terms,
ended up in total agreement with the classical Galilean and Newtonian
method; the other side offered an updated form of an empirical and
divinatory, qualitative, morphological, and utilitarian rationalism that
had fascinated Denis Diderot and many others of the Rousseau school.
The inevitable result was, once again, opposing stands on how to conceive of the man of science and the institutions devoted to scientific
research, where the elitist, selective, and professionalizing state academies stood on one side and the private popular societies run by dilettantes stood on the other.

It is clear even from these brief reflections on those singular events
that, beyond their intrinsic interest, the triumph of the sciences of the
end of the eighteenth century, the crisis of and attacks on the classical
rationality of physical and mathematical mechanics, even the breadth
and depth of the conflict among men of science, seem to have existed
for the express purpose of calling into doubt longstanding and deeply
rooted interpretations of the connection between science and the Enlightenment. This is a topic that anyone who cares to analyze the
eighteenth-century man of science in any depth cannot elude.

In his *The Philosophy of the Enlightenment* (1932), Ernst Cassirer provided a praiseworthy and important reevaluation of the world of the Enlightenment, correcting the romantic and Hegelian condemnation,
which the Marxists shared (though they arrived at their condemnation
by other paths and with other aims in mind), and laying the foundations
for a philosophical reading of the question based in Kant. His interpretation has resisted attacks and continual revision, and even today it
provides a sort of backdrop (at times simply an implicit reference) for
many works published after the Second World War. By defining the philosophy of the Enlightenment essentially as a method, a mentality, and a
form of thought rather than as a coherent system of ideas, Cassirer iden-
tifies its origin and its most authentic cipher as the scientific revolution
and its conquests, and sees its spiritual fathers as Kepler, Galileo, and
Newton. For Cassirer, the identifying characteristic of the culture of the
Enlightenment is the new definition of reason, a definition that differed

from that of previous centuries and coincided with the processes of rationalization typical of the Newtonian scientific paradigm.

In the light of what I have tried to show in the preceding pages, that rigid equation does not withstand the test of historical events in the 1780s. The crisis of the late eighteenth century seems instead to support scholars who have preferred to see the world of the Enlightenment as a particularly rich and complex historical phenomenon whose confines are broader and more indistinct than in Cassirer's hypothesis. Many important works have viewed the Enlightenment as an extraordinary and basically political venture carried on by men determined to transform society through a clash of ideas and to create a new system of values (tolerance, equality, liberty, philanthropy, felicity, cosmopolitanism, etc.) that would be the unmediated expression of a modern civil society finally emancipated from the heavy tutelage of the church, from confessional religions, and from an idea of politics that until then was conceived only *ex parte principis* and never *ex parte civium*. Clearly, the man of science furnished the movement of the Enlightenment with weapons and with important suggestions for elaborating a critical style of thought and a problematics capable of operating within and transforming the real world. Still, it would be an impoverishment of the content and the final aims of that movement to equate the Enlightenment and its image of reason with the Newtonian scientific method.

It is incontestable, however, that if one begins with the historical hypothesis that the Enlightenment represented the process of foundation of a new overall system of values and an original cultural and linguistic universe (anthropologists would prefer to speak of a new system of beliefs and social and cultural practices) rather than a specific form of rationality, it then becomes much easier to analyze the scientific movement and the movement of the Enlightenment as two distinct phenomena, always interacting but autonomous in their underlying motivations. Acceptance of this view would probably clarify the role and function of the men of science who were good Catholics or at least remained organically tied to religious institutions or were animated by an intense need for religious values. We have not devoted much space to them here, in spite of their undeniable importance in eighteenth-century culture and their contribution to the advancement of scientific research.

Unlike positivism, which is too often unduly and polemically connected with the Enlightenment (as in Adorno and Horkheimer's *Dialektik der Aufklärung* [1947] to cite one example), the Enlightenment never consciously, with ideological intent, considered scientific knowledge to be the keystone of all human knowledge. In the tree of knowledge that the *Encyclopédie* based in the human faculties of reason, memory, and imagination, all forms of knowledge were granted equal dignity, and great importance was attached to them all in the utopian realization on this earth of the celestial city. The *philosophes* loved, studied, and propagandized science, but they maintained a distant and even critical attitude toward it. Rousseau was not the only eighteenth-century thinker who contributed to an ever-stronger and more determined tendency toward moral, political, and philosophical criticism of science. During the course of the eighteenth century, and particularly during the 1780s, many men of the Enlightenment from Voltaire to Condillac and Bailly speculated on the origins of science, in particular, on the Galilean and Newtonian revolution. These men elaborated the foundations of a history of science as the social and cultural history of a corpus of knowledge, considered critically on the same plane as other bodies of knowledge. In short, the intellectual experience of the scientist in the age of Voltaire by no means exhausted the breadth of reference and the political will to transform reality of Enlightenment men.

This does not mean that the man of science did not play an extraordinary role in shaping the Enlightenment. Far from it. Even though we need always speak of reciprocal conditioning, there can be no doubt that the scientific community had an effect on all the various forms that the Enlightenment took during the course of the century. As is known, the prestige and the granitic certitudes of the Newtonian mechanical universe inspired the reflections of an important segment of the world of the Enlightenment up to the appearance of the last volume of the *Encyclopédie* in 1764. The famous word portrait of the *philosophe* by Dumarsais, rightly considered a manifestation of the Enlightenment, belongs part and parcel to the first great season of that age. In this portrayal the serene and proud figure of the new philosopher, capable of dominating passions and emotions thanks to the primacy of a critical and methodological reason, stands before a clockwork nature of eternal and reassuring mathematical laws. The *philosophe,* who has turned his back on religion and its mysteries, which he treats with irony and libertine detachment, now recognizes and venerates as divine only humanity and, in particular, civil society, which he even considers, with evident iconoclastic intent, *l'unique Dieu.*

Another portrait, composed in a quite different season of the Enlightenment, reflects a profound change in intellectual climate and historical contexts. It appears in a short work by Jean-Louis Carra published

in 1782 under the title, *Système de la raison ou le prophète philosophe*, a work
that projects a sense of the true omnipotence of humankind, thanks to
the triumph of the sciences, the enthusiasms raised by aerostatic balloons, the diffusion of a vital and dynamic image of nature, and an explicit recognition of the autonomy and strength of the passions with
respect to reason. The new *prophète-philosophe* continued the Enlightenment's historic task of working for the emancipation of man and the creation of new values for a modern civil society, but he also embraced the
neonaturalism of the late eighteenth century and its political and philosophical implications, and he welcomed a competition among the various forms of scientific rationalization that diversified, enlarged, and
complicated the range of faculties and instruments at the disposition of
humankind. If for Dumarsais in the early stages of the Enlightenment
reason alone could and must light the way for the philosopher as he traveled through the shadows toward the light, for Carra he must realize
that the arsenal of weapons available to him was much more vast: by the
end of the century, the new *trinité sacrée* of the Enlightenment extended
to *sensibilité* and to *vérité* the fundamental role that was formerly reserved
for *raison* alone. Even the tone of the argumentation shifts between the
first and last generations of the Enlightenment: where Dumarsais's reflections are serene and detached, Carra's are passionate, strong, and
declamatory. "The first right of man," Carra writes, taking a hint from
Rousseau, "is to be; his second is to think."

> I will predict the progress of reason. . . . The great family of
> man will thus be reunited one day and will be but one society!
> The code of the natural laws will then be the only authority
> needed to lead the multitude. Moral equality will no longer be
> a problem! The distribution of goods will be governed by dis-
> tributive equity and not by despotic caprice! . . . Low vice and
> notorious crimes will no longer be a reason for being respected;
> everything will be in order once and for all, because finally the
> system of reason must have its turn.

Carra the mesmeran spoke in tones of a secular eschatology steeped
in genuine religious feeling. That manner of speaking was by no means
an isolated instance, nor was it common only in the circles of the "popular sciences." We need only read the *Esquisse d'un tableau de l'esprit humain*
of Condorcet, a sworn enemy of the mesmerans, to see another example
of the religious pathos of the "philosopher prophet." The leading figures in the new season of the Enlightenment that accompanied the wan-

ing century differed from those of the recent past. An entire generation of intellectuals who had grown up with the ideals of the *Encyclopédie* had joined Masonic lodges, an experience that radically changed attitudes concerning the representations of history and concerning the bothersome problem of religious attitudes and their potential for becoming an instrument of communication that was not only extraordinarily effective but whose simplicity and immediacy made it an ideal means for kindling an active relationship between high and low in the diffusion of the Enlightenment.

It was this prophetic Enlightenment of the end of the century, imbued with political radicalism and soon to become the true terrain for the cultivation of the revolutionary mentality, that confronted the man of science of the 1780s. As science triumphed, his influence contributed greatly to spreading both hopes and fears of retaliation; his neonaturalism and the image of a changing, transformable natural order encouraged (among other things) the revolutionary idea that social order could be changed and man regenerated, thus creating the citizen. As Robespierre said in a famous statement in 1794: "Everything has changed in the physical order, and everything must change in the moral and political order."

But where the scientist and the man of the Enlightenment of the late eighteenth century influenced one another most was in complex thought patterns that led to a semantic transfer of truth—a concept that was both terrible and extremely suggestive—from the realm of traditional religion to the secular domain. The word "truth" seems to have obsessed men of the Enlightenment of every nationality: men ranging from Condorcet to Lessing, Radishchev, and Filangieri attributed to truth responsibilities and significance cloaked in an intense secular religiosity, and they endowed truth with the power to communicate intellectual conquests, values, and hopes.

Among scientists the process of the appropriation of that magic word occurred rapidly during the last years of the eighteenth century, and their use of it hints at its transformation into ironclad dogma during the following century. Where Galileo had hesitated and retreated in his battle with the theologians and had settled for a double truth, Condorcet, the "philosophical prophet" and scientist, unhesitatingly and proudly proclaimed the truth of science and reason to be unique and eternal, thrusting aside the theologians' time-honored claims. In short, the man of science of the age of the Enlightenment had conquered a full right, with all its consequences, to become—for good or ill—a leading protagonist in human history. The long march that had begun in the ancient world, was interrupted, and then taken up again in the modern world with the scientific revolution had finally ended.

Bibliography

Baker, Keith M. *Condorcet: From Natural Philosophy to Social Mathematics.* Chicago: University of Chicago Press, 1975.

Darnton, Robert. *Mesmerism and the End of the Enlightenment in France.* Cambridge, Mass.: Harvard University Press, 1968.

Ferrone, Vincenzo. *Scienza, natura, religione: Mondo newtoniano e cultura italiana nel primo Settecento.* Naples: Jovene, 1982.

———. *La Nuova Atlantide e i lumi: Scienza e politica nel Piemonte di Vittorio Amedeo III.* Turin: Meynier, 1988.

———. *I profeti dell'Illuminismo: Le metamorfosi della ragione nel tardo Settecento italiano.* Rome and Bari: Laterza, 1989. Available in English as *Newtonian Science, Religion, and Politics in the Early Eighteenth Century: The Intellectual Roots of the Italian Enlightenment.* Translated by Sue Brotherton. Atlantic Highlands, N.J.: Humanity Press, 1995.

Gillispie, Charles Coulston. *Science and Polity in France at the End of the Old Regime.* Princeton: Princeton University Press, 1980.

———, ed. *Dictionary of Scientific Biography.* 16 vols. New York: Scribner, 1970–80.

Guerlac, Henry. *Essays and Papers in the History of Modern Science.* Baltimore: Johns Hopkins University Press, 1977.

Hahn, Roger. *The Anatomy of a Scientific Institution: The Paris Academy of Sciences, 1666–1803.* Berkeley: University of California Press, 1971.

Jacob, Margaret C. *The Newtonians and the English Revolution 1689–1720.* Ithaca: Cornell University Press, 1976.

McClellan, James E., III. *Science Reorganized: Scientific Societies in the Eighteenth Century.* New York: Columbia University Press, 1985.

Rausky, Franklin. *Mesmer o la rivoluzione terapeutica.* Milan: Feltrinelli, 1980.

Roche, Daniel. *Le siècle des Lumières en province: Académies et académiciens provinciaux 1680–1789.* 2 vols. Paris: Mouton, 1978.

———. *Les Républicains des Lettres: Gens de culture et Lumières au XVIIIe siècle.* Paris: Fayard, 1988.

Ross, Sydney. "Scientist: The Story of a Word." *Annals of Science* 18, 2 (1962): 65–85.

Rossi, Paolo. "The Scientist." In *Baroque Personae,* edited by Rosario Villari and translated by Lydia G. Cochrane, 263–89. Chicago: University of Chicago Press, 1995. Originally published as "Lo Scienziato." In *L'uomo barocco,* edited by Rosario Villari, 299–328. Rome and Bari: Laterza, 1991.

Rousseau, G. S., and Roy Porter, eds. *The Ferment of Knowledge: Studies in the Historiography of Eighteenth-Century Science.* Cambridge, U.K., and New York: Cambridge University Press, 1980.

Venturi, Franco. *La caduta dell'Antico Regime 1776–1789*. Pt. 1, *I grandi stati dell'Occidente*. Vol. 4 of *Settecento riformatore*. Turin: G. Einaudi, 1984. Available in English as *The End of the Old Regime in Europe, 1776–1789*. Pt. 1, *The Great States of the West*. Translated by R. Burr Litchfield. 2 vols. Princeton: Princeton University Press, 1991.

Vucinich, Alexander. *A History to 1860*. Vol. 1 of *Science in Russian Culture*. Stanford: Stanford University Press, 1963.

6 / The Artist

Daniel Arasse

When Johann Heinrich Füssli, known in Great Britain as Henry Fuseli, showed *The Nightmare* at the Royal Academy of London in 1783 (Detroit, Institute of Art), it was an event. No one had ever seen a canvas like it. It belonged to none of the organizational categories for the production and reception of paintings of the age (historical paintings, genre paintings, portraits, or landscapes), and it did not seek to please. Admittedly, the work's subject matter bore some relationship to the terrifying subjects that had been enormously successful in England at the end of the eighteenth century, and the Royal Academy's exposition also contained an *Archangel Michael and Satan* by Benjamin West, *The Ghost of Clytemnestra Awaking the Furies* by Downman, and an *Eolus Raising a Storm* by Maria Cosway. But *The Nightmare* had no objective reference to high culture; Füssli's monsters jarred contemporaries' *inner* selves. The painter's intention was to disturb the spectator: Horace Walpole was not fooled; he judged the work "shocking."

Nonetheless no one condemned the painting. To the contrary, it met with a swift success that immediately made Füssli world-famous. Engravings made the image available everywhere in Europe, and throughout his career, until the 1810s and the 1820s, *The Nightmare* dogged Füssli's footsteps as he was invited to copy, refashion, and create variations of his masterpiece. If this painting is one of the most famous works of the epoch it is because it fulfilled a range of expectations, which means that today we have a right to see it as an example of the complexity inherent in the shared inspiration and aims of the artist and the public of the Enlightenment.

Surprising as this may seem, *The Nightmare* is indeed an "enlightened" work. Füssli was denouncing superstitious credences that continued to explain nightmares as the intervention of malevolent supernatural beings (incubi, succubi, and various other sorts of *Kobald*) that supposedly troubled sleepers and possessed and terrified their minds. Füssli believed—following contemporary medical and philosophical theories (as in Kant's *Anthropology from a Pragmatic Point of View*)—that nightmares have precise physiological causes. He used a second version of *The Nightmare* (1790–91, Frankfurt) as the basis for four illustrations for Erasmus Darwin's *The Botanic Garden*, a work that led Darwin to further investigation into the physiological mechanisms of dreams in his *Zoonomia, or, The Laws of Organic Life* (1794–96).

The Nightmare had a strong impact and great popular success not for its philosophical conception but because the raw materials that Füssli used to portray his enlightened idea came right out of the highly traditional folklore and superstition that he was combating. The painting states that monsters are the products of the nightmare, not its cause, yet in the image they are just as real as the body of the sleeping young woman, and they force their horrifying presence on the beholder. One has to look very closely to see that the outlines of the incubus are fluid, almost nonexistent, in comparison to the clearly drawn contours of the sleeping woman's contorted body.

Füssli's dialectic of paradox thus prefigures the logic that provided the base for many of Goya's works—an "enlightened" artist who invented shadows. Above all, *The Nightmare* calls to mind the very famous forty-third plate of Goya's *Los Caprichos* (1799): *El sueño de la razon produce monstruos* (The Sleep of Reason Engenders Monsters). In 1797, an earlier state of the plate included an inscription in which the artist declared his intention was simply to "banish harmful ideas commonly believed, and to perpetuate with this work of *Caprichos* the solid testimony of truth" ("desterran bulgaridades perjudiciales, y perpetuar con esta obra de caprichos, el testimonio solido de la verdad"; quoted in Pérez-Sanchez and Sayre 1989, xcviii). Like Füssli, Goya pictured prejudices and superstitions in order to combat them better.

Mentioning Füssli and Goya in one breath evokes one of the most remarkable paradoxes that confronted an entire clan of Enlightenment artists: there was an indissociable and contradictory connection between the luminous clarity of Reason and its Principles, from which artists drew inspiration, and the inextinguishable force of the Shadows that the men of the Enlightenment—precisely—had sworn to combat. The diurnal side of neoclassicism, in particular in David's formulation, was unambiguous in its confidence in the perfectibility of both human society and the human individual. David's tense, voluntaristic energy was the

Francisco de Goya y Lucientes, The Sleep of Reason Engenders Monsters,
1799. Foto Marburg/Art Resource, NY.

perfect manifestation of that confidence. But his art was only one particular and original aspect of neoclassicism; it by no means exhausts its
riches. Just as we cannot connect David's brand of neoclassicism exclusively with the French Revolution (it began well before 1793, even before
1789), we cannot see the growing vogue for the terrible and the obscure
as a mark of an end-of-the-century disappointment with Reason. Edmund Burke's *A Philosophical Enquiry into the Origins of our Ideas Concerning the Sublime and Beautiful* theorized on the pleasure procured by the
obscure and the terrible. That work appeared in 1757, and as early as
1758 the ultrarational Diderot announced that poetry "must have some-

thing in it that is barbaric, vast, and wild" (Diderot 1966, 103). This is because the century of the Enlightenment was also the age of sensibility and sentiment, and a delicate sensibility could be catastrophically reversed, unleashing obscure passions and impulses. The dialectical dovetailing of Light and Shadows was at the heart of the artistic inspiration of the Enlightenment.

Here too, Füssli's *The Nightmare* is significant. In its first version, a work unconnected with any commission, the artist's motivations were very probably as personal as they were profoundly "tenebrous." On the back side of his canvas, as if secretly, Füssli painted the portrait of a young woman, in all likelihood Lavater's niece, Anna Landolt, with whom Füssli had fallen head over heels in love in Zurich in 1778. Thus, if we think of *The Nightmare* in recto-verso terms, it has every semblance of being a magic charm cast from a distance at an inaccessible loved one: the painter wanted to haunt the nights of the woman he could only possess in his dreams—dreams like the one that he describes in a letter to Lavater on 16 June 1779. Even if on the recto the figures of the young woman, the monster, and the mare are inspired by models from classical antiquity and the Renaissance, and even if Füssli intended the painting as an "invention" founded on what he later (in a lecture before the Royal Academy in 1801) called a "judicious adoption of figures in art," the verso of the canvas reveals that he invested the work with a quasi-magical function—which indicates to what point the intimate subjectivity of the artist of the Enlightenment could harbor impulses that were anything but enlightened.

To return to Goya's *The Sleep of Reason Engenders Monsters,* his monsters are not incubi of dubious reality. The owls and bats engendered by the sleep of Reason are real nocturnal animals in a baleful imagery taken from traditional iconography (in particular, the iconography of emblem books). What is more, Goya asserts in the 1797 plate that his language is "universal." His engraving was to be understood as an allegory, a form that must be "clear, expressive, eloquent," as Gravelot and Cochin state in their *Iconologie par figures,* published in Paris between 1765 and 1781. But the legend accompanying Goya's image also states that the sleeping man whose slumber engenders these monsters is none other than the "author"—Goya in person. He does not take himself to be immune from the follies and superstitions that he condemns but for which he does not claim to know a remedy. *The Sleep of Reason Engenders Monsters* was originally conceived as a frontispiece for a collection of engravings entitled *Sueños* (Dreams). When the collection became *Los Ca-*

prichos, Goya chose as its frontispiece a self-portrait with a scornful expression, as if he wanted to open the terrible nocturnal experiences to which the collection bears witness with an apotropaic image of himself. Goya was to go a good deal farther in his quest to portray the powers of darkness than Füssli ever went. As Jean Starobinski notes, Füssli "deliberately refrained from anything misshapen or ignoble"; Goya, to the contrary, subjected "the creatures of the night" to "a furious attack which itself had something nocturnal about it" and that gave the "Darkness" he caricatured "a rough and massive self-evidence that can no longer be sent back into the void."

This means that we cannot hope to understand the artists of the Enlightenment or claim to describe a collective figure for them if we suppose them to have had a luminous unity of inspiration. Not only were artists animated by differing tendencies according to place and moment, and not only did they make different artistic, philosophical, or political choices; the most contradictory tendencies (between *Lumières* and *Ténèbres;* between Passions and Reason) might exist within one artist. It is that clash that gives the art of the Enlightenment its strongest energy, whether Reason sallies forth to master darkest ignorance and Light chases away the Shadows, or the figures of the Night resist being unveiled and are invested with a fascinating and irresistible vitality, as if they contained the deepest sources of life.

The artists of the Enlightenment may well have made different choices and their styles may well have taken different forms, but in one way or another they all shared a high consciousness of their art and its mission in society. For the Enlightenment, the route to the dignity and the legitimacy of artistic creation passed through the moral and social considerations embodied in the work of art, over and above its purely formal qualities.

In the 1730s, William Hogarth developed a new form of "history painting" in series of paintings—eight scenes for *A Rake's Progress* (1733–35), six for *Marriage à la mode* (1743–45)—to illustrate contemporary morality. As a "Comic History Painter" (his own term), he depicted the ridicules and vices of the aristocracy and the middle classes rather than offering his own values as exemplary. Irony must help to correct mores, and, to make the lesson more efficacious, Hogarth chose engravings as his medium and borrowed his themes from popular plays and novels. That same motivation led Hogarth to do two engravings, *Gin*

Lane and *Beer Street* (1751), in support of a pamphlet of Fielding's on the perils of alcoholism. Hogarth's social morality was conservative, however, and the high price of his engravings hindered their broad distribution among the popular classes. Hogarth promoted the ideas and interests of the enlightened middle class, and the consideration it gave him in return guaranteed his own dignity.

In spite of the ambiguity of Jean-Baptiste Greuze's *arriviste* attitudes and his thirst for social success, the "moral painting" of which he was the herald arose out of an aim similar to Hogarth's. This was the context in which Diderot exclaimed "Courage my friend!" in 1763, and declared his satisfaction with the way Greuze put morality in painting by "moving us, instructing us, correcting us, and encouraging us to virtue" (Diderot 1966, 151). Diderot returned to the topic in 1765, contrasting Greuze (in terms that are in themselves revealing) to Baudouin, Boucher's son-in-law: "Greuze has made himself a painter-preacher of good morals, Baudouin, a painter-preacher of bad; Greuze, a painter of the family and of respectable people; Baudouin, a painter of rakes and houses of ill repute. But fortunately he [Baudouin] [i]s not a skilled draftsman, he lacks color and genius, and [with Greuze] we have genius, drawing, and color on our side, so we're the stronger" (Diderot 1995, 1: 91).

The two paintings *(Saint Roch Interceding for the Plague-Stricken of Marseilles* and *Belisarius Receiving Alms)* that David entered into the Salon of 1781 are equally significant. The *Saint Roch* was commissioned by the Bureau de la Santé Publique to commemorate the epidemic of 1720. Although he was faithful to the traditional iconography of the saint, David stressed the unhappiness and despair of the plague victims more than the saint's intercession. Scholars have seen in this singular treatment a veiled attack against the church, which, it was suggested, was more indifferent to the fate of the poor than to that of the rich, since of the forty thousand victims of the 1720 epidemic only a thousand or so came from social levels above that of the worker or craftsman. On the other hand, in painting Belisarius for his reception into the Académie Royale David chose a theme that was fashionable for its political resonance, especially after the publication of Marmontel's moralizing romance, *Bélisaire*, in 1767. In the late eighteenth century, the figure of Belisarius, the general reduced to beggary by the cynical injustice and ingratitude of Emperor Justinian, was an ideal prop for the social and political propaganda of liberal reformers and moderate conservatives. David's choice was all the more appropriate because comte d'Angiviller, superintendent of the

King's Buildings on Louis XVI's accession to the throne in 1774, was a personal friend of Marmontel's, and Marmontel was secretary of the Académie Française.

A number of other artists in a broad variety of genres might serve as examples of a moral, social, and political commitment underlying the decisions of the "enlightened" artist. The *Encyclopédie* summarizes the concept in the article, "Intéressant," where it states that the artist must be *philosophe et honnête homme* and that the interest of a work of art lies in its moral and social content. This was already the attitude of La Font de Saint Yenne, the inventor of art criticism in the modern sense, in 1734; he demanded that historical paintings be "a school of mores" and take as their subject the virtuous and heroic actions of great men of exemplary humanity, generosity, grandeur, and courage. The idea was not new, and on occasion the intent to put morality into art produced conventional, conservative, even obscurantist works. But as it was formulated at the time, the idea of the artist's social responsibility was understood as a criticism of the decadence and corruption of contemporary society. Like the writer in the works of Jean-Paul Sartre, the artist of the Enlightenment operated "by unveiling," and his work "appealed to the liberty" of its public. Diderot wanted artists to write "as people spoke in Sparta," and Winckelmann, the historian and theoretician of a return to classical antiquity, stated that only Liberty could raise art to its perfection, as was sufficiently demonstrated, he added, by the incomparable beauty of Greek classical art.

This conception of the artist's mission by no means implies any revolutionary political consciousness, and the artistic revolution that was taking place cannot in any way be likened to the coming political revolution in France. Not only, as we shall see, did the political governing class encourage the desire for morality and seriousness in art but as many neoclassical artists were conservative as were progressive or revolutionary.

Antonio Canova's career is exemplary in this respect. In 1779, his *Daedalus and Icarus* was much admired in Rome, but critics invited him to temper his realistic virtuosity in the name of the Greco-Roman ideal. In 1783, his *Theseus and the Minotaur* showed that he had learned this lesson well, and the moral and political resonances of the work bear the stamp of the "enlightened" artist. Canova's first idea for this work had been to show the combat between the hero and the monster, but the final version represents Theseus seated in triumph on the Minotaur's body. Canova's Minotaur was inspired by an engraving of *Le pitture antiche d'Ercolano e contorni,* and its brutal realism contrasted with the idealized perfection of Theseus, whose body perfectly realized the calm grandeur and "tranquil nobility" that Winckelmann had seen as the distinctive sign of classical perfection. The work was hailed as "the first example provided in Rome of the revival of the style, system, and principles of antiquity." To reward him for this masterpiece the Venetian Senate accorded the young Canova an annual pension (in spite of its shaky financial situation). It was evidently honoring the political content of the sculpture more than a successful work of art. As the idealized victor of the monster of Crete, Theseus embodied the patriotism of the Serenissima: having lost its last possessions in Crete in 1715, Venice was forced to cede the Peloponnese to the Turks in 1718, and later, in 1770, Venice was powerless to intervene when the Turks brutally repressed an uprising in Crete.

The ideal of Liberty triumphing over bestiality remained an exception in Canova's work, however. Reaction invaded Venice in the 1780s, and one of its victims was the liberal movement of the Bernabotti, with which some of Canova's patrons were indirectly connected. Canova's idealism became more conservative, almost nostalgic, as if now the eternal Beauty of the ancients could only be grasped as the reflection of an irremediable absence. In any event, when a group of French visitors came to his studio in Rome in 1799, they saw his *Hercules and Lichas* as an allegory in which a French Hercules was destroying the monarchy. Canova responded that he would not have represented that theme for anything in the world, and that the figure of Lichas could just as well signify liberty degenerated. This statement alone should suffice to confirm the extent to which the ideal of Liberty (which, according to Winckelmann, had brought art to its perfection) cannot be equated to the ideal that the French Revolution was working to disseminate in Europe.

It was not on the political level that the artists of the Enlightenment joined together to further seriousness and morality in art. During the latter half of the eighteenth century, the first manifestation of an enlightened attitude in art was a rejection of anything connected with rococo. On occasion that rejection took the form of a nationalist reaction against foreign tastes. In Germany, where rococo and the *rocaille* style were closely connected with the taste that had triumphed under Louis XV, rejection went hand in hand with an anti-French sentiment. In England the change of style that occurred at the beginning of the reign of George III was explicitly encouraged by the architect Robert Adam in the name of a "decent simplicity" proper to the Anglican tradition, which Adam contrasted with the profusion and the magnificence sur-

rounding the ceremonies of the Roman Catholic Church. But the phenomenon was European, and by the 1770s it had reached Italy and
France as well as Germany and England, both in aristocratic milieus and
in the rising middle class. Beyond national and political differences and
social cleavages, rococo was rejected as an art conceived to be a private
luxury. Artists and patrons alike condemned its "frivolous" charms, fa-
voring an ideal of rational and universal beauty founded on the clarity of
pure line. Füssli stated that if art followed the "dictates of fashion, or a
patron's whims" then "its dissolution is at hand"; according to Reynolds,
"The whole beauty and grandeur of the art consists . . . in being able to
get above all singular forms, local customs, particularities, and details of
every kind." The new art aimed at being as universal as Reason; it was to
address its message of grandeur and virtue to the broadest possible public and, beyond, to humanity in all lands and of all times.

Effects of color and texture in painting were particularly suspect.
Since these are "superficial" and addressed to the senses, different individuals might perceive them differently. Standing in opposition to the
gracefulness of colors and the je ne sais quoi that provided the most
highly refined pleasures, line was the lesson of Nature. Rousseau himself, despite his finely developed sensibility, stated that "without line, colors do nothing." Line was not only more "natural" and more universal
than color but also "truer." Schiller complained of color, saying "the
pure outline would give me a more faithful image." For Reynolds, "a firm
and determined outline" shows knowledge of "the exact form which every part of nature ought to have." William Blake judged simplicity of line
not only "the noblest ornament of truth" but one of its essential attributes.

The irresistible spread of neoclassicism was also aided by a feeling
that this style that aimed at universality was a return to the oldest
European tradition in both the linear style of Greek vase paintings and
the simplicity of line of the Italian primitive painters. Goethe admired
Flaxman for his "gift of immersing himself in the innocent mood of the
earlier Italian schools." The rejection of the "affected" graces of the
rococo style was experienced not only as a triumph of Reason but also as
a return to the origins of European art, before it became corrupted
socially. Artists were fond of the myth that painting originated when a
Corinthian potter's daughter traced her lover's profile, projected in sil-
houette against a wall. In this age, drawing enjoyed an incomparable
prestige as the most ancient means of pictorial representation. Hence,
when Quatremère de Quincy urged artists to rekindle "the torch of an-

tiquity," he was inviting them to both a revolution and a resurrection. As Jean Starobinski states, "the moderns were bound to try to forget the methods they had learned, in order to let themselves be ruled by the antique vigor. . . . The first man and the first nations received the whole of art and knowledge, and history had only dimmed the meaning of that first illumination" (Starobinski 1988, 144).

This severe and intellectual approach was a shared characteristic of artists of the Enlightenment, and it contributed to a shift in the artists' theoretical approach to their creations. This point is of capital importance, for the rational reflection that accompanied artistic production at the time led to an increasing recognition of the role that the irrational plays in the work of art and in its creation and reception. This is evident in the two special domains of the definition of creative genius and the reelaboration of the classical notion of the sublime.

The extraordinary development of the academies provided a broad base for this change in theory but was also a manifestation of it. In 1720, there were only nineteen artistic academies in Europe, only a few of which taught art; in 1790, there were more than a hundred, stretching from Philadelphia to St. Petersburg. One significant event was the founding of the Royal Academy of London in 1768, when the monarch's will coincided with a general movement in society that involved both artists and leaders of industry and business. The artists had two associations, the Free Society of Artists and the Society of Artists of Great Britain (which provided the Royal Academy with many of its founding members); the businessmen had a Society for the Encouragement of the Arts, Manufactures and Commerce (now the Royal Society of Arts). The lectures of the Royal Academy (modeled on those of the French Académie des Beaux-Arts) were to have a considerable importance in that they gave the artist-lecturers an opportunity to theorize. When the artist was aware of what provided him with inspiration and guidance, he could situate his creative works in relation to the great examples of the past and the highest demands of art.

The many works on art theory that were produced reflect the liveliness and currency of this intellectual approach (as well as its European scope), and the number of translations and the speed with which they appeared attest to widespread interest. A few examples should suffice: Laugier's *Essai sur l'architecture,* published in France in 1753, was available in English as early as 1755; Daniel Webb's *Inquiry into the Beauties of Painting* (1760) appeared in France in 1765, in Germany in 1766, and in Italy in 1791; Winckelmann's *Geschichte der Kunst des Altertums* (1764) (History of

Ancient Art among the Greeks) was translated into French in 1766. Füssli was the first to translate a work of Winckelmann into English (his *Gedanken über die Nachahmung der griechischen Werke in der Malerei und Bilderhaverkunst* [Reflections on the Painting and Sculpture of the Greeks]).

The artist of the Enlightenment appears as the decidedly modern figure of the creator; he is as distant from the artisan or the pure technical craftsman as he is from the artist as the willing servant of a patron, making his fortune by applying a graceful brush to portraits or fashionable scenes. Winckelmann had invited painters to "dip their brush in intellect," and the enlightened artist did indeed think. If Greuze loudly declared that his brush was dipped "in his heart," Diderot added that in Greuze—an accomplished artist—sensibility and reason went hand in hand: "It would be most astonishing if that artist did not excel. He has wit and sensibility; he is enthusiastic about his art; he does endless studies. . . . Should he meditate a subject he is obsessed by it, followed [by it] everywhere. His very character is affected." Diderot returned to the topic two years later, in 1765: "Chardin and he both speak quite well about their art, Chardin with discretion and objectivity, Greuze with warmth and enthusiasm" (Diderot 1995, 1: 97).

Greuze's enthusiasm, which was both of the intellect and of the senses, is a sign of the times. A fondness for artistic theory renewed the artists' awareness of their activity, for the Enlightenment went as far as seeing reason as the source of the irrational aspects of the creation and reception of works of art. Certainly one of the most decisive contributions of the epoch is that it rooted the programmed rationality of its "diurnal" intentions in a complex conception of creative genius and a decisive reelaboration of the notion of the sublime.

In 1750, Baumgarten's *Aesthetica Acroamatica* overturned traditional concepts with a radical new articulation of the idea of the kind of knowledge that the work of art bears and the experience it proposes. Aesthetics, Baumgarten argues, is a domain over which the "principle of reason," the precondition of all distinct knowledge, has no power. That domain has a value of its own, however: "sense knowledge"—the aesthetic relationship—is "the realm of the confused and indistinct." That is, in perception everything is given in its immediate aspect; it does not allow us to abstract out its single elements. Thus, aesthetic experience belongs to a preconceptual sphere unaffected by logic but that has its own logic, the logic of the "lower cognitive forces." Baumgarten respects the authority of reason, but he conceives of aesthetics as a *gnoseologia inferior,* an "inferior knowledge": the "inferior faculties" of the soul are themselves governed by their own law; although "lower" or "inferior," it is nonetheless Law. The aesthetic relation to the world is thus defined as an "art of thinking beautifully" *(ars pulcre cogitandi)*.

Baumgarten's thought led to a new conception of artistic genius. Since genius possesses an extreme receptivity, force, and broadness of imagination, but also an intellectual perspicacity *(dispositio naturalis ad perspicaciam)*, it is the corollary of a specific gift, that of the *ingenium venustum*. Far from being an assemblage of qualities that can be separated into its constituent parts, the *ingenium venustum* is a "kind of disposition" that "expresses rather a spiritual attitude which imparts its own hue to everything it grasps and assimilates." It is a disposition of the soul with which the artist is born. *Aesthetica* was strongly innovative not only in its desire to found a logic proper to the "lower cognitive forces" within a philosophical system. It was also intended to be a "doctrine of man," an anthropology.

Herder saw in Baumgarten the "real Aristotle of our time." In reality, Baumgarten had only a very limited influence: the artists of the Enlightenment did not read him. His thought nonetheless provides us with a theoretical and historical base because it draws the consequences, in philosophical terms and in the artistic domain, of the rehabilitation of the passions that was in operation during the century—what Cassirer calls "the 'humanization' of sensibility."

Many "philosophical" texts more accessible than the austere German *Aesthetica* reelaborated the notion of the creative genius and described the theoretical mutation that worked to mold artists' growing self-awareness. The evolving thought of the French *philosophes* merits a word here, for in it we can observe the Cartesian tradition and the cult of Reason becoming enriched by the growing prestige of sentiment and the passions.

For Abbé Batteux, whose *Les Beaux-Arts réduits à un même principe* appeared in 1748, the situation should be clear. Responding to Abbé Du Bos, whose *Réflexions critiques sur la poésie, la peinture, et la musique* (1719) left some room for the irrational in poetic inspiration ("One must be inspired by a sort of furor to make such beautiful verse"), Batteux posited that genius and reason are indissociable. Genius is "an active reason that is exerted with art on an object, which industriously searches for all its real faces, all its possibilities. . . . It is an enlightened instrument that searches, digs, pierces secretly." Men of genius invent nothing; they do not "give an object its being" but rather they recognize "that it is as it is."

This strict position was maintained throughout the century. It is essentially Condillac's position in the *Dictionnaire des synonymes* (1758–67):

the genius's merit is limited to "observing, finding, and imitating"; as soon as imagination moves away from "the analogy with nature" it "produces only monstrous and extravagant ideas." For d'Alembert artistic genius resembles "logical" genius: "it discerns hidden beauties with finesse." The article, "Enthousiasme" of the *Encyclopédie* (1755) stresses that, far from being "a sort of furor" or "transport," the moment of enthusiasm resembles "what happens in the soul of the man of genius when reason, by a rapid operation, presents him with a striking and new picture that arrests him, moves him, ravishes him, and absorbs him. . . . The words, *imagination, génie, esprit,* and *talent* are simply terms found to express the various operations of reason." Toward the end of the century, Marie-Joseph Chénier was to adapt d'Alembert's notions to the taste of the day: "It is good sense, reason, that achieves all. . . . And genius is reason sublime."

Still, the article "Génie (Philosophie et littérature)" in the *Encyclopédie* declares that genius is tied to a particular form of sensibility and that it is the province of a certain type of individual, not a talent with which any man might be endowed naturally: "The man of genius . . . has a way of seeing, feeling, [and] thinking that is his alone." Thus, reason is no longer the essential quality of artistic genius; creation hones the product of a sensibility and an imagination in which Reason does not reign.

Diderot occupied a position in this changing picture that is all the more significant for his many contacts with the artists of his age during the biennial Salons of the Académie Royale. He provided accounts of the Salons from 1759 to 1781 for Grimm's *La Correspondance Littéraire,* and through his articles all the enlightened courts of Europe were privy to the new, internalized conception of creative genius. Earlier, in 1746, Diderot stated in his *Pensées philosophiques* that "it is the passions alone, great passions, that can raise the soul to great deeds. Without them, there would be an end to sublimity" (Diderot 1966, 1). Later, although he continued to insist on the role of reason as a balancing factor in creation, Diderot praised sentiment, enthusiasm in particular, and in his account of the 1767 Salon he stated: "The philosopher reasons, the enthusiast feels; the philosopher is sober, the enthusiast is intoxicated." Still, he insists on reconciling that intoxication with the rationality that always presides over creation: in *Le paradoxe sur le comédien* (1773–78), Diderot even judges that when great genius is present in an artist, "it is not his heart, it is his head that does everything" (Diderot 1966, 321). To explain this process Diderot develops the notion of successive stages in the creative process.

The idea was in the air, given that Winckelmann had already advised artists to "sketch with fire and execute with phlegm." Canova's drawings suffice to show that the purest sort of neoclassical practice demonstrate "fire" in sketches. Diderot went farther, however, arriving at the radically new and almost disquieting idea (disquieting to the age of the Enlightenment, that is) that at one stage or another of the creative process the genius was possessed by a sort of specific madness. The madness of genius, far from being pathological, was an integral part of creative energy and the creative impulse. Diderot distinguishes clearly, however, between this creative madness and the *furor poeticus* that inspired the poet of classical antiquity. The ancient poet could only compose if he had been visited by a divine spirit; in his apparent madness the poet or the painter of the Enlightenment was inspired only by his own genius, which became a fundamental and internal attribute of the great artist.

By granting artists a specific capacity for madness, Diderot emphasized an essential aspect of the artistic consciousness of the Enlightenment: the principles of Reason and of its diurnal ideals were clearer in art when they were associated with the obscure but positive forces of the passions and the creative imagination.

The notion of the sublime was another idea in the air during the latter half of the eighteenth century. Superabundantly used, the adjective "sublime" was applied to totally dissimilar works. Diderot alone, in his *Salons,* found both Greuze's *La malédiction paternelle* (The Father's Curse) and Fragonard's *Corrésus et Callirhoé* (Coresus Sacrifices Himself to Save Callirhoe) "sublime," as were Vernet's storms; and Hubert Robert's small paintings of ruins were just as "sublime" as Doyen's large and complex *Miracle des Ardents*. He viewed David's *Saint Roch* with a typically "sublime" mixture of terror and pleasure, and he even stated that Chardin saved his "ideal" from being "miserable" by the sublimity of his technique—his *faire*. Undeniably, the term was all the rage. It would be unfair, however, to accuse Diderot of debasing it. The semantic confusion that surrounded the notion of the sublime only indicates, as Robert Mauzi has suggested, that like the idea of happiness at the same age it compressed intuitions whose principle of unity was more existential than conceptual. Sublime emotion invests most of the works of the latter half of the eighteenth century; sublimity was a specific ferment for the artistic inspiration of the Enlightenment. Piranesi was as sublime as Füssli, Goya as sublime as Blake; Ossian's "primitivism" was sublime, and the scientific nocturnal paintings of Joseph Wright of Derby reflect what has been called the "industrial sublime" of English painting of the time. The notion of the sublime merits analysis as it touches on the essence of the artistic emotion of the Enlightenment.

Before the notion of the sublime was applied to the visual arts, we find the term in Boileau (1674), who took it from the treatise on rhetoric, *On the Sublime,* attributed to Longinus, and used it to designate the extraordinary, the surprising, and the marvelous in discourse. The sublime was not intended to persuade; it was situated beyond reason and it eluded rules; it "removes, ravishes, transports." This resonance persisted in the Enlightenment: when the sublime evoked a transport of exalted reason it was, in the terms of the supposed Longinus, "the echo of a great soul." It was thanks to their superhuman grandeur that David's *Le Serment des Horace* (The Oath of the Horatii), his *Socrate* (Death of Socrates), or his *Brutus* were sublime or that Winckelmann found the *Apollo Belvedere* sublimely attractive. Unlike the Beautiful, which is absolute and objective, the sublime is therefore a subjectively perceived quality found, in the final analysis, less in the object itself than in the strong effect that the object elicits in the viewer. This sublime quite naturally was associated with sentiment and an exalted sensibility: one of the surest signs that the sublime was having its effect was a "torrent of tears." When that point was reached Reason abdicated, succumbing to an emotion that transports beyond all possible reasonable discourse, the manifestation of which is an excessive reaction beyond the rational. This pathetic sublime could become an efficacious weapon in the service of the philosophical struggle of the Enlightenment.

Edmund Burke gave this classical concept a radical change of direction in 1757, when he published *A Philosophical Enquiry into the Origin of Our Ideas Concerning the Sublime and Beautiful,* a work that was reprinted ten times in thirty years, translated into French in 1765 and into German in 1773. If the sublime of "Longinus" operated as a "Trojan horse" within classical theory, Burke's sublime was responsible for a real epistemological mutation. Basing his remarks on an "experimental" method founded in "a diligent examination of our passions in our own breasts" and on "a sober and attentive investigation of the laws of nature"—hence speaking as a philosopher—Burke asserts that the effect produced by the sublime could not be reduced to the one engendered by beauty. "The great" is "rugged and negligent"; it "ought to be dark and gloomy." The "foundation of the sublime" is "whatever is fitted in any sort to excite the ideas of pain, and danger, that is to say, whatever is in any sort terrible, or is conversant about terrible objects, or operates in a manner analogous to terror, is a course of the *sublime;* that is, it is productive of the strongest emotion which the mind is capable of feeling."

Kant later showed that the sublime is not the object of the senses but depends on "the use that the faculty of judgment naturally makes of certain objects." Burke's *On the Sublime and Beautiful* did not, in fact, have any direct, practical influence on artistic production. Like Baumgarten's *Aesthetica,* however, it provides an important benchmark in art theory and was a decisive turning point in the century that deepened the gap between the light refinement of rococo and the grave passion of the Enlightenment. A new field opened up for the artist with the "terrible" sublime: now he could produce works that, far from aiming at the "pleasure" linked to beauty, played on the instinctive impulses of the psyche.

Burke's personality might lead one to think that the sublime and the Enlightenment were radically opposed. The intellectual leader of a reaction that was immediately hostile to the French Revolution (his *Reflections on the French Revolution* was published in 1790), Burke felt an unwavering repugnance for French philosophy. In that work he contrasts collective and general reason with individual reason, which he finds too weak to be of any great help. What was needed was to "draw advantage both from the general bank and from the capital of the nations and the centuries." In other words, Burke chose to be the apostle of "general prejudices" that bore a hidden wisdom. For him human nature was flawed and should be contained by a superior religious or political authority. His political ideas fitted well with his conception of the sublime, which was founded on obscurity more than on the light, investing the individual with terror before a power that surpasses him and that he cannot comprehend. But *On the Sublime and Beautiful,* published when Burke was twenty-eight years old, had a broader impact than its author's political views.

Although Füssli, along with many others, eventually came around to condemning the French Revolution, William Blake, another great creator of the end of the century given to the sublime, remained favorable to it. In 1793, his *Nebuchadnezzar* was a ferocious depiction of the fall of a shameful despotism, and the first book of his *The French Revolution: A Poem in Seven Books* (1791) celebrated the deputies who participated in the Tennis Court Oath in terms that are clearly "sublime":

> . . . Like spirits of fire in the beautiful
> Porches of the Sun, to plant beauty in the desart craving abyss,
>   they gleam
> On the anxious city . . . .

This poem reflects the inspiration behind *Glad Day,* a drawing that Blake made in 1780 to commemorate the social and religious agitation of the Gordon Riots. During the last third of the century, the notion of the sublime as terrible no longer belonged exclusively to Burke: as the (typically sublime) revolutionary rhetoric of Saint-Just suggests, the *Lumières de la Raison* and sublime *Ténèbres* were henceforth indissolubly linked. This followed a notion given in Milton (whom Burke cites), who describes the blinding light of God's throne as covered "with the majesty of darkness" and says of God: "Dark with excessive bright thy skirts appear."

Obscurity proved such a fertile notion that some writers took the polarity of light and dark as the organizing principle of the universe. Blake states: "Opposition is true friendship." Goethe's Mephistopheles states that he is "a part of the darkness that gave birth to light, the proud light who now contends with her mother the Night for her ancient rank and the space she used to occupy." Man was not merely a witness to this struggle in which darkness had the upper hand of light, he was also the circumscribed arena of a (sublime) conflict between solar clairvoyance (Goya's lynx) and hidden shadows.

The most exalted Enlightenment architects showed the full potential of this paradoxical concept. In a general sense, preoccupation with an art founded on universally applicable verities established thanks to the "light" of nature and reason led neoclassical architects to seek increasingly pure forms, which meant (following the principle of a return to origins) more and more primitive or natural forms. The Doric order was particularly in favor as the most ancient expression, stripped to its essence, of an architectural ideal. It was the "geometric purity" of natural phenomena that gave Nicolas Ledoux the idea of basing architecture on the absolute forms of the pyramid, the cube, and the sphere. If, toward the end of the century, Du Fourny stated that "architecture should be regenerated through geometry," it was in part because, to cite Christopher Wren, "geometrical figures are naturally more beautiful than any other irregular; in this all consent, as to a law of Nature." Since it was founded in nature and in reason, the architecture of the Enlightenment rejected rococo just as painting and sculpture had done. As Quatremère de Quincy wrote in 1798, architecture must banish the *bizarrerie* that "gives rise to a system destructive of order and of the forms prescribed by nature." The taste for the bizarre in architecture "usually arises out of weariness of what is best"; it is caused by "the satiety produced by abundance." Wealth and enjoyment were what led to the "disguise of that perfidious art." What was required, to the contrary, in order to attain a "grandeur" that would be both "proportional" and "moral" was to make the "effect of grandeur . . . simple enough to strike us at a glance." We can recognize here the moral conception of art that animated the diurnal side of the artist of the Enlightenment.

But the exaltation of reason might also lead to sublime excesses at the culmination of which the rational rigor of the forms gives a glimpse of the shadow on which reason is based, a shadow conceived as a homogeneous and brutal mass. As Boullée wrote, "The art of moving us by effects of light belongs to architecture, for in all the monuments susceptible of bringing the soul to feel the horror of darkness . . . the artist . . . can dare to say to himself: I make light." Boullée did a project for a monument dedicated to the spirit of the "sublime" Newton in which the lighting "should resemble that on a clear night." The viewer "stands alone" *(isolé de toutes part)* at the center of the spherical construction, "and his eyes can behold nothing but the immensity of the sky." In this project for a cenotaph and the artistic "discovery" that it implied, Boullée felt he had "made [himself] sublime." He probably felt himself equally sublime in designing the many other funerary monuments in which he attempted to rival the Egyptians, inventing not only a "hidden" or "sunken" architecture *(architecture enfouie)* but an "architecture of shadows" *(architecture des ombres)*. With Boullée and his meditation on death and the memory of the living (a neoclassical exercise par excellence), the architecture of the Enlightenment reached the stage of dreaming of an ideal architecture as "a composition made up of the effect of shadows."

Newton's cenotaph was never built. Nor was the architecture of shadows realized. For Boullée the art of architecture lay in conceiving the image of the building rather than in constructing it, and it is in that "production of the mind" that he pushed architectural reason to the extreme—indeed, the sublime—degree of rationality.

We cannot isolate theoretical, intellectual, and moral innovation from the artistic creation we have just been examining, nor from the social, economic, and political milieus for which the artists worked. The rejection of rococo was interpreted as a generic criticism of a corrupted society, but that criticism was not aimed at the established authorities. Quite to the contrary, the authorities backed the criticism and helped to reassert the artist's dignity. Admittedly, patrons have always played a role in artistic production and in the history of forms. But with the Enlightenment and under the impact of themes developed by the *philosophes,* their role reached the point of suggesting a new and more modern conception of relationships among art, culture, society, and political power.

Throughout Europe the eighteenth century was also the century of "enlightened despotism." The enlightened despot put into practice what we might anachronistically call a "cultural policy." That policy was based on the idea, disseminated by men of letters, that the grandeur of a reign depended less on the glory of its military actions than on the quantity and quality of the geniuses who were active during the time. Throughout Europe (monarchical or not) monuments were erected to honor great men and celebrate the glory of the nation. In 1737, Florence honored Galileo with a monument in the church of Santa Croce; in 1740 a monument to Shakespeare was put in Westminster Abbey, and, in 1755, one to Newton went up Trinity College, Cambridge. Descartes had his monument in Stockholm in 1780, and Grotius in Delft in 1781. In 1776, a bust of Winckelmann (who had died in 1763) was placed in the Pantheon in Rome, the first of a series of statues that transformed that Roman monument into a temple to glory—an idea that the French Revolution later recalled.

Monarchs and princes were not content with honoring the dead. They also encouraged the living, and they demonstrated their encouragement through artistic choices that although "personal" were by no means "private," given that they were made by the sovereign. If Frederick the Great, the queen of Sweden, and the prince of Liechtenstein were all fond of the paintings of Chardin, it was probably in part because his "Dutch" style (or what the age took to be Dutch) gave him a reputation as an "enlightened" artist. Amsterdam in the eighteenth century was a stronghold for the diffusion of French philosophic ideas, and to display a taste for Dutch culture was a sign of a "philosophic" mind. It was to Augustus III, king of Poland and elector of Saxony, that Winckelmann dedicated his *Reflections on the Painting and Sculpture of the Greeks* in 1755, a work that directly attacked the rococo taste in favor in Dresden. Augustus nonetheless gave Winckelmann a pension, which enabled him to leave for Rome and to launch his career. In 1757, Charles VII, king of the Two Sicilies (later Charles III of Spain) commissioned engravings for *Le pitture antiche d'Ercolano e contorni,* which he graciously offered to an elite throughout Europe, thus contributing, in a "disinterested" and enlightened manner, to the rapid diffusion of neoclassical motifs in every part of the Continent.

Sovereigns also displayed their enlightened attitudes by founding the first "museums" in the modern sense of the term. In 1769, the Fredericianum in Kassel brought together ancient statues, a library, and natural history collections; starting in 1772, Pius VI ordered the construction and installation of the galleries of the Vatican. These collections were still private but open to visitors, as with the Galleria degli Uffizi in Florence. Things changed in 1779 with the Belvedere Museum in Vienna. The museum's organizer, Christian von Mechel, a friend of Winckelmann's, saw the conception and the disposition of the museum as furnishing "a visible history of art" aimed more at the instruction of the public than at "fleeting pleasure." The idea was revived in Paris in 1792 for the Louvre and in 1795 for the Musée des Monuments Français. In 1798, Aloys Hirt, in a memoir dedicated to the king of Prussia, defined the museum as an instrument of education in the broadest sense. Works of art, he stated, should not be conserved in private palaces but in public museums because "they are a heritage for the whole of mankind."

The development of museums, backed by the sovereigns, probably responded to a growing taste for temporary expositions among an ever-expanding public. In Paris the Salons of the Académie attracted daily as many as seven hundred visitors of mixed social origin—aristocrats, bourgeois, and intellectuals, but also high-ranking state servants, the "gallooned grey suits" whose frequentation shocked the sensibilities of certain great lords who, in 1770, obtained the privilege of visiting the Salon when it was closed to the *grand public.*

The rise of a modern public in the age of the Enlightenment, which is confirmed by the extraordinary popularity of engravings, was also of capital importance. It helps to explain why it was important for the sovereign's political and social image to be reputed "enlightened." Similar preoccupations probably lay behind the decision (in 1787) of the queen of France, Marie Antoinette, to have Elisabeth Vigée-Lebrun paint her portrait with her children: the "mother of a family" was a major figure in both Enlightenment literature and moralistic painting. Some scholars have contrasted the reigns of Louis XV and Louis XVI on this point. As early as 1758, however, Boucher had given his portrait of Madame de Pompadour (London, Victoria and Albert Museum) an "enlightened" air by representing his model, a talented musician, in a natural setting, looking up from a musical score to listen to the song of a bird. Pictured in this manner, the sister of the marquis de Marigny, superintendent of the King's Buildings, seemed almost a devotee of Rousseau before the fact, capable of combining intellectual interests with the simple charms of nature and even of preferring the second to the first. In 1764, when Cochin persuaded Marigny to replace the decor of landscapes, hunting scenes, and erotically tinged mythological scenes in the royal château of Choisy with a series of paintings exalting royal humanitarian sentiments, the château became a center of the renewal of enlightened art. The new decorative program took its subject matter from Roman history, and it was designed to show the pacific and virtuous acts of the emperors more than their military exploits. Two years later, Louis XV probably ordered the removal of such canvases as had been completed, calling once again on Boucher, but a year after Boucher's death, the king accepted the more sober, virtuous program proposed by Marigny.

With Louis XVI this policy was confirmed and enlarged. *L'Ombre du grand Colbert*, published by La Font de Saint Yenne in 1747, and even more, Voltaire's *Le Siècle de Louis XIV* (1751) eventually bore fruit. In 1774, the comte d'Angiviller succeeded Marigny as superintendent, and he systematically promoted an artistic policy that aimed at returning to the grandeur and the glory of the Grand Siècle, redefined in the new spirit of the Enlightenment. Unlike the cycles exalting the glory of the French crown, the works he commissioned rarely refer to the king, celebrating instead the virtues of the nation in general: courage, sobriety, respect of the laws, and, especially, patriotism. It was in response to royal commissions that David painted *The Oath of the Horatii* in 1784 and *Brutus* between 1787 and 1789. In his letters commissioning these works, d'Angiviller revealingly stresses the moral theme more than the historical subject itself. He commissioned statues of great men, among them La Fontaine and Poussin, and, speaking of Marshal Catinat, he emphasized that Catinat was "no less to be recommended for his military talents than for his humanity and his philosophical spirit."

Official commissions systematically encouraged exemplary and didactic programs and moral and virtuous subjects—in short, "enlightened" works and the more optimistic side of the Enlightenment. One might even wonder whether the success of these great "diurnal" themes was not due to their assiduous promotion by the convergent interest of the intellectuals and the political powers. In the thirty last years of the century, the state culture seems to have functioned as an essential lever in the most ambitious sort of enlightened artistic production.

France is a particularly interesting case in point because the revolutionary period throws light on the genuine complexity of this phenomenon. The new people in command took care to continue the policy of official patronage, of course with different themes. Thus, when the Club des Jacobins received a disappointing response to the subscription that it had launched on 1 January 1791 in support of David's *Serment du Jeu de Paume* (Tennis Court Oath)—the club offered an engraving of the painting as a premium—the Constituent Assembly agreed, two days before its adjournment, to take on responsibility for the work. Similarly, in August 1793, the Convention announced the famous competition of Year II to celebrate "the most glorious epochs of the French Revolution," and the first anniversary of the fall of the monarchy was celebrated by a two-fold symbolic manifestation, the inauguration of the Gallery of the Louvre and the destruction of the royal funerary monuments in the Abbey of Saint-Denis. On 9 and 10 Thermidor, Year VI (27 and 28 July 1798), the Directory celebrated the "repatriation" of works of art from Italy with a grandiose Fête des Arts et de la Victoire. In a fine example of ideological manipulation and in spite of opposition from many artists (David and Quatremère de Quincy among them), the government claimed that France, the land of liberty, had a legitimate right to "repatriate" as manifestations of liberty masterpieces of all ages and all countries.

Still, by weakening the traditional structures of artistic production (the Salon was opened to all in 1792 and the Académie Royale was dissolved in 1793) without immediately substituting new institutions for them, the Revolution also highlighted the distance separating the "enlightened" and voluntarist aims of its leaders from the practices, capacities, and taste of the multitude. In the revolutionary Salons the number of artists and works multiplied by a factor of two or three but the "historical paintings" and the "grand genre" that best made the connection with the moral and artistic thought of the Enlightenment did not grow significantly: in 1789, the Salon included 17 "antique paintings" out of a total of 206 works; in 1795, the proportion was 16 out of 535; and between 1769 and 1799 only 147 historical paintings were shown out of a total of 3,076 works. As time went on in revolutionary France, the *petits genres*—portraits, landscapes, genre scenes of a disquieting banality—constituted the overwhelming majority of pictorial production just when the decisive battle between Light and Darkness was being fought.

There were several reasons for the decline of the *grand genre*. Historical paintings were more costly but also, during the short period of the Revolution proper, the accelerating pace of historical events did not permit the time lapse that all grand projects need between decision and realization. The final failure of the *Tennis Court Oath* can probably be attributed to David's many active political responsibilities, but it is also true that barely two years after the Oath itself, unanimity among the revolutionaries was a thing of the past, and several of the leading actors in the events of 20 June 1789 were guillotined under the Terror.

On a deeper level, if great artistic works were not realized during the most intense phase of the Revolution it was partly because of a fundamental contradiction that the artist of the Enlightenment encountered when the principles of reason clashed with the opaque reality of men. In his work the philosopher-artist bore witness to a conflict in which he was also actively involved.

David's level of activity was exceptional, but it is also a good example of this situation. At the start of his career in the Salons, David was a typical "enlightened" artist. Not only did the themes and style of his great historical paintings make him the inventor of an original philosophical neoclassicism; by all that they suggested concerning the mind and the perfect sociability of their models and by the confidence that they manifest in the individual human being's essential goodness and perfectibility, his portraits revealed an essentially enlightened approach to the lesser genre of the portrait.

Along with his political involvement, David took on the social responsibilities that underlay the mission and the dignity of the artist of the Enlightenment. He not only organized the great commemorative celebrations of the advancing Revolution at the demand of the Assembly or the Comité de Salut Public but also worked in the administration of the arts, furnished sketches for the new "national costumes," proposed commemorating each great event of the Republic by striking a medal, and, in May 1794, even responded to a request for caricatures "to awaken the public spirit and make [people] feel how atrocious and ridiculous are the enemies of Liberty and the Republic."

With all this multifaceted activity, the ambitious projects to celebrate "The Triumph of the Enlightened Principles of the Revolution" never saw the light of day. The only paintings that David completed at that time were three canvases painted in shocked reaction to the same type of event: the death of a revolutionary hero. As David himself declared in presenting the portrait of Le Peletier de Saint-Fargeau assassinated, "The true patriot must fervently grasp all means for enlightening his fellow citizens and for ceaselessly presenting before their eyes the sublime traits of heroism and virtue." The themes of these paintings—enlightened patriotism, sublime heroism, virtue—are incontestably those of an artist of the Enlightenment; the way that David treated them confirms his interest in the "universal" meaning of the event rather than the anecdote. In his primordial nudity the young Joseph Bara, fourteen years old at his death, becomes a figure of the new man who has redis- covered the purity of primitive humanity, before all social corruption. The figure of the mature hero (Marat was fifty when he was assassinated) merges two mythical figures of the heroic death: the death of Christ, who died for love of humankind, and the death of the hero of classical antiquity, Seneca in particular, who died for his belief in an ideal of hu- manity. The *Marat assassiné* (Death of Marat) offers the first "philosophi- cal Pietà" in history, a Pietà with no immortality other than in human memory.

The *Joseph Bara* and the *Death of Marat* are perhaps David's master- pieces; they are works in which a shiver of pathos filters through a rig- orously intellectual conception. This makes these paintings all the more symptomatic: at the heart of the formidable struggle between Light and Darkness that the Revolution represented for all the revolutionaries, David's masterpieces exalt the figure of the hero of the Enlightenment— the *Lumières*—slipping into the *Ténèbres* of Death. If the Revolution was experienced as the dawn of Reason making its entry into History, the story of that coming was one of a dual and obscure violence. When advancing Light descended into the opacity of reality, it produced the terrible return of Darkness.

England, in contrast, seemed to have brought together all the condi- tions necessary for a happy flowering of the artist of the Enlightenment. England provided a model of tolerance and liberty for philosophers, and beginning in the 1760s English society welcomed a number of foreign artists who chose to launch their careers in London. In the 1770s, Johannes Zoffany, who was born in Frankfurt and arrived from Rome around 1760, became the most sought-after specialist in "conversation pieces." One might cite others: Benjamin West, born in Pennsylvania, who arrived from Rome in 1763; Angelica Kauffmann, who was born in Switzerland and arrived from Venice in 1766; Philippe Jacques de Loutherbourg, a German who had worked in Paris who arrived in 1771, and Füssli, a Swiss, who lived in London from 1764 to 1766 and returned there to settle permanently in 1778 after a prolonged stay in Italy.

Rome was an almost obligatory relay station in this migration to London. The large English colony there and the English travelers who passed through the city on their "Grand Tour" made a luxurious display of the prestige of an aristocratic and merchant society open to the new style and well disposed to investing large sums in works of art for resi- dences. This was an important phenomenon because it indicated, right from the start, something characteristic of the English version of enlightened attitudes toward art. One key personage in the British colony in Rome, the Scottish painter Gavin Hamilton, worked for art-loving clients, and some of his works influenced no less a painter than David, but the bulk of his revenues came from his activities as a merchant and go-between. As a member of the circle of the cardinal and collector Alessandro Albani and a business associate of Thomas Jenkins, Hamilton participated in archaeological excavations in Tuscany, Rome, Ostia, at Hadrian's Villa, and elsewhere. At times he worked with the English sculptor Joseph Nollekens to "restore" works of art by combining fragments, and he made his fortune furnishing works for some of the most prestigious collections in England—among others, those of Charles Towneley, Lord Shelburne, the Duke of Bedford, and the Earls of Egremont, Leicester, and Lonsdale.

The activities of Gavin Hamilton and Thomas Jenkins also show that neoclassicism was the first artistic movement in history to be systematically promoted as a profitable financial investment. The four sumptuously illustrated volumes of the *Collection of Etruscan, Greek and Roman Antiquities* (1766–67) of Sir William Hamilton, British envoy extraordinary to the court of Naples, were apparently published with the highest, most disinterested motives. In his preface to this work, Sir William argues in favor of the revival of ancient art and declares his desire to encourage artists interested in "inventing" in the ancient style or simply in "copying" monuments by putting at their disposition faithful reproductions of the originals. His volumes did in fact have a considerable impact on such artists as Flaxman, Füssli, and Wedgwood. But the reputation that this publication (which he dedicated to George III) gave to his personal collection permitted Hamilton to sell it to the British Museum in 1772 for a considerable profit. Hamilton's commercial intent was confirmed in 1781–82, when he sold important antiquities to the Duchess of Portland for nearly twice the sum he had paid an associate of Gavin Hamilton and Thomas Jenkins for them.

In England the success of neoclassicism was narrowly connected to a convergence of the "cultural policy" inaugurated by George III and the intellectual and commercial interests of a powerful and enlightened middle class that had been enriched by industrial and economic development.

When he came to the throne in 1760, George III was twenty-two years of age. With the aid of the Tories, the young king worked to restore royal prerogatives but, breaking with the tastes of the Whig aristocracy, he supported the new style, a neo-Palladianism of mixed influences from the Italian Renaissance, Italian mannerism, and Italian baroque. George III, however, declared that the Doric was his "favorite order," and he showed his desire for a coherent artistic policy by according official recognition to two of the most prominent representatives of the new style, the painter Benjamin West and the architect Robert Adam.

The son of Quakers who had emigrated to Pennsylvania in 1725, Benjamin West arrived in Rome in 1760, where he frequented the circles around Cardinal Albani, Pompeo Batoni, Mengs, and Winckelmann. Gavin Hamilton steered West toward neoclassicism and made him understand that a painter could enlarge his reputation and increase his revenues by having engravings made of his works. West was to remember this lesson when he settled in London in 1763. His success in England was swift. Not only did the moral and patriotic themes of neoclassicism harmonize with the conservative values of the power elite, but as an artist of English stock West was celebrated as a "native" capable of competing with the Roman neoclassicists and someone who could provide a model, on British soil, for young English artists.

After painting a number of neoclassical paintings with classical subject matter and a clearly political resonance, West "modernized" his style with *The Death of General Wolfe,* a work celebrating the victory of the English forces over the French in Quebec in 1739 that had assured the British crown a hold on North America. The painting caused a sensation because the people figured in it were in modern dress, thus breaking with the principle (recalled by Reynolds) that "historical painting" must obey the convention of "heroic nudity." The painting was nonetheless an instant success, and the engraving taken from it brought the artist a considerable fortune. In 1771, West repeated the operation with *William Penn's Treaty with the Indians.* By representing the 1682 event as an "enlightened idyll" and taking notable liberties with historical fact, the painting exalted the ideology of a British colonialism that was presumed to deliver the natives from tyranny, convert them to the True Faith, and bring them the benefits of a superior civilization. In the following year, 1772, West was named Historical Painter to the King with an annual stipend of £1,000.

Robert Adam, who was born in Scotland, came to London from Rome in 1758, and in 1761 he was named Joint (that is, second) Architect to the King. His refined neoclassicism was explicitly aimed at helping the reign of George III become a worthy rival of the ages "of Pericles, Augustus, or the Medicis," and Adam encouraged the king to think of himself more as a Roman emperor than as a constitutional monarch. Robert Adam's importance lies not only in the quantity of buildings that he constructed for the crown and the governing elite but also in the fact that with him, the architect directed tne entire framework for living, the "external and internal composition" of the building. By designing the entire decorative program and the furniture (chairs, tables, lamps, candelabras, carpets, mirrors, etc.) for his projects, Adam found himself at the center of a sizable commercial venture involving all the arts as well as the craft and industrial enterprises that produced such items.

Matthew Boulton, Thomas Chippendale, and Josiah Wedgwood all worked for Adam, but it was Angelica Kauffmann who best embodied the success of the English conception of artistic creation. After a Roman sojourn from 1763 to 1765, during which she mixed with Winckelmann, Mengs, Batoni, and Gavin Hamilton and was in close contact with the English colony (Winckelmann reported in a letter that "she paints all the Englishmen who visit Rome"), Kauffmann arrived in London in 1766 in the company of Lady Wentworth, the wife of His Majesty's Resident at Venice. As with Vien in France, Kauffmann's *à la grecque* style offered a soft and decorative version of neoclassicism. By taking her inspiration from Homer and Virgil to evoke an idyllic and heroic age, avoiding the tragic mode and "Spartan" gravity, she totally satisfied the expectations of an elite that for the moment was enjoying a period of peace and relative prosperity. In 1768, at the age of twenty-seven, she was elected a founding member of the Royal Academy—a truly extraordinary privilege—and during the fifteen years she remained in London (from 1766 to 1781), her art brought her a total sum of £14,000, an exceptional amount of money for a woman painter and nearly as much as the royal pension granted to Benjamin West.

Angelica Kauffmann's success clearly shows her skill in satisfying the demands of an aristocratic elite with portraiture and historical painting. Her name is also inseparable from a new artistic practice typical of the form that art took in England of the Enlightenment—mechanical reproduction, which connected artistic production with the industrial revolution. Kauffmann's works were not only reproduced in engravings but were used to decorate all manner of things—fans, furniture, vases, tobacco pouches, ice buckets, tea services, porcelains, etc. Angelica Kauffmann was Matthew Boulton's favorite collaborator. Boulton massproduced neoclassical ceiling decorations for the expanding market that Robert Adam had encouraged, and he invented a method resembling aquatint engraving for reproducing paintings mechanically, a project for which Angelica Kauffmann painted some thirty pictures.

The most original characteristic of artistic production in England of the Enlightenment lay in this sort of association between industry and the artists. The crown and the aristocracy operated in ways similar to their counterparts elsewhere in Europe, but the wealthier representatives of the enlightened middle class (scholars, men of the liberal professions, industrialists, and merchants) patronized art on a large scale. They took their motto from Erasmus Darwin (who was a physician): "To inlist Imagination under the banner of Science." Enlightened entrepreneurs provided artists with a regular outlet for their works, and they organized into clubs, associations and societies—more or less informal groups whose members corresponded with one another and with the most prominent specialists in Europe and America. After founding a botanical society in Lichfield (which translated the *Genera Planetarum* of Linnaeus), Erasmus Darwin went on to found the Derby Philosophical Society and, with Matthew Boulton and the mathematician Charles Small, the Lunar Society of Birmingham. Another figure typical of the epoch and a collector of both art and fossils, Sir Brooke Boothby, was a member of both the Lichfield Botanical Society and the Derby Philosophical Society. It was Boothby who accepted the manuscript of *Rousseau juge de Jean-Jacques* from Jean-Jacques Rousseau in 1776—a work published in Lichfield in 1780. This milieu guaranteed the vitality and, in the last analysis, the coherence of artistic creation of the Enlightenment in the United Kingdom. Boulton put to work artists as different as Reynolds, Kauffmann, Flaxman, West, Wedgwood, and Wright of Derby; Erasmus Darwin commissioned works from Füssli and Blake; Sir Brooke Boothby, from Füssli and Wright of Derby.

It has been said that Wright of Derby's paintings did for the industrial revolution what David's works did in politics for the French Revolution. Joseph Wright, who had close connections with the members of the Lunar Society of Birmingham, specialized in nocturnal scenes that depicted works of art or scientific instruments; then, during the 1770s, he invented the "industrial nocturnal" genre, producing *The Blacksmith's Shop* in 1771, *An Iron Forge* in 1772, and *View of Cromford: Arkright's Cotton Mill at Night* in 1782–83. From that date on, his paintings provide a chronicle of industry and work in the Midlands, and they have a resonance that recalls a very rational and more modern version of Burke's "nocturnal sublime."

The ideals and the success of Josiah Wedgwood provide an even better epitome of the English figure of the artist of the Enlightenment. Named Potter to the King in 1766 and a member of the Lunar Society, Wedgwood played an essential role in the diffusion of neoclassicism in England. His works, based in a simplicity and elegance of line, rejected *chinoiseries* and the exuberance of rococo, and they monopolized the aristocratic market by concentrating on motifs from classical antiquity taken from *Le pitture antiche d'Ercolano e contorni,* from the *Collection of Etruscan, Greek and Roman Antiquities from the Cabinet of the Hon. Wm. Hamilton,* and from the comte de Caylus's *Recueils d'antiquités.* To make sure that his designs were accurate Wedgwood made use of proven artists (Angelica Kauffmann, Wright of Derby, Flaxman, Stubbs, and Blake, among others), and in order to guarantee the quality of his massive production and assure a steady supply of finished pieces, in 1766 he constructed an immense industrial complex, "Etruria," a business venture organized to maximize an "enlightened" alliance between profits and humanity that worked to achieve mass production of works of art.

Among Wedgwood's innovations were breaking down the work process into discrete tasks, systematizing production, firing workers for alcoholism, and having workers punch an early version of a time-clock. He dreamed of making "such Machines of the Men as cannot err." Wedgwood saw industrialization as contributing to the perfectibility of the human species rather than as inhumane, as William Blake thought. At Etruria the workers had decent lodgings, schools, and hospitals reserved for their use; in exchange for complete submission they obtained nourishment, clothing, houses, education, and medical care. As triumphant examples of an enlightened conception of the industrial arts, Wedgwood's factories inspired emotional reactions from painters and poets and elicited the admiration of scientists. They prefigured "singing tomorrows" and an end to the poverty and ignorance of rural society, and they prepared the way for prosperity, popular education, and modern civilization.

In the 1770s Great Britain might seem to have been the European country in which the art of the Enlightenment in its diurnal version, made of confidence in Reason and an optimistic faith in a progress built on applied science, was best realized. The picture is not quite that simple. Even without evoking the downturn in the political and social situation in the 1780s brought on by Great Britain's defeat by its American colonies (with the aid of France) in their War of Independence, and leaving aside the Irish crisis and the Gordon Riots in London, both in

1780—events that revealed a dangerous level of social and religious discontent—the historian of art is obliged to admit a singular fact. It was not the "enlightened" works of Benjamin West, Wright of Derby, Angelica Kauffmann, Johannes Zoffany, or Josiah Wedgwood that proved the most "modern" or that had the most promising future. It was with artists like Blake and Füssli—in short, it was with the preromantic "sublime"—that (with historical hindsight) English artists showed themselves to have been the most inventive creators and artists and the ones who embodied with greatest intensity the personal and philosophical commitment that was the foundation of the dignity of the creator of the Enlightenment.

This is probably because a simple confidence in the perfectibility of the individual and of society was inadequate to achieve one of the fundamental ideals of the Enlightenment—the idea (a "philosophical" idea par excellence) of moral liberty, a quintessentially human spiritual dimension that, without recourse to metaphysics, would permit men to rise above the cosmic or historical violence crushing them. But moral liberty can only be grasped in poignant conflict with its contrary, the opaque weight of natural and social alienation. If he wanted to bring out that dimension of moral freedom in his works, the artist of the Enlightenment (Goya, David, and others) had to accept a paradoxical challenge: turning his back on all refined and "diurnal" elegance, moving far from any decorative conception of art put to the service of a patriarchal and conservative society, he needed, as Jean Starobinski put it, to exalt the light by rendering "all the wildness of the material world, all its mingled wealth of color, light, and shade"; he needed to "depict the invisible presence" of moral liberty within man as he takes up the challenge of the "inevitabilities of matter and event."

Bibliography

Boime, Albert. *Art in the Age of Revolution, 1750–1800*. A Social History of Modern Art, 1. Chicago and London: University of Chicago Press, 1987.

Cassirer, Ernst. *The Philosophy of the Enlightenment*. Translated by Fritz C. A. Koelln and James P. Pettegrove. Humanitas, 7. Boston: Beacon, 1955. Originally published as *Philosophie der Aufklärung*. Tübingen: Mohn, 1932.

Diderot, Denis. *Diderot's Selected Writings*. Edited by Lester G. Crocker. Translated by Derik Coltman. New York: Macmillan; London: Collier-Macmillan, 1966.

———. *Diderot on Art*. Edited and translated by John Goodman. 2 vols. New Haven: Yale University Press, 1995.

Honour, Hugh. *Neo-Classicism*. Pelican, Style and Civilization. Harmondsworth, U.K., and New York: Penguin, 1968.

Jaffe, Kineret S. "The Concept of Genius: Its Changing Role in Eighteenth-Century French Aesthetics." *Journal of the History of Ideas* 4 (1980): 579–99.

Mauzi, Robert. *L'idée du bonheur dans la littérature et la pensée françaises au XVIIIᵉ siècle*. 1960. Paris: A. Colin, 1967.

Pérez-Sánchez, Alfonso E., and Eleanor A. Sayre. *Goya and the Spirit of Enlightenment*. Boston: Bulfinch Press, Little Brown, 1989.

Pommier, Edouard. *L'Art de la Liberté: doctrines et débats de la Révolution française*. Paris: Gallimard, 1991.

Powell, Nicolas. *Fuseli: The Nightmare*. London: Allen Lane, The Penguin Press; New York: Viking, 1973.

Rosenberg, Pierre, and Isabelle Julia. *De David à Delacroix: La peinture française de 1774 à 1830*. Paris, 1974.

Schnapper, Antoine, and Arlette Serullaz. *Jacques-Louis David, 1748–1825*. Paris: Musées nationaux, 1989.

Starobinski, Jean. *1789: Les emblèmes de la Raison*. Paris: Flammarion, 1973. Available in English as *1789: The Emblems of Reason*. Translated by Barbara Bray. Charlottesville: University Press of Virginia, 1982; Cambridge, Mass.: MIT Press, 1988.

Vovelle, Michel. *La Révolution française: Images et récits, 1789–1799*. Librairie du bicentenaire de la Révolution française. 5 vols. Paris: Messidor/Libre Club Diderot, 1989.

7 / The Explorer

Marie-Noëlle Bourguet

Bougainville, Cook, Lapérouse, La Condamine, Pallas, Humboldt: this handful of names is all it takes to evoke the adventure of the century of the Enlightenment. These men completed the exploration of the oceans, launched the exploration of the continents, and provided Europe with the materials—maps, drawings, herbaria, and collections—for an encyclopedic knowledge of the world. Still, this adventure was totally different from the triumphant conquests of the sixteenth and seventeenth centuries: what the explorers brought back from the investigations they carried on at the farthest confines of the planet was not the victorious possession of new lands but a harvest of seeds and plants, a completed image of the globe. They also put an end to a number of myths, among them those of the Austral Lands and the good savage. Their curiosity-filled ambition and their confidence in the usefulness of knowledge made a mark on an epoch determined to combine commerce, science, and progress. The great geographical expeditions of the Enlightenment mark the fragile instant when Europe could believe that its humanist dream, finally extended to a world that it had unveiled (but that it would soon lose) had come true. Was this a beautiful illusion? Perhaps, but it was the story of the avant-garde of the voyagers who left Europe to explore Earth's seas and continents.

Explorer: The Story of a Word

"Explorer: one who goes, who is sent to discover a land in order to find out its extent, its situation, etc." This definition signals the entry (in 1718) of the word "explorer" into the *Dictionnaire de l'Académie française.* The term did not figure in the 1694 edition or in Furetière's dictionary in 1690. One might expect this to be a sign of a new usage in the lan-   *257* guage but the word seems to have been slow to make its way into written French, which remained curiously behind the dictionaries. We have to wait until 1765 to find—but in the medical vocabulary—"the exploration of a wound," and until the last twenty years of the century for the term to be applied to geography. The word appears in Lapérouse, who wrote to the Minister of the Navy on 7 April 1787, while navigating along the coasts of Japan and Tartary: "If we are fortunate enough to explore these coasts with the same care as those of the Americas, I am sure that it will not escape Your Majesty that his ships will have been the first to complete this navigation." Even then, however, the noun "explorer" was not in common use. Other terms were used for the people sent out "to discover" the globe. Lapérouse was referred to as a "navigator," and the scholars on board his ship were astronomers, botanists, and mineralogists. *Voyageur naturaliste* was the title most often used as the official designation of the correspondents of the Jardin du Roi or, later, the Muséum National d'Histoire Naturelle, when they were charged with a mission to far-off places. Citizen Richard, sent in 1793 to explore America, signed his reports in Latin: "Ludovicus Claudus Richard, Itinerator botanicus."[1] There was not an "explorer" among them.

Why was there a gap between usage and the dictionaries? A notice in the *Dictionnaire de Trévoux,* published in 1771, suggests a reason:

> *Explorateur: espion* [spy; informer] is the usual term. There are some rarely used words with something noble and brave about them that is immediately pleasing: usage seems wrong not to receive them. *Explorateur* appears somewhat of that sort. I believe that a little skill in producing it would easily make it successful, and that usage, tyrannical though it is, would deign to bend in its favor. One might add that the word *explorateur* seems to announce functions more noble and more distinguished than the word *espion.* The latter applies to someone who is sent to foreign courts to discover their sentiments, their ways of thinking, their ministerial secrets, etc. "The minister has employed clever *explorateurs* in that court." One can apparently also apply it to someone who is sent to discover a land, to learn about its situation, its size, etc.

The dictionary argues for effacing the military and pejorative connotation that seemed to weigh on the word in order to open up a more glorious semantic career by shifting the explorer from the category of the spy into that of the scholar. It offers the interest of anchoring the modern notion of scientific exploration in a long tradition by connecting it with other old and tenacious meanings that derive from its etymology and its earlier use. It invites us to consider the implications of the link between military reconnaissance and geographical exploration—in short, it invites us to attempt a first portrait of the explorer of the Enlightenment by way of a semantic analysis of the term.

Borrowed from the classical Latin *explorator*, a term that Pliny uses for the scout in the Roman army, the word appeared in the French language by the mid-fifteenth century with its etymological, military meaning: the *explorateur* was a soldier sent on reconnaissance into enemy territory to bring back information on troop numbers and the configuration of the terrain. He was an emissary, a scout, at times a spy. The military treaties of the early modern age tell us in detail about what was expected of such envoys. They distinguish between the simple soldier sent *à la découverte* to scour the countryside for news of the enemy and the officer charged by headquarters with a "reconnaissance" mission within enemy territory, a veritable general inquiry for which all means were admissible, including disguise and secrecy: "Clever officers must be sent, on all sorts of pretext, and they may even be disguised if that is indispensable. They will be instructed about all that they must observe, and on their return all the places and the camps that they have recognized will be noted on a map." It was because this was a clandestine and deceitful practice and one that made reciprocal confidence between countries impossible that Kant denounced the use of spies *(uti exploratoribus)* during military campaigns: "Those infernal arts . . . will not cease with the war . . . but will remain in use even after a peace, which thereby is rendered abortive."[2]

In this military context, which included exploration in the activities of the scout or even the spy in enemy territory, it is less surprising that the word had trouble gaining a foothold in everyday language in the more "noble and brave" sense in the context of the scientific voyage that the dictionaries proposed. For Lapérouse, who was a naval officer charged by Louis XVI with sailing two specially freighted ships around the world, the word "exploration"—which was, incidentally, often associated with terms like "expedition," "campaign of discovery," or "reconnaissance"—remained quite close to its etymology and to the military connotation of its earlier uses, even if the dangers of the ocean replaced the threat of the enemy:

This exploration, in order to be complete, would require an expedition that had no other object, the length of which must be no fewer than two or three years. There is no longer task than a detailed description of a coast sown with islands, cut by a number of gulfs, and whose frequent fogs and always violent and unpredictable currents make an approach possible only with prudence and caution.

Still, the methods and the field of investigation had changed from those of the military scout sent in secret to reconnoiter the enemy territory to those of the geographical explorer. Neither secret nor war strategy was involved: "I will never fly the [French] flag. . . . Although a very good Frenchman, in this campaign I am a cosmopolite, foreign to the politics of Asia." Lapérouse had no conquests in mind: his only interest was to work, following the footsteps of the English, toward a "general reconnaissance of the globe" by mapping coastlines and islands and searching for new sea routes. The explorer's task was to map regions that until that time had escaped Europe's notice.

It is in this sense that we find the word used in English at the very end of the century. In 1793, Thomas Jefferson announced to the French botanist André Michaux that a subscription had been taken up by the American Philosophical Society to enable Michaux "to explore the country along the Missouri, & thence Westwardly to the Pacific ocean." In 1803 Jefferson used the same term—"to explore"—to define the goal of the expedition that the American government was planning to send to the new western and the southern regions of the United States: "I expect to be authorized by Congress to explore and ascertain accurately the geography of the great rivers running into the Mississippi & the Missouri, in order to fix their course & their sources."[3]

We learn from these examples, French and American, that like an army scout, the explorer was an official envoy charged by his government with a mission of discovery in a far-off and little-known region. As such he might find himself caught in the interplay of political rivalries and international conflicts. But when the explorer passed from a military objective (evaluating enemy forces) to a scholarly program (completing the chart of the seas and the inventory of the continents) his mission changed character and took on another dimension. A scout for Europe in the antipodes, the explorer was a reconnaissance man on a front of intellectual conquest that gradually spread over the entire planet.

Exploration, Science, and Empire

The explorer kindles the imagination because he evokes the adventure of an intrepid and solitary hero who departed for an unknown destination and advanced without familiar landmarks. But this romantic image forgets that the explorer was less an adventurer than a scout and that his voyage was the fulfillment of a mission organized and commanded from home base by a prince, a group of merchants, or a learned or missionary institution that had precise objectives born of a provisional geographical knowledge and the expectations of the age. Far from plunging into a void, the explorer knew what he should seek and what he wanted to find. Before following his tracks, we need to look briefly at the political, economic, and mental landscape that provided the background for his departure.

It has often been pointed out that since the Renaissance exploration and conquest have gone together; that European explorers always opened the way for merchants, soldiers, and colonizers; that there were no explorations without some form of domination. On a general level discovery and conquest indeed went hand in hand, as demonstrated by the example a contrario of China, which, in the Ming dynasty, renounced maritime expansion, gave up all curiosity about the world, and failed to follow up on the great expeditions of the fifteenth century that took the Emperor Yung-lo's junks all the way to the Red Sea. But it is one thing to note the nearly structural relationship between science and empire, and another to describe how it worked. Because the connections between discovery and world domination do not seem as simple for the eighteenth century as they do for centuries of conquest like the sixteenth and the nineteenth, the century of the Enlightenment offers a particularly open field of investigation.

Not that the epoch was free from ambition or an appetite for material gain. Behind the voyages of the centuries there lay a mixture of personal and national interests, political objectives, and strategic and commercial stakes. North America is a case in point. At the time of the French presence there, the uncharted territories of the American West attracted colonists in search of furs or mineral deposits, missionaries in search of souls to convert, and local authorities eager to reinforce the control of the French crown. In Louisiana, Bénard de La Harpe and the surveyor Dumont de Montigny took off in 1720 in search of an "emerald rock" situated, according to the Indians, near the Arkansas River; in Canada, Pierre de La Vérendrye and his sons obtained the support of

Governor Beauharnais in 1738 for their projected expedition up the Missouri by dazzling him with projections of the wealth that the discovery of precious-metal mines in the Canadian Northwest would bring to the king of France. When the fall of New France was sealed by the Treaty of Paris in 1763, those vast territories were opened up to the ambitions of the English (soon the Americans), and even to Spaniards and Russians. Trappers, merchants, and adventurers took off for the Great Lakes and the Rocky Mountains with fabulous projects combining the interests of merchant companies and governments. It was when he read about the proposal of the Scottish explorer Alexander Mackenzie in 1802 that a line of forts be established to maintain an English presence from the Great Lakes to the Pacific that Thomas Jefferson decided to launch the first American transcontinental expedition under Meriwether Lewis and William Clark.

As for the Pacific Ocean, beginning in the 1760s, when advances in measuring longitude and in safeguarding the health of ships' crews permitted long voyages to the seas of the Southern Hemisphere, Cook, Vancouver, Lapérouse, and Malaspina—all navigators with official charges—transported to those hitherto inaccessible regions the political rivalries and economic and strategic ambitions of their governments. Louis XVI's instructions to Lapérouse detailed the "objectives relative to politics and commerce" that Lapérouse should make his own:

> As far as it is possible to judge by the reports on those countries that have come to France, the active possession of Spain does not extend north of the ports of San Diego and Monterey. . . . Le sieur de Lapérouse will seek to know the state, the strength, and the objective of these establishments, and to ascertain whether they are the only ones that Spain has founded on that coast. He will also examine at what latitude one can begin to obtain furs . . . what is the likelihood of procuring an establishment on that coast . . . what benefits France might expect from this new branch of commerce.

Lapérouse took care to communicate to Louis XVI his observations on the Russian trade in Alaskan furs and to evaluate the profits that France might get by trading in sea otter skins in the China trade.

Africa was part of the picture as well. The last empty space on the map of the world, the African continent became a new territory for exploration for England at the very end of the century, after the loss of her American colonies. In 1795 Mungo Park, a Scot backed by an association

Nicolas André Monsiau, Louis XVI Giving Instructions in June 1785 to La Pérouse, *1817. Château, Versailles. Giraudon/Art Resource, NY.*

of English businessmen and notables, set off on a voyage to the Niger River with the stated purpose of "rendering the geography of Africa more familiar to my countrymen" and "opening to their ambition new sources of wealth, and new channels of commerce."[4]

But can we reduce these explorations to their directly utilitarian, commercial, and geopolitical objectives? The "Projet d'une campagne de découverte" written in support of Lapérouse's mission states explicitly: "The commercial enterprise . . . is here only secondary" to the geographic and scientific program given in detail in the instructions, copied in the king's own hand, telling the navigator what specific regions of the Pacific Ocean and the coasts of the Americas and Asia he was to explore and listing tasks for the scholars, naturalists, physicians, and astronomers on board. The Société Royale de Médecine drew up a special questionnaire for the physicians and surgeons. One item reads:

We have been told almost nothing about the use of the two hands. The question relative to ambidextrous persons, or to the preference of one hand in respect of the other, has not yet sufficiently occupied the naturalists. It is therefore important to examine whether the peoples to be visited use both of their two hands equally for work, or if they use one preferably, and whether the predominance of the right hand in civilized nations is only the effect of prejudices.

Cuvier wrote an "Instructive Note on the Research to be Done in Relation to Anatomical Difference in the Various Human Races" for the mission of discovery in the South Seas, sponsored by the Institut and the Société des Observateurs de l'Homme, that Bonaparte put in the hands of Captain Baudin. Joseph-Marie de Gérando contributed "Considerations on the Method to be Followed in the Observation of Savage Peoples," the first consciously systematic questionnaire in comparative anthropology, in which he states: "We have above all attempted to present a complete picture that will reunite all the possible points of view according to which the philosopher can contemplate these nations."

All the explorations of the century, even individual enterprises carried on by an adventurer, reserved a prominent place for investigations and inventories. In 1795, when James Mackay, a Scottish trapper in the service of Spain, sent a young Welsh traveler, John Evans, across the American continent, he ordered Evans to keep a log of his travels, devoting a special section in it to natural history, and to collect specimens of the flora and fauna for an eventual scholarly study. Evans was also directed to observe the Indian peoples he might meet, noting their number, habitat, territory, and productions, and to search for the unicorn reported to inhabit the Rocky Mountains. In 1803, when Thomas Jefferson charged George Hunter, a Philadelphia pharmacist with particular expertise in chemistry and mineralogy, with exploring the Louisiana Territory, Jefferson exhorted the leader of the little expedition, William Dunbar, to keep in mind the essentially scholarly objective of their voyage: "The thing to be guarded against is that an indulgence to his [Hunter's] principal qualifications may not lead to a diversion of our mission to a march for gold and silver mines. These are but an incidental object, to be noted if found in their way, as salt or coal or lime would, but not to be sought after."

Can we say that the encyclopedic curiosity displayed in these expeditions was exceptional, or that it served as an alibi for other motivations such as political or commercial espionage? This would be a misunderstanding of the century's intent and its unique quality: a will to know that went beyond visible, direct, immediate utility; an intimate and, in the final analysis, profound conviction that progress was impossible if the map of the world were not complete and a total inventory of its riches were not taken. Knowledge seemed the instrument of progress; it was an opening up, a breakup of the old enclaves, a first form of circulation and commerce. Thanks to knowledge Europe was already peacefully disseminating a universal model of civilization. Louis XVI's instructions to Lapérouse summarize this ideal alliance of science, politics, commerce, and philanthropy:

> At his arrival in each land, he will take steps to win the friendship of the principal chiefs, both by signs of good will and by gifts. . . . He will use all honest means to establish ties with the natives of the land. . . . He will order all the crew to live on good terms with the natives. . . . He will occupy himself with zeal and interest in all means that can better their condition, procuring for their country the vegetables, the fruits, and the other useful trees of Europe and teaching them how to plant them and cultivate them. . . . He will not have recourse to arms except in the last extremity, uniquely for his defense. . . . His Majesty would consider it one of the happiest successes of the expedition if it could be carried out without costing the life of a single man.[5]

In the European imagination, voyagers and navigators were the heroes of a liberal utopia that promised wealth to the entire world and civilization to the savage peoples from one movement of commerce among men.

In the final analysis, if we find political interests in these expeditions, it is in the national dimension that was often given to them, as if the conquest of scientific glory were a necessary demonstration of a nation's grandeur. In France the Académie des Sciences launched a mission in 1735 to measure the terrestrial meridian. This venture took the mathematician Maupertuis to Lapland to measure an arc of the meridian in that latitude and the hydrographer Bouguer, the astronomer Godin, and the *philosophe* scholar La Condamine to the high plateaus of the Andes to measure a degree of the meridian near the equator. The glory of the king of France was bolstered by the progress of science and the solution to the enigma of the "shape" of Earth. A quarter-century later, two occasions for observing the transit of Venus across the Sun, in 1761 and 1769, prompted an international mobilization of scholars and sent them to the four corners of the world. Some 120 scientists participated in the observation of the first transit, 32 of whom were French, 21 German, 21 Swedish, 18 English, 9 Italian, 3 Portuguese, 3 Russian, 3 Danish, and 3 Spanish. In 1769, more than 150 scholars stood ready, a majority of them English this time (80), but observers also included 32 Frenchmen, 4 Germans, 15 Swedes, 7 Spaniards, and 13 Russians. Emulation among these countries was a sign of an international scientific community, but it also showed that the prestige of science contributed to national affirmation.

Spain's evolution illustrates this growing connection between science and nationhood. During part of the century, when Spain still had the largest colonial empire in the world, the Spanish crown was not particularly active in geographical exploration, even in exploration of the territories under its domination. Out of a total of 81 voyagers documented as having visited Peru between 1685 and 1805, only 12 were Spanish, as compared to 41 who were French, 17 English, 7 German, and one each who were Dutch, Swedish, Italian, and American. The Spanish limited themselves to accompanying foreign explorers who went to their colonies, keeping track of their activities but also participating in their projects. Two naval lieutenants, don Jorge Juan and don Antonio Ulloa, escorted the French academicians on their expedition into the Andes to measure an arc of the meridian; in 1769, two Spanish officers were assigned to accompany the astronomer Chappe d'Auteroche when he went to California to observe the second transit of Venus; in 1777, the French naturalist Joseph Dombey was given permission to travel in South America only on the condition that he accept the presence of two young botanists, Hippolito Ruiz (officially the leader of the expedition) and José Antonio Pavon, and agree to share his findings with them at the end of the expedition. In 1782, however, when a devastatingly critical article by Masson de Morvilliers entitled "Que doit-on à l'Espagne?" (What Do We Owe Spain?) appeared in the "Geography" section of the *Encyclopédie méthodique*, the resulting polemics kindled national pride on the Iberian Peninsula, and during the two last decades of the century several geographical and scientific expeditions aimed at demonstrating the scientific capacities of Spain were launched under official royal patronage. Ruiz and Pavon, who had remained in South America after Dombey's return to France, continued their exploration of Chile and Peru until 1788; the botanist José Celestino Mutis was charged with a botanical expedition in New Grenada; the physician Martin de Sessé headed a voyage to explore New Spain in 1787. Above all, the circumnavigation of the South American continent from 1789 to 1794 under the leadership of Alessandro Malaspina, a Genoese, was a response to the voyages of Cook and Lapérouse and was as much aimed at restoring the prestige of Spain as at affirming Spain's presence in Pacific waters.

Mutatis mutandis, the same phenomena could be observed in the eighteenth century in the nations that launched explorations of their new territories. In Russia the czarist regime reinforced its hold over the vast Siberian lands stretching to the Pacific with Bering's expeditions and with two missions to Siberia sponsored by the Academy of Sciences of St. Petersburg, the first (1733–42) under the reigns of Anna and Elizabeth, headed by the physician Johan Georg Gmelin, and the second (1768–74) at the beginning of the reign of Catherine II, under the leadership of the naturalist Peter Simon Pallas. In North America, after the United States had won its independence, the federal government sent explorers to western territories still so little known that even their borders were uncertain. For Jefferson and the American Philosophical Society, founded in 1767, the construction of the national territory, its precise delimitation, and inventorying its features went hand in hand with asserting the young nation's scientific autonomy. Science was an integral part of the process of constructing a nation.

Science could even provide glory without territorial expansion, as the expedition to Arabia launched by the king of Denmark in 1761 shows. The *Danish Courrier* of Copenhagen announced on 12 January 1761: "Although the times are difficult and notwithstanding the heavy burden of the government of our country, His Majesty strives ceaselessly to encourage the development of knowledge and of science while adding to the honor of his people thanks to these useful and meritorious enterprises." The venture had no commercial or strategic objectives. The expedition was made up of five scientists: two Danes (the philologist von Haven and the physician Christian Karl Kramer), one Swede (the naturalist Forsskål, a pupil of Linnaeus's), a Frisian (the young surveyor Carsten Niebuhr), and one German (the artist Georg Wilhelm Baurenfeind). The expedition was to "proceed, wherever it might find itself and for the greater good of science, to new discoveries and observations. It must also collect, and send here, Oriental manuscripts of evident utility, as well as natural history collections and other rare objects from the Levant." Thus, it was a purely scientific expedition: it was by its contribution to the study of ancient languages and archaeology, to astronomy, and to natural history that Denmark intended to maintain its rank among the nations of Europe.

The patriotic dimension of these expeditions posed a problem for recruiting explorers: when their own nation lacked competent personnel, governments often appealed to foreigners. This was the case in Russia. A French geographer, Joseph-Nicolas Delisle (who was also a member of the St. Petersburg Academy of Science) spent twenty years doing cartography and preparing scientific voyages; his brother Louis participated in Bering's expedition and died in Kamchatka in 1741. Bering himself was a Dane who had entered the service of Peter the Great; Gmelin and Pallas, the leaders of missions to Siberia, were both Germans, as were the majority of the participants in those expeditions, though some Russians took part in the second.

The recruitment of foreigners conformed to the cosmopolitan spirit of the Enlightenment but it led to difficulties. When Chappe d'Auteroche, who was French, was sent to Tobolsk at the request of the Academy of St. Petersburg the gloomy picture that he painted of Russia in the report on his trip aroused the fury of Empress Catherine II. The botanist André Michaux, who had been put in charge of a mission of exploration by the United States government in 1793, was forced to interrupt his trip in Kentucky and return to France when it was discovered that this "botanical agent of France" was probably preparing a military campaign to attack Spain's possessions in America. After Cook's death, the Admiralty and Cook's friends quarreled with the two German botanists, Reinhold Forster and his son Georg, who had participated in the second voyage and were publishing its findings on their own. Even the Danish expedition to Arabia, conceived as an exemplary scientific voyage, was imperiled by clashes of overheated national amour propre. In its organization, however, the expedition avoided national prejudices because its five members were reputedly equal, with no official leader, and because the minister, Bernstorff, had even asked the young Niebuhr, rather than von Haven, a Dane, to handle the expedition's finances. When difficulties arose between Forsskål and von Haven, however, the minister expressed concern about the personal ambitions of the young Swede: "Nothing would be more disagreeable for our nation than to see this foreigner attribute to himself all the glory of an initiative that, at the origin, took form in our country, and whose realization depends on the generosity of our king." His worries were not unfounded: Forsskål perfected a secret code for the classification of his herbarium and his other collections, the key for which he communicated only to Linnaeus in an attempt to make the collection difficult to decipher in Copenhagen. Furthermore, in order to give his master a chance to profit from his discoveries, the young scholar requested permission from the Danish government to send duplicates of his samples to various learned institutions in Europe, among them the University of Uppsala, where Linnaeus taught. Forsskål had every intention of combining service to his own career, the interests of Swedish botany, and the prestige of his Danish royal patron. The explorer of the Enlightenment asserted his patriotic fervor by making a scientific contribution that brought glory to his homeland. As Leonard Berchtold wrote in 1789, "A philosophic traveller looks upon his country as a sick friend, for whose relief he asks advice of all the world."[6]

From Dreams to Discovery: The World in Maps

A famous painting by Monsiau shows Louis XVI giving instructions to Lapérouse for his voyage around the world. On the table in the royal *cabinet* there are atlases, open maps, and a globe. It was on maps that explorers, geographers, and politicians imagined their voyages before departure. These maps, with their uncertain contours and their blank spaces set off by legends, offer a picture of the geographical knowledge of the times—a mixture of positive acquisitions, unverifiable information or hearsay, and dreams. Granted, at times these representations were simply fantastic, and first-hand experience proved them totally wrong. Nonetheless, the knowledge they contained determined the decision to embark, the choice of itinerary, and the objectives of the voyage. The collective geographical imagination made it thinkable, hence possible, to take off on a voyage.

Two mysteries still hampered knowledge of the entire globe in the eighteenth century. One was the Northwest Passage, a route that was presumed to enable a ship to sail directly from the Atlantic to the Pacific around or through the North American continent; the other was the existence of a vast southern continent, a large landmass that cartographers and cosmographers since the Renaissance continued to place low in the Southern Hemisphere to give the globe symmetry. These two enigmas authorized all sorts of hypotheses and sent explorers out by land and by sea.

In spite of two centuries of European presence, the North American continent remained in part unknown: from the earliest voyages of discovery from Cartier to Champlain, legends had circulated about the existence of mines of precious metals and a "Western Sea" accessible by river. As late as the 1700s, the geographer Guillaume Delisle placed the Western Sea on his maps, thus further raising expectations. In 1720, the Jesuit François-Xavier de Charlevoix was sent to "make the discovery of the Western Sea," and for three years he made inquiries among the French trappers and lumbermen and the Native Americans. The Canadian colonist Pierre de La Vérendrye and his sons traveled up the Missouri as far as Mandan territory between 1738 and 1743, persuaded they would find a river in those parts that would carry them to the sea. Had not an Indian chief offered to take them to the "great mountains," promising that "from there you can see the sea that you seek"? Native guides and learned maps both propagated the hypothesis of the Western Sea. But how far away was it? Beyond which mountains? No one knew at the time. Working with a shortened vision of the North American continent, neither the geographers in their studies nor the men in the field could conceive of the existence of the gigantic barrier that rose up to the west. The Rocky Mountains were thought to resemble the Appalachians in the east: a range of low summits cut by many easily crossed passes, from which, by simple portages, one could find a river leading to the ocean. This image lay behind all projects for transcontinental expeditions, private or official, French, English, or American. In 1745, when the British Parliament learned that the Russians had arrived on the Pacific Coast following Bering's exploits in Alaska and the Aleutian Islands, it voted a reward of £20,000 for anyone who could find a direct passage to Asia through North America. In 1766, the British colonist Robert Rogers requested financing from the Board of Trade for an expedition that he intended to launch toward the "Oregan" River. When Jefferson sent captains Lewis and Clark to explore the American West in 1804, they carried maps to guide their advance beyond the Missouri that showed the Rocky Mountains as a thin pen-stroke. To call those maps conjectural is to miss the point: they showed the American West as the geographers and voyagers imagined it.

Where the great southern continent was concerned, the philosophers' curiosity added to the geographers' theories and pushed speculation to its limit—all the more so because until the 1760s the distance involved, the fearful mortality of long sea voyages because of deaths due to scurvy, and the imprecision of dead-reckoning navigation all made those regions nearly inaccessible. The image of the world constructed by the discoverers of the Renaissance and the first half of the seventeenth century had remained almost unchanged. On the maps a large part of the Southern Hemisphere was occupied by an immense continent drawn imprecisely on the basis of a few coasts that had been sighted, and the Pacific Ocean was peopled with innumerable islands, sighted once and never found again or discovered several times but noted at different positions and under different names. It took radical innovations to make geographical exploration of the South Seas possible. Astronomic navigation became possible when the astronomers and the mathematicians had made advances in the determination of moon distances and clockmakers had invented timekeepers regular enough to keep an exact mean time on board ship, thus permitting exact calculation of a ship's longitude position. On his second voyage in 1772, James Cook was the first navigator to carry clocks and chronometers—in particular, a copy of the maritime chronometer invented by John Harrison in 1759. Cook's voyages also marked a break with older habits in maritime hygiene and the protection of the sailors' health. Thanks to provisions of fruits, sauerkraut, and vegetables pickled in vinegar, and to a program of port calls that permitted the crew to rest and the ship to take on fresh supplies, Cook lost only seventeen men during the three years and eleven days of his second voyage, and only two from scurvy, out of a crew of 225 sailors. Progress in navigational calculations and hygiene opened the South Seas to European navigators.

In the mid-eighteenth century, philosophers—Buffon, Maupertuis, and, especially, Président de Brosses—had launched a new debate on the southern continent. De Brosses's monumental *Histoire des navigations aux terres australes,* published in 1756, was an appeal for a return to systematic explorations financed by all the princes of Europe. "It is impossible that there not be in such a vast surface some immense continent of dry land . . . capable of holding the globe in equilibrium in its rotation and of serving as a counterweight to the mass of northern Asia."

Curiosity and commercial and political interests were to attract Europeans to those regions, but philosophy played its part as well. The discovery of these lands of the antipodes would resolve the enigma of the origin of man: what sorts of people would the navigators find there, and living in what state of society? The philosophers of the Enlightenment hoped to discover a people who had escaped history, who still lived in a state of nature, and who might prove the original goodness of humankind. "I would prefer an hour of conversation with them than with the finest mind in Europe," Maupertuis proclaimed. In Tahiti, the Hawaiian Islands, and Samoa the navigators were mindful of the debate that raged in discussions from Paris to Berlin.[7]

Figures of the Explorer

Curiosity, ambition, learning, and speculation: these were what decided the explorer's mission and preceded his departure. "In the name of the King. . . . Having charged le sieur Peyssonnel, doctor in medicine, to go to the coasts of Barbary to search for the plants and flowers that he will find there and to make the observations that he will judge appropriate to natural history, we desire and command that you do him no harm and permit him to pass freely." Beyond a name given at the foot of a *brevet* or on a passport, what do we know about the man who was sent to far-off places in search of discoveries?

During the age of the Enlightenment, exploration was not a profession requiring special training or specific competencies. It was not until the Restoration that France had a school for "naturalist-voyagers" at the Muséum d'Histoire Naturelle that recruited students by competition, certified its teaching by examinations, and furnished graduates whom it sent off on missions with an instruction manual, a veritable explorer's guide reissued several times during the century. Until then, voyagers were clerics or officers, botanists or astronomers, trappers or physicians, induced to become explorers by a childhood dream, a chance happening in their careers, someone they met, or a political event. Alexander von Humboldt tells us:

> From my earliest youth I felt an ardent desire to travel to distant regions, seldom visited by Europeans. . . . Though educated in a country which has no direct communication with either the East or the West Indies, living amidst mountains remote from coasts . . . I felt an increasing passion for the sea and distant expeditions. . . . The taste for herborisation, the study of geology, rapid excursions to Holland, England, and France, with the celebrated Mr. George Forster, who had had the happiness to accompany Captain Cook in his second expedition around the globe, contributed to give a determined direction to the plan of travels which I had formed at eighteen years of age.

For the young Lapérouse, born into a family that owned lands in the region of Albi, stories of naval combats that he had heard as a child aroused a taste for the sea—a totally military vocation, however, which was oriented toward geographical exploration by royal command after the American war (the Seven Years' War). The young naval officer wrote to the minister of the Navy: "I will not conceal from you that my every view, up to the present, has been turned toward the military part of my profession . . . and I was more ambitious for M. de Suffren's glory than for Cook's." It was a political event—the Treaty of Paris—that launched Bougainville on the high seas: an aide-de-camp to Montcalm in Canada, he was sent on an expedition to the Falkland Islands *(les Îles Malouines)* that soon was extended into a circumnavigation of the globe.

It took a series of chance happenings to take the young Mungo Park to Africa. The seventh child in a Scottish farming family of thirteen children, Park proved a willing student. Not very tempted by the clergy, he studied medicine at the University of Edinburgh, but botany interested him more. A brother-in-law who was a grain merchant in London put him into contact with Sir Joseph Banks, the president of the Royal Society and a naturalist who had participated in Cook's first voyage. Banks was instrumental in finding Park a post as assistant surgeon on a ship of the East India Company and, when he returned, a mission to explore Africa.

Carsten Niebuhr's career was just as unpredictable. The son of a modest Frisian peasant, he became a surveyor, and in 1757 he obtained a scholarship to study mathematics and astronomy at the University of Göttingen. There he was noticed by one of his professors and recruited for the expedition to Arabia being planned by the king of Denmark, where he served beside scholars with much better credentials than his and greater prestige.[8]

Chance and opportunity were not enough to attract such men, however, without some special advantage. What attracted some of them— buccaneers, trappers, merchants, or missionaries—was a propitious "terrain"; for others—physicians, naturalists, mathematicians, or astronomers—it was scholarly activity; for still others—naval officers and engineers—it was enhanced professional status. We can perhaps get a glimpse of a number of figures of the explorer of the Enlightenment in this variety of situations and competencies, perhaps also a sketchy chronology.

It is only natural to find in the first rank of the explorers—people seemingly predestined for the role—men whose business or vocation took them to the far ends of the earth. On the sea, there were adventurers, seamen, or pirates like the English buccaneer William Dampier. After many expeditions to plunder the Spanish trading posts in the Antilles and the Gulf of Mexico, Dampier, a freelance explorer and a man endowed with curiosity, knocked about Asia and in the China Sea. On his return to England he established contact with the naturalist Hans Sloane and the learned members of the Royal Society, and in 1699 he took to the sea again for a new adventure—a scientific adventure. When he arrived in the Pacific, Dampier sailed along the coasts of New Ireland, discovered New Britain, and explored the strait that now bears his name.

On land there were employees of merchant companies and diplomatic agents. One such was Engelbert Kämpfer, surgeon for the Dutch East India Company, who embarked in 1690 for Japan, where the Dutch had a concession. On two occasions Kämpfer took advantage of the delegation's yearly visit to the emperor's court in Jedo (Tokyo) to see more of Japan, and as he traveled he consulted local maps to learn about the geography of the archipelago, observed the intensive farming techniques of the Japanese, and learned to appreciate their economic self-sufficiency, also taking notes on their laws, mores, and religion. Among the landsmen there were also colonists, trappers, and merchants who, after the fall of New France, set off to conquer the territories of the American Northwest. Peter Pond, a nearly illiterate fur trader from Connecticut, explored the Canadian Northwest in the 1770s; his maps and reports opened the way for the voyages of Alexander Mackenzie in 1789 and 1793.

Finally, there were missionaries. By definition "in the field" and Europe's Christian avant-garde in pagan lands, they were prototypes of this prime category of explorers. Missionaries combined a taste for travel with the training in mathematics, astronomy, botany, and geography they had received in European religious secondary schools and seminaries. Carrying on a long tradition, missionaries went everywhere in the world in the eighteenth century. First among them were the Jesuits, who were present everywhere from the Americas to Asia. In 1689, the Jesuits were on the banks of the Amur River to negotiate the Sino-Russian treaty of Nerchinsk; during the entire eighteenth century, they traveled throughout the Chinese Empire, using their skills in astronomy for the advancement of European cartography as much as for the service of the emperor: "We always had our compass in hand, and we took care to take longitudinal observations from time to time in order to correct our estimates." The *robes noires* ("Black Robes")—Jacques Marquette in the late seventeenth century, Joseph Lafitau and François-Xavier de Charlevoix in the eighteenth century—advanced, side by side with the Canadian *coureurs des bois,* to penetrate deep into the American continent from the Mississippi to Louisiana. Other orders furnished explorers: there were Minims like the botanist Charles Plumier, who was sent to the Antilles by Louis XIV, and Louis Feuillée, an astronomer and naturalist who traveled to the Antilles and to Chile in the early eighteenth century; there were Dominicans like Jean-Baptiste Labat, who stayed in the Antilles from 1696 to 1706 and did much to promote the islands. During the latter part of the century, there seem to have been fewer clergy—the condemnation of the Jesuits and the decline of missionary enthusiasm probably took their toll—but they did not disappear altogether. In North America missionaries like John Heckwelder and David Zeisberger took over from the French fathers to visit the regions beyond the Ohio River. The decline of missionary clergy also reflects a process of secularization in science and the specialization of knowledge, which gradually required the presence of other sorts of voyagers besides the religious.[9]

In the fields of botany and natural history many of the voyagers with more specialized interests were physicians, apothecaries, and pharmacists. Indeed, they were among the century's best-known travelers. It is easy to see why: studies in the natural sciences were connected to the study of medicine. Frenchmen who contributed to the botanic exploration of South America include Jean-Baptiste Fusée-Aublet, the founder of botanical studies in Guyana, Jean-Baptiste Le Blond, Pierre Barère, Joseph de Jussieu, Joseph Dombey, Louis-Claude Richard, and Aimé Bonpland. Most of the naturalists who set off on the maritime expeditions of the end of the century were also trained as physicians: Philibert Commerson sailed with Bougainville, Joseph Boissieu de La Martinière with Lapérouse, and Jacques-Julien Houtou de La Billardière with d'Entrecasteaux. Specialists in natural history became all the more necessary because, in the age of Linnaeus, the needs of botany could not be satisfied by improvised collection with no guiding plan behind it. In England Sir Joseph Banks did his utmost to persuade the East India Company and the Admiralty to add to the expedition's personnel—sailors, hydrographers, and astronomers—genuine naturalists capable of carrying out a methodical collection of the flora of the regions visited and, at the same time, capable of evaluating their resources in view of colonization. In

1768 Banks obtained permission for himself and the Swedish botanist Daniel Solander, a student of Linnaeus's, to participate (at Banks's expense) in Cook's first voyage. Banks's quarrel with Cook prevented him from participating in Cook's second voyage, but he arranged for two German naturalists, Reinhold and Georg Forster, to go along with Cook, and he managed to place a gardener charged with collecting plants as a supernumerary on Cook's third voyage. Above all, it was thanks to Banks that the last great navigations of the century were staffed with professional naturalists: in 1791, Vancouver had on board the naval surgeon Archibald Menzies, and in 1801, the botanist Robert Brown accompanied Flinders. Whether Banks's envoys were "collector-gardeners" or accredited botanists, they had the advantage of preparing for their expeditions by consulting Banks's personal library of treatises on botany and travel accounts and even the herbaria from Cook's expedition.

Increasing specialization was even more apparent in astronomy and cartography, fields requiring a level of technical and mathematical skill that made it imperative to call on genuine experts. The geodesic expedition to Lapland and Peru called upon members of the Paris Académie des Sciences; and the observations of the transit of Venus in 1761 involved three abbé-astronomers: Le Gentil de La Galaisière, who went to Pondicherry, Pingré in Rodriguez Island in the Indian Ocean, and Chappe d'Auteroche in Siberia. On board ship the demands of astronomic navigation made the presence of specialized astronomers increasingly necessary. Abbé La Caille was on board the *Glorieux,* the ship of the Compagnie française des Indes that rounded the Cape of Good Hope under the command of Après de Mannevillette in 1751. In 1785, Lapérouse's expedition used chronometers and instruments that Cook had used on his second voyage (lent by the Admiralty), and Lepaute d'Agelet, a member of the Académie des Sciences and a professor at the École Militaire, served as astronomer on board the *Boussole,* and Louis Monge, the brother of the mathematician, embarked on the *Astrolabe.*

Nonetheless, by the end of the century, a new generation had arrived, a third category of explorer for whom the daily tasks of discovery—taking bearings, drawing charts and maps—were nearly a professional specialization. This meant that special institutions had to be created to provide naval officers with the scientific and technical skills necessary to the new conditions of navigation. In France at the end of the century, expeditions were staffed by men trained in the classrooms of the Académie de Marine, founded in 1752. As Louis XVI's instructions to Lapérouse stated, "His Majesty is persuaded that the officers and the marine guards employed on the two frigates will occupy themselves zealously, in concert with the astronomers, to make all observations that might be of some use to navigation." And in fact, when Lapérouse was obliged to let the astronomer Monge disembark in Tenerife when he proved unable to endure high seas, it was the ship's captain, Fleuriot de Langle, and Law de Lauriston, the ensign, who took over Monge's duties. Officers of the British Admiralty such as Cook and Vancouver or of the Royal French Navy like Lapérouse, Baudin, and Bruni d'Entrecasteaux are among some of the most illustrious names in late-eighteenth-century geographical exploration.

These naval officers were explorers by their training and their professional status; there is another group that should be added to the list, the land travelers of the last third of the century who descended into the craters of the volcanoes of Italy and Sicily, climbed to the summits of the Alps and the Pyrenees, went to the Urals and the Andes, scrutinized rocks, and speculated about the age of Earth. Many of the naturalists and the curious travelers were engineers, mineralogists, and chemists whose special interests sent them on investigations in the field and geological explorations. One of the "inventors" of the Pyrenees was Flamichon, an engineer and geographer charged with mapping the Béarn region who became curious about its physical relief; Palassou, Cordier, and Duhamel were mining engineers sent by the government to seek out exploitable mineral deposits. At the other end of the globe, in the Cordillera of the Andes, Humboldt recalled his former profession as a mining engineer, which made him sensitive to land forms and rocks. As the navigators and the botanists completed the exploration of the seas and the continents, geologists were beginning to probe the history of Earth.[10]

On Land and on Sea: Ways to Travel

The voyagers' lives varied tremendously, as did their competence and the itineraries they chose, but the experience of travel added something of its own that both simplified and sharpened differences among them. Once the known world had been left behind, the explorer was left with his special geographical realm. For some this was the immensity of the ocean with a scattering of islands and coastlines seen from afar; for others it was sands, forests, or mountains. The mariners' and the land travelers' experience was totally different.

The seaman—as paradoxical as it might seem—was sedentary; at great risk, he carried a detached piece of his native land over the surface of the ocean to the ends of the earth. Flying his country's flag, he brought with him—crammed into his small cabin—books and maps, measuring instruments, at times a pet animal. Lapérouse's two frigates, the *Astrolabe* and the *Boussole,* carried provisions for three years, 2 windmills, 5 cows, 200 chickens and other fowl, 30 sheep, and 20 pigs, all tucked in between decks, in the spaces separating one cannon from the other, and even in the lifeboats. When d'Entrecasteaux was sent out in 1791 to search for Lapérouse and his two frigates, which had disappeared, he carried not only the usual store of treatises on astronomy, atlases, and works of natural history (the inventory mentions no fewer than fifteen works by Linnaeus) but also some nineteen volumes of the *Journal des Débats et des Décrets* of the Assemblée nationale! A thousand leagues from home, the ships' crews formed a closed, male, and hierarchical world; a small, ideal Europe with its floating academy of scholars; a society in miniature of mixed age, status, and temperament. The complement of Bougainville's *Boudeuse* included Fesche, a sailor who had been with him in the Falklands and had signed up again, Véron, a young, self-taught astronomer, Saint-Germain, a lawyer who had signed on as a writer, and the young Prince of Nassau-Siegen, who had been packed off to the South Seas by his family to recover from his dissipated habits.

From their perch high on the ship, the navigators watched the seas roll by for months on end, encountering only some atolls. An island or a coast might appear from time to time, to be observed from afar with a spyglass. One of these was the island of Akiaki (which Bougainville called Île des Lanciers) that Bougainville observed on 22 March 1768. He states, "I thought it uninhabited, and on seeing the coconut palms, I would have liked to send boats on land to seek wood, some fruit, perhaps water. An infinite number of birds circled the island and over its shores and seemed to promise plenty of fish off the coast, but the sea was breaking everywhere and no beach offered a place to land." Halts were brief, lasting only long enough to get provisions, give the crew some rest, and repair the ships. Some concession was made, willingly or grudgingly, to the scholars' curiosity: "I can give very little time to the various stops," Lapérouse wrote, "and long periods at sea are not to the taste of our botanists and our mineralogists, who can put their talents to good use only on land."

When they did land, the sailors generally did not scatter or venture very far into the interior. When he arrived at Easter Island in April 1786, Lapérouse wrote: "Our first thought after having landed was to form an enclosure with armed soldiers set around in a circle; we enjoined the inhabitants to leave that space empty, we set up a tent in it, and I had the gifts I was planning to offer them taken off the ship, along with the various animals." He authorized only a rapid foray:

> We had only eight or ten hours to spend on the island and did not want to spend that time fruitlessly. . . . We divided ourselves . . . into two bands: the first, under the orders of the viscount de Langle, was to penetrate as far as possible into the interior of the island, to sow seeds in all places that might seem susceptible of reproducing them, examine the soil, the plants, the crops, the population, the monuments, and in general all that might be of interest in that truly extraordinary people. . . . The others, and I was of their number, limited themselves to visiting the monuments, platforms, houses, and plantations within a league of our base.

During these swift incursions, conducted with the energy and speed of a military reconnaissance, the civilians—learned naturalists, mineralogists, and botanists—took over from the officers. This was their moment for herborizing, collecting rock and animal specimens, and noting the state of the inhabitants and the local resources. Rather than a methodical investigation, the "visit" was a cursory survey. While the *Boudeuse* and the *Étoile* were sailing away from Tahiti, Saint-Germain, the expedition's secretary, summed up the experience with some disappointment: "What can we say about Cythera? Have we seen the interior of the country? Is Mr. de Commerson bringing back a note on the treasures that it holds or might hold in the way of natural history, plants, or mines? Have we taken soundings along the coast? Do we know where there is a good anchorage? Or of what use this voyage has been for the nation?"

Very often the seamen encountered islanders even before they disembarked. Contact was established by gestures, signs, and exchanges of goods. Prudence was always necessary—"No matter how warm a welcome he receives from the savages," Lapérouse's instructions stated, "it is important that he show himself always capable of self-defense." It was often difficult, however, to impose discipline. The story of Bougainville and his men relaxing into their island idyll in Tahiti is a familiar one: "The people offered me one of its women, young and beautiful, and the entire assembly sang the wedding song. What a land! What a people!"

But these happy relations did not last long: the Tahitians themselves let Bougainville understand that he could stay no longer than nine days. Above all, relations were limited, since incomprehension was inevitable on both sides. Although Lapérouse freely allowed the natives to help themselves to nails, mirrors, and hats, their penchant for pillage nonetheless astounded him. Relations could also take a dramatic turn: Cook was killed by the Hawaiians and his dismembered body offered in sacrifice in a sudden unleashing of violence that brutally reversed all the signs. When Cook turned back to the islands because a ship had suffered damages he unwittingly disturbed the symbolic system in which he had been inscribed during his first visit, when he had been welcomed as the sacred personification of the god of seasonal renewal. Even in a dramatic situation, however, the Europeans always had the option to sail away: "I confess that I needed all my reason to keep myself from losing my temper and to stop our crews from massacring them," Lapérouse comments on learning that a landing party sent out for fresh water had been assaulted by a band of islanders that had stoned to death his second in command, Fleuriot de Langle, the botanist Lamanon, and several sailors. Shooting a cannon ball into the water to assuage his anger and save his honor, Lapérouse put out to sea to continue his oceanic explorations.[11]

The explorer who traveled on land faced a totally different situation. Alone or with a few colleagues, at times aided by an interpreter, with little baggage but a bundle of maps, a watch, a compass and a few astronomical instruments, a gun, notebooks, a small supply of vials, and an herbarium, he traveled through unknown lands, stayed among foreign and often hostile peoples, always on the march, exhausted, shaking with cold or fever, with no possibility of turning back. On 10 March 1761, a modest convoy of four sleds left St. Petersburg for Tobolsk carrying Chappe d'Auteroche, his watchmaker, his Lett servant, and his gear—compasses, spyglasses, telescopes, barometers, maps, charts, astronomy books, and a few bottles of wine. On 2 December 1795, Mungo Park left the Gambia coast:

> I was furnished with a horse for myself (a small, but very hardy and spirited beast, which cost me to the value of £7 10s.) and two asses for my interpreter and servant. My baggage was light, consisting chiefly of provisions for two days; a small assortment of beads, amber, and tobacco, for the purchase of a fresh supply, as

I proceeded: a few changes of linen, and other necessary apparel, an umbrella, a pocket sextant, a magnetic compass, and a thermometer; together with two fowling pieces, two pair of pistols, and some other small articles. . . . I had now before me a boundless forest, and a country, the inhabitants of which were strangers to civilized life, and to most of whom a white man was the object of curiosity or plunder. I reflected that I had parted from the last European I might probably behold, and perhaps quitted for ever the comforts of Christian society.

The explorer made better progress if he was able to adapt to the lands and the men he encountered, taking on their mode of life and even their costume. As soon as he arrived in Constantinople, Niebuhr understood the need to dress in oriental style for the rest of his voyage toward Egypt and Yemen: "In Arabia, the many pieces of clothing that make up our dress would by mocked by the populace, and European dress would be extremely uncomfortable." On occasion, the voyager also had to live by his wits and earn his keep (or his life) in exchange for a few services. Toward the end of the seventeenth century, the Italian Gemelli Careri, one of the few travelers to go around the world out of personal curiosity, was obliged to turn his medical knowledge to commercial use; in Peru, Jussieu treated sick Indians while one of his companions, the surgeon Seniergues, bartered the trade goods they had brought from Europe.

Mungo Park made a strong impression on one Muslim schoolmaster by his knowledge of the rudiments of Arabic, and he demonstrated to a Moorish chief who was holding him prisoner his competence as a coiffeur and barber. After being abandoned by his companions, robbed, ransomed, and finding himself once again alone and without resources, he was dependent upon the meager aid the inhabitants of the country granted him. He ate whatever food he was offered, stating that the Africans' way of living was unpleasant to him at first, but that he gradually overcame his repugnance and ended up rather enjoying their food. Park knew enough about his hosts' beliefs to refuse to eat pork, which was nonetheless offered to him: "Though I was very hungry, I did not think it prudent to eat any part of an animal so much detested by the Moors." He learned to travel discreetly and, since his skin color clearly showed him to be white, he passed himself off as an Arab among Muslim Africans. He needed to take precautions in everything, even when carrying on his research, asking questions, or mapping the terrain: "The pocket compass soon became an object of superstitious curiosity. Ali was very desirous to be informed, why that small piece of iron, the needle, pointed to the Great Desert. . . . I told him that my mother resides far beyond the sands of the Sahara, and that whilst she was alive the little piece of iron would always point that way." Park even had to accept a reversal of roles, letting himself be looked at, touched, and interrogated by the natives with as much curiosity as he showed in them. The Moorish women undressed him and examined him in scrupulous detail; the slaves in whose company he found himself surprised him by their questions: "They repeatedly asked me if my countrymen were cannibals. They were very desirous to know what became of the slaves after they had crossed the salt water." In short, anyone who penetrated into a continent's interior had to be ready to fit in with the ways of the lands he traveled through and to melt into the landscape. A talent for adaptation—one might even say for blending in—was a precondition of survival.[12]

Journal, Map, and Herbarium: Recording Discoveries

If navigators and land travelers differed by the spaces they occupied and the geography they investigated, they shared the experience of time, both as duration and as ongoing daily routine. All these expeditions were long, often taking several months, even several years—at least two to three years for the navigators who sailed around the world (two years and seven months for Bougainville; more like four years for Lapérouse's projected itinerary, for Cook's ships in their third voyage, and for Vancouver's ships to complete their circumnavigation). Duration was more flexible for land voyages: Chappe d'Auteroche spent fifteen months in Russia; Peyssonnel took more than a year to visit "regencies" in Algeria and Tunisia; Mungo Park returned to Great Britain from Africa in 1797 after an absence of two years and seven months. But land explorations could also be very long: Adanson spent more than four years in Senegal as an agent for the Compagnie des Indes; after exploring Yemen, Niebuhr visited the Orient, getting as far as India, and returned to Denmark after six years; Pallas and his companions spent six years traveling in Siberia from the Ural Mountains to Lake Baikal; between 1799 and 1804, Humboldt and Bonpland traveled all over Central and South America from the Andes to the Orinoco and from the Antilles to New Mexico; La Condamine, who left for Peru in 1735, returned to France, after a side trip to the Amazon, only in 1745. And when the astronomer Le Gentil was unable to observe the first transit of Venus across the Sun in 1761, he took advantage of his unexpected opportunity to remain in India, and he decided to stay in Pondicherry to be sure not to miss the next one in 1769.

These long years of travel took both a physical and a moral toll on the explorers. After two and a half years on the high seas, Lapérouse admitted his weariness and his ruinous condition to his friend Le Coulteux in a letter written from Botany Bay, as his ships were about to leave for the last stage of his mission: "Whatever professional advantages this expedition may have brought me, you can be certain that few would want them at such cost, and the fatigues of such a voyage cannot be put into words. When I return you will take me for a centenarian. I have no teeth and no hair left and I think it will not be long before I become senile." Feelings of distance and isolation were even harder to bear. On 16 November 1785, as he was about to set off across the Pacific, Lapérouse wrote to Fleurieu: "Do not forget, my dear friend, to write to us in Kamchatka, Manila, China, and Île de France [Mauritius]: you can never imagine how much pleasure your letters give us and how necessary they are to us. Add to them, I beg of you, all the gazettes you can." A note written by André Thouin, gardener-in-chief to the king, shows that Paris had not forgotten the voyagers sent to the ends of the earth. On 7 February 1786 a package was sent off containing a bundle of mail including personal letters for the members of the expedition, recent copies of the *Journal de Paris*, and a note from Thouin to his colleague Collignon full of practical advice and news of other naturalists on missions. All of this, "forming a large package," was addressed to "Mr. le comte de Lapérouse, à Canton en Chine." We will never know what happened to this package or to many others that failed to reach their destinations. "By an extraordinary stroke of bad luck," Humboldt wrote, "we remained in the Spanish colonies two years without receiving a single letter from Europe." Sometimes mail arrived too late. Niebuhr did not receive a list of questions that Professor Michaelis had drawn up for the Arabian expedition that left Denmark in 1761 until 1764, when the mission to Yemen had been completed and all his companions were dead.

When there were wars or political upheavals at home, the voyagers' total ignorance of what was happening in Europe might lead them, unwittingly, into danger: the ships that left France in 1791 to search for Lapérouse arrived off Java flying the white flag with the gold fleur-de-lys, only to learn that the Republic had been proclaimed and Louis XVI put to death. As a loyal officer of the Marine Royale, d'Auribeau, who was the leader of the expedition after d'Entrecasteaux had died, preferred to give himself up to the Dutch rather than fly the new flag, and the scholars on board, suspected of republicanism, were imprisoned. The naturalist La Billardière managed to get back to France in 1796, but his collections were confiscated by the British.

When they had been away from Europe for months or years and had received only very occasional news of home, the explorers found themselves plunged into a time without landmarks in which one day followed another. It was a time filled with the daily occupations of discovery: taking bearings, adding to the maps and charts, observing the lands they passed by or through. Their logbooks, by sea and by land, bear witness to this. The better part of their day was spent on tasks of a repetitive and detailed routine—tasks that might be irritating, even harassing, or interrupted by moments of danger and fear—rather than in the heroic and tumultuous adventures attributed to them by legend.

The journal or logbook with its daily registration of discoveries was the first of these tasks. Humboldt wrote of his trip to the Orinoco, "I have compelled myself, throughout my voyage . . . to write day by day—in the canoe or in camp—what seems to me noteworthy." Keeping a journal, a practice that had long been habitual among the navigators and that was made obligatory for French naval officers by the ordinances of 1689 and 1765, was an explicit requirement for both the officers and the scholarly explorers of the major expeditions. Lapérouse's instructions stated:

> Le sieur de Lapérouse will have a double register kept on each frigate in which there will be noted, day by day, at sea and on land, astronomical observations . . . all observations relative to the state of the sky and the sea, the winds, the currents, the variations in atmosphere, and all that pertains to meteorology. . . . At the end of the voyage . . . le sieur de Lapérouse will collect all the journals of the expedition that have been kept on the two frigates by the officers and the marine guards, by the astronomers, scholars, artists, pilots, and all other persons.

Similar instructions were given to voyagers who explored new lands: "Each member of the expedition will keep a journal, a copy of which will he will send to Copenhagen as often as he has occasion to do so," Minister Bernstorff admonished the five scholars whom the king of Denmark sent to Arabia.[13]

These journals and logbooks filled with measurements and learned observations, with details, with dates and places, were a preliminary registration process. They were as neutral and as complete as possible. Nonetheless, they reflect a first process of selection from among the mass of daily facts, events, and experiences. Geography naturally predominates, as the first concern of the explorer charged with advancing into unknown regions and seas whose maps and charts he was to correct or compose. This task seemed so essential to all voyagers that the astronomer Pingré, sent to Rodriguez Island to observe the transit of Venus, did not want to leave the island without having penetrated into the interior to take triangulations to map the island.

Day after day, the navigators noted what route they had followed and took bearings of the coasts and islands they saw. On 11 March 1793, d'Auribeau, second in command on the *Recherche,* was sailing along the coast of New Zealand following the route Lapérouse had taken. He reports: "From midday to 4 o'clock: sky overcast, the sea very smooth, moderate breeze from the west, steering E1/4SE to stand directly to North Cape, skirting the Northern coast at 2 to 3 Leagues distance." In these far-off seas, which had already been visited by a few English and Dutch navigators and by Cook himself during his first voyage, many geographical observations needed correction. D'Entrecasteaux noted:

> We explored Cape Maria Van Diemen fully and took observations North and South of it, about 4 or 5 leagues off. This cape is the farthest NW of New Zealand and was named by Tasman. I observed that at the West point of this cape there are four islets, of which two are quite substantial and two somewhat smaller; they are marked on Mr Cook's chart only as reefs, but we clearly made out their extent which, I repeat, is quite considerable.

There were also errors of longitude to be corrected: "That famous navigator [Cook] did not have a chronometer on his first voyage and without that aid . . . a difference in longitude of half a degree is in no way surprising." When all that an explorer had to go on when he arrived in a hitherto unexplored place was a set of maps drawn by geographers working in their studies and based on poorly verified fact and legend, he had to begin anew, in the field. As Humboldt says, not without a hint of irony:

> We showed copies of the maps of Surville and La Cruz to old soldiers, who had been posted in the mission since its first establishment. They laughed at the supposed communication of the Orinoco with the Rio Idapa, and at the "White Sea," which the former river was represented to cross. . . . Those good people

could not comprehend how men, in making the map of a country which they have never visited, could pretend to know things in minute detail, of which persons who lived on the spot were ignorant. The lake Parima, the Sierra Mey, and the springs which separate at the point where they issue from the earth, were entirely unknown at Esmeralda.

Could the explorer at least make use of the inhabitants' geographical knowledge? "The Indians had given us the names of the ten islands that make up their archipelago," Lapérouse noted in December 1787, when he was sailing around Samoa. "They had placed them approximately on a piece of paper, and although we were persuaded that one could hardly count on the chart they had drawn, we did not doubt that there was some sort of confederation among those ten islands, well known to one another." But the navigator was unable to read the schematic picture that the islanders had drawn of the area they knew so well. The islanders' mental chart, woven out of familiar itineraries and known landmarks and circumscribed by where their dugout canoes had sailed, was not the same as the geographers' mental map, which was constructed on the basis of topographical and astronomic observations and presupposed a global view of the larger area.

All voyagers experienced this gap between traditional representations and learned approaches. As they advanced toward the Rocky Mountains, Canadian and American travelers questioned the native Americans. All that La Vérendrye had to help him locate the rapids was a hydrographic map drawn by an Indian named Ochagach. It represented the distance from Lake Superior to the "River of the West" by a series of portages, and distances were estimated in the number of days it would take to travel. Lewis and Clark were led by a series of Indian guides who replaced one another from tribe to tribe as the party advanced, taking the expedition from hill to hill, peak to peak, toward a horizon always announced and always inaccessible. Even in Europe explorers of another type, mountain climbers who tried to get information from the inhabitants of the lower valleys about the best routes to the top of the Alps or the Pyrenees, had similar misadventures. Ramond, a naturalist who explored the Pyrenees at the end of the eighteenth century, stated: "The most unpredictable of these difficulties is the ignorance that I encountered in the people of those parts concerning the real position of Mont Perdu [Mount Perdido]. It is visible only from high places, and it disappears as soon as one returns below. I was obliged to resolve to find my way by luck."[14]

Islands, archipelagos, coasts, or mountains that the explorer discovered and whose position and outlines he noted on a map needed to be given a name. At times this was a term, more or less distorted, taken from the native name: "Mississippi" meant "the great river"; the expression "O'Tahiti," which the English were first to adopt, signified "there is Tahiti." More often, the discoverer replaced local designations with a name taken from his own culture, projecting onto these distant spaces an imaginary universe peopled with saints, kings, and heroes. Bougainville, who had a penchant for classical antiquity, baptized "Nouvelle-Cythère" the paradise island that the English (unbeknownst to him) had called by its native name, Tahiti. Cook named the archipelago of the Society Islands in honor of the Royal Society and the Sandwich Islands (the Hawaiian Islands) after the First Lord of the Admiralty. When Cook anchored off Desolation Island during his third voyage, he renamed it Kerguelen Island in honor of the French navigator who had discovered it in 1772. Lapérouse, too, left a string of French names behind him along the coasts of Asia and America, and he gave Necker's name to an island in the middle of the Pacific Ocean. The map became a memoir of a discovery, of its dates, and of its principal actors.

Exploration followed a ritual so immutable and repeated so faithfully day after day that the Tarqui Indians could find no better parody, during a celebration that La Condamine attended, than to mime an astronomer scanning the heavens with his telescope. Collecting botanical specimens may have been less ostentatious, but it nonetheless occupied a good deal of time. On Monday, 22 October 1804, William Dunbar, sent to explore the American Southwest, wrote meteorological observations in his journal, as he did every day: "Thermometer before sun-rise, 65°. Wind S.S.E. cloudy. A few drops of rain before day." Annotations on the flora followed: "Saw also many patches of an aquatic plant resembling little Islands, some floating on the surface of the river, and others adhering to or resting on the shore and logs." Once a plant had been collected, its description permitted its identification and its relation to known species:

> Examined the plant & found it to be a hollow jointed stem with
> roots of the same form. . . . I have not been able to detect the

flower, so as to be able to determine the class and order to which the plant belongs, it is not probably new; I at first supposed it might be the same which is described by Mr. Bartram as occupying large portions of the surfaces of rivers in East Florida, but upon examination I found it to be entirely different.

Men of the Enlightenment were curious about plants for two reasons. First, despite the difficulty the voyagers encountered when they tried to subject the exuberance of tropical species to categories of classification conceived for European flora, and despite the enormous challenge represented by Linnaeus's requirement that for certain identification each plant sample had to include a flower and a fruit, the science of botany raised the hope of achieving a systematic nomenclature of the natural world, something that satisfied the century's taste for inventory and taxonomy. Second, economic and utilitarian interests urged a search for new plants to be acclimatized in Europe and throughout the world. During his stay in Louisiana, the missionary François Le Maire investigated the virtues of herbs and simples: "I wrote by the last ship to Mr. Isnard, successor to Mr. Tournefort in the chair of botany at the Jardin Royal, that I was working to send him some medicinal plants from here to remedy the damage done by the severe winter of 1709." Edible plants were of special interest: in 1792, at the request of Sir Joseph Banks, William Bligh, the former captain of the *Bounty,* transported seedlings of breadfruit tree from Tahiti to the Antilles; Archibald Menzies, the botanist who sailed with Vancouver, was charged with making a survey of the vegetation in the regions he visited and with observing the use the natives made of them and evaluating their potential utility should the homeland decide to colonize.

The naturalist-explorers worked indefatigably in the field. On 28 May 1767, Philibert Commerson, the botanist on board the *Étoile,* wrote to his brother from Montevideo: "Often I don't know where to begin, I forget to eat and drink, and our captain, my excellent friend, carries his attentions to the point that I am provided with light only until midnight, because he realized that, to the detriment of my health, I took nearly the whole night away from sleep for a thorough examination of all that was before me." This is probably an accurate picture: between one landfall and another—in Brazil, Mauritius, Tierra del Fuego, Tahiti, and New Guinea—Commerson accumulated an herbarium of over two hundred volumes. At nearly the same time, Joseph Banks and Daniel Solander were working equally hard on board the *Endeavor.*

> Now do I wish that our freinds in England could by the assis-
> tance of some magical spying glass take a peep at our situation:
> Dr Solander setts at the Cabbin table describing, myself at my
> Bureau Journalizing, between us hangs a large bunch of sea
> weed, upon the table lays the wood and barnacles; . . . without
> being conjurors [they] might guess that we were talking about
> what we should see upon the land which there is now no doubt
> we shall see very soon.[15]

Although their quarters on board were cramped, the botanists had the
advantage of being able to spend time while on the high seas arranging
the specimens they has amassed on their visits on land, classifying them
with the aid of the botanical treatises they had brought along, and placing them in their herbaria. This task was harder for the land voyagers,
who had to limit their collections severely for lack of transport facilities.
One of them states, "Mr. Dombey, who travels much less conveniently
through Peru and Chile, has collected a dozen samples for each species
of new plant." Land travelers, who carried fewer books and lacked
means for comparison, could not always identify their samples with certainty. Dombey apologized to Thouin in advance:

> Doubtless many errors have slipped into our descriptions. One
> needs at least a few years to familiarize oneself with the botany
> of two leagues of these forests, which are nearly impenetrable,
> and most of whose trees are dioecious [bearing both male and
> female flowers]. . . . I warn you that my manuscripts are full of
> errors. . . . You understand that, without great experience,
> lacking books and good instruments, I must have fallen into
> great errors.

These difficulties did not prevent Dombey and his companions from
shipping home from Peru seventy-eight crates filled with plants, seeds,
and other natural history samples. Humboldt and Bonpland brought
back from the Americas more than 60,000 plants and an herbarium containing some 6,200 species. Forsskål amassed twenty crates of samples
during his trips to the Mediterranean, Egypt, and Yemen.[16]

Fauna was not forgotten in this superabundance of flora the explorers collected in their attempt to inventory the world's plant life. Animals, in fact, often fascinated them even more than plants, as evidenced
by notations in their journals on their encounters and their astonish-

ment. Humboldt says of his and Bonpland's first experience of the nocturnal life of the jungle:

> The night was calm and serene and there was a beautiful moonlight. The crocodiles [were] stretched along the shore. . . . Everything passed tranquilly till eleven at night; and then a noise so terrific arose in the neighboring forest, that it was almost impossible to close our eyes. . . . These were the little soft cries of the sapajous, the moans of the alouate apes, the howlings of the jaguar and cougar, the peccary, and the sloth, and the cries of the curassao, the parraka, and other gallinaceous birds. When the jaguars approached the skirts of the forest, our dog . . . began to howl and seek for shelter beneath our hammocks.

By day the naturalists carried on quieter and more scientific observations. Although there was no mythical unicorn to be found in the Rocky Mountains, Lewis described more than 250 animal species, more than a hundred of them hitherto unknown. He painstakingly noted their aspect and their measurements; Jefferson's quarrel with Buffon on the degeneration of species in the New World was not far off. Still, for obvious reasons of commodity, few specimens were brought back. Even Lewis could do little more than pick up some fossils and stuff a few birds, following the method Jefferson had shown him. In Siberia Pallas found mammal remains conserved in the ice. Forsskål collected corals and shells in the Mediterranean area and in Arabia, and in spite of the heat and difficult travel conditions he attempted to conserve fish and snakes in alcohol-filled jars. When he arrived in France in 1804, Humboldt gave a llama skeleton to the Muséum d'Histoire Naturelle, and he gave Cuvier fossilized elephant tusks to examine. During his voyage with Bonpland, Humboldt even tried to send living animals back to Europe.

> The capuchin of the Esmeraldas (Simia chiropotes), which so much resembles man in the expression of its physiognomy; and the sleeping monkey (Simia trivirgata), which is the type of a new group; had never yet been seen. . . . We destined them for the menagerie of the Jardin des Plantes at Paris. . . . The monkeys and birds died at Guadaloupe, but fortunately the skin of the Simia chiropotes, the only one found in Europe, was sent a few years ago to the Jardin des Plantes, where the *couxio* (Simia satanas), and the stentor or alouate of the steppes of Caracas (Simia ursina) had already been received.[17]

Man, past and present, physical and moral, also figured in the naturalists' gigantic collection efforts. In Chile, in California, at Easter Island, and at Sakhalin Island, Rollin, the ship's surgeon on the *Boussole,* took anatomical and anthropological measurements, and Lapérouse made notations in his journal on the native vocabulary as he sailed along the coasts of Tartary. Humboldt brought back from America skulls that he had taken from a sanctuary when the natives were not looking, and he communicated his observations on Indian languages to his brother Wilhelm, a grammarian and linguist. Dombey observed the alimentary and medical practices of the Amerindians and was one of the first to take an interest in Peruvian archaeology and to collect Inca vases and pots. Pallas described in detail the way of life of Siberian tribes: the Ostyaks, Kirghiz, and Samoyed. During his first voyage, Cook amassed in the *Endeavor* stuffs and practical and artistic objects that he had gathered during his stay in Tahiti; Banks collected terms for a first vocabulary of the Tahitian language and learned something about local customs. Péron, the naturalist and zoologist on Captain Baudin's expedition to the Austral Seas, gathered a variety of items including a skeleton from Mozambique and a mummified arm. In particular, he collected more than two hundred objects "relative to the natural history of man" from Timor Island and various Pacific islands: shields, assegais (javelins), weapons, personal decorations, and utensils. As with flora and fauna, only an enterprise of collection and inventory seemed capable of laying the foundations for a natural history of man.

The explorers also had in mind other things than natural history collections when they arrived at the edges of the known world. The primitivism of philosophers from Buffon to Rousseau and from Helvétius to Diderot who set up the "savage" as a witness to man's origins had put its mark on the navigators' perceptions of the places they were discovering and their attitudes toward the peoples they found there. The notations in their journals reveal the extent to which they viewed moving through space as a voyage through time leading back to the earliest ages of humanity. For Bougainville the sojourn in Tahiti marked the height of this return to the past and to the time of origins: he found there a people who had "those elementary acquisitions in the arts that suffice for man near the state of nature, working little, enjoying all the pleasures of society, the dance, music, conversation, and, to end the list, love, the only god to which, I believe, this people sacrifices." For the European, travel was an opportunity to return to the sources of human history.

Twenty years or so later, Lapérouse also believed that he had found the earthly paradise in the Samoan Islands:

> What imagination would fail to portray happiness in a site as rav-
> ishing as this, a climate that requires no clothing; breadfruit
> trees, coconuts, bananas, guavas, oranges, etc. that need no cul-
> tivation presented these fortunate inhabitants a healthy and
> agreeable nourishment; chickens, pigs, and dogs lived on the
> excess of these fruit and permitted them to vary their foods.
> They were so rich and had so few needs that they disdained our
> iron tools and our stuffs.

For the seamen, these images evoked the Garden of Eden in the first
days of Creation, before sin and the Fall: "We said to one another: 'These
islanders are the happiest inhabitants of the earth; they spend their days
in leisure, surrounded by their women, and, having no care but to decorate themselves, raise birds, and, like the first man, effortlessly pick the
fruits that grow over their heads.' " But the navigators were also well
aware that these fantasies were an illusion born in Europe and projected
onto the antipodes: "We did not see any weapons, but their bodies were
covered with scars, which showed that they were often at war or quarrel-
ing. . . . Man, nearly savage and in anarchy, is a fiercer being than the
wolves and the tigers of the forests." Lapérouse had already had occasion
to declare that the dream of the Golden Age was gone. Although his subject was the inhabitants of the northern coasts of the American continent, he took the opportunity to comment on European philosophers:

> They make their books by their fireside, and I have been voyag-
> ing for thirty years: I am witness to the injustices and the trickery
> of these peoples who are described to us as being so good be-
> cause they are so close to nature. But that nature is sublime only
> in its masses; it neglects all the details. It is impossible . . . to en-
> ter into society with the man of nature because he is barbarous,
> wicked, and clever.

The world that was revealed to the explorer's eyes lost its enchantment:
man was not naturally good, either at home or in far-off lands.[18]

The Return Trip

If Lapérouse's diatribe reached those to whom it was addressed, it was
because he had decided to leave one of his companions, the young Barthélemy de Lesseps who had joined the expedition as an interpreter, at
Petropavlosk, on the Kamchatka coast, halfway through the voyage, fear-
ing that the results of his discoveries and his reflections on them might

be destroyed in a shipwreck. Lesseps carried the journals and reports of the first part of the voyage on an extraordinary east-west crossing of Asia (the opposite direction from the usual itinerary) that took him from the solitudes of Siberia to Russia, St. Petersburg, and, eventually, Versailles. Lesseps was to be the only member of the Lapérouse expedition who returned, the sole remainder of the party that disappeared in the mysterious shipwreck at Vanikoro, along with the accounts of the two frigates' last navigations in the South Seas. As Lesseps's cross-continental trek shows, the explorers' most obsessive fear must have been a voyage with no return; a tragic end to their adventure that would bring it to naught, except perhaps for its contribution to utopian imaginings or for new attempts to follow in their wake. This was the case when d'Entrecasteaux was sent on an expedition to search for Lapérouse in 1791.

Many voyages of exploration were in fact one-way trips. Some explorers paid with their lives for the risks they had run. Cook, Marion-DuFresne, and Fleuriot de Langle were victims of confrontations with natives. All trace of Lapérouse was lost after the shipwreck at Vanikoro, and Bruni d'Entrecasteaux died of exhaustion off the small island where his predecessor had disappeared. The naturalist Louis Ventenat, suspected of republicanism, was imprisoned by the Dutch and died at Île de France, on his way home, in 1794. Commerson died on Île de France in 1773 without knowing that he had just been elected an associate member of the Académie des Sciences. Many land travelers suffered the same fate: of the five members of the Danish expedition, only three reached San'a, the capital of Yemen and only Carsten Niebuhr returned to Copenhagen (in 1767, after two years of wandering); Chappe d'Auteroche was stricken in an epidemic on his way to California; Mungo Park drowned going down the Niger River on his second voyage to Africa, perhaps the victim of an ambush.

Some failed to return for other reasons. There were voyagers who could not make up their minds to go back to Europe, or who did so after so many years that their return went unnoticed. While Bouguer and especially La Condamine gave brilliant talks in Paris about their Peruvian expedition and settled down to write about their experiences, the academician and astronomer Godin settled in South America as a professor of mathematics, a journalist, and a fortifications consultant, then moved to Spain. Throughout his life, he published nothing about his voyage. His health compromised, Joseph de Jussieu, another member of the Peru expedition, remained in South America, accumulating notes and herbaria but never getting around to organizing them. After thirty-six years he finally returned, prostrated, his nerves shattered, a shadow of his former self. Some returned but could not readapt to ordinary life. Whereas Humboldt triumphantly toured all the capitals of Europe and threw himself into the multiple activities of a cosmopolitan man of learning, Bonpland, his traveling companion, obsessed by the memory of his voyages, was dissatisfied with his quiet life in the gardens of La Malmaison. Leaving to Humboldt the task of organizing their materials and writing an account of their voyage, he returned to South America in 1814, where he led an adventurous life full of ups and downs and died in poverty.

Others found themselves dispossessed of credit for their discoveries. On his return to France, Dombey had a brief moment of fame among a public curious about science and the exotic that had followed the travelers' itinerary in the gazettes. The *Gazette de France* announced on 29 May 1785: "The Academy of Science has learned that le sieur Dombey, botanist-physician returning from Peru, arrived at Cádiz on 22 February, with seventy-eight crates full of objects relating to natural history." Difficulties soon arose, however. A first shipment of crates was captured by English corsairs and their contents, sold at auction in Lisbon, were bought by Spain. A second shipment containing specimens gathered by Dombey's two companions was lost in a storm, after which the Spanish authorities placed an embargo on his collections and divided them up without giving him the time to label his plants. Furthermore, he was forced to promise not to publish anything before the return of the two young Spaniards, Ruiz and Pavon, who had remained in South America to complete their collections. Whether Dombey was worn out by his long trials, defeated by his financial troubles, or simply unable to do so, he gave up all thought of publishing or protesting. All that was left to him— aside from his herbarium—was his correspondence with Thouin and Antoine-Laurent de Jussieu, some reflections on agronomy, and the descriptions of some plants that had been grown in the Jardin du Roi from seeds he brought back. Spain got all the glory from the expedition, and when Ruiz and Pavon did return, four years later, they published their works on the flora of Chile and Peru with no mention of the man who had been their guide in the field.

Still other explorers remain relatively unknown or else their discoveries have been misunderstood. On his return from North Africa in 1725, what Peyssonnel hoped to get out of his voyage—made at his own expense with no backing but a royal passport—was recognition of his qualities as a scientist and perhaps to be given responsibility for another and more official expedition. To that end, he sent letters and memoirs to the learned men of his time, to the Académie des Sciences in Paris, and to the Royal Society in London. It was all in vain: his relation of his voyage remained in manuscript, and if his letters were read in enlightened circles, we have little echo of it. Abbé Bignon found Peyssonnel's notes on Tunisia *"médiocrement curieuses"*; Réamur and Bernard de Jussieu paid little heed to his description of corals, even though he was the first to note their animal nature. With no other reward than a title of *médecin herboriste du roi*, Peyssonnel left France in 1727 to settle in Guadalupe, where he married and remained until his death in 1759, returning to Europe for only one brief trip. At the time, his works were mentioned only in England, in *Philosophical Transactions* for 1751 and 1759; Daubenton mentions his name in the article, "Corail" of the *Encyclopédie;* at the end of the century, Abbé Poirot mentions him in his own account of a voyage in Africa. It was not until the 1830s that even a portion of Peyssonnel's narration and his letters were published and Flourens rediscovered his study on corals. By then a totally different question—colonial conquest in Algeria—had renewed French interest in North Africa.

The history of Forsskål's botanical and zoological collections from the Mediterranean area and Arabia offers a pathetic and almost absurd example of the human and material costs of these expeditions, even of their wastefulness. At each step in the voyage that had set off toward Yemen in 1761, Forsskål, like his companions, sent off crates of plants, seeds, and animals that he had prepared. Some of the shipments from Constantinople and Cairo were stolen en route by corsairs, and the rest did not arrive in Copenhagen (in extremely bad condition) until 1763. One package sent from Suez got lost on the way; others deposited in the customs house of Mokha were rifled by suspicious local authorities, who opened the jars, emptied out the alcohol, and threw out the fish and snake specimens. A dozen crates finally did arrive in Europe, after a long detour by way of India and China, three years after Forsskål's death. The director of the natural history museum of Copenhagen, perhaps out of bitterness toward a more famous rival, perhaps out of simple negligence, did not even open them, thus letting Forsskål's collections decompose. They were not studied until 1772, when a few botanical and zoological studies were published. The manuscript of his journal was mislaid and found only in the early twentieth century. Out of seven boxes of manuscripts and twenty crates of specimens, all that is left today is a collection of insects, corals, shells, and fish—plus the name of a plant that Linnaeus named for Forsskål, a nettle, in memory of his disciple's fierce stubbornness. The science of his day remained in ignorance of the bulk of his discoveries—some 24 new genera and 300 new species—thus reducing the voyager's indefatigable activity to nothing or almost nothing. Everything had to be done over again.[19]

From Voyage to Narration

Beyond the voyages themselves, episodes that were at times idyllic and often tragic, we need to evaluate what the explorers accomplished and what effect their achievements had on the culture and the science of the Enlightenment as it turned toward the nineteenth century.

After their return from their adventures, the explorers usually prepared a narrative of the voyage to inform the public of their discoveries. As Abbé Prévost pointed out, writing was a duty. "A true voyager must work for posterity as much as for himself and make his writings useful to everyone," he recommended. And indeed, with 3,540 titles, French and non-French (more than twice the number published in the preceding century), travel literature, which had accounted for only a very small share of book production, became a rapidly growing genre in the eighteenth century.

In the forty final years of the century, when the trend was toward voyages to the far north and the far south, the diligence of explorers hastening to published their accounts gives a measure of the public's appetite for reading about distant lands. The German edition of the first volumes of Pallas's *Reise durch verschiedene Provinzen des russischen Reichs* was published in St. Petersburg in 1771, when the naturalist was still pursuing his discovery of Siberia. The author explains, "Count Vladimir Orlof, director of the Academy, exhorted us to publish as soon as possible the journals of our voyages in order to respond to the eagerness . . . of the scholars of Europe." The work was swiftly translated into Russian, English, and Italian; a French edition in five volumes with an atlas, *Voyage du professeur Pallas dans les différentes parties de la Russie et de l'Asie septentrionale*, was published in 1788, and a second edition, "less expensive and more portable" appeared in 1793, when the French Revolution was raging.

Abbé Prévost further noted that the voyager "should be skilled in writing a report that's not only truthful but includes, without distinction, all objects of curiosity and knowledge." As soon as the explorer returned, a new period began for him, a time for recalling to memory and for writing. Pen in hand, he faced new perils: how to relate a personal adventure and describe an unknown world; how to turn the fiction of the narration into a true report and a work of science? When he returned from Africa in 1797, Mungo Park spent several months in London, and he gave the society that had commissioned his trip a brief report. It was judged insufficient: the society expected something more detailed. Park returned to Scotland and set to work on a task for which he had no preparation. The book was published in 1799 and was translated into French the same year. Was the book's success due to the novelty of the information it contained about the interior of a practically unknown continent, or to the personal tone of the narration, the quality of Park's powers of observation, and the abundance of his adventures? Park promised his readers, "I shall . . . proceed . . . to a regular detail of the incidents which happened, and the reflections which arose in my mind, in the course of my painful and perilous journey, from its commencement, until my return to the Gambia."

The explorer-writer might organize his materials according to two methods and two highly different types of exposition and writing, the narrative and the tableau, borrowed, respectively, from the classical genres of the travel journal and the descriptive memoir. On his return, the academician La Condamine chose to narrate his discovery of the Andes and the Amazon in the form of a daily log, a *journal de route* in which his observations were fitted, one by one, into a chronological narrative, thus inviting the reader to follow his itinerary and join him in his findings. By the words and rhythms of his narrative La Condamine attempted to transmit the sensations of a traveler gradually gaining altitude in the Cordillera of the Andes:

> The higher I went, the sparser the woods became; soon I saw nothing but sands and, higher still, bare, carbonized rocks, which ran along the northern lip of the volcano of Pichincha. When I reached the top of the ridge, I was struck by an astonishment mixed with admiration to see a long valley, five or six leagues wide, cut by streams that joined to form a river. As far as the eye could see, I saw cultivated fields alternating with plains and meadows; green hillsides, villages and hamlets surrounded by thick hedges and garden plots. The city of Quito, in the distance, closed this pleasant perspective.

At the beginning of his narrative La Condamine explains why he devoted so much space to himself and to his adventures. Autobiography is a law of the genre and what the public expects: "One will doubtless find that I have often spoken of myself in this relation. This is a privilege granted to voyagers: one only reads them to know what they have done and seen." It was perhaps to project the anxieties that he undoubtedly felt as he crossed Russia that Chappe d'Auteroche used suspense to construct his *Voyage en Sibérie:* would he arrive in Tobolsk in time to observe the transit of Venus? Similarly, Bougainville chose the narrative form of the journal for his *Voyage autour du monde,* published in 1771. That way he could communicate to his readers the emotion the sailors felt as the ships approached the islands, and he could invite them to immerse themselves in a contemplation of nature suddenly unveiled: "The verdure charmed our eyes, and the cocoa-trees everywhere exposed their fruits to our sight, and over-shadowed a grass-plot adorned with flowers; a thousand birds were hovering about the shore, and seemed to announce a coast abounding in fish, and we all longed for a descent."

A few explorers gave their personal adventure and their relation of it a much broader scope, sharing their awareness that any contribution to knowledge is rooted in subjective experience and draws sustenance from it. For the naturalist Ramond as he explored the Pyrenees, the narrative was not a literary form chosen because it could render the picturesque but a privileged method of exposition for giving an account of the relationship between the investigator and his terrain—a relationship that is both physical and intellectual, made of empathy mixed with hostility, suffering, and incomprehension and that could not, with impunity, be removed from the final narration. The explorer's biography is neither useless dross nor vulgar exoticism; it is the raw material out of which the scientist constructs his science. When this happens, the journal or the travel narrative becomes a truly scientific genre appropriate to discovery and field research.[20]

Unlike his colleague La Condamine, Bouguer chose to write a brief treatise offering a global and orderly view of Peru, beginning with its geography and climate, moving on to the nature of the terrain and the origin of the mountains, and ending with the inhabitants and their customs. Here the explorer acts as a simple witness, a mirror carried along the way, neutrally and exhaustively registering the observable world and effacing himself from his description as much as possible. Nature is talked about rather than seen; it is exposed by means of raw forms, as an immediate given in which the voyager does not admit to his own presence: "These forests almost always form a sort of copse close to the sea. . . . The space between the trees is covered with a prodigious quantity of parasite plants and bushes. Some wrap around the trunks and the branches; others descend vertically in a direct line, like cords attached at the top. The last empty spaces are occupied by reeds of all sizes." In this sort of reporting, the only hint we have of the traveler's personal adventure is in an organization that parallels the route he followed. Alexander von Humboldt's *Voyage aux régions équinoxiales* (Personal Narrative of Travels to the Equinoctial Regions of America) offers the most finished model of this sort of writing combining the itinerary and the synthetic picture, although Humboldt's emphasis on a systematic and orderly presentation and his exhaustive detail lead the travel account in the direction of descriptive statistics. The *Description d'Egypte,* a monumental publishing venture contemporary to Humboldt's work but that continued into the Restoration, marks the apogee of the encyclopedic genre that attempted to circumscribe geographical, natural, and human reality spatially and subject it to method. This work illustrates the connection between travel and statistics all the better for following the *Statistique générale de la France* published at the turn of the century on the basis of investigations conducted by the first *préfets* of the French *départements.*

As these last examples show, all intermediary genres between the narrative and the tableau were possible, and they varied according to the writer's skill and character. The astronomer Pingré wrote his *Voyage à Rodrigue* in a traditional manner, alternating an anecdotal narrative of events, as he navigated from one island to another, with a series of descriptive memoirs on his principal ports of call—Rodriguez, Île de France, Île Bourbon (Réunion). Each description was organized in the same order and covered the history of the place and its geography, climate, botanical and zoological particularities, population, economy, administration, and so forth. Peyssonnel, like Tournefort before him, adopted another traditional genre, narration by letters, a device that cuts the narrative into temporal segments and permits varying subject matter according to whether the addressee is a botanist, a geographer, or a man of letters.

Although discovery narratives varied enormously in style and form, their content, which reflected what the voyagers thought worthy of being related and, perhaps, published, showed some common characteristics. When Peyssonnel, a physician and a naturalist, traveled to the Barbary Coast, he fulfilled the official purpose of his mission by sending Jussieu and Chirac several shipments of seeds and plant samples that he had gathered in the countryside or obtained in the markets. On his return, Peyssonnel wrote several memoirs on topics related to natural history and medicine, which he addressed to the learned institutions of his time. Both the letters he sent to a number of prominent personalities, which soon circulated semi-officially in the learned world, and the manuscript narrative that he wrote, probably in the hope of publishing it, contain only very small traces of his scientific interests. Medicine and botany combined account for only 5 percent of their texts; geography, to the contrary, "both ancient and modern," occupies around 30 percent of the text; customs, more than 35 percent; and history, archaeology, and belles lettres—that is, "Arabic manuscripts, inscriptions, medals, and statues"—nearly 25 percent. Peyssonnel's writings were among the first in the century to show an implicit distinction in genre between the explorer's scientific work and the narrative of his voyage.

A similar duality led the astronomer Pingré to take out of his account, which was devoted to anecdotes about his adventures and to documentary reporting, all technical references to the observation of Venus, the purpose of his mission to Rodriguez Island. Technical details were to be reserved for a communication delivered before the Académie des Sciences. When Pallas published his narrative he also put out a series of articles and learned works (no fewer than seventy titles) in all the disciplines he touched on during his exploration—botany, zoology, geography, geology, philology. Humboldt also pruned his works in the interest of not overburdening with scientific matter an account addressed to a broad public. For the same reason, Humboldt used a number of drawings and engravings of landscapes to illustrate his *Voyage aux régions équinoxiales du nouveau continent.* In these early stages of what later became an explosive development and specialization of knowledge, there was a growing tendency to distinguish the account of a voyage from the scientific memoir and to establish a difference in status between the two, which reserved for the first the domains of knowledge that were less codified and closer to the voyager's experience, personal curiosity, and subjectivity—that is, the geography, history, and customs of the peoples he encountered.[21]

Precisely for these reasons, the travel narrative was a literary genre that appeared suspect to some readers fascinated with geographical novelties. The duc de Croÿ stated that he preferred to get his information directly, from a study of maps, logbooks, and scientific memoirs, and he reproached Bougainville for a desire to please that made him give in to current fashion in writing his *Voyage autour du monde.* What did this mean? It is true that Bougainville carefully rewrote the original text of

his logbook. Instead of a few pages, three whole chapters (out of the sixteen in the volume) are devoted to his sojourn in Tahiti. This may have
been Bougainville's way of concealing the relative geographical and
commercial failure of the voyage and of inducing the public to forget
that in his oceanic wanderings he discovered no southern continent, no
lands of spices, no new route to China. Just as certainly, when he relegated his remarks on war, human sacrifice, and the hierarchy of Tahitian
society to the end of the chapter, and when he placed his account of
meeting other, decidedly hostile and bellicose islanders in the later continuation of his *Voyage*—but who would pay attention to it there, after his
account of his stay in the enchanted isles?—Bougainville took a stand in
contemporary intellectual debate and responded to the expectations of
a public that read such works as an illustration of ideas currently in
vogue. If we looked to the emotional and philosophical charge of such
narratives, we could see the mark they made on the culture and collective imagination of the philosophers and the simply curious, who did not
need to leave home to gather matter for reflection on the nature of man
and society, the origin of languages, and religions.

But could readers find anything that would help them understand human societies in the picturesque bric-a-brac of the voyagers' narratives?
Some publishers attempted to put order into multiple and scattered
works by offering collections of extracts and summaries in geographical
or historical order. J. F. Bernard published a *Recueil des voyages du Nord* in
Amsterdam between 1715 and 1718, and a *Recueil des voyages dans l'Amérique méridionale* in 1738. The most ambitious enterprise—it was intended to provide a "complete system of history and modern geography
that will represent the actual state of all nations"—was the *Histoire générale des voyages* written at least in part by Abbé Prévost for d'Aguesseau,
the first sixteen volumes of which appeared between 1746 and 1761. But
beyond such collections, what was there?

"The voyagers only give events. . . . They do not make a full study of
the customs of peoples," Jean-Nicolas Démeunier wrote in 1776. Because the century had a passion for classification and thought that no
order could exist without an outline, Démeunier attempted to subject
the customs and ways of living of various peoples to the rules of a taxonomic order, just as the naturalists were doing for plants and rocks.
L'Esprit des usages et des coutumes des différents peuples is an encyclopedic
catalogue of over 2,500 examples taken from all over the earth and all
the centuries of history. The work's aim was a stroke of genius: rather

than pursuing the facile game of formal analogies, comparing customs that resembled one another but were remote in space or time—the game exemplified by Lafitau in his *Moeurs des sauvages amériquains comparées aux moeurs des premiers temps* (1724)—Démeunier sought to find a meaning, a "spirit" (as Montesquieu had done for law in his *Esprit des lois*), in humankind's most customary habits and gestures. That is, he sought the function, real or symbolic, with which customs are endowed in the society that practices them. In the eighteen sections of his work, this ambitious compiler swept through all aspects of human life from eating habits to funerary rites, including alliance customs, power structures, and various forms of war. By distributing under each heading the heteroclite knowledge that the authors of classical antiquity, the historians, and the voyagers had accumulated about all the peoples of the world, Démeunier demonstrates the extreme flexibility of the human mind, which can attribute a variety of meanings to one gesture or, inversely, can express one idea in apparently contradictory customs. "Peoples often invert customs," Démeunier states, summarizing a broad, nongeographical elaboration (structuralist before its time) of the materials the voyagers had gathered. Démeunier's statement also marks the limits of his enterprise, since revealing the function of the widest imaginable variety of customs left unanswered the question of their local origin. Démeunier himself had an inkling of this problem. Calling for new voyages and field studies, he stated: "The most singular customs would appear simple if it were possible for the philosopher to examine them in place."

Another form of reconstruction of the voyagers' contributions to knowledge, still within the framework of a taxonomic order, and another way to escape geographical limits was in "supplements" and utopian fictional narratives, genres that grew increasingly popular. Such literary doubles provided a continuation or a parallel to published reports, at times dissolving them in commentary. Bougainville's notation in his journal on his departure from Tahiti was already an invitation to an imaginary voyage: "Legislators and philosophers, come see here, fully established, what your imaginations have not even dreamed of. . . . This is the true Utopia." In 1772 Diderot published a *Supplément au voyage de Bougainville,* making use of the "reality" of Bougainville's narration to add his own philosophic reflections, and imperceptibly shifting Bougainville's ethnographic description in the direction of utopian reverie. Diderot uses the themes of incest and sexual liberty—the only elements in Tahitian life that he found worthy of attention—as a means for bringing the narration back to his own interests and for launching a virulent critique of European morality and society.

Similarly, the *Fragments du dernier voyage de Lapérouse,* published anonymously in 1797, when the mystery of the disappearance of the *Astrolabe* and the *Boussole* had not yet been solved, presented another form of the literary double. The work uses the subterfuge of a stolen notebook that arrives in France after a series of happenstance events to support a utopian narrative combining, as the rules of the genre demand, moralistic pronouncements and minute "true" details (the names of islands that Lapérouse visited, the names of crew members, mentions of real exotic plants, etc.). The disappearance of Lapérouse is explained by his deliberate decision to settle on a Pacific isle to avoid foundering in a worse storm than any he had ever confronted on the high seas—the wreck of France in the Revolution.

These false narratives, which are as chatty as the logbooks are taciturn, made the newly discovered islands into fashionable places for imaginary travel. Just when the great voyages of the end of the eighteenth century were providing concrete solutions to the enigma of the "Austral Continent," myth took refuge in the archipelagos scattered across the Pacific Ocean, the new land of dreams and the new Utopia. Genuine geographical exploration was abandoned in favor of history, philosophy, and political satire.[22]

The Garden Back Home

"The immense book of nature has so to speak been opened in the Jardin des Plantes." In this proclamation to the Convention in 1793, Lakanal announced the nation's appropriation of the former Jardin du Roi and the foundation of the Muséum d'Histoire Naturelle. He invited scholars and curious citizens to leave their *cabinet de lecture* to stroll the pathways of the botanical garden and examine the collections in the museum, where, spread before their eyes, would be the skins of exotic animals, rare rock samples, and plant specimens that had been brought back. The collections that voyagers had made in the four corners of the earth during the eighteenth century had literally exploded the inventory of the physical world, imposing the image of an inexhaustible nature of infinite variety. To limit ourselves to the vegetable kingdom, a few thousand species were known in the sixteenth century; some 10,000 had been classified in Tournefort's time; the number of known species rose to over 50,000 by the beginning of the nineteenth century. Gardeners and botanists did their best to master these superabundant, proliferating, and widely diverse materials.

The first way to do so was by nomenclature and classification, which permitted scientists to submit nature to an intelligible order in which each animal or plant species had a rightful place. Although the herbaria that botanists brought back from the regions they had visited were usually kept, in their initial condition, with each voyager's papers and manuscripts (as at the British Museum with the herbaria of Hans Sloane and Sir Joseph Banks, and at the Muséum d'Histoire Naturelle in Paris with those of Tournefort, Vaillant, Commerson, the Jussieus, Michaux, and Dombey), scholars also worked to redistribute duplicate samples from these "historical" herbaria, placing them in a "general herbarium" of the world, an inventory (ideally, complete) of all the species the voyagers' efforts had made known. In 1793, when Lamarck submitted to his colleagues a "Plan of the Work to be Done to Put in Order the Herbaria of the Cabinet d'Histoire Naturelle," it stated:

> A label with a number at the top will be attached to each plant; next [the label] will present the name of the plant's genus and species according to Linnaeus or according to the more recent author who may have treated it since. . . . At the bottom of the same label the native habitat of the plant will be mentioned, with the specific herbarium from which it was taken or the garden from which it came or, finally, the person who donated it to the Cabinet, with mention of the year in which the plant was entered into the herbarium.

Botanists debated what order of classification to adopt for this general herbarium: rather than Linnaeus's sexually based system, which was useful for scholars but overly abstract and not comprehensive enough, Lamarck advised using "the order of natural families of Mr. de Jussieu" as a better way to explain plant interrelationship according to similarities among their general characteristics.

By the end of the century, the Jussieuan system of classification was adopted for the botanical gardens that contained plants whose seeds or cuttings had been brought back by the voyagers. Among these were the Trianon Garden, remodeled by Bernard de Jussieu in 1759, and the garden of the École Botanique of the Cabinet du Roi, whose plantings Antoine-Laurent de Jussieu renewed. Each plant was set next to the plants taxonomically closest to it. As an image of the botanical tables projected onto the ground, the garden offered an opportunity to see the order in a nature that may indeed be multiple and infinitely varied but that was rationalized, dominated by classification, rendered readable at last. The few lacunae could be seen only in the places or pages the botanist had left blank when he constructed the systematic table of his herbarium or in the empty spots that the gardener left in his plot of ground to signal plant species that might exist and perhaps did exist somewhere in the world but were as yet unknown. These gaps were all that recalled that the inventory of the planet was still incomplete.

But in this order proposed for deciphering the book of nature, the geographic origin of the plants was little but a mention at the bottom of a label. In reality, however, geographical proximity and taxonomic proximity rarely go together. Plants very close to one another by the classification criteria of Linnaeus, Jussieu, or Lamarck might be found in the natural state poles apart from one another. The table of nature and the map of the world were not easily superimposed.

Gardeners realized this and attempted to minimize geographical differences by acclimatizing plants from all over the world. In France, as early as 1719, the Jardin Apothicaire in Nantes was placed under the supervision of the Jardin Royal in Paris as "a depository and a nursery . . . for the upkeep and cultivation of plants from foreign lands." The gardens of Rochefort and La Rochelle were used as annexes for their ocean climate and were specifically charged with acclimatizing exotic plants. The Jardin du Roi served as a relay point in botanical exchanges from one region of the world to another: starting with one coffee tree seedling imported to Amsterdam from Indonesia and cultivated in a greenhouse in the Jardin du Roi constructed for that purpose in 1714, Antoine de Jussieu introduced the coffee plant into Martinique, the Antilles, and all the French colonies.

Institutions were also created in the colonial territories. At Île de France, Pierre Poivre worked in the Jardin des Pamplemousses to naturalize spices from the Moluccas (Spice Islands) and to cultivate useful or curious plants for introduction into European gardens. Seeing that the forests surrounding Le Réduit were in decline, the naturalist Fusée-Aublet tried to acclimatize oaks from Europe in the island's botanical garden. In New Spain the botanical garden in Mexico City was responsible for acclimatizing European species and preparing indigenous plants for transplantation. In North America the nursery created by André Michaux in New Jersey in 1786 was devoted to the cultivation of trees thought to be candidates for transplantation in Europe, as requested by

Abbé Nolin, the director of the nursery in Rambouillet, who was concerned by advancing deforestation in France and who sent Michaux a list of American trees he would like to see adopted in France.

Efforts to introduce new species in Europe were already producing changes in the traditional European flora. A number of ornamental or exotic plants were introduced in Europe: bougainvillaea from Tahiti, honeysuckle from Virginia in 1731, and, in 1737, *Magnolia grandiflora,* imported by La Galissonnière, the governor of Canada. Useful plants were imported as well: Michaux states that during his stay in North America between 1785 and 1796, he sent more than 60,000 young trees and ninety cases of seeds, which were distributed throughout France by provincial botanical gardens and nurseries.

But in the final analysis, leaving aside the greenhouses and official gardens and counting only the plants that were truly naturalized in their new environment and integrated into local flora, the end result was slim. Linnaeus could rightly cite the case of the *Erigeron canadiensis* (horseweed) that came from North America toward the middle of the seventeenth century, was introduced in some botanical gardens, and became a weed inhabiting uncultivated areas, but in 1801, the catalogue of the Jardin des Plantes established by Louiche Desfontaines lists only 120 plant species of American origin that were more or less acclimatized in France. At the beginning of the nineteenth century, the botanical unification of the world remained a dream—even more, an open question.

The problem of how species were distributed over the surface of the planet remained unsolved. Rather, the question had barely begun to be posed. How to account for the spatial distribution of botanical species; for the presence of plants in one place and their absence from others, even in comparable latitudes? Lamarck's "Plan" had already suggested that the general herbarium be complemented by special herbaria arranged by the geographical origin of the plants: "Thus I propose forming four special herbaria, to wit, (1) an herbarium of the plants indigenous to Europe; (2) an herbarium of the plants of Asia; (3) an herbarium of the plants of Africa; (4) an herbarium of the plants of America." But this first reclassification by continent was still very loose, revealing the insufficiency of the data collected. The botanist-explorers had focused so intently on their task of naming and classifying each individual plant collected that they neglected to make field observations of the environment, the climate, and the soil (and were not asked to do so). They had not thought to describe the local flora in general. Simple, cumulative collection had sufficed for the construction of the table of genera and species. But already Humboldt, observing the influence of temperature and altitude on vegetation, had felt the need to inscribe the various types of flora he encountered within their natural milieus. On 27 Frimaire, Year XII (1804), he declared to the professors of the Muséum, whom he intended to inherit the herbarium he had assembled in the Americas with Bonpland: "This collection, aside from having been described in place . . . has the further advantage of not presenting a single object for which one cannot indicate the height above sea level at which it grows." Humboldt's *La géographie des plantes,* published in 1807, sketches out a geographical approach to the distribution of vegetation. The problem of the relationship between geography and botany had been raised.

But if science was to move on from collecting to mapping, it would require a new program of exploration, a return to the field to study and attempt to understand the relationship, in every part of the world, between the soil, the climate, the fauna and flora, and even the humans found there. As Humboldt stated:

> The maritime expeditions and circumnavigatory voyages have conferred just celebrity on the names of the naturalists and the astronomers who have been appointed by various governments to share the dangers of those undertakings; but . . . it is not by sailing along a coast that we can discover the direction of chains of mountains, and their geological constitution, the climate of each zone, and its influence on the forms and habits of organized beings. . . . The great problem of the physical description of the globe is the determination of . . . the eternal ties which link the phenomena of life, and those of inanimate nature.[23]

It is with this return to the terrain of geography that I would like to conclude. It might seem paradoxical, however, if we think of the end result of the discoveries that founded the glory of the maritime and terrestrial explorations of the century of the Enlightenment. After the voyages of Cook, Lapérouse, and Vancouver, it was common knowledge that there is no continent in the temperate zones of the Southern Hemisphere and no northern passage by which ships can pass between the Atlantic and Pacific Oceans. The first expeditions into the uncharted lands of America and Siberia and the first incursions into Africa led Europeans to look to the interior of the continents. Expeditions were sent to the Alps, the Urals, and the Andes, and the study of their relief raised questions about the history of the planet. But the Amazon Basin, the territories west of the Mississippi, the high regions of central Asia, and, above all, the interior of Africa still remained untouched by exploration at the beginning of the nineteenth century.

Nonetheless, all that geographical knowledge was the fruit of explorations that, during that age, remained fugitive and occasional. Even the expeditions motivated by the construction of the state—Russian expeditions in Asia and United States expeditions into the American West, where discovery and appropriation of the territory went hand in hand—could still barely be distinguished, in their concrete modalities, from scientific expeditions that did not include occupation of the soil (or, on occasion, involved only a symbolic possession-taking) and that left few traces other than a harvest of samples and plants dried between the pages of an herbarium. Here and there the ships' wakes and the voyagers' itineraries left a tenuous and discontinuous network of connections on the surface of the oceans and the lands. Although the description of the contours of the face of Earth was now nearly complete, its spaces, its thickness, its depth, and its history remained to be discovered, and with them the story of how fauna, flora, and societies had taken root in each region.

The explorers of the Enlightenment left a program, inscribed in the crisscrossing lines of their maps and charts, in the organization of their collections, and in the narratives of their voyages, for those who would follow their footsteps in the nineteenth century and would return to the places to which those explorers had shown the way.

Notes

1. "Explorateur," "Exploration," in *Trésor de la langue française: Dictionnaire de la langue du XIXᵉ et du XXᵉ siècle*, vol. 8 (Paris: Centre National de la Recherche Scientifique, 1980–94); Lapérouse to the Minister of the Navy, in *Le voyage de Lapérouse, 1785–1788: Récits et documents originaux présentés par John Dunmore et Maurice de Brossard*, 2 vols. (Paris: Imprimerie nationale, 1985), 1: 265; Paris, Archives Nationales, AJ 15/511, no. 420: "Catalogue des oiseaux guyanais donnés au musée public de Paris par Louis-Claude Richard," 1793.

2. "The couriers and the explorers . . . are sent to reconnoitre in order to give information on the route and on the way to proceed on the road and at times, when such is possible, to learn the situation of the enemy" (*Livre des Eschez Amoureux* [ca. 1450], quoted in Pierre Laurent, "Contribution à l'histoire du lexique français," *Romania* 15 [1925]: 38–39); [Frederick II], *Instruction militaire du roi de Prusse pour ses généraux . . .* , trans. M. Faesch (n.p.: F.-J. de Chastellux, 1761), 31; Immanuel Kant, *Perpetual Peace*, with an introduction by Nicholas Mur-

ray Butler (New York: Columbia University Press, 1939), sec. 1, paras. 6, 8. On the connected notions of espionage, reconnaissance, and exploration, see Alain Dewerpe, *Espion: Une anthropologie historique du secret d'État contemporain* (Paris: Gallimard, 1994), esp. 38–39, 229–44.

3. *Le voyage de Lapérouse,* passim, esp. 1: 260 (Lapérouse to Fleurieu, 3 January 1787), 266 (7 April 1787), 257 (Lamanon to the Minister, 1 January 1787); Thomas Jefferson to André Michaux, 30 April 1793, quoted in *The Letters of the Lewis and Clark Expedition,* ed. Donald Dean Jackson (Urbana: University of Illinois Press, 1962), 669; Thomas Jefferson to Andrew Ellicot, 23 December 1803, in John Francis McDermott, "The Western Journals of George Hunter, 1796–1805," *Proceedings of the American Philosophical Society* 103, 6 (1959): 770–73 (quotation, 771).

4. Philippe Jacquin, "A la recherche de la Mer de l'Ouest: L'exploration française en Amérique du Nord," *Voyager, explorer,* special issue of *Dix-huitième Siècle* 22 (1990): 139–48, esp. 144; James P. Ronda, "Dreams and Discoveries: Exploring the American West, 1760–1815," *William and Mary Quarterly,* 3d ser., 46 (1989): 145–62; *Le voyage de Lapérouse,* 1: 31–32; Mungo Park, *Travels in the Interior Districts of Africa,* new ed., 2 vols. (London: John Murray, 1817), 1: 3 (consulted in French as Mungo Park, *Voyage dans l'intérieur de l'Afrique* [Paris: Maspero, 1980], a reprint of the French edition of the Year VIII, 34).

5. *Le voyage de Lapérouse,* 1: 14, 37–38; Maurice Zobel, "Les naturalistes voyageurs français et les grands voyages maritimes du XVIIIème et XIXème siècles" (thèse de doctorat, médecine, Université de Paris, 1961). On this expedition, see also Catherine Gaziello, *L'expédition de Lapérouse, 1785–1788: Réplique française aux voyages de Cook* (Paris: CTHS, Distribution Documentation Française, 1984). George W. Stocking, "French Anthropology in 1880," *Isis* 55, 2 (1964): 134–50; Jean Copans and Jean Jamin, eds., *Aux origines de l'anthropologie française: Les Mémoires de la Société des Observateurs de l'Homme en l'an VIII* (Paris: Le Sycomore, 1978), 127–76; Ronda, "Dreams and Discoveries," 151–52; McDermott, "The Western Journals of George Hunter," 772.

6. On the expeditions to Peru and Lapland, see Roger Mercier, "Les Français en Amérique du Sud au XVIIIème siècle: La mission de l'Académie des sciences, 1735–1745," *Revue Française d'Histoire d'Outre-mer* 56, 205 (1969): 327–74; Claude J. Nordmann, "L'expédition de Maupertuis et Celsius en Laponie," *Cahiers d'Histoire Mondiale* 10, 1 (1966): 74–97; Jean-Pierre Martin, *La figure de la terre: Récit de l'expédition française en Laponie suédoise (1736–1737)* (Cherbourg: Isoète, 1987); Mary Terrall, "Representing the Earth's Shape: The Polemics Surrounding Maupertuis's Expedition to 'Lapland,'" *Isis* 83 (1992): 218–37; Rob Iliffe, "'Aplatisseur du monde et de Cassini': Maupertuis, Precision Measurement and the Shape of the Earth in the 1730s," *History of Science* 31 (1993): 335–75; Antonio Lafuente and José L. Peset, "La question de la figure de la terre: L'agonie d'un débat scientifique au 18e siècle," *Revue d'Histoire des Sciences* 37, 3–4 (1984): 235–54. On the observation of the passage of Venus, see

Harry Woolf, *The Transits of Venus: A Study of Eighteenth-Century Science* (Princeton: Princeton University Press, 1959). On voyages to South America, see Anne-Marie Brénot, "Les voyageurs français dans la vice-royauté du Pérou au XVIIIᵉ siècle," *Revue d'Histoire Moderne et Contemporaine* 35 (1988): 240–61; [Nicolas Masson de Morvilliers], "Espagne," in *Encyclopédie méthodique: Géographie moderne,* 3 vols. (Paris: Panckoucke, 1783–88), quoted in *Ciencia y contexto histórico nacional en las expediciones illustradas a América,* ed. Fermín del Pino Díaz (Madrid: Consejo Superior de Investigationes Científicas, 1988), 20, 181–86; *La spedizione Malaspina in America e Oceania, 1789–1794* (Genoa: Sagep Editrice, 1987). On the Danish expedition to Arabia, see Thorkild Hansen, *La mort en Arabie: Une expédition danoise, 1761–1767* (Arles: Actes Sud, 1988), 17, 84–85. See also Carsten Niebuhr, *Reisebeschreibung nach Arabien und andern umliegenden Ländern,* 2 vols. (Copenhagen, 1774–78) (available in French translation as *Voyage en Arabie et d'autres pays circumvoisins,* 2 vols. [Amsterdam, 1776–80]); Numa Broc, *La géographie des philosophes: Géographes et voyageurs français au XVIIIᵉ siècle* (Paris: Ophrys, 1975), 159–62, 383–91; G. Brown Goode, "The Origin of the National Scientific and Educational Institutions of the United States," *Papers of the American Historical Association* 4, 2 (1890): 38. On the relation between science and cosmopolitanism in eighteenth-century voyages, see Léopold Berchtold, *Essay to Direct and Extend the Inquiries of Patriotic Travellers,* 2 vols. (London, 1789), 1: 85 (available in French translation as *Essai pour diriger et étendre les recherches des voyageurs qui se propose l'utilité de leur patrie* [Paris, 1797], 1: 93), quoted in Elisabeth Chevallier, "Une méthode universelle pour voyager avec profit, par Léopold Berchtold," *Voyager, explorer,* special issue of *Dix-huitième Siècle* 22 (1990): 13–24 (quotation, 13); Jean-Paul Faivre, "Savants et navigateurs: Un aspect de la coopération internationale entre 1750 et 1840," *Cahiers d'Histoire Mondiale* 10, 1 (1966): 98–108; Lorraine Daston, "The Ideal and Reality of the Republic of Letters in the Enlightenment," *Science in Context* 4, 2 (1991): 367–86; Sverker Sörlin, "National and International Aspects of Cross-Boundary Science: Scientific Travel in the 18th Century," in *Denationalizing Science,* ed. Elizabeth Crawford et al. (Dordrecht: Kluwer Academic Publishers, 1993), 43, 72.

7. Broc, *La géographie des philosophes,* 154–58, 173–75, 183; Lucie Lagarde, "Le passage du Nord-Ouest et la Mer de l'Ouest dans la cartographie française du 18ᵉ siècle: Contribution à l'étude de l'oeuvre des Delisle et Buache," *Imago Mundi* 41 (1989): 19–43; Jacquin, "A la recherche de la mer de l'ouest," 147; Ronda, "Dreams and Discoveries," 150–51; *Le voyage de Lapérouse,* 1: 150–84; Charles de Brosses, *Histoire des navigations aux Terres Australes,* 2 vols. (Paris: Durand, 1756), 1: 13; Pierre Louis Moreau de Maupertuis, *Lettre sur le progrès des sciences* (1752; Paris: Aubier-Montaigne, 1980), 150. On this debate, see Michèle Duchet, *Anthropologie et histoire au siècle des Lumières: Buffon, Voltaire, Rousseau, Helvétius, Diderot* (Paris: Maspero, 1971).

8. Jean-André Peyssonnel, *Voyage dans les régences de Tunis et d'Alger,* ed. Lucette Valensi (Paris: La Découverte, 1987), 13; *Instructions pour les voyageurs et pour*

les employés dans les colonies sur la manière de recueillir, de conserver et d'envoyer des objets d'histoire naturelle, rédigées sur l'invitation de S.E. le ministre de la Marine et des Colonies par l'administration du Muséum royal d'histoire naturelle (Paris, 1824). Portraits of explorers can be found in André Leroi-Gourhan, ed., *Les explorateurs célèbres* (Geneva: Mazenod, 1947), and Yves Laissus, "Les voyageurs naturalistes du Jardin du Roi et du Muséum d'histoire naturelle: Essai de portrait-robot," *Revue d'Histoire des Sciences* 34, 3–4 (1981): 260–317. See also Alexander von Humboldt, *L'Amérique espagnole en 1800 vue par un savant allemand,* presented by Jean Tulard, Temps et Continents (1965; Paris: Calmann-Lévy, 1990), 31–32; quoted from Alexander von Humboldt, *Personal Narrative of Travels to the Equinoctial Regions of America During the Years 1799–1804,* trans. and ed. Thomasina Ross, 3 vols. (London: George Bell & Sons, 1877), 1: 1; *Le voyage de Lapérouse,* 1: 61; Park, *Travels in the Interior Districts of Africa,* 2: 62; Hansen, *La mort en Arabie,* 39–45.

9. Gérard Blanc, "Dampier, ou la relation des îles aux Tortues," *Voyager, explorer,* special issue of *Dix-huitième Siècle* 22 (1990): 159–70, esp. 160; Denise Brahimi, "Quelques éléments sur la vie d'Englebert Kaempfer" (unpublished); Numa Broc, "Voyageurs français en Chine," *Voyager, explorer,* special issue of *Dix-huitième Siècle* 22 (1990): 39–49; Laissus, "Les voyageurs naturalistes," 265–66; Paul Fournier, *Les voyageurs naturalistes du clergé français avant la Révolution* (Paris: Le Chevallier, 1932); Ronda, "Dreams and Discoveries," 148–49.

10. Laissus, "Les voyageurs naturalistes"; Jean-Marc Drouin, "De Linné à Darwin: Les voyageurs naturalistes," in *Éléments d'histoire des sciences,* ed. Michel Serres (Paris: Bordas, 1989), 321–35; Sylvie Lacroix, "Sir Joseph Banks et l'envoi des naturalistes dans les explorations anglaises (1765–1820)," *Voyager, explorer,* special issue of *Dix-huitième Siècle* 22 (1990): 121–26; Jean-Michel Racault, "L'observation du passage de Vénus sur le soleil: Le voyage de Pingré dans l'océan Indien," *Voyager, explorer,* special issue of *Dix-huitième Siècle* 22 (1990): 107–20, esp. 107; *Le voyage de Lapérouse,* 1: 34, 261 (de Langle to the Minister, 18 January 1787); Serge Briffaud, "Naissance d'un paysage: L'invention géologique du paysage pyrénéen à la fin du XVIIIᵉ siècle," *Revue de Synthèse* 4, 3–4 (1989): 420–52, esp. 424–26.

11. *Le voyage de Lapérouse,* 1: 51, 260 (Lapérouse to the Minister, 3 January 1787), 2: 67–69, 455 (Lapérouse's journal); Hélène Richard, *Le voyage de d'Entrecasteaux à la recherche de Lapérouse: Une grande expédition scientifique au temps de la Révolution française* (Paris: CTHS, 1986); Étienne Taillemite, ed., *Bougainville et ses compagnons autour du monde,* 2 vols. (Paris: Imprimerie nationale, 1977), 1: 305, 320 (Bougainville's journal); 2: 109 (Saint-Germain's journal); Jean-Pascal Le Goff, "Les fleurs d'Akiaki: Un épisode du voyage de Bougainville," *Voyager, explorer,* special issue of *Dix-huitième Siècle* 22 (1990): 171–84, esp. 172; Louis Antoine de Bougainville, *Voyage autour du monde par la frégate "La Boudeuse" and la flûte "L'Étoile"* (1771), quoted in Eric Vibart, *Tahiti: Naissance d'un paradis au siècle des Lumières,* La Mémoire des siècles, 202 (Paris: Complexe, distribution Presses Universitaires de France, 1987), 85; Marshall Sahlins, "Captain James Cook; or

the Dying God," *Islands of History* (Chicago: University of Chicago Press, 1985), 104–35.

12. Francine-Dominique Liechtenhan, "Custine avant Custine: Un jésuite en Russie," *Revue de la Bibliothèque Nationale* 33 (1989): 36–46; Hansen, *La mort en Arabie*, 98; Broc, *La géographie des philosophes*, 46–47; Laissus, "Les voyageurs naturalistes," 299; Park, *Travels in the Interior Districts of Africa*, 1: 43–44, 48, 185, 193, 484; Denise Brahimi, "Mungo Park en Afrique: L'explorateur exploré," *Voyager, explorer,* special issue of *Dix-huitième Siècle* 22 (1990): 147–58.

13. *Le voyage de Lapérouse,* 1: 165 (Letter of 7 February 1788), 250 (letter of 16 November 1785), 34–36; Laissus, "Les voyageurs naturalistes," 295–97; Hansen, *La mort en Arabie*, 349, 66; Richard, *Le voyage d'Entrecasteaux,* 171–213; Humboldt, *L'Amérique espagnole,* 60. On the correspondence between André Thouin and the naturalist-voyagers, see Yvonne Letouzey, *Le Jardin des Plantes à la croisée des chemins avec André Thouin, 1747–1824* (Paris: Muséum National d'Histoire Naturelle, 1989). Lapérouse, quoted in John Dunmore, *Pacific Explorer: The Life of Jean-François de La Pérouse* (Palmerston North, New Zealand: Dunmore Press, 1985), 279.

14. Racault, "L'observation du passage de Vénus," 114; *Extracts from New Zealand Journals Written on Ships under the Command of d'Entrecasteaux and Duperrey, 1793 and 1824,* transcribed and translated by Isabel Ollivier (Wellington: Alexander Turnbull Library Endowment Trust, with Indosuez New Zealand Limited, 1986), 38–41 (d'Auribeau's journal), 26–27 (d'Entrecasteaux's journal); Humboldt, *L'Amérique espagnole,* 176–77, *Personal Narrative,* 2: 468; *Le voyage de Lapérouse,* 2: 458–59 (journal of Lapérouse); Louis Ramond, *Extraits d'une lettre du citoyen Ramond . . . au citoyen Hauÿ . . . lue à l'Institut, séance du 21 vendémiaire an VI* (n.p., n.d.), 30 pages, quoted in Briffaud, "Naissance d'un paysage," 445.

15. "The Exploration of the Red, the Black, and the Washita Rivers, by William Dunbar," in *Documents Relating to the Purchase and Exploration of Louisiana* (Boston and New York: Mifflin & Co., 1904), 15; François Le Maire, "Relation de la Louisiane," Paris, Bibliothèque centrale du Muséum d'histoire naturelle, MS 948, fol. 3v; Lacroix, "Sir Joseph Banks," 121–25; Joseph Banks, *The Endeavor Journal,* ed. J. C. Beaglehole, 2 vols. (Sydney, London, etc.: Angus & Robertson, 1962), 1: 396; Laissus, "Les voyageurs naturalistes," 312.

16. Catherine Lang, "Joseph Dombey (1742–1794): Un botaniste au Pérou et au Chili: Présentation des sources," *Revue d'Histoire Moderne et Contemporaine* 35 (1988): 262–74; E. T. Hamy, *Alexandre de Humboldt et le Muséum d'histoire naturelle: Étude historique publiée à l'occasion du centenaire du retour en Europe de Humboldt et de Bonpland,* offprint from *Nouvelles archives du Muséum,* 4th ser., 8 (1904), 32 pages. On natural history collecting in the expeditions, see Marie-Noëlle Bourguet, "La collecte du monde: Voyage et histoire naturelle (fin 17e siècle–début 19e siècle)," in *Le Muséum au premier siècle de son histoire,* ed. Claude Blanckaert, Roger Chartier, Claudine Cohen, and Pietro Corsi (Paris: Éditions du Muséum, forthcoming).

17. Humboldt, *L'Amérique espagnole*, 66, 193, and *Personal Narrative*, 2: 162–63; 3: 110; Paul Russel Cutright, "Meriwether Lewis: Zoologist," *Oregon Historical Quarterly* 69, 1 (1968): 5–28; Hamy, *Alexandre de Humboldt*.

18. Rollin, "Mémoire ou dissertation sur les habitants des Îles de Pâque et de Mowée . . . ", "Mémoire phisiologique et pathologique sur les Américains . . . ", and "Dissertation sur les habitants de l'île de Choka et sur les Tartares orientaux, par M. Rolin, chirurgien ordinaire de la Marine et chirurgien-major de la frégate 'La Boussole,'" in *Le voyage de Lapérouse*, 1: 228–39; "Journal de Lapérouse," in ibid., 2: 147, 388–91, 447; Lang, "Joseph Dombey," 263; E. T. Hamy, "Les collections anthropologiques et ethnographiques du voyage de découvertes aux terres australes (1801–1804)," *Bulletin de Géographie Historique et Descriptive* 1 (1906): 20–34; Taillemite, *Bougainville et ses compagnons*, 1: 327 (Bougainville's journal).

19. Jean-Baptiste-Barthélemy, baron de Lesseps, *Journal historique du voyage de M. de Lesseps . . . depuis l'instant où il a quitté les frégates françoises au port Saint-Pierre et Saint-Paul du Kamtschatka, jusqu'à son arrivée en France le 17 octobre 1788*, 2 vols. (Paris: Imprimerie Royale, 1790); *Le voyage de Lapérouse*, 1: 185–91; Mercier, "Les Français en Amérique du Sud," 337–42; Hamy, *Alexandre de Humboldt*, 11–22; Lang, "Joseph Dombey," 262–67; Peyssonnel, *Voyage dans les régences de Tunis et d'Alger*, 10–16; Hansen, *La mort en Arabie*, 301–15.

20. Roger Chartier, "Les livres de voyage," in Roger Chartier and Henri-Jean Martin, eds., *Histoire de l'édition française*, 4 vols. (Paris: Fayard, Promodis, Éditions du Cercle de librairie, 1989–91), 2: 266–68. The distribution of titles of such books reflects both the geographic activity of the century and the public's curiosity about all parts of the world, near and far. Europe figures in more than half of these works, but America and Asia each account for 13 percent of titles, Africa for 7 percent, the South Seas for 2 percent, and general geography for 12 percent. Peter Simon Pallas, preface to *Voyages du professeur Pallas dans plusieurs provinces de l'Empire russe et dans l'Asie septentrionale . . .* (Paris: Maradan, Year II [1794]). The publication of this edition enabled the geographer Edme Mentelle to enrich the course that he was presenting at the École Normale in the Year III with Pallas's new information on Siberia. See Daniel Nordman, ed., *L'École Normale de l'an III: Leçons d'histoire, de géographie, d'économie politique* (Paris: Dunod, 1994), 280–309, 331–32. Antoine François Prévost, *Histoire générale des voyages ou Nouvelle collection de toutes les relations de voyages . . .*, 20 vols. (Paris: Didot, 1746–91), 11 (1753): 560; Park, *Travels in the Interior Districts of Africa*, 1: 41; Charles-Marie de La Condamine, *Journal du voyage fait par ordre du Roi, à l'Équateur, servant d'introduction historique à la mesure des trois premiers degrés du méridien* (Paris: Imprimerie Royale, 1751), xxvi, 14–15; Mercier, "Les Français en Amérique du Sud," 352–56; Jean Chappe d'Auteroche, *Voyage en Sibérie* (Paris: Debure père, 1768); Bougainville, *Voyage autour du monde* (Paris: 1771), 179, quoted in Le Goff, "Les fleurs d'Akiaki," 172 and quoted here from Bougainville, *A Voyage Around the World*, trans. John Reinhold Foster (Dublin, 1772), 207. On Ramond, see Briffaud, "Naissance d'un paysage," 426.

21. Pierre Bouguer, *La figure de la terre, déterminée par les observations de Messieurs Bouguer, et de La Condamine . . . Avec une relation abrégée de ce voyage . . .* (Paris: Jombert, 1749), xxi; Mercier, "Les Français en Amérique du Sud," 344; Alexander von Humboldt, *Voyages aux régions équinoxiales du nouveau continent, faits en 1799, 1800, 1801, 1802, 1803, et 1804,* 13 vols. (Paris: Schoell, 1816); *Description de l'Égypte, ou Recueil des observations et des recherches qui ont été faites en Égypte pendant l'expédition de l'armée française,* 21 vols. (Paris: Imprimerie impériale, 1809–28). On the relationship between travel and statistics, see Marie-Noëlle Bourguet, *Déchiffrer la France: La statistique départementale à l'époque napoléonienne* (Paris: Éditions des archives contemporaines, 1988). Racault, "L'observation du passage de Vénus," 111 (Pingré's report is unpublished); Peyssonnel, *Voyage dans les régences de Tunis et d'Alger,* 19, 35; E. T. Hamy, *Peyssonnel et Antoine de Jussieu,* offprint from *Bulletin de Géographie Historique et Descriptive* 2 (1907), 7 pages. On the relation between voyages and writing, see (on Bougainville) Marie Pierre Dion, *Emmanuel de Croÿ (1718–1784): Itinéraire intellectuel et réussite nobiliaire au siècle des Lumières* (Brussels: Éditions de l'Université de Bruxelles, 1987), 226–36; and (in general) Pierre Berthiaume, *L'aventure américaine au XVIIIe siècle: Du voyage à l'écriture* (Ottawa: Presses de l'Université d'Ottawa, 1990); Mary Louise Pratt, *Imperial Eyes: Travel Writing and Transculturation* (London and New York: Routledge, 1992).

22. Jean-Nicolas Démeunier, *L'esprit des usages et des coutumes des différents peuples,* Les Cahiers de Gradhiva, 4, 2 vols. (1776; Paris: J. M. Place, 1988), 1: ix, 40; Taillemite, *Bougainville et ses compagnons,* 1: 327–28 (Bougainville's journal); quoted from *A Voyage Around the World,* 532; Denis Diderot, *Supplément au voyage de Bougainville* (Paris: Garnier-Flammarion, 1972), manuscript copies of which circulated in the salons of Paris and all Europe from 1773 on (available in English in Denis Diderot, *Rameau's Nephew and Other Works,* trans. Jacques Barzun and Ralph H. Bowen [Indianapolis: Bobbs-Merrill, 1956], 179–228); Bertrand d'Astorg, *Variations sur l'interdit majeur: Littérature et inceste en Occident* (Paris: Gallimard, 1990), 30; [Jacques Cambry], *Fragments du dernier voyage de La Pérouse* (Quimper: Imprimerie de P. M. Barazer, Year V [1797]), reprinted in Jacques Gury, "En marge d'une expédition scientifique: 'Fragments du dernier voyage de La Pérouse' (1797)," *Voyager, explorer,* special issue of *Dix-huitième Siècle* 22 (1990): 195–236.

23. E. T. Hamy, *Les derniers jours du Jardin du Roi et la fondation du Muséum d'histoire naturelle* (Paris: Imprimerie nationale, 1893); Drouin, "De Linné à Darwin," 321–35; Asa Gray, "Notices of European Herbaria, Particularly Those Most Interesting to the North American Botanist," *American Journal of Science and Arts* 40, 1 (1841): 1–18; Jean-Baptiste de Monet, chevalier de Lamarck, "Plan du travail à faire pour mettre en ordre les herbiers du Cabinet d'histoire naturelle," Paris, Archives Nationales, AJ 15/512, no. 503; Henri Daudin, *De Linné à Jussieu: Méthodes de la classification et idée de série en botanique et en zoologie (1740–1790)* (Paris: F. Alcan, 1926; reprint, Paris: Éditions des archives contemporaines, 1983);

Yves Laissus and Jean Torlais, *Le Jardin du Roi et le Collège royal dans l'enseignement des sciences au XVIIIème siècle* (Paris: Hermann, 1986), 287–341; Racault, "L'observation du passage de Vénus," 119; del Pino Díaz, *Ciencia y contexto histórico nacional,* passim; William J. Robbins and Mary Christine Howson, "André Michaux's New Jersey Garden and Pierre-Paul Saunier, Journeyman Gardener," *Proceedings of the American Philosophical Society* 102, 4 (1958): 351–70; *Les botanistes français en Amérique du Nord avant 1850,* Colloques internationales du CNRS (Paris: CNRS, 1957), passim, esp. 171–77; Hamy, *Alexandre de Humboldt,* 11. On the history of plant travel, see Marie-Noëlle Bourguet, "La collecte du monde"; Marie-Pierre Dumoulin-Genest, "L'introduction et l'acclimatation des plantes chinoises en France au 18e siècle" (thèse de doctorat, École des Hautes Études en Sciences Sociales, Paris, 1994), 3 vols. On early biogeography, see Alexander von Humboldt, *Essai sur la géographie des plantes,* ed. Charles Minguet, Philippe Babo, and Jean-Paul Duviols (1807; Namur: Éditions Érasme, 1990); Humboldt, *L'Amérique espagnole,* 282, and *Personal Narrative,* 1: xi; Janet Browne, *The Secular Ark: Studies in the History of Biogeography* (New Haven: Yale University Press, 1983); Malcolm Nicolson, "Alexander von Humboldt and the Geography of Vegetation," in *Romanticism and the Sciences,* ed. Andrew Cunningham and Nicholas Jardine (Cambridge, U.K., and New York: Cambridge University Press, 1990), 169–85; Jean-Marc Drouin, *Réinventer la nature: L'écologie et son histoire* (Paris: Desclée de Brouwer, 1991).

8 / The Functionary

Carlo Capra

> Where, then, is the city?
> It has been nearly taken over by the
> functionaries.
>
> *Saint-Just*

> Civil Servants and the members of
> the executive constitute the greater
> part of the middle class, the class in
> which the consciousness of right and
> the developed intelligence of the
> mass of the people [are] to be found.
>
> *Hegel*

Definitions

According to the lexicographers, the terms "functionary" (*fonctionnaire*) and "bureaucracy" (*bureaucratie* [from *bureau*, meaning office]) first appeared in France during the late eighteenth century. The first term was coined by Turgot, the second by Vincent de Gournay (to whom we also owe *"laisser faire, laisser passer"*). The terms that were in use in Europe under the ancien régime—*officiali, oficiales, officiers*, "officers," *Beamte*—referred either to an "office," understood as the exercise of powers conferred by the sovereign or, in the case of terms such as "King's servants," *königliche Bediente*, or *dvoriane*, to the "service" that such persons performed for the monarch. The fact that these neologisms began to circulate after 1780 might be taken to indicate that the phenomena to which they referred had become evident only then or shortly before, thus supporting the notion of a "bureaucratic revolution" (Bosher 1970,

123ff.) or an "administrative revolution" (Torrance 1978, 56) parallel to and connected with the many other upheavals (demographic, agricultural, industrial, political) that scholars place in the same time period. "The rapid growth of state administration and its transformation into a recognisable modern bureaucracy was closely related to the demographic explosion, subsequent urbanization, and economic and social development" (Pilbeam 1990, 107). Where France is concerned, Tocqueville's thesis of an underlying continuity in administration between the absolute monarchy and the post-Revolution governments has been contested in a number of recent studies, some of whose authors have placed the birth of modern bureaucracy in the Directorate (Clive H. Church), others under the Consulate and Napoleonic Empire (Pierre Légendre, Jean Tulard).

These interpretations do not basically disagree with Max Weber's famous thesis that modern bureaucracy ("monocratic" or "bureaucratic administration") was simply another facet of a process of rationalization connected with capitalism:

> On the one hand, capitalism in its modern stages of development requires the bureaucracy, although both have arisen from different historical sources. Conversely, capitalism is the most rational economic basis for bureaucratic administration and enables it to develop in the most rational forms, especially because, from the fiscal point of view, it supplies the necessary money resources. (Weber 1974, 219 [Fischoff translation, 224])

Weber's parenthetical phrase ("although both have arisen from different historical sources") opens the way to a different chronology of the phenomenon of bureaucracy that should not be limited to the European context. In China, competitive examinations for the recruitment of functionaries (the rule in western Europe for barely two centuries) was introduced some fourteen hundred years ago. Conversely, if we look closely at the administrative systems of Europe at the end of the eighteenth century, it is difficult to find more than a partial or embryonic presence of the components of Weber's "ideal types" of the modern "bureaucratic apparatus."

The assumption that underlies my own analysis is that rather than the transition to capitalism, it is the increase in states' military and fiscal needs, the tendency toward an increasingly tight control over national territory and toward a stricter social discipline, and changes in the criteria for the legitimation of power that provide the framework for a historical consideration of bureaucracy and the functionary, at least in Europe, the area that concerns us here. This means that the process we are investigating was slow and uneven rather than rapid and linear; at times it accelerated, at times it halted, and it went through phases of stagnation and sedimentation. It did not necessarily take place in the same way in all countries. Thus, if some of the traits of the bureaucratic viewpoint and operational style were already present, for example, in the *officiali* who served the princes or the city-states of Renaissance Italy, other characteristics developed in the great absolute monarchies, when "royal administration develop[ed] into something that might be called an administrative structure of central government based on stable and worked-over offices, regulations and rules of procedure" (Kamenka 1989, 93), and still others had to wait for the great watershed moment of the French Revolution.

Undeniably, the century of the Enlightenment represented a significant stage in that long and tortuous process, not so much for the growth of the apparatus of state (though that growth was notable in a number of cases) as for the birth of an ideology of the public welfare that led even some of the "enlightened despots" to proclaim themselves "the first servants of the state." It would take too long to trace here the rise of that ideology from pietism to enlightened Catholicism of the Muratorian sort, from natural law theory to Austro-German cameralism, from Lockeian contractualism to the *bienfaisance* advocated (in an absolutist vein) by Abbé de Saint-Pierre and the marquis d'Argenson. Nonetheless, the more modern sorts of public servants such as the inspectors and the engineers of the Ponts et Chaussées, in which some French historians see the first true incarnation of the functionary (Mousnier 1974–80, 2: 79–80, 545ff.; Antoine 1989, 329) can easily be seen as coexisting with such typical structures of the ancien régime (in the French context) as the venality and heredity of offices, the dominance of personal loyalty over the impersonal concept of service, the existence of sinecures, the private use of public funds, and more.

It seems clear that we must give up overly neat distinctions and excessively rigid criteria of classification if we want to make sense of the composite and multifaceted reality of the eighteenth century. But we also need to define our field of investigation if we are to avoid being too generic. First, given that today the term "functionary" is applied to individuals active in both public administration and private enterprise, we need to justify our exclusion of the latter. A first reason lies in the low numbers of a clerical class in private enterprise before the nineteenth century. This is not to say that all employees were state employees: we need only think of municipal and local administrations or of the employees of hospitals and ecclesiastical institutions. A second reason is the particular dignity that characterized responsibilities connected with royal or public service, a prestige that is well expressed by the definition of an office given in the early seventeenth century by Charles Loyseau as a *dignité ordinaire avec fonction publique* (dignity of attendance with a public function).

The complex organizations that were intended to turn a profit for the private capital invested in them but nonetheless (for various reasons) enjoyed state protection and support provide an important exception to the strictly public nature of the functionary. These included commercial companies with special privileges and monopolies, the Bank of England (founded in 1694), and the tax-farming companies. It is telling that the term "civil servant," now synonymous with the public employee, was originally used in connection with employees of the British East India Company. The French Ferme Générale had nearly 30,000 permanent employees around 1774 and between 5,000 and 6,000 *buralistes* (temporary employees), and it produced about a third of the monarchy's revenues. It was the first organization to use and develop (more fully than elsewhere) such innovations as formal career stages, codified employee evaluations, and a uniform pension plan based on regular contributions from both the employee and the company. As Vida Azimi, the author of a recent and well-documented study, observes, "One should not stop at the private character of that institution. Tax farming is the old form of the concession, which is one particular form of organization of a public service" (Azimi 1987, 3). The same might be said of the Ferma Generale in Lombardy (1751–70) or the *Régie* instituted by Frederick II of Prussia in 1766, both of which were typical examples of the sort of "parallel bureaucratic structure" (Johnson 1975, 201) that were intended to come together, with no substantial alteration, in the state administration and even to serve as a model for other state agencies.

Nor can we exclude from the broader definition of the category of public servants the personnel of the princely courts, even though it would be difficult to fit into Weber's definition of the functionary the veritable army of noble dignitaries, chamberlains, major-domos, equerries, almoners, masters of the hunt and huntsmen, foot guards and horse guards, ushers, stewards, cup-bearers, cooks, valets, musicians, singers, painters, and others who peopled the palaces of Versailles, the

Hofburg, and the lesser courts set up in imitation of them. Still, there were consequences to the crucial role of the courts in the domestication of the nobility, the projection to the outside world of an image of grandeur and power, and the elaboration of a model of taste and behavior:

> The exercise of sovereignty continued to be structured in a patrimonial sense up to the end of the absolute monarchy. Even the functionaries in the public administration were naturally thought of as the "servants" of their lords and were expected to work for the interest of the prince and not towards that of the "state." This is demonstrated by the personal ties that often existed between Court officials and administrative officials and by the lack of any financial separation of the two spheres. (von Kruedener 1973, 3–4)

The notables whom Max Weber classified under the heading of patriarchal power require special consideration. Weber cites the example of the English justices of the peace, men equipped with "increasingly complex police and criminal court powers" whose appointments were "formally . . . revocable but in practice . . . for life" who were chosen "from among the landowners of the district and qualified by virtue of their groundrent and were willing to serve without remuneration and who maintained a knightly style of life" (Weber 1974, 2: 363 [Fischoff translation, 1059]). Singly, in small groups in "petty sessions," or in "quarter sessions" (assemblies that met four times a year), justices of the peace not only judged minor crimes but resolved disputes and arbitrated local controversies; fixed wages; supervised weights and measures, care of the high roads, and aid to the poor; and granted or revoked tavern-keepers' licenses. According to a recent study, "The quintessential justice embodies both the patriarchal and patrician paternalist—both the local father who symbolizes the community and responds to its immediate needs, and the more Victorian and distant paterfamilias whose rule accords with the just but impersonal laws of nature" (Landau 1984, 5–16). The gradual predominance of the second rule during the course of the eighteenth century, together with an emphasis on impartiality and disinterestedness, made the justice of the peace a model for the "civil servant" to come (ibid., 359–62). We cannot call him a functionary, however, because his activities were voluntary and he was a dilettante (few justices of the peace had any legal preparation). Still, "patrician" authority of the sort that the justice of the peace wielded was an important instrument of social control in peripheral areas in the eighteenth century—and not only in England—along with the "patrimonial" power of the feudal lords, still very much alive in most of the Continent.

Other exclusions seem less problematic. First among these are the military and the clergy, categories devoted to public service in a variety of ways but too specific in their forms of recruitment, mental attitudes, and lifestyles to be bracketed with functionaries. Nonetheless, the borderline between military and civil functions was unclear, and in Russia and Prussia, for instance, men often moved from the one to the other. What is more, ministers of the cult were often also public functionaries. This tendency was clear in Lutheran lands, where ministers in the Consistory had a genuine function of governance, but it is also found in Catholic lands in the form of the Josephist "good priest." Although they were not as numerous as in earlier centuries, the many priests and abbés who held a variety of posts in the state administrations should of course be considered as functionaries. The Papal States (the subject of an interesting study by Renata Ago) are a case apart. There the upper levels of the bureaucracy were almost exclusively made up of prelates.

Although it was during the eighteenth century that the theory of the separation of powers first arose and was first applied in practice (for example, by the Austrian monarchy and its Italian offshoots, not to mention Britain), one cannot separate the judicial sphere from the administrative one. For one thing (despite Montesquieu), the idea of jurisdiction as the exercise of an authority, delegated or direct, employed both to settle controversies or punish transgressions and to prevent their occurrence by the use of all the measures that enter into the notion of "police" remained deeply rooted in ancien-régime Europe. For another thing, throughout much of the eighteenth century, juridical training continued to be the cultural terrain that aspiring functionaries preferred, whether they used their training subsequently or not. It should also be observed that, precisely during the eighteenth century, the idea that the instruction of the citizenry and the training of personnel for public administration were among the primary tasks of government gained ground in many lands among university professors and schoolteachers, who began to take on "state"-related connotations in Prussia and under the Austrian monarchy when obligatory elementary education was introduced. This meant that the margin of autonomy left to teachers and professors was diminished correspondingly (to increase once again in the age of liberalism). As Charles E. McClelland has observed, "The professor was more and more a civil servant (though a peculiar one) and less and less a member of a *Korporation*" (McClelland 1980, 92).

Finally, we need to touch on the important question of the venality of offices—or, more accurately, on the fact that they were considered the officeholder's personal property, hence inheritable. In a *bon mot* often quoted, the comte de Pontchartrain, *contrôleur des finances* under Louis XIV, stated: "Every time it pleases Your Majesty to create an office, God creates some imbecile who will buy it." The monarch's powers of creation in this connection (if not those of his direct and divine superior) diminished during the course of the eighteenth century, but on the eve of the Revolution France still had 50,000 hereditary offices, more than 4,000 of which (according to Necker's calculations) were in the hands of the nobility (Behrens 1985, 50–51). Some of these were true sinecures: the post of *secrétaire du roi* was the classic *savonnette à vilains* (commoners' soap), and for that very reason it was a much sought-after and costly post. In the majority of cases, however, a title corresponded to actual duties that required specific qualifications—a degree in jurisprudence for judges; military experience for the officials of the *maréchaussée* (a mounted police force).

Although in principle the notion that a position could be considered as hereditary property seems poles apart from the modern vision of a bureaucracy based on professionalism and merit, the system assured the officeholder an independence that would otherwise have been extremely difficult to achieve in a society as rigidly hierarchical as France under the ancien régime. For example, in the interests of encouraging his *grands maîtres des eaux et forêts* to resist pressures put upon them to allow indiscriminate exploitation of the nation's forestry resources, Louis XIV restored to that post the status of *officier* that it had previously entailed (Waquet 1978, 323–24). Nor was the formation of veritable dynasties of magistrates and administrators necessarily an impediment to the acquisition of a "protobureaucratic" mentality (Giesey 1983, 207) in which personal and family ambitions mingled with a proud professional awareness and a sincere devotion to the service of the king. For example, the six *intendants de finance* and the four *intendants de commerce* were powerful personages in the French eighteenth century. All these men held patrimonial offices, often handed down from father to son; all were noble; all were trained in jurisprudence and drawn from the pool of administrators of the *maîtres des requêtes,* who also provided most of the provincial *intendants.* They had access to the King's Council, exercised contentious jurisdiction, and held regularly scheduled collegial gatherings with or without the *contrôleur général,* whom they viewed more as a colleague or a rival than a superior. Under them, "the common clerks were in inferior positions, listed as appendages to their masters, the magistrates, for such clerks no matter what their responsibilities, could not have dignity or authority in the eyes of the higher orders" (Bosher 1970, 57).

Still, in a contradiction typical of the twilight years of the ancien régime, these representatives of an aristocratic and patrimonial conception of officeholding were at the same time technocrats with a modern and dynamic vision of administration. Examples of this are the Trudaines, father and son, who made a signal contribution to the development of civil engineering and road construction (about which more below), or the three generations of the Lefèvre d'Ormesson family, reform-minded directors of the Département des Impositions (Mosser 1978).

This means that in practice the customary distinction between *officiers* and *commissaires* needs to be nuanced and cannot serve as a criterion for discriminating between a "patrimonial" sort of administration in France and a modern bureaucracy. The problem is less relevant for the other countries of Europe, in which the venality of offices, if not formally abolished (as in the Papal States in 1694 and in Austrian Lombardy in 1749), began to disappear or, at the most, regarded only lower-level posts and municipal responsibilities (for example, in Spain and the kingdom of Naples).

Numbers

These necessary preliminaries out of the way, we need to try, first, to evaluate the number of the public servants in Enlightenment Europe. Joseph Massie's estimate of 16,000 public employees in England in the 1760s is usually accepted as accurate (Brewer 1989, 65). Thus, the ratio of functionaries to the population at large for that date would be on the order of 1:500. Forty years earlier, at the beginning of the age of Walpole, there had been some 12,000 public employees in England (excluding the royal house) (Holmes 1982, 255). The real boom in public employment, however, came between the end of the Stuart dynasty and the Peace of Utrecht (1713), when England was obliged to arm, both militarily and financially, for a long confrontation with the France of Louis XIV. The shift from a farm-contract system to direct management of customs duties (traditionally the pillar of British finance), the complex organization necessary for the collection of the new excise tax on alcoholic beverages (later extended to salt and other widely consumed products), and the administrative demands of strengthening the navy and mobilizing a respectable land army (nearly 150,000 men under arms toward the end of the War of the Spanish Succession) explain the ten-fold increase in state personnel that G. E. Aylmer, in his authoritative study, estimates at 1,200 men during the Cromwellian interregnum (Aylmer 1973, 169). The assignment of at least three-quarters of this personnel to collect and manage money is hardly surprising: the Excise Office had more than 6,000 employees toward the end of the century and another 6,000 worked in the Customs Offices.

Few scholars have hazarded global estimates for France. The figure of over 300,000 employees and *officiers* proposed some time ago by Herman Finer (Fischer and Lundgreen 1975, 462) seems greatly exaggerated. As late as the mid-nineteenth century, the personnel in public administration varied between 135,000 and 250,000, according to what criteria are adopted (Wright 1985, 2211). We need to add to the more than 50,000 *officiers* many of the 35,000 or so full-time employees and tax agents referred to by Necker (Necker 1784, 1: 194ff.). If we also take into account the staffs of the ministries of the secretaries of state and their various offices—670 persons in 1788 (Church 1981, 326)—the thirty-two provincial intendancies, with their secretariats and subdelegations, the personnel of the law courts, the 4,000 horsemen of the *maréchaussée,* and the more than 2,000 agents of the lieutenant general (chief of police) of Paris, we will not be too far off the mark if we put the number of public servants, broadly defined but excluding workers in the municipal and feudal administrations, in pre-Revolution France at something like 100,000 persons, or a ratio of 1:270 to the population as a whole.[1]

Administrative "density" was presumably not much lower (around 1:350) in Spain at the end of the century according to tax census figures for 1787 and 1797, which list, respectively, 36,485 and 27,243 *empleados del rey* out of a population of approximately 11 million (Domínguez Ortiz 1981, 394). In Spain as in France, however, it is hard to ascertain the confines of public employment, given that "neither the administrative career nor the organization of work underwent spectacular changes during the course of the eighteenth century" (Fernández Albadalejo 1985, 2321) except for extending Castilian laws to the Aragonese kingdoms and shifting power from the old royal councils to state secretariats similar to modern ministries. For example, offices continued to be venal under the Bourbon monarchy, although sales were not regulated by law, as in France, and were limited to posts with no jurisdictional powers. In fact, when the crown reacquired such posts it was, for the most part, in order to resell them at a higher price (Tomás y Valiente 1982, 151–77).

In the kingdom of Prussia the numerical increase of the bureaucracy—contrary to the common impression—remained within reasonable limits. At the end of the reign of Frederick William I (1740), government offices employed no more than about 2,000 persons, and even after the annexation of Silesia in 1750, only some 1,000 persons were added (Johnson 1975, 16–17), although this estimate seems to exclude judicial offices. Some of the duties that elsewhere were taken on by the civil administration were handled by military personnel, given that Prussia—in the famous phrase attributed to Mirabeau—was not so much a state that disposed of an army as an army that disposed of a state. During the latter part of the reign of Frederick II and the reign of Frederick William II, the institution of the *Régie*, new territorial conquests, judicial reform, and new efforts to bolster the school system undoubtedly much increased personnel, although it is difficult to make an accurate estimate because studies nearly always concentrate on the highest level of functionaries. One estimate puts the number of *Höhere Beamte* at 1,700 and that of *Subalternenbeamte* at 4,000 to 5,000 around 1806, when the total population neared 9 million, for a ratio of about 1:1,500 (Wehler 1987, 261–62). Another scholar (Wunder 1986, 55) reckons that at the same date there were at least 23,000 public employees, which would lower the ratio to 1:400. In Württemberg, which had a total population of 634,000 in 1794, 1,326 people worked for the state, giving a ratio of 1:554 (Wunder 1986, 47).

For the Austrian monarchy, we now have the painstaking studies of P. G. M. Dickson, who estimates that royal employees numbered some 10,000 in 1762, including Hungary but excluding Belgium and Austrian Lombardy (Dickson 1987, 1: 309). Since the population of the central territories of the Austrian monarchy was at the time about 14 million, the ratio of public servants to the general population was thus even lower than in Prussia. If, however, we add to the royal employees the employees of the administrations of the states *(Stände)* in the territories *(Länder)*, the ratio becomes 1:1,000. Numbers grew rapidly in the succeeding decades, reaching 130,000 employees for the entire empire of the Austrian monarchy in 1841 (Heindl 1991, 140).

The Italian states, to the contrary, show a notably higher ratio of governmental employees to the population. In Piedmont under the House of Savoy after the reforms of Victor Amadeus II, when the population was about 1.5 million, "the magistracy alone employed nearly two thousand persons, and as many were officials in the administrative and financial sectors"; "a few hundred political officials and [officials] of the cultural institutions and the court" should be added to that number (Balani 1981, 597). In the Grand Duchy of Tuscany at the beginning of the reign of Pietro Leopoldo, there were some 3,500 *stipendiati* out of a general population of less than a million.[2]

In Russia, to conclude this rapid and partial review, the increase in the czarist bureaucracy outstripped the rise in population, rapid as that was. There were 10,500 bureaucrats in 1755, 16,500 in 1765, and 38,000 in 1800; the ratio of public employees to the overall population was halved with respect to a century earlier, from 1:2,000 to 1:1,000 (Pintner 1980, 292).

Although all these figures represent estimates rather than precise data, we can state that at the end of the century of the Enlightenment, state bureaucracies in Europe represented a fraction of the population at large that varied between 1:300 to 1:1,000—a ratio that becomes fully significant when we think that today in the major European countries the same coefficients are about 1:15 or 1:20. When contemporaries lamented the excessive intrusion of the state in their lives, however, they were comparing these figures to past times. We also should keep in mind that functionaries were more highly concentrated in the capital cities and provincial centers than they were later, which made their presence all the more visible and burdensome. In Berlin in 1786, state employees counted for 3,500 persons out of a city population of some 150,000; Madrid had 6,372 functionaries for a general population of under 200,000; Vienna, which had roughly the same population as Madrid, had 4,500. It is hardly surprising that contemporary observers noted the phenomenon: in 1789, Johann Pezzl described the "army" of employees wending their way to work early in the morning in Vienna (Heindl 1991, 227); Louis-Sébastien Mercier, who is obviously exaggerating, claimed that a third of the Paris population was intent on "pouring ink onto paper under the banners of the tax office" (Mercier 1782–83, 7: 176–77).

Social Origin, Terms of Employment

Functionaries provide too broad a sphere of reference and the current state of studies is too uneven to permit a systematic treatment of such determinant aspects as the social extraction of the functionaries; their recruitment and professional training; their hierarchical stratification;

their wages, promotions and careers; their work schedules and discipline. The best we can do is to hazard a few generalizations and offer some illustrative examples.

Rulers of the early modern era tended to surround themselves with collaborators of bourgeois origin because those social strata had a near monopoly on humanistic juridical culture and because the princes mistrusted a nobility "of the sword" still clinging to political ambitions. Both of these reasons collapsed between the seventeenth and the eighteenth centuries. The aristocracy of Europe gave up its direct attack on the state in favor of an attempt to occupy it. In that aim it moved to acquire the requisite preparation in the universities, the Jesuit colleges, or, in England, the public schools, and to round off this education with long and costly foreign travel—the "grand tour" or the *Kavalierstour.* This change in the noble classes took various forms. In Spain nobles simply took over the major public responsibilities; France saw the constitution of a sizable nobility "of the robe" that became increasingly integrated with the old aristocracy; in England and, between 1720 and 1772, in Sweden, the crown's absolutist designs were defeated as political power shifted to parliaments mainly representative of the aristocracy. As a result, henceforth in nearly all European lands in the eighteenth century, the upper levels of public administration were largely in the hands of the nobility of both recent and ancient origin. In Bourbon Spain the grandees were excluded from the most influential posts, but this favored the middle and lesser nobility rather than the bourgeoisie, to the point that such authoritative scholars as Domínguez Ortiz and Molas Ribalta speak of the birth of an "administrative nobility" (Molas Ribalta 1980, 93). The overwhelming majority of the members of the Council of Castile, in Janine Fayard's in-depth analysis, belonged to "families of *hidalgos solariegos* or *notorios,* [men] who had modest landholdings in the north of the Iberian Peninsula; while a third of them were sons of *regidores* or *veinticuatros* [holders of hereditary seats on the city councils]." Only 8 percent of them were titled (Fayard 1979, 343). The new Bourbon dynasty brought a certain lowering of social rank, still within the aristocracy. Above all, the predominance of jurists trained in the *Colegios Mayores* of Salamanca, Valladolid, and Alcalá declined (from 77 percent of total membership in the Council of Castile in the seventeenth century to 47 percent in the eighteenth century). The rise of the *manteistas*—men trained in other schools—signaled the entry, under Charles III, to the upper levels of the Spanish administration of magistrates and bureaucrats (nicknamed *golillas* for their white ruffs) who were devoted to the absolute monarchy and whose minds were open to the new ideas (Lynch 1989, 253ff., 293ff.).

In France the problem of the social composition of the royal bureaucracy is inevitably intertwined with debate on the social origins of the French Revolution and the existence (or absence) of an "aristocratic reaction." Studies of the most prestigious branches of public service clearly demonstrate the absolute predominance of titled nobility in their ranks. Pierre Goubert notes: "Under Louis XVI all the ministers were nobles of ancient or very ancient origin, as were all the councilors of state, all the intendants (but one), all the bishops, and all the abbots. . . . Before talents with no escutcheon or too fresh ennoblement doors closed one by one" (Goubert in Braudel and Labrousse 1970, 2: 95). Others deny that access to such posts was restricted, emphasizing instead a continuity in noble predominance from the times of Louis XIV, even stressing the relatively greater opportunities for "new men" during the last decades of the ancien régime (see for example Doyle 1976, 13ff.).

Without becoming too involved in this controversy, we should note that the fact that some administrative and judicial organs of the state had the same proportion of "new men" at the beginning and at the end of the eighteenth century in no way means that ever-larger crowds of hopeful candidates continued to have the same chance of success (Lucas 1976, 107ff.). Moreover, the problem of social mobility affects the intermediate levels of the administration and the magistracy more than their uppermost levels. The case of Besançon, studied by Maurice Gresset, shows that with the formation of veritable dynasties of magistrates during the eighteenth century it became more and more difficult for members of the legal profession to shift to seats in the local parlement—which helps to explain the massive support for the Revolution among the Besançon *avocats* in 1789 (Gresset 1978).

In England under the House of Hanover most of the new functionaries came from "that job-hungry class, the non-armigerous parish gentry of small estates" (Holmes 1982, 250). In Sweden, an impoverished nobility made a determined search for governmental posts in the "age of liberty" inaugurated by the constitutions of 1719–20. In 1750, nobles occupied two-thirds of the 500 or so high-level posts, although that proportion diminished notably during the second half of the century (Roberts 1986, 74). Nobles occupied more than 60 percent of middle- and high-level posts in the central administration of the Austrian government throughout the decade of Joseph II's rule (1780–90). If, however, we follow Waltraud Heindl's observation that "those who belonged to the lesser nobility had much more in common, in their lifestyle and the level of their earnings, with the bourgeoisie than with the high aristocracy" and we consider only titled nobility, the proportion of nobles falls to under 20 percent (Heindl 1991, 147–48).

There was no country in which aristocratic social status was more closely connected with service to the sovereign than Russia, both because of the weakness of a noble class that was dependent on the czar for the assignment of lands *(pomest'e)* and the repression of peasant flight and revolt and because of the absence of a bourgeoisie to provide an alternative. Peter the Great's famous Table of Ranks of 1722 listed fourteen levels in the civil administration, parallel to the ranks in the army and the navy. The eighth level automatically conferred nobility. Although the great majority of such persons was already of noble extraction, there were several commoners and foreigners who joined the Russian elite in that manner. According to S. M. Troitskii (quoted in Meehan-Waters 1980, 80–82), the social composition of the Russian bureaucracy in the mid-eighteenth century was as follows:

	TOTAL LISTED	NOBLE ORIGIN	NON-NOBLES
I (levels 1–5)	145	127 (88%)	18 (12%)
II (levels 6–8)	562	432 (77%)	130 (23%)
III (levels 9–14)	1,344	463 (34%)	881 (66%)
IV (no level)	3,328	138 (4%)	3,190 (96%)
Total	5,379	1,160 (22%)	4,219 (78%)

As we can see, at that date the great majority of state employees fell outside the fourteen ranks of service, but the proportion of ranked employees increased constantly, to reach 72 percent of all employees a century later (Pintner 1980, 192).

The profound influence that the Table of Ranks had on the mindset of the Russian aristocracy is clear from the gradual replacement of the old term for government employees, *dvoriane* (servants), by the term *chinovniki* (from *chin*, meaning title, or rank). Although obligatory and lifelong service in the bureaucracy or in the army (with frequent instances of switching from the one to the other) was later attenuated under Peter the Great's successors and, in practice, abrogated by Peter III in 1762, the custom never totally disappeared. For one thing, the overwhelming majority of the aristocracy did not have enough serfs to assure them a spendthrift life of leisure; for another, unlike nobility, the civil service ranks were never hereditary, which meant that every career began at the lowest level. The great Russian novels of the nineteenth century reflect many of the components of the aristocratic-bureaucratic mentality—a sense of rootlessness induced by the continual transfers required by service to the czar, an acceptance of hierarchy and a military sort of discipline, and an ambivalent attitude toward the Western models imposed from on high. "Reinforced by social and political realities, the individual nobleman's sense of vagueness and insecurity as to his status played a significant part in fostering his transformation into a member of the intelligentsia" (Raeff 1966, 41).

The aristocratic republics of Italy and the city-states of Switzerland and Germany, where there was a constitutional distinction between political responsibilities reserved to the patriciate and lower-level offices that were open to a second order (in Venice, that of the *cittadini originari*), are of course special cases. Some of the German states provide the best examples of territories that maintained the sixteenth-century tradition of assigning to a class of jurists of bourgeois extraction the privilege of furnishing the prince with his most highly qualified collaborators. Out of the 180 high- and middle-level functionaries in Hesse-Kassel studied by Charles Ingrao, 130 had commoner fathers, although thirty-two of them were later ennobled (Ingrao 1987, 24). In the Electorate of Hannover, on the other hand, nobles predominated in the upper ranks of the administration, with only 12 percent of the posts occupied by commoners. "The monopoly position of the Hannoverian aristocracy depended in large measure on the absence of the prince-elector and on his respect of longstanding social relations" (Lampe 1963, 237). In the kingdom of Prussia as well, the recruitment of bourgeois fostered by the "Sergeant King," Frederick William I, encountered major obstacles under his successor, Frederick II, who was persuaded that "the nobility, the first rank of the state, by definition has the first place in the defense of the state as well as the guardianship of its dignity abroad and its constitution at home" (quoted in Schieder 1989, 252). Thus, for example, whereas in 1737 only 17 percent of the staff of the Central Directory and the ranks of the war and domain councilors of the provincial boards were noble, that proportion rose during the following decades to between 25 percent and 32 percent (Johnson 1975, 254). Only one of the twenty men named to the Generaldirektorium between 1740 and 1786 was not of noble birth (Rosenberg 1958, 162). In the *Landräte,* those who occupied an intermediate position among the notables and functionaries with administrative, judiciary, and fiscal responsibilities and operated in the rural districts *(Kreise)* were by definition noble, elected by the local *Junker* from lists of names approved by the sovereign.

In Piedmont under the House of Savoy, the nobility also gained ground during the latter half of the eighteenth century, but for the most part the nobles involved had titles acquired recently through holding office, and at the start of that period there were few nobles (16 percent among the major officeholders; barely 2 percent among the minor ones [Balani 1981, 598]). As Giuseppe Ricuperati states, the long period of Savoy absolutism resulted in "the creation of a service nobility with a strong sense of the state, an ideology of competence, and a notable capacity for experiencing the relationship between politics and culture as a professional ethic." The nobility in public service formed a social class different from both the bourgeoisie and the ancient nobility, a class that "tended, within only a few generations, not only to gain control of political careers, but also of collateral careers in everything from the army to diplomacy, the court, and the church" (Ricuperati 1990, 853, 870). A process that was in some ways analogous had begun in the Grand Duchy of Tuscany with the disappearance of the old patrician families who had monopolized the most lucrative and prestigious positions in the magistrature and the permanent governmental positions between the early seventeenth century and the end of the Medici dynasty in 1737. Those families had filled 31 percent of permanent posts in 1736; 20 percent in 1773; and 12 to 13 percent in 1784. The "new patricians and nobles" listed in the *libri d'oro* drawn up on the basis of the law of 1750 resisted somewhat better (Litchfield 1986, 315).

In short, throughout central and western Europe, public office, along with ecclesiastical and military careers, represented an important source of revenue for the aristocracy, particularly in its less wealthy ranks, and an ideal opportunity for energetic younger sons. Commenting on the continuity of aristocratic power, Hamish M. Scott has recently remarked that "the elite had adjusted to the precursor of this change, the expanded state structures of the early modern period, and had come to play a dominant role within them (Scott 1995, 2: 278). For the bourgeoisie, public service constituted one of the principal roads to ennoblement, but as generations passed, officeholders (of every extraction) of fairly high rank tended to become amalgamated into a social group with recognizable features of its own. In Prussia that group obtained juridical sanction with the *Allgemeines Landrecht,* the law code promulgated in 1794; and elsewhere as well it gained privileges and recognition tied to public function rather than to birth.

A second phenomenon (after social mobility) widespread in cosmopolitan Europe of the eighteenth century was geographical mobility, or the migration of civil functionaries and their military counterparts from one country to another. At times such transfers were genuine "loans": Pompeo Neri, a Tuscan, was sent to Milan to direct operations for the tax surveys of the Austrian monarchy under Maria Theresa from 1749 to 1757; Ignaz von Felbiger, a native of Silesia, was transferred from the Prussian administration to its Austrian equivalent, where he played a crucial role in organizing a public school system in 1774. Although the Habsburg Empire had long imported personnel from foreign lands, in Russia this was a new phenomenon linked to the policy of modernization and westernization launched by Peter the Great. Bureaucratic elites circulated just as often, however, within German or Italian lands: nearly a third of the high and middle functionaries of Hesse-Kassel came from other areas of Germany (Ingrao 1987, 29), and there was a large proportion of foreigners in the bureaucracy of Württemberg as well (Vann 1984, 178). The president and six out of ten councilors on the Supreme Economic Council instituted by Maria Theresa in Milan in 1765 came from other parts of Italy or from north of the Alps; the two principal ministers of Carlo di Borbone in Naples were the marchese di Montealegre, a Spaniard, and Bernardo Tanucci, a Tuscan. The frequency of such transfers cannot be explained solely by the fact—which Ernesto Sestan noted some years ago—that technical administrative competence was a rare, hence exportable, commodity in the eighteenth century (Sestan 1955, 20–21). Reform-minded sovereigns also felt the need to make use of personnel who had no connections with the local governing elites and their interests, and who would not be mired in a defense of the current political and institutional structure. Pompeo Neri and Bernardo Tanucci provide the best demonstrations of that hypothesis: in their native Tuscany they supported a continuity with the past regime and with "republican" traditions, but in Lombardy and Naples, respectively, they became intransigent defenders of the absolute monarchy and of reform.

The Preparation of the Functionary

Both the nobles and the commoners who aspired to public service required an adequate preparation, both generic and specific. As previously noted, juridical studies continued to play a central role in the training of upper-level functionaries and magistrates. There was a close connection between university teaching and a career in the bureaucracy everywhere but in England, where "training for the law in the 18th century was done elsewhere, in service with an attorney and at the Inns of Court, and placement and advancement in the royal administration depended on patronage and connections and hardly at all on a university education" (Stone 1975, 51). According to a viewpoint by now generally accepted, the European universities of the eighteenth century had for some time ceased to be vital centers for intellectual life, limiting their activities to passing on a hallowed traditional culture based on cultivation of the authors of classical antiquity and on Roman law.

Serious attempts at renewal were taking place in a number of places, however, for example, in the institution of courses on public law or in broadening the study of the national law. Although many German universities were stagnating in a desolating penury of means and ideas, Göttingen, a university founded in 1734 by the Elector of Hannover, soon became a leading center of humanistic and historical culture, and the proportion of university graduates in the upper levels of the Hannoverian administration rose from 56 percent in 1714–36 to 81 percent in 1737–60 (McClelland 1980, 50). The universities of Halle and Frankfurt an der Oder instituted chairs in administrative science, and enrollments rose considerably in response to the manifest needs of Frederick William I to recruit to the Generaldirektorium instituted in 1723 functionaries who would be "loyal and honest, with an open mind, who understand business and have practiced it, who possess good notions of commerce, manufacturing, and related matters, and who also know how to write" (*Die Behördenorganisation*, 1901, 577). Prussia was also in the forefront in the institution of regular examinations for the hiring of state functionaries. Examinations, adopted in Prussia in 1755 for judicial offices and in 1770 for administrative posts "made university studies the rule for aspiring functionaries" (Hellmuth 1985, 111). The same thing was true in Austria after 1766.

In Italy the University of Pisa played an important role in preparing a new governing class. In Naples the university reform put into effect in 1736 by Celestino Galiani was followed by the creation of a university chair of Commerce and Mechanical Arts for Antonio Genovesi in 1754. In Pavia a *piano disciplinare* in 1771 and a *piano scientifico* in 1773, both modeled on previous reforms in Vienna, produced a genuine revolution in instructional content that was aimed at promoting "the culture of

minds and the rectification of hearts, and, in consequence, the formation and propagation of enlightened and open-minded subjects who
will support the salutary regulations" (in the words of the royal dispatch
of 24 November 1764 cited in Capra 1984, 407–8). The connection between higher education and bureaucratic career opportunities was particularly close in Piedmont, where the reform of the University of Turin
under Victor Amadeus II was accompanied by the inauguration of a system of state secondary schools unique in Europe. As Donatella Balani
shows, roughly half of the more than 4,000 graduates of the Faculty of
Law in Turin between 1720 and 1798 found a place in the public offices,
and the numbers of students who enrolled mirrored the needs of the
state administration (Balani 1981, 690ff.).

France followed a different route, concentrating less on the reform
of existing institutions and more on the creation of special schools to
train the technical personnel required for the new tasks of government.
For the École des Ponts et Chaussées, founded in 1747, we have Luigi
Blanco's detailed and well-documented study (1991), which also discusses the training, ideology, and activities of the corps of engineers.
Other schools worthy of mention are the École Navale, opened at the
Louvre in 1748, and the École de Génie founded in the same year at
Mézières. After 1750, Vienna could boast of the Theresianum, a secondary school for nobles who wanted to devote themselves to the service of
the state. Even in Russia, every effort was made, beginning with the reign
of Peter the Great, to constrain the nobility to seek education, for example by welcoming noble youths into the select regiments of the Guards
and into the cadet corps instituted in 1721 in St. Petersburg. It remained
the rule, however, for the great majority of civil employees to be
schooled in an on-the-job apprenticeship as a supernumerary hoping to
gain entry to the permanent staff when an opening appeared, or else as a
trainee (*Auscultator* in Prussia). Often the necessary practical and theoretical knowledge was still passed on from father to son or from uncle to
nephew. The portrait of the *empleado* that Antonio Gil y Zárate drew in
1843, with some nostalgia for the good old days, was valid for other countries as well as Spain:

> Widespread custom ensured that the employee was usually
> born of an employee. As soon as the son of a functionary got out
> of school he was placed at his father's side as a voluntary appren-
> tice *[meritorio]*. There he was trained in writing, he perfected his
> accounting skills, and he learned the bureaucratic regulations.

After six years or more a post would finally open up, and the neophyte would join the permanent staff as a scribe with a stipend of three hundred ducats. (Correa Calderón 1950, 1023)

The protection of the powerful was just as important as family ties. The Bureau des Dépêches of the French Ministry of Finance can serve as an example. Its director and *premier commis* after 1778 was Charles Hersemulle de la Roche:

In his bureau were his son-in-law, Etienne-Marie Denois, who was also the son of a *premier commis* of a Secretary of State for War; de Boconvilliers, a nephew of de la Roche; Pardon, whose name was linked to that of de la Roche in a marriage of the previous generation, making them probably cousins; Meslin, in whom one of the King's aunts, Madame Victore, took a patronizing interest; Vassal, son-in-law of a *premier commis*, Cochereau, and with two "protectors," Madame Adelaide, another royal aunt, and de Villevault, a Master of Requests; de Glatigny, whose father was *valet de chambre* to the Queen; Nay, a nephew of Cadet de Chambine, *premier commis* of the Bridges and Roads; François Delorme, a relative of a *premier commis* in the War Department; and Charles Coster, from a large and powerful family with several members in royal service. (Bosher 1970, 61)

"No fewer than forty-seven families contributed three or more members to duty at the Naval Board" in England between 1660 and 1800 (Brewer 1989, 81). The fact that recommendations and protection were indispensable in order to gain access to a career in public service (or even the fact that such posts were for sale) did not mean that preparation and merit were totally ignored. Rather, people sought to combine the two. As Raffaele Ajello observes, "If it did not want to compromise the efficiency of its administration, hence the survival of its power, the government could not permit itself to ignore criteria of specific competence" (Ajello 1981, 348).

How Bureaucracies Functioned

The Russian Table of Ranks is a unique example of a hierarchy uniformly extended to the entire bureaucratic apparatus without distinction of function or agency. Elsewhere heterogeneity was the rule in qualifications and relations of subordination, and the idea of fitting personnel into predetermined roles and levels had hardly begun. In the

French ministries during the latter half of the eighteenth century, a hierarchy began to take shape as "the ministries and intendancies employed in their bureaus clerks of various ranks, ranging from first and second secretary, bureau chief, *commis* first class, and *commis* second class down to scribe and copyist" (Mousnier, 1974–80, 2: 546 [Pearce translation, 567]). Old and new ways were inextricably mingled in the largest of the French ministries, the Contrôle Général des Finances, which combined the functions of ministries of the Interior, Finance, the Treasury, the Economy, Public Works, and more. At the end of the ancien régime, the *contrôleur général* supervised some 360 employees: 30 *premier commis* with about the same number of *chefs* under them, around 205 *commis,* and perhaps 30 *garçons de bureau.* Not all the ministry personnel was included within its 38 *bureaux,* however, since there were also persons who received special stipends for such specific tasks as collecting population data or compiling a dictionary of commerce (a task that Trudaine entrusted to Abbé André Morellet, Cesare Beccaria's translator, who never, in fact, completed the work).

On the one hand, the working methods of the functionaries in the Ministry of Finance differed notably from those of their colleagues in other ministries, where collegial practices were still the rule: "Of a more modern sort, [Finance employees] were inspired by a spirit that was more administrative than judiciary, avid for reports, inquiries, circulars, letters of response, studies, analyses, all weighed and summarized by the *commis* in the solitude of their offices rather than in conferences among legal experts" (Antoine 1970, 327). On the other hand, the structure of the Ministry of Finance bore no resemblance to the usual hierarchical pyramid. Some of its offices were in Versailles but more were in Paris, where they were scattered throughout the city: "Each *premier commis* [they usually headed one or two bureaus] normally rented his own premises, established and furnished his bureaux and then applied to the Minister for reimbursement" (Bosher 1970, 53). Until the reforms instituted by Necker in 1777, relations between the minister and the personnel under him were in great part mediated by the *intendants* of finance and of commerce.

It should be noted that the employees of the Contrôle Général were only in part responsible for the management of the finances of the French state. The greater part of their work actually consisted in the supervision and registration of the activities of *officiers* who were not ministerial employees—treasurers, receivers and payers of funds who held title to venal offices and had a large measure of independence as money managers in private transactions and even in loans to the crown. They also supervised such agencies as the Ferme Générale for the collection of indirect taxes, the Administration Générale of the royal demesne, and the Régie Générale des Aides (for excise taxes), the last two of which were created by Necker between 1777 and 1780 by combining a number of previously existent offices and organisms.

The English governmental agency for the administration of the excise taxes—that is, taxes on alcoholic beverages and on a large number of other consumer goods from salt to candles and soap—provided a genuine model for bureaucratic organization and inspired the reforms of the last two decades of the century. "Not only was the Excise the biggest government department, it was also the one which had most contact with the public" (Brewer 1989, 102). The agency was headed by nine commissioners, who had weekly meetings with the Lords of the Treasury and who had under them a staff of more than 200 persons in 1770. In London, 723 officers worked under the supervision of a corps of inspectors and sent payments directly to the office of a receiver general. The agency's organization was somewhat more complex outside London, where (still in 1770) 53 deputy tax collectors and an equal number of clerks operated as centers of collection for payments taken up by 2,704 officers working under the watchful eye of 253 supervisors.

Any candidate for a post in this bureau had to pass fairly rigorous examinations requiring a better than elementary command of mathematics and geometry: "Tom Paine, perhaps the most famous of all excise officers, studied for 14 months before becoming a supernumerary in 1761" (Brewer 1989, 104). The officers, who were called "gaugers," were obliged to cover many miles on foot or on horseback to inspect the locales (about 100,000 in all England at the end of the eighteenth century) where taxed articles were manufactured or sold, collect the sums due, and give out receipts. They also kept detailed ledgers that were sent periodically, together with the supervisors' record books, to the central offices. This system of controls was set up to make collusion and fraud difficult and to permit realistic estimates of how much each agent collected (promotions or penalties were based on collection revenues). Frequent personnel transfers from one division to another discouraged the formation of personal ties between tax collectors and manufacturers or local businessmen. The efficient operation of this system, along with a natural increase in production and commerce and periodic rises in taxation, explain why the Excise Office was the most dynamic source of revenue for the monarchy of Great Britain in the eighteenth century. Its contributions rose from approximately 30 percent of all revenues during the first decade of the century to average nearly 50 percent between 1740 and 1780.

A quite different atmosphere reigned in the Customs Service in Britain, "carrying as it did a medieval supercargo of redundant officials and expensive sinecurists" (Roseveare 1969, 95). For precisely that reason, its posts were much sought after, and normally they were reserved for the kin or the clients of ministers in office or the great aristocrats. One candidate for a post wrote to his protector that he would be content with a stipend of £70 to £100 a year, but that he would ask for £200 or £300 a year if "actually required to labour" (ibid., 96). These figures become more meaningful if we compare them to the stipends of the excisemen, which ranged from £50 a year for agents to £90 yearly for supervisors and £120 per annum for the exactors—sums that were only minimally increased by other benefits that their colleagues in the Treasury enjoyed as a matter of course.

It would be an easy task to collect figures to demonstrate that the retribution level in public service was, on average, rather low, that levels of pay differed notably (given like ranks) among the various agencies, and that they covered a far broader range than is true today. In Piedmont, the gap between the highest levels and lowest ranks in the bureaucratic pyramid was on the order of a ratio of 15:1 or 20:1 (Balani 1981, 607). In Vienna stipends ranged from 20,000 to 30,000 florins a year for the highest ministerial posts to 500 florins and even less for the lowest-paid clerks. In the French Ministry of War stipends ranged from 200 francs a year for the lowest-paid employees (doorkeepers and porters) to sums that varied from 4,000 to 8,000 francs a year at the highest levels. In 1776, the minister of war, the comte de Saint-Germain, promulgated an ordinance reorganizing stipends in his ministry and establishing a hierarchy in which a *chef de bureau* (a title equivalent to the previous *premier commis*) earned 15,000 livres tournois a year; the three grades of *commis ordinaire* earned from 1,000 to 5,000 livres tournois a year; and an *élève* (student) earned 600 livres tournois a year (Church 1981, 33). Saint-Germain's project met with insuperable opposition, in particular because it stipulated that such stipends would be inclusive of all the various entries that traditionally constituted a large and often preponderant part of the functionary's "pay envelope"—"gratifications," fees and payments demanded of anyone who requested an attestation or other document, honoraria paid to judges, and a number of exemptions and privileges. In the state of Milan at the beginning of the eighteenth century, such supplements,

> on the average, nearly doubled the stipends for the highest posts—that is, Governor, Grand Chancellor, senators, and police superintendents . . . but they increased pay six-fold in lower-level posts. Combining all posts, high and low, in all branches of administration, we can state that the expenditure relative to employment, which amounted to 459,134 lire for stipends alone, rose to 1,283,256 lire when honoraria, repayment of costs, and all the other minor entries accepted and registered in the Half Year books are added. (Pugliese 1924, 383)

This system offered the advantage that the government could shift to the population, in particular to those who made use of the public services, the better part of the cost of maintaining the "officials." Obviously, it also favored all manner of abuse and extortion on the part of these officials, as demonstrated *ad abundantiam* by the studies of Federico Chabod regarding Milan and of Roberto Mantelli regarding the kingdom of Naples under Spanish rule. The system was also inextricably connected with the patrimonial conception of offices, which considered them as an investment to be exploited. One of the first reforms put into effect in Lombardy during the reign of Maria Theresa, the *nuova pianta* for the Milanese magistracy introduced by Gianluca Pallavicini in 1749, eliminated the venality of offices, assigned decorous stipends to public employees, and reduced other emoluments to moderate and fixed sums henceforth redistributed to all personnel from a central account (Mozzarelli 1972, 134–40).

Analogous measures were put into effect in the other territories of the Habsburg monarchy, where, however, salaries remained notably lower than in Milan, and the lack of provisions for adjustment to the cost of living led, in the final decades of the century, to serious discomfort. After 1748, Samuel von Coccej energetically spearheaded efforts to raise stipends, eliminate judges' honoraria, and introduce a system of merit-based recruitment within the Prussian judicial system. Similar reforms had to wait in the other German states, where throughout the eighteenth century stipends continued to be paid largely in goods (with rations of grain, wood, and wine that functionaries could then resell). Nonetheless, in the Napoleonic era and the years immediately following, Baden, Württemberg, and Bavaria had the first codifications of a

Beamtenrecht that stipulated, among other things, "just cause" for firings and the recognition of a privileged juridical status for all state dependents (not just for nobles): "The honor of the [state] employees had to be stimulated and constantly encouraged to unlimited commitment, not by means of punishments, but by means of rewards" (Wunder 1986, 28).

Everywhere, a change in the character of pensions provides a significant indication of the shift toward a modern conception of public service. No longer considered a grace conceded by the sovereign on a case-by-case basis, pensions became a right regulated by law and connected with length of service. While in France and England pensions were based on the workers' voluntary contributions, the "norm" promulgated in 1781 by Joseph II (which was soon imitated by other governments) assured all state employees a third of their stipends after fifteen years of service, half after twenty-five years, and their entire stipend after forty years. Other dispositions covered illness and the payment of a pension to the spouse after the beneficiary's death. The Austrian administration also regulated promotions on the basis of length of service, a principle that in time had the effect of lowering the employees' spirit of initiative but that offered the advantage of discouraging influence by means of clientage relations or personal connections.

Jakob Van Klaveren has analyzed the structural character of corruption within the apparatus of the state in ancien-régime Europe in economic terms. For him it was an exploitation, following the laws of the market, of the particular form of enterprise represented by public office; an exploitation made possible by the large measure of autonomy left to the employees of the oligarchical republics and the more temperate monarchies. Other scholars have related corruption to insufficient retribution for public service. More recently, Jean-Claude Waquet has proposed an explanation in functional terms. According to his thesis, which he illustrates with numerous examples taken from the history of the Grand Duchy of Tuscany between the seventeenth and eighteenth centuries, corruption "fulfilled a double function. It shared out money, which public servants, being for the most part from noble extraction, needed badly. At the same time it redistributed power in favour of a born elite class who had never completely accepted the fact of its deprival" (Waquet 1984, 236 [McCall translation, 191]). Waquet himself warns against mechanically applying this analysis to other political and institutional situations, however, and he insists on the importance of recognizing that behaviors which we might consider corrupt were regarded less stringently by both contemporary society in general and the people who were involved in them.

Where progress was made in combating corruption during the eighteenth century (in Prussia, England, in the Austrian monarchy, and even in Tuscany under Lorraine rule), we can say that two things had changed. On the one hand, more rigid disciplinary norms were adopted and severe punishments were set in place. Governments grew more vigilant in rooting out corruption, to the point of creating genuine spy systems, as in Prussia with its notorious *Fiskalen* or in Austria after the institution of a secret police under Joseph II. On the other hand, public employees themselves internalized a new ideology of the public good and formed a concept of honor unlike aristocratic honor and, in Joseph von Sonnenfels's words, centered on a "consideration of the rectitude of the citizen" (von Sonnenfels 1819, 1: 370ff.). The most famous expression of this bureaucratic and state-centered ethic is the "pastoral letter" sent out by Joseph II in December 1783. It states:

> I have sought to inspire in all the servants of the state the love that I feel for the general welfare and zeal for its service. . . . From this it follows that in all enterprises, without exception, every person must carry out his own responsibilities with maximum zeal, without measuring his own labor either in hours or in days or in pages; but rather he must expend all his energies, when he has a task before him, to execute it according to expectations and according to his duty. . . . Anyone who has no love for the service of his country and his fellow citizens, who fails to feel himself inflamed by a special zeal to do good, is not made for [public] service. . . . Self-interest of all sorts is the ruin of all affairs and the most unpardonable offense in a functionary of the state. (Walter 1950, 123–26)

Reality of course fell far short of this ideal, as we shall soon see. Nonetheless, historians agree that the formation of a bureaucracy that was by and large honest, disciplined, and devoted to public service, and that was remote from any notion of "representing" a certain territory or social class (a move that began in the latter half of the eighteenth century), was one of the pillars of the imposing structure of the Austrian monarchy before the First World War, guaranteeing its "static grandiosity" against the many forces for its disintegration. The same was true, mutatis mutandis, for the Germany that Otto Hintze proudly defined in a 1911 study as "the classic bureaucratic country of the European world" (Hintze 1964, 66–125). More recently, another scholar has declared:

> By the late eighteenth century the German bureaucracies comprised a generally honest, hard-working group of university-trained professionals. Although their numbers included a high percentage of commoners at all levels, they were well integrated into their state's power and social structure by a merit system that rewarded talent over birthright. (Ingrao 1990, 230)

Working Conditions

In the eighteenth century the workplace was usually separated from the home. We have only fragmentary information on functionaries' work hours, but they were nothing like those of the manual laborers' interminable day. In England in the Treasury, where discipline was particularly relaxed, the daily schedule established in 1752 was from nine o'clock in the morning to three o'clock in the afternoon, five days a week. Many clerks made an appearance only after eleven, however, and some were absent from the office often and deliberately (Roseveare 1969, 106). The same was true in the Navy Office, where even the chief clerks had to be admonished "to Sign all certificates and other Papers at your Office, and not at Taverns and Coffee houses, as hath been heretofore practiced" (Baugh 1965, 60–61). In France the working day in the ministries was traditionally seven or eight hours long, but even there observance of the norm was highly elastic as late as Balzac's day (Thuillier 1976, 28ff.). In the chanceries of Vienna work hours were from nine to twelve o'clock in the morning and from three to six o'clock in the afternoon, six days a week, but observance of this schedule became less rigid as one rose in the hierarchy. After the reform of 1771 employees of the offices of the Milan Magistrato Camerale were expected to spend seven hours a day at work (Mozzarelli 1981, 456).

What really counted, even in the eyes of the most demanding governments, was not so much regular presence in the workplace as the immediate and willing fulfillment of the assigned tasks. Even Joseph II, who claimed that work was not to be measured "either in hours, days, or pages," allowed for "repose from business, which is felt doubly earned when one is conscious of having done his duty" (quoted in Walter 1950, 125). In Cremona, Vincenzo Lancetti, an employee in the Ministry of War of the kingdom of Italy during the Napoleonic era and the author of an interesting (but unpublished) treatise, "Delle qualità e dei doveri degli impiegati pubblici," praised the "sweet satisfaction . . . of an employee who leaves his cubicle clear of papers every day." Lancetti nonetheless thought it inappropriate to require functionaries to put in regular office hours:

> It is always useful for ministries to establish the hours in which they remain open and accessible. . . . But it smacks of the schoolroom or the monastery to demand that all levels of employees in the ministries, especially the principal ones, must absolutely and constantly be present from a given hour to another equally fixed hour, whether they have equivalent work or not.

The good employee, Lancetti observed, will remain in the office at night should work require it, but "when he is freed from it will know how to profit from such moments and, without reproach, will absent himself" (Capra 1986, 66). Lancetti defined alacrity as "that spontaneous and resolute will to pursue the tasks that are yours, that sitting at your post without too many preambles of going to and from, visits, conversations, chats, snacks, newspapers, strolls, [and] all the things that consume one-third of the hours dedicated to work" (ibid.).

Lancetti's description of daily office routine, which we might find all too familiar, is corroborated by other contemporary documents. One is an enumeration of the "general defects" of the employees of the Tuscan government compiled by the grand duke, Pietro Leopoldo, before he left Florence in 1790:

> Negligence in being unwilling to apply themselves to business and in being little in the office; in relying entirely on subordinates for the details of business; in coming to the office more for appearance's sake and as little and as late as they can and spending their time there in useless chatter and gossip or in attending to their own affairs; in giving themselves airs, promising protection, and fooling people, especially in Florence, by pretending always to be busy with many affairs and occupations, and making promises to everyone with an air of importance and mystery calculated to win themselves acclaim, to make others bow to them and do them favors and work things around to attracting the honor of everything that is done to themselves and excusing themselves, with the public and with individuals, even against all truth, and blaming whatever might not please some individ-

ual on the governing power or on other employees. (Pietro
Leopoldo 1969–74, 1: 57)

In the Austrian monarchy the employees of the provincial inten-
dancy of Bozzolo seemed to embody the austere ideal of Joseph II. The
director, Luigi Berti, stated in 1787: "All the clerks come [to the office]
in the morning . . . at eight o'clock at the latest . . . they remain there
until two o'clock in the afternoon; they return at five o'clock and are
there until midnight." According to Berti, all of these men were

> capable and correct and educated. Their conduct is exemplary,
> not by force, but out of natural inclination and character. . . . If
> they have a moment to breathe on a holiday they use it to take a
> walk together. They keep away from the idlers in the city and
> from revelers and take their society by being in the office, get-
> ting together to discuss business with their Intendant. (Capra
> 1984, 524)

There is abundant proof of a less heroic reality, however—one closer to
the "bureaucratic ideal so typical of the Austria that we know," which
showed less zeal for "the enlightened will to renew the state" than for "a
system of careful neglect, which at the same time involved a scrupulous
and careful respect of the law . . . and an indolent immobilism that
avoided any effective reform or constitution" (Magris 1976, 30). The
protagonist of Joseph Richter's *Herr Kaspar* (1787) found a little paradise in a government office in which no one was in danger of working
himself to death:

> Around him he saw nothing but friendly, merry faces; his wor-
> thy colleagues, instead of working, gathered in a circle, sniffing
> snuff and recounting to one another the news of the city or play-
> ing a hand of piquet. The superiors often did not see them for
> weeks at a time, and when the weather was fine the entire chan-
> cery might take off time to play bowls.

At a certain point it occurs to Kaspar to settle down to work. His colleagues are astonished, and "not two hours had passed before half the
city had heard of the miracle: the chancery had a clerk who worked"
(Richter 1787, 196–98).

To my knowledge this is one of very few eighteenth-century novels
with a public functionary as its protagonist. The bureaucrat had not yet
become a literary character: the century of the Enlightenment had no
equivalent to the *employés* of Balzac, Courteline's *ronds-de-cuir,* Grillpar-

zer's Bancbano, or Gogol's Akaky Akakievich, not to mention Vittorio Berezio's Monsù Travet or Emilio De Marchi's Demetrio Pianelli in Italy or, later, Roth's "Hauptmann Joseph Trotta von Sipolje" (in *Radetzky-marsch*) and Musil's "Man Without Qualities," Section Chief Tuzzi.

If we want to reconstruct the "administrative anthropology" or the "living bureaucratic experience" of which Guy Thuillier has written so suggestively regarding nineteenth-century France, we must look to memoirs rather than to caricatures like those of Louis-Sébastien Mercier (Thuillier 1987, 39–52). We have nothing for the eighteenth century that is as detailed or as captivating as the diaries of Samuel Pepys and John Evelyn, but we do have autobiographies and accounts by function-aries or ex-functionaries like Tom Paine's *The Case of the Officers of Exise;* the *Souvenirs* of Jacob Nicolas Moreau, a *conseiller* for the Court des Comptes of Provence beginning in 1764 and *avocat de finance* after 1759; the *Autobiographie* of Ernst Ferdinand Klein, a prominent figure in the Prussian bureaucracy; or the *Educazione diretta agl'impieghi e cariche per mezzo delle passioni che vi conducono* of Francesco Maria Gianni, who rose rapidly "from the bureaucracy into politics" in Tuscany under Pietro Leopoldo (Diaz 1966). The daughter of an Austrian functionary, Jo-hann Georg Obermayer, has left us a lively description of her father's studies, career, and lifestyle from his first and memorable encounter with Kaunitz, who took him into the Chancery of the Court and the State, to his acquisition of the title of "major official" that conferred new social dignity on him and enabled him to lead an existence of ease and intellectual refinement. "My father adored Emperor Joseph like a god," his daughter and biographer reported, "and shared nearly all the liberal opinions of that epoch" (von Weckbecker 1929, 39). She also harbored suspicions concerning the sudden demise of the incorruptible Ober-mayer, a man cordially detested by his colleagues, whom he often repri-manded.

The Functionary in Society

The formalism of the functionary, his unthinking attachment to rou-tine, his cult of regulations and paperwork, his servility toward his supe-riors and superciliousness toward his subordinates and the public—in short, the negative aspects of bureaucracy in all ages—began to arouse criticism, even denunciation, which became more frequent during the French Revolution and in the Napoleonic era. Jacques Peuchet was one person who vigorously protested (in 1789) the arrogance and corruption of the *commis* and complained of the "tone of mystery and intrigue that reigns in the affairs most essential for the well-being and the tranquility of the citizenry" (Thuillier 1987, 53ff.).

There was another side of the question, however: a contemporary, Pietro Verri, commented in a "Dialogo fra l'imperatore Giuseppe II ed un filosofo" on the "ministerial despotism" instituted by Joseph II:

> It is true that the ministers are disheartened and that their office has become precarious and uncertain; that all of them, when they receive their stipends, tremble at the thought that it might be for the last time, and that before they express their opinions they take good care to scrutinize the physiognomy of their presiding officers in order to avoid displeasing them because they control everyone's destiny. But no one is working to make sure that the new regulations succeed, and no one takes to his innermost heart the glory and felicity of your reign; everyone works only enough to continue to receive his stipend. . . . All the cards are marked with ongoing numbers, and they are not distributed; all the proposals are written and sent to the censor's bureau. But the proposals are not sincere, nor are the shipments. Everything is servilely refashioned and no one dares proffer an ingenuous opinion, since everything depends on the unlimited despotism of your presiding officers. . . . The organization of a governmental bureau is surely a good, but it is a secondary good, the first good being the good will, the rectitude, and the enlightenment of the ministers, whose qualities surely require a nonthreatening independence of opinion. (Verri 1854, 74–75)

What comes through in this statement of a notion that Verri shared, differences aside, with the physiocrats, with Turgot, and with Tory opinion in England is an ideal counter-image of the functionary as a member of the "natural" ruling class of a country—the landowning class. That class alone held rights of citizenship, thanks to its material ties to the soil; it was the only class with a disinterested love of the homeland and sufficient education and enlightenment to take part in the country's governance. "This social level," Pietro Verri writes in his "Meditazioni sull'economia politica," which "is not obliged to think about the food supply and comforts that it already possesses, will be the seedbed from which we will have the best-educated young people to be judges, men of letters, [and] captains; young people who do not lack the means to be educated, and who need not be paid for public service the amount that must be paid to anyone who has only his stipend on which to live" (Verri 1964, 208–9).

This vision of a public administration of notables, which we have seen partially realized in the English justices of the peace and the Prussian *Landräte* and which inspired the creation of the French provincial assemblies in 1787, was destined to fade with the ancien régime in which it had taken shape, along with the Rousseauistic vision of magistrates as the immediate expression of popular sovereignty, ready at any moment, like Cincinnatus, to exchange their pens for the plow or for the sword.

It would take too long to go into the reasons for this historical defeat, which obviously were not limited to a serious undervaluation of the technical and administrative requirements implicit in such conceptions. What we need to do instead is to conclude this survey with a reminder of the positive and progressive contributions that functionaries made, by their presence and their efforts, not only to the execution of the tasks assigned to them by their superiors but also to imagining and planning reforms.

First, it is worth recalling that if in France the *philosophes* organized as a faction—*parti*—extraneous and fundamentally hostile to the apparatus of the monarchy, in the lands in which enlightened absolutism had its finest hours—the Austrian monarchy, Spain under the Bourbons, the German and Italian states—intellectuals, many of whom were in the princely employ, had a quite different destiny and made quite different choices. In Germany such intellectuals included men as different as Kant, Goethe, Herder, and Wieland; in Austria, Martini and Sonnenfels; in Italy, Verri, Beccaria, Galiani, Filangieri, and Galanti; in Spain, Campomanes, Olavide, and Jovellanos. If these men's relations with their sovereigns and the principal ministers were not always idyllic (as we have seen in the case of Pietro Verri or in the case of Goethe, who, after his ten-year experience in administrative posts, stated that anyone [except the ruler] who spends his time on administrative affairs must be a philistine, a knave, or a fool), it is just as true that at least for a while they thought they were contributing to the creation of a more civil and more just society. Historical investigation has been broadening its scope, moving from a concentration on figures famous for their literary and philosophical works to the magistrates, administrators, and technicians whose writings centered on concrete questions and were not intended for the public at large, or else to the anonymous functionaries and clerks whose preparation, activities, and preferences were the *conditio sine qua non* for the realization of reform programs.

Traditional German historiography praised the Prussian bureaucracy as the bearer of universal values and an ethical conception of the state, but after the Second World War historians turned toward the interpretation championed by Hans Rosenberg, which stresses instead the Prussian bureaucracy's defense of class interests and its successful struggle with the monarchy, between the eighteenth and the nineteenth centuries, to impose a "formal transformation of monarchical autocracy into a system of bureaucratic-aristocratic authoritarianism" (Rosenberg 1958, 173). That this interpretation—fertile as it was—was unilateral has been demonstrated by more recent studies like those of Möller, Hellmuth, and Tortarolo, who have shown the breadth of many civil servants' intellectual interests and their authentic vocation for reform. We learn, for example, that 20 percent of the authors of the articles published in the *Berlinische Monatsschrift,* the most important periodical of the Berlin Enlightenment, were public functionaries, and another 26.7 percent were professors in secondary schools or universities (Möller 1974, 252). According to one contemporary observer, 138 out of 172 men of letters who worked in Berlin, the capital city of Prussia, but were not born there, occupied public posts (Tortarolo 1989, 273). Moreover, Tortarolo (among others) has demonstrated the "strong, often bitter, will for reform common to the generation of the young functionaries" as they worked to prepare the *Allgemeines Landrecht* of 1794 (Tortarolo 1989, 217 and passim).

In the other German states, as Charles W. Ingrao states, "Over the last two decades historians have come to appreciate the bureaucracy's role as an agent for progressive change" (Ingrao 1987, 12). Helen Liebel proposed the phrase "enlightened bureaucracy" in opposition to the exclusive concentration of many historians of the past on the orientations and the directives of sovereigns presumed to be "enlightened." In Baden, the state that Liebel examines, "the bureaucrats ultimately succeeded in imposing a kind of limited monarchy on the *Markgraf,* and in this sense they won a victory that made possible the later strong emergence of liberalism in the German southwest" (Liebel 1965, 13). Liebel's interpretation undeniably reflects an "anti-tyrannical" bias, but other studies (Gerteis 1983, for example) have shown the broad diffusion of protoliberal attitudes in the ranks of the bureaucracy of the southwest German states.

In the Austrian monarchy during the last twenty years of the century, it is clear that the relaxation of censorship regulations conceded in 1781 by Joseph II contributed to the rapid development "within the Fourth Estate" (an essential part of which was the most forward-looking portion of the bureaucracy) of a movement in public opinion that "had overtaken enlightened despotism by which it had first been aroused. It was beginning to question the fundamental assumptions of aristocratic privilege, of Christianity, and of absolute monarchy itself" (Wangermann 1969, 12). Wangermann has painstakingly reconstructed the career and the ideas of one typical representative of that movement, Gottfried van Swieten, the son of a famous physician and advisor to Maria Theresa, Gerard van Swieten. Thanks to the protection of Chancellor Kaunitz, Gottfried van Swieten, a deist in religion and a constitutionalist in politics, was named president of the Commission for Education and Censorship. In a number of instances he succeeded, with the aid of his colleagues, in getting measures passed that were much more "liberal" than the emperor would have liked, for example, regarding the number and nature of university courses, which Joseph II thought ought to "serve exclusively for the formation of state functionaries" (Wangermann 1978, 23ff.).

We would never reach the end of the available examples if we were to extend them, as we should, to the Italian and Iberian states, to Russia, and to the Scandinavian countries, but also to the European territories least touched by enlightened absolutism, France and England first among them. The parabola that Waltraud Heindl has so efficaciously described in a recent study on Austrian bureaucracy from the 1780s to 1848—the trajectory of a force that until it reached its highest point in and after the French Revolution was dynamic and progressive and only later became a source of political and social immobilism—can stand, mutatis mutandis, for a large part of the Old Continent. The customary coupling of a bureaucratic mentality and a misoneistic and conservative attitude is no longer acceptable for the age of the Enlightenment, an epoch of transition from the "official" of the ancien régime to the modern functionary.

Notes

1. Church himself (1981, 72) seems to suggest a figure of the sort when he evaluates later figures for the bureaucracy at 250,000, or "five times the total size of the effective non-venal administration in 1788."

2. The figure for 1766 is taken from Litchfield (1986, 124), where the ratio is inexplicably given as 1: 470.

Bibliography

Ago, Renata. *Carriere e clientele nella Roma barocca.* Rome and Bari: Laterza, 1990.

Ajello, Raffaele. "Il modello napoletano nella storia del pubblico funzionario." In *Profili storici: La tradizione italiana,* 329–79. Pt. 1 of *Il pubblico funzionario: Modelli storici e comparativi.* Vol. 4 of *L'educazione giuridica.* Perugia: Libreria universitaria, 1975–.

Antoine, Michel. *Le Conseil du roi sous le règne de Louis XV.* Geneva: Droz, 1970.

———. *Le gouvernement et l'administration sous Louis XV: Dictionnaire biographique.* Paris: CNRS, 1978.

———. *Louis XV.* Paris: Fayard, 1989.

Aylmer, Gerlad Edward. *The State's Servants: The Civil Service of the English Republic, 1649–1660.* London and Boston: Routledge and Kegan Paul, 1973.

———. "From Office-Holding to Civil Service: The Genesis of Modern Bureaucracy." *Transactions of the Royal Historical Society,* 5th ser., 30 (1980): 91–108.

Azimi, Vida. *Un modèle administratif de l'Ancien Régime: Les commis de la Ferme générale et de la Régie générale des aides.* Paris: CNRS, 1987.

Balani, Donatella. "Ricerche per una storia della burocrazia piemontese nel Settecento." In *Profili storici: La tradizione italiana,* 592–639. Pt. 1 of *Il pubblico funzionario: Modelli storici e comparativi.* Vol. 4 of *L'educazione giuridica.* Perugia: Libreria universitaria, 1975–.

Baugh, Daniel A. *British Naval Administration in the Age of Walpole.* Princeton: Princeton University Press, 1965.

Die Behördenorganisation und die allgemeine Staatsverwaltung Preussens im 18. Jahrhundert. Vol. 3 of *Acta Borussica,* edited by Gustav von Schmoller, D. Krauske, and V. Loewe. Berlin: Verlag von Paul Parey, 1901.

Behrens, C. B. A. *Society, Government and the Enlightenment: The Experiences of Eighteenth-Century France and Prussia.* London: Thames and Hudson; New York: Harper & Row, 1985.

Blanco, Luigi. *Stato e funzionari nella Francia del Settecento: Gli "ingénieurs des ponts et chaussées."* Bologna: Il Mulino, 1991.

Bosher, J. F. *French Finances, 1770–1795: From Business to Bureaucracy.* Cambridge, U.K.: Cambridge University Press, 1970.

Braudel, Fernand, and Ernest Labrousse, eds. *Histoire économique et sociale de la France.* 4 vols. in 8 pts. Paris: Presses Universitaires de France, 1970–82.

Brewer, John. *The Sinews of Power: War, Money and the English State, 1688–1796.* London: Unwin Hyman; New York: Alfred A. Knopf, 1989.

Capra, Carlo. "Il Settecento." In *Il Ducato di Milano dal 1535 al 1796,* by Domenico Sella and Carlo Capra. Turin: UTET, 1984.

———. "'Il dotto e il ricco ed il patrizio vulgo . . .': Notabili e funzionari nella Milano napoleonica." In *I cannoni al Sempione: Milano e la Grande Nation,* 37–72. Milan: CARIPLO, 1986.

Chabod, Federico. "Usi e abusi nell'amministrazione dello Stato di Milano a mezzo il Cinquecento." In *Carlo V e il suo impero,* 451–521. Turin: Einaudi, 1985.

Church, Clive H. *Revolution and Red Tape: The French Ministerial Bureaucracy, 1770–1850.* Oxford: Clarendon Press, 1981.

Correa Calderón, Evaristo. *Costumbristas españoles: Estudio preliminar y selección de textos.* Vol. 1. Madrid: Aguilar, 1950–51.

Diaz, Furio. *Francesco Maria Gianni: Dalla burocrazia alla politica sotto Pietro Leopoldo di Toscana.* Milan and Naples: Ricciardi, 1966.

Dickson, P. G. M. *Finance and Government under Maria Theresia, 1740–1780.* 2 vols. Oxford: Clarendon Press, 1987.

Domínguez Ortiz, Antonio. *Sociedad y Estado en el siglo XVIII español.* Barcelona, Caracas, and Mexico City: Ariel, 1981.

Doyle, William. "Was there an Aristocratic Reaction in Pre-Revolutionary France?" In *French Society and the Revolution,* edited by Douglas Johnson, 3–28. Past and Present Publications. Cambridge, U.K.: Cambridge University Press, 1976.

Fayard, Janine. *Les membres du Conseil de Castille à l'époque moderne (1621–1746).* Geneva: Droz, 1979.

Fernández Albadalejo, Pedro. "Spagna." In *L'amministrazione nella storia moderna.* Vol. 2, 2309–64. Milan: Giuffrè, 1985.

Fischer, Wolfram, and Peter Lundgreen. "The Recruitment and Training of Administrative and Technical Personnel." In *The Formation of National States in Western Europe,* edited by Charles Tilley, 456–561. Princeton: Princeton University Press, 1975.

Gerteis, Klaus. *Bürgerliche Absolutismuskritik im Südwesten des Alten Reiches vor der Französischen Revolution.* Trier: Trierer Historische Forschungen Verlag, 1983.

Giesey, Ralph E. "State Building in Early Modern France: The Role of Royal Officialdom." *Journal of Modern History* 55 (1983): 191–207.

Goubert, Pierre. *Les Français et l'ancien régime.* 2 vols. Paris: Armand Colin, 1984; reprint, 1991. (References are to *L'ancien régime: La società; I poteri.* Milan: Jaca Book, 1984.)

———. "La société traditionnelle." *Histoire économique,* edited by Braudel and Labrousse. 2: 567–600.

Gresset, Maurice. *Gens de justice à Besançon: De la conquête par Louis XIV à la Révolution (1674–1789).* 2 vols. Paris: Bibliothèque Nationale, 1978.

Heindl, Waltraud. *Gehorsame Rebellen: Bürokratie und Beamte in Österreich, 1780 bis 1848.* Vienna, Cologne, Graz: Böhlau Verlag, 1991.

Hellmuth, Eckart. *Naturrechtsphilosophie und bürokratischer Werthorizont: Studien zur preussischen Geistes- und Sozialgeschichte des 18. Jahrhunderts.* Veröffentlichungen des Max-Planck-Instituts für Geschichte, 78. Göttingen: Vandenhoeck & Ruprecht, 1985.

Hintze, Otto. "Der Beamtenstand." In *Soziologie und Geschichte.* Vol. 2 of *Gesam-*

melte Abhandlungen, edited by G. Oestreich. Göttingen: Vandenhoeck & Ruprecht, 1962–67.

―――. "Il ceto dei funzionari." In *Stato e società.* Bologna: Zanichelli, 1980.

Holmes, Geoffrey S. *Augustan England: Professions, State and Society, 1680–1730.* London and Boston: Allen and Unwin, 1982.

Ingrao, Charles W. *The Hessian Mercenary State: Ideas, Institutions and Reform under Frederick II, 1760–1785.* Cambridge, U.K., and New York: Cambridge University Press, 1987.

―――. "The Smaller German States." In *Enlightened Absolutism: Reform and Reformers in Later Eighteenth-Century Europe,* edited by H. M. Scott, 221–43. London: Macmillan; Ann Arbor: University of Michigan Press, 1990.

Johnson, Hubert C. *Frederick the Great and His Officials.* New Haven and London: Yale University Press, 1975.

Kamenka, Eugene. *Bureaucracy.* Oxford and Cambridge, Mass.: Blackwell, 1989.

Kreudener, Jürgen von. *Die Rolle des Hofes in Absolutismus.* Stuttgart: G. Fischer, 1973.

Lampe, Joachim. *Aristokratie, Hofadel und Staatspatriziat in Kurhannover: Die Lebenskreise der Höheren Beamten an der kurhannoverschen Zentral- und Hofbehörden, 1714–1760.* Göttingen: Vandenhoeck & Ruprecht, 1963.

Landau, Norma. *The Justices of the Peace, 1679–1760.* Berkeley, Los Angeles, and London: University of California Press, 1984.

Légendre, Pierre. *Histoire de l'administration de 1750 à nos jours.* Paris: Presses Universitaires de France, 1968.

Liebel, Helen P. "Enlightened Bureaucracy versus Enlightened Despotism in Baden, 1750–1792." *Transactions of the American Philosophical Society,* n.s., 55, 5 (1965): 1–132.

Litchfield, R. Burr. *Emergence of a Bureaucracy: The Florentine Patricians, 1530–1790.* Princeton: Princeton University Press, 1986.

Lucas, Colin, "Nobles, Bourgeois and the Origins of the French Revolution." In *French Society and the Revolution,* edited by Douglas Johnson, 88–131. Past and Present Publications. Cambridge, U.K.: Cambridge University Press, 1976.

Lynch, John. *Bourbon Spain 1700–1808.* Oxford and Cambridge, Mass: Blackwell, 1989.

Magris, Claudio. *Il mito absburgico nella letteratura austriaca moderna.* Turin: Einaudi, 1976.

Mantelli, Roberto. *Il pubblico impiego nell'economia del Regno di Napoli: Retribuzioni, reclutamento e ricambio sociale nell'epoca spagnuola (secc. XVI–XVII).* Naples: Istituto italiano per gli studi filosofici, 1986.

McClelland, Charles E. *State, Society and University in Germany, 1700–1914.* Cambridge, U.K., and New York: Cambridge University Press, 1980.

Meehan-Waters, Brenda. "Social and Career Characteristics of the Administrative Elite." In *Russian Officialdom: The Bureaucratization of Russian Society from the Seventeenth to the Twentieth Century,* edited by Walter McKenzie Pintner and Don Karl Rowney. Chapel Hill: University of North Carolina Press, 1980.

Mercier, Louis Sébastien. *Tableau de Paris.* Nouvelle édition corrigée et augmentée. 8 vols. Amsterdam, 1782–83.

Möller, Horst. *Aufklärung in Preussen: Der Verleger, Publizist und Geschichtsschreiber Friedrich Nicolai.* Berlin: Colloquium Verlag, 1974.

Molas Ribalta, Pedro. "La chancilleria de Valladolid en el siglo XVIII: Apunte sociológico." In *Historia social de la Administración española: Estudios sobre los siglos XVII y XVIII,* 87–116. Barcelona: Consejo Superior de Investigaciones Científicas, 1980.

Mosser, Françoise. *Les intendants des finances au XVIIIᵉ siècle: Les Lefèvre d'Ormesson et le Département des impositions, 1715–1777.* Mémoires et documents publiés par la Société de l'École des Chartes, 23. Geneva: Droz, 1978.

Mousnier, Roland. *Les institutions de la France sous la monarchie absolue.* 2 vols. Paris: Presses Universitaires de France, 1974–80. New ed., Paris: Presses Universitaires de France, 1990—. Available in English as *The Institutions of France under the Absolute Monarchy, 1598–1789: Society and the State.* Translated by Arthur Goldhammer. 2 vols. Chicago: University of Chicago Press, 1984.

Mozzarelli, Cesare. *Per la storia del pubblico impiego nello stato moderno: Il caso della Lombardia austriaca.* Milan: Giuffrè, 1972.

———. "Il modello del pubblico funzionario nella Lombardia austriaca." In *L'età moderna,* 439–59. Pt. 2 of *Il pubblico funzionario: Modelli storici e comparativi.* Vol. 4 of *L'educazione giuridica.* Perugia: Libreria universitaria, 1975–.

Necker, Jacques. *De l'administration des finances de la France.* 2 vols. Paris, 1784.

Pietro Leopoldo of Habsburg-Lorraine. *Relazioni sul governo della Toscana.* Edited by Arnaldo Salvestrini. 3 vols. Florence: Olschki, 1969–74.

Pilbeam, Pamela M. *The Middle Classes in Europe, 1789–1914: France, Germany, Italy and Russia.* London: Macmillan; Chicago: Lyceum Books, 1990.

Pintner, Walter McKenzie. "The Evolution of Civil Officialdom." In *Russian Officialdom: The Bureaucratization of Russian Society from the Seventeenth to the Twentieth Century,* edited by Walter McKenzie Pintner and Don Karl Rowney, 190–226. Chapel Hill: University of North Carolina Press, 1980.

Pugliese, Salvatore. "Condizioni economiche e finanziarie della Lombardia nella prima metà del secolo XVIII." *Miscellanea di Storia Italiana* 52 (1924).

Raeff, Marc. *Origins of the Russian Intelligentsia: The Eighteenth-Century Nobility.* New York: Harcourt, Brace and World, 1966.

Rao, Anna Maria. *Il Regno di Napoli nel Settecento.* Naples: Guida, 1983.

Richter, Joseph. *Herr Kaspar: Ein Roman wider die Hypochondrie.* Vienna, 1787.

Ricuperati, Giorgio. "Gli strumenti dell'assolutismo sabaudo: Segreterie di stato e Consiglio delle finanze nel XVIII secolo." *Rivista storica italiana* 102 (1900): 796–863.

Roberts, Michael. *The Age of Liberty: Sweden, 1719–1722*. Cambridge, U.K.: Cambridge University Press, 1986.

Rosenberg, Hans. *Bureaucracy, Aristocracy and Autocracy: The Prussian Experience, 1660–1815*. Cambridge, Mass.: Harvard University Press, 1958; Boston: Beacon Press, 1966.

Roseveare, Henry. *The Treasury: The Evolution of a British Institution*. London: Penguin Press; New York: Columbia University Press, 1969.

Schieder, Theodor. *Friedrich der Grosse: Ein Köningtum der Widersprüche*. Frankfurt am Main: Propyläen, 1983. (References are to *Federico il Grande*. Turin: Einaudi, 1989.)

Scott, Hamish M. "Conclusion: The Continuity of Aristocratic Power." In *The European Nobilities in the Seventeenth and Eighteenth Centuries*, edited by Hamish M. Scott. 2 vols. London and New York: Longman, 1995.

Sestan, Ernesto. "Il riformismo settecentesco in Italia: Orientamenti politici generali." *Rassegna storica toscana* 1, 2–3 (1955): 19–37.

Sonnenfels, Josef von. *Grundsätze der Polizey, Handlung und Finanzwissenschaft*. 1770–71. 8th ed., 3 vols. Vienna: Heubner und Volke, 1819–22.

Stone, Lawrence. "The Size and Composition of the Oxford Student Body, 1580–1909." In *The University and Society*, edited by Lawrence Stone. Vol. 1, 3–110. Princeton: Princeton University Press, 1975.

Thuillier, Guy. *La vie quotidienne dans les Ministères au XIXᵉ siècle*. Paris: Hachette, 1976.

———. *La bureaucratie en France aux XIXᵉ et XXᵉ siècles*. Paris: Economica, 1987.

Tomás y Valiente, Francisco. *Gobierno e instituciones en la España del Antiguo Régimen*. Madrid: Alianza Editorial, 1982.

Torrance, John. "Social Class and Bureaucratic Innovation: The Commissioners for Examining the Public Accounts, 1780–1787." *Past and Present* 78 (1978): 56–81.

Tortarolo, Edoardo. *La ragione sulla Sprea: Coscienza storica e cultura politica nell'illuminismo berlinese*. Bologna: Il Mulino, 1989.

Van Klaveren, Jakob. "Die historische Erscheinung der Korruption, in ihrem Zusammenhang mit der Staats- und Gesellschaftsstruktur betrachtet." *Vierteljahrschrift für Sozial- und Wirschaftsgeschichte* 44 (1957): 289–324.

Vann, James Allen. *The Making of a State: Württemberg 1593–1793*. Ithaca and London: Cornell University Press, 1984.

Verri, Pietro. *Scritti vari*. Edited by Giulio Carcano. 2 vols. Florence: Le Monnier, 1854.

———. *Del piacere e del dolore ed altri scritti di filosofia ed economia*. Edited by Renzo De Felice. Biblioteca di classici italiani 16. Milan: Feltrinelli, 1964.

Walter, Friedrich, ed. *Die Zeit Josephs II. und Leopolds II. Aktenstücke*. Pt. 4 of *Von der Vereinigung der Österreicheschen und Böhmischen Kanzlei bis zur Einrichtung der Ministerialverfassung (1749–1848)*. Vol. 2 of *Die Österreichische Zentralverwaltung*. Vienna: A. Holzhausens Nachfolger, 1950.

Wangermann, Ernst. *From Joseph II to the Jacobin Trials: Government Policy and Public Opinion in the Habsburg Dominions in the Period of the French Revolution.* Oxford Historical Series, 2d ser. London: Oxford University Press, 1959.

———. *Aufklärung und Staatsbürgerliche Erziehung: Gottfried van Swieten als Reformator des österreichischen Unterrichtswesens, 1781–1791.* Österreich Archiv. Vienna: Verlag für Geschichte und Politik; Munich: Oldenbourg, 1978.

Waquet, Jean Claude. *Les Grands-Maîtres des eaux et forêts de France de 1689 à la Révolution.* Mémoires et documents publiés par la Société de l'École des Chartes, 25. Geneva: Droz, 1978.

———. *De la corruption: Morale et pouvoir à Florence aux XVIIe et XVIIIe siècles.* Paris: Fayard, 1984. Available in English as *Corruption: Ethics and Power in Florence, 1600–1770.* Translated by Linda McCall. University Park, Penn.: Pennsylvania State University Press, 1992.

Weber, Max. *Wirtschaft und Gesellschaft.* Tübingen: J. C. B. Hohr (P. Siebeck), 1922. Available in English as *Economy and Society: An Outline of Interpretive Sociology.* Translated by Ephraim Fishoff et al. Edited by Guenther Roth and Claus Wittich. 3 vols. New York: Bedminster Press, 1968. (Consulted in Italian as *Economia e società.* 2 vols. Milan: Edizioni di comunità, 1974.)

Weckbecker, Emilie von. "Der Lebenslauf des Rates in der Hof- und Staatskanzlei Johann Georg Obermayer (1733–1801)." In *Von Maria Theresia zu Franz Joseph: Zwei Lebensbilder aus dem alten Österreich,* edited by Wilhelm Weckbecker. Berlin: Verlag für Kulturpolitik, 1929.

Wehler, Hans Ulrich. *Vom Feudalismus des Alten Reiches bis zur Defensiven Modernisierung der Reformära, 1799–1815.* Vol. 1 of *Deutsche Gesellschaftsgeschichte.* Munich: Beck, 1987.

Wright, Vincent. "Francia." In *L'amministrazione nella storia moderna.* Archivio, n.s., 3. Vol. 2, 2169–242. Milan: Giuffrè, 1985.

Wunder, Bernd. *Privilegierung und Disziplinierung: Die Entstehung des Berufsbeamtentums in Bayern und Württemberg (1780–1825).* Studien zur modernen Geschichte, 21. Munich and Vienna: Oldenbourg, 1978.

———. *Geschichte der Bürokratie in Deutschland.* Frankfurt am Main: Suhrkamp, 1986.

9 / The Priest

Dominique Julia

An eighteenth-century parish priest tells us:

> It was toward the happiness of being a *curé* that his every desire
> was bent; it was to acquire the talents and the virtues necessary
> to that important ministry that he applied himself ceaselessly. "I
> know no functions on this Earth more worthy of a man," he of-
> ten said with enthusiasm, "than that of a *curé*. To instruct one's
> brothers, comfort them in their trials, console them in their
> woes; encourage their virtues, show them the true use of their
> goods, smooth out the road of life for them, ward off the hor-
> rors of the grave for them and give them sweet hope for com-
> pany as they descend into it—those are the tasks of a good *curé*."
> Such was the idea that Monsieur de Sernin had formed regard-
> ing his ministry. What felicity for the state whose ministers
> adopt such a notion of their duties! For indeed it is to the minis-
> trations of the heads of parishes that the mores and the peace of
> the people are entrusted. It is upon them alone that families'
> internal happiness depends. The laws can do little more than
> contain hardened criminals and maintain external order, but it
> is to the parish priests that internal order, whose infinite details
> escape the laws, is entrusted. . . . A good *curé*, in a word, is the
> least imperfect image of a God of peace and mercy.[1]

The theme of the *bon curé* was certainly not new in the eighteenth
century. Still, everyone from the authors of religious works to the *philosophes* showed new interest in it, emphasizing the *social* task entrusted to
the parish priest more than mystical union with Christ's sacrifice. Téo-
time, Voltaire's "good priest" and a doctor of souls, is primarily a teacher
defending public prosperity and public order, charged with maintain-

ing virtue and acceptable conduct among his flock. Jean-Jacques Rousseau's Savoyard Vicar espouses dogmas that are "truly useful" and speaks to his parishioners' hearts: "metaphysical discussions which are out of my reach and yours and which, at bottom, lead to nothing" are no more for him than "wasting in disputation of the divine essence the brief time that is given us to honor it." For him, true religion is "pleasing to God and useful to men." A good parish priest is "a minister of goodness" and a man of peace; he is the father of his parishioners, whom he leads to happiness by bringing them back, by his preaching and his counsel, to the sublime moral message of the Gospel, detached from all the superstitious encrustation that the history of churches has left on it.

The Savoyard Vicar was not the only example: one might also cite Bernardin de Saint-Pierre's village vicar or the parish of the Auxerre Arcadia described by Rétif de La Bretonne in *La vie de mon père* and *Monsieur Nicolas*. When we read these philosophical and literary models, we get the impression that clerical activities were wholly directed toward social utility and obeyed a logic of the construction of civil and political society.[2] The religious beliefs that these parish priests were supposed to foster mattered less than the results of their practical administration of parish life and the hermeneutics of their sermons: as educators, they had succeeded in *civilizing* an entire people.

This was, incidentally, the very parable that Pierre de Clorivière intended to relate in his account of the life of Father de Sernin. Monsieur de Sernin was sent to a parish situated in a forest at least seven leagues from any other inhabited place, and he had been forewarned about "the rough and ferocious character of the men he would be guiding," given that most of his parishioners were poachers who, "paying no heed to their families, spent their days and nights in the woods." With the support of the provincial *intendant,* the new *curé* succeeded in extracting his parishioners from the miserable poverty in which they lived. Guns were deposited in the rectory, then transferred to the nearest brigade of the *maréchaussée;* and tools, seeds, fertilizer, and draft animals were distributed. "Within a year, one could see a land horrible for its sterility and for the ferocious inhabitants that it contained change into a smiling, fertile place populated by hard-working, virtuous men." Monsieur de Sernin preached a simple doctrine: "To enlighten men in all things that might be useful to them in time and for eternity was, he often repeated, the only way to keep them in order and make them happy."[3] But was there any sort of historical reality behind this literary fiction that places the parish priest in the category of functionary of morality charged (along with the police) with assuring peace to villages and concord to households? Before answering that question we need to clarify the social status of the priest in the early modern age.

The Constraints of the Benefice System

The historian is naturally tempted to go back to the decrees of the Council of Trent and its dual concern to give a dogmatic response to Luther's challenge to the sacrament of ordination and to reform abuses within the Roman Catholic Church. The decree on dogma of 15 July 1563 insists on the sacrificial character of the priesthood: it states that the priesthood, instituted by Christ, had an essential mission that lay in the priest's dual powers of *consecration* and absolution (the decree deliberately makes no mention of the power to preach precisely because the reformers claimed that the ministry should be limited to preaching alone). Ordination, transmitted by a true *sacrament* (a point that Luther rejected when he affirmed that ordination rites were a purely human invention), contributed to giving the church its *hierarchical* structure, given that spiritual powers come from on high and are transmitted by Christ, not by delegation from the community. By the same token, the priest is *superior* to the lay person. The Council's decree of 17 September 1562 was derived logically from that doctrinal statement:

> There is nothing that leads others to piety and to the service of God more than the life and example of those who have dedicated themselves to the divine ministry. For since they are observed to be raised from the things of this world to a higher position, others fix their eyes upon them as upon a mirror and derive from them what they are to imitate. Wherefore, clerics, called to have the Lord for their portion, ought by all means so to regulate their life and conduct that in dress, behavior, gait, speech, and all other things nothing may appear, but what is dignified, moderated, and permeated with piety.[4]

It was not an easy matter to effect a reform of the priestly state. The task was entrusted to the bishops. The numbers of men who entered the priesthood were not determined by shifts in the theological discourse on priestly vocations alone. Equally important (perhaps even more so) were the objective conditions that defined access to ecclesiastical posts; that is, the typology and the economic hierarchy of benefices, procedures for the transmission of benefices, and the demographic evolution in the clerical group itself. From this point of view, the extreme complexity of the benefice system (about which pastors could do relatively little) contributed in large measure to retarding the implantation of the Catholic Reformation and to reducing and diversifying its impact, not only from one state to another but from one diocese to another. Benefice structures inherited from the late Middle Ages persisted and even grew throughout the early modern period. Maintaining large numbers of foundations for masses, canonries, chaplaincies, and clerical communities had at least two consequences. First, it did not encourage the emergence of a purely ministerial clergy, since care of souls was not specific to the clerical state and anyone who held a benefice could easily get a substitute who would take over the responsibilities that went along with his revenues. Next, and especially, it played the patronage game, ecclesiastical and lay, to reinforce the place of local and family strategies in clerical careers, leaving the bishops little room for any real power or control.

This means that we need to analyze the statistics on numbers of ordinations less in terms of priestly "vocation" than in function of the quantity and specific characteristics of the vacant posts. The tendency to occupy a clerical post is stronger when it is considered quasi-patrimonial. Before we move on to an interpretation of the highs and lows of the statistical curve, however, we need to look carefully at both the structure of the benefice market and the scale of revenues in individual dioceses.[5]

In Brittany, for example, an entire clerical society of chaplains had remained intact—men who were not necessarily wealthy but who nonetheless enjoyed close connections with the local nobility.[6] Similarly, a good many priestly societies—*méparts, consorces, familiarités,* communities of *filleul* priests—continued to survive in Burgundy, Franche-Comté, and Auvergne, maintaining in those areas a plethora of priests who were born in the parish in which the association was situated (their first rule of membership) and who carried on parish activities. In France that particular structure declined markedly during the eighteenth century, partly because the revenues that the priestly societies managed in common eroded in the long term; partly because the bishops gradually imposed their authority over them. In 1726, Massillon, the bishop of Clermont, acting with the backing of the Parlement de Paris, moved to oblige all future *filleul* priests in his diocese to serve as a vicar for at least three years before being received into the community of the priest's native parish, and he obliged the communities themselves to recognize the full and entire authority of the *curé*—the parish priest—who was not necessarily chosen from among their number and who was to preside at all their assemblies. The bishop was attempting to remedy the public scandal of quarrels stirred up by "idle" priests who limited "their occupations and their zeal to arguing with the parish priests, disputing the rights inherent in their post" and who saw themselves as "the masters of churches in which they are merely the subordinate and auxiliary ministers."[7]

But if in many places in France those priestly societies seemed relics of a former age (in the diocese of Clermont more than half of the communities of *filleul* priests listed in 1729–78 out of 145—were represented by the *curé* alone or by the *curé* and only one or two *filleuls*), they continued to be pillars of the ecclesiastical structures of the Italian Mezzogiorno. In the south of the Italian Peninsula, and particularly on the Adriatic face of the Apennines (Molise, Basilicata, Capitanata, the Tèrra di Bari, and the Tèrra di Otranto) such communities, known as *chiese ricettizie,* might represent between half and two-thirds of all parishes, demonstrating the firm grip of family systems on the local ecclesiastical organization.[8] Given that the jurists of the kingdom of Naples considered the *chiese ricettizie* as secular patrimonies, they were de facto private associations of priests who came from one parish and who elected one of their number to function as rector and parish priest, the bishop merely verifying that the candidate was eligible to the post. Such associations exploited holdings held in common that at times were worth considerable amounts, each member of the group managing a portion for a time. Although fewer than a third of the parishes of the kingdom of Naples (29 percent) were *chiese ricettizie,* during the first half of the nineteenth century, they represented 55 percent of the annual net revenues of all parishes, and we can reasonably estimate that in the eighteenth century they gathered 70 to 75 percent of all parish revenues. Both by their autonomy and by their wealth, associative institutions of this sort offered a constant challenge to the pastoral efforts of the bishops. As Domenico Rossi, bishop of Potenza—a diocese in which 93.4 percent of all parishes were served by *chiese ricettizie*—stated in a report *ad limina* in 1771:

> The bishop has available no benefice of free advowson with which he can reward deserving priests; from which it follows that clerics, as soon as they have become priests, having nothing to hope from their prelate, study no more and give themselves over to idleness and vices. The second harm is that the canons,

having more regard for their flesh and blood than for merit, often give preference to the least worthy persons.[9]

It would be an easy matter to find similar characteristics throughout the part of northern Spain from the Pyrenees to the Atlantic Ocean, from the Aragonese crown lands to Galicia, including Old Castile and León. There, a number of things combined both to limit the bishops' power to intervene and to maintain a continual supply of "clerics" who had little interest in priestly ordination. Village communities played an essential role in sponsoring priests; benefices were treated as private property and were reserved to the inhabitants of the parish or the region; large numbers of chaplaincies "of blood" were available only to members of the founder's lineage; there was a thick network of "capitulary" parishes whose care of souls *insolidum* belonged to the body of officiating benefice holders, men who often received the better part of their revenues from distributions "for assiduity" from common funds.[10] To cite only one example, throughout the eighteenth century in the diocese of Santiago de Compostela, ordinations to the minor orders remained more than twice as numerous as ordinations to the priesthood.[11] What persisted here was an open conception of the clerical state that left room for degrees of clericalization between the layman and the priest. The church was defined primarily by how deeply it was rooted in a given place, whose inhabitants felt that in exchange for the ecclesiastical patrimony built up by their ancestors and the tithes collected yearly that endowed the benefices, the spiritual services that corresponded to those benefices should be offered to clerics with close ties to the local kinship and sociability networks.

These few examples show to what point the figure of the priest in the eighteenth century was an integral part of varying social, economic, and cultural contexts and how fallacious it would be to attempt to reduce that figure to one model alone. At every step along the way, we need to reinsert the priest into the whole of the local or regional society, ecclesiastical and secular, analyzing the precise impact of the range of revenues from benefices, the dominant types of patronage, and the canonical procedures used to access posts. Clearly, in France the right to appeal to Rome or to the vice-legate in Avignon to obtain a desired benefice, either by *prévention*—that is, by being the first to reserve a date on the registers of the Datary when the title holder to the benefice had died—or by resignation *in favorem,* made it easier to short-circuit the right of the *collateur ordinaire* to make appointments and helped to keep within a lineage a benefice that was considered to be family patrimony, transmitted from uncle to nephew, brother to brother, or cousin to cousin.

In Spain the system of apostolic "reservations" that gave the Holy See the power to name a very large number of benefices during eight months of the year meant that the papal nuncio, who held the full powers of papal legate with spiritual authority, was flooded with similar requests from clerics who had little desire to subject themselves to the reformed regulations that the diocesan bishops—the Ordinaries—of the land were trying to impose. One might well wonder just how many parish posts were filled by an open competition that took place— precisely—during the months reserved to the Holy See in lands called "of obedience" and in the lands of the German Concordat. It has been calculated, for example, that in the ex-diocese of Toul, only 30 percent of parish posts were filled by competition between 1750 and 1789 in areas subject to that procedure, whereas the pope had six months to make appointments in the Three Bishoprics (Toul, Metz, and Verdun) and eight months in Lorraine. This means that benefice holders used the resource of resignation *in favorem* to prevent the bishop from making his own choices for those posts.[12] The canonist Durand de Maillane, an expert in the matter, even states about "resignations pure and simple" that when a benefice holder put one into the hands of his *collateur ordinaire* (advowee) or the bishop, it was "for the most part simply a sort of secret resignation *in favorem*, thanks to the advowee's compliance in following, although freely and without simony, the intention of the resigning cleric in favor of a person whom he suggests."[13] I do not recall these rules regarding the workings of the benefice system in order to deny the impact of the Catholic Reformation but rather to emphasize the limits and constraints under which it operated. If a region had a high or low density of priests, it does not signify, a priori, that it was more or less "Christian" than its neighbor (besides, by what gauge are we to measure its vitality?). It simply implies that long-term structures that had disappeared elsewhere persisted in certain places.[14]

Training Priests: The Institution of Seminaries

One of the major tasks assigned by the canons of the Council of Trent was to assure better training for the priesthood by the institution of seminaries specifically for that purpose. Canon 18, promulgated during the twenty-third session, stipulated that "all cathedral [and] metropolitan churches . . . each according to its means and the extent of its diocese" were "to provide for, to educate in religion, and to train in ecclesiastical discipline, a certain number of boys of their city and diocese . . . in a college located near the said churches or in some other suitable place." The seminarians, who must be at least twelve years old and "know how to read and write competently," were to be chosen predominantly from the sons of the poor ("those of the wealthy class" were not excluded but must "be maintained at their own expense"), and they must show proof of sufficient "character" and "inclination" to "justify the hope that they will dedicate themselves forever to the ecclesiastical ministry." The seminary was a boarding institution in which the students, who were tonsured on their entry, always wore clerical garb, but the Council also thought of it as a secondary school in which the students, divided into classes "according to their number, age, and progress in ecclesiastical discipline," would study "grammar, singing, ecclesiastical computation, and other useful arts" and would be instructed "in Sacred Scripture, ecclesiastical books, the homilies of the saints, the manner of administering the sacraments, especially those things that seem adapted to the hearing of confessions, and the rites and ceremonies." Inspired directly by the medieval model of the university college for scholarship students, here put to the service of ecclesiastical discipline, the seminary was wholly subject to the bishop's jurisdiction and was to be financed by a contribution taken from a portion of the revenues of all the benefices of the diocese, "even those of regulars, though they enjoy the right of patronage, even if exempt," and from all other ecclesiastical revenues. "Should he deem it necessary," the local bishop had the right to seek the aid of the secular arm "for the payment of this portion."[15]

It was one thing to express a desire and quite another to realize it, and defining an institutional model was not tantamount to applying it. What are we to understand about the seminary in the eighteenth century? The response varies widely from one Catholic state to another and one diocese to another. The best we can do here is to sketch out some of the prime characteristics of the sort of schooling that assured the "institution" of the priest.

The Tridentine model of the seminary was a relative failure for several important reasons. The first was financial: it proved impossible to levy any general tax on benefices, especially in a period of crisis in land revenues, and all moves to consolidate priories or abbeys were met with resistance. This means that except in the rare cases in which the bishops themselves contributed a notable part of their own resources to found a

seminary, such institutions lacked a solid financial base. With a resounding unanimity, the cathedral chapters refused to contribute to the creation of seminaries, under the pretext that they already saw to the
training of choirboys. When a bishop did on occasion manage to impose
his will, the canons of the cathedral insisted that the seminarians attend
all the offices of the choir. This was true in Cádiz, Cordova, Grenada,
Málaga, and Murcia. Second, not all bishops were fully persuaded of the
utility of the Tridentine seminaries. They preferred the predominant
model of the university college for scholarship students, and they
thought it quite adequate for the formation of their clergy. This explains
why such important dioceses as Salamanca, Seville, Toledo, and Santiago de Compostela had no seminary until the late eighteenth century
or even the nineteenth century.[16] Similarly, the council of the ecclesiastical province of Cambrai, meeting in Mons in 1586, decided to open
a "provincial" seminary in the University of Douai in which twenty scholarship students from the archdiocese would study theology, along with
twelve scholarship students from each suffragan bishopric, the money
being guaranteed (as the fathers of the Council of Trent desired) by a
tax on every benefice. Finally, in its second General Congregation of
1565, the Society of Jesus, after due deliberation, refused to take over the
seminaries proposed by the bishops (exceptional cases aside), and the
spread of the Jesuits' network of secondary schools *(collèges)* provided
formidable competition to the efforts of bishops who were obliged to
recognize that the Society's formula was successful. Thus, the "Tridentine" seminaries, given their extremely limited resources and small number of scholarships, were unable to take in more than an infinitely small
portion of the future diocesan clergy.

During the seventeenth century, several major changes considerably modified the institutional composition of the seminaries. First, a
multitude of lay congregations arose, particularly in France, in the aim
of restoring the eminent dignity of a priestly state that had been degraded by the drunkenness and debauchery of the benefice holders.
Under the guidance of their founders—Cardinal de Bérulle for the Oratory and Jean-Jacques Olier for the Compagnie de Saint-Sulpice—the
congregations developed a priestly spirituality that insisted on the mystical union of the priest to the sacrifice of Jesus Christ, "host and victim of
God," which the priest makes present in the Eucharist. Stressing the
sanctity of the priestly state, which demanded perfection and a necessary rupture with the world, these congregations took on as their mission helping the bishops in all the ecclesiastical functions that the

prelates were willing to entrust to them (missions, preaching, etc.). In particular, they strove to "institute" priests, as the proposal for the foundation of the French Oratory states, "in the use of the knowledge that schools and books do not teach, and in the purely ecclesiastical virtues, and in the way to carry out with prudence, intelligence, and efficacy the ecclesiastical functions for which each [priest] usually has no master or guide but his own capacities and experience."[17] These congregations were also voluntarily constituted outside the benefice system, because both the Order of Oblates of St. Ambrose, founded under the guidance of Carlo Borromeo, bishop of Milan, and the Congregation of Oratorians promised never to seek benefices "either directly or indirectly," even though they were permitted to accept them and, "in that manner, retire without offense to the corps [and] without confusion on the part of the world."[18] Similarly, Vincent de Paul's decision to impose simple vows, poverty among them, on the Lazarists can be attributed to a desire to keep missionary energies within an apostolic way of life. Experience had taught Vincent that his companions were strongly tempted to retire to a benefice after a few years spent in the Congregation of the Mission. This rule was enforced by the Bull *Ex Commisse Nobis* in 1655.

It should be noted that among the many priestly congregations that flourished in the seventeenth and eighteenth centuries and took on the explicit mission of improving the training of priests, the French congregations differed notably from their Spanish counterparts (for instance, the Pios Operarios founded by Francisco Ferrer in the kingdom of Aragon in the 1720s)[19] and from the Italian congregations (the Oblates of St. Ambrose or one of their branches, the missionary Oblates of Rho, founded in 1721),[20] which were usually diocesan. The Italian congregations had a strong, centralized structure under the direction of a general superior. Although subject to the bishops, who called on them for the exercise and use of ecclesiastical functions, they were nonetheless not totally dependent on the bishops for everything regarding their governance and regulation. This allowed them to unify their practices, aided by the circulation of men from house to house within the same spiritual family.

After a number of false starts, the congregations devised a formula for the training of priests, taking in candidates for orders for a stated period before each step in ordination and using a number of exercises to help these candidates internalize their priestly state—exercises that included a method for saying and repeating prayers, individual and collective "examinations," spiritual conferences, readings, and confession.

The congregations particularly stressed the observance of rules and of a rigorous schedule that enveloped each seminarian in an intimate identification with the priestly Christ from morning to night. As the bishops urged pastoral reform in their discourses, they gradually came to see a long sojourn in the seminary as an essential means for persuading their clergy to acquire the regularity of life necessary to the exercise of their ministry. Thus, the bishops moved increasingly from the simple idea of holding a "retreat" for the candidates before each step in ordination to the notion of obligatory attendance in the seminary for a period of time that varied according to place and time but tended to grow longer and have fewer interruptions in the form of returns to the secular world. Specific formulas varied enormously with human and monetary resources.

In France, where the centralization of the congregations made them more unified than elsewhere in Europe, we can see several rather different types of seminary in the early eighteenth century. A first model was the seminary for simple preparation for clerical functions. The future priest attended one of these institutions after studying theology elsewhere (generally in a *collège* or a university), and he remained in the seminary for a period of time that was set by the bishop and varied for each ordination. In the seminary he was to become imbued with the spirit and the virtues appropriate to the state to which he aspired and to be trained in the functions that awaited him: liturgy, preaching, administration of the sacraments, catechism. As Jean-François de Montillet, the archbishop of Auch, wrote in 1770 in the pastoral Instruction that accompanied a collection of the synodal statutes of the diocese, the studies that were to be pursued in this type of institution were not centered on theological questions:

> This is not their time. Those things have to be learned before coming here; [now is the time for questions] of Scripture; for the holy rules of the Church in the administration of the sacraments (especially those of penitence); for ceremonies, rubrics, ritual, and diocesan constitutions; above all, for the study of the great intellectual discipline of the saints and he who made the saints—that is, of that eminent science that teaches how to speak to God, to pray and meditate; the study of the conduct of behavior, of sentiments, of language, of the inner and outer as-

pect of a worthy priest in all the various conditions in which divine Providence may place him.[21]

During the latter half of the eighteenth century, the seminaries of Cambrai, Le Mans, and Saint-Malo were of this same type. In the archdiocese of Cambrai, aspirants to ordination were gathered in the Château de Beuvrage, near Valenciennes, where they spent from seven and a half months to a year: 83.5 percent of the seminarians were between twenty-two and twenty-six years of age on entering the institution; they had behind them three (32.7 percent) or four (49.3 percent) years of study, either at the University of Douai (62.6 percent), at the nearby University of Louvain (22.8 percent), or with the Jesuits in Mons (9 percent).[22] Future priests in the diocese of Le Mans, whose bishop required them to spend three years in theological studies, were equally divided between the diocesan *collèges* (at Le Mans in particular, but also at Domfront) and establishments outside the diocese (the philosophy seminary connected with the University of Angers; *collèges* or clerical communities in Paris), but they often attended the seminary at Le Mans between their philosophical studies and their theological training.[23] In the diocese of Saint-Malo before the expulsion of the Jesuits from France in 1762, the majority of the deacons who presented themselves to be examined for the priesthood after attending the diocesan seminary of Saint-Méen, run by the Lazarists, had studied theology either in the lay *collège* at Dinan or (more often) in the Jesuit schools that surrounded the diocese, often in Rennes but also at Vannes.[24] What we see here is a division of roles between boarding seminaries that purveyed a spiritual preparation for the clerical life and *collèges* that offered day students an intellectual program.

The same division existed in a second type of seminary, the boarding institution in which young men lived *during* the time that they studied philosophy or theology outside the seminary, either in the *collège* or the university of the city. This model was particularly well developed at the end of the seventeenth century. Several variations existed: at times the seminary was joined to what had been a *collège* but had passed into the hands of a congregation. This is what happened, for example, with all the seminaries that were taken over by the Society of Jesus after 1682, when the twelfth General Congregation, at the urging of several bishops and of Father de La Chaize, the king's confessor, agreed to give the general discretionary powers to stipulate the conditions for acceptance into these establishments. Behind this move was an interest in combating the progress (considered baneful) of Jansenism within the French clergy. At other times, a seminary was founded when the city's *collège* was given over to a congregation, which then took over both institutions. In a third variation, the professors of philosophy and theology who gave public courses might operate in total independence from the directors of the seminary. This often occurred in university cities, notably in Paris, the leading center for theological studies. Parisian seminarians went twice a day to courses in theology given either at the house of their order at the Sorbonne or at the Collège de Navarre, returning to their respective communities, which were run by the priestly congregations (Sulpicians, Lazarists, Oratorians, and priests of the Community of St. Nicolas du Chardonnet).

Still, it is clear that the seminary became more and more of a school during the eighteenth century. There were two reasons for this: first, in the dioceses with a thinner network of secondary schools, the episcopal seminaries were obliged to fill in the gap and teach philosophy and theology; second, the violence of the theological conflicts brought on by the Jansenist crisis prompted a number of bishops to bring back under their direct tutelage courses of study that congregations they suspected of heterodoxy were offering in their episcopal seat (this occurred in Angers and Nantes, where the secondary schools were run by the Oratory). The expulsion of the Jesuits in 1762 accelerated this change toward a more "total" curriculum in the seminaries because chairs of theology in the former *collèges* of the Society of Jesus were often eliminated and the teaching of theology transferred to the episcopal seminary. This occurred in Aix-en-Provence, Cahors, Carcassonne, Le Puy, Pau, and Toulouse, to cite only a few examples.

Between the seventeenth century and the eighteenth century, the scholarly demands made of candidates to the priesthood became stricter. In 1668, the general assembly of the Congregation of the Mission stated that "for the choice of the authors who are taught [in the seminaries], one must take into account the capacities of the seminarians, the time they can remain at the seminary, the availability of books, the wishes of the bishop, and many other similar circumstances. One might nevertheless, in some of our seminaries, teach authors a little more demanding than those currently in use."[25] This was a recognition that at that date the teaching of theology in the Lazarist seminaries was far from being well developed and that the better part of the students' training was directed toward an apprenticeship in spiritual exercises and the practice of ecclesiastical functions. In the eighteenth century the examinations given candidates for orders seem to have grown more and more demanding. In Limoges all the seminarians were interrogated three times a year before the dates fixed for ordinations (Christmas, Lent, and Pentecost).

Examinations were conducted by two or three of the seminary's directors and in the presence of the bishop's *grands vicaires;* they pertained to "the treatises of scholastics and of morality that they have seen and to the orders to which they aspire," which meant that the candidates had "sometimes six or seven treatises about which they must respond." It was the task of the superior to order seminarians whom he considered insufficiently prepared not to present themselves, while their spiritual director "had the responsibility of getting them to swallow the pill quietly so it could be done without noise and without fuss."[26] Certain diocesan *ordos* of the end of the century gave out yearly lists of the questions regarding dogma and morality on which the candidates would be interrogated.

Beyond these general indications, however, we need to establish a specific scale of what moved the examiners to accept or reject a candidate for orders (and for the seminary's entrance examinations, when they existed). In the diocese of Saint-Malo, for which examination registers are available, most rejections seem to have been for insufficient levels of knowledge. There was one 27-year-old subdeacon, for instance, who excused his weak responses about the Book of Genesis by his poor memory, saying that "even if he spent six years learning it, his memory would have furnished him no more." The diocesan examiners, who rejected him, responded dryly that "he would remain a subdeacon for more than twelve years if he made no better effort than that." In one counterexample, a candidate was admitted despite his weak responses with the notation that "if he stays in the country without going to a school where he can exert himself he will always be a deacon."[27] The highest number of rejections came before tonsuring or before taking minor orders, the examiners preferring not to allow the aspirant cleric to go farther "in the orders" so as to avoid admissions, as the Bible states, *ad duritiam cordis.*

The predominance of the school model is perhaps clearest in the change in the *petits séminaires*—boarding schools that took in children who were still in the "humanities" classes, hence as young as twelve years old. During the seventeenth century, opinion was still widely divided about the appropriateness of cultivating the priestly vocation in childhood. Father Charles Faure, the superior general of the canons regular of Sainte-Geneviève, saw in this custom a way to counter parents' passion for sending to the major seminaries the "dullest minds and the most ill-fashioned bodies in their families." If instead they were to send "children of such a tender age that they [the parents] have little or no knowledge of their mind and their capacities," it might be possible, "with time, having a large number, to choose the best minds; those most appropriate for the major seminaries."[28] Vincent de Paul wrote what was perhaps the most vigorous criticism of the Council of Trent's decree, which he intended to respect, however, "as coming from the Holy Spirit." He stated:

> Experience nonetheless shows that in the way it has been carried out regarding the age of seminarians it does not work either in Italy or in France, some withdrawing before time, others having no inclination for the ecclesiastical state, others withdrawing into the communities, and still others fleeing the places to which obligation ties them by their having been raised there and preferring to seek their fortunes elsewhere. There are four [seminaries] in the kingdom: at Bordeaux, at Reims, at Rouen, and, formerly, at Angers. None of those dioceses receives any good effect from them, and I fear that except for Milan and Rome, things are the same in Italy.[29]

The priestly congregations thus felt somewhat hesitant about taking over the minor seminaries: "It is neither our vocation nor our grace," Father Tronson stated in 1692, when the bishop of Autun expressed a desire to see the Compagnie de Saint-Sulpice take over the direction of a minor seminary.[30] It is true, moreover, that priestly vocations in the seventeenth century were more often cultivated within the Marian congregations and other pious associations that regularly gathered the most devout students in the urban secondary schools for repeated spiritual exercises. We should note that a number of the "little" seminaries of the age were more like elite boarding schools to which the governing classes sent sons whom they destined to a prestigious ecclesiastical career. Examples of these were seminaries at Pontlevoy, Sorèze, Juilly (in its early days), or the seminary of Saint-Vincent in Senlis. The "worldly" vocation of such schools rapidly gained the upper hand over early clerical orientation—thanks in part to the sociological makeup of their clientele—and courses on more agreeable topics won out over spiritual exercises. A similar evolution took place in northern and central Italy in the seminary-secondary schools founded by the bishops in the eighteenth century. When they received paying boarding students who belonged to the nobility or the bourgeoisie, they tended to align their teaching to that of the *seminaria nobilium,* as in Pistoia, Reggio Emilia, and Siena.[31]

Beginning in the 1680s, however, another model of the "little" seminary appeared that was promised a bright future—a model in which "poor" clerics were supported by the charity of bishops or nobles enlisted by the bishops. This movement began in Paris when a deacon from Gascony, François de Chanciergues, established a dozen communities of young students in the *collèges,* and the idea soon spread to the provinces. The purpose was to offer opportunities to study free (not the case in the major seminaries) as a way of encouraging vocations from the more modest levels of society and filling problem posts—vicarages, country parishes with modest revenues, teaching positions—that the young of the wealthy urban classes seemed disinclined to occupy.

Here the "little" seminary was a means for furnishing country areas with properly prepared priests. In exchange for their scholarship (sometimes called *titulum seminarii*), the poor clerics promised to take whatever employment was chosen for them. This meant that the seminary had the task of evaluating (as soon as possible) the vocation of the seminarians who came from craft or peasant milieus by examining their "their talents, their dispositions, and the motives that led them to enter the ecclesiastical state . . . to prevent them from entering into [that state] against the will of God when they are not right for it [and] to detach them from their place of origin and from their families, from a desire for worldly wealth, and from worldly pleasures." As Henri Arnauld, bishop of Angers, stated in the set of regulations that he promulgated in 1686 for a "society of poor schoolboys established in the city of Angers in order to form them to the ecclesiastical spirit according to the will of the Council of Trent and the designs of the great St. Charles [Borromeo]," one of the major defects in vocations arising from the poorer parts of the population was that

> the poor consult only the will of their parents, for whom they have an extreme attachment because they depend upon them for their subsistence, [and] they make it a necessity to follow blindly the instructions [their parents] give them for the reception of holy orders, which they regard only with low and inter-

ested views, as a mechanical profession useful for earning a living and for putting them at a higher rank than that of their
birth.[32]

It is hardly surprising that from that time on competition based on
scholastic excellence was one of the criteria most frequently used to admit poor students into the *petits séminaires*. Priests in country parishes
picked out the brightest students in their "rectory" schools and guided
them toward the diocesan "little" seminary, which took them in only after a thoroughgoing examination of their capacities. Not only was the
cost of board and lodging much lower than in the boarding *collèges* (frequently it was set according to the family's financial resources) but there
was often a system of progressive exemptions if the seminarian had a
good school record, thus injecting meritocracy into the heart of priestly
training. After the expulsion of the Jesuits, the French bishops favored
the formula of the *petit séminaire-collège* all the more because they attributed the decline in vocations (a genuine and fairly widespread phenomenon beginning in the mid-eighteenth century) to lower standards
of religious training in the *collèges*. The boarding school that offered
teaching in the humanities was thought to be the best way to preserve
the future servants of the church from a rising tide of philosophical attack. This was the start of a system that blossomed during the nineteenth
century.

Did the situation in France just described exist in other European countries? In the Italian Peninsula the early model for the seminary set in
place in Milan by Carlo Borromeo had an impact that made it a point of
reference for all new institutions.

The life of the seminarians in Milan began with a week of spiritual
exercises, and their daily routine included pious exercises that took
place either in the seminary chapel or in the cathedral. Inside the arch-
diocesan school the seminarians began their studies with the rudiments
of grammar, then moved on to more properly ecclesiastical subjects,
working under the supervision of "prefects" who reported to the rector
at regular intervals about the comportment of the students under their
charge. By means of a disciplinary system that left no room for individual initiative and that tended to avoid all contact with the outside world,
the school aimed at inculcating an ideal of separation from the world
that would leave a durable trace throughout the priest's ministry. At the
same time, the minute care taken in examining candidates at each step

in the ordination process was intended not only to check on the candidates' level of preparation but also to test their moral and intellectual aptitudes for the ministry. For Carlo Borromeo, individuals should be put on a hierarchical scale of five classes according to the importance of the pastoral responsibilities in the ecclesiastical posts to be filled.[33]

We need to be clear, however, about the real diffusion of the Borromean model. Although more than seventy "Tridentine" seminaries were founded between 1563 and 1570, about fifty between 1571 and the end of the sixteenth century, and another forty-five during the first half of the seventeenth century, how many of them truly conformed to the Milanese example? How many of them had a durable existence, and how many seminarians did they really train? To answer such questions we would need to know how each institution operated. It now seems that for some time they trained only a small minority of priests. Two examples will have to suffice.

At the end of the seventeenth century, when the archbishops of Naples, Innico Caracciolo and Giacomo Cantelmo Stuart, launched a stringent policy of *sacerdotalizzazione* to raise standards among their diocesan clergy, they imposed strict economic conditions (making it obligatory to hold a hereditary title on being tonsured in order to reduce false vocations), intellectual conditions (examinations before taking each order), and disciplinary conditions. In order to supervise their reform efficaciously they set up an organism, the Congregazione degli Ordinandi, which was charged with verifying the worth of the estate of candidates for examination and their intellectual qualifications, and with making sure that their behavior conformed to the required standards. When it came to ascertaining the level of the future priests' spiritual training, however, the archbishop had to rely on the cooperation of pious associations, "congregations" that met for lay or ecclesiastical spiritual exercises under the direction of instituted groups of secular priests living in community—the Jesuits primarily, but also the Pii Operai and the Oratorians. Out of 381 candidates for orders (at all levels) from the city of Naples during the period 1692–1702, 257 (or 67.4 percent) had frequented the "congregations" more or less regularly; seminarians accounted for only 62 (or 16.3 percent) of the candidates. Still, this was a clear sign of progress in the spiritual education of future priests.[34] In reality, the increase in the number of the clergy that continued throughout Italy until the mid-eighteenth century, thanks not only to familial strategies but also to the communities' increased demand for priestly services[35]—a demand that engendered hopes for a career with a benefice within the various social levels concerned and that far outstripped the demand for priests[36]—required a considerable effort on the part of the bishops for financing and construction.

In Lombardy, which Xenio Toscani has studied in depth, priestly ordinations doubled (even tripled in certain cases) between the last decade of the seventeenth century and the 1730s, and they remained at a very high level until the 1750s. In forty years the global numbers of clergy of the Lombard dioceses nearly doubled. This means that the seminaries, which, at the end of the seventeenth century, could train only 10 to 15 percent of would-be priests, fell behind in their aim of providing spiritual preparation. This explains the construction fever that seized the Lombard bishops: in Brescia, the number of places in the seminary grew from sixty to 120 in the period 1710–11, and at the time of Cardinal Querini's death in 1755 it could hold 150 boarding students; in Cremona between the end of the seventeenth century and the 1730s, the seminary's boarding capacity rose from forty to eighty places; capacity doubled as well in Lodi in the 1720s to fifty boarding seminarians. The best that the architectural boom could do, however, was to keep up with the growth in ordinations. Few dioceses (one of these was the minuscule diocese of Colma, which had only fifty parishes surrounding the episcopal seat and whose seminary prepared 60 percent of diocesan priests) could still boast of training most of its aspirant priests within the walls of its episcopal seminary. Most priests were trained by country parish priests, in the secondary schools, or by the religious orders in schools that were opened in monasteries. This explains the development (which the bishops encouraged) of congregations and groups of secular priests who provided the clergy with spiritual exercises. Many *case per esercizi spirituali al clero* were founded at the time, and they played an important auxiliary role in encouraging a more austere priestly spirituality and fostering the emergence of a new type of priest.[37] Although they were unable to continue to impose a school experience in which all candidates for the priesthood boarded in the seminary, the Lombard bishops nonetheless succeeded in improving the cultural and spiritual training of clerics considerably and, by that token, in improving ecclesiastical discipline.

Priestly "Modesty"

If I have insisted on the importance of the seminary, it is because, despite variations in the model that naturally produced widely differing degrees of inculcation of the ecclesiastical spirit, the seminaries shared one important characteristic. Their insistence on the observation of rules taught candidates for the priesthood to abstain from worldly affairs and bred in them gravity and modesty—the external aspects of an internal state that was the priest's intimate adherence to the priesthood of Jesus Christ, the perfect worshiper of God. The *Examens particuliers* of Monsieur Tronson, the director of the seminary of Saint-Sulpice (a work first published in 1690 and frequently reprinted after that date), can serve as an example for the inculcation of modesty and as an emblem for the function of a clerical style through an appropriate pedagogical system.[38]

This text perceives the world as a permanent danger against which the individual must set up a series of barriers. Not only must nonessential visits, which awaken "thoughts of the world, ideas of amusements, the souvenir of our past failings" be reduced to an absolute minimum; not only were women prohibited in this universe (the cleric must never find himself alone with "a person of different sex" and he will avoid looking at a woman, "for in order to remedy the passion of love one must not let one's gaze pause on the creatures who might touch or soften the heart"); but the cleric must constantly practice a spiritual hygiene that allows him to go about the world without seeing it. Walking through the city streets to attend theology courses given in the public schools or taking a constitutional at the institution's country house must be accompanied by pious exercises to ward off all distractions. Canon Baston, who was a student in one of the communities of the seminary of Saint-Sulpice around 1770, relates that the seminarians walked to courses at the Sorbonne in twos or threes, taking turns reciting the rosary out loud: "By means of that innocent ruse, going from the seminary to the *collège* and from the *collège* to the seminary usually took place without having seen anything. It seemed as if we had gone from one room to another. We had met no one."[39]

At every moment a seamless space separated the seminarian from the outside world. But within that enclosed space there were still natural needs that introduced profane acts. In order to exorcize temptation, getting up, meals, and going to bed were presented and must be experienced as exercises in mortification in which the cleric was harshly reminded of his sinful condition. An entire symbolic system was put into place to sacralize the simplest—but the most "dangerous"—moments of daily life. The cassock was a "robe of honor" but underclothing, the "results" and "effects" of sin, must be regarded as "the remains of the beasts and the skins of the animals lower than which our disobedience has reduced us"; its use was tolerated only when accompanied by "moaning over the loss of our innocence." Not only must "obedience," "modesty," and "religion" regulate the external aspects of going to bed, but as he undressed the cleric must enter "into a great desire to strip himself" of himself and of all things "in order to honor the nudity of Our Lord in his Passion" and "enter into that great despoliation of all the old man of which St. Paul speaks: *Expoliantes vos veterem hominem cum actibus eius* [Strip off the old man with his deeds]." The bed was a "sepulchre"; sheets were "our winding-sheets"; sleep was "the very image of death." All this was aimed at eliminating the phantasms of an errant imagination.

Going beyond that essential break with the world, Monsieur Tronson's *Examens particuliers* develops a dialectic of sight that appears in a good many other spiritual texts from the *Ejercicio de perfección* of Alfonso Rodriguez to Bérulle. The priest must not fix his eyes on a world in which he risks perdition, but he must never forget that the world is watching him. This explains the greater insistence on the priest's composed external personage. Appearance is here a form of access to the essence of the priestly Christ that the priest's entire comportment must interpret for his contemporaries. This ecclesiastical "modesty," which elicited an irresistible revulsion in a nineteenth-century observer as sensitive as Stendhal, was an attempt to inculcate a *habitus*. Although it borrowed many of the traits of the social code of Erasmian *civilitas*, clerical modesty was aimed not only at repressing all unseemly spontaneity of the body but, above all, at maintaining the priest in an equilibrium that protected him from extremes and placed him at an equal distance from negligence and affectations, sadness and laughing out loud, worldly gossip and a gloomy or disdainful silence. Through the precepts dispensed to him, the priest of the eighteenth century appears here as a sort of *neutral* being best defined as "neither/nor." He was expected to be self-effacing and to minimize the salient features of his personality; the educators of the clergy of the early modern period saw eliminating every individual trait, combined with separation from the world, as the Christ-like priest's condition of visibility. Paradoxically, this educational model reached its apogee in France only in the nineteenth century, when the post-Concordat bishops joined in support of a formula for the seminary that offered a long period of all-embracing priestly training—intellectual, spiritual, and pastoral. The innumerable new editions of Tronson's *Examens particuliers* throughout the century are further evidence of this. But wasn't this model already anachronistic in a changing world?

Sociability and Priestly Culture

Whatever gap there may have been between the model and the clerics' appropriation of it, the training provided by the seminary undoubtedly led to improved moral standards among the clergy. In the seventeenth century the reports of pastoral visits and the dossiers of the officialities, the diocesan courts, show us a universe of violent, debauched, and uncontrollable priests who gambled, hunted, drank, and kept concubines. Notations of the sort become much rarer in France of the eighteenth century. We can safely estimate at around 5 percent the proportion of diocesan secular priests implicated in deviant practices after 1720.[40] Admittedly, mid-eighteenth-century police inspectors arrested a hundred or so ecclesiastics every year "found in debauchery" with public prostitutes. Half of these were holders of large benefices, often men who were only passing through Paris, and it would be unfair to infer a general state of sacerdotal morality from flagrant instances of illicit paid sex involving dissolute clerics.[41]

Also, certain dioceses were more backward than others when it came to the reform of pastoral morality and practices. In Brittany in the diocese of Tréguier between 1700 and 1730, 147 of the 530 priests (nearly a third of the total) got drunk on a regular basis, 41 were involved in sexual debauchery, 27 committed violent acts, 11 perpetrated various dishonest acts, and 8 were absentees. That made a total of 234 clerics culpable of moral failings, without counting those who fell short of expectations on the pastoral level or who exercised their ecclesiastical functions poorly. After 1730, however, the efforts of reforming bishops of Tréguier—notably Monsignor Olivier Jegou de Kervilio, who was bishop from 1694 to 1731 and visited his diocese yearly from 1695 to 1729—began to show results. The dossiers of the officiality demonstrate that cases of priests on trial for moral questions had by then become extremely infrequent and problems of conduct were exceptional. Moreover, by that time a deviant priest would immediately meet with severe punishment.

A new type of priest had been born—better trained, more spiritually inclined, perhaps more isolated from his flock.[42] It was to this model of the "good priest," what is more, that Ernest Renan, who was born in Tréguier in 1823, paid homage when, speaking of his childhood, he evokes the "wise and good" priests who were his first spiritual preceptors, crediting them with "whatever may be good in me." He acknowledges that later on he had teachers "far more brilliant and learned," but none who "inspired such feelings of veneration." "The fact is," Renan concludes, "that, according to my experience, all the allegations against the morality of the clergy are devoid of foundation. I passed thirteen years of my life under the charge of priests, and I never saw anything approaching to a scandal; all the priests I have known have been good men."[43]

Not only was the priest a man separated from the world; he was invited at regular intervals to renew the spirit of his vocation. In some dioceses the annual retreat, which was strongly recommended, took the form of a general retreat held at the episcopal seminary at specific times of the year. There, all or some of the ecclesiastics engaged in the ministry met, under the guidance of a preacher, to meditate and pray in community for eight days. This practice, which seems to have spread throughout France as the century advanced, could only have reinforced priestly solidarity.

Another exercise brought together priests of the same district at regular intervals—once a month or once every two months—to discuss specific topics. These "ecclesiastical conferences" (also called "diaconal assemblies" or "assemblies of vicars forane") were held under the supervision of the dean (when the territorial divisions of the diocese were respected) or of a "director" who brought together in his parish ten to twenty of his colleagues from the area. These meetings generally centered on three themes: explication of Holy Scripture, a "spiritual" subject (very often the duties and virtues of ecclesiastics), and "practical" theology and morality, which amounted to analysis of cases of conscience and was an activity that tended to take up more and more time as the meeting went on.[44] The monthly or bimonthly topics were announced in advance by the episcopal curia, and the announcement was often accompanied by an imposing bibliography to guide the participants in their preparation for the conference. The "results" or "conclusions" of each conference appeared in the form of a theological dissertation addressed to the episcopal chancery, which duly noted the copies. Such gatherings provided a means of intellectual surveillance of the clergy, and they might be consulted at a later date when priests who had participated in them came up for promotion.

These "papers" corrected by the vicars general tended to generate a uniform discourse, however: after all, had not the bishop of Saint-Malo stated in 1750 that the purpose of the conferences was to procure "uniformity of doctrine and conduct" and "a love of studies"? And indeed, the bookish erudition displayed by the redactors of these dissertations punctuated with opportunely chosen citations led to a stereotyped language that had become impermeable to both the personal experience of the participants and the real lives of their parishioners. The aim of developing a jurisprudence common to all confessors produced a series of abstract "cases" all treated in the same manner. The hierarchy was not always fooled by this fine unanimity, however: as the dean of the chapter of Cambrai put it, speaking of the "diaconal assemblies" of the diocese: "After a Latin prayer, said by each parish priest in turn, they reason about what regards their parishes, and the dean tells them what the archbishop wants to have them told or reports what the parish priests have charged him to say. After the meeting, they go to dine together."[45] Once this group language had been thus codified, the function of clerical sociability seems to have predominated over strictly intellectual activity.

Jean Meslier, the *curé* of the parish of Étrepigny, in the Ardennes, was an exception to this rule, and he offers a demonstration *a contrario* of the impact of the conferences. At his death, Meslier left a particularly explosive "memoir" of his thoughts and his sentiments in which he denounced all religions—the Christian religion first and foremost—as impostures and iniquitous mysteries that kept the population in idolatry and superstition. Still, his reflections on the "uncertainty of the Gospel" and on the "so-called Holy Scriptures," which "contain no more-than-human erudition or wisdom" and his denunciation of "spiritual" and "mystical" interpretations reflect not only the questions discussed in the ecclesiastical conferences of the diocese of Reims but even the bibliography that the archiepiscopal authorities had furnished in support of those conferences. Here, the task of compilation that the ecclesiastical conference required served as a point of departure for the elaboration of a particularly heterodox line of thought.[46] There should be no need to add that Jean Meslier did not think it opportune to communicate his sentiments to his fellow priests or that he kept absolutely silent about his thoughts. He states that he was "very happy" to die "as peacefully" as he had lived, not wanting to expose himself in his lifetime, "to either the indignation of the priests or the cruelty of tyrants who, by their lights, would find no torment harsh enough to punish such alleged temerity."[47] Thus, putting in place mechanisms to control practice ended either in linguistic conformism throughout the corps or in the adoption of a double life in which an official personage masked an inner experience that he could not talk about openly.

The ecclesiastical conferences serve as evidence that the ignorance of earlier times was followed by a clerical culture drawing mainly on St. Thomas Aquinas and the fathers of the church, on contemporary commentators on Scripture, and on works of moral theology. Both the synodal statutes and the episcopal ordinances continually made additions to the list of books that were expected to be on the good priest's shelves, and the official reports of pastoral visits attest that during the eighteenth century these norms were respected. In the archdeaconry of Autun in 1729, research shows that all parish priests owned the few indispensable volumes and many priests owned many more books: nine priests owned twenty to fifty volumes, and five owned one hundred to three hundred books.[48] A more detailed analysis, this time of the probate inventories of ecclesiastics' libraries in the cities of the provinces in western France (Normandy, Maine, Anjou, Brittany), shows that a rapid change occurred during the eighteenth century. At the end of the seventeenth century, 30 percent of the priests in this sample owned fewer than ten volumes and a few had none; only 5 percent had a library of more than a hundred works. During the course of the first third of the eighteenth century, however, the priests who had received the necessary intellectual formation in the seminaries gathered sizable libraries: in 1730, libraries of more than a hundred volumes account for 45 percent of the sample, for 60 percent in 1755–60, and for 75 percent in 1790. At the latter date, nine ecclesiastics out of ten had more than fifty volumes, and one out of three owned more than a hundred books. In one century the exception had become the rule.

At the same time, however, the composition of priestly libraries had clearly changed: the Flemish and Spanish commentators on Scripture (Maldonat, Estius, Cornelius a Lapide), the *Summa theologica* of St. Thomas, and the fathers of the church had given way to more practical manuals and widely circulated works written in French—printed anthologies of reports on ecclesiastical conferences, collections of homilies, works on how to administer the sacraments, and books of moral theology, meditations, or priestly spirituality. These libraries contained very few books of secular culture, though. In the libraries of fewer than three hundred volumes, religious books accounted for between 80 and 90 percent of all books. These figures provide a good indication of the growing gap between clerical culture and the culture of the lay elites of the worlds of officeholders and the *bourgeoisie à talents,* where the number of religious works owned clearly declines, especially after 1760.[49]

Probate inventories of priests' libraries in Piedmont from the first half of the nineteenth century (which reflect the situation during the eighteenth century) show a similar configuration. Out of the fifty-seven inventories found, twenty-six (45.7 percent) concern libraries of over a hundred volumes; eleven (or 19.3 percent), collections of fifty to a hundred volumes; another eleven, those of fewer than ten volumes.[50] This means that here too the book had become part of the usual equipment of parish priests in both city and country. Once again, however, the books were for the most part religious. If we set aside four libraries that contained more than four hundred volumes and reflected broader interests, the proportion of religious works reached 84 percent of all books. Beyond the "classics"—St. Augustine's *Confessions* and *The City of God,* St. Thomas's *Summa theologica,* and the letters of St. Jerome (which were found in many libraries but represented only 5 percent of all books)—there were two principal categories in Piedmontese libraries. First, there were compendia of theology (20 percent of all works) that the priest had probably used in the seminary and brought with him to his benefice. For the most part these were treatises on moral theology, such as those of Daniel Concina and Idalfonso da Bressanvido or of French authors like Paul-Gabriel Antoine, Pierre Collet, and Louis Habert. Second, there were books of devotion, spiritual exercises, or the lives of the saints (again, 20 percent of all works). We find among the second group all the best-sellers of pious literature of the Catholic Reformation from the *Introduction à la vie dévote* of Francis of Sales to the *Esercizi di perfezione cristiana (Ejercicio de perfección)* of Alfonso Rodriguez; from the *Combattimento spirituale* of the Theatine Lorenzo Scupoli to the works of the Jesuit Paolo Segneri. The impact of a spirituality derived from Ignatius of Loyola's *Spiritual Exercises* is obvious here. Catechisms, confession manuals, and collections of homilies completed the collections and helped the pastor in his daily practice.[51]

One cannot help being struck by the professional similarity between priests' libraries in France and in Piedmont, a similarity further accentuated by three specific characteristics. First, in a region in which the French language was more widely spoken than in the rest of the Italian Peninsula, the proportion of books in these libraries printed in France reached 18.7 percent. Second, there are many translations of French spiritual authors or sacred orators (Francis of Sales, for instance, or Bourdaloue). This was also how Jansenist thought was diffused in Italy, since Italian translations of Joseph Duguet, Pierre Nicole, and the Catechism of Montpellier by the Oratorian François Pouget are present in a number of libraries. Third, even in remote and isolated areas, parish priests showed a lively interest in contemporary ecclesiastical culture. The extremely detailed notes in the reports on the general visit in 1749–51 of Leopold Ernest Firmian, coadjutant bishop of Trent, confirm the Piedmontese data. The clergy in his diocese owned works ranging from commentaries on the Old and New Testament by Father Noël Alexandre or dom Augustin Calmet to the texts of Muratori and Tartarotti.[52] In its way, the composition of clerical libraries attests that, urged on by the mechanisms of diocesan discipline, the "new" priests by and large internalized the norms inculcated in them in the seminary to prepare them for the just exercise of their functions.

An Order of Practice

But if the priests, who were charged by their social and cultural separation from the rest of society with expressing the frontier between the sacred and the profane and with maintaining an orthodox diffusion of religious representations and beliefs, became the focus of the church's distinction between itself and other social groups, they also participated in an administration of practices whose logic was no longer religious but henceforth was regulated by the criterion of social utility.[53] I shall give only a few examples here, taken from different levels.

Country priests, who by now were more cultivated, might help the *intendant* of the province in his task of making an inventory of agricultural products (as happened in Franche-Comté in 1774), or they might aid in the systematic count of baptisms, marriages, and deaths requested, through the offices of the *intendant,* by Abbé Expilly for his *Dictionnaire des Gaules.* If the country priests continued to walk through the fields of the parish, performing blessings and leading processions during Rogation Days to ask "protection for the goods of the earth" as their flocks demanded, they themselves were no longer satisfied with cultivating the rectory's kitchen garden, developing instead agricultural experiments to improve cereal yields and livestock quality. By rational exploitation of the lands of their own benefices "they enlightened the farmers of their parishes . . . the most serious [of whom] followed their example."[54] In 1774, the rectors of the Breton diocese of Saint-Pol-de-Léon, responding to an investigation concerning beggars that was transmitted to them by their bishop, Jean-François de la Marche, who was reacting in his turn to the solicitations of Turgot, the *contrôleur général des finances,* expressed their hostility toward the medieval system of alms. In the eyes of the parish priests, the most customary causes of beggary were "idleness," a "repugnance toward work, especially hard work," and a fondness for "taking to the roads." Although the priests recognized that poverty had economic causes—the high price of wheat, divided inheritances that made for farms too small to exploit profitably—and a demographic cause—large families—they put their hopes in a police force that would pursue "foreign" beggars in the parish (perhaps the troops could arrest them, even send them to the colonies?) and in putting the poor to work, even from childhood, either in the general hospitals of the province or in parish hospitals managed by the rector.[55] One parish priest even went so far as to suggest "withholding marriage from all those whom one can predict will not be able to support its temporal responsibilities." He adds, "I have always regarded the marriage of beggars with a certain repugnance, and when I examine the results of those marriages, it seems to me that the state loses in them and religion does not gain anything."[56] Here, the priest was an agent of public order who participated fully in the rationality and the utilitarianism of the Enlightenment, both of which were aimed at furthering productivity.

It is hardly surprising that parish priests in the early nineteenth century were among those who worked for the diffusion of a vaccine to combat smallpox, epidemic in France, the Low Countries, and the French territories on the Italian Peninsula.[57] In order to persuade their flocks, some parish priests had themselves vaccinated; others led their parishioners to the vaccinator or organized free vaccinations in the rectory. They saw this as a true state duty since priests, being "ministers of a God of truth," were honor-bound to destroy popular error concerning the "humors" inoculated. In 1805, one *curé* in the *département* of the Ourthe reported to the secretary of the *préfecture* about the first vaccination session held in his village. He states:

> That day, Monsieur! when the antidote to smallpox was welcomed with enthusiasm and received with joy by the parishioners, was, it seems to me, the day of triumph of that admirable victor over the most dreadful and the most murderous of illnesses, and the hope of Monsieur le Préfet will not have been vain. Light has finally pierced our cottages and the shadows of prejudice have been dissipated.[58]

Still, his flock could put up a lively resistance to the parish priest's control over liturgy and religious practices. One example of this was the custom of ringing the church bells during thunderstorms, a practice that the population demanded and judged "benign." Eighteenth-century parish priests grew increasingly hostile to practicing the exorcisms that ritual demanded on that occasion. If they requested that this liturgical ceremony be suppressed it was because they were perfectly aware of the misunderstanding that it set up: the people expected that exorcism would have an immediate effect; success or failure depended on the operator's power (that is, the priest's power), and any refusal to perform such operations was greeted with death threats. Failure could turn the community against its priest, who lost all prestige: he was no "hail chaser."

When some eighteenth-century parish priests were confronted by the magical signification attributed to ceremonial canons that made them a sort of shaman, they argued the power of reason and knowledge and called their parishioners "ignorant," "superstitious," "fanatical," and riddled with "prejudices."[59] In his response to an inquiry sent him by his bishop in 1783, one parish priest in the diocese of Tarbes explained how he had cleverly tried to introduce Benjamin Franklin's discovery to his village:

> During thunderstorms, one rings the bells. The belltower and the bell-ringers have been struck by lightning twice in less than fifty years. We ourselves would be struck down by the inhabitants if we attempted to impede this bell-ringing. I would like to inspire in them greater confidence in an electrical lightning rod that I am having put up on our very high belltower, but in order to have it seem to them endowed with some virtue, it has to be consecrated by some sort of blessing (something in which the physicists have so far shown insufficient signs of interest). What is more, we still continue to do the exorcisms and the prayers, missal in hand: in this way, we have thus far been personally guaranteed against lightning.[60]

This "enlightened" parish priest, who evidently considered technology more operative, relegated benediction to the storeroom of useless accessories. In the broad movement that aimed at eliminating the "indecencies" that were soiling worship and at modeling the comportment of parishioners, it is not surprising to note that cultural criteria played an extremely important role in the parish priests' moral evaluations of their flocks. When the parish priests of the dioceses of Reims (in 1774) and Tarbes (in 1783) were invited by their respective bishops to define "the predominant characteristic of the parishioners, their good qualities, their vices, and their most common faults," the responses they gave contained two major points striking to anyone who reads them today.[61]

For one thing, the grid by which the pastors read the problem was evidently directly borrowed from the categories found in the treatises on morality that they absorbed in the seminary. That reading matter offered a systematic catalog of vices listing, in descending order of gravity, drunkenness and frequentation of the taverns (a veritable and omnipresent obsession that was also a power struggle within the community, the tavern-keeper being to some extent the "anti-*curé*" who acted as the focal point for a sociability directly competing with the church), financial interest, gossip, calumny, lawsuits and quarrels, violence, slyness or bad faith, youthful libertine habits, and oaths and blasphemies. The responding priests grouped the "vices" in their answers in ways that even more strikingly bear the mark of the confession manual. Good qualities are much less frequently mentioned: in the eyes of their parish priests, the parishioners were basically "hard-working," "charitable" and "almsgiving," "pious" or endowed with "religion." Equally striking, however, is the eminently civil character of the responses, which insist on cultural traits typically found in relations between a pastor and his flock, such as the subservience of the faithful. On the positive side, the parishioners are called "gentle," "polite," "honest," "affable," "sociable," "manageable," "docile," and "submissive," although here and there a priest wonders how sincere that behavior might be: "They make a show of much submission and respect toward their pastor, especially when he speaks to them." On the other hand, the parishioners are often called "haughty," "proud," "hard," "intractable," "independent," "republican," "having brusque and free manners," "rude," "savage, as is typical in hamlets," "unsociable because they are continually wandering, following their flocks in the mountains," and "naturally fierce." The shepherds and peasants of the Pyrenees had obviously not acquired the code of manners of Erasmian civility. Worse, they had "no education" and were "without any taste for instruction." Under such conditions the parish priest's first priority was to work for *éducation* and *civilisation*. The *curé* of Beaudean, in the diocese of Tarbes, was engaged in a struggle against the "feudal despotism" of the local lord who had always opposed the installation of a school (which the pastor managed to start anyway). The priest explains:

> When I arrived, the inhabitants of Beaudean were, and still are
> in part, in a state that I would find it difficult to describe because

the degradation of extreme servitude is not a characteristic but
a brutalization. I am obliged by my state to give these unhappy
people some notions of morality. I was forced to begin by teaching these unfortunates that they were men and were living in
society; that they were called to all the advantages procured by
civilization. . . . I have made little progress because I have been
continually occupied by the oppressive hand that held my parishioners in irons. Still, as well as I have been able to see into
these souls degraded and shrunken by a long and harsh slavery,
I believe my parishioners capable of much good. Their hearts
are good, and basically they have intelligence; religious and incapable of malice, they will long lack all the virtues that demand
courage and energy.[62]

Thus, the life of Monsieur de Sernin was not fictional. As an educator
and a "civilizer," the priest participated in a movement that took the social ethic for its frame of reference in practice. What the change in the
portrait of the eighteenth-century priest attests to—in its own way—is
the re-use of religious structures in the service of an order that they no
longer determined and that gradually introduced its own criteria into
those structures.

At the end of the century, when Austrian Josephism defined the
priest as *curé*, state functionary, and an agricultural expert capable of
advising his parishioners about the technical aspects of land management, this movement simply carried a common experience to its extreme. Historians have perhaps insisted too much on the conflict
between Joseph II and the papacy (a conflict that really had more to do
with the suppression of the religious orders). If one thing is evident in
the eighteenth century, it is the papacy's recognition of the preeminence of the modern state, as witnessed by Benedict XIV's policy of
working for concordats with the Two Sicilies (1741), Spain (1753), and
Lombardy (1757). By accepting the state's taxation of ecclesiastical
holdings and the abandonment of the anachronistic privileges of the
Roman Curia to grant benefices, the pope was betting on a religious
reform aimed at correcting the misdeeds of a surplus of idle and uncontrollable clerics and carried out under the tutelage of the states. Nonetheless, the order that came to be defined at that time was no longer the
order defined by the Council of Trent but rather that of the national
sovereignty of the absolutist monarchies of the early modern age, in

whose service religious beliefs and institutions now functioned, whether or not those charged with making them function were aware that a change had occurred.

Both the administration of religious rites and religious symbols became more and more fixed, frozen in an operation of social control that made the faithful the *object* of policy. Although the parish priests of Saint-Pol-de-Léon, discussed above, thought that a hospital-workhouse, backed up by efficacious police pressure from the *maréchaussée,* could provide an answer to the social scourge of beggary, they never speak of the beggars as *subjects.* Unique for its style is the response of the *curé* of the island of Molène, who displays his identification with his people by using the pronoun "we." Writing to his bishop, Jean-François de la Marche, he begs him:

> Have pity on your poor people, who cry out and moan in miserable poverty. I am quite persuaded that there is no place in your diocese as unprovided with foodstuffs as this. They come to my house unable to carry on, weeping and saying that they are dying of hunger, as are their children. More than once I have given them the bread that was on my table without having any other. But the misfortunes of the people also make the poverty of the priest. I have had for all the tithing only fifty *boisseaux* of barley, Brest measure, which will soon be gone. What will these unhappy people do until the end of the year? We have no one to whom we can turn and who takes an interest in us except only you, Monsignor.[63]

Notes

1. [Pierre Picot de Clorivière], *Le modèle des pasteurs ou précis de la vie de M. de Sernin, curé d'un village dans le diocèse de T**** (Paris, 1779), 11–12.

2. On the theme of the good parish priest, see Pierre Sage, *Le "Bon prêtre" dans la littérature française d'Amadis de Gaule au Génie du Christianisme* (Geneva and Lille: Droz, 1951).

3. [Picot de Clorivière], *Le modèle des pasteurs,* 25–2645, 52.

4. Quoted from *Canons and Decrees of the Council of Trent,* trans. H. J. Schroeder (St. Louis and London: Herder, 1941), 152. See also *Les Conciles oecuméniques,* vol. 2, pt. 2 of *Les Décrets: de Trente à Vatican II, texte original et édition française,* gen. ed. Giuseppe Alberigo (Paris: Éditions du Cerf, 1994), 1498–99 (session XXII, 17 September 1562, Reform decree, Canon 1).

5. On this question, see Dominique Julia, "Système bénéficial et carrières

ecclésiastiques dans la France d'Ancien Régime," in *Historiens et sociologues au-jourd'hui: Journées d'études annuelles de la Société Française de Sociologie,* Université de Lille I, 14–15 June 1984 (Paris: CNRS, 1986), 79–107.

6. See Charles Berthelot du Chesnay, *Les prêtres séculiers en Haute-Bretagne au XVIIIᵉ siècle* (Rennes: Presses Universitaires de Rennes II, 1984).

7. See L. Welter, "Les communautés de prêtres dans le diocèse de Clermont au XVIIᵉ et XVIIIᵉ siècle," *Revue d'Histoire de l'Église de France* 35 (1949): 5–35.

8. There have been several recent works on the *chiese ricettizie.* Some of the more important studies are the following: Gabriele De Rosa, "Pertinenze ecclesiastiche e santità nella storia sociale e religiosa della Basilicata del XVIII al XIX secolo," and Augusto Placanica, "Chiesa e società nel Settecento meridionale: Vecchio e nuovo clero nel quadro della legislazione riformatrice," *Ricerche di storia sociale e religiosa* 7–8 (1975): 7–68, 121–89, respectively; Mario Rosa, *Religione e società nel Mezzogiorno tra Cinque e Seicento* (Bari: De Donato, 1976); Vincenzo De Vitiis, "Chiese ricettizie e organizzazione ecclesiastica nel Regno delle Due Sicilie dal Concordato del 1818 all'Unità," in *Per la storia sociale e religiosa del Mezzogiorno d'Italia,* ed. Giuseppe Galasso and Carla Russo, 2 vols. (Naples, Guida, 1980–82), 2: 349–473.

9. Quoted in De Rosa, "Pertinenze ecclesiastiche," 26.

10. See Christian Hermann, *L'Église d'Espagne sous le patronage royal (1476–1834): Essai d'ecclésiologie politique* (Madrid: Casa de Velázquez, 1988), 23, 260–61. In the diocese of Naples during the third quarter of the seventeenth century, 40 percent of tonsured clerics were between seven and fourteen years of age. In this case access to the clerical state does not reflect a carefully deliberated choice of the priesthood on the part of the candidate but only the family's desire to possess a benefice. Furthermore, 59 percent of tonsured clerics from the city of Naples failed to go farther than minor orders (unlike the tonsured clerics from rural areas, two-thirds of whom became subdeacons). See Giacomo Garzya, "Reclutamento e mobilità sociale del clero secolare napoletano fra il 1650 e il 1675," in *Per la storia sociale e religiosa del Mezzogiorno d'Italia,* ed. Giuseppe Galasso and Carla Russo, 2 vols. (Naples, Guida, 1980–82), 1: 241–306.

11. See Baudilio Barreiro Malon, "El clero de la diócesis de Santiago: Estructura y comportamientos (siglos XVI–XIX)," *Compostellanum* 23 (1988): 469–508.

12. See Jean-Marie Ory, "La carrière ecclésiastique dans le diocèse de Toul, 1750–1790," *Annales de l'Est,* 5th ser., 36 (1984): 18–49.

13. Pierre Toussaint Durand de Maillane, *Dictionnaire de droit canonique et de pratique bénéficiale,* 3d ed., 5 vols. (Lyon, 1776), 2: 276.

14. On the impact of family strategies on the prodigious increase in the number of clerics during the seventeenth century, in particular in the Mediterranean area, see Pietro Stella, "Strategie familiari e celibato sacro in Italia tra '600 e '700," *Salesianum* 41 (1979): 73–109.

15. *Canons and Decrees of the Council of Trent,* 175–77.

16. See Francisco Martín Hernández, *1563–1700*, vol. 1 of *Los seminarios españoles: Historia y pedagogía* (Salamanca: Ediciones Sígueme, 1964–); Francisco Martín Hernández and José Martín Hernández, *Los seminarios españoles en la epoca de la Ilustración: Ensayo de una pedagogía eclesiástica en el siglo XVIII* (Madrid: Consejo Superior de Investigaciones Científicas, 1973); *Canons and Decrees of the Council of Trent*, 171–77.

17. "Projet de l'érection de la congrégation de l'Oratoire de Jésus," (1610), in *Correspondance du Cardinal Pierre de Bérulle*, ed. Jean Dagens, Bibliothèque de la Revue d'Histoire Ecclésiastique, 17–19, 3 vols. (Paris: Desclée de Brouwer; Louvain: Bureaux de la Revue, 1937), 1: 119.

18. Ibid., 1: 118.

19. See Martín Hernández and Martín Hernández, *Los seminarios españoles en la epoca de la Ilustración*, 56–83.

20. On the missionary Oblates of Rho, see Xenio Toscani, "La letteratura del buon prete di Lombardia nella prima metà del Settecento," *Archivio Storico Lombardo* 102 (1976): 158–95.

21. *Recueil des statuts synodaux du diocèse d'Auch: Instruction pastorale de Monseigneur l'archevêque d'Auch sur l'état sacerdotal* (Toulouse, 1770), 42. The document specifies that candidates must attend the seminary for one year in all, divided into four stays of three months before each ordination. Candidates also had to demonstrate that they had completed three years of theological studies.

22. Gilles Deregnaucourt, *De Fénelon à la Révolution: Le clergé paroissial dans l'archevêché de Cambrai* (Lille: Presses Universitaires de Lille, 1991), 173–81, 204.

23. Alex Poyer, "Devenir curé dans le diocèse du Mans au XVIIIe siècle" (thèse de doctorat de troisième cycle, Université de Rennes II, 1986), 65.

24. Berthelot du Chesnay, *Les prêtres séculiers*, 145.

25. "Avis et résolutions de l'Assemblée générale tenue en l'année 1668 touchant les séminaires," in *Recueil des principales circulaires des supérieurs généraux de la Congrégation de la Mission*, 3 vols. (Paris: Procure Général de la Congrégation de la Mission, 1877), 1: 90.

26. Louis Tronson, *Correspondance de M. Louis Tronson*, 3 vols. (Paris: V. Lecoffre, 1904), 1: 416 (Thomas Bourget, director of the seminary in Limoges, to M. Tronson, director of the seminary of Saint-Sulpice in Paris, 8 April 1695).

27. Berthelot du Chesnay, *Les prêtres séculiers*, 147.

28. See Père du Molinet, "Histoire des chanoines réguliers de la Congrégation de France de l'an 1630 jusqu'en l'an 1640," Bibliothèque Sainte-Geneviève, MS no. 612, fol. 273.

29. Vincent de Paul to Bernard Codoing, superior of the house of the Mission in Rome, 13 May 1644, in St. Vincent de Paul, *Correspondance* vol. 1, pt. 2 of *Correspondance, Entretiens, Documents . . .* , ed. Pierre Coste, 3 vols. in 15 pts. (Paris: Gabalda, 1920–), 408–11.

30. Tronson, *Correspondance*, 1: 162 (letter to Monsieur Le Vayer de Pressac, 14 December 1692).

31. See Carlo Fantappiè, "Istituzioni ecclesiastiche e istruzione secondaria nell'Italia moderna: I seminari-collegi vescovili," *Annali dell'Istituto Storico italogermanico in Trento* 15 (1989): 189–240.

32. The rule, written by Joseph Grandet, was published in Georges Letourneau, *Mémoires de Joseph Grandet . . . Histoire du séminaire d'Angers, depuis sa fondation en 1659 jusqu'à son union avec Saint-Sulpice en 1695,* 2 vols. (Angers: Germain et G. Grassin, 1893), 2: 487–503.

33. On the Borromean model of the seminary, see Maurilio Guasco, "La formazione del clero: I seminari," in *La Chiesa e il potere politico dal Medioevo all'età contemporanea,* ed. Giorgio Chittolini and Giovanni Miccoli, vol. 9 of *Storia d'Italia, Annali,* ed. Ruggiero Romano and Corrado Vivanti, 9 vols. (Turin: Einaudi, 1978–86), 649–58.

34. See Giacomo Garzya, "Reclutamento e sacerdotalizzazione del clero secolare della diocesi di Napoli: Dinamica di una nuova politica pastorale nella seconda metà del Seicento," in *Per la storia sociale e religiosa del Mezzogiorno d'Italia,* ed. Giuseppe Galasso and Carla Russo, 2 vols. (Naples, Guida, 1980–82), 2: 81–157.

35. See Xenio Toscani, "Il reclutamento del clero (secoli XVI–XIX," in *La Chiesa e il potere politico dal Medioevo all'età contemporanea,* ed. Giorgio Chittolini and Giovanni Miccoli, vol. 9 of *Storia d'Italia, Annali,* ed. Ruggiero Romano and Corrado Vivanti, 9 vols. (Turin: Einaudi, 1978–86), 573–628.

36. For evidence of a surplus of priests in relation to both population increase and available benefices, see the remarks on Friuli in Claudio Donati, "Dalla 'regolata devozione' al 'giuseppinismo' nell'Italia del Settecento," in *Cattolicesimo e Lumi nel Settecento italiano,* ed. Mario Rosa (Rome: Herder, 1982), 77–98.

37. On this point, see Xenio Toscani, *Il clero lombardo dall'Ancien Régime alla Restaurazione* (Bologna: Il Mulino, 1979), and "Ecclesiastici e società civile nel '700: Un problema di storia sociale e religiosa," *Società e Storia* 5 (1982): 683–716.

38. I am following here the argument in Émile Goichot, "'Sacerdos Alter Christus': Modèle spirituel et conditionnement social dans les 'Examens particuliers,'" *Revue d'Histoire de la Spiritualité* 51 (1975): 73–98.

39. *Mémoires de l'Abbé Baston, chanoine de Rouen,* ed. Julien Loth and Charles Verger, 2 vols. (Paris, 1897), 1: 55.

40. This is the figure that Gilles Deregnaucourt arrives at in his study of the dossiers of the officiality of Cambrai: *De Fénelon à la Révolution,* 329–40.

41. See Erica-Marie Benabou, "Amours 'vendues' à Paris à la fin de l'Ancien Régime: 'Clercs libertins,' police et prostituées," in *Aimer en France: 1760–1860,* Actes du Colloque international de Clermont-Ferrand, ed. Paul Viallaneix and Jean Ehrard, 2 vols. (Clermont-Ferrand: Association des Publications de la Faculté des Lettres et Sciences Humaines, 1984), 493–502.

42. Georges Minois, *La Bretagne des prêtres en Trégor d'Ancien Régime* (n.p.: Éditions Beltan, 1987), 196–97, 254–70.

43. Ernest Renan, *Souvenirs d'enfance et de jeunesse* (1883), ed. Jean Pommier (Paris: A. Colin, 1959), 53, 129; quoted from *Recollections of My Youth*, trans. C. B. Pitman (New York: G. P. Putnam's Sons, 1883), 54, 9, 117.

44. There has been an abundant new literature on the ecclesiastical conferences in recent years. See Jean-Marie Gouesse, "Assemblées et associations cléricales: Synodes et conférences ecclésiastiques dans le diocèse de Coutances aux XVIIᵉ et XVIIIᵉ siècles," *Annales de Normandie* 24, 2 (1974): 37–71; Michel de Certeau, *L'écriture de l'histoire* (Paris: Gallimard, 1975), 208–10 (available in English as *The Writing of History*, trans. Tom Conley [New York: Columbia University Press, 1988]); Berthelot du Chesnay, *Les prêtres séculiers*, 427–32; Deregnaucourt, *De Fénelon à la Révolution*, 340–44.

45. Quoted in Deregnaucourt, *De Fénelon à la Révolution*, 344.

46. See Dominique Julia and Denis McKee, "Les confrères de Jean Meslier: Culture et spiritualité du clergé champenois au XVIIᵉ siècle," *Revue d'Histoire de l'Église de France* 69 (1983): 61–86.

47. *Oeuvres complètes de Jean Meslier*, ed. Jean Deprun, Roland Desné, and Albert Soboul, 3 vols. (Paris: Anthropos, 1970), 1: 33 (introduction to the *Mémoire*).

48. Thérèse-Jean Schmitt, *L'organisation ecclésiastique et la pratique religieuse de l'archidiaconé d'Autun de 1650 à 1750* (Autun: n.p., 1957), 133. See also Julia and McKee, "Les confrères de Jean Meslier."

49. See Jean Quéniart, *Les hommes, l'Église et Dieu dans la France du XVIIIᵉ siècle* (Paris: Hachette, 1978), 69–77, 260–73.

50. Luciano Allegra, *Ricerche sulla cultura del clero in Piemonte: Le biblioteche parrocchiali nell'Arcidiocesi di Torino sec. XVII–XVIII* (Turin: Deputazione subalpina di Storia Patria, 1978).

51. Instructional books and catechism and confessional manuals represented 9.9 percent of all books; books of sermons, 8.8 percent; books on biblical studies and ecclesiastical history and the texts of reports from synods and councils, 7.4 percent. In secular literature, belles lettres accounted for 5 percent of books; history, geography, and philosophy, 3 percent; scientific and technical subjects, 2.5 percent. All these figures exclude the four ecclesiastical libraries with over four hundred volumes, which would falsify the overall results.

52. See Claudio Donati, *Ecclesiastici e laici nel Trentino del Settecento (1748–1763)* (Rome: Istituto storico per l'età moderna e contemporanea, 1975), 174–78.

53. De Certeau, "The Formality of Practices: From Religious Systems to the Ethics of the Enlightenment (the Seventeenth and Eighteenth Centuries)," chap. 4 in *The Writing of History*, 147–205.

54. From the statement of a parish priest in the Jura, quoted in Michel Vernus, *Le presbytère et la chaumière: Curés et villageois dans l'ancienne France (XVIIᵉ et XVIIIᵉ siècles)* (Rioz: Éditions Togirix, 1986), 112.

55. Fanch Roudaut, Daniel Collet, and Jean-Louis Le Floc'h, *1774: Les recteurs léonards parlent de la misère* (Quimper: Société archéologique du Finistère,

1988). Certain rectors suggested that hospitals might also be founded using the wealth of the religious orders.

56. Response of the *curé* of Plocider, in ibid., 129.

57. See Yves Marie Bercé, *Le chaudron et la lancette: Croyances populaires et médecine préventive, 1789–1830* (Paris: Presses de la Renaissance, 1984), 121–35; Pierre Darmon, *La longue traque de la variole: Les pionniers de la médecine préventive* (Paris: Perrin, 1986), 201–7; Carl Havelange, *Les figures de la guérison (XVIIIᵉ– XIXᵉ siècles): Une histoire sociale et culturelle des professions médicales au pays de Liège* (Liège: Bibliothèque de la Faculté de Philosophie et Lettres de Liège, 1990), 251–67.

58. Quoted in Havelange, *Les figures de la guérison,* 261.

59. See Dominique Julia, "La réforme posttridentine en France d'après les procès verbaux de visites paroissiales: Ordre et résistances," in *La società religiosa nell'età moderna,* Atti del Convengo di studi di storia sociale e religiosa, Capaccio-Paestum, 18–21 May 1972 (Naples: Guida, 1972), 311–415. Parish priests in the diocese of Trent were also hostile toward ringing bells: see Donati, "Dalla 'regolata devozione' al 'giuseppinismo,' " 96–97.

60. Response of a parish priest in Auriebat to the bishop's questionnaire, Tarbes, Bibliothèque Municipale de Tarbes, MS no. 60, 609–19.

61. For the inquiry in the diocese of Reims in 1774, see Dominique Julia, "Le clergé paroissial du diocèse de Reims," I: "De la sociologie aux mentalités"; II: "Le vocabulaire des curés: Essai d'analyse," *Études Ardennaises* 47 (1967): 19–35; 55 (1968): 41–66, respectively. For the episcopal inquiry in Tarbes in 1783, see Bibliothèque Municipale de Tarbes, MSS nos. 59–64. All expressions enclosed in quotation marks refer to these two investigations.

62. Response of Alexis Doleac, *curé* of Beaudean, Tarbes, Bibliothèque Municipale de Tarbes, MS no. 60, 33–43.

63. Response of Joseph Bégoc, *curé* of Molène, quoted in Roudaut, Collet, and Le Floc'h, *1774: Les recteurs léonards parlent de la misère,* 103–4.

10 / The Woman

Dominique Godineau

Madame d'Épinay gathering in her salon the greatest minds of the age; the marquise de Pompadour, patroness of arts and letters; Madame Roland, *égérie des Girondins;* the marquise de Merteuil in *Les liaisons danger euses,* or Marceline in *Le mariage de Figaro* bitterly bewailing women's condition—all these women, real and imaginary (and many more, for the list goes on) spring immediately to mind when the eighteenth century is mentioned.

Does this mean that the century of the Enlightenment was also the century of the woman, as one scholar has declared?[1] In many ways the expression seems justified, for not only did women crowd the public scene and not only do female characters teem in literature but *la Femme* was at the center of a plethora of writings in which philosophers, physicians, and writers considered the physiology, reason, upbringing and education, and social role of women. The woman—alive, imaginary, or the object of study—was incontestably omnipresent. Women were everywhere: whether one walked through the popular quarters of the cities, peeked through the door of a crafts workshop, sat at a tavern table or penetrated a literary circle; whether one was introduced at court or watched a public manifestation, flipped through a novel, romance, or essay, or found a place at the theater, women were inescapably present.

In this sense, the century of the Enlightenment was indeed the century of the woman—but a woman who remained subordinate, minor. With no civic or political identity, she was excluded from the centers of power and existed juridically only through men. Her professional, civic, and political rights were not recognized. The emblematic female figures should not lead us astray: if women reigned in the literary, philosophical, and political salons; if the greatest philosophers of the time deigned to exchange ideas with them and were sensitive to their points of view, the fact

remains (and is useful to recall from the start), no woman author appears
in the pages of the *Encyclopédie*. Madame de Merteuil and Marceline, symbols of revolt against women's condition, do not weigh as heavily in the
balance as the chief female role model of the Enlightenment—Sophie,
the submissive companion of Rousseau's Emile, a woman created for him
and whose principal function is to assure the well-being and the happiness
of her husband. And when, at the end of the century, the revolutionaries
attempted to turn the ideas of the Enlightenment into reality and to construct a new city in which everyone would share in sovereignty as a responsible citizen, women were excluded. It was then that the contradictions of
that "paradoxical century" in which women enjoyed a "'mixity' without
parity," exploded with full force.[2]

There is a trap concealed in speaking of the woman of the Enlightenment, for there was no one "woman" but many. The woman of the Enlightenment might be woman as the Enlightenment imagined her; that
is, as she appears in the philosophical texts (written, for the most part,
by men). She is the woman of the male Enlightenment, and her totally
theoretical portrait does not completely correspond to that of contemporaries. The woman of the Enlightenment is also the woman of
eighteenth-century literature, the woman of writers such as Choderlos
de Laclos and Beaumarchais, writers who often found just the right
words to describe the condition of the women of their time. Or was the
woman of the Enlightenment perhaps the woman who participated in
the movement of the Enlightenment by her own writings or by her capacity for creating an intellectual circle about her? We might also describe the woman of the Enlightenment simply as the woman who lived
during that century. In this definition, there is not one woman but various types of women who belonged to different social milieus: the
woman of the court, the aristocrat, the bourgeoise, the woman of the
people, the peasant, etc. Similarly, it would be a mistake to ignore national differences: although the Enlightenment was a phenomenon
common to the Western world, every country had its own culture in
which women led noticeably different lives.

Still, our aim here is not to draw up an exhaustive catalog of the various types of "women of the Enlightenment" but rather to point out the
major trends in the century. We need to consider the contrary movements that put women at the heart of society, writing, and thought, and
at the same time tended to push them to the periphery and relegate

them to an inferior place. That conflict, which derives from the relationship between the sexes and reflects the dynamics of that relationship, continued throughout the age. To treat the woman of the Enlightenment is thus—also, and above all—to analyze that relationship, clarify its complexity, grasp how it was constructed and how it weighed on the lives of women (and men) and, in a broader sense, on the evolution of society. More than anything else, we need to know what image the men of the Enlightenment had of their female companions.

Men's Gaze

Female Nature

The eighteenth century saw the triumph of the idea that women have a specifically female nature. That triumph was essentially the work of the physicians and the *philosophes*. More than ever before, they speculated on what makes a woman and on what differentiates and separates woman from man. They spoke in the name of the human race, and they thought themselves neutral observers of gender differences. But they wrote as men, and it was their own gender that they used as a standard of measurement and analysis for the female. Thus, the article "Femme" in Diderot's *Encyclopédie* presents woman as "the female of the man"; when we turn a few pages to the entry for "Homme," however, we find a general definition of the entire human species. This points to one of the principal problems of the Enlightenment: how could one reconcile a difference between the sexes and a philosophy of universality? All authors agreed that women are half of humankind, but once that statement was made their positions diverged.

One current of thought can be seen in the heirs of Poullain de la Barre. His writings (notably, *De l'égalité des deux sexes: Discours physique et moral où l'on voit l'importance de se défaire des préjugés* [1673]) marked a turning point in male/female thought. Rather than stating, as had been the case up to then, that either the male or the female sex was superior, he introduced the notion of equality into the *querelle*. As a convinced Cartesian, he rejected prejudice in favor of reason, and he based his opinions on a coherent philosophical system rather than on personal preferences. Asserting that "the mind has no sex," he insisted that reason, which defines membership in the human species, was proper to men and women alike. He saw their common humanity as primordial in the face of differences deriving as much from culture and education as from nature. Women should thus enjoy the same rights and the same education as men (which would allow them to eliminate the faults they were accused of), and they should pursue the same professional, intellectual, and political functions as men. Poullain replaces the history of female dependency within the history of institutions, and he analyzes role division as the result of a historical process. Although there was little reaction to his treatises in his own day, they were republished in the eighteenth century (and even translated into English) and were read by— among others—Montesquieu and Choderlos de Laclos. Philosophers like Helvétius and Condorcet picked up his theories. Still, they did not represent the dominant ideology of the men of the Enlightenment.

The opposing and clearly predominant attitude had two illustrious spokesmen, one a *philosophe* and the other a physician: Jean-Jacques Rousseau and Pierre Roussel. The first devoted the last part of his book, *Émile, ou, de l'éducation* (1762) to "Sophie ou la Femme"; the second published a *Système physique et moral de la femme* (1775), a work that studied the body and the being of women. Both Rousseau and Roussel had a considerable influence on the thought of the Enlightenment. Reducing current opinion to system, they sparked a dynamic movement that produced a harvest of writings, medical and/or philosophical, on the specificity of the female. For all these authors, the woman represented, admittedly, half of the human species, but a half that was fundamentally different. From difference they passed on rapidly to inequality, and from inequality to inferiority. But let us return to their reasoning to see how it worked out logically.

Everything began with the obvious fact that men and women are physically different. It is Nature who has willed this difference, and she could not possibly act without reason. Admittedly, points in common between men and women exist. They "belong to the species," Rousseau writes; differences are differences "of sex." In other words: "In everything not connected with sex, woman is man." The problem was that in woman everything derives from sex: "The male is male only at certain moments. The female is female her whole life or at least during her whole youth. Everything constantly recalls her sex to her."[3] This opinion cannot be credited to Rousseau's misogyny, given that Diderot thought exactly the same thing. In *Sur les femmes* (1772), he states: "The woman bears within herself an organ susceptible of terrible spasms, which, *disposing* of her. . . ."[4] The rhythm of her life, Diderot adds, is imposed by sexual functions—menstruation, pregnancy, menopause. As for Roussel, he states that "the woman is not a woman only in one place, but in all the facets by which she may be considered."[5] The uterus is the female organ par excellence, the one that commands all other organs. It dominates and determines the woman, who is therefore defined by her sex, not by her reason, as with man.

Women's Reason

The woman could not have the same type of reason as the man. Like the rest of her person, her reason was subject to her genital organs. This explained much of her weakness, hence her inferiority. On the one hand, she was an eternal invalid, regularly subject to ills proper to her—a true handicap that meant that she could not possibly lead an active life in society. On the other hand, that dominating uterus made her into a being of excessive sensitivity, prey to an unbridled, exalted imagination. Diderot, for example, not only notes that the uterus "disposes of her" but adds that "it arouses in her imagination phantoms of every sort."[6] Physicians like Roussel explained women's heightened sensitivity by the finer ramifications of their blood vessels and their nerves. This was the time when Condillac's sensationalism saw reason as arising from sensations: since women were more sensitive, did this give them an advantage? No, because the very excessiveness of their sensitivity blocked the development of reason: too many sensations prevented ideas from maturing by halting the passage from sensation to concept. Thus women's development stopped at the first stage, that of the imagination—an uncontrollable, dangerous imagination that was both negative, peopled with "phantoms of every sort," and childlike. "O women! What extraordinary children you are!" Diderot exclaimed.[7]

If women were incapable of carrying conceptualization very far, their reason had to turn toward the concrete and the practical. "It is for them to apply the principles man has found, and to make the observations which lead man to the establishment of principles." Rousseau wrote about Sophie: "Woman observes, and man reasons."[8] As abstraction was not her province, her reflection could only be brought to bear on the particular, not the general. She ought not to philosophize on Man, but "must . . . make a profound study of the mind of man . . . [of] the minds of the men around her, the minds of the men to whom she is subjected by either law or opinion."[9] When woman exercised her reason it should be turned toward others—toward her husband and her children. Reason allowed her to assure their happiness and their well-being, hence to fulfill her role as a woman.

Women's Role

The anatomical and intellectual differences between the sexes corresponded to a difference in their social roles. "Woman's status," Rousseau and the physicians asserted, is to be a mother, and they added that her anatomy predestined her to that role. What followed from that maternal function and her physiological weakness was a less active life, a "passive state" (Roussel) dictated by nature. The woman of the men of the Enlightenment was thus sedentary, and her principal activities took place on the domestic scene. What is more, the physicians added, she is not made for physical exercise: her bones are not as hard as men's, her pelvic basin and her hips give her a less determined gait. While her husband might reflect on human destiny or leave the home to lead a life in society, she was to remain within, take care of the children, and make the dwelling as agreeable as possible. Each sex had its own functions, willed by nature: men's functions were public, women's were private; and it would be subversive to confuse the two. When Enlightenment thought examined gender differences and the relationship between men and women it became profoundly determinist and functionalist. "Sophie ought to be a woman as Emile is a man—that is to say, she ought to have everything which suits the constitution of her species and her sex in order to fill her place in the physical and moral order."[10]

The century of triumphant reason was thus not free of paradoxes. In a society where the sexes mixed (at least in France) on nearly all occasions, where women were at the heart of social life, both in the street and in the literary circles, a reigning ideology incontrovertibly divided the qualities, the space, and the social roles of the sexes. Men of the Enlightenment regularly exchanged ideas and concepts with women, but they questioned the intellectual capacities of "the Woman." Whereas the Enlightenment fought prejudice as the enemy of reason, the philosophers had no intention of abandoning their own prejudices where women were concerned. And while they placed the notion of universality and the principal of equality founded in natural law at the center of their discourse, they defended the idea of a "feminine nature" that was separate and inferior. Belief in the perfectibility of the human species was one of the foundations of Enlightenment thought: the advancement of reason constituted one of the motive forces of history. But women were situated outside history. Entirely determined by their physiology, they lived under the sign of the immutable; their reason, their functions, and their "nature" did not evolve. "At all times," Rousseau insists, their duties are the same.

These contradictions derived in great part from a difficulty in apprehending gender differences. This was a philosophical difficulty, and it arose from articulating one sort of discourse on the universal level and a different discourse on the "other" when the speaker was a man speaking of women. At that point a primary difficulty arose in conceiving that the other was not a powerful enemy intent on bringing you death. At the turn of a page a genuine fear of woman suddenly emerges. Fear of her "unlimited desires" (Rousseau); fear that the attraction she held for men would lead them to their death. Happily, nature had given women simplicity, shame, and modesty as their portion in order to restrain their insatiable appetites. The female body, whose functions remained a mystery to science, terrified with its difference and its violence. The pages that *philosophes* and physicians blackened concerning women are filled with contradictions, oscillating with no transition between the two contrary images of a soft, maternal woman and an excessive, savage woman. One begins to wonder if their long developments on the weakness and modesty of women are more of an exorcism destined to reassure the author than a confident affirmation. These anxieties are more clearly evident in another sort of text—in so-called popular literature—where they are stripped of all ambiguity.

Women in Literature

Women occupy a good deal of space in the eighteenth-century novel. It created complex characters as its heroines. The war between the sexes became a familiar mechanism in dramatic action. The woman is pitied and/or magnified in this literature, but she is not merely a caricature or a stereotype: she is a real person, whose condition, problems, and psychology the writers describe.

The tone is different in the works written for (but not by) "the people" that had a renewed popularity in the eighteenth century. A peddler's literature (known in France under the name of the Bibliothèque bleue from the color of the books' blue paper covers) diffused an image of the woman that is dominated by clichés and presents a surprisingly hate-filled portrait. Women are spiteful, cruel, sly, vain, lazy, easily angered, loose-tongued, greedy, spendthrift, and dominating; they seem to have been created to make men's lives miserable. A disciple of Satan,

Woman brought death to Earth: when God created Eve out of Adam's rib, *Le miroir des femmes* (1717) tells its readers, he took care to plunge Adam into a deep sleep, "so that he would not see coming out of his own body the being who was to drag him with her into the coffin."[11] Under a beautiful and fascinating—hence even more dangerous—earthly exterior, woman was death, and her embrace was fatal to man. To conjure away death, then, woman must be subjected, domesticated (all the more so because man was obliged to live with her). If a man wanted to avoid being reduced to nothing by his marriage, he must dominate his spouse, repress her desires and her insatiable sexual appetite, and annihilate her personality. In that way, active "woman/death" became a "woman dead out of personal and social nonexistence."[12] On that condition, it was possible to live with her. The Bibliothèque bleue depicts marriage as veritable warfare—no "war in lace" but a combat in which the man must defeat the woman if he himself does not want to be vanquished. This extremity reveals the conflict between men and women and the male anxieties it elicited much better than the carefully polished phrases of the philosophers. The couple was one of the prime sites for this clash and, as it happens, the Enlightenment challenged traditional marriage to promote a new conception of the relationship between husband and wife.

Married Women

The desire to reduce wives to submission can of course be found in the condition that was legally imposed on them. In all Western countries, wives were juridical minors with a nearly nonexistent civic identity. They generally did not have the right to initiate a lawsuit or sign a contract. Their wealth was usually managed by their husbands, at times without their having any say in the matter. French customary law placed the wife under the authority of her husband, without whose accord she could not act. In some regions daughters were stripped of their paternal inheritance. Everywhere women were excluded from the direction of craft associations, as they also were—obviously—from all political bodies, municipal, regional, or national.

These are all flagrant and well-known injustices. Although it is useful to recall them, they fail to express the full complexity of the condition of women in the age of the Enlightenment. If we want to do that we need to leave the "Woman" of the philosophers, physicians, novelists, and jurists and seek out the women of the eighteenth century. Rich or

poor, educated or illiterate, they made use—each in her own manner—
of the fissures in the social fabric to participate in the public world in
spite of the discourses, prejudices, and laws.

Marriage Challenged

A young woman learns from her serving maid that she will soon be married. She weeps. Her father is surprised: "What's so formidable about
marrying a decent, well-born man, with a nice fortune in the bargain?"
She replies: "Well, I suppose he is, if you say so; but it's dreadful to be
handed over like this to a perfect stranger." After explaining to her that
the only bad marriages are love matches, the father concludes: "Poor
people need all the love they can get, if they're to jog on together; but a
couple that's better off only need to be civil to each other to live comfortably; their money does the rest. Come now; make up your mind to it, and
show a little spirit, and a smile or two; you'll see, it won't be so bad."[13]

The fact that this dialog imagined by Louis-Sébastien Mercier in his
Tableau de Paris (Paris, 1783–86) is stereotyped does not detract from its
verisimilitude. In wealthy circles, marriage was still by and large treated
as a social or economic transaction decided by the men of the family.
The future husband was chosen in function of his social position and his
revenues by parents who hoped to make a fine alliance or guarantee
their daughter a secure future. It mattered little if the happy bridegroom was an old man, if his fiancée loved someone else, or if she simply
did not like him: she had nothing to say about it, for her parents were
persuaded that they were working for her good. Toward the end of the
century, the daughters of enlightened families—nobles or commoners—
might nonetheless have had somewhat more to say. Although they were
anxious to find appropriate matches for their daughters, neither the father of Victorine de Chastenay (born in 1771) nor the father of Manon
Phlipon (the future Madame Roland, born in 1754) opposed their
daughters' reiterated refusals to marry the suitors presented to them.
Both the nobleman and the master engraver were followers of the *philosophes* and had certainly read some of the abundant literature—essays,
novels, or plays—denouncing arranged marriages.

Traditional marriage was in fact one of the favorite targets of the
Enlightenment. "Marriage nowadays is a yoke, and a heavy one," Mercier wrote.[14] What was wrong with it? First, it was criticized for being perverted by social and financial considerations (Mercier demanded the
suppression of dowries, according to him the prime source of conjugal

discord). Plays were written about ill-assorted couples whose union would be a disaster. Young girls were pitied for being sacrificed to family politics by being given to repugnant old men, to libertines who would dilapidate their fortunes, or to misers who would make them live in poverty. If they were resigned to their fate they would be unhappy; if not, they would deceive their husbands. Such marriages were rejected in the name of young women's freedom and in the name of proper conduct, both of which they threatened.

This sort of thinking launched a forceful attack on the indissolubility of marriage. Divorce existed in a number of Protestant countries, but in Catholic Europe spouses who ended up hating one another were condemned to remain together to the death. Separation "of goods and of bodies" was a possible recourse, but the separated spouses could not remarry. Because they were infertile they were considered "useless to the state" or "given over to libertinage," as Mercier states in "Séparation" in his *Tableau de Paris*—once again summarizing the century's thoughts but also demanding the authorization of divorce. Little by little, the religious concept of the indissolubility of marriage was countered by the idea of marriage as a contract, freely consented to by both parties, but which, because it was a contract, might be broken. This notion peaked during the French Revolution when the Constitution of 1791 stated that "the law considers matrimony simply as a civil contract." This was a truly revolutionary definition. On the one hand, it made the woman a juridical subject; on the other, it opened the way for the law authorizing divorce (20 September 1792).

The Couple in the Enlightenment

A new vision of the couple emerged from such reflections on marriage. The couple of the Enlightenment was to be constructed on sentiment and not on convention. In theory, marriage was not an arena for confrontation between the man and the woman but a place of harmony and personal development constructed by both partners. This is Kant's definition, for example. In a section of his *The Metaphysics of Morals* (1797) entitled "Marriage Right," he states: "Marriage is the union of two persons of different sex for lifelong possession of each other's sexual attributes."[15] Another German philosopher, Fichte, stated in 1796 that marriage "has no purpose outside itself, which is its own purpose—that is, a reciprocal, natural, and moral relationship of hearts."[16] The notions of a contract freely consented to and of mutual satisfaction gave women a more worthy place. What is more, such notions were not exclusive to a small circle of enlightened spirits but were ideas that spread throughout society and reflected a profound change in thinking. A sixteenth-century proverb stated: "A good horse and a bad horse need the spur / A good woman and a bad woman need the stick," but Leroux's *Diction-naire comique,* published in 1786, notes that "one must be the companion and not the master of one's wife."[17] Again, the century of the Enlightenment is full of paradoxes: it gives us both the sinister image of marriage of the Bibliothèque bleue and the much more optimistic and soothing image of couples as companions.

And what about Rousseau? Where are we to place Emile and Sophie, the couple who were the beacon and the model for the Enlightenment? Sophie is indeed the companion of Emile. Their marriage is not one ruled by convention: her parents, although they offer wise counsel, leave her free to choose the partner her heart dictates. Love and affection precede their union; the "right of nature" prevails. Once married, Emile does not treat his wife as "his horse," but rather as his companion, and both cooperate in founding a happy family. But, one might object, Sophie's position is as an inferior and the relationship is founded on inequality! If Dame Discord has no place in their home, if loud cries and bickering are not to be heard, it is because Sophie, who has learned "early to endure even injustice and to bear a husband's wrongs without complaining," obeys him without saying a word and seeks only to please him.[18] Is Sophie the "woman/death" of popular literature? Certainly, but in spite of his excesses and his crudeness, Rousseau is not out of harmony with his century, for all thinkers, progressive though they may have been, agreed that it is natural for the man to dominate and command within the couple. To be a companion to one's husband by no means meant being his equal. That love, confidence, even complicity might reign within the marriage of the Enlightenment did not have as a corollary—far from it!—that inequality was banished.

The twenty-second in the series of thirty-seven holidays that Robespierre proposed to the Convention on 7 May 1794 was dedicated to "Love" and the next four to family virtues, among which "Conjugal Faith" came first, followed by "Paternal Love," "Maternal Tenderness," and "Filial Piety." The term "Faith" *(la Foi)* seems surprising. Naively perhaps, one might have expected "Love." But the term that was used expresses the sentiment that current criteria thought should prevail between spouses. The Directory kept some of Robespierre's holidays, notable a yearly *Fête des Époux.* On that occasion the Directory notables—men of the last

flickering glimmers of the Enlightenment—offered normative discourses on their vision of the ideal couple. A study of these texts permits a
better grasp of what Robespierre had in mind.[19] Happy marriages, they
tell us, are "the fruit of reflection." Conjugal love is a reasoned love. Passion, barely tolerated when the couple is forming, must be banished if it
is no more than a "passing pleasure" or an "intense sensation that leaves
behind only nothingness and remorse" and is not accompanied by esteem, virtue, and concordant character. Passion is merely ephemeral,
and when it fades it must be replaced by confidence and friendship, the
true cement of the couple. "Love unites spouses," one of these discourse
tells us, "but it is friendship that guides them." Friendship, founded
on esteem, frankness, "enlightened tenderness," and fidelity, must be
sage—that is, guided by reason. The orators (all of them male) occasion-
ally addressed young women directly, pointing out to them what their
future place would be as subordinates but not slaves. The wife is "the
companion of man in his youth, his friend in his mature age, his nurse in
his old age."

What did women expect from marriage? Women published less
than men, but we can nonetheless learn something about their aspirations from texts of a quite different sort—judicial and police archives
that tell us about the couple among "the people."

The Couple among the People

Couples formed much more freely among the common people than in
wealthy circles because mutual attraction was more important than
money. Young women worked and, at least in the cities and towns, they
were not totally dependent upon their parents, whose roof they might
even leave to live alone. Occasions for people to meet one another were
frequent, and the absence of rigid financial strategies facilitated unions—
legitimate or not—for although it was not the norm, living together was
far from unknown and was on the rise in the bigger cites in the eighteenth century. Marriage was not an act to be taken lightly, but it was
subject to different rules. A woman of the common people expected
happiness from marriage, and happiness was often equated with "establishment." In a life that was otherwise precarious, marriage was synonymous with stability, both in emotional and in socioeconomic terms.
The laws of love were not the only ones ruling unions on the lower levels
of society, however: although actual money arrangements did not enter
into the formation of the couple, both men and women nonetheless

hoped for economic betterment from a union founded on their common capacity for work.

Suits that have been conserved in the archives indicate, in reverse, how men and women in lower-class couples were expected to divide social roles. Through their expressions of bitter disillusionment and tenacious grudges and through the witnesses' indignation, a portrait of the good wife and the good husband begins to take shape. The good wife was a hard worker; she was also expected to manage the household's money, doing her best with the available resources to see to it that the family always had something to eat. Men showed little interest in the difficulties of this female role of providing nourishment, which in part explains why women played a prominent rule in food riots. It was not only hunger or maternal instinct that brought them to the front of the crowd but also an unbearable feeling of failure when they were unable to carry out their social role. The husband had special duties as well. He was not to beat his wife, deceive her, speak harshly to her, or endanger the honor of the couple by his behavior. He must not dilapidate their savings but rather provide his wife with enough to live on. If the wife hoped that marriage would give her a degree of economic stability, she also expected her husband to esteem her and be attentive to her and to their children. If this tacit pact was broken too often and too violently, she might leave the conjugal roof with her children, despite the economic difficulties that lay in wait for her, and try to remake her life elsewhere. Like her husband, the woman of the people insisted on preserving a degree of autonomy. On certain questions she felt that he could mind his own business and that she was not answerable to him. She considered it her right, once her family duties had been seen to, to leave the house to attend to personal business, chat with her women friends, or drink a glass in the tavern—a mixed space where the presence of a woman, alone or in the company of men or women friends, was not at all shocking.

Working Women

From Working Women . . .

Louis-Sébastien Mercier noted the relative independence of the women (and girls) of the people, the artisan class, and the petty bourgeoisie, and he attributed their freedom to a professional activity that permitted them to have "more of a say in their households" and "always to manage a bit of money"—something that he claims was not true of women in the

higher levels of society. The remark is pertinent. A majority of the
women of the century of the Enlightenment worked, in town or in
the fields. This was not choice but economic necessity: in an age when
the frontier between indigence and poverty was thin, women's work was
obligatory to the survival of the household. Women's work was simply
part of the social and familial landscape; it was the norm in popular milieus, and it played an essential role in economic life.

Contemporaries knew this well. On every street-corner they met a
throng of women selling merchandise, new or second-hand, or poor
women selling anything and everything in order to survive—old clothes
and second-hand hats, little pastries or herb teas, flowers or tobacco.
The market woman and the washerwoman, legendary for their short
tempers and their sharp tongues, were familiar figures, as was the serving maid, often fresh from the country (in a city like Paris, women accounted for 80 percent of domestic servants). Women also earned a
living sewing, and on occasion contemporary chroniclers lashed out at
men who took up needle and thread, thus depriving women of work
considered their specialty. There should be no need to recall that peasant women (and peasants were a majority of the population) worked
hard on the family farm, where agricultural tasks were also divided according to gender.

Collective memory retains these traditional images of women at
work; from there it is an easy logical jump to deducing that service activities were the only spheres of economic life that involved woman workers.
This somewhat hastily overlooks the many crafts and artisanal workers,
many of whom were employed in textile operations but some of whom
worked wood or metal (as polishers, needle-makers, etc.). Others worked
in paper manufacturing or bookmaking, or made fans, tobacco pouches,
and much more. These women worked either at home (sometimes with
their husbands) or else in workshops, along with male workers in the
same trade. In the small artisanal workshop the wife of the master was also
a constant female presence. She participated fully in the life of the workshop, took charge of sales, and directed operations when her husband
was absent on business. Often she kept the books or worked side by side
with the others.

. . . to Unequal Status

Although women were indispensable to the economy, they did not have
the same place in it as men. Less well qualified, they were confined to the

secondary tasks of preparation or finishing; consequently, they were
paid less. Anyone—man or woman—who proposed putting a stop to
this vicious circle and allowing women to earn a decent living by granting them a professional qualification equal to men's met with swift male
reactions. In Paris during the Revolution a typographical school for
women was opened: until then, the women workers in printshops pasted
book covers or bound books and earned on average a seventh of what
male typography workers earned. When the word went out that women
might be initiated into the "noble" (and very well-paid) jobs in the printing profession, all the typographers in Paris protested, violently attacking the director of the school and any of their colleagues who dared
teach their skills to women.

With the exception of certain professions in commerce or fashion
reputed to be "feminine," women were excluded from the guild system.
The master's wife, without whom the workshop would have functioned
only with great difficulty, did not exist in the eyes of the trade guild. If
her husband died and she remarried, her new husband inherited the
master's post. As for woman workers, even if they had been trained as
apprentices, they never became journeymen, and the all-male journeymen's organization rejected them as a matter of course.

Thus, in spite of their highly visible presence in nearly every
sphere of the economy, women were excluded from the representative
organs of the working world and were ignored juridically. Once again,
we see an ambiguity characteristic of the Enlightenment, which put
women at the center of its culture but at the same time pushed them to
the periphery.

The Education of Enlightenment Women

The Debate

Some writers insisted that the companion to the enlightened man could
not be an imbecile. She needed a minimum of instruction if she were to
understand him, discuss things with him, and raise their children. Other
writers went farther to insist that the lack of instruction for women was
one of the principal causes of the inequality between men and women,
adding that women's education needed to be improved to rid them of
their defects and give them back their true nature and their rightful
place in society. For whatever reason, the question of female education
caused a good deal of ink to flow. The debate was not new. The seven-

teenth century had produced a number of texts pleading the cause of female education—with moderation in the cases of Mademoiselle de Scudéry, Madame de Sévigné, or Fénelon; militantly and with feminist overtones in the works of Poullain de la Barre and Mary Astell (*A Serious Proposal to the Ladies*, 1694). The Enlightenment, which placed instruction at the heart of its thought, gave the question new currency, and writings on the topic proliferated, particularly in the latter half of the eighteenth century. Men, women, philosophers, writers famous and unknown, all gave the public the fruit of their reflections, offered suggestions, and drew up proposals. The provincial academies, which were always quick to echo the latest topics, debated "How Can the Education of Women Render Men Better?" (Besançon, 1775), or "What Would Be the Best Means for Perfecting the Education of Women?" (Châlons-sur-Marne, 1783). It was to respond to the latter question that Laclos wrote his essay, *De l'éducation des femmes.*

Female voices were not absent from this debate. Madame de Miremont devoted several years to composing a voluminous *Traité de l'éducation des femmes* (seven volumes were published from 1779 to 1789). It was a favorite topic of the feminine press that arose at that time.[20] In *The Nonsense of Common-Sense* (1737), Lady Montagu, a friend of Mary Astell, defended the education of women. Eliza Haywood, the editor of *The Female Spectator* (1744–46), later of *Epistles for the Ladies* (1749–50), invited her female readers to seek instruction. Both *The Lady's Magazine* and *Le Journal des Dames* (1759–78) gave special attention to the education of girls. In Germany, Sophie von La Roche created female revues with a pedagogical cast (*Lettres à Rosalie* in 1772; *Pomona* in 1783). La Roche earned a certain celebrity as the author of a novel, *Geschichte des Fräuleins von Sternheim* (1771), a work that posed the problem of the young woman's education. Several other women chose the novel as a vehicle for the denunciation of the failings of female education and a way to propose a more satisfactory system, among them Madame de Graffigny (*Lettres d'une Péruvienne* [1752]) and Marie-Jeanne Riccoboni (*Histoire d'Ernestine* [1762]).

Convent education, often accused of making young women ignorant, was a favorite target of criticism. Education within the family, as with Emile and Sophie, was deemed preferable, but some authors, aware that this solution was possible only in privileged circles, imagined genuine schools for girls. Mixed schools were rejected, not only for reasons of "good mores" but also because neither the contents nor the goals of education were the same for boys and for girls. Boys learned for themselves;

girls, in view of their future social and domestic role. "Thus the whole education of women ought to relate to men," Rousseau wrote.[21] The goal of female education was to create efficacious and agreeable wives and mothers capable of raising their children properly. Knowing how to run a household; being able to read, write, and count; having some rudiments of history, geography, literature, and foreign languages—and, of course, of religion, dance, music, and perhaps drawing—was amply sufficient for women. What good would it do them to know Greek or Latin or study scientific axioms? They might become ridiculous pedants, deplorable housewives, and embittered old maids, like the bluestocking who aroused so much laughter in England. These constraining views were denounced with growing vigor by women who demanded a real change in the content of female instruction, who preached the equality of knowledge, and who called upon their sisters to perfect their learning in all domains.

Differences in Instruction

Beyond the debates and the projects, what in fact was the level of instruction of women of the Enlightenment? Undeniably, if we look at all social classes, women profited from the educational system that had been put into place in the preceding century. At the end of the seventeenth century, 14 percent of French women could sign their names; a hundred years later, the proportion had nearly doubled (27 percent). Admittedly, gender inequality persisted: at that later date, 48 percent of French men could sign their names (a ratio of 177 men for every 100 women). The gap between men and women had diminished, however, because a hundred years earlier that ratio was 207 men to 100 women. In the century of the Enlightenment, female literacy was thus progressing more rapidly than male. Similarly, in 1755, 60 percent of English men and 35 percent of English women signed marriage registers in the Church of England; thirty-five years later, the percentage for men was the same but that for women had risen to 40 percent.

The same phenomenon can be found throughout the Western world. In 1630, 178 men for every 100 women signed promises of marriage in contracts drawn up before a notary in Amsterdam (57 percent of men; 32 percent of women); in 1780, the proportion was 133 men for 100 women (85 percent; 64 percent). In country areas near Turin, where literacy figures started very low, women caught up even more spectacularly: in 1710, 350 men for 100 women (21 percent of men; 6

percent of women) signed their marriage contracts; eighty years later, there were "only" 216 male signatories for every 100 females (65 percent; 30 percent). In New England, where the literacy gap between men and women was less marked, women's progress is less striking: 182 men for every 100 women signed their wills in the mid-eighteenth century (84 percent; 46 percent); a century earlier, 196 men for every 100 women had signed their names (61 percent; 31 percent).[22]

These figures conceal a number of disparities, however, both regional and social. In southern France, for instance, literacy in general was lower than the national average, and the gap between men and women was much bigger than north of the famous imaginary line drawn from Saint-Malo to Geneva. It should be unnecessary to point out that a daughter from the privileged classes received immeasurably more instruction than a girl of the people.

If her family were fairly wealthy, a girl born to privilege would be entrusted to one of those much-criticized convent schools, where she probably did not, in fact, learn much. But if her family had been won over to the ideas of the century she might have an excellent education within the family circle. Victorine de Chastenay, in the final twenty years of the ancien régime, was one of this fortunate few. Starting at the age of five, Victorine received lessons in history, geography, and grammar. Her father followed her progress closely and invited her to share in the arithmetic tutorials he himself was receiving at home. For the next six years, she studied geometry and algebra with her brother's tutor. The two children also studied Latin and, less intensively, English. Music, drawing, and catechism completed the program. Monsieur de Chastenay, who adored botany, persuaded his daughter to keep an herbarium. If we can believe her later report, little Victorine was a gifted child, a "prodigy" who "loved studies with a passion."[23] Still, her teachers were her brother's, hired for him and in function of his studies. Even if, as she says, she was their favorite and even if *une jeune demoiselle latiniste* was a novelty and a source of pride for her professor, her teachers' observations were directed primarily to her brother. Victorine was able to profit from the instruction given to him. Even with her parents' open minds and the studious atmosphere that reigned in their home, would she have had such a complete education if there had been no boy in the family?

Be that as it may, Victorine's education bore fruit. Her thirst for knowledge led her to devour the books in the family library: at ten she was reading the *Histoire d'Angleterre* of Father d'Orléans, *Les Révolutions romaines* of Vertot, *La Constitution d'Angleterre* of Delolme, Plutarch's *Lives,* Racine's *Britannicus,* and more. At twelve, she was translating Horace and started to keep a diary. In the early days of the Revolution she was barely sixteen, and turned, "obviously," to Montesquieu, Locke, and Mably. As an accomplished daughter of the Revolution, she considered herself "a young philosopher for whom fancy dresses, light pleasures, and vain amusements mattered little" in comparison with reading and study, which she continued to enjoy throughout her life.

Other young girls, both noble and commoner, profited from a solid education within the family during the last third of the century. Being born into an intellectual milieu quite naturally improved the chances of receiving above-average instruction: Germaine Necker (de Staël) springs immediately to mind, as do Caroline Michaelis (Böhmer-Schlegel-Schelling) and Maria Therese Heyne (Forster-Huber), both the daughters of professors at Göttingen. Children born into a less brilliant milieu might also have an excellent education if their parents were "enlightened" and not too poor. Manon Phlipon (Roland), the daughter of a well-off Paris engraver, belonged to the upper levels of the arts as a craft, on the border of the *bourgeoisie à talents.* She could read at the age of four, and at seven years of age began to have lessons from writing masters and teachers of geography, history, dance, music, and Latin. She read Appian, Plutarch, Fénelon, Tasso, Voltaire, and the Bible.

The *collèges*—the secondary schools that trained the century's adolescent boys—did not accept girls. Where, then, did girls go if they could not enjoy the benefits of instruction in the home and their parents, for ideological or financial reasons, rejected a convent education? They went to one of the many private, lay *pensions* that opened in the cities. English boarding schools and French *maisons d'éducation* provided girls of the petty nobility or the bourgeoisie a fairly traditional education aimed at making them good mothers of Christian families.

As for the daughters of the more popular classes (the lower ranks of crafts and commerce and the peasantry), they might receive elementary instruction in the religious *petites écoles,* which were not costly and sometimes were free for students from poorer families. Aside from religion and morality, they learned to read, even to write and do simple arithmetic. This course of studies founded on religion was supplemented by various types of needlework, thus to some extent preparing them (though this was not professional training) for their future life as workers.

Women of Culture

Better educated than her grandmothers, the woman of the Enlightenment did not want to be left behind in that century full of intellectual
novelties. She wanted to take the instruction she had been given to make
her a good wife and use it for her own personal enrichment. She, too,
wanted to participate in the Enlightenment and not be a stranger to her
century. How was she to slip into a culture not directly designed for her?
By never ceasing to learn, by keeping up with what was being talked
about and written, and—why not?—by eliciting talk or by writing.

Reading

The woman of the Enlightenment was a voracious reader. Fashionable
novels (writers were well aware that women made up a sizable part of
their public), classical Greek and Roman authors, treatises on education, revues, political pamphlets, philosophical writing, history books—
nothing escaped her. The young Victorine de Chastenay is a striking example. Women's letters teem with references to the latest book they have
read and the reflections that their reading has inspired. The daughters
of the century found reading a refuge from morose or troubled times.
Caroline Michaelis-Böhmer and Victorine de Chastenay use almost
the same words to speak of the solace they find in books, one to combat boredom in the small mining town where her husband practiced
medicine, the other to beguile away the time waiting for the Terror to
abate.

   In the eighteenth century, pictorial representations of solitary reading show more women readers than men, a sign that reading was becoming a female activity as well as a private one.[24] But whereas male reading
was the sign of intellectual activity, the woman who read was easily considered a proud pedant or an idle female. In either case she was trans-
gressing her traditional role—by seeking access to male knowledge; by
stealing the time that she should have been devoting to running her
household, to her husband, or to her children; by creating an intimate
space between herself and the book that excluded man. Female reading
was dangerous. A serious book on her table was a sign that the female
reader sought to become learned and wanted to take man's place. A
novel in her hand or on her knee was a sign that she was given to letting
herself go in dreams, abandonment, even lasciviousness.

   This association can be clearly seen in paintings and in the commentaries that those paintings elicited. We can also see it in the suit that one

Montjean, a Paris artisan who made "fashion garments," brought against his wife. In 1774 the irate husband began to keep a diary in which he related the dissolution of his marriage.[25] He complains that his wife no longer wanted to work but only wanted to "go walking, eating oysters, or drinking wine"—or to read novels: she "wanted to be by the window reading a book." Aside from what this document tells us about relations between men and women in an artisan milieu, it also shows that for both men and women, reading novels was connected with a certain idleness and with the lifestyle of the privileged classes, with which this woman, who came to feel her condition as the wife of an artisan unbearable, sought to identify. To be seen with a book in her hand was for her a sign of social distinction. It is characteristic of the times that female reading— along with leisurely strolls and nibbling at oysters—was part of a desire for social promotion and its concomitant imitation of the upper classes.

The female reader is not always the solitary figure in a domestic setting that paintings show. A network of intellectual sociability surrounded the book in which women fully participated. In the larger German cities the proprietors of reading rooms, sensitive to the needs of their female fellow citizens, created special corners where women could slake their thirst for reading at their leisure. Both men and women generally attended the many small reading societies formed by a wealthy and cultivated company, thus minimizing a gender-based division of roles. Later, during the French Revolution, tenants who lived in apartment buildings might jointly subscribe to a journal that they then read in common.

The Salon

When the Enlightenment is mentioned, the image of the *salonnière* often springs to mind. The woman who kept a salon seems to have been at the heart of its intellectual movement: she played a leading role in the emergence and diffusion of thought, and she encouraged a meeting between thinkers and the world of money and power. The eighteenth-century salon was, in fact, one of the new places for sociability in which nobles, wealthy bourgeois, men of letters, and men of science of all nationalities met. It was a meeting-place, a place for knowledge, a place for creation, for exchange, for social apprenticeship, and for cultural circulation. It was also a place for an intellectual mixing of the sexes. Typically, the salon was directed by a woman or, as the century advanced, by one of those new Enlightenment couples founded on mutual respect: Helvétius, Condorcet, Lavoisier and their wives.

A salon was a heavy responsibility. It required keeping a careful watch over the composition of the assembled group, avoiding extremes, giving each guest an opportunity to shine, etc. If the *salonnière* did her job well, she derived a number of satisfactions from it: the social satisfaction of making a name for herself in cultural circles and seeing her salon sought after by the most fashionable company; the intellectual satisfaction of conversing with the greatest minds of the times, hearing them express innovative ideas, responding to them as an equal, offering them an opportunity to meet potential patrons. They might have the exhilarating pleasure of participating in the adventure of the Enlightenment, even of furthering that adventure.

There were also illusions involved in the salons, and some of the *salonnières* were not fooled by them. There was the illusion that during the time and within the space of the salon distinctions of rank, wealth, or gender were abolished, as if by enchantment. Within the salons, women held the role that the enlightened philosophers had dreamed of for them: worthy companions (here, of the mind), attentive, sufficiently educated and intelligent to carry on a conversation and to guide the man (the author, the thinker) by their encouragements or their pertinent criticisms and to aid him, by their attentions, to construct his work. But although the *salonnières* of the Enlightenment may have played this facilitating role, they never possessed real intellectual power. Once again, we return to the paradox of the century: the salons were undeniably places for the promotion of women. They permitted women to participate in the cultural sociability of the times and even to play a brilliant and universally recognized intellectual role, but that role nonetheless remained inscribed within certain limits and never fundamentally overturned relations between the sexes.

History has retained the names of the women who had the most fashionable salons: Madame de Tencin, Madame de Lambert, Madame Geoffrin, Madame du Châtelet, Madame du Deffand, Mademoiselle de Lespinasse, Madame d'Épinay, Madame Necker, and more. In their houses one might encounter Montesquieu, Voltaire, Diderot, d'Alembert, Grimm, Marmontel, Buffon, and the entire *Encyclopédie* group. In Paris and in the French provinces, other women received a less star-studded cast of secondary writers and liberal nobles and bourgeois, all of whom contributed—on a more modest scale, to be sure—to giving the century its luminosity.

Although the salon reached its highest point in France, it was not exclusively French. Intellectual and fashionable gatherings instigated by a woman multiplied throughout eighteenth-century Europe. In Italy they were called *conversazioni,* a word that gives a good indication of their aim. One could find well-known salons in Germany as well, for example that of the writer Sophie von La Roche, one of the most faithful habitués of which was Goethe. In Germany, however, such gatherings—which were not always led by women—were closer to literary teas than to the gatherings in the Paris salons. In them small groups of carefully selected friends met to read together and to discuss literature, but they had neither the social mixing nor the political, philosophical, and economic dimensions of their Parisian counterparts. In spite of that, German literary gatherings mark an evolution in relations between men and women. In like fashion, even though Anglo-Saxon usages tended to keep the sexes apart, by the mid-eighteenth century the English bluestockings had overturned those rules and instituted French-style salons.

Writing

Some women were tempted to move on from reading and salon conversation to writing. Correspondence, notes taken on books they had read, personal translations of an ancient or foreign author, diaries (like the one Victorine de Chastenay began at the age of twelve)—these first feminine forays into writing made some women want to make their writings public. In all Western countries the number of published works written by women increased during the eighteenth century,[26] a sign not only of better education for women but also of their desire to be more than "companions" whose talents benefited only those closest to them. If some women thought it prudent to remain within the shadow of anonymity or hide behind a pseudonym or behind the author they translated, others had no hesitation about openly confronting opinion. The novels of Sophie von La Roche and Marie-Jeanne Riccoboni were genuine literary successes, saluted as such by the writers of the time, and works—not a negligible detail—that brought them financial independence. The works of Madame de Genlis and Madame d'Épinay were standard references in the educational field. To reduce production by women writers to novels or well-known pedagogical texts, however, would be to forget the many philosophical, political, and scientific essays written by women. Madame du Châtelet (who, incidentally, translated Newton) published an *Institutions de physique.* The monumental *History of England from the Accession of James I* (8 vols., 1763–78) of Catharine Macaulay soon became a model of the genre and won her the admiration of *philosophes.* The hostility that Olympe de Gouges endured and the difficulties she encountered in becoming accepted as a playwright in Paris during the 1780s echoed those of Luisa Bergalli in Venice in the 1750s.

The Political Scene

Before the Revolutions

Anne of England, Maria Theresa of Austria, and Catherine of Russia were women who left a mark on the politics of their countries and their century. But with the exception of these sovereigns and a few royal mistresses like Madame de Pompadour, women were excluded from the political centers of power. This of course did not prevent them from participating in the public life of their countries. The salons of the eighteenth century were also political circles. Olympe de Gouges, Catharine Macaulay, and many others put their pens to the service of their ideas. As for women of the people, they were traditionally in the first ranks of all public disturbances—food riots, religious upheavals, and anti-fiscal and political uprisings. Protectresses of the community, they rose to defend its rights. Thanks to their mobility, their constant presence in the streets, their familiarity with public spaces, and their role in the neighborhood, they soon learned of any violation of the tacit rules governing the balance between public power and its subjects. They were quick to rise to protest any situation they judged intolerable, dragging their men along with them.

A number of historical studies centered on various European countries have made women's role in uprisings familiar to us, along with the relationship between men and women in riots.[27] But the relationship between women and the power structure was not limited to the latter's fearful surveillance of the women it considered potential rioters. In a more subtle fashion, the monarchy needed their approbation as well. The populace was expected to attend the great festive ceremonies that marked important events (a military victory, a royal marriage or birth, etc.). The crowd that, by its presence, magnified the symbolic connection between the king and his people was made up of both women and men. At times women alone took it upon themselves to embody that connection: when they came to congratulate the king on the birth of a dauphin, the Dames de la Halle de Paris were received at Versailles as representing the people. The political participation of women was a complex phenomenon that needs further study, and we should guard against overly hasty conclusions. That women had a de facto political existence through their writings, their presence, and their revolts should not lead us to forget that they were denied that existence juridically, a fact that placed concrete limitations on their field of action. Similarly, if the monarchical system took their reactions into account, that does not by any means signify that they participated in power.

Enlightenment thought reformulated the political connection and the social contract. But while the *philosophes* wrote page after page on the best form of government, on nationhood, citizenship, natural rights, and more, most of them had nothing to say about women. What was women's place to be in the ideal city of the Enlightenment? At home: this seemed so evident that it was not worth saying. But if we search a bit farther it becomes clear that it was not so easy to eliminate a bothersome question with a stroke of the pen or by ignoring it. Contradiction lay in wait for the best of them. Thus, Diderot states in the *Encyclopédie* that the word "*citoyen*," which he defines as applying to one who holds political rights in a free society, is a noun used only in the masculine: "This title is conceded to women, to young children, and to servants only inasmuch as they are members of the family of a citizen, strictly speaking; but they are not truly citizens." The *pas vraiment* reveals the philosopher's embarrassment: to state abruptly that the word had no feminine form (at a time when *citoyenne* existed in the language, albeit in the more restricted sense of a woman living in a city) resolved nothing. Quite the contrary. The revolutions of the final decades of the century posed the problem with a new acuity.

The Revolutionaries

The end of the eighteenth century was punctuated by a series of revolutions placed under the sign of the Enlightenment. From Amsterdam to Paris via Boston, the Western world challenged traditional order. The place and the role of women, society's view of them, and relations between the sexes did not escape these overwhelming changes unscathed. Nowhere, however, were women legally accorded the full political rights of citizenship. The new political order, the point of arrival of the Enlightenment, seemed reserved to men. But that order was constructed by both men and women, and women not only did not remain insensitive to events but participated in them actively and had no intention of being left out of the new city.

In the insurgent mobs women of the people continued to play their traditional role, even starting a number of riots. When the Orangists of Rotterdam revolted against the Patriots in 1784, a mussel-vendor, Kaat Mussel, was noted among their leaders. On 5 October 1789, it was Parisian women who went to seek out Louis XVI at Versailles. Six years later, in 1795, it was again women who were the most virulent in preaching revolt against the "Thermidorian" power, which they held responsible for letting the people die of hunger and betraying the popular revolution. And when insurrection broke out on 1 May 1795, it was women who first took to the streets, inciting the men to join them. On that occasion, the authorities wrote that women were acting as *boutefeux* (firebrands, fomenters of trouble), and the deputies forbade women from gathering in the streets in groups of more than five.[28] Hunger was not the only motivation for female mobs: in October 1789 women protesters proclaimed that they wanted bread, "but not at the price of liberty"; in May 1795, a seamstress stated that the deputies must bow before insurgents who represented "the sovereign people." "Liberty," "sovereignty"—here indeed were Enlightenment words. They serve to remind us that women, even women from modest milieus, were not unaware of the ideas of the century and that they contributed to the revolutionary attempt to realize them.

What is more, women did not limit themselves to rising up only in times of crisis. In France they frequented political assemblies, and they formed women's clubs where the newspapers and the decrees of the Assembly were read and where the club members discussed politics and shared their opinions with the representatives of the nation. A large number of the petitions and addresses that the deputies received, encouraging them, expressing reflections to them, and making political demands of them, came from women. Some women publicized their opinions in broadsheets, pamphlets, or posters tacked up in public places. It was because of one of her posters attacking the Montagnard Convention that Olympe de Gouges was arrested in the autumn of 1793. Beginning in 1789, she had published some thirty political writings in the form of pamphlets, tracts, books, and plays. From 1788 to 1799, women wrote some 150 published political works.

Nor was France, all due allowances made, an exceptional case. Before her famous *A Vindication of the Rights of Woman* (1792), the British feminist Mary Wollstonecraft had responded to Burke's attacks on the French Revolution in *A Vindication of the Rights of Men* (1790). In 1794, she published *An Historical and Moral View of the Origin and Progress of the*

French Revolution. Her compatriot Catharine Macaulay also defended the French Revolution in a number of works. Although German women published no theoretical studies, they translated the French revolutionaries and introduced the Revolution into novels, where they also expressed their own reflections on that event—Sophie Mereau in *Das Blüthenalter der Empfindung* (1794), Maria Therese Heyne-Forster-Huber in *La Famille Seldorf* (1795), and Sophie von La Roche in *Schönes Bild der Resignation* (1795–96) and *Erscheinungen am See Oneida* (1798).[29]

The salons became political gatherings. Their semi-private character made them a more neutral place to meet people than the official organisms and clubs. What could not be debated in the feverish atmosphere of the official gatherings could be discussed in the more muffled atmosphere of the salon. It was in the salon of the comtesse d'Yves, for instance, that Belgian democrats and traditionalists met in 1789.

The Revolution of Two Women of the Enlightenment

Madame Roland had one of the most famous salons in Paris. In 1791 the entire patriotic milieu could be found there: men as different as Robespierre, Pétion, Abbé Grégoire, Brissot, Abbé Fauchet, Thomas Paine, and Condorcet. Madame Roland's house was a place where newly elected provincial deputies could learn about the inner workings of politics and meet the leading lights of the Paris scene. Very soon it became a place in which Girondist politics were worked out and speeches were discussed before being presented to the Jacobins and the Assembly. The hostess did not merely receive her company but directed the discussions and exerted a real influence on the guests. By her education, her reading, her Rousseauistic religion, and her belief in the superior worth of accomplishments, she was an excellent representative of the spirit of the Enlightenment. Even before the Revolution, she worked in close cooperation with her husband, helping him write his academic discourses and technical treatises, his reports on manufacturing, or his articles for the *Encyclopédie méthodique*. The Revolution gave a new direction to this conjugal collaboration. Manon Roland profoundly inspired her husband's politics, and when he became a minister she wrote some of his most important official texts.

Although a true politician, Manon Roland did not consider herself a spokesperson or a representative of her sex. "I do not believe that our customs as yet permit women to show themselves," she wrote in a letter in April 1791. "They must inspire good and nourish and enflame all sentiments useful to the homeland, but not seem to compete in political activities. They will be able to act openly only when all the French can be called free men." She herself hardly ever wrote except anonymously or under her husband's name. For that reason, despite her undeniable modernity, Madame Roland represents a fairly traditional figure of a political woman whose importance, somewhat like that of certain queens and royal favorites, was muted, linked to her personal place and her influence within male governing milieus.

Nonetheless, Manon Roland was guillotined on 8 November 1793 for her opinions and for her political role. Only a few days after her death, *La Feuille de Salut Public,* a semi-official organ, published an article addressed "To Women Republicans," which was reprinted on 19 November in *Le Moniteur Universel.* It stated that "the Roland woman, a *bel esprit* fond of great projects" and "a monster in all ways" had "sacrificed nature by attempting to raise herself above it; the desire to be learned led her to forget the virtues of her sex, and that forgetfulness—always dangerous— brought her to her death on the scaffold." This clear warning needed no further commentary: let other educated women watch their step! The same article also attacked Olympe de Gouges, guillotined on 3 November, for her "exalted imagination," which had led her to want to be "a statesman" and to forget "the virtues proper to her sex."

Olympe de Gouges was certainly not a *femme savante.* Her education had been somewhat succinct (she herself admitted that she did not know how to write very well). That had not prevented her from plunging into a career as a woman of letters and a dramatist. Imbued with the spirit of the Enlightenment, she fought to defend the natural rights of all human beings. Her fight against slavery, her struggle for equality of the sexes, and her defense of authors' proprietary rights were known to all, for unlike Madame Roland, Olympe de Gouges always made her opinions public, had no compunction about signing her own name, and publicized herself with a vigor that brought her a good many vexations even before the Revolution. Above all, she wrote in the name of all women, presenting herself as their spokesperson and calling on them to revolt against an unjust situation, and she demanded that natural rights apply to all her sex (notably in her *Déclaration des Droits de la Femme et de la Citoyenne*). Intransigent in her principles, she refused to operate in the shadows to wait for some future evolution to achieve political recognition for women.

A New Relationship between the Sexes?

Aside from these two portraits of real women, there is another and totally theoretical portrait of particular interest—that of the woman of the
future society who emerged from revolution. This new woman inhabited
both sides of the Atlantic. In both America and France women rejected
the image of flirtatious coquettes uniquely concerned with their jewels,
their appearance, and their attractiveness to men: that sort of woman,
born of a perverted relationship between the sexes, reflected an entire
people's servitude. In a republic women should no longer be frivolous,
weak, and passive but worthy, energetic, and active. And men would have
to look at their companions with new eyes, appreciate them, and love
them for their moral qualities rather than their physical beauty. In December 1793 a young Parisian, Joséphine Fontanier, defended this new
relationship between the sexes in a discourse delivered before an assembly of sans-culottes:

> The time has come to an end when woman, humbled and de-
> graded by the false and frivolous adoration paid to her and with
> which [men] claimed to honor her, was regarded as at best
> a being of second rank, destined uniquely to give flowered
> crowns to her husband, to be an ornament in society as roses are
> the ornament of gardens. Ah, citizens! Would you dare to claim
> the name of republicans if you still thought beauty to be the first
> quality of a woman? . . . No, no, citizens, let us leave to the
> courts of despots and to the corrupt cities . . . that false way of
> appreciating one-half of the human race. . . . Let us look with
> scorn—or rather, with compassion—at those frivolous women,
> those ephemeral beings who know nothing and want nothing
> but to shine. . . . No more frivolous ideas for us; henceforth in-
> different to the color of a ribbon, the fineness of a gauze, the
> shape or the price of our earrings; our virtues will be our only
> ornament and our children our jewels.[30]

American women insisted on the importance of a republican education that would develop their innate qualities and assure them independence, self-respect, and self-reliance. French women added that
relations between the sexes ought no longer be marked with the stamp
of "marital despotism"—a stamp that they compared, quite literally, to

the king's seal or a noble's crest. They demanded women's right—and duty—to "participate in public affairs."

For society as a whole, however, the *républicaine* was above all a mother whose essential task was to raise her children as good citizens. At that point, the debate that had begun during the latter half of the eighteenth century on the woman and her specific functions took on a totally new resonance.

Citoyennes?

The French Revolution created a new political space in which every citizen recovered natural rights. But was it open to both men and women? Did women come to possess political rights? The answer is no, they did not. But then how to justify this violation of the principle of universality, the basic principle of the Declaration of the Rights of Man, on which the new society was in turn founded? The solution lay in recourse to an innate difference between the sexes and in the notion of a specifically female nature.

Rousseau is cited constantly by revolutionaries hostile to women's participation in politics. Roussel is rarely mentioned, but his theories served as the basis of their arguments. By her physical constitution, woman is physically and intellectually more fragile than man and—therefore—incapable of enjoying political rights. Furthermore, she is called by nature to functions that differ from men's and that "have to do with the general order of society," as Deputy Amar stated in a report on 30 October 1793 preceding the prohibition of women's political clubs. That did not mean that women were excluded from the revolutionary city, Amar continued, but that their role in it was domestic and related to mores. They were "made for softening the behavior of men" and for raising future citizens in the cult of "public virtues," good, and liberty. In 1798, Kant stated that it was woman who led man to morality and culture.[31] American women agreed with Kant. Rather than demanding a public function, they stated that the revolutionary rupture had given a new and civic meaning to their familial and maternal role. Furthermore, they insisted, women are the guarantors of the morality and virtue of the country, which cannot survive without those qualities.

French women, who lived in a society in which women had a richer social life, were not content with that sort of "private citizenship." They did not reject the notion of a distribution of social roles between the sexes, but they did not see why it was incompatible with public activities, even with the exercise of political rights. In 1793 a group of Paris women asked: "And why must women, gifted with the faculty of hearing and expressing their thoughts, be excluded from public affairs? The Declaration of Rights is common to both sexes, and the difference consists in duties: some are public and some are private. Men are particularly called to fulfill the first. . . ."

Like these women, all partisans of the political existence of women stressed what men and women have in common: reason, which defines the human being and which brings rights. Against the conception of two diametrically opposed natures, they claimed the legacy of Poullain de la Barre. "We are not another species on this Earth different from yours: the mind has no sex; nor do virtues," Mademoiselle Jodin wrote in 1790 in *Vues législatives pour les femmes*. The conclusion was clear: men and women should enjoy the same rights.

This was a question of principle and of logic more than one of justice. The exclusion of women from citizenship rights was a violation of the "principle of equal rights" and an "act of tyranny" that involved all of society, not just its female victims, as Condorcet wrote in an article, "Sur l'admission des femmes au droit de cité," published in the *Journal de la Société de 1789* (July 1790). Indeed, "the principle of equality of rights" presupposed that "either no individual of the human species has any true rights or all have the same ones." As a man of the Enlightenment, Condorcet placed himself on the terrain of reason against prejudice, vain declamations, or the "universal opinion" that Amar appealed to in 1793. Condorcet reminded those who argued women's unique physiology that the female body has no monopoly on illness, and that to remove a thinking being's rights because of an alleged physical weakness was ridiculous: "Why should beings exposed to pregnancies, to transient indispositions, not be able to exercise the same rights that it has never occurred to anyone to take away from persons with the gout who take cold easily every winter?"

Condorcet's arguments are reiterated in all texts favorable to women's political existence. Olympe de Gouges appeals to the "force of reason" against "inconsequence" and insists that there has never been a constitution (the alternative is tyranny) that has not been a cooperative venture of both men and women. The president of the women's club of Dijon exclaimed, calling upon both principle and currently operative relations between the sexes, "Wherever women will be slaves [without full rights], men will be bowed down under despotism."

The French Revolution, a point of rupture and a moment of total challenge, closed the era of the Enlightenment. Women acquired a juridical and civic existence (though not for long), but citizenship was refused to them. This did not stop them from acting as citizens, thus adding the word *citoyenne*, in its political sense, to the dictionaries and to history. By creating a political space founded on the principle of equality, the Revolution stressed the Enlightenment paradox of "'mixity' without parity." That paradox might have been accommodated in a world founded on the principle of inequality; now that was impossible. The simple fact that it had become *possible* to imagine the equality of men and women exacerbated tensions. The image of the "woman/death" (the death of the Revolution, of society, of the man) invaded discourse. The fear of seeing the relationship between the sexes challenged took on unheard-of proportions. Men feared having to share power—a fear often conceived in terms of losing political, social, intellectual, or domestic power. They feared men might be enslaved and that confusing gender roles would bring on chaos. Some attempted to conjure away these anxieties by an insistent reiteration of the conceptions of the physician-philosophers of the Enlightenment who were the sources of women's exclusion.

It is perhaps precisely because, in a society tending toward democracy, "'mixity' without parity" was no longer tenable that the Code Civil of 1804 hammered in the notion that parity was out of the question and that a strict division of men's and women's spheres reduced "mixity" even farther in the nineteenth century. And yet—one final paradox—it was the revolutionary rupture that gave feminism a chance to develop in that age.

Notes

1. Paul Hoffmann, *La femme dans la pensée des Lumières* (Paris: Ophrys, 1977).

2. Arlette Farge, "Il secolo al femminile: Ruolo e rappresentazione della donna," in *Europa Moderna: La disgregazione dell'Ancien Régime* (n.p.: Banca Nazionale del Lavoro, n.d.), 177–89.

3. Jean-Jacques Rousseau, *Émile, ou, de l'éducation* (Paris: Garnier/Flammarion, 1966), 465, 470; quoted here and below in this chapter from *Emile, or, On Education*, trans., with introduction and notes, Allan Bloom (New York: Basic Books, 1979), 358, 357, 361.

4. Denis Diderot, *Sur les femmes*, in *Oeuvres de Diderot*, Bibliothèque de la Pléiade, 25 (Paris: Gallimard, 1951), 952.

5. Pierre Roussel, Système physique et moral de la femme, 2d ed. (1775; Paris: Crapar, Caille et Ravier, 1805), 1.

6. Diderot, *Sur les femmes,* 952.

7. See Michele Crampe-Casnabet, "A Sampling of Eighteenth-Century Philosophy," in *Renaissance and Enlightenment Paradoxes,* ed. Natalie Zemon Davis and Arlette Farge, vol. 3 of *A History of Women in the West,* ed. Georges Duby and Michelle Perrot, 5 vols. (Cambridge, Mass.: Belknap Press of Harvard University Press, 1990–92), 315–47. See also Yvonne Knibiehler, "Les médecins et la 'nature féminine' au temps du Code Civil," *Annales E.S.C.* 31 (1976): 824–45.

8. Rousseau, *Emile,* 386, 387.

9. Ibid., 387.

10. Ibid., 362, 357.

11. *Le miroir des femmes,* ed. Arlette Farge, Bibliothèque bleue (Paris: Montalba, 1982).

12. Ibid., 35.

13. Louis-Sébastien Mercier, "Comment se fait un mariage," in *Tableau de Paris: Nouvelle édition corrigée et augmentée,* 12 vols. (Amsterdam, 1782–88); quoted from "Mariage à la mode," in *The Waiting City: Paris 1782–88,* trans. and ed. Helen Simpson (London: George G. Harrap, 1933), 117–18.

14. Louis-Sébastien Mercier, "Filles nubiles," in *Tableau de Paris: Nouvelle édition corrigée et augmentée,* 12 vols. (Amsterdam, 1782–88); quoted from "Marriageable," in *The Waiting City: Paris 1782–88,* trans. and ed. Helen Simpson (London: George G. Harrap, 1933), 49.

15. Immanuel Kant, *The Metaphysics of Morals,* trans., with introduction and notes, Mary Gregor (Cambridge, U.K., and New York: Cambridge University Press, 1991), 96.

16. Johann Gottlieb Fichte, *Grundlage des Naturrechts nach Principien der Wissenschaftslehre,* 2 vols. (Iena and Leipzig: Christian Ernst Gabler, 1796–97), quoted in Marie-Claire Hoock-Demarle, *La femme au temps de Goethe* (Paris: Stock, 1987), 123, 163.

17. Quoted in Jean-Louis Flandrin, *Familles: Parenté, maison, sexualité dans l'ancienne société* (Paris: Hachette, 1976; Seuil, 1984), 121. See also Flandrin, *Families in Former Times: Kinship, Household, and Sexuality,* trans. Richard Southern, Themes in the Social Sciences (Cambridge, U.K., and New York: Cambridge University Press, 1979), 122, 123.

18. Rousseau, *Emile,* 370.

19. The texts of some twenty of these discourses are conserved in the Bibliothèque Nationale, Paris, with the call number Lb42.

20. See Martine Sonnet, "A Daughter to Educate," and Nina Rattner Gelbart, "Female Journalists," in *Renaissance and Enlightenment Paradoxes,* ed. Natalie Zemon Davis and Arlette Farge, vol. 3 of *A History of Women in the West,* ed. Georges Duby and Michelle Perrot, 5 vols. (Cambridge, Mass.: Belknap Press of Harvard University Press, 1990–92), 101–31, 420–35, respectively. See also Martine Sonnet, *L'éducation des filles au temps des Lumières* (Paris: Cerf, 1987).

21. Rousseau, *Emile,* 365.

22. These figures are taken from Roger Chartier, "Les pratiques de d'écriture," in *De la Renaissance aux Lumières*, ed. Roger Chartier, vol. 3 of *Histoire de la vie privée*, ed. Philippe Ariès and Georges Duby, 5 vols. (Paris: Seuil, 1985–87), 114–20; quoted from "The Practical Impact of Writing," in *Passions of the Renaissance*, vol. 3 of *A History of Private Life*, 111–59.

23. Victorine de Chastenay, *Mémoires de Madame de Chastenay, 1771–1815* (Paris: Perrin, 1986).

24. Chartier, "The Practical Impact of Writing," 144–47.

25. The Montjean journal is studied in Arlette Farge, *La vie fragile: Violence, pouvoirs et solidarités à Paris au XVIIIe siècle* (Paris: Hachette, 1986), 101–18; quoted from *Fragile Lives: Violence, Power and Solidarity in Eighteenth-Century Paris*, trans. Carol Shelton (Cambridge, Mass.: Harvard University Press, 1993), 85, 89.

26. Claude Dulong, "From Conversation to Creation," in *Renaissance and Enlightenment Paradoxes*, ed. Natalie Zemon Davis and Arlette Farge, vol. 3 of *A History of Women in the West*, ed. Georges Duby and Michelle Perrot, 5 vols. (Cambridge, Mass.: Belknap Press of Harvard University Press, 1990–92), 395–419.

27. See the summary in Arlette Farge, "Protesters Plain to See," in *Renaissance and Enlightenment Paradoxes*, ed. Natalie Zemon Davis and Arlette Farge, vol. 3 of *A History of Women in the West*, ed. Georges Duby and Michelle Perrot, 5 vols. (Cambridge, Mass.: Belknap Press of Harvard University Press, 1990–92), 489–505.

28. Dominique Godineau, *Citoyennes tricoteuses: Les femmes du peuple à Paris pendant la Révolution française* (Aix-en-Provence: Alinéa, 1988).

29. Marie-Claire Hoock-Demarle, *La rage d'écrire: Femmes-écrivains en Allemagne de 1790 à 1815* (Aix-en-Provence: Alinéa, 1990), 87–157.

30. Paris, Archives Nationales, F1c III Seine 17.

31. Immanuel Kant, *Anthropologie in Pragmatischer Hinsicht* (Königsberg: F. Nicolovius, 1789); available in English as *Anthropology from a Pragmatic Point of View*, trans., with introduction and notes, Mary J. Gregor (The Hague: Nijhoff, 1974).

Index

427